INEQUALITY: CAUSES AND CONSEQUENCES

RESEARCH IN LABOR ECONOMICS

Series Editor: Solomon W. Polachek

IZA Co-Editor: Konstantinos Tatsiramos

Recent Volumes:

Volume 33: Research in Labor Economics
Edited by Solomon W. Polachek and Konstantinos Tatsiramos

Volume 34: Informal Employment in Emerging and Transition
Economies
Edited by Hartmut Lehmann and Konstantinos Tatsiramos

Volume 35: 35th Anniversary Retrospective
Edited by Solomon W. Polachek and Konstantinos Tatsiramos

Volume 36: Research in Labor Economics
Edited by Solomon W. Polachek and Konstantinos Tatsiramos

Volume 37: Labor Market Issues in China
Edited by Corrado Giulietti, Konstantinos Tatsiramos and
Klaus F. Zimmermann

Volume 38: New Analyses in Worker Well-Being
Edited by Solomon W. Polachek and Konstantinos Tatsiramos

Volume 39: Safety Nets and Benefit Dependence
Edited by Stéphane Carcillo, Herwig Immervoll, Stephen P.
Jenkins, Sebastian Königs and Konstantinos Tatsiramos

Volume 40: Factors Affecting Worker Well-Being: The Impact of Change
in the Labor Market
Edited by Solomon W. Polachek and Konstantinos Tatsiramos

Volume 41: Gender Convergence in the Labor Market
Edited by Solomon W. Polachek, Konstantinos Tatsiramos and
Klaus F. Zimmermann

Volume 42: Gender in the Labor Market
Edited by Solomon W. Polachek, Konstantinos Tatsiramos and
Klaus F. Zimmermann

RESEARCH IN LABOR ECONOMICS   VOLUME 43

INEQUALITY: CAUSES AND CONSEQUENCES

EDITED BY

LORENZO CAPPELLARI
Università Cattolica Milano and IZA

SOLOMON W. POLACHEK
State University of New York at Binghamton and IZA

KONSTANTINOS TATSIRAMOS
University of Nottingham and IZA

United Kingdom − North America − Japan
India − Malaysia − China

Emerald Group Publishing Limited
Howard House, Wagon Lane, Bingley BD16 1WA, UK

First edition 2016

Copyright © 2016 Emerald Group Publishing Limited

Reprints and permissions service
Contact: permissions@emeraldinsight.com

British Library Cataloguing in Publication Data
A catalogue record for this book is available from the British Library

ISBN: 978-1-78560-811-7
ISSN: 0147-9121 (Series)

ISOQAR
REGISTERED

ISOQAR certified
Management System,
awarded to Emerald
for adherence to
Environmental
standard
ISO 14001:2004.

Certificate Number 1985
ISO 14001

INVESTOR IN PEOPLE

CONTENTS

EDITORIAL ADVISORY BOARD   *vii*

PREFACE   *ix*

INEQUALITY OF OPPORTUNITY IN EUROPE:
IS THERE A ROLE FOR INSTITUTIONS?
  Daniele Checchi, Vito Peragine and Laura Serlenga   *1*

HOUSEHOLD LIFETIME INEQUALITY ESTIMATES
IN THE U.S. LABOR MARKET
  Luca Flabbi, James Mabli and Mauricio Salazar   *45*

ESTIMATING THE INTERGENERATIONAL
ELASTICITY AND RANK ASSOCIATION IN THE
UNITED STATES: OVERCOMING THE CURRENT
LIMITATIONS OF TAX DATA
  Bhashkar Mazumder   *83*

INCOME SHOCKS OR INSURANCE – WHAT
DETERMINES CONSUMPTION INEQUALITY?
  Johannes Ludwig   *131*

THE ROLE OF ESTABLISHMENTS AND THE
CONCENTRATION OF OCCUPATIONS IN WAGE
INEQUALITY
  Elizabeth Weber Handwerker and James R. Spletzer   *167*

INEQUALITY AND CHANGES IN TASK PRICES:
WITHIN AND BETWEEN OCCUPATION EFFECTS
  Nicole Fortin and Thomas Lemieux   *195*

v

INTERGENERATIONAL TRANSMISSION OF SKILLS
AND DIFFERENCES IN LABOR MARKET OUTCOMES
FOR BLACKS AND WHITES
    Tsunao Okumura and Emiko Usui   *227*

THE COLLEGE WAGE PREMIUM OVER TIME:
TRENDS IN EUROPE IN THE LAST 15 YEARS
    Elena Crivellaro   *287*

RISING WAGE INEQUALITY, REAL WAGE
STAGNATION AND UNIONS
    Stephen Machin   *329*

IS THERE AN ADVANTAGE TO WORKING? THE
RELATIONSHIP BETWEEN MATERNAL
EMPLOYMENT AND INTERGENERATIONAL
MOBILITY
    Martha H. Stinson and Peter Gottschalk   *355*

DOES INCOME INEQUALITY IN EARLY CHILDHOOD
PREDICT SELF-REPORTED HEALTH IN
ADULTHOOD? A CROSS-NATIONAL COMPARISON
OF THE UNITED STATES AND GREAT BRITAIN
    Richard V. Burkhauser, Markus H. Hahn,   *407*
    Dean R. Lillard and Roger Wilkins

EDITORIAL ADVISORY BOARD

PREFACE

Inequality has been rising in many countries over the last decades and the process seems to have accelerated with the Great Recession. Not only is income distribution more unequal today than 40 years ago, but also the transmission of income differences through generations remains substantial. In other words, many countries fail to experience upward economic mobility as was prevalent in the past. This volume contains 11 original papers which deal with the causes and consequences of inequality. The topics covered include the way inequality is measured, the level of equal opportunities across countries, the impact of education, the effect of changing occupational structure, the consequences of changing productivity within the firm, the roles of stagnating average real wages, the decline of union membership, the effect of maternal labor supply on labor market outcomes of their children, and the link between income inequality and health.

In the first paper, Daniele Checchi, Vito Peragine, and Laura Serlenga provide an empirical investigation of income inequality and equality of opportunities in Europe. One of the key messages of the paper is that standard income inequality and equality of opportunities measures do not necessarily provide the same type of country rankings — especially when comparing formerly non-market economies with coordinated market economies, like Nordic ones. The authors also find that equality of opportunity measures do not exhibit significant variation over time, as income inequality measures do, suggesting that they reflect embedded features of national socio-economic systems. Institutions play a role in shaping the varying degrees of equal opportunities across countries, in particular educational systems, labor market institutions, and parental leave opportunities during child rearing.

The interaction of family responsibilities and institutions can also shape inequality. In the second paper, Luca Flabbi, James Mabli, and Mauricio Salazar offer two key perspectives on the issue of income inequality derived from a model of household search. First, by explicitly modeling individual behavior, they distinguish between inequality in income and inequality in welfare over the life cycle. Second, by also modeling the economic interaction of spouses, they identify different sources of inequality. Using their structural model for policy simulations, they show that increasing dispersion of the wage offer distribution affects earnings inequality but not welfare inequality. This suggests that agents may enact behaviors that at least partially neutralize the effects of exogenous shocks to the wage distribution. Also differences in labor supply between men and women result in different patterns of wage inequality.

Using appropriate data also plays a role in understanding inequality, particularly regarding intergenerational changes (how much children's income is associated with the income of their parents). Intergenerational income associations are important measures because they can be informative about the degree of income mobility, with higher intergenerational income association implying lower mobility. In the third paper, Bhashkar Mazumder discusses alternative approaches to the estimation of intergenerational income associations (elasticities vs. rank correlations) casting the discussion in the framework of recent U.S. evidence from tax records, which shows lower estimates of both compared with previous findings, implying more intergenerational income mobility than commonly thought. The author reconciles these discrepancies by showing that the tax records used do not have the right structure which is needed for the estimation of intergenerational associations. These include: a sufficient length of income strings on children and fathers centered around the early 40s, and an age range where life-cycle biases are typically considered negligible. Using longer panel data from household surveys (PSID), the author shows that the data limitations of the tax records used in recent papers can explain a big part of the discrepancies in results. The paper also stresses the conceptual advantages of rank-based measures over elasticities. The main conclusion is that available tax data do not provide the adequate structure of information for estimating intergenerational income associations.

While the bulk of the inequality literature concentrates on incomes or earnings, starting with the late 1990s economists have been interested in exploring also the inequality of consumption and its connection with income inequality. Consumption is a key welfare determinant and its distribution across households may inform about "deep parameters" of the underlining behavioral model. In the fourth paper, Johannes Ludwig revisits the theme focusing on the U.S. case where consumption inequality did not follow the rise of income inequality. Using PSID data up to 2010 and imputing consumption data, the author identifies two main channels which can explain why consumption inequality did not increase. First, increasing income inequality came through the more volatile component of the income process, which can be smoothed away through credit when making consumption plans. Second, an increased ability of households in insuring themselves against any type of income shocks, permanent or transitory, again points to the relevance of financial markets. Nevertheless, despite a household's ability to cushion income shocks in the short run, the causes of income inequality are important to understand long-run consequences. The next six papers deal with potential sources of inequality.

It is well known that wages vary across employers. For example, large establishments typically pay more. Less well known is a new strand of research documenting how increasing inequality between these employers is responsible for greater overall wage inequality. Also less well known is that establishments are becoming more concentrated in occupations as routine occupations are being replaced by technology and an additional number of occupations are being outsourced in order to cut compensation costs. In the next paper, Elizabeth Weber Handwerker and James R. Spletzer utilize new employer—employee linked data to show first the importance of establishment effects in widening the wage distribution, and second the growing divergence of wages between establishments which in part results from an increasing within establishment occupational concentration at least in the 2000—2011 time period. Both bring attention to efficiency changes within establishments related to the overall wage distribution.

In the next paper, Nicole Fortin and Thomas Lemieux examine the link between wage inequality and task prices, which are difficult to measure because changing task prices are often blurred by endogenous selection into tasks. In the model they present, wage levels depend upon tasks and task prices, while tasks depend on workers' skills. This implies that wage inequality depends on both the level and dispersion of task prices. Using detailed data on task contents of jobs, the authors' findings suggest that automation has reduced average wages and increased their dispersion. The study advances the current literature on routine jobs and wage inequality by showing that changes in task prices due to changing content of tasks are an important ingredient of changes in the overall wage distribution.

Differences in labor market outcomes between groups are partly related to the intergenerational transmission of skills. In the next paper, Tsunao Okumura and Emiko Usui investigate the contribution of intergenerational transmission of skills to the black/white earnings gap. The authors first set out a theoretical model that allows for skills, multidimensionality and their transmission across generations. They then take this model to the data drawn from the NLSY79, showing that a large portion of the within-generational earnings gap is in fact coming from the previous generation, being accounted for by the process of skill transmission. However, the intergenerational process cannot explain the whole of the earnings gap within a generation, particularly at the lower end of the earnings distribution.

Secularly, changing skill levels and task prices can affect the college wage premium. In the next paper, Elena Crivellaro offers a cross-country analysis of the college wage premium in Europe. She considers several factors that might affect relative wages, particularly the supply and demand of skilled labor as well as labor market institutions. To address endogeneity of the supply of skills, she proposes an IV strategy based on educational reforms that arguably shifted the supply of college graduates. These reforms together with the evolution of inequality-reducing labor market institutions, such as the minimum wage, contributed to a decline of the college wage premium over time.

The decline of union power may also be a factor. In the next paper, Stephen Machin explores the connection between rising wage inequality, stagnation of average real wages, and the decline of unions. The author shows that the rise of wage inequality observed in many countries (e.g., United States, United Kingdom, Germany) was concurrent with the stagnation of average wages, defined as the absence of real wage growth. This phenomenon is worrying from a welfare perspective especially because stagnation occurred in the bottom and middle quantiles of the wage distribution, but not at the top. This happens in an era of the demise of unions where new workers do not unionize implying a decoupling between average wages and productivity.

Maternal labor supply can also be a factor. In the next paper, Martha H. Stinson and Peter Gottschalk investigate the effect of maternal labor supply on labor market outcomes of their children when they grow up. Answering this question is challenging because of both endogeneity issues and data limitations. Having access to rich longitudinal data, that allows measuring both the parental earnings when the child is very young and the adult earnings of the child, they find no significant effect of maternal labor supply during the first five years of a child's life on earnings, employment, or mobility. However, having a working mother during children's high school years has a positive effect on employment for daughters.

The consequences of rising inequality can be felt far into the future. In the final paper, Richard V. Burkhauser, Markus H. Hahn, Dean R. Lillard, and Roger Wilkins confirm earlier results that income inequality experienced as a child is related to health status many years later when the child becomes an adult. Using the Cross-National Equivalent File (CNEF) data from the United States and Great Britain, they show that men and women are more likely to report poor health if inequality was wide during their first five years of life. Further, for the United States this result remained robust when controlling for demographic characteristics, permanent income, and yearly socioeconomic status. The implication is that the effects of inequality transcend the simple intergenerational transmission usually studied which makes the study of inequality all the more important.

As with past volumes, we aim to focus on important issues and to maintain the highest levels of scholarship. We encourage readers who have prepared manuscripts that meet these stringent standards to submit them to *Research in Labor Economics* (RLE) via the IZA website (http://rle.iza.org) for possible inclusion in future volumes.

Lorenzo Cappellari
Solomon W. Polachek
Konstantinos Tatsiramos
Editors

INEQUALITY OF OPPORTUNITY IN EUROPE: IS THERE A ROLE FOR INSTITUTIONS? ☆

Daniele Checchi[a], Vito Peragine[b] and Laura Serlenga[c]

[a] University of Milan and IZA
[b] University of Bari
[c] University of Bari and IZA

ABSTRACT

This paper studies the cross-country differences in conventional measures of inequality of opportunity in Europe in the space of individual disposable incomes. Exploiting two recent waves of the EUSILC database reporting information on family background (2005 and 2011), we provide estimates of inequality of opportunity in about 30 European

☆ Paper presented at the conference on Social Mobility (Bocconi University, October 2014) and IZA conference on "Inequality: causes and consequences" (Bonn, March 2015). We are grateful to the participants for helpful comments, and in particular Luca Flabbi and Anders Björklund for helpful suggestions. The comments of the two referees have helped us to significantly improve the paper. We are solely responsible for any remaining errors.

Inequality: Causes and Consequences
Research in Labor Economics, Volume 43, 1−44
Copyright © 2016 by Emerald Group Publishing Limited
All rights of reproduction in any form reserved
ISSN: 0147-9121/doi:10.1108/S0147-912120160000043008

countries for two sufficiently distant data points, allowing a check of consistency for country rankings. In addition, we exploit two observations available for most of the countries to explore the relationship between many institutional dimensions and inequality of opportunity, finding evidence of negative correlation with educational expenditure (especially at the pre-primary level) and passive labour market policies.

Keywords: Inequality; inequality of opportunities; institutions

JEL classifications: D63; E24; J5

1. INTRODUCTION

The literature on inequality of opportunity has significantly expanded in recent years.[1] There are different reasons for embracing the opportunity perspective. The first is that most of those who worry about inequality do so because they think that it is unjust, or at least partially unjust. In addition, existing surveys show that most people judge income inequalities arising from different levels of effort as less objectionable than those due to exogenous circumstances as gender, race, family origin, etc. The implicit idea is that what matters for a just society is the distribution of opportunities, rather than the distribution of outcomes. Hence, it is interesting to measure that portion of outcome inequality that can be attributed to exogenous circumstances and hence reflects unequal opportunities.

In addition to normative reasons, the analysis of opportunity inequality can have an instrumental value. First, social attitudes towards redistributive policies may be affected by the knowledge, or the perception, of the origin of income inequalities (Alesina & La Ferrara, 2005). By recognising that a small (large) amount of existing inequalities is due to unequal opportunities, one may decrease (increase) the support for redistributive policies. Second, opportunity inequality, rather than income inequality, can be related to aggregate economic performance: it has been suggested (Bourguignon, Ferreira, & Walton, 2007; World Bank, 2006) that the existence of strong

---

1. For comprehensive reviews of the inequality of opportunity literature, see the recent surveys by Ramos and Van de Gaer (2015), Roemer and Trannoy (2015) and Ferreira and Peragine (2015).

and persistent inequalities in the initial opportunities open to individuals can generate true inequality traps that represent severe constraints to perspectives of future growth of an economy, by preventing entire groups from participation into economic and social life.[2] Finally, the analysis of opportunity inequality may help the understanding of the generation of income inequality, since it constitutes the layer hardest to remove through public intervention. Nevertheless, the knowledge of the factors determining opportunity inequality can help to identify the more deprived groups in a society, thereby revealing new points of emphasis in social and redistributive policies. These considerations are relevant for many countries and for the debate on social protection and social policies in Europe.[3]

After the theoretical contributions by Roemer (1993, 1998) and Fleurbaey (1995, 2008), a recent and growing literature in the last 15 years has tried to assess the degree of inequality of opportunity in different countries, and to evaluate the opportunity-equalizing effects of public policies. A number of different measurement and evaluation methodologies have been proposed and an even broader array of empirical applications has been undertaken. However, cross-countries comparisons are less frequent in the literature, probably because of data limitations.[4] Ferreira and Gignoux (2011), by using different data sets, present comparative evidence on inequality of opportunity over six Latin-American countries, showing

---

2. For an empirical analysis of the relationship between inequality of opportunity and growth in a sample of US states, see Marrero and Rodríguez (2013), they decompose total inequality into inequality of opportunity and inequality of effort, showing that GDP per capita growth rate is negatively correlated with the former and positively with the latter. A similar line of research has been followed by Ferreira, Lakner, Lugo, and Ozler (2014), with a cross-country analysis involving a sample of 84 countries.

3. To further stress the point, it is worth recalling that the OECD is launching a Centre for Opportunity and Equality, "... a new platform for promoting and conducting policy-oriented research on the trends, causes and consequences of inequalities in society and the economy, and a forum to discuss how policies can best address such inequalities." (from the flyer of presentation).

4. Some papers provide regional disaggregation of the opportunity inequality measures (Checchi and Peragine (2010) for Italy, Marrero and Rodríguez (2013) for US states) but the differences are difficult to interpret when confronted with a homogeneous institutional framework at the national level. There is a parallel literature on cross-country comparisons of intergenerational mobility (see for example Corak (2013)) that we leave aside here, because it focuses on a specific set of circumstances (typically parental income and/or education) neglecting the contribution to inequality of all other components. Comparisons of opportunity inequality and intergenerational mobility indices can be found in Brunori, Ferreira, and Peragine (2013).

that race and region of birth are more relevant in explaining opportunity deprivation than in attaining poverty status. Brunori, Palmisano, and Peragine (2015), use a set of surveys to compute measures of inequality of opportunities over 11 Sub-Saharan African countries, showing that ethnicity and region of birth are the most relevant factors in explaining inequality of opportunity in consumption. While in both Ferreira and Gignoux (2011) and Brunori et al. (2015) cross-countries comparability is severely limited by estimates based on country-specific surveys, Checchi, Peragine, and Serlenga (2010) present cross-country evidence on 25 European countries using a harmonised data set (the EUSILC survey conducted in 2005), finding that ex-ante equality of opportunity exhibits positive correlation with public expenditure in education, whereas ex-post equality of opportunity is also positively associated to union presence and fiscal redistribution. Marrero and Rodríguez (2012) analyse the same data set, showing that opportunity inequality in household equivalised incomes is negatively correlated with development (proxied by GDP per capita), and positively correlated with long-term unemployment and early school leaving, all measured at 1998 values.[5] Despite using different definitions for the outcome variable,[6] both papers agree on the fact that Nordic countries and Slovenia are characterised by low inequality of opportunity, while Mediterranean countries (Italy, Greece, Spain and Portugal), Anglo-Saxons (Greta Britain and Ireland) and poorer Eastern EU (Estonia, Latvia, Poland, and Lithuania) are among the countries with highest inequality of opportunity.

Our contribution to the literature is mainly empirical. With respect to previous literature we propose a more careful modelling strategy to account for employment opportunities, by including the potential incomes of those who are unemployed (computed according to a selection equation à la Heckman) and focus on individual disposable incomes. In addition, we show that measures of opportunity inequality are more persistent (namely,

---

5. Marrero and Rodríguez (2012) consider as circumstances parental education and occupation (separately taken for each parent), family economic conditions when young and country of origin; conversely they do not take into account gender and age as additional categories for defining *types*.

6. Marrero and Rodríguez (2012) use disposable equivalent income for those households whose head is between 26 and 50 (though it is not mentioned how they estimate net from gross incomes when the former is not available). Checchi et al. (2010) use post-tax individual earnings (including imputed incomes for unemployed) for individuals aged between 30 and 60, grossifying net incomes based on fiscal legislation that was in order in the previous year.

less cyclical) than measures of total inequality, at least in our sample of European countries. The standard country ranking based on total inequality, where Nordic countries are lowest and Mediterranean and Anglo-Saxons are highest, is only partially confirmed when considering opportunity inequality. Finally, when we correlate total inequality and opportunity inequality to institutions, exploiting the availability of two data points per country, we find significant correlations with educational variables (expenditure in education, especially in pre-primary education) and labour market policies variables (passive labour market policies). An appendix shows the robustness of our findings when we change inequality measures (from Gini index to Mean Log Deviation) as well as definition of opportunity inequality, moving from an ex-ante perspective (which is the one adopted throughout the present paper) to the ex-post one.

This paper is organised as follows. Section 2 briefly reviews the concept of opportunity inequality and discusses some measurement issues. Section 3 describes the data and provides our estimates of total inequality and inequality of opportunity for the periods and countries considered. Section 4 correlates total inequality and opportunity inequality to institutional measures, proposing alternative estimation strategy to check the robustness of our results. Section 5 concludes by discussing the policy implications of our findings and suggesting directions for future research.

2. MEASURING OPPORTUNITY INEQUALITY: A SIMPLE MODEL

Consider a distribution of income x in a given population. Suppose that all determinants of x, including the different forms of luck, can be classified into either a set of *circumstances* C that lie beyond individual control, or as responsibility characteristics, summarised by a variable[7] e, denoting *effort*. Circumstances belong to a finite set Ω. For example, suppose that the only circumstance variables are race, which can only take values in the set {black, white}, and parental education, that only takes values in the set {college education, high school education}. In this case the set Ω would be the following: $\Omega = (\{black, parents with high school education\}, \{black,$

---

7. Effort could also be treated as a vector. However, we follow the literature and treat it as a scalar.

parents with college education}, {white, parents with high school education}, {white, parents with college education}).

Effort may be treated as either a continuous or a discrete variable belonging to the set Θ. The outcome of interest is generated by a function $g : \Omega \times \Theta \to R$ such that:

$$x = g(C, e) \tag{1}$$

This can be seen as a reduced-form model in which incomes are exclusively determined by circumstances and effort, such that all individuals having the same circumstances and the same effort obtain the same income. Neither opportunities themselves, nor the process by which some particular outcomes are chosen, are explicitly modelled in this framework. The idea is to infer the opportunities available to individuals by observing joint distributions of circumstances, effort and outcomes. Roughly speaking, the source of unfairness in this model is given by the effect that circumstance variables (which lie beyond individual responsibility) have on individual outcomes.

Thus, we have a population of individuals, each of whom is fully characterised by the triple (x, C, e). For simplicity, treat effort e, as well as each element of the vector of circumstances, C, as discrete variables. Then this population can be partitioned in two ways: into types T_i, within which all individuals share the same circumstances, and into tranches T_j, within which everyone shares the same degree of effort. Denote by x_{ij} the income generated by circumstances C_i and effort e_j. Suppose in addition that there are n types, indexed by $i = 1, ..., n$, and m tranches, indexed by $j = 1, ..., m$. In this discrete setting,[8] the population can be represented by a matrix $[\mathbf{X}_{ij}]$ with n rows, corresponding to types, and m columns, corresponding to tranches:

To the $n \times m$-dimensional matrix $[\mathbf{X}_{ij}]$ in Table 1, let there be associated an $n \times m$ dimensional matrix $[\mathbf{P}_{ij}]$ where each element p_{ij} represents the proportion of total population with circumstances C_i and effort e_j.

Given this model, the measurement of inequality of opportunity can be thought of as a two-step procedure: first, the actual distribution $[\mathbf{X}_{ij}]$ is transformed into a counterfactual distribution $[\tilde{\mathbf{X}}_{ij}]$ that reflects only and fully the unfair inequality in $[\mathbf{X}_{ij}]$, while all the fair inequality is removed. In the second step, a measure of inequality is applied to $[\tilde{\mathbf{X}}_{ij}]$. The construction of the counterfactual distribution $[\tilde{\mathbf{X}}_{ij}]$ should reflect the principle of *equality of opportunity*.

---

8. In an alternative formulation, that would treat effort as a continuous variable, $F_i(x)$ would denote the advantage distribution in type i and q_i denote its population share. The overall distribution for the population as a whole would be $F(x) = \sum_{i=1}^{n} q_i F_i(x)$.

Table 1. Distribution of Outcomes according
to Circumstances and Effort.

	e_1	e_2	e_3	...	e_m
C_1	x_{11}	x_{12}	x_{13}	...	x_{1m}
C_2	x_{21}	x_{22}	x_{23}	...	x_{2m}
C_3	x_{31}	x_{32}	x_{33}	...	x_{3m}
⋮	⋮	⋮	⋮	⋮	⋮
C_n	x_{n1}	x_{n2}	x_{n3}	...	x_{nm}

Within this framework, the opportunity egalitarian principle can be decomposed into two distinct and independent sub-principles: the *Reward Principle*, which is concerned with the apportion of outcome to effort and, in some of its formulations, requires to respect the outcome inequalities due to effort;[9] and the *Compensation Principle*, according to which all outcome inequalities due to C are unfair and should be compensated by society. Any satisfactory measure of opportunity inequality should respect both the compensation and the reward principles. The existing literature has developed two main versions of the compensation principle and two consequent approaches to the measurement of opportunity inequality, namely, the *ex-ante* and the *ex-post* approach.

According to the *ex-ante approach*, there is equality of opportunity if the set of opportunities is the same for all individuals, regardless of their circumstances. Hence, in the ex-ante version, the compensation principle is formulated with respect to individual opportunity sets: it requires reducing the inequality between opportunity sets. In the model introduced above, a given row i, that is the income distribution of a given type, is interpreted as the opportunity set of all individuals with circumstances C_i. Hence, the focus is on the rows of the matrix above: the counterfactual distribution should eliminate the inequality within the rows (*reward*) and reflect the inequality between the rows (*ex-ante compensation*).

---

9. See Ferreira and Peragine (2015) for a discussion of the different formulations of the reward principle proposed in the literature. One of such formulations, *Utilitarian Reward*, states that society should express full neutrality with respect to inequalities due to effort; since in the ex-ante approach the income distribution of types is interpreted as the opportunity set of individuals in that type, it follows that, according to Utilitarian Reward, the social evaluation of the opportunity set is based on the means of the type distribution.

On the other side, according to the *ex-post approach*, there is equality of opportunity if and only if all those who exert the same effort end up with the same outcome. The compensation principle, in the ex-post version, is thus defined with respect to individuals with the same effort but different outcomes: it requires reducing income inequality among the individuals with the same effort. This means that opportunity inequality within this approach is measured as inequality within the columns of the matrix. Hence, the corresponding counterfactual distribution should reflect the inequality within the columns (*ex-post compensation*) but should eliminate the inequality between the columns (*reward*).

Different measures, which are either consistent with the ex-ante or the ex-post approaches, have been proposed in the literature (see Ferreira & Peragine, 2015; Ramos & Van de Gaer, 2015): they express different and sometimes conflicting views on equality of opportunity and in fact the rankings they generate may be different.[10] In addition, their informational requirements are quite different: while for the ex-ante approach, one needs to observe the individual outcome and the set of circumstances, for the ex-post approach, a measure of individual effort is required. Therefore, in addition to normative considerations, the choice of the methodology to adopt should reflect also the data availability. In our case, as will be discussed in the next section, the database we use does not contain a satisfactory measure of effort: for this reason in the rest of this paper, we focus on the ex-ante approach.[11]

In particular, the measure we use, *Between-Types Inequality*, was variously proposed by Peragine (2002), Checchi and Peragine (2010) and Ferreira and Gignoux (2011). It relies on a counterfactual distribution $[\tilde{\mathbf{X}}_{BT}]$, which is obtained by replacing each individual income x_{ij} by the average income of the type she belongs to (μ_i), abstracting from individual level of effort.[12] This smoothing transformation is intended to remove all inequality within types. Formally (Table 2):

---

10. See Fleurbaey and Peragine (2013) for a discussion of the clash between ex-ante and ex-post equality of opportunity.

11. However, in the appendix we also provide estimates of inequality of opportunity based on an ex-post approach: for this computation, we adopt Roemer's statistical measure of effort, according to which the individual effort is identified as the rank of individual within the relevant type income distribution.

12. Hence, the between-types measure satisfies *ex-ante compensation* and *utilitarian reward*. See Ferreira and Peragine (2015).

Between-types counterfactual distribution is

$$\left[\tilde{\mathbf{X}}_{\text{BT}}\right] : \forall j \in \{1, \ldots, m\}, \forall i \in \{1, \ldots, n\}, \tilde{x}_{ij} = \mu_i = \frac{\sum_{j=1}^{m} p_{ij} x_{ij}}{\sum_{j=1}^{m} p_{ij}}$$

Table 2. Measuring between-Types
Inequality ($n = m = 3$).

	e_1	e_2	e_3
C_1	μ_1	μ_1	μ_1
C_2	μ_2	μ_2	μ_2
C_3	μ_3	μ_3	μ_3

Once the smoothed distribution $\left[\tilde{\mathbf{X}}_{\text{BT}}\right]$ is obtained, any inequality measure I applied to such distribution, $I(\tilde{\mathbf{X}}_{\text{BT}})$ is to be interpreted as a measure of inequality of opportunity. Following Aaberge, Mogstad, and Peragine (2011), in this paper we use the Gini coefficient.[13]

3. THE EMPIRICAL ANALYSIS: INCOME INEQUALITY AND OPPORTUNITY INEQUALITY IN EUROPE

3.1. Data Description

To obtain information on circumstances and incomes in representative samples of the population, we use data from the 2005 and 2011 waves of the European Survey on Income and Living Conditions (EUSILC), which is annually run by national Central Statistics Offices and collects information on the income and living conditions of different household types. The survey contains information on a large number of individual and household characteristics as well as specific information on poverty and social exclusion. The present study has been made possible by the inclusion in

---

13. In the Appendix, following Checchi and Peragine (2010), we also compute the mean logarithmic deviation, which is an additively decomposable inequality index (Theil, 1979a, 1979b) and therefore allows obtaining an exact decomposition of overall inequality (I) into two terms: the between-types inequality (I_{BT}), to be interpreted as inequality of opportunity, and the within-types inequality (I_{WT}), interpreted as inequality due to effort.

both 2005 and 2011 of specific modules providing information for attributes of each respondent's parents during her childhood period when aged 14–16. These additional modules report information on family composition, number of siblings, the educational attainment, occupation as well as the labour market activity status of respondent's mother and father and the presence of financial problems in the household. The 2005 survey includes 26 countries, while the 2011 survey consists of 31 countries.[14] The main advantage of these surveys is the relatively large number of countries which allow the cross-country comparative analysis of inequalities.

In order to study the role of circumstances in determining individual destiny, we study *individual incomes and labour market positions*, instead of equivalised household incomes used by other authors (Marrero & Rodríguez, 2012). There are two reasons for this choice: on one side, family members experience different sets of circumstances (they have different gender, age, sometimes country of origin), and averaging among members attenuates the impact of individual circumstances; on the other side, mating, family formation and fertility are individual choices that may reflect effort, which we do want to keep separate from circumstances.

To account for cross-country differences in labour market transition, we restrict the sample to individuals aged between 30 and 60 who are either working full or part-time, unemployed or fulfilling domestic tasks and care responsibilities. Our outcome variable is the *disposable income*.[15] In

---

14. The 2005 sample consists of Austria (AT), Belgium (BE), Cyprus (CY), Czech Republic (CZ), Germany (DE), Denmark (DK), Estonia (EE), Greece (EL), Spain (ES), Finland (FI), France (FR), Hungary (HU), Ireland (IE), Iceland (IS), Italy (IT), Lithuania (LT), Luxemburg (LU), Latvia (LV), Netherlands (NL), Norway (NO), Poland (PL), Portugal (PT), Sweden (SE), Slovenia (SI), Slovakia (SK) and Great Britain (UK). In the 2011, Bulgaria (BG), Switzerland (CH), Croatia (HR), Malta (MT) and Romania (RO) are added to the previous list, counting 31 countries in total. We have retained the additional countries available for 2011 because they do not bias the analysis of temporal variation (where they are excluded by construction) but improve the estimate precision when considering the correlation with institutions.

15. The *net individual income* definition includes "(net) employee cash or near cash income" (variable PYN010) plus "(net) cash benefits or losses from self-employment" (variable PYN050 – negative values set equal to zero) plus "(net) non-cash employee income" (this variable not available for all countries – variable PYN020). Capital incomes are excluded because they are only measured at household level, and it would be arbitrary to attribute them to household members. The *disposable income* definition adds "(net) unemployment benefits" (variable PYN090), "(net) survivor' benefits" (variable PYN110), "(net) sickness benefits" (variable PYN120), "(net) disability benefits" (variable PYN130) and "(net) education-related allowances" (variable PYN140). The appendix describes the procedure utilised to pass from net to gross incomes (or vice versa) when one of the two definitions was absent in the original files.

addition, being aware of the fact that welfare indicators estimated from micro-data can be very sensitive to the presence of extreme incomes (Cowell & Victoria-Feser, 1996a, 1996b, 2002), we censored the countries' income distributions by dropping the highest percentile.[16]

3.2. Circumstances

We consider gender, age, country of origin and family background as circumstances affecting individual incomes irrespective of individual responsibility. Gender is often neglected as circumstance, probably because other authors restrict their analysis to household heads, who are typically men. However, being woman implies a disadvantage in the labour market independently of the responsibility of the individual. Similarly, in the case of age, young people lack experience, but have greater potential, whereas on average old people are characterised by the opposite condition. Since ageing is again out of individual responsibility, we consider five-year age groups.[17] Nationality identifies as native those who declare the country of birth being the same of the country of residence. The family background offers a large set of possible information, regarding education and occupation of fathers and mothers, as well as subjective perception of the family financial conditions of the interviewees when they were young. In order to maintain a minimal sample size for each definition of type, we restrict to parental education as measured by the highest educational attainment in the parent couple.[18]

Consequently, the set of circumstances identifies *96 types*, as a result of 2 genders × 2 origins × 6 age groups × 4 parental education

---

16. Van Kerm (2007) discusses how ordinal comparisons of countries are found to be robust to variants of data adjustment procedures such as trimming and winsorizing.

17. Given two surveys, which are six-year distant one from the other, we can potentially distinguish between age groups (being 30- to 35-year old) from birth cohorts (being born between 1980 and 1985). In a previous version of the paper, we replicated the analysis of correlation with institutions treating the two cross-sections as pseudo-panels, controlling for cohort effects. This has the advantage of increasing the degrees of freedom (and therefore the precision of the estimates), however, at the cost of arbitrariness in matching individual with institutional measures. Since the results were not significantly different from what presented in the next section, we have not reported them. Available from the authors.

18. The choice between parental education and parental occupation is driven by the fact that the former is statistically more relevant in affecting children incomes than the latter, given the intergenerational persistence in educational attainments. See Table A3.

categories.[19] It is important to note that the empirical estimates of "between-types" inequality of opportunity are to be interpreted as lower-bound estimates. A formal proof of the lower-bound result is contained in Ferreira and Gignoux (2011), but the intuition is straightforward: the set of circumstances, which is observed empirically and used for partitioning the population into types, is a strict subset of the set of all circumstance variables that matter in reality. The existence of unobserved circumstances guarantees that these estimates of opportunity inequality could only be higher if more circumstance variables were observed.[20] Table A2 shows reports summary statistics of both individual and parental characteristics.

3.3. Labour Market Participation

Standard analysis of income inequality abstracts from the problem of different pattern of labour market participation by referring to mean (or equivalised) household incomes, thus implicitly assuming income redistribution within the household. This solution is unsatisfactory for the problem of measuring inequality of opportunity at individual level, since part of the effect of circumstances on incomes works through labour market participation. We have considered possible alternatives to cope with this problem: including anyone out of the labour market with zero as income; replacing missing incomes with the mean of each type (corresponding to reweighting of population groups with positive incomes to account for individuals out of the labour market). All strategies avoid the explicit modelling of the selection into remunerated occupations, and for this reason, we preferred to follow an approach à la Heckman. We have estimated a selection equation into employment using parental occupation and marital status as exclusion restrictions, and an income generating process based on circumstances and own educational attainment, country by country. In our view, this represents a closer approximation to the notion of permanent

---

19. With respect to parental education, group 1 refers to individuals whose parents have at best achieved low levels (pre-primary, primary or lower secondary education), group 2 corresponds to individuals who have at least one of the parents with intermediate levels of education (upper secondary education and post-secondary non-tertiary education), group 3 are individuals with at least one of parent with college degrees (first or second stage of tertiary education) and group 4 includes all cases with missing information on parental information (which constitute a large fraction, especially in the samples of Nordic countries).
20. The distance between upper and lower bounds is analysed by Niehues and Peichl (2011).

income than other alternatives. In Table A3, we report pooled regressions, estimated separately for each survey, in order to get an idea of (average) magnitude and significance of the coefficients. Therefore, we account for the existence of unemployed *imputing to all individuals with zero income their expected income (namely, the conditional income corrected by the probability of self-selection into employment)*.

3.4. Income and Opportunity Inequality Rankings in Europe

Given this data set, we have computed alternative measures of income inequality. Starting with the estimates of overall income inequalities, we notice that the ranking based on Gini index from our data is quite consistent with the ranking provided by OECD and Eurostat (see the data in Table A4): the Spearman rank correlation between our inequality measure (Gini) and the one calculated by OECD is 0.70 in 2005 and 0.66 in 2011, and a bit lower when compared to Eurostat. This is considerable when recalling that OECD and Eurostat are based on household equivalised incomes, while we are using personal incomes (excluding unemployed for comparability reasons). The rank correlation drastically declines if we use an alternative inequality measure given by the Mean Log Deviation (MLD − see Table 3). This is not surprising, since the MLD put more weight in the calculation on low incomes, while the Gini weights more the bulk of the distribution. For this reason, in the sequel we will discuss our results in terms of Gini indices, while relegating the MLD ones in the appendix.

By looking at Fig. 1, we get a comprehensive view of country differences in terms of disposable income inequality. There is a group of "low inequality" countries, which includes Nordic countries (Sweden, Norway and Denmark) and continental countries (Netherlands and Belgium). There is a second group of "high inequality" countries, gathering market economies (Great Britain, Ireland, as well as Switzerland and Luxemburg) and Baltic countries (Latvia, Lithuania, Estonia plus Poland). A residual third group includes the Mediterranean countries (Italy, Greece, Portugal and Spain) and the central European ones.[21]

---

21. A particular case is represented by Germany, which registers an unusual high level of income inequality in 2005. Looking at the density distribution (see Fig. A1) it shows a large fraction of low incomes, which could represent the initial effect of flexibilisation introduced by the Hertz reform at the beginning of the initial decade (also known as "one-euro jobs").

Table 3.   Spearman's Rank Correlation between Alternative Inequality
Measures.

	Gini Disposable Incomes (OECD)	Gini Disposable Incomes (Eurostat)	Gini Disposable Incomes (Our Sample)	MLD Disposable Incomes (Our Sample)
2005				
Gini household equivalent disposable incomes (OECD)	1.000			
Gini household equivalent disposable incomes (Eurostat)	0.898***	1.000		
Gini individual disposable incomes (our sample)	0.701***	0.537***	1.000	
MLD individual disposable incomes (our sample)	0.294	0.076	0.708***	1.000
2011				
Gini household equivalent disposable incomes (OECD)	1.000			
Gini household equivalent disposable incomes (Eurostat)	0.891***	1.000		
Gini individual disposable incomes (our sample)	0.660***	0.661***	1.000	
MLD individual disposable incomes (our sample)	0.346	0.426**	0.707***	1.000

Statistical significance: ***$p < 0.01$, **$p < 0.05$, *$p < 0.1$.

Our choice of considering also the unemployed and those who are out of the labour market with their potential income has an impact in measuring inequality, which varies according to labour market participation in the country. In Fig. 1 we compare the inequality indices computed excluding (horizontal axis) and including these individuals (vertical axis). The vertical distance from the 45° line measures the extent of correction, which in some cases (Greece, Poland and Romania) is significant. In our view, this reinforces the need of accounting for this fraction of population, who are temporarily (or permanently) out of the labour market, also due to circumstances. For this reason, in the sequel of the paper, *we rely on inequality measures that include these individuals.*

3.5. Measuring Inequality of Opportunities

We move now to the calculation of inequality of opportunity. As illustrated in Section 2, we have replaced individual incomes for each type with their

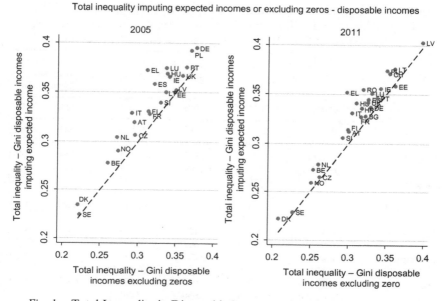

Fig. 1. Total Inequality in Disposable Incomes — EUSILC 2005 and 2011.

means and we have computed the inequality over this counterfactual distribution. This is the inequality that we would observe if all differences in effort were cancelled: this inequality is totally unfair being attributable to circumstances out of individual responsibility (between-group inequality).[22]

The ex-ante inequality of opportunity is reported in Table 4 and shown in Fig. 2 (sorting countries according to the mean of the index over the two surveys). It accounts for a large fraction of total inequality: on average it is beyond two fifths of total inequality.[23] What is more interesting is that country ranking is not necessarily identical to the one obtained with total inequality. Rich countries (Switzerland and Luxemburg) rank highest in terms of inequality of opportunities, but also Greece and Great Britain are

---

22. If we predict individual income using dummies associated to types, the parametric and the non-parametric methods provide identical results. Results do not necessarily coincide in the ex-post approach.

23. Table A5 provides the same measure using the mean log deviation, computed according to both the ex-ante and the ex-post approaches. The fraction of inequality of opportunity on total inequality is on average 0.15 in the ex-ante and 0.20 in the ex-post approach.

Table 4. Total Inequality and Inequality of Opportunities – EUSILC –
Disposable Incomes, Imputing Expected Incomes to Zero Incomes,
Estimated at Country Level Correcting for Self-Selection.

	Total Inequality – Gini		Opportunity Inequality – Gini		Opportunity Inequality Ratio – Gini	
	2005	2011	2005	2011	2005	2011
Austria	0.319	0.312	0.167	0.154	0.524	0.494
	(0.0028)	(0.0029)	(0.0011)	(0.0010)		
Belgium	0.278	0.273	0.143	0.134	0.514	0.491
	(0.0028)	(0.0028)	(0.0012)	(0.0012)		
Bulgaria	na	0.328	na	0.132	na	0.402
		(0.0027)		(0.0010)		
Switzerland	na	0.371	na	0.218	na	0.588
		(0.0031)		(0.0010)		
Czech Republic	0.307	0.265	0.126	0.123	0.41	0.464
	(0.0037)	(0.0021)	(0.0015)	(0.0008)		
Germany	0.395	0.336	0.212	0.18	0.537	0.536
	(0.0022)	(0.0019)	(0.0005)	(0.0006)		
Denmark	0.234	0.222	0.089	0.073	0.38	0.329
	(0.0023)	(0.0025)	(0.0007)	(0.0008)		
Estonia	0.35	0.358	0.137	0.129	0.391	0.36
	(0.0032)	(0.0032)	(0.0013)	(0.0011)		
Greece	0.372	0.352	0.19	0.169	0.511	0.48
	(0.0026)	(0.0027)	(0.0013)	(0.0014)		
Spain	0.358	0.344	0.168	0.124	0.469	0.36
	(0.0016)	(0.0017)	(0.0007)	(0.0007)		
Finland	0.33	0.314	0.102	0.096	0.309	0.306
	(0.0021)	(0.0025)	(0.0006)	(0.0008)		
France	0.328	0.327	0.138	0.129	0.421	0.394
	(0.0021)	(0.0022)	(0.0009)	(0.0008)		
Croatia	na	0.336	na	0.125	na	0.372
		(0.0025)		(0.0011)		
Hungary	0.369	0.341	0.146	0.133	0.396	0.39
	(0.0024)	(0.0022)	(0.0011)	(0.0008)		
Ireland	0.365	0.356	0.17	0.132	0.466	0.371
	(0.0026)	(0.0031)	(0.0012)	(0.0014)		
Italy	0.329	0.331	0.154	0.143	0.468	0.432
	(0.0014)	(0.0015)	(0.0006)	(0.0005)		
Lithuania	0.35	0.376	0.117	0.092	0.334	0.245
	(0.0032)	(0.0028)	(0.0012)	(0.0012)		
Luxembourg	0.374	0.351	0.211	0.197	0.564	0.561
	(0.0033)	(0.0026)	(0.0019)	(0.0014)		
Latvia	0.352	0.403	0.134	0.119	0.381	0.295
	(0.0036)	(0.0032)	(0.0015)	(0.0010)		

Table 4. (*Continued*)

	Total Inequality – Gini		Opportunity Inequality – Gini		Opportunity Inequality Ratio – Gini	
	2005	2011	2005	2011	2005	2011
Netherlands	0.304 (*0.0024*)	0.279 (*0.0020*)	0.182 (*0.0007*)	0.148 (*0.0005*)	0.599	0.53
Norway	0.290 (*0.0029*)	0.259 (*0.0031*)	0.131 (*0.0007*)	0.112 (*0.0010*)	0.452	0.432
Poland	0.392 (*0.0015*)	0.374 (*0.0018*)	0.146 (*0.0009*)	0.142 (*0.0008*)	0.372	0.38
Portugal	0.375 (*0.0034*)	0.346 (*0.0032*)	0.142 (*0.0020*)	0.1 (*0.0017*)	0.379	0.289
Romania	na	0.355 (*0.0027*)	na	0.153 (*0.0014*)	na	0.431
Sweden	0.224 (*0.0025*)	0.229 (*0.0022*)	0.098 (*0.001*)	0.092 (*0.001*)	0.438	0.402
Slovenia	0.339 (*0.0024*)	0.306 (*0.0018*)	0.102 (*0.0012*)	0.086 (*0.0008*)	0.301	0.281
Great Britain	0.367 (*0.0022*)	0.341 (*0.0028*)	0.155 (*0.0008*)	0.165 (*0.001*)	0.422	0.484

Values in brackets report estimates of the standard errors computed via bootstrapping (400 replications).

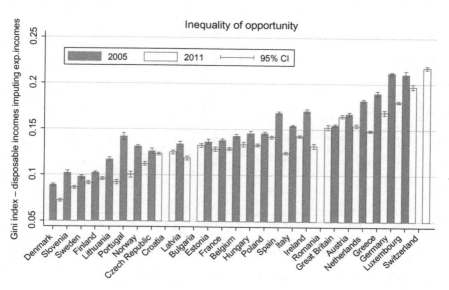

Fig. 2. Inequality of Opportunity – EUSILC 2005 and 2011.

in the group of high opportunity inequality countries. At the other extreme, the Nordic (and now the Baltic) countries rank low. The continental European countries (in particular Italy, France and Spain) are in an intermediate position, with Germany and Netherlands recording high measures of inequality of opportunity.

The relationship between total inequality and inequality of opportunity can be better analysed with the help of Fig. 3. Despite the underlying level of total inequality, some countries seem characterised by a smaller fraction of inequality of opportunity (countries significantly below the regression lines are Slovenia, Lithuania and Finland), whereas other countries score worse in terms of the same index (apart from Switzerland and Luxemburg, countries constantly above the regression line are Germany, Netherlands and Greece). In general, countries with higher income inequality are also characterised by a higher level (portion) of inequality of opportunity. This finding could be interpreted as a generalisation of the so-called "Great Gatsby" curve (Corak, 2013), showing a negative relationship between income inequality and social mobility.

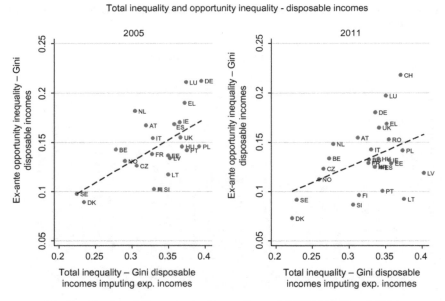

Fig. 3. Total and Opportunity Inequality — EUSILC 2005 and 2011.

We finally compare the changes over time of our inequality measures in Fig. 4. The 2005 survey (recording information on 2004 incomes) reflects a period of substantial growth, while the 2011 survey (data referred to 2010 incomes) is significantly affected by the consequences of the financial crisis. We notice that total inequality exhibits larger cyclical fluctuations when compared to inequality of opportunity, with a general trend to declining values (due to income compressions generated by the crisis). It is also interesting to notice that in few countries the inequality of opportunity remain almost stable over the time interval (Czech Republic, Poland and Hungary, but also Finland and Slovenia at a lesser extent). This may suggest that inequality of opportunity measures capture underlying mechanisms of income generation, which are deeply rooted in the country social systems.

4. THE EMPIRICAL ANALYSIS: INEQUALITY OF OPPORTUNITY AND INSTITUTIONS

There is a wide literature that aims at classifying countries according to the ways in which markets and institutions operate, and the extent of state intervention (think of the "variety of capitalism" literature, distinguishing

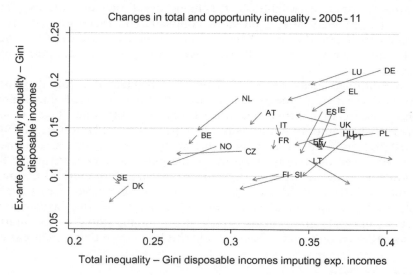

Fig. 4. Changes of Inequality Measures − EUSILC 2005−2011.

between coordinated market economies and liberal market economies – Hall & Soskice, 2001). In our case, we are interested in channels through which circumstances affect the generation of income. There are large arrays of channels through which this may operate: educational attainments, family networking, gender/age/ethnic group discrimination, to quote the most evident ones.[24] Different countries have different institutions regulating these dimensions, with different degree of effectiveness. We ask ourselves whether there is any correlation between institutional framework and observed variations (cross-country and over-time) in inequality attributable to circumstances.

In this section, we analyse the potential association between institutional characteristics and opportunity inequality. Since total inequality (and especially inequality of opportunity) are persistent variables, and institutional variables are in many cases even more persistent, it is impossible to provide a clear-cut analysis of causal impacts. Past level of inequality may have affected the access to education, which in turn may shape current level of inequality via the effect of parental education: reverse causation represents a clear issue in our case, and therefore we cannot go beyond simple correlation analysis. However, the availability of two observations for most of the countries allows us to increase the precision of our estimates, since country effects (either fixed or random) control for omitted variables. Let us finally recall that institutions come in clusters (namely, they tend to be collinear) and therefore it is often difficult to isolate the contribution of one specific feature keeping other institutions constant (especially when we can rely on two data points per country only).

Institutional measures are themselves problematic, for they are mostly derived from categorical variables that describe procedures (presence/absence of a provision, alternatives available, and stages to be accomplished) and do not measure their effectiveness. However, we may (partially) account for this by resorting to proxy variables, obtained from observed behaviour of people acting under a given institution. To provide an example, we know that for historical and/or cultural reasons, countries differ in childcare availability. Counting the number of available kindergartens would be a possible candidate for this institutional feature, but data are difficult to collect on a comparable cross-country basis. Resorting to the fraction of children attending kindergarten

---

24. See the classification proposed by Dardanoni, Fields, Roemer, and Sánchez Puerta (2006).

constitutes a reasonable alternative, which is much simpler to be collected from international/national statistical offices. As with most of institutional measures, this variable is potentially endogenous, since we ignore whether children do not attend kindergartens because they are not available, because their mothers prefer housewifery and/or because most of the population still live in enlarged families (where grandparents take care of nursing). Nevertheless, the literature suggests that early schooling may contribute to reducing the role of parental background in competence formation (e.g. Cunha & Heckman, 2007; Heckman, Krueger, & Friedman, 2002). Therefore, other things constant we expect that countries where children attend kindergarten more be also characterised by lower inequality of opportunity, since income differences generated by circumstances should be lower. In the same vein, we know that the stratification of the educational system may reinforce the impact of parental education, since low-educated parents may prevent their kids from aspiring to more academic-oriented careers (see, e.g. Brunello & Checchi, 2007; Hanushek & Wößmann, 2006). The quality of education may also play a role, since it may compensate the disadvantage of students coming from poor environment. Unfortunately, data on school quality are not easily available (unless one is ready to consider students achievements as a proxy for "revealed" quality). More modestly, we have considered the student/teacher ratio as proxy for quality of education. We have put our best effort to collect information on educational features that were available for the largest set of countries in our sample. In order to minimise the endogeneity risk, we take the institutional measures averaged over the previous five years (2000–2004 for individuals surveyed in 2005 and 2006–2010 for individuals surveyed in 2011). Descriptive statistics are reported in Table 5, while data sources are in Table A6.

When we consider labour market institutions, we expect that wage compressing institutions may reduce within-group variance in earnings (and therefore incomes), with limited impact on between-group inequality. Here, data availability, especially for new entrants in the EU, is limited (since some of them do not belong to OECD, which is our main source of information). We consider here the traditional measures of the degree of institutionalisation: the presence of unions (proxied by union membership over dependent employment, the degree of bargaining coverage, the degree of bargaining centralisation), the degree of employment protection, the presence of minimum wages (relative to mean wages), the unemployment benefit and the tax wedge (which are often correlated, since the latter

Table 5. Descriptive Statistics – 2000–2004 and 2006–2010.

Variable	Obs	Countries	Mean	Std. Dev.	Min	Max
Inequality measures						
Total inequality (Gini) – disposable incomes (excluding richest 1% – imputing expected income to unemployed)	49	26	32.959	4.539	22.222	40.285
Ex-ante inequality of opportunities (Gini) – disposable incomes (excluding richest 1% – imputing expected income)	49	26	13.951	3.421	7.260	21.822
Educational institutions						
Expenditure per student, primary (% of GDP per capita)	55	28	20.529	4.662	10.963	31.072
Expenditure per student, secondary (% of GDP per capita)	56	29	25.603	5.411	14.144	38.640
Expenditure per student, tertiary (% of GDP per capita)	53	27	31.984	11.600	15.955	69.811
Government expenditure on education as % of GDP (%)	56	29	5.403	1.164	3.285	8.385
Expenditure on education as % of total government expenditure (%)	54	28	12.324	2.418	4.531	16.813
Primary education, duration (years)	58	29	5.475	1.073	4.000	8.000
Adjusted savings: education expenditure (% of GNI)	58	29	5.074	1.179	2.899	8.173
Pupil–teacher ratio in primary education	51	26	13.981	2.945	9.640	19.495
Pupil–teacher ratio in secondary education	50	26	11.097	1.697	7.252	15.213
Percentage of students in secondary education enrolled in vocational programmes	58	26	24.911	10.255	6.477	46.810
Gross enrolment ratio, pre-primary, both sexes (%)	57	29	86.716	17.131	47.525	123.083
Expenditure on pre-primary as % of government expenditure on education (%)	54	27	8.961	3.534	0.059	19.777
Labour market institutions						
Union density	58	29	35.395	21.343	7.232	89.609
Coverage rate	57	29	62.846	25.269	11.156	100.000
Bargaining centralisation	56	28	0.386	0.152	0.102	0.928
Employment protection legislation	42	23	2.422	0.666	1.198	4.550
Minimum wage/mean wage	58	29	0.590	0.304	0.287	1.000
Unemployment subsidy replacement rate	56	29	35.454	15.799	5.945	61.774
Tax wedge	56	29	25.162	7.906	8.167	40.593
Active labour market policy/GDP	54	28	0.591	0.439	0.044	1.872
Passive labour market policy/GDP	54	28	0.909	0.663	0.130	2.456
Social expenditure/GDP	57	29	2.184	0.864	1.048	3.678
Parental leave – weeks of absence	42	21	59.482	49.340	16.000	214.000

partially finances the former), the existence of active and passive labour market programmes, the generosity of the welfare state (proxied by social expenditure over the gross domestic product) and the possibility of intra-household redistribution of housewifing (proxied by the availability of parental leaves).

In accordance with the literature, we expect that when the labour market is heavily regulated, wages are less related to individual features, since unions press for job-related pay scales (Visser & Checchi, 2009). In addition, employment protection reduces labour turnover, reducing individual income variability (and therefore aggregate wage inequality). Both measures have been proven reducing total income inequality in the aggregate (Checchi & García Peñalosa, 2008). Minimum wages also contribute to the containment of total inequality, which may reflect into the abatement of inequality of opportunity (Salverda & Checchi, 2015). When we consider the role of welfare provisions, we do not have a priori theoretical expectation on their correlation with inequality of opportunity, since taxes and subsidies aim to contain income inequality (through taxation) and to provide income insurance against unforeseeable events (through subsidies), but in few cases they include compensatory measures which attenuate the impact of circumstances. However, as long as fiscal redistribution sustains low incomes (that may be correlated to disadvantaged conditions), we could find some positive correlation with such inequality.

Despite fully recognising the clustered nature of institutions, we start initially with bivariate correlation between different measures of inequality of opportunity and institutional proxies. In Table 6 we report total inequality as reference in column (1) and ex-ante inequality of opportunity in columns (2). We observe that total inequality is reduced in country/years where/when public expenditure in education is high, as well as pre-primary education attracts more pupil and/or vocational education prevent school drop-out. Conversely inequality of opportunity is negatively correlated with fewer dimensions of public expenditure in education. When we consider labour market institutions, correlations are consistent with theoretical expectations: unions and centralised bargaining reduce total inequality, and similar correlation obtains for minimum wage, active and passive labour market policies and social expenditure. Vice versa inequality of opportunity seems rather independent from labour market institutions, except when exhibits negative correlation with union membership and unemployment benefit replacement rate.

Table 6. Pairwise Correlations – 26 Countries – Income Inequality Measured in 2005 and 2011 – Institutions Measured by Average of Previous Five Years.

	(1) Total Incomes Inequality (Gini)	(2) Opportunity Inequality (Gini)
Educational institutions		
Expenditure per student, primary (% of GDP per capita)	−0.075	−0.286*
Expenditure per student, secondary (% of GDP per capita)	−0.494***	−0.474***
Expenditure per student, tertiary (% of GDP per capita)	−0.746***	−0.162
Government expenditure on education as % of GDP (%)	−0.680***	−0.616***
Expenditure on education as % of total government expenditure (%)	−0.267*	−0.443***
Primary education, duration (years)	−0.155	−0.030
Adjusted savings: education expenditure (% of GNI)	−0.588***	−0.638***
Pupil−teacher ratio in primary education	0.064	0.006
Pupil−teacher ratio in secondary education	−0.008	0.276*
Percentage of students in secondary education enrolled in vocational programme	−0.492***	−0.026
Gross enrolment ratio, pre-primary, both sexes (%)	−0.331**	0.107
Expenditure on pre-primary as % of government expenditure on education (%)	0.043	−0.241*
Labour market institutions		
Union density	−0.652***	−0.365***
Coverage rate	−0.533***	−0.091
Bargaining centralisation	−0.338**	−0.037
Employment protection legislation	−0.031	−0.122
Minimum wage/mean wage	−0.465***	−0.107
Unemployment subsidy replacement rate	−0.217	−0.441***
Tax wedge	−0.435***	−0.166
Active labour market policy/GDP	−0.600***	−0.152
Passive labour market policy/GDP	−0.315**	−0.035
Social expenditure/GDP	−0.443***	−0.100
Parental leave − weeks of absence	−0.027	−0.0845

Statistical significance: ***$p < 0.01$, **$p < 0.05$, *$p < 0.1$.

When we take these correlations to more stringent tests using multivariate analysis (and even controlling for either random or fixed country effects), only few institutional dimensions survive. Some of them have limited variation and are likely to be absorbed by country effects. A serious problem is the limited number of degrees of freedom, due to missing values.[25] In order not to lose information, we have imputed missing values using the sample means over each year, introducing a dummy variable controlling for imputation. In Table 7, we report the OLS regressions when pooling countries and controlling for either random or fixed country effects.[26] Educational expenditure (and its share devoted to pre-primary education) are the only educational variables retaining statistical significance with inequality of opportunity, irrespective of the specification: other things constant, an increase in the allocation of public educational expenditure to pre-primary education reduces the inequality of opportunity. In addition, an increase in union density and/or in passive labour market expenditure seems reducing opportunity inequality, but the effects are statistically weaker.

Notice that total inequality and inequality of opportunity obtain statistical significance in correlation with different regressors. Total inequality (which reflects both between-group and within-group components[27]) is significantly correlated with union density and labour market policies, both of the active and passive variety. Among the educational variables, only the fraction of students in the vocational track (an often used proxy for the degree of secondary school stratification) exhibits negative correlation.

We could therefore conclude that inequality of opportunity seems associated to institutional dimensions that operate before the entrance in the labour market and/or when (temporary) excluded by the same market (as in the case of recipients of unemployment benefits). In particular, the expenditure in education seems the most effective instrument available to governments. Fig. 5 well summarise this point: on the left panel, we observe that countries with the highest level of public expenditure in education are also the countries with the lowest level of inequality of opportunity; symmetrically (but rather independently – the correlation of the two

---

25. Notice that we cannot include time invariant variables (like duration of primary education, coverage or bargaining centralisation) because they are alternative to country fixed effects. In addition, when we use only non-missing information on all available institutional variables, we are left with 29 observations and 15 countries, which renders the model estimated in Table 7 meaningless.

26. Table A7 replicates the estimates using the MLD as inequality measures, both under ex-ante and ex-post approaches. Results are similar with those commented in the text and will not be discussed further.

27. Though the Gini index is not neatly decomposable in these two components, the Mean Log Deviation reported in the Appendix is, but results are very similar.

Table 7. Inequality and Institutions – 26 Countries – 2005 and 2011 – Disposable Incomes (Imputing Expected Incomes to Zero Incomes).

	Total inequality (Gini)			Ex-ante opportunity inequality (Gini)		
	1	2	3	4	5	6
	Pooled	Random effects	Fixed effects	Pooled	Random effects	Fixed effects
Education expenditure (% of GNI)	-0.25	-0.695	-0.85	-1.702**	-1.417**	-0.485
	[0.836]	[0.777]	[1.055]	[0.775]	[0.628]	[0.592]
Pupil–teacher ratio in primary education	-0.146	-0.228	-0.432	-0.24	-0.081	-0.006
	[0.186]	[0.200]	[0.310]	[0.142]	[0.125]	[0.102]
% Students in secondary education enrolled in vocational programmes	-0.106**	-0.099*	0.214*	0.057	0.02	0.029
	[0.046]	[0.053]	[0.118]	[0.037]	[0.044]	[0.081]
Expenditure on pre-primary as % of govern. expenditure on education	-0.208	-0.215	-0.073	-0.309***	-0.317**	-0.380**
	[0.132]	[0.156]	[0.240]	[0.097]	[0.131]	[0.140]
Union density	-0.094**	-0.101**	-0.25	-0.090**	-0.088*	-0.022
	[0.038]	[0.042]	[0.187]	[0.038]	[0.045]	[0.095]
Parental leave – weeks of absence	-0.016	-0.006	0.065**	-0.023*	-0.01	-0.006
	[0.016]	[0.016]	[0.025]	[0.013]	[0.011]	[0.011]
Unemployment subsidy replacement rate	-0.029	0.000	0.054	-0.060*	-0.021	0.132*
	[0.044]	[0.047]	[0.078]	[0.033]	[0.034]	[0.064]
Active labour market policy/GDP	-8.478***	-6.184***	5.144	1.6	2.012*	1.868
	[1.768]	[1.456]	[3.705]	[1.624]	[1.128]	[1.364]
Passive labour market policy/GDP	3.216***	2.455**	-0.731	-0.893	-0.785	-1.977**
	[1.136]	[1.017]	[1.414]	[0.892]	[0.605]	[0.826]
Minimum wage/mean wage	1.089	0.789	23.374	3.578*	3.355	27.171
	[1.612]	[1.593]	[26.470]	[1.868]	[2.277]	[17.443]
Observations	49	49	49	49	49	49
Number of country	26	26	26	26	26	26
R^2 (within)	0.749	0.201	0.591	0.714	0.654	0.839
Hausman test (p-value)		9.48 (0.57)			19.62 (0.05)	

Robust standard errors in brackets – ***$p < 0.01$, **$p < 0.05$, *$p < 0.1$ errors clustered by country – constant and year included.

expenditure variable is −0.22), the right panel shows that favouring pre-primary education among other items of public expenditure is also associated to low opportunity inequality. We find therefore additional supportive evidence to the argument put forward by Heckman et al. (2002) that pre-primary education is a powerful instrument to attenuate social disperities.

Conversely, standard labour market institutions contribute to the attenuation of income inequality. It is worth remembering that these inequalities are measured at individual level, and are therefore more pronounced than those recorded when intra-household redistribution takes place (as in the case when equivalised incomes are considered).

5. CONCLUDING REMARKS

In this paper, we present measures of total income inequality and inequality of opportunities in 26 European countries by using the EU-SILC database, for two survey years, 2005 and 2011. Inequality has been measured by

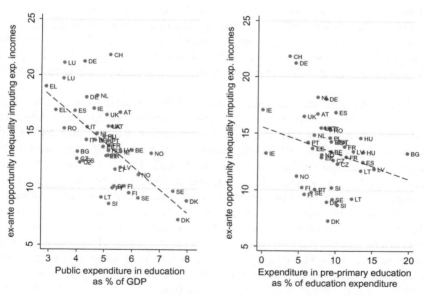

Fig. 5. Educational Expenditure and Inequality of Opportunity.

taking into account both individuals with positive incomes and individuals without income, by imputing them their potential incomes: as a consequence, total inequality tends to be higher than usually recorded by official statistics, for a large set of countries. We have shown that standard income inequality and inequality of opportunities do not necessarily offer the same type of country orderings, even if Nordic countries score low under both measures. At the other tail of the ranking, rich countries (like Switzerland and Luxemburg) score highest, but also Netherlands and Germany are characterised by high inequality of opportunity.

We have also shown that total income inequality exhibits larger fluctuations than inequality of opportunities, indicating that the latter is more persistent than the former. This could be taken as evidence of income formation being deeply affected by the set of circumstances we have selected (gender, age, nationality and parental education).

Different social and economic mechanisms may generate the income and opportunity inequalities we observe: the working of the educational system contributes to attenuating the influences of some circumstances, which can be effective pre-market (like family background, ethnicity or even gender). Once the individual enters the labour market (an event which is also dependent on the same set of circumstances), other types of institutions (like unions or labour policies) may contribute to contain income inequalities.

Our search for correlation between inequalities and institutional variables shows that labour market institutions are negatively associated to total inequalities, while educational expenditure (and pre-primary education expenditure in particular) is negatively associated with inequality of opportunities.

Two *caveats* should be kept in mind while evaluating our results. The first *caveat* concerns the selection of circumstances. We have assumed that the selected circumstances affect income formation, but we formally do not prove it. In principle, we should include in the set of circumstances only factors that causally affect income formation. Take, for example, the variable "country of origin". This variable implies a negative premium in income formation in most countries. However, being born in a different country may be the reflection of an intentional choice (migration) or the effect of parental choice, or even the outcome of accidental events (marriage). The impossibility of distinguishing among these alternatives renders our exercise a purely descriptive one, where inequality is decomposed according to arbitrary (though plausible) assumptions.

The second *caveat* relates to the treatment of effort in the equality of opportunity framework and, specifically, in the ex-ante approach.

According to this approach, once the circumstances are identified, any other factor affecting income is treated as socially acceptable. This includes effort, but also unobservable ability or simply luck. Moreover, we have used a reduced form model, where the individual choice of effort is only implicit and not explicitly modelled. This strategy is obviously constrained by data availability, but is exposed to possible criticisms. As openly discussed by Ravallion (2015), any social evaluation of inequalities, both total or opportunity ones, should be sensitive to the individual effort and to the disutility of effort associated with a given income level. After all, we measure income inequality because we are ultimately interested in the distribution of welfare among individuals. And, the argument goes, the disutility of effort, together with the income attained, is a component of the individual welfare. While this point is well taken, its full recognition requires an explicit theoretical model of the choice of effort which goes beyond the reduced form approach followed in this paper (and in most of the literature developed so far), requiring a richer data set to identify individual effort. The search for better ways to model and to measure intentions and efforts is our future line of research. In this respect, the EUSILC surveys do not offer a large array of measures for potential effort, and we have to resort to national data sets, undermining the comparability of the results.

REFERENCES

Aaberge, R., Mogstad, M., & Peragine, V. (2011). Measuring long-term inequality of opportunity. *Journal of Public Economics, 95*, 193–204.

Alesina, A., & La Ferrara, E. (2005). Preferences for redistribution in the land of opportunities. *Journal of Public Economics, 89*, 897–931.

Bourguignon, F., Ferreira, F. H. G., & Walton, M. (2007). Equity, efficiency and inequality traps: A research agenda. *Journal of Economic Inequality, 5*, 235–256.

Brunello, G., & Checchi, D. (2007). Does school tracking affect equality of opportunity? New international evidence. *Economic Policy, 52*, 781–861.

Brunori, P., Ferreira, F. H. G., & Peragine, V. (2013). *Inequality of opportunity, income inequality and economic mobility: Some international comparisons.* World Bank Policy Research Working Paper No. 6304.

Brunori, P., Palmisano, F., & Peragine, V. (2015). *Inequality of opportunity in sub saharan Africa.* ECINEQ wp 2015.

Checchi, D., & García Peñalosa, C. (2008). Labour market institutions and income inequality. *Economic Policy, 23*, 601–649.

Checchi, D., & Peragine, V. (2010). Inequality of opportunity in Italy. *Journal of Economic Inequality, 8*, 429–450.

Checchi, D., Peragine, V., & Serlenga, L. (2010). *Fair and unfair income inequalities in Europe.* IZA Discussion Paper No. 5025/2010.

Corak, M. (2013). Income inequality, equality of opportunity, and intergenerational mobility. *Journal of Economic Perspectives, 27*, 79–102.

Cowell, F. A., & Victoria-Feser, M. P. (1996a). Poverty measurement with contaminated data: A robust approach. *European Economic Review, 40*, 1761–1771.

Cowell, F. A., & Victoria-Feser, M. P. (1996b). Robustness properties of inequality measures. *Econometrica, 64*, 77–101.

Cowell, F. A., & Victoria-Feser, M. P. (2002). Welfare rankings in the presence of contaminated data. *Econometrica, 70*, 1221–1233.

Cunha, F., & Heckman, J. (2007). The technology of skill formation. *American Economic Review, 97*, 31–47.

Dardanoni, V., Fields, G. S., Roemer, J. E., & Sánchez Puerta, M. L. (2006). How demanding should equality of opportunity be, and how much have we achieved? In D. G. Gary Fields & S. Morgan (Eds.), *Mobility and inequality: Frontiers of research from sociology and economics*. Stanford, CA: Stanford University Press.

Ferreira, F. H. G., & Gignoux, J. (2011). The measurement of inequality of opportunity: Theory and an application to latin America. *Review of Income and Wealth, 57*(4), 622–657.

Ferreira, F. H. G., Lakner, C., Lugo, M. A., & Ozler, B. (2014). *Inequality of opportunity and economic growth: A cross-country analysis*. Policy Research Working Paper Series No. 6915, The World Bank.

Ferreira, F. H. G., & Peragine, V. (2015). Individual responsibility and equality of opportunity. In M. Adler & M. Fleurbaey (Eds.), *Handbook of well being and public policy*. Oxford: Oxford University Press.

Fleurbaey, M. (1995). Three solutions for the compensation problem. *Journal of Economic Theory, 65*, 505–521.

Fleurbaey, M. (2008). *Fairness, responsibility and welfare*. Oxford: Oxford University Press.

Fleurbaey, M., & Peragine, V. (2013). Ex-ante versus ex-post equality of opportunity. *Economica, 80*, 118–130.

Hall, P., & Soskice, D. (2001). *Varieties of capitalism: The institutional foundations of comparative advantage*. Oxford: Oxford University Press.

Hanushek, E., & Wößmann, L. (2006). Does educational tracking affect performance and inequality? Differences-in-differences evidence across countries. *Economic Journal, 116*, C63–C76.

Heckman, J. J., Krueger, A. B., & Friedman, B. M. (2002). *Inequality in America: What role for human capital policies?* Cambridge, MA: MIT Press.

Marrero, G. A., & Rodríguez, J. G. (2012). Inequality of opportunity in Europe. *Review of Income and Wealth, 58*(4), 597–621.

Marrero, G. A., & Rodríguez, J. G. (2013). Inequality of opportunity and growth. *Journal of Development Economics, 104*, 107–122.

Niehues, J., & Peichl, A. (2011). Upper and lower bounds of inequality of opportunity: Theory and evidence for Germany and the U.S. mimeo.

Peragine, V. (2002). Opportunity egalitarianism and income inequality: A rank-dependent approach. *Mathematical Social Sciences, 44*, 45–64.

Ramos, X., & Van de Gaer, D. (2015). Empirical approaches to inequality of opportunity: Principles, measures, and evidence. *Journal of Economic Surveys*, doi: 10.1111/joes.12121.

Ravallion, M. (2015). *Inequality when effort matters*. NBER wp n.21394.

Roemer, J. E. (1993). A pragmatic theory of responsibility for the egalitarian planner. *Philosophy and Public Affairs, 22*, 146–166.

Roemer, J. E. (1998). *Equality of opportunity.* Cambridge, MA: Harvard University Press.

Roemer, J., & Trannoy, A. (2015). Equality of opportunity. In A. Atkinson & F. Bourguignon (Eds.), *Handbook of income distribution* (Vol. 2B). Amsterdam, North Holland.

Salverda, W., & Checchi, D. (2015). Labour-market institutions and the dispersion of wage earnings. In A. Atkinson & F. Bourguignon (Eds.), *Handbook of income distribution* (Vol. 2B, pp. 1535–1728). Amsterdam, North Holland.

Theil, H. (1979a). The measurement of inequality by components of income. *Economics Letters, 2,* 197–199.

Theil, H. (1979b). World income inequality and its components. *Economics Letters, 2,* 99–102.

Thévenon, O., & Solaz, A. (2013). *Labour market effects of parental leave policies in OECD Countries.* OECD Social, Employment and Migration Working Papers, No. 141, OECD Publishing, Paris. doi:10.1787/5k8xb6hw1wjf-en

Van Kerm, P. (2007). *Extreme incomes and the estimation of poverty and inequality indicators from EU-SILC.* IRISS Working Paper Series No. 2007-01.

Visser, J., & Checchi, D. (2009). Inequality and the labour market: Unions. In W. Salverda, B. Nolan, & T. Smeeding (Eds.), *Oxford handbook of economic inequality.* Oxford: Oxford University Press.

World Bank. (2006). *World development report 2006: Equity and development.* Washington, DC: The World Bank and Oxford University Press.

APPENDIX

The original data files report information on gross or net incomes according to country-specific collection rules. The survey conducted in 2011 was the first one requiring all countries (31) to report information on gross values, while only two-thirds (20 countries) provided information on net incomes.[28]

We have taken advantage of the existence of both gross and net values in 2005 to estimate a tax schedule (net values regressed on a polynomial of the gross values up to 4th grade, plus control for gender and marital status) for two countries (Germany and Great Britain). Under the assumption of invariance of the tax legislation, these schedules have then been used to obtain net income values for 2011. Conversely, for other five countries (Greece, Spain, Italy, Latvia and Portugal), we exploited the existence of gross and net values in 2011 to impute gross values in 2005. For five more countries (Denmark, Finland, Hungary, Netherlands and Norway), we have used information on the country tax legislation to obtain net values from gross ones, again under the assumption of constant legislation (see tables 8–12 in Checchi et al., 2010).

The imputed values are italicized in Table A1, which reports mean incomes (in Euros). As a result, we are able to compute inequality indices for 57 countries/year using gross incomes, and 50 countries/year using disposable incomes.

Table A2 provides descriptive statistics for the output variables (gross and disposable income) and for the available circumstances. Samples are rather similar across the two waves as far as gender and age composition, while parental education is improving over surveys in almost all countries. Variations in median incomes and fraction of population with zero gross income (a proxy for the unemployment rate) reflect different growth trajectories and cyclical fluctuations.

Table A3 estimates the income generating function, controlling for self-selection into positive values for disposable incomes, pooling all countries together; country fixed effects are included, in order to control for country differences (in means). In the calculation of inequality measures, we have estimated an identical model for each occurrence country/survey, in order to improve the fit of the model to the country-specific data. The conditional income multiplied by the probability of selection constitutes our imputed expected incomes for individuals who record zero incomes. Since additional

---

28. Cyprus provided information on net incomes for only 62 individuals over 4,589, and we have therefore considered these cases equivalent to missing.

Table A1. Information on Availability on Gross and Net Values —
Mean Incomes.

Country	2005		2011	
	Gross income	Disposable income	Gross income	Disposable income
Austria AT	20594.0	15576.8	26584.6	19576.1
Belgium BE	21395.2	15985.6	25850.1	19573.0
Bulgaria BG	na	na	2776.9	2396.6
Switzerland CH	na	na	47821.7	41383.3
Cyprus CY	15033.2	na	19821.1	na
Czech Republic CZ	4718.6	3463.4	8342.1	6169.3
Germany DE	22097.8	16061.0	25259.7	*19212.4*
Denmark DK	35916.8	*26050.4*	44467.0	*31187.5*
Estonia EE	3536.4	2943.0	6104.4	5294.6
Greece EL	*10729.3*	9063.6	11552.7	9370.8
Spain ES	*9850.6*	9812.1	12967.8	11830.3
Finland FI	22850.4	*20390.3*	29434.4	*25667.3*
France FR	19192.6	16486.3	22368.3	19304.1
Croatia HR	na	na	5789.5	4885.8
Hungary HU	3493.3	*2739.2*	4606.7	*3543.3*
Ireland IE	21644.0	18480.1	22182.4	19348.5
Iceland IS	33299.2	na	26366.8	na
Italy IT	*16395.5*	13124.6	20077.1	15363.0
Lithuania LT	2763.8	2070.0	4363.6	3563.2
Luxemburg LU	30754.4	26200.2	36022.4	29931.5
Latvia LV	*2255.6*	2178.7	4753.7	4073.4
Malta MT	na	na	11322.1	na
Netherlands NL	24814.4	*21649.2*	33934.9	*27639.7*
Norway NO	32261.2	*29502.2*	49110.3	*41660.4*
Poland PL	2756.0	2234.9	5481.0	4349.5
Portugal PT	*8185.9*	7077.7	9826.2	7978.5
Romania RO	na	na	2147.4	1752.1
Sweden SE	23653.7	18367.7	29136.8	23356.2
Slovenia SI	10516.0	7930.6	13993.8	10647.3
Slovakia SK	3029.9	na	6714.1	na
United Kingdom UK	25413.5	19205.9	22306.7	*17012.2*

information (like own education, parental occupation and marital status)
do not enter the set of circumstances, the imputed incomes for the unemployed and they have not contain additional information beyond their
circumstances.

Table A4 compares inequality measures from alternative sources
(OECD, Eurostat and our own sample), and it is used to compute the correlation matrix reported in Table 3 in the text.

Table A2. Descriptive Statistics – EUSILC – Population Aged 30–60.

2005	AT	BE	BG	CH	CY	CZ	DE	DK	EE	EL	ES	FI	FR	HR	HU
Obs	5,703	5,418			4,740	4,338	13,371	7,017	4,626	6,070	15,672	12,999	10,144		7,428
Median gross income (>0)	23,800	27,932			17,226	5,362	25,365	37,834	3,806	14,541	12,449	24,011	21,303		3,840
Median disposable income (>0)	16,949	17,287				3,951	16260	28,212	2,914	11,900	12,000	22,368	16,941		3,145
Female	0.52	0.52			0.53	0.53	0.57	0.52	0.54	0.52	0.53	0.51	0.52		0.52
Age (years)	44.67	44.85			44.87	45.61	45.52	45.35	45.53	44.66	44.48	46.67	44.96		44.98
Foreign	0.09	0.08			0.09	0.01	0.05	0.04	0.15	0.06	0.05	0.02	0.09		0.02
Parental education: primary	0.06	0.05			0.01	0.02	0.09	0.52	0.06	0.01	0.03	0.54	0.04		0.03
Parental education: secondary	0.54	0.58			0.79	0.21	0.14	0.19	0.41	0.86	0.83	0.30	0.65		0.48
Parental education: college	0.36	0.21			0.14	0.70	0.48	0.20	0.37	0.08	0.06	0.09	0.22		0.41
Pop. with zero gross incomes	0.20	0.27			0.21	0.18	0.17	0.08	0.17	0.32	0.30	0.11	0.18		0.24

2011	AT	BE	BG	CH	CY	CZ	DE	DK	EE	EL	ES	FI	FR	HR	HU
Obs	6,097	5,892	6,989	7,433	4,544	8,538	12,342	5,781	5,233	5,990	15,174	9,550	10,859	6,808	13,067
Median gross income (>0)	28,200	31,013	3,068	50,460	20,800	9,377	29,512	46,181	6,520	15,740	17,080	30,519	24,060	8,068	5,304
Median disposable income (>0)	19,946	20,700	2,454	43,648		7,214	17,608	33,506	5,113	12,902	13,800	27,613	19,658	5,762	4,322
Female	0.53	0.52	0.51	0.54	0.55	0.52	0.54	0.53	0.52	0.52	0.52	0.50	0.52	0.52	0.54
Age (years)	45.36	45.03	46.19	45.73	45.57	45.56	46.50	46.66	45.77	45.26	45.07	46.52	45.70	47.05	46
Foreign	0.10	0.11	0.00	0.10	0.12	0.01	0.06	0.05	0.13	0.08	0.07	0.03	0.07	0.11	0.00
Parental education: primary	0.02	0.09	0.06	0.10	0.01	0.24	0.10	0.53	0.07	0.10	0.04	0.51	0.05	0.12	0.02
Parental education: secondary	0.37	0.47	0.49	0.22	0.72	0.46	0.10	0.15	0.32	0.71	0.81	0.24	0.73	0.53	0.61
Parental education: college	0.47	0.23	0.35	0.52	0.19	0.23	0.54	0.19	0.41	0.12	0.07	0.14	0.10	0.29	0.27
No incomes	0.16	0.23	0.16	0.10	0.17	0.17	0.17	0.07	0.19	0.31	0.31	0.10	0.14	0.36	0.22
Yearly change median gross income	2.87	1.76			3.19	9.76	2.56	3.38	9.39	1.33	5.41	4.08	2.05		5.53
Yearly change median disposable inc	2.75	3.05				10.55	1.34	2.91	9.82	1.36	2.36	3.57	2.51		5.44

2005

2005	IE	IS	IT	LT	LU	LV	MT	NL	NO	PL	PT	RO	SE	SI	SK	UK
Obs	5,988	3,575	24,795	5,041	4,234	3,766		10,941	6,855	19,611	5,252		6,412	12,305	6,709	10,608
Median gross income (>0)	27,066	32,911	20,570	2,894	36,780	2,436		28,278	35,064	3,909	8,010		25,672	10,541	3,648	28,291
Median disposable income (>0)	20,327		15,836	22,78	29,190	2,165		27,282	33,635	2,431	6,838		18,450	8,024		19,639
Female	0.53	0.51	0.51	0.55	0.51	0.55		0.52	0.51	0.53	0.52		0.52	0.51	0.53	0.52
Age (years)	45.48	44.75	44.45	45.62	44.24	45.07		44.71	44.73	45.58	45.28		45.32	45.29	45.49	44.68
Foreign	0.03	0.02	0.04	0.06	0.09	0.16		0.05	0.05	0.00	0.01		0.09	0.11	0.00	0.10
Parental education: primary	0.29	0.58	0.01	0.03	0.04	0.03		0.54	0.51	0.04	0.06		0.54	0.66	0.03	0.26
Parental education: secondary	0.55	0.16	0.84	0.64	0.55	0.51		0.30	0.13	0.57	0.89		0.32	0.19	0.39	0.47
Parental education: college	0.10	0.21	0.12	0.24	0.29	0.34		0.09	0.20	0.34	0.02		0.07	0.13	0.50	0.15
No incomes	0.29	0.06	0.25	0.20	0.27	0.22		0.15	0.09	0.39	0.26		0.09	0.06	0.21	0.23

2011

2011	IS	IT	LT	LU	LV	MT	NL	NO	PL	PT	RO	SE	SI	SK	UK	IS
Obs	4,233	3,648	20,652	5,296	6,632	6,296	4,654	11,179	4,927	15,238	5,755	7,699	6,469	12,926	6,712	7,245
Median gross income (>0)	29,483	25,905	23,385	4,677	39,169	4,787	16,412	35,465	51,118	7,035	10,191	2,880	30,967	14,925	7,500	24,197
Median disposable income (>0)	20,960		17,944	3,791	31,163	3,889		31,864	45,198	4,844	7,899	2,092	24,082	11,102		14,721
Female	0.53	0.51	0.52	0.54	0.52	0.55	0.52	0.53	0.51	0.52	0.53	0.52	0.52	0.51	0.53	0.54
Age (years)	44.08	45.67	45.32	47.58	44.57	45.95	46.52	46.22	45.50	45.96	46.03	46.18	45.67	45.58	45.62	4559.00
Foreign	0.07	0.04	0.06	0.06	0.10	0.14	0.06	0.05	0.05	0.00	0.06	0.00	0.10	0.12	0.00	0.09
Parental education: primary	0.26	0.57	0.03	0.06	0.01	0.05	0.08	0.52	0.50	0.09	0.02	0.09	0.61	0.65	0.02	0.18
Parental education: secondary	0.35	0.13	0.75	0.55	0.53	0.39	0.68	0.19	0.12	0.45	0.92	0.78	0.13	0.24	0.35	0.45
Parental education: college	0.27	0.23	0.17	0.28	0.33	0.40	0.18	0.18	0.21	0.40	0.03	0.10	0.16	0.07	0.55	0.19
No incomes	0.35	0.07	0.21	0.24	0.23	0.21	0.36	0.11	0.07	0.30	0.25	0.30	0.08	0.16	0.17	0.22
Yearly change median gross income	1.44	-3.91	2.16	8.33	1.05	11.92		3.85	6.48	10.29	4.10		3.17	5.97	12.76	-2.57
Yearly change median disposable inc	0.51		2.10	8.86	1.10	10.25		2.62	5.05	12.18	2.43		4.54	5.56		-4.69

Table A3. Income Generating Process with Self-Selection into Employment – EUSILC.

Dependent variable	1 Log disposable income	2 Selection into positive incomes	3 Log disposable income	4 Selection into positive incomes
Survey year	2005	2005	2011	2011
Female	−0.426***	−0.691***	−0.376***	−0.555***
	[0.044]	[0.076]	[0.038]	[0.067]
Foreign born	−0.140***	−0.308***	−0.178***	−0.278***
	[0.035]	[0.068]	[0.028]	[0.060]
Age group = 36−40	0.087***	0.088***	0.099***	0.091***
	[0.012]	[0.026]	[0.010]	[0.020]
Age group = 41−45	0.160***	0.106***	0.173***	0.118***
	[0.017]	[0.026]	[0.012]	[0.034]
Age group = 46−50	0.186***	0.083**	0.204***	0.122***
	[0.018]	[0.035]	[0.013]	[0.038]
Age group = 51−50	0.151***	−0.024	0.184***	0.014
	[0.026]	[0.049]	[0.017]	[0.041]
Age group = 56−60	−0.018	−0.437***	0.077***	−0.329***
	[0.064]	[0.053]	[0.025]	[0.057]
Personal attainment = primary education	0.196	0.192	0.086	0.203**
	[0.122]	[0.129]	[0.063]	[0.099]
Personal attainment = lower secondary education	0.369***	0.293***	0.244***	0.303***
	[0.123]	[0.104]	[0.064]	[0.104]
Personal attainment = (upper) secondary education	0.577***	0.562***	0.511***	0.606***
	[0.131]	[0.112]	[0.070]	[0.106]
Personal attainment = post-secondary non tertiary education	0.712***	0.715***	0.665***	0.798***
	[0.159]	[0.093]	[0.068]	[0.122]
Personal attainment = first or second stage of tertiary education	0.962***	0.938***	0.919***	1.007***
	[0.145]	[0.096]	[0.073]	[0.105]
Highest parental education = lower than secondary	−0.034**		−0.046***	
	[0.014]		[0.013]	
Highest parental education = upper secondary	0.055***		0.041***	
	[0.014]		[0.011]	
Highest parental education = tertiary	0.037**		0.044***	
	[0.018]		[0.009]	
Highest parental occupation = blue-collar		0.009		0.04
		[0.033]		[0.033]
Highest parental occupation = white-collar		0.043		0.084**
		[0.028]		[0.033]
Highest parental occupation = salariat		0.028		0.079***
		[0.030]		[0.029]
Married		−0.119*		−0.070*
		[0.066]		[0.042]
Observations	205,392		230,356	
Censored values	32,679		31,696	
Countries	23		27	
p-Value rho = 0	0.46		0.11	

Robust standard errors clustered by countries in brackets – ***p < 0.01, **p < 0.05, *p < 0.1.

Table A4. Alternative Measures of Total Income Inequality – Disposable Incomes.

Year	Equivalised Household Disposable Incomes after Taxes and Transfers – Population 18–65 (Gini OECD)		Equivalised Household Disposable Incomes after Taxes and Transfers – (Gini Eurostat)		Personal Disposable Incomes (after Taxes and Transfers) Excluding Zero Incomes – (Gini our Sample)	
	2005	2011	2005	2011	2005	2011
Austria	0.259	0.283	0.263	0.274	0.295	0.301
Belgium	0.277	0.262[a]	0.280	0.263	0.261	0.254
Bulgaria			0.250	0.350		0.323
Cyprus			0.287	0.292		
Czech Republic	0.259	0.256	0.260	0.252	0.296	0.262
Denmark	0.227	0.250	0.239	0.278	0.221	0.208
Estonia	0.328	0.324	0.341	0.319	0.349	0.362
Finland	0.266	0.268	0.260	0.258	0.314	0.300
France	0.288	0.310	0.277	0.308	0.315	0.317
Germany	0.304	0.298	0.261	0.290	0.377	0.346
Greece	0.343	0.341	0.332	0.335	0.312	0.298
Hungary	0.300	0.293[b]	0.276	0.268	0.339	0.311
Iceland	0.279	0.250	0.251	0.236		
Ireland	0.321	0.308	0.319	0.298	0.342	0.343
Italy	0.325[c]	0.324	0.328	0.319	0.292	0.305
Latvia			0.362	0.351	0.350	0.398
Lithuania			0.363	0.330	0.337	0.362
Luxembourg	0.287	0.275	0.265	0.272	0.337	0.332
Malta			0.270	0.272		
Netherlands	0.285	0.287[a]	0.269	0.258	0.272	0.261
Norway	0.284[c]	0.260	0.282	0.229	0.274	0.252
Poland	0.333	0.306	0.356	0.311	0.370	0.351
Portugal	0.370	0.339	0.381	0.342	0.364	0.338
Romania			0.310	0.332		0.320

Table A4. (*Continued*)

Year	Equivalised Household Disposable Incomes after Taxes and Transfers – Population 18–65 (Gini OECD)		Equivalised Household Disposable Incomes after Taxes and Transfers – (Gini Eurostat)		Personal Disposable Incomes (after Taxes and Transfers) Excluding Zero Incomes – (Gini our Sample)	
	2005	2011	2005	2011	2005	2011
Slovak Republic	0.280	0.258	0.262	0.257	0.330	0.293
Slovenia	0.241	0.245	0.238	0.238		
Spain	0.307	0.348	0.322	0.340	0.321	0.327
Sweden	0.236[c]	0.268	0.234	0.244	0.223	0.227
Switzerland		0.278		0.297		0.355
United Kingdom	0.335	0.346	0.346	0.330	0.359	0.433

Sources: Data from OECD are downloaded from http://stats.oecd.org/ (section "Social protection and well-being/income distribution and poverty") – Data from Eurostat are based on the SILC database and are downloaded from http://ec.europa.eu/eurostat/web/income-and-living-conditions/data/main-tables).

[a]Refers to 2010.
[b]Refers to 2012.
[c]Refers to 2004.

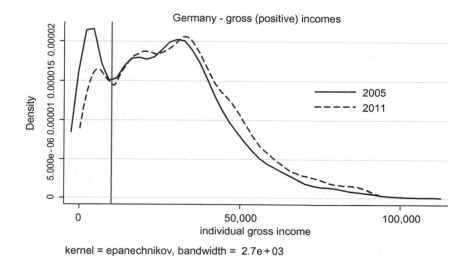

Fig. A1. Income Distribution in Germany — EUSILC 2005 and 2011.

Fig. A1 highlights the anomalous increase in inequality recorded in the German sample for 2005, where a significant mass of individual earned a low income below 5,000 Euros (mostly earnings from dependent employment). This hump is gradually absorbed in the subsequent waves.

Table A5 provides total inequality, inequality of opportunity and their ratio using a different measure of inequality, the Mean Log Deviation, which has the desirable property of exact decomposition (i.e. the total inequality minus inequality of opportunity provides an estimates of the inequality due to effort). The opportunity inequality can be computed according to two approaches, as illustrated in Section 2, the *ex-ante* (which is the perspective adopted in the main text) and the *ex-post*. This latter measure is obtained according to Roemer's statistical solution: given the non-observability of effort, we need to deduce the degree of effort from some observable behaviour. Following Checchi and Peragine (2010), we assume that all individuals at the pth quantile of the income distribution in their types have exerted a comparable degree of effort. Given the assumed monotonicity of the income function, this corresponds to the quantile in the effort distribution of the type. Thus, we define the tranche p in a population as the subset of individuals whose income is at the pth rank of the income distributions of their respective types. Specifically, in order to retain

Table A5. Total Inequality and Inequality of Opportunities – EUSILC – Disposable Incomes, Imputing Expected Incomes to Zero Incomes, Estimated at Country Level Correcting for Self-Selection.

	Total Inequality – MLD		Ex-Ante Opportunity Inequality – MLD		Ex-Ante Opportunity Inequality Ratio – MLD		Ex-Post Opportunity Inequality – MLD		Ex-Post Opportunity Inequality Ratio – MLD	
	2005	2011	2005	2011	2005	2011	2005	2011	2005	2011
Austria	0.22 (0.0061)	0.209 (0.0058)	0.046 (0.0008)	0.039 (0.0005)	0.039	0.209	0.06 (0.0004)	0.048 (0.0003)	0.273	0.23
Belgium	0.166 (0.0067)	0.18 (0.0082)	0.034 (0.0006)	0.031 (0.0006)	0.031	0.205	0.035 (0.0001)	0.03 (0.0001)	0.211	0.167
Bulgaria		0.214 (0.0041)		0.028 (0.0005)	0.028			0.036 (0.0002)		0.168
Switzerland		0.316 (0.0058)		0.079 (0.0009)	0.079			0.12 (0.0008)		0.38
Czech Republic	0.241 (0.0041)	0.144 (0.0033)	0.029 (0.0005)	0.024 (0.0009)	0.024	0.12	0.035 (0.0002)	0.03 (0.0001)	0.145	0.208
	0.241 (0.0041)	0.144 (0.0033)	0.029 (0.0005)	0.024 (0.0009)	0.024	0.12	0.035 (0.0002)	0.03 (0.0001)	0.145	0.208
Germany	0.394 (0.0067)	0.211 (0.0025)	0.075 (0.0004)	0.053 (0.0004)	0.053	0.19	0.113 (0.0005)	0.065 (0.0002)	0.287	0.308
Denmark	0.166 (0.0063)	0.153 (0.008)	0.014 (0.0003)	0.01 (0.0009)	0.01	0.084	0.015 (0.0001)	0.009 (0.0002)	0.09	0.059
Estonia	0.254 (0.0064)	0.269 (0.0065)	0.029 (0.0006)	0.027 (0.0006)	0.027	0.114	0.029 (0.0001)	0.026 (0.0001)	0.114	0.097
Greece	0.268 (0.0064)	0.233 (0.0038)	0.061 (0.0007)	0.049 (0.0009)	0.049	0.228	0.078 (0.0004)	0.064 (0.0004)	0.291	0.275
Spain	0.245 (0.0029)	0.226 (0.0029)	0.049 (0.0004)	0.026 (0.0003)	0.026	0.2	0.064 (0.0002)	0.03 (0.0001)	0.261	0.133
Finland	0.290 (0.0061)	0.257 (0.0056)	0.018 (0.0003)	0.016 (0.0003)	0.015	0.062	0.026 (0.0001)	0.02 (0.0001)	0.09	0.078

France	0.224 (0.0042)	0.24 (0.0048)	0.031 (0.0004)	0.027 (0.0004)	0.027	0.138	0.036 (0.0001)	0.034 (0.0002)	0.161	0.142
Croatia		0.213 (0.0039)		0.026 (0.0004)	0.026			0.034 (0.0001)		0.16
Hungary	0.284 (0.0058)	0.249 (0.0035)	0.035 (0.0006)	0.028 (0.0004)	0.028	0.123	0.053 (0.0003)	0.045 (0.0002)	0.187	0.181
Ireland	0.258 (0.0045)	0.243 (0.0060)	0.049 (0.0008)	0.028 (0.0007)	0.028	0.19	0.064 (0.0003)	0.032 (0.0002)	0.248	0.132
Italy	0.218 (0.0022)	0.23 (0.0026)	0.039 (0.0003)	0.033 (0.0002)	0.033	0.179	0.05 (0.0001)	0.042 (0.0001)	0.229	0.183
Lithuania	0.225 (0.0048)	0.268 (0.0056)	0.022 (0.0005)	0.015 (0.0004)	0.015	0.098	0.026 (0.0001)	0.018 (0.0001)	0.116	0.067
Luxembourg	0.277 (0.0062)	0.246 (0.0051)	0.073 (0.0012)	0.062 (0.0008)	0.062	0.264	0.093 (0.0005)	0.075 (0.0003)	0.336	0.305
Latvia	0.223 (0.0056)	0.343 (0.0068)	0.028 (0.0007)	0.023 (0.0005)	0.023	0.126	0.032 (0.0001)	0.025 (0.0001)	0.143	0.073
Netherlands	0.223 (0.0040)	0.188 (0.0037)	0.058 (0.0005)	0.036 (0.0002)	0.036	0.26	0.088 (0.0005)	0.054 (0.0003)	0.395	0.287
Norway	0.247 (0.0067)	0.193 (0.0070)	0.029 (0.0004)	0.022 (0.0005)	0.022	0.117	0.045 (0.0005)	0.029 (0.0004)	0.182	0.15
Poland	0.283 (0.0028)	0.265 (0.0028)	0.038 (0.0004)	0.034 (0.0004)		0.134	0.042 (0.0001)	0.041 (0.0001)	0.148	0.155
Portugal	0.250 (0.0051)	0.212 (0.0041)	0.034 (0.0011)	0.019 (0.0008)	0.019	0.136	0.044 (0.0002)	0.023 (0.0001)	0.176	0.108
Romania		0.27 (0.0048)		0.039 (0.0006)	0.04			0.071 (0.0006)		0.263
Sweden	0.119 (0.0043)	0.129 (0.0045)	0.017 (0.0003)	0.015 (0.0004)	0.143	0.116	0.018 (0.0002)	0.017 (0.0001)	0.151	0.132
Slovenia	0.392 (0.0078)	0.213 (0.0044)	0.031 (0.0008)	0.014 (0.0002)	0.079	0.066	0.091 (0.0008)	0.018 (0.0001)	0.232	0.085
Great Britain	0.262 (0.0042)	0.202 (0.003)	0.038 (0.0004)	0.043 (0.0005)	0.145	0.213	0.046 (0.0001)	0.050 (0.0002)	0.176	0.248

Table A6.   Data Sources or Institutional Variables.

	Sources
Educational Institutions Variables	
Expenditure per student, primary (% of GDP per capita)	World Bank (http://data.worldbank.org/indicator)
Expenditure per student, secondary (% of GDP per capita)	World Bank (http://data.worldbank.org/indicator)
Expenditure per student, tertiary (% of GDP per capita)	World Bank (http://data.worldbank.org/indicator)
Government expenditure on education as % of GDP (%)	Unesco (http://data.uis.unesco.org/)
Expenditure on education as % of total government expenditure (%)	Unesco (http://data.uis.unesco.org/) − updated using World Bank growth rates when missing
Primary education, duration (years)	World Bank (http://data.worldbank.org/indicator)
Adjusted savings: education expenditure (% of GNI)	World Bank (http://data.worldbank.org/indicator)
Pupil−teacher ratio in primary education	headcount based − Unesco (http://data.uis.unesco.org/)
Pupil−teacher ratio in secondary education	headcount based − Unesco (http://data.uis.unesco.org/)
Percentage of students in secondary education enrolled in vocational programmes	both sexes − Unesco (http://data.uis.unesco.org/)
Gross enrolment ratio, pre-primary, both sexes (%)	both sexes − Unesco (http://data.uis.unesco.org/)
Expenditure on pre-primary as % of government expenditure on education (%)	Unesco (http://data.uis.unesco.org/)
Labour market institutions	
Union density	ICTWSS database (Visser 2013 − http://www.uva-aias.net/208)
Coverage rate	ICTWSS database (Visser 2013 − http://www.uva-aias.net/208)
Bargaining centralisation	ICTWSS database (Visser 2013 − http://www.uva-aias.net/208)
Employment protection legislation	Strictness of employment protection − overall − version 1 − source: OECD http://www.oecd.org/employment/emp/oecdindicatorsofemploymentprotection.htm)
Minimum wage/mean wage	Minimum relative to mean wages of full-time workers − set equal to 1 if minimum wage provision is absent − source: OECD (except Iceland) http://stats.oecd.org/Index.aspx?DataSetCode=RMW

Table A6. (*Continued*)

	Sources
Unemployment subsidy replacement rate	Unemployment insurance and unemployment assistance benefits – gross replacement rate for a full-time adult worker – source: OECD historical series – combination of GRR(APW) until 2001 and GRR(AW) afterward – available in odd years, inter-year means introduced in even years – http://www.oecd.org/els/benefitsandwagesstatistics.htm)
Tax wedge	Average tax wedge (sum of social contributions and income taxes to the average wage) – average between single worker and one-earner married couple with two children – source: OECD http://www.oecd.org/tax/tax-policy/taxing-wages.htm)
Active labour market policy/gdp	OECD http://stats.oecd.org/Index.aspx?DatasetCode=LMPEXP
Passive labour market policy/gdp	OECD http://stats.oecd.org/Index.aspx?DatasetCode=LMPEXP
Social expenditure/gdp	cash benefit + benefit in kind in percentage of GDP – source: OECD (available on quinquennial base then interpolated) http://www.oecd.org/social/expenditure.htm
Parental leave – weeks of absence	weeks of paid leave for child birth – source: Thévenon and Solaz (2013) – further documentation at http://www.oecd.org/social/soc/oecdfamilydatabase.htm

a sufficient number of individuals in each cell, we redefined types using gender, age and parental education (48 types) and we partitioned the type distributions in five quintile. Values in brackets report the estimate of the standard errors obtained from bootstrapping (400 replications).

Table A7 represents the counterpart of Table 7, replacing Gini index with MLD as dependent variable. Columns (7)–(9) introduce the ex-post measure of inequality of opportunity. The main results are confirmed (or even strengthened): expenditure in education over GDP and the share of expenditure in pre-primary education are negative and statistically significant regressors for inequality of opportunity, and similarly occurs for passive labour market policies.

Table A7. Inequality and Institutions – 26 Countries – 2005 and 2011 – Disposable Incomes (Imputing Expected Incomes to Zero Incomes).

	1	2	3	4	5	6	7	8	9
	Total inequality (MLD)			Ex-ante opportunity inequality (MLD)			Ex-post opportunity inequality (MLD)		
	Pooled	Random effects	Fixed effects	Pooled	Random effects	Fixed effects	Pooled	Random effects	Fixed effects
Education expenditure (% of GNI)	-0.894	-1.067	-4.088	-0.981**	-0.835**	-0.443	-1.591***	-1.512***	-1.439
	[1.282]	[1.334]	[3.214]	[0.384]	[0.335]	[0.314]	[0.563]	[0.571]	[0.921]
Pupil–teacher ratio in primary education	-0.119	-0.205	-1.651	-0.137*	-0.083	-0.095	-0.182	-0.241	-0.545
	[0.283]	[0.310]	[1.185]	[0.070]	[0.075]	[0.060]	[0.115]	[0.171]	[0.325]
% Students in secondary education enrolled in vocational programmes	-0.061	-0.056	0.613**	0.027	0.017	0.043	0.055	0.056	0.092
	[0.097]	[0.101]	[0.269]	[0.020]	[0.024]	[0.032]	[0.037]	[0.042]	[0.068]
Expenditure on pre-primary as % of govern. expenditure on education	-0.394	-0.432*	-0.448	-0.175***	-0.203***	-0.283***	-0.279**	-0.339***	-0.532***
	[0.232]	[0.249]	[0.725]	[0.055]	[0.070]	[0.051]	[0.109]	[0.126]	[0.175]
Union density	-0.069	-0.073	0.189	-0.037*	-0.038	0.004	-0.052	-0.057	0.223
	[0.062]	[0.064]	[0.513]	[0.021]	[0.023]	[0.045]	[0.032]	[0.036]	[0.163]
Parental leave – weeks of absence	0.015	0.019	0.150*	-0.008	-0.001	0.000	-0.007	-0.003	-0.01
	[0.029]	[0.031]	[0.085]	[0.007]	[0.006]	[0.006]	[0.012]	[0.013]	[0.024]
Unemployment subsidy replacement rate	0.078	0.089	0.196	-0.016	0.009	0.095***	0.002	0.017	0.189***
	[0.072]	[0.076]	[0.182]	[0.015]	[0.019]	[0.024]	[0.029]	[0.029]	[0.060]
Active labour market policy/GDP	-7.949**	-7.180**	18.440*	1.202	1.310**	1.259	2.183**	2.051**	2.981
	[3.633]	[3.427]	[9.982]	[0.759]	[0.586]	[0.816]	[1.011]	[0.817]	[2.105]
Passive labour market policy/GDP	3.118	2.872	-4.678	-0.605	-0.593*	-1.428***	-1.318***	-1.244**	-3.029***
	[2.135]	[2.099]	[3.747]	[0.394]	[0.320]	[0.355]	[0.463]	[0.565]	[0.989]
Minimum wage/mean wage	2.572	2.412	43.307	1.622	1.585	19.897**	2.509	2.538	33.613*
	[3.205]	[3.148]	[67.202]	[1.031]	[1.211]	[7.499]	[1.676]	[1.808]	[18.882]
Observations	49	49	49	49	49	49	49	49	49
R^2 (within)	0.372	0.172	0.571	0.696	0.695	0.887	0.598	0.511	0.777
Number of country	26	26	26	26	26	26	26	26	26
Hausman test (p-value)		10.51 (0.48)			53.43 (0.00)			11.30 (0.41)	

Robust standard errors clustered by country errors in brackets – ***$p < 0.01$, **$p < 0.05$, *$p < 0.1$ – constant and survey control included.

HOUSEHOLD LIFETIME INEQUALITY ESTIMATES IN THE U.S. LABOR MARKET[☆]

Luca Flabbi[a], James Mabli[b] and Mauricio Salazar[c]

[a]UNC-Chapel Hill, IDB and IZA
[b]Mathematica Policy Research
[c]UNC-Chapel Hill

ABSTRACT

This paper provides household lifetime inequality indexes derived from representative U.S. labor market data. We obtain this result by using estimates of the household search model proposed by Flabbi and Mabli (2012). Inequality indexes computed on the benchmark model shows that inequality in utility values is substantially different from inequality in earnings and wages and that inequality at the cross-sectional level is significantly different from inequality at the lifetime level. Both results deliver original policy implications that would have not been captured

[☆]We would like to thank the Editors, the conference participants and, in particular, two anonymous referees for very useful comments. The views expressed in this paper are those of the authors and should not be attributed to the Inter-American Development Bank or Mathematica Policy Research.

Inequality: Causes and Consequences
Research in Labor Economics, Volume 43, 45–82
ISSN: 0147-9121/doi:10.1108/S0147-912120160000043020

without using our approach. In particular, we find that a counterfactual policy experiment consisting in a mean-preserving spread of the wage offers distributions increases lifetime inequality in wages and earnings but not in utility. When comparing inequality at the individual level between men and women, we find inequality in wages and earnings to be higher for husbands than wives but inequality in utility to be higher for wives. A counterfactual decomposition shows that the job offers parameters are the main source of the gender differential.

Keywords: Household search; lifetime inequality; structural estimation

JEL classifications: J64; D63; C63

1. INTRODUCTION

Income inequality is a fundamental indicator of an economy's overall performance, efficiency and, of course, equity. Because labor income comprises the majority of household income for most households, income inequality is inherently tied to features of the labor market. Accordingly, a lot of emphasis has been devoted to measurement issues both in terms of the theory behind appropriate indicators and in terms of data collection. We propose here a measure of inequality with two relevant yet relatively understudied features: the use of a lifetime perspective and the focus on the household.

By lifetime inequality, we mean a measure of inequality able to take into account labor market dynamic. Although a standard measure of inequality based on cross-sectional wages is informative, it cannot take into account that the position of an individual in the wage distribution is temporary. Labor market dynamic implies that she may lose the job and become unemployed (employment risk) or that her wage may change (wage risk) or that she may simply decide to follow other opportunities (labor market mobility). A lifetime measure should provide a summary measure of inequality that is able to take into account these events. Various empirical approaches have been used to tackle the issue. Starting from the seminal Gottschalk and Moffitt (1994), many contributions have focused on decomposing the overall wage variability in a transitory (over time) component and in a permanent component. In a similar vein, Buchinsky and

Hunt (1999) and subsequent contributions focus on assessing the stability of an individual in the wage distribution by using transition probabilities. Yet another and larger group of contributions focuses on insurance against risk by working with consumption data and risk-sharing mechanisms. Contributions in this line of research are popular and influential both in the micro literature[1] and in the macro literature.[2]

We follow a different strategy by defining *lifetime* as the dynamic implied by participating over time (but in steady state) in a given labor market characterized by frictions and wage and employment risk. All the main structural parameters of the labor market are estimated from the data. In this respect, we focus more on the modeling and estimating of the labor market than the contributions listed before. This emphasis explicitly allows for wage and employment mobility as a result of optimal individual behavior but it comes at the cost of losing the life-cycle dynamic that some of the previous contributions were able to consider.[3] Our approach belongs to a still small but growing literature which includes the seminal Flinn (2002) comparing inequality and mobility in the U.S. and Italian labor market; Bowlus and Robin (2004) developing an innovative non-stationary model of job mobility; and Flabbi and Leonardi (2010) decomposing the increase in inequality in the United States in the 1990s.

---

1. Early seminal contributions are Attanasio and Davis (1996) and Blundell and Preston (1998). Low, Meghir, and Pistaferri's (2008) is one of the most complete models in this line of research.

2. Kaplan (2012), Heathcote, Storesletten, and Violante (2008), Heathcote, Perri, and Violante (2010), Krueger and Perri (2006) are all contributions in the macro literature modelling risk and concerned with the difference between income and consumption inequality.

3. One particularly important concern is human capital accumulation. Some recent contributions in the macro literature with heterogeneous agents (e.g., Badel & Huggett, 2014; Huggett, Ventura, & Yaron, 2011) confirm the result of the traditional human capital literature: accumulated human capital when entering the labor market has a major impact on the variation of realized earnings over the life cycle. This modeling feature is extremely difficult to incorporate in our context where the final objective is the structural estimation of the model parameters. The structural estimation literature has been able to incorporate some education choice behavior (e.g., Flinn & Mullins, 2015) but only one paper has managed to convincingly incorporate human capital accumulation over time in a structurally estimated search model: Bagger, Fontaine, Postel-Vinay, and Robin (2014). However, even in this case the human capital evolution remains quite mechanical. Moreover, computational issues make it extremely difficult to extend this approach to a household search context.

What sets our contribution apart within this smaller literature is the focus on the household. No previous contributions[4] provide estimates of lifetime household inequality. The importance of the focus on the household is straightforward: individuals engaged in stable relationships share resources and make important decisions together. As a result, evaluating inequality at the household level may be a better indicator of individual welfare, of the state of an economy or of the performance of a labor market than inequality at the individual level. The importance of the household has long been recognized by the literature. In particular, the third line of research listed above (see notes 1 and 2) has pointed out the importance of considering that decisions are taken at the household level and the relevance of sharing rules within the household. In our approach, we will be able to address only the first of the two issues since we will assume a unitary model of the household. However, in taking into account that decisions are made at the household level we will need to develop a model of dual search in the labor market, a problem that provides a contribution in its own right and that has been introduced in the search literature only recently.[5]

We develop and estimate a standard but fairly complete search model of the labor market. We allow for search both on-the-job and during unemployment and we also allow for a simple labor supply decision. The main feature of the model is allowing for the interaction between labor market decisions of the two spouses. The two spouses search (and work) simultaneously in two labor markets. Each of the two markets is allowed to be characterized by gender-specific parameters. We estimate the model by simulated methods of moments on the 2001–2003 panel of the *Survey of Income and Program Participation* (SIPP).

We compute three indicators of lifetime and cross-sectional household inequality on the benchmark model. Each indicator is used to compute inequality in wages, earnings, and utility. Comparing lifetime and cross-sectional inequality measures we find substantial differences in the magnitude

---

4. The only exception is our own Flabbi and Mabli (2012). This previous version of our work has now been updated and split into two contributions: the current paper focusing on inequality and Flabbi and Mabli (2015) focusing on the comparison between estimating a search model at the household level and at the individual level.
5. Dey and Flinn (2008) is the first contribution estimating an household search model; Guler, Guvenen, and Violante (2012) provide an exhaustive treatment of the impact of preferences in an household search model with a unitary household.

of the inequality indices and in the ranking between wages, earnings, and utility inequality they imply.

We then perform a series of counterfactual and policy experiments. The first set of experiments shows the sensitivity of household inequality to the different labor market parameters. In particular we look at the impact of labor market frictions, dispersion of job offers and frequency of part-time offers. We find substantially different implications when judging the policies based on lifetime measures or on cross-sectional measures. The second set of experiments is motivated by a result found in the benchmark specification: women (wives) exhibit different levels of inequality than men (husbands). In particular, wives' wages and earnings inequality is lower but lifetime inequality is higher than husbands' inequality. In the experiments, we decompose the sources of these differentials in impact due to: labor market frictions, job offers, and preferences.

The paper is organized as follows. The next section presents the model. Section 3 presents the Data. Section 4 briefly describes the identification strategy, specifies the estimator, and presents the estimates. Section 5 contains the main contribution of the paper and it is devoted to the inequality exercise. We describe how we estimate lifetime values and then define the inequality indexes used in the analysis. We follow with a discussion of the benchmark case, before providing in separate subsections the counterfactual and policy experiments. Section 6 concludes.

2. MODEL

2.1. Environment

We develop a search model of the labor market where decisions are made at the household level.[6] It is a natural extension of the usual single-agent decision problem to a joint-search problem of two agents looking for jobs simultaneously. The major simplification we introduce to keep the problem tractable is assuming a unitary model of the household: households consist of two agents sharing consumption, pooling income, and maximizing a common utility function. Consistently with the data we will use in

---

6. The environment is the same as the one labeled as *household search extended model* in Flabbi and Mabli (2012). We refer to the paper for a more detailed description of the model.

estimation (married couples), we call individuals belonging to one type *wives* and to the other type *husbands*. Wives' parameters are denoted by the subscript W and individuals belonging to the set of wives are indexed by j. Husbands' parameters are denoted by the subscript M and individuals belonging to the set of husbands are indexed by i. Notice that the model imposes another major simplifications: we are only looking at married couples, that is, we do not model household formation and dissolution. As a result, the only assortative mating that the model may explain and generate is the one over labor market states. As we will see, this is implied by the fact that the labor market status of one spouse has an impact on the optimal decision rule about job offers received by the other spouse.[7]

The model is in continuous time in a stationary environment. Shocks follow Poisson processes with exogenous parameters. There are three types of shocks in the market. First, job offers while unemployed characterized by the arrival rate parameter λ_A. $A = M, W$ denotes parameters pertaining to husbands and wives. Second, there is also on-the-job search, leading to offers characterized by the rate γ_A. Once offers are accepted, can be terminated endogenously or exogenously. Endogenous termination may occur because one spouse may decide to quit the current job as a result of a change in the labor market status of the other spouse. Exogenous terminations are introduced in order to take into account other sources of job termination (e.g., firings or firm closings). They are modeled as an exogenous Poisson process with parameter η_A. Exogenous termination is the third and final shock characterizing the environment.

We also add labor supply, a nonstandard feature in the search literature[8] that we introduce in order to match the employment distribution for women given the relatively large number of women present in the final estimation

---

7. Some contributions are starting to merge labor and marriage markets in the presence of frictions: Chiappori, Costa-Dias, and Meghir (2015) propose a model where both markets are present but with a different timing in the decision process, first the marriage market and then the labor market; Flabbi and Flinn (2015) is a preliminary contribution where individuals are allowed to contemporaneously search in both markets and when married, to continue a joint search in the labor market; finally, Greenwood, Guner, Kocharkov, and Santos (2015) develop a unified model of marriage and divorce but they limit labor supply decisions to married women.

8. Blau (1991) is the only example of an estimated search model including this feature, that is, the joint offer of wage-hours pairs. Flabbi and Moro (2012) estimate a search model allowing for the choice between part-time and full-time work but the choice is contingent to a wage offer and it is bargained with the employer.

sample. Labor supply also generates a richer household interaction environment. To make the estimation tractable, we introduce the intensive margin of labor supply by assuming that job offers require either a full-time hours schedule or a part-time hours schedule.[9] The distribution of wage offers is conditional on the hours schedule requirement. We denote this by writing the wage offer distribution to gender A in part-time and full-time jobs as $F_A^{pt}(w)$ and $F_A^{ft}(w)$. The indexes pt and ft denote that all the parameters characterizing the wage offers distributions are conditional on the hours schedule requirement. The exogenous proportion of part-time offers is denoted by p. Notice that, as common in a search model setting, households are ex-ante identical and the only source of heterogeneity are the job offers, which are extracted from gender-specific wage offer distributions.

The instantaneous utility functions of household i, j depend on the idiosyncratic components and on the time-invariant household-specific non-labor income y_{ij}. For identification purposes, we assume a Constant Relative Risk Aversion (CRRA) utility function. Household instantaneous utility is therefore defined as:

$$u\left(c_{ij}, l_i, l_j; \delta, \beta, \alpha\right) = (1 - \alpha_M - \alpha_W)\frac{c_{ij}^{\delta} - 1}{\delta} + \alpha_M\frac{l_i^{\beta_M} - 1}{\beta_M} + \alpha_W\frac{l_j^{\beta_W} - 1}{\beta_W} \quad (1)$$

where

$$c_{ij} = w_i h_i + w_j h_j + y_{ij}$$
$$l_i = 1 - h_i$$
$$l_j = 1 - h_j$$
$$h_{i,j} \in \left\{h^{pt}, h^{ft}\right\}$$

We choose a CRRA specification because it nests the two main utility function specifications used in the applied micro literature: linear and log utility. It is also a utility function frequently used in the macro literature.

---

9. This characterization is consistent with the usual assumption in implicit contract theory where firms post job package offers (see, e.g., Hwang, Mortensen, & Reed, 1998). Wage-hours packages are embedded in a labor market search framework by Gørgens (2002). Other examples of empirical search model featuring job offers including not only a wage but an additional job characteristics are: Dey and Flinn (2008) and Aizawa and Fang (2013) adding health insurance; Flabbi and Moro (2012) adding job flexibility; and Meghir, Narita, and Robin (2015) adding formality status.

2.2. Value Functions

As a result of this environment, each spouse can be in three different states: unemployment, part-time employment, and full-time employment. Since each spouse can be in three states, each household can be in nine different states, each subject to a different set of shocks. We report the list of each state together with the notation for the value function and the parameters characterizing the shocks in Table 1. Notice that each household is also characterized by a time-invariant household-specific y_{ij}. For convenience, we drop the conditioning on y_{ij} in Table 1 and in the rest of this subsection. The value function V denotes the cases when both spouses are employed; T the cases when one spouse is employed and the other is unemployed; U the case where both spouses are unemployed.

The full expressions of the value functions in recursive form are available in a slightly more general form in Flabbi and Mabli (2012). Here, we will just focus on one example to point out the richness of the interaction between spouses' labor market states allowed by the model. It is particularly instructive to look at the value of a household where one spouse is working full-time (say, the husband) and the other spouse is unemployed and searching. The value function for such household is denoted by $T_M[w_i, h^{ft}]$ where w_i and h^{ft} denote, respectively, the husband's wage and the hours worked. The index M denotes that the spouse in the

Table 1. Household Labor Market States.

State	Value Function	Shocks
FT, FT	$V[w_i, h^{ft}, w_j, h^{ft}]$	$\gamma_M, \eta_M^{ft}, \gamma_W, \eta_W^{ft}$
FT, PT	$V[w_i, h^{ft}, w_j, h^{pt}]$	$\gamma_M, \eta_M^{ft}, \gamma_W, \eta_W^{pt}$
FT, U	$T[w_i, h^{ft}]$	$\gamma_M, \eta_M^{ft}, \lambda_W$
PT, FT	$V[w_i, h^{pt}, w_j, h^{ft}]$	$\gamma_M, \eta_M^{pt}, \gamma_W, \eta_W^{ft}$
PT, PT	$V[w_i, h^{pt}, w_j, h^{pt}]$	$\gamma_M, \eta_M^{pt}, \gamma_W, \eta_W^{pt}$
PT, U	$T[w_i, h^{pt}]$	$\gamma_M, \eta_M^{pt}, \lambda_W$
U, FT	$T[w_i, h^{ft}]$	$\lambda_M, \gamma_W, \eta_W^{ft}$
U, PT	$T[w_i, h^{pt}]$	$\lambda_M, \gamma_W, \eta_W^{pt}$
U, U	U	λ_M, λ_W

Notes: The states acronym are defined as follows: FT = employed full-time; PT = employed part-time; U = unemployed. The first position and the indexes i and H refer to husbands. The second position and the indexes j and W refer to wives.

household who is currently working is the husband. The value function is characterized by the following equation:

$$
\left(\rho + \gamma_M + \eta_M^{ft} + \lambda_W\right) T_M\left[w_i, h^{ft}\right] = u\left(w_i h^{ft} + y_{ij}, 1 - h^{ft}, 1\right)
$$

$$
+ \gamma_M(1 - p_M) \int \max\left\{T_M\left[w_i, h^{ft}\right], T_M\left[w', h^{ft}\right]\right\} dF_M^{ft}(w)
$$

$$
+ \gamma_M p_M \int \max\left\{T_M\left[w_i, h^{ft}\right], T_M\left[w', h^{pt}\right]\right\} dF_M^{pt}(w) + \eta_M^{ft} U
$$

$$
+ \lambda_W(1 - p_W) \int \max\left\{
\begin{array}{c}
T_M\left[w_i, h^{ft}\right], V\left[w_i, h^{ft}, w', h^{ft}\right], \\
T_W\left[w', h^{ft}\right]
\end{array}
\right\} dF_W^{ft}
$$

$$
+ \lambda_W p_W \int \max\left\{
\begin{array}{c}
T_M\left[w_i, h^{ft}\right], V\left[w_i, h^{ft}, w', h^{pt}\right], \\
T_W[w', h^{pt}]
\end{array}
\right\} dF_W^{pt}(w)
$$

(2)

A household where the husband works full-time and the wife searches enjoys flow utility $u\left(w_i h^{ft} + y_{ij}, 1 - h^{ft}, 1\right)$ and it may receive three shocks: an on-the-job offer to the husband, a job offer to the wife, and a termination shock to the husband's job. Each job offers may be either part-time or full-time.

What is interesting in the dual-search process detailed by our household search framework is that under our utility function assumption[10] a shock to one of the spouse may generate a change of the other spouse's labor market state. For example, consider the fifth row in Eq. (2) where the wife is receiving a full-time offer. If this full-time offer is accepted, the husband may react by staying in the current job but he may also react by quitting the current job (leading to household state $T_W\left[w', h^{ft}\right]$). This contemporaneous change of state result cannot be dealt with or without the joint modeling of both spouses' search processes as we do in the current formulation of the model.

2.3. Optimal Decision Rules

The optimal decision rule of the dual-search problem in the household search context retains the reservation value property of the usual individual

---

10. See Dey and Flinn (2008) and Guler et al. (2012) for a formal proof. We provide a more detailed discussion of this result in Section 2.3.

search model with linear utility with the only difference that the critical value is now defined on the utility value.[11] Based on the choices and the value functions, utility reservation values can be derived in the same way as reservation wage values are derived in a standard linear-utility individual-search model: by finding the instantaneous utility values such that the household is indifferent between the relevant alternatives. The equations defining the reservation utility values and the formal definition of the equilibrium are notational heavy and are not reported. The extended version of the equations and the full equilibrium definition is available in Flabbi and Mabli (2012).

What is interesting to discuss for the objectives of this paper is the source of the dependence between spouses' labor market choices and states. If agents are risk neutral then the household search model equilibrium is equivalent to the individual search model equilibrium. The intuition for the result is very simple. With linear utility, the marginal utility of income is constant and therefore the decision of one spouse about job offers does not depend on the other spouse contributing income to the household by working or not.

Instead, if agents are endowed with our CRRA utility function, that is, a utility function with curvature and risk aversion, then the income flow to the household is relevant in making decisions. For example, assume a household where the husband is looking for a job and the wife is working at a given wage. The wife's wage has now an impact on the husband's decision rule: the higher the wife's wage, the higher the income flow to the household the lower the cost of search. This channel makes the husband pickier in accepting job offers. At the same time, the higher the wife's wage, the lower the expected gain from search. This second channel makes the husband less picky in accepting job offers. These simple channels generate two main results:

1. In the presence of CRRA utility, the labor market state of one spouse has an impact on the optimal labor market choices of the other spouse;
2. The direction of this impact with respect to a standard individual search model or a household search model with linear utility is ambiguous.

---

11. This is due to the presence of a labor supply decision function of the hours worked regime. For extensive discussion and formal proofs, see Blau (1991) and Hwang, Mortensen, and Reed (1998). For a similar application, see Flabbi and Moro (2012).

Both results are clearly pointed out in Dey and Flinn (2008). An extensive discussion, including conditions applied to more general formulations of the utility function and formal proofs, is in Guler et al. (2012). Finally, an extensive and intuitive graphical discussion of the result is reported in Flabbi and Mabli (2012).

3. DATA

We use data from the 2001–2003 panel of the *Survey of Income and Program Participation* (SIPP) to estimate the model. The main objective of the SIPP is to provide accurate and comprehensive information about the principal determinants of the income of individual households in the United States. The SIPP collects monthly information regarding individual's labor market activity including earnings, average hours worked, and whether the individual changed jobs within an employment spell. The main advantage of using the SIPP is the ease in creating labor market histories for all individuals in the sample and in linking detailed spousal labor market information across time. The second characteristic is clearly a fundamental requirement in our empirical application and it is not available at this level of precision in other commonly used panel data for the United States. The main disadvantage is the relatively short time span over which the panel data are available. However, our model has enough structure to be able to identify and precisely estimate the main structural parameters even if the time dimension of the panel is short.

3.1. Sample Restrictions

Although the target sample size for each SIPP panel is quite large, the size of our sample is reduced by several restrictions. After imposing all selection criteria, our sample consists of 3,984 individuals for a total of 1,992 married couples.

We select married couples in which each spouse is aged between 25 and 50 (inclusive) at the beginning of the panel. We only consider married couples in which each spouse is present in the household throughout the panel, meaning that we exclude any couples that are separated or not living together at any point in the panel.[12] Additionally, neither spouse must participate in the armed services throughout the sample period.

We exclude couples if either spouse has a *broken* labor market history, such as being in the sample at the beginning and the end of the panel, but absent in between. We exclude spouses if either spouse is out of the labor force for the entire panel period or if either spouse transitions between out of the labor force and unemployment, but does not work in the panel period. Instead, we choose to include spouses in the sample who answer that they are out of the labor force at some point in the panel, but have an employment spell or unemployment spell at other points in the sample.

Hours and earnings information must be observable at every point in the panel for any employed individual. Couples in which at least one individual does not supply hours worked per week are excluded from the sample. We recode hours worked per week into part-time and full-time categories but we use the full hours worked variation to derive hourly wages when they are not directly reported in the hourly format. Individuals are coded as working part-time if they work less than 35 hours per week and full-time if they work at least 35 hours per week.

We only impose a small adjustment on the raw wage data: We exclude couples in which there exist at least one spouse whose wage lies in the top 0.75 percent or the bottom 0.75 percent of the wage distribution conditional on gender. All wages are adjusted for inflation to the 2001 CPI.

3.2. Descriptive Statistics

Descriptive statistics of the estimation sample are reported in Tables 2 and 3. Since we separately estimate the model for couples with and without children younger than 18 years, we present the descriptive statistics conditioning on the presence of children. We add this control in estimation to partially take into account the systematic difference in labor market behavior induced by the presence of children. A better solution would have been to directly model fertility decisions but this is clearly a nontrivial extension to the model.

---

12. Notice that the loss of information due to this restriction is limited since we require couples to be married only for our relative short period of observation (2 years).

Table 2. Descriptive Statistics: Cross-Sectional Components.

	Yes Children Younger than 18				No Children Younger than 18			
	N = 3,340				*N = 644*			
	Total	Spouse labor market status			Total	Spouse labor market status		
		Employed		Unemployed		Employed		Unemployed
		FT	PT			FT	PT	
Females								
Labor market status								
Employed FT	0.558	0.556	0.550	0.613	0.755	0.779	0.625	0.438
Employed PT	0.265	0.275	0.217	0.113	0.168	0.159	0.313	0.188
Unemployed	0.177	0.170	0.233	0.275	0.078	0.062	0.063	0.375
Hourly wages								
Employed FT								
Mean	15.02	15.13	14.94	13.08	15.79	16.11	11.28	12.11
CV	0.517	0.516	0.537	0.504	0.510	0.506	0.479	0.371
Employed PT								
Mean	12.72	12.71	13.35	12.27	12.87	12.98	11.01	14.30
CV	0.605	0.608	0.605	0.501	0.555	0.578	0.432	0.385
Weekly earnings								
Mean	528.1	528.0	543.9	516.9	607.1	623.7	404.1	459.0
CV	0.640	0.644	0.632	0.553	0.584	0.578	0.563	0.425

Table 2. (*Continued*)

Males

	Yes Children Younger than 18 N = 3,340				No Children Younger than 18 N = 644			
	Total	Spouse labor market status			Total	Spouse labor market status		
		Employed		Unemployed		Employed		Unemployed
		FT	PT			FT	PT	
Labor market status								
Employed FT	0.916	0.912	0.950	0.878	0.901	0.930	0.852	0.720
Employed PT	0.036	0.035	0.029	0.047	0.050	0.041	0.093	0.040
Unemployed	0.048	0.053	0.020	0.074	0.050	0.029	0.056	0.240
Hourly wages								
Employed FT								
Mean	18.91	18.37	20.09	18.74	19.29	19.43	19.78	16.37
CV	0.509	0.490	0.471	0.616	0.490	0.507	0.384	0.513
Employed PT								
Mean	15.57	13.68	16.96	18.73	12.52	9.68	14.90	29.00
CV	0.681	0.491	0.556	0.916	0.601	0.374	0.629	0.000
Weekly earnings								
Mean	795.3	771.8	849.3	785.9	800.6	808.9	799.3	700.3
CV	0.526	0.508	0.484	0.634	0.520	0.536	0.441	0.502

Source: Data are from the 2001–2003 panel of the Survey of Income and Program Participation (SIPP).
Notes: The cross-sectional moments are computed from the first point-in-time sample extracted from the panel. CV stands for coefficient of variation.

Table 3. Descriptive Statistics: Longitudinal Components.

	Yes Children Younger than 18				No Children Younger than 18			
	N = 3,340				*N* = 644			
	Total	Spouse labor market status			Total	Spouse labor market status		
		Employed		Unemployed		Employed		Unemployed
		FT	PT			FT	PT	
				Females				
Labor market transitions:								
From employed FT to								
Employed FT	0.902	0.909	0.879	0.796	0.926	0.934	0.800	0.857
Employed PT	0.050	0.048	0.091	0.061	0.037	0.031	0.200	0.000
Unemployed	0.047	0.042	0.030	0.143	0.037	0.035	0.000	0.143
From employed PT to								
Employed FT	0.090	0.093	0.077	0.000	0.111	0.087	0.400	0.000
Employed PT	0.812	0.807	0.923	0.889	0.889	0.913	0.600	1.000
Unemployed	0.097	0.100	0.000	0.111	0.000	0.000	0.000	0.000
From unemployed to								
Employed FT	0.084	0.088	0.000	0.091	0.080	0.111	0.000	0.000
Employed PT	0.071	0.073	0.000	0.091	0.080	0.056	0.000	0.167
Unemployed	0.845	0.838	1.000	0.818	0.840	0.833	1.000	0.833

Table 3. (Continued)

	Yes Children Younger than 18				No Children Younger than 18			
	N = 3,340				N = 644			
	Total	Spouse labor market status			Total	Spouse labor market status		
		Employed		Unemployed		Employed		Unemployed
		FT	PT			FT	PT	
Males								
Labor market transitions:								
From employed FT to								
Employed FT	0.960	0.954	0.974	0.958	0.948	0.947	0.978	0.889
Employed PT	0.016	0.019	0.012	0.012	0.017	0.018	0.022	0.000
Unemployed	0.024	0.027	0.014	0.031	0.034	0.035	0.000	0.111
From employed PT to								
Employed FT	0.300	0.333	0.231	0.286	0.313	0.400	0.200	0.000
Employed PT	0.650	0.636	0.769	0.571	0.688	0.600	0.800	1.000
Unemployed	0.050	0.030	0.000	0.143	0.000	0.000	0.000	0.000
From unemployed to								
Employed FT	0.438	0.469	0.556	0.318	0.375	0.286	0.667	0.333
Employed PT	0.013	0.000	0.000	0.045	0.063	0.000	0.333	0.000
Unemployed	0.550	0.531	0.444	0.636	0.563	0.714	0.000	0.667

Source: Data are from the 2001–2003 panel of the Survey of Income and Program Participation (SIPP).
Notes: The transitions proportions are computed from the first point-in-time sample extracted from the panel to the point-in-time sample extracted three months later.

Moreover, the short time dimension of the data does not provide a lot of information about this process.[13]

Table 2 contains descriptive statistics of the cross-sectional features of the data. We compute them at the beginning of the observation period (beginning of 2001) and then three months apart for the following 24 months. The values of the statistics are very stable across time and in Table 2 we just report values for the first point-in-time sample. The first and fifth columns report unconditional moments while the other columns report moments conditional on the other spouse's labor market status.

Gender differentials are in line with the literature and the aggregate evidence: men are much more likely to work full-time (91.6% compared with 55.8% for women in household with children) and earn on average higher wages than women. The gender gap in full-time jobs is about 23%, almost equal to the gender wage gap at the median reported by the Bureau of Labor Statistics. The gender gaps are not significantly reduced on the sample without young children, pointing out the well-known persistence of the phenomenon. There is indication of a full-time premium in accepted wages: average hourly wages are higher in full-time jobs than in part-time jobs on all the samples. As a result, the gender gap in earnings is larger than the gender gap in wages, reaching 40% overall on the sample of couples with young children.

We describe cross-sectional inequality at the individual level by reporting coefficient of variations (CV) computed on hourly wages and weekly earnings. Hourly wages inequality is quite similar between men and women while overall inequality in weekly earnings is slightly higher for women. This is mainly due to the higher proportion of women working part-time and point out to the importance of labor supply decisions in determining gender differentials in the labor market.

But the most relevant result emerging from the descriptive statistics is that the labor market status of one spouse varies with the labor market status of the other spouse. For example, in the sample with children, 26.5% of women are employed part-time overall but only 11.3% of the women married to an unemployed husband are employed part-time. Not only the labor market status but also the average wage varies with the labor market status

---

13. We use 18 years as cut-off point because it usually denotes the age when children leave home therefore significantly changing the child-care requirements on the household. We have experimented with different cut-off points without experiencing qualitative changes in the results.

of the husband. Women's average wages decrease from 15.13 dollars an hour, to 14.94 dollars an hour, to 13.08 dollars an hour if, respectively, the husband works full-time, works part-time or is unemployed. Wage variation is also sensitive to the husband's labor market status: the coefficient of variation is decreasing as we move from the husband working full-time, to working part-time, to unemployment. Husbands are less sensitive than wives to the spouse's labor market status but there are still non-negligible effects: the full-time employment rate decreases from 91.2% on the sample of men married to women working full-time to 87.8% on the sample married to unemployed women. The variation in average wages is more modest (average wages are 18.37 dollars an hour in the first sample and 18.74 dollars an hour in the second) but the variation in wage dispersion is very sensitive to the wife's labor market status (the coefficient of variation in hourly wages is much smaller if the wife is working than if the wife is unemployed). The sample of couples without young children confirms the sensitivity of one's labor market status to the spouse's labor market status. In some cases, the differences are larger than in the sample of couples with young children: for example, full-time employment range from 77.9% on women married to men employed full-time to 43.8% on women married to unemployed men. Notice, however, that if the sensitivity is similar the impact of the other spouse's labor market status may be different: on the sample of couples without young children we see women working more frequently full-time if the husband does the same while the opposite is true on the sample with young children.

Table 3 contains descriptive statistics of the labor market dynamics information contained in the data. We summarize the information reporting transition probabilities between the labor market state at the beginning of the period and the labor market state three months later. Again, we present the evidence conditioning and not conditioning on the other spouse's labor market status. There is persistence across labor market states, in particular on full-time employment: for example, 90% of women and 96% of men employed full-time are still employed full-time three months later. However, transition across labor market states are not rare, in particular for men: 45% of men who are unemployed at the beginning of the period are employed three months later. This proportion is much lower on the female sample: only 15% of unemployed women are employed three months later.

The evidence conditioning on the spouse's labor market status confirms the sensitivity observed in Table 2. For example, in the sample with children an employed woman married to an unemployed husband is much more likely to become unemployed (a frequency of 14.3% as opposed to about 4% if the husband is employed) and a woman working part-time is much more likely to do so three months later if also the husband is employed part-time. Males transitions are also sensitive to their wives labor market status: if they work part-time, they are 20 percentage points more likely to do so three months later if the wife works part-time than if the wife is unemployed. Qualitatively similar results are found in the sample without young children. However, a larger number of transitions are not observed due to the smaller sample size: for example, we observe zero transitions from part-time employment to unemployment on both the males and females samples.

In conclusion, both Table 2 and Table 3 show the sensitivity of one spouse labor market status to the other's spouse labor market status. Accounting for this sensitivity is one of the motivations to use a household search model as we do in the current paper. It is also an empirical feature allowing for the identification of some important model's parameters.

4. ESTIMATION AND IDENTIFICATION

4.1. Identification

The identification discussion is based on a data set of linked information for husbands and wives, including accepted hourly wages, hours worked, labor market state dummies, transitions and wage growth over time and some individuals characteristics such as demographics and the presence of children. We present just the main intuition while we refer to Flabbi and Mabli (2012) for further details.

As a preliminary step, we have to add a few more functional form assumptions on top of those already presented in Section 2. First, due to the well-known non-identification result of Flinn and Heckman (1982), we need to assume a *recoverable* wage offers distribution if we want to estimate the entire wage offer distribution and not simply fit the accepted wage distribution. Following the most common assumption in the recent literature, we assume a lognormal distribution. The parameters of the distribution are conditional both on gender and hours requirement and they are denoted as $\left(\mu_A^{ft}, \sigma_A^{ft}\right)$ and $\left(\mu_A^{pt}, \sigma_A^{pt}\right)$.

Second, we consider how to integrate in the identification and estimation procedure two household heterogeneity characteristics: non-labor income

and the presence of children. Both imply a different optimal decision rules
for each labor market state combination and therefore we introduce them
in a very stylized way: they are both exogenous and they are time-invariant.
Non-labor income assumes three values directly estimated from the data
and the presence of children is used to split the sample in order to obtain a
separate set of structural parameters for household with or without
children. The age limit we impose on the children is 18 years old, that is,
we code as households with children all the households that have children
18 years old or younger.[14]

As a result of these additional parametrization, the parameters to be
estimated can be sorted in three groups:

1. Mobility and cost of search parameters;
2. Wage offer distributions parameters;
3. Utility parameters.

Due to lack of identification, the discount rate parameter ρ is not estimated
but fixed to 5% a year.

The mapping from the structural parameters to the data is too
complicated to be solved analytically and therefore an analytical proof of
identification cannot be provided. A detailed heuristic discussion of the
identification of the model is provided in Flabbi and Mabli (2012). The
intuition is as follows.

The mobility parameters and the wage offer distribution parameters are
identified following the usual results from individual search models. As
shown by Flinn and Heckman (1982), they are identified from information
on, respectively, transitions between labor market states and accepted
wages distributions.

The utility parameters identification is more interesting since search
model usually assume linear utility. Labor supply information provides
identification for the relative weight given to leisure in the utility function
while the dependence between spouses' labor market decisions provide
identification about the relative risk aversion coefficients. The second result
is obtained from the theoretical implication discussed in Section 2.3: Labor
market decisions of one spouse depend on labor market decisions of the
other spouse only if the utility function is non-linear. As a result, the degree

---

14. Flabbi and Mabli (2012) use a different parameterization by introducing the excluding
restriction that the presence of children has an impact only on the weight given to leisure in
the utility function α_A.

on non-linearity implied by risk aversion can be identified by the intensity of the dependence between spouses' labor market decisions.

4.2. Estimation Method

Due to the possibility of *simultaneous* changes in the labor market states of both spouses in a given household, we cannot estimate by maximum likelihood. We choose instead the method of simulated moments. Following Dey and Flinn (2008) and Flabbi and Mabli (2012), we extract moments from point-in-time samples that focus on steady states aggregated moments and transitions probabilities.

The estimation procedure works as follows. First, we select the moments with which to estimate the parameters of the model. We calculate these moments in our original sample and reserve them for use in the criterion function. Second, we write a procedure that generates the simulated moments given a set of parameter estimates. Each time the simulation is run, the value functions are solved using fixed point methods and the optimal decision rules are obtained. Third, we randomly assign each couple an initial labor supply configuration and we simulate labor market histories, where each labor market history denotes a sequence of transitions between labor market states for a pair of spouses. Fourth, we compute in the simulated sample the same moments we want to target in the data. Fifth, we use a criterion function[15] to minimize the distance between sample and simulated moments. The minimizer of the criterion function is the estimator we propose.

The moments are chosen closely following the identification strategy outlined in Section 4.1. Transitions are important to identify mobility parameters; therefore, we include all the transitions between labor market states. Recall that there are 16 possible household states since each spouse can be in four different states. Transitions between all the 16 states are possible with only one exception: if both spouses are out of the labor force. Accepted wages are crucial to identify wage offers parameters. We include

---

15. The criterion function is the usual quadratic form composed of the vector of the distance between sample and simulated moments weighted by a diagonal matrix. The weighting matrix we use is also standard in similar application and it is built by placing the inverse of the sample moment standard deviation on the main diagonal. See Flabbi and Mabli (2012) for additional details.

first, second, and third moments of all the relevant wage offers distributions. Finally, interaction between spouses' labor market states is important
to identify the utility parameters: we include the above moments conditioning on the other spouse labor market states. For wages, we also add the
correlation between spouses' wages.

Since we allow all the structural parameters (with the exception of the
relative risk aversion parameter which is common to the household) to be
different for husbands and wives, all the moments listed above are gender-
specific. Finally, since we allow the presence of children to impact the structural parameters, all the moments listed above are computed for household
with and without children. Overall, we have a total of 121 moments to estimate a total of 23 parameters for households with children and the same
number of moments and parameters for households without children. The
complete list of sample moments and of simulated moments at estimated
parameters is reported in the appendix of Flabbi and Mabli (2012).

4.3. Estimation Results

We report the estimation results in Tables 4 and 5. Table 4 reports the
structural parameters estimates and Table 5 some relevant predicted values.
The first two columns pertain to the sample of households with children
younger than 18 years old; the last two columns to the sample of households without children younger than 18 years old.

The structural parameters estimates confirm the systematic differences
by gender found in the literature. As the individual search model estimated
by Flabbi (2010) on CPS data and by Bowlus (1997) on NLSY data, the
household search model we estimate on SIPP data shows that there are
differences by gender in all the structural parameters of the model, with the
stronger differences concerning the wage offers distribution. As reported in
Table 5, women are more likely to receive part-time job offers and when
they receive full-time offers they are at lower wages, on average. With
respect to labor supply estimates, the model estimates a rate of part-time
offers three-times larger for women than men. This finding is in line with
the previous literature.[16]

The point estimates of the utility parameters contain some interesting
results. The weight on leisure (α) is estimated to be higher for women than

---

16. See, for example, Altonji and Paxson (1988) and Flabbi and Moro (2012).

Table 4. MSM Estimation Results: Parameter Estimates.

	Yes Children Younger than 18		No Children Younger than 18	
	Wives	Husbands	Wives	Husbands
λ	0.2356	0.2993	0.2568	0.3198
	(0.0168)	(0.0299)	(0.0156)	(0.0227)
γ	0.0857	0.1179	0.0932	0.1216
	(0.0041)	(0.0117)	(0.0057)	(0.0130)
η_{pt}	0.0127	0.0191	0.0171	0.0193
	(0.0020)	(0.0006)	(0.0008)	(0.0014)
η_{ft}	0.0153	0.0149	0.0186	0.0172
	(0.0034)	(0.0009)	(0.0016)	(0.0006)
μ^{pt}	2.1986	2.0361	2.2046	2.0225
	(0.0502)	(0.0881)	(0.0578)	(0.0886)
μ^{ft}	1.9497	1.9369	2.0265	1.9783
	(0.0259)	(0.0382)	(0.0366)	(0.0651)
σ^{pt}	0.4566	0.6871	0.4649	0.6518
	(0.0216)	(0.0399)	(0.0194)	(0.0425)
σ^{ft}	0.4103	0.6637	0.3794	0.6461
	(0.0267)	(0.0164)	(0.0105)	(0.0188)
p	0.1819	0.0588	0.1626	0.0511
	(0.0141)	(0.0045)	(0.0044)	(0.0056)
α	0.2082	0.1248	0.1564	0.1175
	(0.0075)	(0.0060)	(0.0081)	(0.0113)
δ	0.0439	0.0475		
	(0.0024)	(0.0017)		
β	0.0488	0.0547	0.0472	0.0470
	(0.0029)	(0.0035)	(0.0019)	(0.0020)
N	3,340	644		

Source: Data are from the 2001–2003 SIPP.
Notes: Standard errors in parentheses are computed by bootstrap with 30 replications.

men on both samples but more so on the sample of household with young children present. This is consistent with evidence indicating that the impact of the presence of children is asymmetric by gender and confirms the importance of estimating the model on households with and without children. It also indicates the limitations of our approach in this respect: leisure is essentially a different good if the sample includes households with or without children. In the sample without children what we call leisure is closer to actual leisure time while in the sample with children is likely to also include child-care work.

The coefficient of relative risk aversion, defined in our parametrization as $(1 - \delta)$, is estimated to be close to 1 on all the sample and specification.

Table 5. MSM Estimation Results: Implied Values.

	Yes Children Younger than 18		No Children Younger than 18	
	Wives	Husbands	Wives	Husbands
		Wage offers		
$E[w]$	8.073	8.709	8.471	8.931
	(0.284)	(0.325)	(0.276)	(0.487)
$V[w]$	12.985	42.285	12.624	41.373
	(1.769)	(4.156)	(1.146)	(4.721)
$E[w|pt]$	10.003	9.701	10.102	9.346
	(0.429)	(0.891)	(0.597)	(0.905)
$V[w|pt]$	23.193	56.789	24.621	46.229
	(2.386)	(13.540)	(4.126)	(12.241)
$E[w|ft]$	7.644	8.647	8.154	8.908
	(0.248)	(0.336)	(0.318)	(0.523)
$V[w|ft]$	10.715	41.378	10.295	41.111
	(1.835)	(4.604)	(1.237)	(5.159)
		Durations		
$E[t_o|U]$	4.244	3.341	3.893	3.127
	(0.272)	(0.251)	(0.209)	(0.251)
$E[t_o|E]$	11.674	8.479	10.734	8.222
	(0.470)	(1.262)	(0.571)	(1.038)
$E[t_e|pt]$	78.634	52.331	58.343	51.817
	(9.511)	(1.966)	(2.680)	(4.605)
$E[t_e|ft]$	65.498	67.295	53.620	58.301
	(10.357)	(4.115)	(5.457)	(2.098)

Source: Data are from the 2001–2003 SIPP.
Notes: Standard errors in parentheses are computed by bootstrap with 30 replications. w are hourly wages; pt and ft part-time and full-time; t_o durations in months before job offer shock; t_e durations in months before job termination shock; E expected value; V variance.

It is an estimated value higher than the one obtained by Dey and Flinn (2008) but lower than the preferred value used by Guler et al. (2012). Overall, it is in general lower but comparable with values found in the micro literature (Chetty, 2006). Our parametrization nests the linear case since the utility function becomes linear in consumption when $\delta = 1$. A specification test for linearity is strongly rejected for both samples.[17]

---

17. The null for the specification test is $\delta = 1$. The *P*-values on both the sample with children and the sample without children is smaller than 0.0001.

The fit of the model on the moments we explicitly target in the estimation procedure is overall quite good.[18] We have chosen to fit a relatively large set of moments with a relatively parsimonious specification so it should not be too surprising that we fit some data features better than others. The model does a very good job in fitting the husband's wage distributions, the equilibrium labor market state proportions, the transitions probabilities and most of the cross-moments. However, it generates an acceptable but worse fit on the wives' wage distributions. This is a fairly common finding in the literature: Dey and Flinn (2008) have similar problems in fitting the cross-sectional moments of wives and both Flabbi (2010) and Bowlus (1997) obtain a better fit of the male wage distribution than of the female wage distribution.[19]

5. INEQUALITY

The estimation of the model structural parameters allows us to simulate labor market careers for households and individuals. This labor market careers can then be used to compute inequality measures both cross-sectionally and over time. We call *lifetime inequality* the inequality that summarizes the entire labor market careers of given agents. We give a formal definition below. The final objective of this section is, on top of building a measure of lifetime inequality, to provide a decomposition of the sources of inequality and to assess the impact of policy variables on the level of inequality through counterfactual policy experiments.

5.1. Simulations and Lifetime Variables

The simulation procedure works as follows. We start by fixing the parameter vector: the parameter vector is set at the point estimates of the estimated model when computing moments and indexes in the *benchmark* model; it is set at a proper combination of the point estimates when computing moments and indexes in the *counterfactual* and *policy experiments*

---

18. For a more detailed discussion of the model fit, see Section 5.2 in Flabbi and Mabli (2012).
19. Bowlus (1997) estimates the model separately for High School and College graduates: she obtains a worse fit for women than men on the High School sample and a better fit on the College sample but the High School sample has a larger sample size.

models. Each household begins in a given labor market state. Random numbers are generated to determine the length of time until each spouse receives a shock. When the shock is a job offer, the actual content of the job offer (wage level, part-time/full-time regime) is also drawn using a random number generator and it is drawn from the appropriate exogenous wage offers distribution. Recall that wage offers distribution are conditional on gender, part-time/full-time regime and presence of children in the household. The duration a household spends in each labor market state is recorded, along with the wages and hours associated with labor market states in which at least one spouse is employed. This process is repeated until the labor market history (the sum of the durations spent in all states) reaches 480 months (40 years).

One of the objectives of the paper is to propose inequality measures that take into account not only the current position of an individual in the accepted wage distribution but also her transitions over labor market states and the evolution of her wage over the entire labor market career. We attempt to satisfy this objective by proposing a summary measure of the evolution over time that we label *lifetime* value. The concept is then applied to a variety of indicators describing inequality in wages, earnings, and utility.

Lifetime values are created for each household and individual in the sample by integrating over discounted values of being in each labor market state over the full length of the labor market career. For example, the lifetime utility measure for the household i, j is defined as:

$$LU_{ij} = \sum_{s=1}^{S} \exp(-\rho t_s) \int_{t_{s-1}}^{t_s} u(c_{ij}, l_i, l_j; \delta, \beta, \alpha) \exp(-\rho v) \mathrm{d}v \tag{3}$$

where s denotes a spell in which the labor market status of both partners is unchanged. When building this lifetime index for individuals or for wages and earnings we simply change appropriately the argument of the integral and the length of the spells. Our *lifetime inequality* comparisons will be based on computing inequality measures on indexes defined as LU_{ij} in Eq. (3).

We use this measure of lifetime utility to describe household lifetime inequality for two reasons. First, it is a very intuitive measure able to capture the dynamic implied by participating over time in a given labor market characterized by frictions and wage and employment risk since the simulated labor market careers are timed as actual, observed labor market careers. Second, this is the measure used by the previous literature on the subject[20] and therefore, by using it, we can provide household-level measures that are comparable with the individual-level measures computed by previous contributions.

5.2. Inequality Measures

We want to use inequality indicators that are flexible in terms of sensitivity to different parts of the distribution. For this reason, we use indicators belonging to the Generalized Entropy class of inequality indexes which is defined in Shorrocks (1984) as:

$$GE(\nu) = \frac{1}{\nu(1-\nu)} \left[\frac{1}{n} \sum_{i=1}^{n} \left(\frac{y_i}{\bar{y}} \right)^{\nu} - 1 \right] \tag{4}$$

where y_i is the variable of interest in a population of individuals $i = 1, 2, \ldots n$; $\bar{y}$ is the sample mean; and v is a parameter.

This class has two important properties useful for our objective: (i) the sensitivity to the top of the distribution is governed very parsimoniously by one parameter, the parameter v: the more positive is v the higher the sensitivity of the index to differences in the top of the distribution; (ii) all indexes are in the same scale making the comparisons among them very convenient. Among the indexes belonging to this class, we will focus at most on the following three: GE (2) which equals to half the square of the coefficient of variation, GE (1) which is the Theil entropy index, and GE (0) which is the mean log deviation.[21]

5.3. Benchmark Model Results

Table 6 reports the inequality indexes computed over variables extracted from simulations of the benchmark model. The benchmark model is the model run at the estimated parameters reported in Table 4. The top panel reports results on the sample of household with children younger than 18

---

20. See for example, Flinn (2002), Bowlus and Robin (2004), and Flabbi and Leonardi (2010).
21. This class of inequality measures is also used by two other papers looking at lifetime inequality measures in a search context: Flabbi and Leonardi (2010) and Flinn (2002).

Table 6. Household Inequality in the Benchmark Model.

	Household			Wives		Husbands	
	Utility	Wages	Earnings	Wages	Earnings	Wages	Earnings
Yes Children Younger than 18							
Lifetime variables							
GE (0)	0.0235	0.0141	0.0159	0.0251	0.0309	0.0282	0.0302
GE (1)	0.0236	0.0145	0.0163	0.0241	0.0289	0.0297	0.0317
GE (2)	0.0240	0.0152	0.0171	0.0242	0.0282	0.0325	0.0347
Cross-section variables							
GE (0)	0.0286	0.1014	0.1056	0.0504	0.0563	0.1387	0.1436
GE (1)	0.0262	0.0907	0.0943	0.0491	0.0541	0.1313	0.1342
GE (2)	0.0250	0.0914	0.0953	0.0516	0.0554	0.1444	0.1465
No Children Younger than 18							
Lifetime variables							
GE (0)	0.0225	0.0113	0.0124	0.0145	0.0142	0.0251	0.0269
GE (1)	0.0226	0.0117	0.0129	0.0150	0.0144	0.0266	0.0284
GE (2)	0.0230	0.0124	0.0137	0.0158	0.0148	0.0292	0.0312
Cross-section variables							
GE (0)	0.0302	0.0958	0.1009	0.0565	0.0593	0.1444	0.1510
GE (1)	0.0270	0.0859	0.0899	0.0564	0.0565	0.1361	0.1405
GE (2)	0.0253	0.0865	0.0905	0.0601	0.0573	0.1481	0.1520

Notes: Inequality Indexes are computed over variables obtained by simulating the model at the estimated benchmark values reported in Table 4. Lifetime variables are defined in Eq. (3). *GE* (*v*) are indicators belonging to the Generalized Entropy class (see Eq. (4)). Specifically, *GE* (2) is half the square of the coefficient of variation, *GE* (1) is the Theil entropy index, and *GE* (0) is the mean log deviation.

and the bottom panel on household without children younger than 18. In each panel, the top rows report results on lifetime variables (see Eq. (3) for the definition) and the bottom rows results on cross-sectional variables.

There are major differences in the patterns of the inequality measures obtained on lifetime variables and on cross-sectional variables. First, in the cross-section, inequality at the utility level is lower than inequality at the wages and earnings level. This equalizing effect is not present when considering the lifetime horizon. It means that the durations in each state and the role played by shocks reverse this channel over time.

Second, when increasing the sensitivity to the top of the distribution — that is, moving from *GE* (0) to *GE* (2) — inequality increases in lifetime terms but decreases in the cross-section. However, the differences between indexes are not very large so we do not see this as a major result.

Third, inequality in wages and earnings between household and inequality in wages and earnings between individuals are ranked differently in the cross-section than over the lifetime.[22] Over the lifetime, the household has an equalizing effect both for husbands and wives: looking for example at *GE* (2) on earnings, household inequality is 0.0171 compared with 0.0282 wives inequality and 0.0347 husband inequality. At the cross-sectional level, the household has an equalizing effect only for husbands: *GE* (2) on earnings is 0.0953 for households, 0.0554 for wives and 0.1465 for husbands. This indicates that the assortative mating patterns can be very different in a static environment with respect to a dynamic environment.

Fourth, the results on the sample household without children younger than 18 repeat similar patterns but with different magnitudes. The most relevant difference in magnitudes refers to lifetime wages and earnings inequality for wives: it is much larger in the sample with children than in the sample without children. The use of part-time and difference preferences for leisure are among the important sources of this difference.

Overall, we think that these results deliver two main conclusions that support the motivation behind our approach: (i) inequality at the utility level is different than inequality on earnings and wages; (ii) inequality at the cross-sectional level is different than inequality at the lifetime level and may therefore deliver different policy implications. We explore this issue in the next two sections.

5.4. Counterfactual Experiments Results

5.4.1. Labor Market Structure and Household Inequality

We perform five policy experiments to estimate the impact of labor market changes and reforms on household inequality. We simulate the impact of changes in search frictions and job termination rates; the impact of an increase and a decrease in the proportion of part-time offers; and the impact of an increase in the dispersion of wages offers at same mean. Results are reported in Table 7. Since the inequality indexes are not very

---

22. It is straightforward to obtain measures of husbands and wives inequality by directly using their respective wages. It is more difficult to obtain measure of utility inequality for husbands and wives because utility is defined only at the household level. In Section 5.4.2, we will propose a summary measure of utility at the individual level to compare the gender gap on inequality but it requires very strong assumptions not fully consistent with usual models of household interaction.

LUCA FLABBI ET AL.

Table 7. Household Inequality: Impact of Labor Market Structure.

Experiments	Mean	GE (2)		
	Utility	Utility	Wages	Earnings
Yes Children Younger than 18				
Lifetime variables				
Benchmark	379.5	0.0240	0.0171	0.0152
Reduce frictions (RF)	394.2	0.0186	0.0148	0.0132
RF and increase turnover	385.3	0.0208	0.0128	0.0117
Increase part-time offers	379.0	0.0244	0.0164	0.0145
Decrease part-time offers	379.5	0.0239	0.0174	0.0160
Mean-preserving spread wage	394.3	0.0202	0.0456	0.0409
Cross-section variables				
Benchmark	1.889	0.0250	0.0953	0.0914
Reduce frictions (RF)	1.951	0.0209	0.0868	0.0831
RF and increase turnover	1.905	0.0239	0.0923	0.0882
Increase part-time offers	1.892	0.0260	0.0993	0.0945
Decrease part-time offers	1.881	0.0259	0.0899	0.0881
Mean-preserving spread wage	1.987	0.0262	0.2243	0.2082
No Children Younger than 18				
Lifetime variables				
Benchmark	422.2	0.0230	0.0137	0.0124
Reduce frictions (RF)	439.8	0.0172	0.0114	0.0108
RF and increase turnover	429.9	0.0194	0.0098	0.0092
Increase part-time offers	421.1	0.0233	0.0133	0.0123
Decrease part-time offers	423.6	0.0222	0.0139	0.0128
Mean-preserving spread wage	442.6	0.0206	0.0265	0.0243
Cross-section variables				
Benchmark	2.104	0.0253	0.0905	0.0865
Reduce frictions (RF)	2.179	0.0203	0.0769	0.0732
RF and increase turnover	2.126	0.0231	0.0879	0.0833
Increase part-time offers	2.111	0.0247	0.0885	0.0832
Decrease part-time offers	2.102	0.0248	0.0850	0.0833
Mean-preserving spread wage	2.215	0.0264	0.1540	0.1464

Notes: *GE* (2) is half the square of the coefficient of variation. Each experiment changes a specific set of parameters by 50% leaving the rest at the benchmark values. Specifically, *Reduce frictions*: increase $(\lambda_{W,M}, \gamma_{W,M})$; *Reduce frictions and increase turnover*: increase $(\lambda_{W,M}, \gamma_{W,M})$ and $\left(\eta_{W,M}^{PT}, \eta_{W,M}^{FT}\right)$; *Increase Part-time Offers*: increase $(p_{W,M})$; *Reduce part-time offers*: decrease $(p_{W,M})$; *Mean-preserving spread wage*: change $\left(\mu_{W,M}^{PT}, \sigma_{W,M}^{PT}, \mu_{W,M}^{FT}, \sigma_{W,M}^{FT}\right)$ so that the coefficient of variation in wage offers increases but the mean is unchanged.

sensitive to v and to guarantee better readability, we report only the GE (2) index. In each experiment, we change a specific set of parameters by 50% leaving the other parameters at the benchmark values. This new combination of parameters will generate different optimal decisions that we take into account when performing the simulations. The benchmark is the estimated model reported in Table 4.

We first focus on the top panel of Table 7, where we report results for the sample with children younger than 18 year old. The first row reports the benchmark values. The second row evaluates the impact of a reduction in search frictions, that is, we increase the arrival rates of wage offers $(\lambda_{W,M}, \gamma_{W,M})$ by 50%. Reducing frictions reduces lifetime inequality. The effect is mainly through shorter unemployment periods as shown by the relative more stable values in wages and earnings inequality. In the third row we check if the positive impact of a reduction in frictions may be offset by an increase in turnover generated by an increase in exogenous job terminations, that is, we increase both the dismissal rates $\left(\eta_{W,M}^{PT}, \eta_{W,M}^{FT}\right)$ and the arrival rates $(\lambda_{W,M}, \gamma_{W,M})$. Results show that the decrease in inequality induced by lower search frictions is not offset by an increase in terminations rates. The policy conclusion is that a more efficient search and matching process decrease *utility* inequality both at the *lifetime* level and at the cross-sectional level. The process also increases average household utility, as shown by the values reported in the first column.

The second set of policies looks at the impact of part-time (rows 4 and 5 for lifetime variables and 10 and 12 for cross-section variables). As we mentioned, the introduction of a labor supply margin in the model is unusual but we think it is justified to better match the labor market behavior of women. Women tend to work less hours than men and they highly value job flexibility.[23] The possibility of working part-time is still one of the most important institutional arrangements able to provide this flexibility. While previous works have tried to determine the presence of a "part-time penalties,"[24] we can evaluate here the impact of the presence of part-time on overall inequality. Row 4 shows the impact of an increase in part-time offers as described by a 50% increase in the parameters $(p_{W,M})$. Results

23. See for example, Altonji and Paxson (1988) and Flabbi and Moro (2012).
24. For example, Blank (1990) estimates large wage penalties for working part-time using Current Population Survey data.

shows that household inequality in earnings experiences a small increase, which is mainly due to a higher number of husbands accepting part-time jobs. If we decrease part-time offers by 50%, the increase in inequality in earnings for women is almost exactly balanced by a decrease in inequality in earnings for men leading to a value very similar to the benchmark. Lifetime inequality in utility and wages increases slightly. Our conclusion is that lifetime inequality is not very sensitive to changes in the proportion of part-time offers.

The last policy we look at tries to mimic a demand-driven increase in the dispersion of wage offers distributions. Such a policy could be interpreted as a very stylized version of the "skill-biased technological change" viewed by many scholars as an important source of the significant increase in inequality in the United States in recent decades.[25] We implement the policy by changing the wage offers distribution parameters $\left(\mu_{W,M}^{PT}, \sigma_{W,M}^{PT}, \mu_{W,M}^{FT}, \sigma_{W,M}^{FT}\right)$ so that the coefficient of variation in full-time and part-time wage offers increases by 50% but the mean remains unchanged. The mean-preserving spread has a very large impact on wages and earnings inequality: cross-sectional indexes more than double with respect to the benchmark model, and lifetime indexes are more than two times larger than in the benchmark. However, optimal behavior is smoothing the impact on utility, leading to only a relatively modest increase in cross-sectional utility inequality and to actually a *decrease* in lifetime utility inequality. This is possible because a larger dispersion in wage offers is combined with a higher (endogenous) value of unemployment and a quicker chance to move up the wage distribution. The decrease in lifetime inequality is paired with the largest increase in average utility among the five experiments: mean lifetime utility increases from 379.5 in the benchmark model to 394.3 in the Mean-Preserving Spread Experiment. The experiment is therefore very instructive on a couple of dimensions: (i) it shows that even large increases in wage and earnings inequality may not lead to an increase in utility inequality; (ii) it shows once again the importance of a lifetime perspective since the previous result is missed in the cross-sectional measures.

The bottom panel of Table 7 reports results for the same policies but applied to the sample of households without children younger than 18. The main messages are confirmed, including the increase in average lifetime

---

25. Katz and Murphy (1992) is an influential earlier contribution; Acemoglu (2002) provides theoretical background; Card and DiNardo (2002) empirically assess its empirical impact on inequality; Eckstein and Nagypal (2004) document skill-premia over a long time span.

utility and the decrease in lifetime utility inequality induced by the mean-preserving spread experiment.

5.4.2. Decomposition of Gender Differentials in Inequality

We have seen that inequality in wages and earnings is quite different between husbands and wives and it may be instructive to use the model to find the sources of this differential. It would be also interesting to do the same on inequality based on utility measures. However, our household search model specification assumes household utility and not individual utility. Our proposed solution, at some cost in terms of theoretical coherence with the model, is to "re-assign" utility to the two spouses from the household model in the following way.[26] We impute individual utility — say, to the wife — from the household utility as:

$$u(c_j, l_j; \delta, \beta_W, \alpha_W) = (1 - \alpha_W)\frac{c_j^{\delta} - 1}{\delta} + \alpha_W \frac{l_j^{\beta_W} - 1}{\beta_W} \tag{5}$$

where

$$c_j = w_j h_j + y_{ij}/2$$
$$l_j = 1 - h_j - s_j$$
$$h_j \in \{h^{pt}, h^{ft}\}$$

Eq. (5) is a simple specialization of Eq. (1) where we focus on leisure and labor income of only one of the spouse and we split non-labor income in half.

There are two problematic issue in this formulation. First, in Eq. (5) we assign non-labor income to each individual spouse by splitting equally the household non-labor income between them. It is an arbitrary assumption but it is entirely driven by data limitation since we do not observe non-labor income individually assigned in the data. Second, the risk aversion coefficient δ is a coefficient estimated for the pooled household consumption and not for individual consumption. This assumption generate a contradiction with the theoretical model that we cannot solve. However, using the parameter in this way allows us to gain a reasonably meaningful formulation to compare utility inequality at the individual level. As a result, we have decided to report this expression when presenting our decomposition of the gender differential in inequality.

---

26. This approach is used in Flabbi and Mabli (2012) to compare estimates derived from a household search model with those derived from an individual search model. This section borrows heavily from that paper.

We propose the decomposition by performing the following experiments. Each experiment changes a specific set of parameters to be equal between husbands and wives. Parameters are always set at husbands' values. The first experiment, labeled Frictions, involves all the mobility parameters: λ, γ, η. The second experiment, labeled Job offers, involves all the job offers parameters: μ, σ, p. Finally, the third experiment, labeled Preferences, involves the gender-specific preference parameters: α, β.

Table 8 reports the results. For readability, we only report the *GE* (2) index, that is, half the square of the coefficient of variation. We first notice that in the benchmark model, inequality in wages and earnings is always

Table 8. Household Inequality: Gender Differentials Decomposition.

Set of Parameters	Wives *GE* (2)			Husbands *GE* (2)		
	Wages	Earnings	Utility	Wages	Earnings	Utility
Yes Children Younger than 18						
Lifetime variables						
Benchmark	0.0242	0.0282	0.1071	0.0325	0.0347	0.0825
Frictions	0.0213	0.0266	0.1185	0.0324	0.0340	0.0861
Job offers	0.0355	0.0405	0.0973	0.0331	0.0350	0.0885
Preferences	0.0175	0.0164	0.1169	0.0333	0.0355	0.0859
Cross-section variables						
Benchmark	0.0516	0.0554	0.0384	0.1444	0.1465	0.0354
Frictions	0.0556	0.0617	0.0381	0.1524	0.1504	0.0359
Job offers	0.1630	0.1673	0.0400	0.1595	0.1602	0.0352
Preferences	0.0672	0.0602	0.0409	0.1638	0.1658	0.0368
No Children Younger than 18						
Lifetime variables						
Benchmark	0.0158	0.0148	0.1213	0.0292	0.0312	0.0907
Frictions	0.0133	0.0125	0.1177	0.0289	0.0311	0.0889
Job offers	0.0300	0.0327	0.1031	0.0298	0.0318	0.0887
Preferences	0.0148	0.0125	0.1167	0.0280	0.0299	0.0888
Cross-section variables						
Benchmark	0.0601	0.0573	0.0394	0.1481	0.1520	0.0369
Frictions	0.0632	0.0563	0.0379	0.1460	0.1516	0.0350
Job offers	0.1521	0.1585	0.0409	0.1574	0.1615	0.0361
Preferences	0.0697	0.0543	0.0389	0.1570	0.1601	0.0366

Notes: *GE* (2) is half the square of the coefficient of variation. Each experiment changes a specific set of parameters to be equal between husbands and wives. Parameters are always set at husbands' values. Frictions includes all the mobility parameters λ, γ, η; Job offers includes all the job offers parameters μ, σ, p; Preferences includes the preference parameters α, β.

higher for husbands than wives. This is a standard finding in the gender wag gap literature. In utility terms, instead, we find the opposite ranking with wives' inequality indexes always higher than husbands'. This differential is stronger at the lifetime level than at the cross-sectional level.

We then proceed with the decomposition of the differentials (rows 2–4 of each panel) in its three components. What we find is that the job offers are the main source of the gender differentials in wages and earnings inequality: when wives values are set equal to husbands values (and individuals are allowed to re-optimize choices with the other parameters left at the benchmark gender-specific values), wives' inequality indexes become very similar to husbands' inequality indexes. This includes both the inequality indexes on wages and earnings (originally higher for men) and the inequality indexes on utility (originally higher for women). Interestingly, preferences will lead to a higher differential in cross-sectional inequality but not in lifetime inequality.

Finally, it is important to notice that in lifetime inequality terms, wives' indexes indicate more dispersion than husbands' indexes. In this case, the job offers parameters have an equalizing effect. However, in interpreting these results, it is important to keep in mind the caveat we have used in assigning individual utility from estimated obtained by a unitary model of the household.

6. CONCLUSIONS

This paper provides household lifetime inequality indexes derived from representative U.S. labor market data. We obtain this result by using estimates of the household search model proposed by Flabbi and Mabli (2012). Focusing on lifetime measures is important in order to take into account the importance of mobility across labor market states and the impact of wage and employment risk. Focusing on household measures is essential to take into account that labor market decisions are taken at the household level and that couples share risk and resources.

Inequality indexes computed on the benchmark model shows that inequality in utility values is substantially different from inequality in earnings and wages and that inequality at the cross-sectional level is different from inequality at the lifetime level. Both results deliver original policy implications that would have not been captured without using our approach. In particular, we find that a counterfactual policy experiment mimicking a skill-biased technological change leads to an increase in lifetime inequality in wages and earnings but to a decrease in lifetime inequality in utility. The lack of increase in lifetime utility inequality is not captured by cross-sectional measures that, instead, indicate a large increase in inequality across the board.

When comparing inequality at the individual level between men and women, we find inequality in wages and earnings to be higher for husbands than wives but inequality in utility to be higher for wives. A counterfactual decomposition shows that the job offers parameters are the main source of the differential: when wives' job offers parameters are set equal to husbands' job offers parameters, the gender differential in inequality indexes almost disappears.

REFERENCES

Acemoglu, D. (2002). Technical change, inequality and the labor market. *Journal of Economic Literature*, *40*(1), 7–72.

Aizawa, N., & Fang, H. (2013). *Equilibrium labor market search and health insurance reform*. NBER Working Paper No. 18698.

Altonji, J., & Paxson, C. (1988). Labor supply preferences, hours constraints, and hours-wage trade-offs. *Journal of Labor Economics*, *6*(2), 254–276.

Attanasio, O., & Davis, S. (1996). Relative wage movements and the distribution of consumption. *Journal of Political Economy*, *104*, 1227–1262.

Badel, A., & Huggett, M. (2014). Interpreting life-cycle inequality patterns as an efficient allocation: Mission impossible? *Review of Economic Dynamics*, *17*(4), 613–629.

Bagger, J., Fontaine, F., Postel-Vinay, F., & Robin, J.-M. (2014). Tenure, experience, human capital, and wages: A tractable equilibrium search model of wage dynamics. *American Economic Review*, *104*(6), 1551–1596.

Blank, R. (1990). Are part-time jobs bad jobs? In G. Burtless (Ed.), *A future of lousy jobs? The changing structure of U.S. wages*. Washington, DC: Brooking Institution.

Blau, D. (1991). Search for nonwage job characteristics: A test for reservation wage hypothesis. *Journal of Labor Economics*, *9*(2), 186–205.

Blundell, R., & Preston, I. (1998). Consumption inequality and income uncertainty. *Quarterly Journal of Economics*, *113*, 603–640.

Bowlus, A. (1997). A search interpretation of male-female wage differentials. *Journal of Labor Economics*, *15*(4), 625–657.

Bowlus, A. J., & Robin, J.-M. (2004). Twenty years of rising inequality in US lifetime labor values. *Review of Economic Studies*, *71*(3), 709–743.

Buchinsky, M., & Hunt, J. (1999). Wage mobility in the United States. *Review of Economics and Statistics*, *81*(3), 351–368.

Card, D., & DiNardo, J. E. (2002). Skill-based technological change and rising wage inequality: Some problems and puzzles. *Journal of Labor Economics*, *20*(4), 733–783.

Chetty, R. (2006). A new method of estimating risk aversion. *American Economic Review*, *96*, 1821–1834.

Chiappori, P.-A., Costa-Dias, M., & Meghir, C. (2015). *The marriage market, labor supply and education choice.* NBER Working Paper No. 21004.

Dey, M., & Flinn, C. (2008). Household search and health insurance coverage. *Journal of Econometrics, 145*, 43–63.

Eckstein, Z., & Nagypal, E. (2004). The evolution of U.S. earnings inequality: 1961–2002. *Federal Reserve Bank of Minneapolis Quarterly Review, 28*(December), 10–29.

Flabbi, L. (2010). Gender discrimination estimation in a search model with matching and bargaining. *International Economic Review, 51*(3), 745–783.

Flabbi, L., & Flinn, C. (2015). *Simultaneous search in the labor and marriage markets with endogenous schooling decisions.* Mimeo, UNC-Chapel Hill and NYU.

Flabbi, L., & Leonardi, M. (2010). Sources of earnings inequality: Estimates from an on-the-job search model of the U.S. labor market. *European Economic Review, 54*(6), 832–854.

Flabbi, L., & Mabli, J. (2012). *Household search or individual search: Does it matter? Evidence from lifetime inequality estimates.* IZA Discussion Paper No. 6908.

Flabbi, L., & Mabli, J. (2015). *Household search or individual search: Does it matter?* Mimeo, UNC-Chapel Hill and Mathematica Policy Research.

Flabbi, L., & Moro, A. (2012). The effect of job flexibility on female labor market outcomes: Estimates from a search and bargaining model. *Journal of Econometrics, 168*, 81–95.

Flinn, C. (2002). Labour market structure and inequality: A comparison of Italy and the U.S. *Review of Economic Studies, 69*, 611–645.

Flinn, C., & Heckman, J. (1982). New methods in analyzing structural models of labor market dynamics. *Journal of Econometrics, 18*, 115–168.

Flinn, C., & Mullins, J. (2015). Labour market search and schooling investment. *International Economic Review, 56*(2), 359–398.

Gottschalk, P., & Moffitt, R. (1994). The growth of earnings instability in the U.S. labor market. *Brookings Papers on Economic Activity, 2*, 217–254.

Gørgens, T. (2002). Reservation wages and working hours for recently unemployed US women. *Labour Economics, 9*(1), 93–123.

Greenwood, J., Guner, N., Kocharkov, G., & Santos, C. (2015). Technology and the changing family: A unified model of marriage, divorce, educational attainment and married female labor-force participation. *American Economics Journal: Macroeconomics, forthcoming.*

Guler, B., Guvenen, F., & Violante, G. (2012). Joint-search theory: New opportunities and new frictions. *Journal of Monetary Economics, 59*(4), 352–369.

Heathcote, J., Perri, F., & Violante, G. (2010). Unequal we stand: An empirical analysis of economic inequality in the United States. *Review of Economic Dynamics, 13*(1), 15–51.

Heathcote, J., Storesletten, K., & Violante, G. (2008). Insurance and opportunities: A welfare analysis of labor market risk. *Journal of Monetary Economics, 55*, 501–525.

Huggett, M., Ventura, G., & Yaron, A. (2011). Sources of lifetime inequality. *American Economic Review, 101*, 2923–2954.

Hwang, H., Mortensen, D., & Reed, R. (1998). Hedonic wages and labor market search. *Journal of Labor Economics, 16*(4), 815–847.

Kaplan, G. (2012). Inequality and the lifecycle. *Quantitative Economics, 3*, 471–525.

Katz, L. F., & Murphy, K. M. (1992). Changes in relative wages, 1963–1987: Supply and demand factors. *Quarterly Journal of Economics, 107*(1), 35–78.

Krueger, D., & Perri, F. (2006). Does income inequality lead to consumption inequality? Evidence and theory. *Review of Economic Studies, 73*(January), 163–193.

Meghir, C., Narita, R., & Robin, J.-M. (2015). Wages and informality in developing countries. *American Economic Review, 105*(4), 1509–46.

Low, H., Meghir, C., & Pistaferri, L. (2008). *Wage risk and employment risk over the life-cycle.* IZA Discussion Paper No. 3700.

ESTIMATING THE INTERGENERATIONAL ELASTICITY AND RANK ASSOCIATION IN THE UNITED STATES: OVERCOMING THE CURRENT LIMITATIONS OF TAX DATA ☆

Bhashkar Mazumder

Federal Reserve Bank of Chicago and
University of Bergen

ABSTRACT

Ideal estimates of the intergenerational elasticity (IGE) in income require a large panel of income data covering the entire working lifetimes for two generations. Previous studies have demonstrated that using short panels

☆ I thank Andy Jordan and Karl Schulze for outstanding research assistance. I thank participants at seminars at IZA, the New York Fed, the Chicago Fed, the University of Bergen, the University of Tennessee, and the University of Michigan as well as Nathaniel Hendren for helpful comments. I also thank a referee for valuable comments and guidance. The views expressed here do not reflect those of the Federal Reserve Bank of Chicago or the Federal Reserve system.

Inequality: Causes and Consequences
Research in Labor Economics, Volume 43, 83–129
ISSN: 0147-9121/doi:10.1108/S0147-912120160000043012

and covering only certain portions of the life cycle can lead to considerable bias. I address these biases by using the PSID and constructing long time averages centered at age 40 in both generations. I find that the IGE in family income in the United States is likely greater than 0.6 suggesting a relatively low rate of intergenerational mobility in the United States. I find similar sized estimates for the IGE in labor income. These estimates support the prior findings of Mazumder (2005a, b) and are also similar to comparable estimates reported by Mitnik et al. (2015). In contrast, a recent influential study by Chetty, Hendren, Kline, Saez (2014) using tax data that begins in 1996 estimates the IGE in family income for the United States to be just 0.344 implying a much higher rate of intergenerational mobility. I demonstrate that despite the seeming advantages of extremely large samples of administrative tax data, the age structure, and limited panel dimension of the data used by Chetty et al. leads to considerable downward bias in estimating the IGE. I further demonstrate that the sensitivity checks in Chetty et al. regarding the age at which children's income is measured, and the length of the time average of parent income used to estimate the IGE suffer from biases due to these data limitations. There are also concerns that tax data, unlike survey data, may not adequately reflect all sources of family income. Estimates of the rank—rank slope, Chetty et al.'s preferred estimator, are more robust to the limitations of the tax data but are also downward biased and modestly overstate mobility. However, Chetty et al.'s main findings of sizable geographic differences within the US in rank mobility are unlikely to be affected by these biases. I conclude that researchers should continue to use both the IGE and rank-based measures depending on their preferred concept of mobility. It is also important for researchers to have adequate coverage of key portions of the life cycle and to consider the possible drawbacks of using administrative data.

Keywords: Intergenerational mobility; tax data

JEL classification: J62

1. INTRODUCTION

Inequality of opportunity has become a tremendously salient issue for policy makers across many countries in recent years. The sharp rise in inequality has given rise to fears that economic disparities will persist into future generations. This has led to a heightened focus on the literature on intergenerational economic mobility. This body of research, which is now several decades old, seeks to understand the degree to which economic status is transmitted across generations. A critical first step in understanding this literature and correctly interpreting its findings is having a sound understanding of the measures that are being used and what they do and do not measure. This paper focuses on two prominent measures of intergenerational mobility, the intergenerational elasticity (IGE), and the rank–rank slope, and discusses several key conceptual and measurement issues related to these estimators.

The IGE has a fairly long history of use in economics dating back to papers from the 1980s. It is generally viewed as a useful and transparent summary statistic capturing the rate of "regression to the mean." It can, for example, tell us how many generations (on average) it would take the descendants of a low-income family to rise to the mean level of log income. In recent years, many notable advances have been made in terms of measurement and issues concerning life cycle bias (e.g., Böhlmark & Lindquist, 2006; Grawe, 2006; Haider & Solon, 2006; Jenkins, 1987; Mazumder, 2005a; Solon, 1992).[1] As a result of these contributions, most recent US estimates of the IGE in family income are generally around 0.5 or higher.[2]

Thus far, no study of intergenerational mobility in the US has yet been conducted that has used very long time averages of family income of parents and has also utilized averages of family income in both generations centered at age 40, where life cycle bias is minimized.[3] This paper fills this void in the literature by using PSID data that meet these requirements. Using up to 15 year averages of income in the parent generation yields estimates of the IGE with respect to family income of sons that are greater than 0.6. I also find that the IGE with respect to the labor income of male

---

1. Reviews of this literature can be found in Solon (1999) and Black and Devereux (2011).
2. Solon's (1992) estimate is 0.483. Hertz (2005) reports an IGE of 0.538. Hertz (2006) finds the IGE to be 0.58. Bratsberg et al. (2007) estimate the IGE of family income on earnings to be 0.54. Jäntti et al.'s. (2006) estimate of the same measure is 0.517. Mitnik et al.'s. (2015) estimate of the standard IGE is between 0.55 and 0.74. Note that all of these studies (like Chetty et al., 2014) report some variant of the IGE with respect to *family income*. Of course, many other studies have used a different income concept such as labor market earnings.
3. The closest is Mitnik et al. (2015), who use nine-years of parent income and children between the ages of 35 and 38.

household heads is greater than 0.6 and very similar to the estimate found by Mazumder (2005a) using social security earnings data.[4]

These results stand in stark contrast with the results in a recent highly influential study by Chetty, Hendren, Kline, Saez (2014), who use large samples drawn from IRS tax records and produce estimates of the IGE in family income of just 0.344 suggesting significantly greater intergenerational mobility. Furthermore, Chetty et al. argue that none of the previous biases identified in the literature on IGE estimation apply to their data. Given the importance of the IGE as one of the key conceptual measures of intergenerational mobility, it is worth revisiting the measurement issues in the context of their sample. This exercise is not only useful for revisiting the specific results of Chetty et al., but also holds more general lessons for other research seeking to exploit administrative data to measure intergenerational mobility.

The IRS-based intergenerational sample used by Chetty et al. is fundamentally limited in a few key respects that ultimately stems from the fact that the data only begin in 1996. First, children's income is only measured in 2011 and 2012. This is at a relatively early point in the life cycle for cohorts born between 1980 and 1982 (ages 29 to 32) and during a period when unemployment was quite high in the US. This age range is one in which we would expect substantial life cycle bias in producing IGE estimates (Haider & Solon, 2006). Moreover, relative to a more ideal data structure, where cohorts of children could be chosen such that they were observed over the 31 years spanning the ages of 25−55, Chetty et al. are limited to using only 6 percent of the life cycle. Second, parents' income is also measured for only a short period (five years) covering just 16 percent of the life cycle and at a relatively late period in life. Roughly 25% of observations of fathers' income in their sample are measured at age 50 or higher. The literature has shown that starting around the age of 50 a substantial share of the variance in income is due to transitory fluctuations. This leads to substantial attenuation of the IGE relative to what would be found if one used lifetime income for the parents (Haider & Solon, 2006;

---

4. Chetty et al. (2014) suggest that the high estimates in Mazumder (2005a) are solely due to data imputations of fathers' SSA earnings that are topcoded in some years and are not the result of using longer-time averages of father earnings. Below, I reiterate arguments against that claim that were originally discussed in Mazumder (2005a) but subsequently ignored by Chetty et al., 2014 in their appendix E discussion. I also point to other studies in the literature that are supportive of the findings in Mazumder (2005a). It is notable that this study yields similar estimates to Mazumder (2005a) while requiring no imputations of income.

Mazumder, 2005a). Third, recent research has established that administrative data can sometimes lead to worse measurement error than survey data, particularly at the bottom end of the income distribution (e.g., Abowd & Stinson, 2013; Hokayem et al., 2012, 2015).

It is important to make it very clear that the main focus of Chetty et al. is not their national estimates of the IGE. Instead, the authors make an important contribution to the literature by producing the first estimates of a different measure of mobility, rank mobility, at a very detailed level of US geography. Notably, they provide evidence of substantial heterogeneity across the United States. As I discuss below, the biases that affect their national estimates of the IGE likely have little effect on their main conclusions regarding geographic differences.

The limitations of the tax data for intergenerational analysis can be sharply contrasted with the PSID sample used in this paper. In the PSID sample, family income is observed in both generations over a vastly larger portion of the life cycle and the time averages are *centered* over the prime working years in both generations. I estimate the IGE using this closer to "ideal" sample and then show how the estimates change if I impose the same kinds of data limitations that exist in the IRS data. The results show that the data limitations lead to IGE estimates that are roughly half the size of the estimates with the complete data and similar in magnitude to the estimates of Chetty et al. A very similar pattern of results is also found by Mitnik et al. (2015).[5]

Chetty et al. also find the IGE to be very sensitive to how they choose to impute the income of children who report no family income during 2011 and 2012. However, it is the limited panel dimension of their data and their reliance on administrative data which makes their analysis susceptible to this problem. Had they been able to observe the income of children during later periods of the life cycle and other sources of income, then such imputation becomes unnecessary.[6] This is important because it is their concern about the robustness of the IGE that led Chetty et al. to using rank-based

---

5. Mitnik et al. (2015) use IRS data that begins in 1987 enabling children to be observed into their late 30s and for parent income to be measured over nine years. Not only do Mitnik et al. also produce similar sized estimates to the PSID results when using a comparable methodology (0.55–0.74), but they also show that they can match the Chetty et al. estimates if they restrict their analysis to 29- to 32-year olds and use five year averages of parent income.
6. Mitnik et al. (2015) introduce a new approach to estimating the IGE that enables them to overcome this sensitivity to years of missing income when using a small window to measure child income. I discuss this in Section 3.

estimators.[7] This contrasts with other studies, some predating Chetty et al.'s work, that have also used rank-based measures to study intergenerational mobility but for conceptual reasons.[8]

Given the recent shift in the literature to using rank-based measures, it is useful to distinguish the measurement concerns with the IGE from the conceptual differences between the two estimators. In short, both measures can provide useful insights about different mobility concepts. Since certain questions are best answered by the IGE, researchers should continue to use that estimator as at least one tool in their arsenal. Nevertheless, rank-based estimators are also valuable. In addition to providing information on a different concept of mobility, positional mobility, rank-based measures are also useful for distinguishing upward versus downward movements, making subgroup comparisons, and for identifying nonlinearities. I would argue that even if Chetty et al. had found the IGE to be perfectly robust in their tax data, it would still be preferable to use rank-mobility measures to understand geographic differences. This is because an IGE estimated in, say, Charlotte, North Carolina would only be informative about the rate of regression to the mean income in *Charlotte*. If ranks are fixed to the national distribution, then rank mobility measures enable a more meaningful comparison across cities.

Finally, I use the PSID to estimate the rank–rank slope. The estimates (0.4 or higher) are only moderately larger than what is found with the IRS data (0.341) or what is found with the PSID data when imposing the tax data limitations. Although the rank–rank slope may be more robust to the data limitations of the IRS sample than the IGE, it is still not perfect and suggests that the rate of intergenerational mobility even by rank-based measures may be overstated by the tax data. This is broadly in line with findings for Sweden (Nybom & Stuhler, 2015). In the future as the panel length of US tax data increases, these biases will recede in importance. However, it is uncertain whether researchers will be able to obtain tax data in future decades.

I conclude that researchers should continue to use the IGE if that is the conceptual parameter of interest. Even when the ideal data are not available, researchers can still attempt to assess the extent of the bias based on

---

7. Dahl and DeLeire (2008) also shift to rank-based measures based on concerns regarding the robustness of the IGE but their concerns revolve around a different measurement issue than Chetty et al. which I discuss in Section 3.

8. See Bhattacharya and Mazumder (2011), Corak et al. (2014), Mazumder (2014) and Bratberg et al., 2015.

prior research.[9] The rest of this paper proceeds as follows. Section 2 describes conceptual differences between the IGE and the rank–rank slope. Section 3 discusses measurement issues with the IGE and outlines an "ideal" dataset. It then compares this ideal dataset with Chetty et al.'s IRS-based sample and samples that can be constructed with publicly available PSID data. Section 4 describes the PSID data. Section 5 presents the main results and Section 6 concludes.

2. CONCEPTUAL ISSUES

The concept of regression to the mean over generations has a long and notable tradition going back to the Victorian era social scientist Sir Francis Galton who studied, among other things, the rate of regression to the mean in height between parents and children. Modern social scientists have continued to find this concept insightful as a way of describing the rate of intergenerational persistence in a particular outcome and to infer the rate of mobility as the flip side of persistence. In particular, economists have focused on the IGE. The IGE is the estimate of β obtained from the following regression:

$$y_{1i} = \alpha + \beta y_{0i} + \varepsilon_i \tag{1}$$

where y_{1i} is the log income of the child's generation and y_{0i} is the log of income in the parents' generation.[10] The estimate of β provides a measure of intergenerational persistence and $1 - \beta$ can be used as a measure of mobility. For simplicity, if we assume that the intergenerational relationship actually follows a simple autoregressive process then one can use β to extrapolate how long it would take for gaps in log income between families to recede.[11] For example, consider a family whose log annual income is around 9.8 ($18,000). We might be interested in knowing roughly how

---

9. See, for example, Gouskova et al. (2010), who show that their IGE estimates rise from around 0.4 to over 0.6 when taking into account these biases.

10. Often the regression will include age controls but few other covariates since β is not given a causal interpretation but rather reflects all factors correlated with parent income.

11. Recent research has cast doubt on the simple AR(1) model arguing that there may be independent effects emanating from prior generations such as grandparents and great-grandparents (Lindahl, Palme, Massih, & Sjögren, 2015). Nevertheless, the AR(1) assumption provides a useful first approximation and conveys the general point about why the magnitude of the estimates might matter.

many generations it would take (on average) for the descendants of this family's log income to be within 0.05 of the national average log income of 11.2 ($73,000). If, for example, the IGE is around 0.60 as claimed by Mazumder (2005a) then it would take seven generations (175 years). On the other hand if the IGE is around 0.34 as claimed by Chetty et al. (2014), then it would take just four generations. Clearly, the two estimates have profoundly different implications on the rate of intergenerational mobility by this metric. If the rate of regression to the mean is, in fact, what we are interested in knowing, then the IGE is what we ought to estimate. For example, some papers find that the IGE is particularly useful for calibrating structural models of interest (e.g., De Nardi & Yang, 2015; Lee & Seshadri, 2015). The concept of regression to the mean is also widely used in other aspects of economics such as the macroeconomic literature on differences in per-capita income across countries (e.g., Barro & Sala-i-Martin, 1992).

The rank−rank slope on the other hand is about a different concept of mobility, namely, *positional* mobility. For example, a rank−rank slope of 0.4 suggests that the expected difference in ranks between the adult children of two different families would be about 4 percentiles if the difference in ranks among their parents was 10 percentiles. How are the two measures related? Chetty et al. (2014) point out that the rank−rank slope is very closely related to the intergenerational correlation (IGC) in log income. They and many others have also shown that the IGE is equal to the IGC times the ratio of the standard deviation of log income in the child's generation to the standard deviation of log income in the parents' generation:

$$IGE = IGC \frac{\sigma_{y1}}{\sigma_{y0}} \qquad (2)$$

This relationship is sometimes taken to imply that a rise in inequality would lead the IGE to rise but not affect the IGC and that therefore, the IGC may be a preferred measure that avoids a "mechanical" effect of inequality. By extension one might also prefer the rank−rank slope if one accepts this argument. Several comments are worth making here. First, in reality the parameters are all jointly determined by various economic forces. In the absence of a structural model, one cannot meaningfully talk about holding "inequality" fixed. For example, a change in β might cause inequality to rise, rather than the reverse, or both might be altered by some third force such as rising returns to skill. The mathematical relationship shown in Eq. (2) does not substitute for a behavioral relationship and so we cannot truly isolate forces driving inequality from the IGE. Second, even if it was the case that the IGC or rank–rank slope was a measure that was "independent of inequality," that doesn't mean that society shouldn't continue to be interested in the rate of regression to the mean. It may well be the case that it is precisely because of the rise in inequality that societies are increasingly concerned about intergenerational persistence and so incorporating the effects of inequality may actually be critical to understanding the rates of mobility that policy makers want to address. Mitnik et al. (2015), for example, argue in favor of the IGE precisely because it incorporates distributional changes.

In addition to providing useful information about positional mobility, the rank–rank slope has other attractive features. Perhaps its most useful advantage over the IGE is that it can be used to measure mobility differences across subgroups of the population with respect to the national distribution. This is because the IGE estimated within groups is only informative about persistence or mobility with respect to the *group-specific mean*, whereas the rank–rank slope can be estimated based on ranks calculated based on the national distribution. Chetty et al. (2014) were able to use this to characterize mobility for the first time at an incredibly fine geographic level. Mazumder (2014) used other "directional" rank mobility measures to compare differences in intergenerational mobility between blacks and whites in the United States. However, for characterizing intergenerational mobility at the *national level* both the IGE and the rank–rank slope are suitable depending on which concept of mobility a researcher is interested in studying.

3. MEASUREMENT ISSUES AND THE IDEAL INTERGENERATIONAL SAMPLE

3.1. Measurement Issues

The literature on intergenerational mobility has highlighted two key measurement concerns that I briefly review. The first issue is attenuation bias that arises from measurement error or transitory fluctuations in parent income. In an ideal setting, the measures of y_1 and y_0 in Eq. (1) would be measures of lifetime or permanent income, but in most datasets, we only have short snapshots of income that can contain noise and attenuate estimates of the IGE. Solon (1992) showed that using a single year income as a proxy for lifetime income of fathers can lead to considerable bias relative to using a five-year average of income. Using the PSID, Solon concluded that the IGE in annual labor market earnings was 0.4 "or higher." Mazumder (2005a) used the SIPP matched to social security earnings records and showed that using even a five-year average can lead to considerable bias and estimated the IGE in labor market earnings to be around 0.6 when using longer time averages of fathers earnings (up to 16 years). Mazumder argues that the key reason that a five-year average is insufficient is that the transitory variance in earnings tends to be highly persistent and appeals to the findings of US studies of earnings dynamics that support this point. Using simulations based on parameters from these other studies, Mazumder shows that the attenuation bias from using a five-year average in the data is close to what one would expect to find based on the simulations. In a separate paper that is less well known, Mazumder (2005b) showed that if one uses short-term averages in the PSID and uses a Hetereoscedastic Errors in Variables (HEIV) estimator that adjusts for the amount of measurement error or transitory variance contained in each observation, then the PSID-adjusted estimate of the IGE is also around 0.6.

This latter paper is a useful complement because unlike the social security earnings data used by Mazumder (2005a) the PSID data are not top-coded and doesn't require imputations. Chetty et al. (2014) have contended that the larger estimates of the IGE in Mazumder (2005a) were due to the nature of the imputation process rather than due to larger time averages of fathers' earnings. Specifically, in cases where earnings were above the social security taxable maximum they were imputed by using the mean earnings level by race and education level from other data sources. Mazumder acknowledges that this moves a step in the direction toward "instrumenting" for fathers earnings based on demographic characteristics but argues that it is not obvious that this imparts an upward bias and may well lead to a downward bias.[12] Mazumder also shows that when using up to seven year averages and dropping fathers who are ever topcoded, which is about half of the sample, that the resulting IGE of 0.439 ($N = 1,144$) is not very different from the IGE of 0.472 ($N = 2,240$) for the full sample. Mazumder

---

12. See footnote 13 in Mazumder (2005a). That footnote explains why in the presence of life-cycle bias, an IV estimate of the IGE for sons who are younger than 40 and fathers who are older than 40 leads to downward bias. The mean age of sons in Mazumder (2005a) is 32 and the mean age of fathers in 1984 is 47. Chetty et al. (2014) ignore this point when they discuss Mazumder (2005a) in their appendix E.

further argues that this robustness check of dropping fathers who are ever topcoded may impart a downward bias due to a potential selection effect of eliminating father son pairs whose IGE may be higher because they are selected from the top of the income distribution.[13] In any event, a number of other studies in addition to Mazumder (2005b), which also do not require imputed data, and in some cases use administrative tax data, demonstrate that longer time averages lead to substantially higher IGE estimates. These studies include: Nilsen et al. (2012), Gregg et al. (2013), Mazumder & Acosta, 2015, and Mitnik et al., 2015.

The second critical measurement concern in the literature concerns life cycle bias best encapsulated by Haider and Solon (2006). One aspect of this critique concerns the effects of measuring children's income when they are too young. Children who end up having high lifetime income often have steeper income trajectories than children who have lower lifetime income. Therefore, if income is measured at too young age, it can lead to an attenuated estimate of the IGE in lifetime income. Haider and Solon show that this bias can be considerable and is minimized when income is measured at around age 40. A related issue is that transitory fluctuations are not constant over the life cycle but instead follow a u-shaped pattern over the life cycle (Baker & Solon, 2003; Mazumder, 2005a). This implies that measuring parents' income when they are either too young or (especially) too old can also attenuate estimates of the IGE. While there are econometric approaches one can use to correct for life cycle bias, one simple approach is to simply center the time averages of both children's and parents' income around the age of 40. Using this approach with the PSID, Mazumder and Acosta estimate the IGE to be around 0.6. Mitnik et al. (2015) also use this approach with IRS data covering older cohorts who are observed as late as age 38 and find that both sources of bias are quantitatively important. Further, Nilsen et al. (2012), Gregg et al. (2014), and Nybom and Stuhler (2015) using data from other countries show that both time averaging and

---

13. Mitnik et al. (2015), for example, find that the IGE is higher at the upper half of the income distribution. Chetty et al. (2014) in their appendix E do not address this selection argument in their discussion of Mazumder's table 6 and imply that the results of the robustness check are explained by an upward bias due to IV. Mazumder (2005a) points out that if he uses longer time averages than 7 years and also drops fathers who are ever topcoded that this results in dramatically smaller samples that are likely to be highly selected and are likely to be uninformative about the effects of topcoding. One possible way to gauge the potential upward or downward bias of using imputing topcoded values would be to run simulations with fake data where one can use a range of parameter values to assess the magnitude of the bias.

life cycle bias play a role in attenuating IGE coefficients. Importantly, these studies find that these biases matter even when using administrative data.[14]

3.2. Comparisons of Intergenerational Samples

To better understand the limitations with currently available intergenerational samples in the US with respect to these measurement issues, it is useful to think about what an ideal sample would look like. In an ideal setting, we would want to construct an intergenerational sample where income is measured for both generations throughout the entire working life cycle, say between the ages of 25 and 55.[15] For example, suppose our data ends in 2012 (as in Chetty et al.); then for full life cycle coverage for the children's generation, we would want cohorts of children who were born in 1957 or earlier. For the 1957 cohort, we would measure their income between 1982 and 2012. For the 1956 cohort, we would measure income between 1981 and 2011 and so on. Suppose that for the parents' generation, the mean age at the time the child is born is 25. Then for the 1957 cohort, we would collect income data from 1957 to 1987, from 1956 to 1986 for the parents of the 1956 birth cohort and so on. With such a dataset in hand we would be confident that we would have measures of lifetime income that are largely error-free and would also be free of life cycle bias.

Unfortunately, for most countries, including the United States, it is difficult to construct an intergenerational dataset with income data going back to the 1950s.[16] Still, we can come somewhat close to this ideal sample with publicly available survey data in the Panel Study of Income Dynamics (PSID).[17] The PSID began in 1968 and started collecting income data

---

14. Chetty et al. speculate that perhaps they find that time averaging and life cycle bias don't matter because of their use of administrative data which they suspect to be less error prone than survey data.

15. The precise end points are debatable but for measurement purposes, one might want to ensure that most sample members have finished schooling and that most sample members have not yet retired. In theory, however, it may be better to consider earnings even at young ages when adolescents may have chosen to forego earnings for human capital accumulation that pays off later in life. In any case, the main point of the argument in this section would still hold if one used a much broader age range.

16. The SIPP-SER data used by Mazumder (2005a, 2005b) and Dahl and DeLeire (2008) meet some but not all of these requirements.

17. The code used to construct the main estimates in this paper will be made available to researchers either through the author's website or through personal communication.

beginning in 1967 for a nationally representative sample of about 5,000 families. The 1957 cohort would have been 11-years old at the time the PSID began; so, this cohort along with those born as early as 1951 would have been under the age of 18 at the beginning of the survey. The approach I take in this paper is to construct time averages of both parent and child income centered around the age of 40 in order to minimize life cycle bias. For parents, these time averages include income obtained between the ages of 25 and 55 and for children these averages include income obtained between the ages of 35 and 45.

Relative to the ideal sample, the PSID sample is close in several regards. Since it covers the 1967–2010 period, it is able to utilize large windows of the life cycle for both generations. For example, for the 16 cohorts born between 1951 and 1965, in principle, income can be measured in all years that cover the age range between 35 and 45. For the cohorts born between 1967 and 1975, their parents' income can also be measured through the ages of 25 and 55. Of course, attrition from the survey diminishes the size of the actual samples with observations in all of these years but at least the potential for such coverage is there.[18]

Now let us contrast this with the limitations faced by Chetty et al. (2014) in their analysis of currently available IRS data. First the tax data are currently only digitized going back to 1996, which is far from what the ideal dataset would require (1957), or even what is available in the PSID (1967). Therefore, there is no birth cohort for whom the income of parents can be measured for the entire 31-year time span between the ages of 25 and 55. Furthermore, the authors chose to limit the analysis to just a five-year average between 1996 and 2000. A possible explanation for this choice is that lengthening their time averages further would have necessitated measuring income when parents were at an older than ideal age. I will return to this point later when I explain why their sensitivity analysis suffers from bias. The mean age of fathers in their sample in 1996 is reported to be 43.5 with a standard deviation of 6.3 years. This implies that over the five years from 1996 through 2000, roughly 24 percent of the father-year observations used in constructing the average would be when fathers are over the age of 50.[19] This is an age at which the transitory variance in income is quite high (Mazumder, 2005a). They also report that prior to

---

18. As discussed later, I use survey weights to address concerns about attrition.
19. This example assumes the data are normally distributed. In 2000, more than a third of the observations would be when fathers are over the age of 50.

1999 they record the income of non-filers to be zero. Therefore, for about 3 percent of observations in three of the five years used in their average they impute zeroes to the missing observations.[20]

For the children in the sample, the data limitations are even more severe. Chetty et al. use cohorts born between 1980 and 1982 and measure their income in 2011 and 2012 when they are between the ages of 29 and 32. For this age range, simulations from Haider and Solon (2006) suggest that there would be around a 20 percent bias in the estimated IGE compared to having the full life cycle. A further complication is that their measures are taken in 2011 and 2012 when unemployment was relatively high and labor force participation quite low. They report that they drop about 17 percent of observations from the poorest families due to their having zero income *over those two years.* If their sample had covered 29- to 32-year old in other time periods spanning other periods of the business cycle, then using such a short window would have been somewhat less of a concern.

Finally, there is a concern about whether administrative income data adequately captures true income, particularly at the low and the high ends of the income distribution. For example, at the lower end of the distribution, tax data could miss forms of income that go unreported to the IRS. At the higher end, tax avoidance behavior could lead to an under-reporting of income. Hokayem et al. (2015) find that administrative tax data can do a worse job than survey data in measuring poverty. Abowd and Stinson (2013) argue that it is preferable to treat both survey data and administrative data as containing error. I also discuss below how a preferred concept of family income that includes all resources available for consumption, including transfers and income of other family members, would render tax data inadequate.

It is useful to visualize just how different the data structure of the Chetty et al. sample is from an ideal intergenerational sample. This is shown in Fig. 1. For each of three samples, there are two columns of 31 cells representing the ages from 25 to 55 in each generation and we assume that just one parent's income can be measured. The degree of coverage over the life course is represented by the extent to which the cells are colored. Panel A shows that if we measured income in both generations using data spanning, the entire life course for two generations then all

---

20. See footnote 14 of Chetty et al. (2014). They show that measuring income over 1999 to 2003 has no effect on their rank mobility estimates but they do not show how the IGE estimates change. Measuring income from 1999 to 2003 potentially worsens the attenuation bias in the IGE resulting from measuring fathers at late ages.

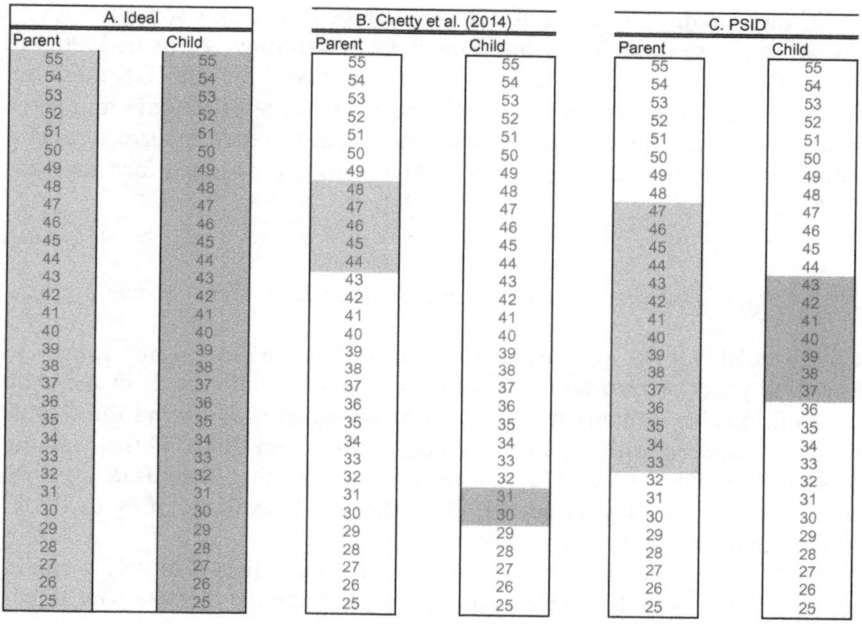

Fig. 1. Comparison of Life Cycle Coverage across Intergenerational Samples.

the cells in both generations would be colored in. Panel B contrasts this with a typical parent–child observation in the Chetty et al. sample.[21] This makes it clear just how small a portion of the ideal life cycle is covered. Just 6 percent of the child's life cycle and just 16 percent of the parent's life cycle would be covered. Panel C contrasts this with an example of a result that will be produced with the PSID in the current study. There are many cohorts for whom both child and parent income can be measured over several years centered around the age of 40 when life cycle bias is minimized. The figure presents an example of a 7-year average of child income and a 15-year average of parent income. Such a sample would cover 23 percent of the child's life cycle and 48 percent of the parent's life cycle.

---

21. This example takes a child born in 1981 whose income is observed at age 30 and 31 during the years 2011 and 2012. I assume that the father was 29 years old when the child was born so that the father's income is measured between the ages of 44 and 48 during the years 1996 to 2000. This example closely tracks the mean ages of the sample as reported by Chetty et al. (2014).

To their credit, Chetty et al. (2014) attempt to conduct some sensitivity checks to assess these issues but their data, which only begins in 1996, are not well suited to doing effective robustness checks for the IGE measure. Below I will replicate their sensitivity checks with the PSID data and show how the current IRS data limitations lead them to reach incorrect conclusions regarding the sensitivity of their IGE estimates to these measurement problems.

3.3. Estimating the IGE when Children Have Zero Income

Chetty et al. (2014) also argue that the IGE estimator is not robust to imputing years of zero family income observed for individuals in the child generation. They obtain an estimate of 0.344 when they restrict the sample to those children with positive income in 2011 and 2012. If they impute $1,000 of income to individuals with zero income, then their IGE estimate rises to 0.413. If they assign $1, then their IGE estimate rises to 0.618. There are three points worth making here.

First, the issue of having to deal with missing values is largely a consequence of the poor life cycle coverage of their sample. To see why this is the case, imagine a hypothetical researcher in the year 2035 that attempts an intergenerational analysis for the 1980 birth cohort using the tax data. In 2035, one would have complete information on family income throughout the ages of 25–55 and would not have to worry that some of these individuals reported no income in 2 of the 31 years of the life cycle, during a period when unemployment was relatively high. There would be as many as 29 other years of income data available to calculate lifetime income. In fact, based on the prior literature, a researcher could probably obtain a fairly unbiased estimate of the IGE for the 1980 birth cohort by the early 2020s if they could obtain even a few years of income around the age of 40. In the PSID one can track cohorts born as far back as the 1950s who may be observed over many years, at many ages, and at different stages of the business cycle.

Second, recent work by Mitnik et al. (2015) point to an alternative approach for estimating the IGE that is not sensitive to situations in which researchers may have only a short span of data on children's income and encounter cases of zero income. Specifically, they estimate the elasticity of the expected income of children rather than the elasticity of the geometric mean of income, which the literature has traditionally focused on. They argue that this is the estimand that researchers should actually be interested in estimating.[22] They present striking evidence that unlike the traditional IGE estimator, their alternative estimator of the IGE is relatively immune to the treatment of missing income of children when income is measured over only a short window of the life cycle. However, it is unclear, and ultimately an empirical question as to whether the Mitnik et al. approach to estimating the IGE would yield substantially different results from the traditional approach if one had access to the entire lifetime income stream of children. In such a situation there would likely be very few cases of zeroes. This would be a fruitful avenue for future research to explore.

A third remark relates to the *concept* of family income one wants to use. Economists (e.g., Mulligan, 1997) have sometimes argued that an ideal measure of intergenerational mobility would seek to measure lifetime consumption in both generations since consumption is perhaps the measure closest to utility which is what economists like to focus on. In this case, ideally we would like to measure *total family resources* which includes income obtained from transfers and from other family members. This is an example where survey data that have access to transfer income would be preferable to tax data that may not. Including transfers may not only be a preferred measure but may also help alleviate the problem of observing zero earnings or zero income as is common in administrative data. It is also not obvious why the preferred measure of family income would be one that only includes labor market earnings, transfers and capital income that happen to be reported on tax forms. This may help explain why Chetty et al. estimate an IGE of 0.452 when they limit their sample to individuals between the 10th and 90th percentiles. The lack of coverage of all forms of transfer income may be less problematic for this range since it excludes the bottom of the income distribution.

3.4. *Estimating the IGE when Parents Have Zero Income*

It is worth pointing out that the prior discussion is in many ways very distinct from the problem of having a measure of zero income for *parents*. Chetty et al. (2014) and Mitnik et al. both cite Dahl and DeLeire (2008) in their discussions of the robustness of the IGE but Dahl and Deliere

---

22. Chetty et al. (2014) argue that the preferred estimator of Mitnik et al. (2015) can be interpreted as a "dollar-weighted" estimator of the IGE and the traditional IGE can be viewed as a "person-weighted" estimator and suggest that each answers a different question.

actually confront an entirely different issue. Dahl and Deliere utilize social
security earnings data. For the years 1951 through 1983, they cannot distinguish between years of zero earnings due to non-coverage in the SSA sector
from "true" zeroes due to non-employment. When they construct measures
of parent average earnings over the ages of 20–55 and include all years of
earnings they obtain estimates of the IGE of only around 0.3 for men.
However, their estimates may be including many years when actual earnings are positive but are erroneously treated as zero because fathers were
working in the non-covered sector. Since this measurement error is on the
right-hand side it can severely attenuate the estimate of the IGE.

They attempt to correct for this in some specifications by restricting the
sample to parents who were not in the armed forces or self-employed and
who therefore would likely be in the covered sector. But, importantly, the
class of worker variable is only observed in one year, 1984, which is at a
relatively late point in the life cycle for most of their sample of fathers.
Therefore, their long-term averages still include many years of zero earnings for workers who were actually in the non-covered sector in the 1950s,
1960s, or 1970s but who had shifted to the covered sector by 1984. Not surprisingly, using the class of worker status observed in 1984 to restrict the
sample still yields very low estimates of the IGE. However, when they
restrict the number of years of zero earnings in other very sensible ways to
more directly address the issue, they obtain estimates of around 0.5–0.6.
For example, when they use the log of average earnings beginning with the
first five consecutive years of positive earnings up to age 55 they obtain an
estimate of 0.498.

A clear advantage of the IRS tax data compared to the SSA data is that
there is no requirement of working in sectors covered by SSA. However,
there may be concerns related to whether individuals file their taxes and
whether the IRS samples contain those who don't file. As mentioned earlier, Chetty et al. assign zero income to parents who are in their sample but
did not file taxes in years prior to 1999. This can also lead to attenuation
bias in estimating the IGE.

4. PSID DATA

I restrict the analysis to father–son pairs as identified by the PSID's
Family Identification Mapping System (FIMS) and use all years of available family income between the ages of 25 and 55 between the years of

1967 and 2010.[23] For the main analysis, I consider a measure of family income that excludes transfers and excludes income from household members that are not the head of household or the spouse. This provides a measure of family income that is probably most comparable to the concept used by Chetty et al. (2014). In addition, I also constructed a measure of family income that also includes transfers received by the household head or spouse, but these results are not presented.[24] Finally, I construct a measure that uses only the labor income of the father and son to be more comparable to papers that emphasize the IGE in labor market income (e.g., Mazumder, 2005a, 2005b; Solon, 1992). Labor income is not simply earnings from an employer but also incorporates self-employment. Observations marked as being generated by a "major" imputation are set to missing. Yearly income observations are deflated to real terms using the CPI. In the PSID, the household head is recorded as having zero labor income if their income was actually zero or if their labor income is missing, so one cannot cleanly distinguish true zeroes with labor income. All of the main analysis only uses years of non-zero income when constructing time averages of income. When using family income, instances of reports of zero income are relatively rare so the results are virtually immune to the inclusion of zeroes. Therefore, the concerns about the sensitivity of results around how to handle years of zero income is effectively a non-issue when using family income.

The main analysis only uses the nationally representative portion of the PSID and includes survey weights to account for attrition. All of the analysis was also done including the SEO oversample of poorer households and includes survey weights. While the samples with the SEO are larger and offer more precise estimates, there is some concern about the sampling methodology (Lee & Solon, 2009). Finally, all estimates are clustered on fathers.

The approach to estimation in this study is slightly different than in most previous PSID studies of intergenerational mobility. Rather than relying on any one fixed length time average for each generation and relying on parametric assumptions to deal with life cycle bias (e.g., Lee & Solon, 2009), I estimate an entire matrix of IGE's for many combinations of

---

23. The focus on sons contrasts with Chetty et al. (2014) who pool sons and daughters and Mitnik et al. (2015) who mainly produce separate estimates by gender.
24. These results were broadly similar to the baseline findings using the narrower measure of family income.

lengths of time averages that are all centered around age 40. I will present the full matrix of estimates along with weighted averages across entire rows and columns representing the effects of a particular length of the time average for a given generation. For example, rather than simply comparing the IGE from using a 10-year average of fathers' income to using a five-year average of fathers' income *for one particular time average of sons' income*, I can show how the estimates are affected for every time average of sons' income.

5. RESULTS

5.1. IGE Estimates

Table 1 shows the estimates of the IGE in family income that is conceptually similar to that used by Chetty et al. (2014). The first entry of the table at the upper left shows the estimate if we use just one year of family income in the parent generation and one year of family income for the sons when they are closest to age 40 and also are within the age-range constraints described earlier. This estimate of the IGE is 0.414 with a standard error of 0.075 and utilizes a sample of 1,358. One point immediately worth noting is that this estimate which uses just a single year of family income around the age 40 is higher than the 0.344 found by Chetty et al. (2014). Moving across the row, the estimates gradually include more years of income between the ages of 35 and 45 for the sons. At the same time, the sample size gradually diminishes as an increasingly fewer number of sons have will income available for a higher length of required years. For the most part, the estimates don't change much and most are in the range of 0.35–0.42. At the end of the row, I display the weighted average across the columns, where the estimates are weighted by the sample size. For the first row, the weighted average is 0.381.

Moving down the rows for a given column, the estimates gradually increase the time average used to measure family income in the parent generation and as a consequence also reduces the sample size. For example, if we move down the first column and continue to just use the sons' income in one year measured closest to age 40 and now increase the time average of parent income to two years, the estimate rises to 0.439 as the sample falls to 1,317. Using a five-year average raises the estimate to 0.530 ($N = 1,175$). Increasing the time average to 10 years increases the estimate to 0.580

Table 1. Estimates of the Father-Son IGE in Family Income.

Time Avg. Fath. Inc.	Time Average of Sons' Income (Years)										Wgt. Avg.
	1	2	3	4	5	6	7	8	9	10	
1	0.414	0.372	0.405	0.375	0.397	0.361	0.317	0.315	0.354	0.415	0.381
	(0.075)	(0.067)	(0.069)	(0.068)	(0.064)	(0.070)	(0.063)	(0.068)	(0.080)	(0.091)	
	1,358	1,184	1,050	932	786	595	440	351	267	183	
2	0.439	0.420	0.434	0.402	0.429	0.443	0.391	0.379	0.419	0.453	0.423
	(0.066)	(0.059)	(0.062)	(0.062)	(0.068)	(0.088)	(0.067)	(0.069)	(0.082)	(0.089)	
	1,317	1,145	1,015	901	758	572	419	331	251	170	
3	0.478	0.445	0.450	0.414	0.440	0.440	0.401	0.380	0.416	0.449	0.441
	(0.067)	(0.060)	(0.064)	(0.064)	(0.071)	(0.088)	(0.062)	(0.066)	(0.078)	(0.088)	
	1,268	1,099	970	862	719	537	389	306	230	154	
4	0.478	0.455	0.467	0.435	0.453	0.463	0.419	0.388	0.431	0.422	0.453
	(0.068)	(0.061)	(0.069)	(0.069)	(0.079)	(0.105)	(0.063)	(0.067)	(0.085)	(0.091)	
	1,216	1,051	926	819	678	497	354	273	203	133	
5	0.530	0.493	0.500	0.468	0.479	0.477	0.428	0.398	0.441	0.454	0.485
	(0.071)	(0.065)	(0.075)	(0.076)	(0.088)	(0.113)	(0.065)	(0.069)	(0.090)	(0.098	
	1,175	1,015	892	788	649	471	332	255	188	123	
6	0.517	0.482	0.492	0.458	0.473	0.476	0.420	0.389	0.434	0.452	0.477
	(0.071)	(0.066)	(0.077)	(0.078)	(0.091)	(0.120)	(0.064)	(0.067)	(0.091)	(0.092)	
	1,120	966	843	741	606	431	299	228	165	105	
7	0.529	0.485	0.492	0.459	0.464	0.462	0.379	0.369	0.399	0.402	0.474
	(0.077)	(0.073)	(0.086)	(0.089)	(0.105)	(0.144)	(0.065)	(0.078)	(0.109)	(0.104)	
	1,063	915	795	696	564	396	271	202	143	87	
8	0.552	0.518	0.546	0.521	0.545	0.595	0.368	0.345	0.430	0.468	0.523
	(0.086)	(0.082)	(0.091)	(0.096)	(0.110)	(0.166)	(0.092)	(0.114)	(0.166)	(0.156)	
	1,005	863	747	648	520	354	232	168	114	67	
9	0.573	0.537	0.558	0.536	0.560	0.629	0.435	0.391	0.494	0.624	0.548
	(0.090)	(0.087)	(0.096)	(0.101)	(0.115)	(0.179)	(0.090)	(0.117)	(0.183)	(0.159)	
	956	818	710	614	488	326	208	147	97	54	

Table 1. (Continued)

Time Avg. Fath. Inc.	Time Average of Sons' Income (Years)										Wgt. Avg.
	1	2	3	4	5	6	7	8	9	10	
10	0.580	0.529	0.545	0.521	0.550	0.633	0.421	0.388	0.502	0.698	0.544
	(0.095)	(0.092)	(0.101)	(0.106)	(0.124)	(0.197)	(0.092)	(0.124)	(0.201)	(0.192)	
	895	766	660	569	449	298	185	129	83	45	
11	0.630	0.567	0.590	0.576	0.602	0.691	0.460	0.380	0.461	0.650	0.588
	(0.099)	(0.099)	(0.107)	(0.113)	(0.134)	(0.220)	(0.093)	(0.140)	(0.234)	(0.245)	
	818	696	595	510	399	255	149	98	59	31	
12	0.648	0.592	0.623	0.589	0.624	0.747	0.474	0.386	0.400	0.604	0.612
	(0.109)	(0.108)	(0.117)	(0.123)	(0.151)	(0.258)	(0.119)	(0.164)	(0.247)	(0.271)	
	743	633	541	465	358	224	121	78	46	24	
13	0.667	0.612	0.649	0.625	0.605	0.533	0.462	0.287	0.395	0.363	0.612
	(0.122)	(0.107)	(0.110)	(0.113)	(0.114)	(0.117)	(0.115)	(0.215)	(0.301)	(0.164	
	656	554	470	399	307	184	96	57	31	13	
14	0.714	0.692	0.714	0.681	0.659	0.629	0.511	0.457	0.986	0.761	0.685
	(0.129)	(0.104)	(0.116)	(0.120)	(0.122)	(0.115)	(0.182)	(0.311)	(0.411)	(0.368)	
	590	495	415	349	263	146	70	36	15	7	
15	0.680	0.664	0.662	0.616	0.651	0.597	0.532	0.576	1.527	0.954	0.656
	(0.134)	(0.099)	(0.109)	(0.108)	(0.123)	(0.129)	(0.216)	(0.393)	(0.258)	(0.700)	
	533	448	374	309	228	120	54	24	11	6	
Wgt. avg.	0.539	0.501	0.517	0.485	0.501	0.510	0.405	0.374	0.432	0.469	

($N = 895$). Using a 15-year average raises the estimate further to 0.680 ($N = 533$). The weighted average for each row is displayed in the last column and the weighted average for each column is displayed in the bottom row.

A few points are worth making. Since expanding the time average in either dimension reduces the sample size, it risks making the sample less representative. The implications on the estimates, however, are quite different for whether we increase the time average for the sons' generation or for the fathers'. For the parent generation, increasing the time average tends to raise estimates. This is consistent with a story in which larger time averages reduce attenuation bias stemming from mis-measurement of parent income (Mazumder, 2005a, 2005b; Solon, 1992). This also accords with standard econometric theory concerning mis-measurement of the right-hand side variable. On the other hand, econometric theory posits that mis-measurement in the dependent variable typically should not cause attenuation bias. Indeed, increasing the time average of sons' family income has little effect. But crucially, this is because we have *centered the time average* of family income in each generation so that the life cycle bias which induces "non-classical" measurement error in the dependent variable (Haider & Solon, 2006) may already be accounted for.

By this reasoning, one might consider the estimates in the first column to be the most useful since they allow one to see how a reduction in measurement error in parent income affects the estimates while simultaneously minimizing life cycle bias and keeping the sample as large as possible. A more conservative view would be to use the weighted average in the final column that takes into account the possible effects of incorporating more years of data on sons' income while also giving greater weight to estimates with larger samples. Fig. 2 shows the pattern of estimates from the two approaches as I gradually use longer time averages. With either approach, time averages of 10–15 years yield estimates of the IGE in family income that are consistently greater than 0.6. Table A1 and Fig. C1 show the analogous set of estimates using larger samples that include the SEO oversample.

The key idea of the study is to see how these IGE estimates would compare to what one would obtain by imposing the current data limitations of the IRS sample. To do this, one can use the second column and fifth row of Table 1 as a baseline estimate. That estimate of 0.493 uses a two-year average of family income of sons centered around age 40 and a five-year average of parent income centered around age 40. If I now impose a sample restriction such that I use a two-year average of sons taken over the ages of

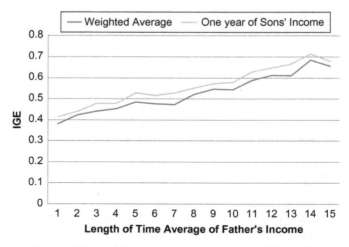

Fig. 2. Effects of Time Averaging on Father–Son IGE in Family Income.

29–32 and use a five-year average of parent income centered around the age of 46, then the estimate I obtain is 0.282 (s.e.=0.099). This is only 57 percent of the value when using similar time averages centered at age 40. Furthermore, if the true IGE is actually 0.7, then it is only 40 percent of the true parameter. If I include the SEO subsample then the estimate rises a bit to 0.325 (s.e.=0.081). For that sample, the data limitations yield estimates that are 62 percent of the comparable estimates when using time averages centered at age 40. Neither of the two estimates are statistically different from the Chetty et al. estimate of 0.344. This suggests that it is the data limitations in the tax data that lead Chetty et al. to produce estimates that are vastly lower than what has been reported in most of the previous literature.

Interestingly, Mitnik et al. (2015) report a strikingly similar pattern of results. Their baseline estimates use children's income measured between the ages of 35 and 38 and 9-year averages of parent income. Using a non-parametric approach on a sample that includes all children, their estimates of the traditional IGE range from 0.55 to 0.74 depending on how they impute the income of children who report no income.[25] When they move from this baseline sample to one that mimics the sample used by Chetty

25. See their table 11.

et al. (children between the ages of 29 and 32 and using a five-year average of parent income), their estimate falls to 0.28. If they instead use their preferred IGE estimator, then their main estimate is 0.50 and their estimate when mimicking the sample used by Chetty et al. is 0.37.

Table 2 shows a set of IGE estimates that only use the labor income of fathers and sons. On the whole, the estimates in Table 2 are fairly similar to those in Table 1 as is shown in Fig. 3, which plots the weighted average across the columns. For example, when using a 12-year average of fathers' income, the IGE when using labor income is 0.611 and when using family income the estimate is 0.612.

These estimates are broadly similar and slightly higher than those found by Mazumder (2005a), who used the labor market earnings of fathers and sons from social security earnings data. Mazumder (2005a) relied on several data imputation approaches to deal with issues related to social security coverage and topcoding. However, with the PSID, none of these kinds of imputations are necessary. These findings, along with similar results in Mazumder (2005b), Mazumder and Acosta (2015) and Mitnik et al. (2015) which also do not require imputations, suggest that the results of Mazumder (2005a) are likely not due to the use of imputations as argued by Chetty et al. (2014) but instead are due to the longer time averages available in the SSA data and the PSID. This also suggests that Mazumder (2005a) may have been correct in arguing that the use of imputations may not have imparted an upward bias.[26]

5.2. Robustness Checks

A drawback of the PSID data is that there can be substantial attrition. One may be concerned that the samples that use longer time averages of parent income could be very different from the ones that use shorter time averages. Perhaps, it is the case that the higher estimates that I attribute to using longer time averages in Table 1 are instead due to a change in the composition of families.

To address this, I conduct two robustness exercises. First, I use a set of *fixed* samples to show how IGE estimates change as I increase the time average of parent income while holding the composition of families constant. To narrow the focus of the exercise, I consider the case of using one

---

26. Sees Section 3 for a more detailed discussion of this issue.

Table 2. Estimates of the Father-Son IGE in Labor Income.

Time Avg. Fath. Inc.	Time Average of Sons' Income (Years)										Wgt. Avg.
	1	2	3	4	5	6	7	8	9	10	
1	0.299 (0.072) 955	0.308 (0.069) 824	0.308 (0.063) 696	0.335 (0.064) 581	0.358 (0.065) 466	0.333 (0.066) 360	0.373 (0.069) 264	0.395 (0.070) 202	0.384 (0.085) 156	0.359 (0.084) 104	0.359
2	0.412 (0.063) 928	0.412 (0.061) 799	0.407 (0.061) 674	0.405 (0.065) 562	0.407 (0.074) 450	0.369 (0.075) 345	0.439 (0.059) 250	0.422 (0.059) 191	0.427 (0.077) 147	0.412 (0.081) 96	0.383
3	0.436 (0.061) 900	0.422 (0.061) 773	0.401 (0.059) 649	0.395 (0.064) 539	0.393 (0.073) 431	0.368 (0.076) 329	0.440 (0.056) 236	0.430 (0.055) 180	0.441 (0.072) 137	0.421 (0.080) 88	0.473
4	0.420 (0.064) 864	0.412 (0.063) 741	0.408 (0.062) 622	0.392 (0.067) 514	0.387 (0.076) 411	0.359 (0.077) 310	0.435 (0.058) 218	0.404 (0.058) 163	0.409 (0.073) 123	0.395 (0.082) 80	0.491
5	0.472 (0.069) 841	0.462 (0.066) 720	0.440 (0.067) 609	0.416 (0.071) 502	0.397 (0.080) 401	0.367 (0.082) 300	0.445 (0.059) 209	0.416 (0.059) 155	0.437 (0.077) 116	0.437 (0.091) 76	0.516
6	0.485 (0.071) 797	0.473 (0.068) 683	0.450 (0.068) 574	0.432 (0.074) 469	0.402 (0.083) 371	0.360 (0.082) 274	0.455 (0.059) 190	0.434 (0.061) 139	0.471 (0.084) 101	0.488 (0.102) 63	0.490
7	0.486 (0.077) 760	0.468 (0.074) 652	0.440 (0.075) 546	0.420 (0.082) 445	0.385 (0.091) 349	0.332 (0.087) 255	0.441 (0.073) 174	0.401 (0.080) 123	0.432 (0.104) 88	0.430 (0.106) 52	0.497
8	0.510 (0.085) 725	0.487 (0.081) 622	0.473 (0.079) 518	0.459 (0.087) 419	0.451 (0.094) 327	0.407 (0.080) 235	0.414 (0.092) 158	0.352 (0.108) 110	0.382 (0.135) 80	0.409 (0.117) 45	0.559
9	0.511 (0.086) 699	0.476 (0.081) 597	0.461 (0.079) 500	0.445 (0.088) 404	0.452 (0.094) 314	0.408 (0.080) 225	0.427 (0.092) 149	0.356 (0.109) 103	0.392 (0.136) 73	0.406 (0.122) 41	0.583

10	0.513 (0.088) 657	0.474 (0.084) 561	0.468 (0.081) 470	0.461 (0.092) 377	0.475 (0.102) 290	0.426 (0.085) 203	0.446 (0.101) 130	0.413 (0.122) 89	0.443 (0.161) 62	0.516 (0.144) 34	0.593
11	0.578 (0.093) 597	0.503 (0.091) 512	0.491 (0.087) 425	0.494 (0.096) 340	0.528 (0.106) 255	0.429 (0.092) 176	0.461 (0.116) 107	0.437 (0.143) 69	0.483 (0.203) 48	0.526 (0.186) 24	0.616
12	0.596 (0.102) 539	0.506 (0.108) 461	0.526 (0.105) 380	0.496 (0.113) 302	0.565 (0.131) 226	0.413 (0.118) 151	0.427 (0.158) 85	0.376 (0.158) 53	0.346 (0.233) 34	0.391 (0.157) 15	0.611
13	0.690 (0.111) 477	0.589 (0.114) 401	0.628 (0.112) 327	0.636 (0.127) 254	0.701 (0.153) 185	0.551 (0.143) 118	0.494 (0.176) 66	0.556 (0.208) 38	0.790 (0.316) 22	0.323 (0.323) 7	0.615
14	0.744 (0.116) 427	0.651 (0.122) 356	0.676 (0.119) 285	0.715 (0.138) 218	0.793 (0.161) 161	0.699 (0.158) 96	0.638 (0.216) 48	0.695 (0.266) 25	1.526 (0.259) 10	5.971 (0.916) 4	0.702
15	0.751 (0.122) 386	0.623 (0.127) 319	0.649 (0.125) 251	0.652 (0.138) 189	0.719 (0.163) 135	0.641 (0.179) 78	0.547 (0.266) 35	0.659 (0.282) 18	1.335 (0.253) 7	4.240 (0.000) 3	0.713
Wgt. avg.	0.574	0.517	0.458	0.469	0.504	0.471	0.519	0.535	0.564	0.592	

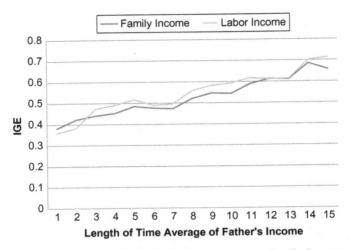

Fig. 3. Father–Son IGE in Labor Income versus Family Income.

available year of income for sons when they are closest to the age of 40.[27] I then consider, for example, the 1,063 families where I have seven years of available family income of fathers and see how the estimates change as I gradually increase the time average of parent income from one to seven years. This is shown in column 3 of Table 3. If I use one year of parent income, the IGE is estimated to be 0.358. If I use a three-year average, the estimate rises to 0.446. If I use a five-year average, the IGE rises further to 0.504 and rises to 0.529 when averaging all seven years. In column 4, I show how the estimates change for the 895 families with 10 years of income and in column 5, I present the pattern of estimates for the 533 families with 15 years of income. Columns 1 and 2 consider the effects of time averaging for smaller time averages of three and five years where the samples are even larger. In nearly all cases, the estimates rise monotonically as more years are used to increase the time average. Mitnik et al. (2015) present a similar set of exercises using their IRS samples in their appendix and show a similar pattern when they increase time averages of parent income up to nine years. This is comforting because one clear advantage of administrative tax data is that attrition from a survey is not a concern.

---

27. These are the samples that are in column 1 of Table 1.

Table 3. Estimates of the Father–Son IGE in Family Income Using Fixed Samples.

Time Avg. Father Inc.	Samples Use Sons with One Year of Income and Fathers with the Following Available Years of Income				
	3	5	7	10	15
1	0.397 (0.070)	0.393 (0.074)	0.358 (0.078)	0.388 (0.100)	0.291 (0.131)
2	0.438 (0.068)	0.430 (0.071)	0.401 (0.076)	0.429 (0.097)	0.366 (0.122)
3	0.478 (0.067)	0.473 (0.070)	0.446 (0.075)	0.497 (0.095)	0.453 (0.124)
4		0.484 (0.069)	0.460 (0.072)	0.522 (0.091)	0.479 (0.114)
5		0.530 (0.071)	0.504 (0.075)	0.579 (0.094)	0.568 (0.121)
6			0.515 (0.075)	0.581 (0.092)	0.580 (0.118)
7			0.529 (0.077)	0.595 (0.094)	0.622 (0.120)
8				0.583 (0.094)	0.619 (0.119)
9				0.584 (0.095)	0.635 (0.123)
10				0.580 (0.095)	0.643 (0.122)
13					0.662 (0.132)
15					0.680 (0.134)
N	1,268	1,175	1,063	895	533

A second exercise directly examines the characteristics of families in which longer time averages of parent income are available. I consider seven characteristics of fathers: income, age; education; percent black, percent white; percent married; and percent ever divorced.[28] As before I consider how these characteristics differ for the samples presented in column 1 of Table 1. The results are shown in Table B1. The table shows, for example, that the mean education level of fathers in the sample of 533 families with 15 years of parent income is 13.0. This compares to a mean of 12.9 years

---

28. I also consider mother's education.

for fathers with five years of income. The lower panel of the table shows that the difference is not statistically significant (p-value $= 0.50$). While the families with longer time averages may be slightly more educated they are also more likely to be black and more likely to be divorced, suggesting some evidence of negative selection. Overall, there is no clear pattern of selection with respect to socioeconomic status.

If one compares the samples with 10-year averages to those with 1 or 5 years, there are no statistically significant or economically meaningful differences in father characteristics. The fact that the estimates of the IGE are already well above 0.5 even when using 10-year averages suggests that the main points of the paper likely hold. In summary, there are no especially striking patterns that suggest that the longer time averages are due to changing characteristics of parents.

Despite these checks, I would still be somewhat cautious in arguing that the considerably smaller samples, with say 11−15 years of parent income, do not suffer from *any* concerns related to selection. One concern is that if the attenuation bias with using short-term averages is truly due to measurement error and serial correlation in transitory fluctuations as argued by Mazumder (2005a), then one would not expect the IGE to increase nearly linearly with the length of the time average as Fig. 1 shows, but instead would exhibit a more concave pattern as the simulation results in Mazumder (2005a) depict. This is one argument in favor of using administrative data where attrition is typically not an issue. Although the currently available US tax data does not yet have a long enough panel length to resolve this issue, future studies using administrative data in the US and other countries should continue to shed light on the nature of the earnings process and what it might imply for IGE estimates using longer-time averages.

5.3. Sensitivity Checks in Chetty et al. (2014)

Chetty et al. (2014) argue that their national estimates of the IGE are unaffected by the age at which children's income is measured. They also argue that their estimates are unaffected by the length of the time average used to measure parent income. They perform sensitivity checks to demonstrate this empirically and present the results visually in figures. In this section, I describe why those sensitivity checks suffer from bias and show how one can demonstrate this using the PSID. In short, their sensitivity checks introduce new attenuation bias from using parent income at older ages.

This bias appears to fully offset the reductions in attenuation bias that would otherwise have been apparent when using older children or when extending the time average of parent income.

They first discuss the sensitivity of the IGE to the age at which child income is measured, Chetty et al. claim that while there is some life cycle bias early in the career that this stabilizes once children have reached the age of around 30. They conduct an empirical exercise that is shown in their appendix figure IIA. They implement this sensitivity check by using an additional tax dataset that includes much smaller intergenerational samples from the Statistics of Income (SOI). With the SOI data, they can examine the IGE between parents and children for earlier birth cohorts going back to 1971. However, they continue to use family income in 2011 and 2012 for children and in 1996–2000 for the parents. This implies, for example, that when they examine the 1971 cohort to measure the IGE for 41-year olds, they are actually using parent income that is measured when the child was between the ages of 25 and 29 and unlikely to be living at home. Perhaps more importantly, this also requires that they use the income of fathers when they are likely to be especially old. For example, the income of a father who was 28 when his child was born in 1971 would be 53- to 57-years old when his income was measured in 1996–2000. Using parent income at such late ages when transitory fluctuations are a substantial part of earnings variation can lead to substantial attenuation bias that could off-set the reduction in life cycle bias from measuring child income at age 40 (Mazumder, 2005a). Overall, it could make it appear as though there is no life cycle bias when in fact it may actually be substantial.

With a long-running panel dataset like the PSID, one can replicate this sensitivity check but can also show how the results differ if one *simultaneously keeps the age at which father's income is measured, constant*. To implement this exercise, I first replicate the findings in Chetty et al. by gradually increasing the age at which sons' income is measured from 22 to 41 while simultaneously increasing the parent age range at which the five-year average of parent income is measured to match the analogous age range implied by the tax data.[29] I then fix this problem by using a five-year time average of parent income that is always centered at the age of 40 while

---

29. To fix ideas, for those sons who are aged 32, one would use the income of fathers when the child is between the ages of 15 and 19 as in Chetty et al. For those who are 33 one would use the income of fathers when the child is between 16 and 20 and so on.

simultaneously raising the age of sons when their income is measured from 22 to 41.

Fig. 4 shows the results of this exercise. The dark gray line replicates the sensitivity check that suffers from bias. Life cycle bias appears to level off around the age of 30 and may even appear to decline slightly in the late 30s. The light gray line demonstrates that this sensitivity check is flawed once you hold parent age constant around the age of 40. While both lines track each other reasonably well before the age of 30, they start to diverge after the age of 32. This is precisely around the time when the dark gray line utilizes data on parents when the child is no longer in the home, when the parents are entering their 50s and when their income becomes noisy. With the light gray line, however, we continue to use centered time averages of parents around the age of 40 to eliminate this downward bias. The bottom line is that there is in fact substantial life cycle bias that cannot be uncovered by the sensitivity checks in the Chetty et al. version of the tax data because of inherent data limitations.

There is also a second pertinent sensitivity analysis that Chetty et al. present in their figure 3B. Here, they consider how their results change when they increase the time average of parent income. They do this by adding additional years beyond the 1996−2000 time frame and showing that their rank−rank slope estimates do not increase, though they never show the results of this exercise for the IGE. The key problem with this approach is that can only extend the length of the time averages *forward* in time. This

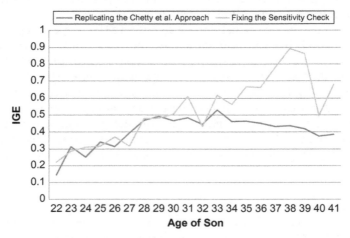

Fig. 4.   Re-examining the Sensitivity of the IGE to Son's Age.

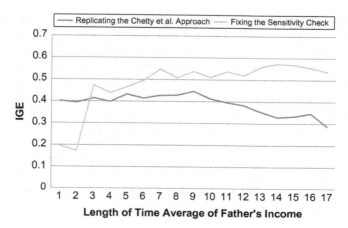

Fig. 5. Re-examining the Sensitivity of the IGE to Longer Time Averages of Parent Income.

necessarily results in increasing the attenuation bias from using later ages in the life cycle of parents. This can again have an offsetting effect due to attenuation bias. For example, the mean age of fathers in their sample in 2003 exceeds 50 so once they start lengthening time averages to include data in 2003 and beyond, they are actually including income observations containing a large transitory component. As before, this also implies that they are actually utilizing many years of income when the child is likely no longer living at home. With the PSID, one can avoid this pitfall. Specifically, one can increase the length of the time average while still holding constant the mean age of fathers by using centered time averages.

As before, I first use the PSID to replicate the results of the sensitivity check in Chetty et al and then show that time averaging does in fact reduce the attenuation bias once one removes the mechanical effect of increasing parent age.[30] The results are shown in Fig. 5. First, I am able to replicate the spirit of the finding in Chetty et al.'s figure 3B. The dark gray line

---

30. Specifically, I use just a 2 year average of sons' income over the ages of 29 to 32 and then start with a single year of fathers' income that is measured when the son is 15 and then gradually add years of fathers' income from subsequent years. For a five year average, this uses the income of fathers when the son is between the ages of 15 and 19. This mimics the 1981 birth cohort in Chetty et al. whose parent income is measured between 1996 and 2000. A ten year average then utilizes the income of fathers when the son is between the ages of 15 and 24.

shows that as I extend the time average of fathers' income by using years
when the fathers are getting older, I find that the time averages appear to
have no effect on increasing estimates of the IGE. The IGE stays flat at
first and then actually starts to decline when the time averages get very
large. However, when I use a centered time average of fathers' income
around the age of 40, a lengthening of the time average generally leads to
greater IGE estimates suggesting that larger time averages of parent income
do tend to reduce attenuation bias. It is worth noting here that Mazumder
(2005a) was able to use SSA data to extend his time averages of fathers
earnings backwards in time and also use centered time averages. Finally,
Mitnik et al. (2015) also show that in their tax data that longer time
averages of parent income and measuring child income at later ages lead to
higher IGE estimates.

5.4. Rank–Rank Slope Estimates

In this section, I present an analogous set of results for the rank–rank
slope. For this analysis, I use the same measure of family income that is
used to generate Table 1. The results are shown in Table 4. With the
rank–rank slope, some new patterns emerge. First, it appears that increasing the length of the time averages centered at the age of 40 for sons does
appear to increase the slope estimates. For example, looking over the first
10 rows, it appears that in nearly every case the slope estimates are higher
when sons' income is averaged over 8, 9, or 10 years rather than just 1 or 2
years. This was not the case with the IGE. In Table 1, it was typically the
reverse pattern. It is not obvious why this is the case but perhaps there is
some aspect of life cycle bias that is more pronounced when using ranks
than when using the IGE. This may be a fruitful issue for future research
to investigate.

Second, the effect of using longer time averages of parent income is
much more muted with the rank–rank slope than with the IGE. In
Table 1, the weighted average of the IGE across all the rows goes from
around 0.38 when using a single year of family income to about 0.66 when
using 15 year averages of family income – a 72 percent increase. The analogous increase in the rank–rank slope is a rise from 0.31 to 0.40 or just a
29 percent increase. A takeaway from Table 3 is that the rank–rank slope
may be around 0.4 or higher rather than the 0.34 reported by Chetty et al.
If we do the same exercise of imposing the limitations of the tax data on
our PSID sample, the estimate drops from 0.33 when using centered time

Table 4. Estimates of the Father-Son Rank–Rank Slope in Family Income.

Time Avg. Fath. Inc.	Time Average of Sons' Income (Years)										Wgt. Avg.
	1	2	3	4	5	6	7	8	9	10	
1	0.282	0.304	0.326	0.309	0.333	0.322	0.295	0.290	0.307	0.423	0.310
	(0.032)	(0.036)	(0.039)	(0.040)	(0.043)	(0.050)	(0.059)	(0.065)	(0.071)	(0.080)	
	1,358	1,184	1,050	932	786	595	440	351	267	183	
2	0.290	0.312	0.341	0.329	0.362	0.376	0.352	0.339	0.356	0.448	0.334
	(0.032)	(0.035)	(0.038)	(0.040)	(0.043)	(0.050)	(0.059)	(0.065)	(0.073)	(0.083)	
	1,317	1,145	1,015	901	758	572	419	331	251	170	
3	0.296	0.317	0.341	0.328	0.362	0.379	0.373	0.352	0.375	0.451	0.338
	(0.032)	(0.035)	(0.039)	(0.041)	(0.043)	(0.049)	(0.055)	(0.065)	(0.072)	(0.086)	
	1,268	1,099	970	862	719	537	389	306	230	154	
4	0.296	0.320	0.347	0.333	0.366	0.391	0.396	0.363	0.389	0.435	0.343
	(0.032)	(0.036)	(0.039)	(0.041)	(0.044)	(0.050)	(0.055)	(0.067)	(0.078)	(0.096)	
	1,216	1,051	926	819	678	497	354	273	203	133	
5	0.309	0.333	0.362	0.348	0.378	0.399	0.413	0.374	0.402	0.482	0.357
	(0.032)	(0.036)	(0.040)	(0.042)	(0.045)	(0.052)	(0.058)	(0.069)	(0.083)	(0.097)	
	1,175	1,015	892	788	649	471	332	255	188	123	
6	0.299	0.319	0.348	0.333	0.362	0.385	0.404	0.365	0.399	0.504	0.344
	(0.034)	(0.037)	(0.042)	(0.044)	(0.047)	(0.054)	(0.063)	(0.072)	(0.088)	(0.095)	
	1,120	966	843	741	606	431	299	228	165	105	
7	0.283	0.302	0.328	0.311	0.336	0.350	0.370	0.316	0.339	0.436	0.318
	(0.035)	(0.039)	(0.044)	(0.046)	(0.049)	(0.057)	(0.067)	(0.076)	(0.095)	(0.104)	
	1,063	915	795	696	564	396	271	202	143	87	
8	0.282	0.303	0.336	0.321	0.348	0.362	0.332	0.279	0.280	0.396	0.317
	(0.037)	(0.042)	(0.046)	(0.049)	(0.052)	(0.062)	(0.075)	(0.088)	(0.112)	(0.123)	
	1,005	863	747	648	520	354	232	168	114	67	
9	0.292	0.309	0.342	0.333	0.365	0.394	0.403	0.327	0.318	0.493	0.334
	(0.038)	(0.043)	(0.048)	(0.050)	(0.053)	(0.062)	(0.071)	(0.091)	(0.125)	(0.113)	
	956	818	710	614	488	326	208	147	97	54	

Table 4. (Continued)

Time Avg. Fath. Inc.	1	2	3	4	5	6	7	8	9	10	Wgt. Avg.
10	0.287	0.304	0.330	0.319	0.352	0.379	0.397	0.330	0.314	0.539	0.325
	(0.039)	(0.044)	(0.049)	(0.051)	(0.054)	(0.064)	(0.074)	(0.098)	(0.138)	(0.134)	
	895	766	660	569	449	298	185	129	83	45	
11	0.299	0.315	0.345	0.338	0.364	0.394	0.413	0.315	0.267	0.518	0.336
	(0.040)	(0.046)	(0.051)	(0.054)	(0.057)	(0.069)	(0.080)	(0.112)	(0.162)	(0.169)	
	818	696	595	510	399	255	149	98	59	31	
12	0.310	0.326	0.354	0.336	0.363	0.386	0.390	0.303	0.236	0.587	0.339
	(0.042)	(0.049)	(0.054)	(0.057)	(0.062)	(0.077)	(0.093)	(0.125)	(0.179)	(0.196)	
	743	633	541	465	358	224	121	78	46	24	
13	0.335	0.355	0.392	0.384	0.385	0.357	0.311	0.133	0.076	0.264	0.354
	(0.046)	(0.051)	(0.055)	(0.057)	(0.065)	(0.088)	(0.118)	(0.162)	(0.232)	(0.295)	
	656	554	470	399	307	184	96	57	31	13	
14	0.356	0.391	0.433	0.428	0.432	0.445	0.400	0.322	0.446	0.618	0.403
	(0.048)	(0.050)	(0.055)	(0.057)	(0.066)	(0.088)	(0.127)	(0.191)	(0.285)	(0.244)	
	590	495	415	349	263	146	70	36	15	7	
15	0.350	0.382	0.428	0.426	0.447	0.436	0.418	0.399	0.635	0.423	0.401
	(0.050)	(0.051)	(0.057)	(0.057)	(0.068)	(0.095)	(0.137)	(0.242)	(0.231)	(0.382)	
	533	448	374	309	228	120	54	24	11	6	
Wgt. avg.	0.300	0.321	0.350	0.337	0.364	0.377	0.371	0.329	0.346	0.457	

averages (two years for sons and five years for fathers) to 0.28 when using sons between the ages of 29 and 32 and fathers between the ages of 44 and 48. Again, these results suggest that even the rank—rank slope estimates using the tax data are likely attenuated, albeit to a lesser degree than the substantial attenuation with the IGE estimates. These results are also very similar if one includes the SEO oversample of poorer households or just uses labor income of fathers and sons (results available upon request).

In Figs. 6 and 7, I return to sensitivity analysis exercises from Chetty et al. (2014) in the context of the rank—rank slope and replicate those exercises with the PSID, first allowing father's age to shift higher mechanically but then correcting for this by holding father's age constant using centered time averages around the age of 40. Fig. 6 doesn't point to a very clean story. In this case, the dark gray line is often larger than the light gray line suggesting that estimates are often slightly lower when using the centered time averages. On the other hand both lines, but especially the light gray one, appear to trend higher over the course of the 30s suggesting that perhaps life cycle bias does not taper off around age 30. Fig. 7 is also interesting. The dark gray line is flat to declining and very similar to what Chetty et al. find but has the problem of conflating two different biases. The light gray line, which fixes the mechanical increase in fathers' age when taking longer time averages does show evidence of larger estimates but only when the time averages are very long. Overall, estimates of the rank—rank slope are also likely biased down due the limitations of the tax data but to a much lesser extent than the IGE.

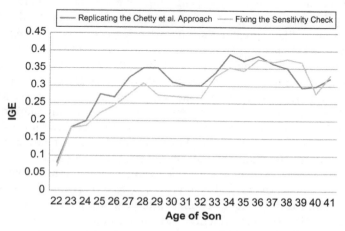

Fig. 6.   Re-examining the Sensitivity of the Rank—Rank Slope to Son's Age.

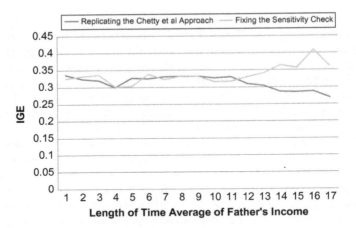

Fig. 7.   Re-examining the Sensitivity of the Rank—Rank Slope to Longer Time
Averages of Parent Income.

6. CONCLUSION

The literature on intergenerational mobility over the past few decades has
shown how attenuation bias and life cycle bias can substantially affect estimates of the IGE. Most previous estimates of the IGE in family income in
the United States are around 0.5. Utilizing PSID data, I generate the first
estimates of the IGE in the US using long time averages of parent income
and using income centered at age 40 in both generations. I find that the
IGE for sons is likely greater than 0.6 with respect to both family income
and labor market earnings suggesting less mobility than most previous estimates and similar to estimates in Mazumder (2005a).

In contrast, using very large samples of tax records that begin in 1996,
Chetty et al. (2014) estimate that the IGE is actually much lower at 0.344.
Further they claim that these estimates are not subject to attenuation bias or
life cycle bias. If accurate, this finding is important because it implies that
income gaps between families in America will dissipate relatively quickly
over time. It is important to understand whether the evidence of greater
mobility from their tax data sample is accurate or spurious. Revisiting the
results from this study may also hold more general lessons for researchers
who use administrative data to estimate intergenerational mobility.

I first describe the fundamental data limitations of using intergenerational samples based on US tax data that only begin in 1996. The key

point is that the panel length is currently too short to do a good job overcoming the issues concerning attenuation bias and life cycle bias. I demonstrate that a long-lived survey panel such as the PSID that may only have a few thousand families is actually more useful for estimating the national IGE than having millions of tax records if the data are limited in their ability to cover long stretches of the life course. Specifically, I show that when I use the PSID but impose the same age structure and use the shorter time averages of parent income to mimic Chetty et al., that I obtain similar IGE estimates of around 0.3. I also demonstrate that the sensitivity checks used by Chetty et al. to address concerns about (1) the age at which sons' income is measured and (2) the length of time averages of parent income, are flawed because they impose an offsetting attenuation bias by increasing the age at which parent income is measured. Correcting for this confounding, I show that the life cycle bias and attenuation bias almost surely exist in the tax data when estimating the IGE.

Further confirmation of this is provided by Mitnik et al. (2015), who find evidence of these biases in a different IRS sample that extends further back in time and enables an analysis of older children and the use of longer time averages of parent income. The fact that several other papers that also use administrative data in other countries (Gregg et al., 2013; Nilsen et al., 2012; Nybom & Stuhler, 2015) also show that these biases matter, suggest that Chetty et al.'s findings are more the exception than the rule.

On the other hand, the results with the PSID with respect to the rank–rank slope suggest that these biases are much smaller and that the rank–rank slope is relatively more robust (though not entirely immune) from these measurement concerns. It is important, however, to remember that the IGE is conceptually different from the rank–rank slope and may continue to be of substantial value to researchers and policy-makers especially in an era of rising inequality when income gaps in society may be expanding. In that context, focusing only on positional mobility solely because measurement is easier, may not be appropriate.

Another point worth emphasizing is that survey data may be advantageous for measuring certain sources of income that simply may not be tracked in tax records. These sources of income may provide better measures of the true resources available to families, especially for those at the low end of the income distribution. Given the growing use of administrative data and the excitement over new sources of such data, this characteristic of survey data may start to become overlooked. This is an argument for continuing to produce estimates of intergenerational mobility using survey data despite their smaller sample sizes, at least as a complement to using administrative data.

Finally, it is important to make clear that Chetty et al. (2014) make a notable contribution to the literature by demonstrating that there may be large geographic differences in intergenerational mobility across the United States. It is likely that these large geographic differences will remain even after correcting for the biases in the tax data. Nevertheless, it may be useful for future research to more directly examine this issue and verify that the central findings in their paper are robust to these biases.

REFERENCES

Abowd, J., & Stinson, M. (2013). Estimating measurement error in annual job earnings: A comparison of survey and administrative data. *Review of Economics and Statistics*, *95*(5), 1451–1467.

Baker, M., & Solon, G. (2003). Earnings dynamics and inequality among canadian men (1976–1992): Evidence from longitudinal income tax records. *Journal of Labor Economics*, *21*(2), 289–321.

Barro, R., & Sala-i-Martin, X. (1992). Convergence. *Journal of Political Economy*, *100*(2), 223–251.

Bhattacharya, D., & Mazumder, B. (2011). A nonparametric analysis of black–white differences in intergenerational income mobility in the United States. *Quantitative Economics*, *2*(3), 335–379.

Black, S. E., & Devereux, P. J. (2011). Recent developments in intergenerational mobility. In O. Ashenfelter & D. Card (Eds.), *Handbook of labor economics* (Vol. 4, pp. 1487–1541). Amsterdam: Elsevier.

Böhlmark, A., & Lindquist, M. (2006). Life-cycle variations in the association between current and lifetime income: Replication and extension for Sweden. *Journal of Labor Economics*, *24*(4), 879–896.

Bratberg, E., Davis, J., Nybom, M., Schnitzlein, D., & Vaage, K. (2015). *A comparison of intergenerational mobility curves in Germany, Norway, Sweden and the U.S.*, Working Paper No. 01–15, University of Bergen.

Bratsberg, B., Røed, K., Raaum, O., Naylor, R., Jäntti, M., Eriksson, T., & Österbacka, E. (2007). Nonlinearities in intergenerational earnings mobility: Consequences for cross-country comparisons. *Economic Journal*, *117*(519), C72–C92.

Chetty, R., Hendren, N., Kline, P., & Saez, E. (2014). Where is the land of opportunity? The geography of intergenerational mobility in the United States. *Quarterly Journal of Economics*, *129*(4), 1553–1623.

Corak, M., Lindquist, M., & Mazumder, B. (2014). A comparison of upward intergenerational mobility in Canada, Sweden and the United States. *Labour Economics*, *30*, 185–200.

Dahl, M., & DeLeire, T. (2008). *The association between children's earnings and fathers' lifetime earnings: Estimates using administrative data*. Institute for Research on Poverty, University of Wisconsin-Madison.

De Nardi, M., & Yang, F. (2015). *Wealth inequality, family background, and estate taxation.* NBER Working Paper No. 21047.

Gouskova, E., Chiteji, N., & Stafford, F. (2010). Estimating the intergenerational persistence of lifetime earnings with life course matching: Evidence from the PSID. *Labour Economics, 17*(2010), 592–597.

Grawe, N. D. (2006). Lifecycle bias in estimates of intergenerational earnings persistence. *Labour Economics, 13*(5), 551–570.

Gregg, P., Jonsson, J. O., Macmillan, L., & Mood, C. (2013). *Understanding income mobility: The role of education for intergenerational income persistence in the US, UK and Sweden.* DoQSS Working Paper No. 13-12.

Gregg, P., Macmillan, L., & Vittori, C. (2014). *Moving towards estimating lifetime intergenerational economic mobility in the UK.* DoQSS Working Paper No. 14-12.

Haider, S., & Solon, G. (2006). Life-cycle variation in the association between current and lifetime earnings. *American Economic Review, 96*(4), 1308–1320.

Hertz, T. (2005). Rags, riches, and race: The intergenerational economic mobility of black and white families in the United States. In S. Bowles, H. Gintis, & M. Osborne Groves (Eds.), *Unequal chances: Family background and economic success.* Princeton, NJ: Princeton University Press.

Hertz, T. (2006). *Understanding mobility in America.* Center for American Progress.

Hokayem, C., Bollinger, C., & Ziliak, J. (2015). The role of CPS nonresponse in the measurement of poverty. *Journal of the American Statistical Association, 110*, 935–945.

Jäntti, M., Bratsberg, B., Røed, K., Raaum, O., Naylor, R., Osterbacka, E., ... Eriksson, T. (2006). *American exceptionalism in a new light: A comparison of intergenerational earnings mobility in the nordic countries, the United Kingdom and the United States.* IZA Discussion Paper No. 1938, Institute for the Study of Labor (IZA).

Jenkins, S. (1987). Snapshots versus movies: 'Lifecycle biases' and the estimation of intergenerational earnings inheritance. *European Economic Review, 31*(5), 1149–1158.

Lee, C.-I., & Solon, G. (2009). Trends in intergenerational income mobility. *The Review of Economics and Statistics, 91*(4), 766–772.

Lee, S. Y., & Seshadri, A. (2015). *Economic policy and equality of opportunity.* Unpublished Working Paper, University of Wisconsin.

Lindahl, M., Palme, M., Massih, S. S., & Sjögren, A. (2015). Long-Term Intergenerational Persistence of Human Capital: An Empirical Analysis of Four Generations. *Journal of Human Resources, 50*(1), 1–33 (see http://jhr.uwpress.org/content/50/1/1.full.pdf+html).

Mazumder, B. (2005a). Fortunate sons: New estimates of intergenerational mobility in the United States using social security earnings data. *The Review of Economics and Statistics, 87*(2), 235–255.

Mazumder, B. (2005b). The apple falls even farther from the tree than we thought: New and revised estimates of the intergenerational inheritance of earnings. In S. Bowles, H. Gintis, & M. Osborne-Groves (Eds.), *Intergenerational inequality.* Princeton, NJ: Russell Sage Foundation.

Mazumder, B. (2014). Black-white differences in intergenerational economic mobility in the United States. *Economic Perspectives, 38*(1).

Mazumder, B., & Acosta, M. (2015). "Using occupation to measure intergenerational mobility" with Miguel Acosta. *The ANNALS of the American Academy of Political and Social Science, 657*, 174–193.

Mitnik, P. A., Bryant, V. L., Weber, M., & Grusky, D. B. (2015). *New estimates of intergenera-*
tional mobility using administrative data. SOI Working Paper, Statistics of Income
Division, Internal Revenue Service.

Mulligan, C. B. (1997). *Parental priorities and economic inequality.* Chicago, IL: University of
Chicago Press.

Nilsen, O. A., Vaage, K., Aavik, A., & Jacobsen, K. (2012). Intergenerational earnings mobility revisited: Estimates based on lifetime earnings. *Scandinavian Journal of Economics,*
114(1), 1–23.

Nybom, M., & Stuhler, J. (2015). Biases in Standard Measures of Intergenerational
Dependence.

Solon, G. (1992). Intergenerational income mobility in the United States. *American Economic*
Review, 82(3), 393–408.

Solon, G. (1999). Intergenerational mobility in the labor market. In O. Ashenfelter & D. Card
(Eds.), *Handbook of labor economics* (Vol. 3, pp. 1761–1800). Amsterdam: Elsevier.

APPENDIX A

Table A1. Estimates of the Father–Son IGE in Family Income Using SEO Subsample.

Time Avg. Fath. Inc.	Time Average of Sons' Income (Years)										Wgt. Avg.
	1	2	3	4	5	6	7	8	9	10	
1	0.451	0.403	0.434	0.414	0.426	0.393	0.357	0.363	0.383	0.401	0.415
	(0.054)	(0.048)	(0.049)	(0.051)	(0.047)	(0.050)	(0.047)	(0.054)	(0.066)	(0.077)	
	2,133	1,842	1,611	1,400	1,158	867	623	490	364	251	
2	0.485	0.450	0.468	0.438	0.457	0.451	0.406	0.402	0.418	0.430	0.453
	(0.053)	(0.045)	(0.047)	(0.049)	(0.052)	(0.061)	(0.048)	(0.053)	(0.063)	(0.069)	
	2,062	1,774	1,550	1,345	1,109	828	590	460	340	234	
3	0.526	0.476	0.491	0.457	0.476	0.473	0.439	0.428	0.446	0.461	0.480
	(0.056)	(0.049)	(0.054)	(0.053)	(0.059)	(0.068)	(0.051)	(0.054)	(0.065)	(0.074)	
	1,989	1,706	1,483	1,287	1,054	780	548	427	313	213	
4	0.531	0.487	0.508	0.476	0.487	0.493	0.449	0.435	0.464	0.443	0.492
	(0.058)	(0.051)	(0.058)	(0.059)	(0.066)	(0.080)	(0.052)	(0.056)	(0.072)	(0.079)	
	1,865	1,594	1,389	1,200	975	709	491	379	278	186	
5	0.586	0.526	0.544	0.510	0.514	0.508	0.457	0.446	0.482	0.483	0.527
	(0.062)	(0.056)	(0.066)	(0.067)	(0.076)	(0.092)	(0.058)	(0.062)	(0.082)	(0.093)	
	1,780	1,519	1,320	1,137	917	661	452	346	253	167	
6	0.575	0.515	0.535	0.499	0.506	0.503	0.437	0.425	0.476	0.481	0.518
	(0.063)	(0.056)	(0.068)	(0.069)	(0.079)	(0.097)	(0.057)	(0.062)	(0.086)	(0.094)	
	1,677	1,429	1,235	1,057	848	597	398	300	215	137	
7	0.593	0.528	0.548	0.514	0.516	0.513	0.420	0.418	0.446	0.428	0.528
	(0.067)	(0.063)	(0.076)	(0.079)	(0.093)	(0.119)	(0.060)	(0.071)	(0.099)	(0.102)	
	1,579	1,343	1,155	984	783	543	357	263	186	115	
8	0.595	0.544	0.576	0.546	0.554	0.587	0.422	0.411	0.480	0.514	0.553
	(0.073)	(0.069)	(0.077)	(0.081)	(0.090)	(0.125)	(0.079)	(0.097)	(0.137)	(0.136)	
	1,490	1,266	1,087	918	724	490	313	225	154	95	

Table A1. (*Continued*)

Time Avg. Fath. Inc.	Time Average of Sons' Income (Years)										Wgt. Avg.
	1	2	3	4	5	6	7	8	9	10	
9	0.616	0.560	0.588	0.560	0.571	0.622	0.479	0.461	0.546	0.660	0.577
	(0.077)	(0.073)	(0.081)	(0.085)	(0.094)	(0.135)	(0.077)	(0.102)	(0.153)	(0.140)	
	1,405	1,190	1,025	862	674	447	276	195	129	74	
10	0.633	0.558	0.587	0.555	0.575	0.645	0.476	0.451	0.547	0.691	0.582
	(0.082)	(0.079)	(0.087)	(0.092)	(0.105)	(0.157)	(0.086)	(0.109)	(0.170)	(0.155)	
	1,321	1,123	961	803	623	410	245	172	112	63	
11	0.674	0.584	0.618	0.587	0.599	0.669	0.471	0.385	0.470	0.606	0.608
	(0.087)	(0.086)	(0.093)	(0.099)	(0.114)	(0.179)	(0.084)	(0.119)	(0.195)	(0.183)	
	1,182	1,003	849	703	540	342	194	130	81	44	
12	0.700	0.610	0.650	0.601	0.620	0.720	0.482	0.381	0.415	0.617	0.633
	(0.097)	(0.095)	(0.103)	(0.110)	(0.131)	(0.214)	(0.108)	(0.143)	(0.215)	(0.226)	
	1,068	903	764	632	478	297	158	103	63	34	
13	0.714	0.619	0.656	0.621	0.598	0.526	0.454	0.291	0.392	0.389	0.625
	(0.111)	(0.097)	(0.099)	(0.104)	(0.104)	(0.106)	(0.144)	(0.187)	(0.251)	(0.161)	
	942	794	667	546	414	248	126	78	45	21	
14	0.769	0.698	0.721	0.678	0.651	0.616	0.507	0.436	0.909	0.859	0.700
	(0.118)	(0.094)	(0.106)	(0.112)	(0.112)	(0.104)	(0.170)	(0.274)	(0.354)	(0.353)	
	831	694	581	471	350	193	88	48	21	8	
15	0.752	0.675	0.677	0.626	0.653	0.598	0.546	0.569	1.318	1.094	0.682
	(0.123)	(0.090)	(0.099)	(0.100)	(0.112)	(0.114)	(0.200)	(0.335)	(0.334)	(0.642)	
	745	624	521	419	304	163	70	34	16	7	
Wgt. avg.	0.587	0.526	0.549	0.515	0.522	0.524	0.435	0.415	0.461	0.479	

APPENDIX B

Table B1. Summary Statistics of Fathers by Available Years of Income.

	N	Income ($)	Age	Father Education	Mother Education	Black	White	Married	Ever Divorced
1	1,358		41.6 (0.1)	12.9 (0.1)	12.2 (0.1)	5.1% (0.01)	94.1% (0.01)	97.2% (0.01)	24.0% (0.01)
2	1,317		41.9 (0.1)	12.9 (0.1)	12.2 (0.1)	5.1% (0.01)	94.1% (0.01)	97.2% (0.01)	24.5% (0.01)
3	1,268	79,233 (1,601)	41.5 (0.1)	12.9 (0.1)	12.2 (0.1)	5.1% (0.01)	94.2% (0.01)	97.2% (0.01)	25.1% (0.01)
4	1,216	79,805 (1,565)	41.7 (0.1)	12.9 (0.1)	12.3 (0.1)	5.3% (0.01)	94.0% (0.01)	97.2% (0.01)	25.9% (0.01)
5	1,175	79,477 (1,520)	41.4 (0.1)	12.9 (0.1)	12.3 (0.1)	5.2% (0.01)	94.0% (0.01)	97.2% (0.01)	26.3% (0.01)
6	1,120	80,877 (1,630)	41.6 (0.1)	12.9 (0.1)	12.3 (0.1)	5.3% (0.01)	94.0% (0.01)	97.2% (0.01)	26.5% (0.01)
7	1,063	80,962 (1,659)	41.3 (0.1)	12.9 (0.1)	12.3 (0.1)	5.2% (0.01)	94.0% (0.01)	97.2% (0.01)	26.9% (0.01)
8	1,005	81,612 (1,675)	41.5 (0.1)	12.9 (0.1)	12.3 (0.1)	5.5% (0.01)	93.7% (0.01)	97.3% (0.01)	27.5% (0.01)
9	956	81,175 (1,682)	41.2 (0.1)	12.9 (0.1)	12.3 (0.1)	5.4% (0.01)	93.8% (0.01)	97.4% (0.01)	27.5% (0.01)
10	895	82,609 (1,744)	41.4 (0.1)	12.9 (0.1)	12.4 (0.1)	5.1% (0.01)	94.0% (0.01)	97.3% (0.01)	27.9% (0.01)
11	818	82,650 (1,780)	40.9 (0.1)	12.9 (0.1)	12.5 (0.1)	5.3% (0.01)	93.7% (0.01)	97.1% (0.01)	29.1% (0.02)
12	743	82,005 (1,823)	41.0 (0.1)	13.0 (0.1)	12.5 (0.1)	5.2% (0.01)	93.8% (0.01)	96.8% (0.01)	29.0% (0.02)

Table B1. (Continued)

	N	Income ($)	Age	Father Education	Mother Education	Black	White	Married	Ever Divorced
13	656	81,503	40.6	13.0	12.5	5.2%	93.7%	96.4%	30.0%
		(1,909)	(0.1)	(0.1)	(0.1)	(0.01)	(0.01)	(0.01)	(0.02)
14	590	81,444	40.7	13.0	12.5	5.7%	93.1%	96.1%	31.4%
		(2,012)	(0.0)	(0.1)	(0.1)	(0.01)	(0.01)	(0.01)	(0.02)
15	533	82,272	40.3	13.0	12.5	5.9%	92.7%	95.9%	32.5%
		(2,131)	(0.0)	(0.1)	(0.1)	(0.01)	(0.01)	(0.01)	(0.02)
Two-sample test in difference of means									
5v. 10 T-Stat		-1.35	0.38	-0.32	-0.45	0.10	0.03	-0.12	-0.80
P-Val		0.18	0.71	0.75	0.65	0.92	0.98	0.91	0.42
5v. 15 T-Stat		-1.07	13.49	-0.68	-1.64	-0.56	0.98	1.34	-2.57
P-Val		0.29	0.00	0.50	0.10	0.58	0.33	0.18	0.01

APPENDIX C

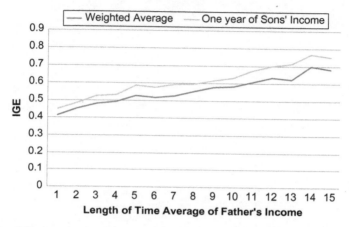

Fig. C1. Effects of Time Averaging on Father-Son IGE in Family Income Including SEO Sample.

INCOME SHOCKS OR INSURANCE – WHAT DETERMINES CONSUMPTION INEQUALITY? ☆

Johannes Ludwig

Ruhr Graduate School in Economics and Ruhr-Universität Bochum

ABSTRACT

Contrary to the implications of economic theory, consumption inequality in the United States did not react to the increases in income inequality during the last three decades. This paper investigates if a change in the type of income inequality — from permanent to transitory — or a change in the ability to insure income shocks is responsible for this. A measure of household consumption is imputed into the Panel Study of Income Dynamics to create panel data on income and consumption for the period 1980–2010. The minimum distance investigation of covariance relationships shows that both explanations work together: the share of transitory

☆The author is grateful to Mathias Klein, Michael Roos, two anonymous referees as well as to the participants of the 8th Ruhr Graduate School Doctoral Conference in Economics and the IZA Workshop on Inequality 2015 for helpful comments and suggestions.

Inequality: Causes and Consequences
Research in Labor Economics, Volume 43, 131–166
ISSN: 0147-9121/doi:10.1108/S0147-912120160000043009

shocks increases over time, but the capability to insure against permanent and transitory income shocks also improves. Together, these phenomena can explain the lack of an increase in consumption inequality.

Keywords: Consumption inequality; transitory and permanent inequality; consumption insurance

JEL classifications: D12; D31; E21

1. INTRODUCTION

A lot of research has been devoted to the problem of rising income inequality in the United States since the beginning of the 1980s. Far fewer authors have analyzed the development of consumption inequality over the same time frame. In case it is examined, consumption inequality has mostly been found to increase surprisingly little (see, e.g., Heathcote, Perri, & Violante, 2010; for a different view, see Aguiar & Bils, 2015; Attanasio, Hurst, & Pistaferri, 2015). From a theoretical perspective, this lack of a response to increasing income inequality is striking: When the variance of income increases in a permanent income-setting, households should adjust their consumption expenditure, and consumption inequality should increase proportionally.

Two explanations for this phenomenon have been suggested: Krueger and Perri (2006) assume that households have increased their ability to insure consumption expenditures against shocks to income with the help of credit. Blundell, Pistaferri, and Preston (2008) argue that it is the type of the income shock that has changed — from less insurable permanent shocks to better insurable transitory shocks. The aim of this paper is to test these two explanations against each other and investigate whether changes in insurance possibilities or changes in income shocks explain the transition of income inequality to consumption inequality during the last three decades.

The development of consumption inequality over time is of its own interest, since consumption is generally considered to be a better indicator for current household welfare compared to current income (Meyer & Sullivan, 2013b). Most researchers use only income as an indicator, but to be able to determine the welfare consequences of increasing income inequality it is necessary to know how changes in income inequality translate into consumption. Moreover, estimating consumption insurance parameters is also relevant for computational macroeconomists, since Kaplan and Violante (2010) have argued that the parameters estimated by Blundell et al. should become a benchmark for macroeconomic incomplete-markets models.

Krueger and Perri (2006) were the first to highlight the different dynamics of income and consumption inequality in the United States since the 1980s. To explain this phenomenon they develop a model where financial markets react endogenously to increasing income inequality by extending credit supply to households that are hit by large shocks. Thus, when income inequality increases over time, credit supply reacts and households do not need to decrease spending on consumption. In this way, households are able to insure consumption against larger and larger income shocks. Krueger and Perri use repeated cross-section data on income and consumption from the Consumer Expenditure (CE) Survey to estimate inequality trends in the period 1980−2003 and then try to match the trend in consumption inequality via simulation. They simulate several models with different specifications for the financial sector and show that the development of consumption inequality is determined by the amount of insurance that the financial sector offers.

Blundell et al. (2008), on the contrary, emphasize that the type of income shock is crucial for the reaction of consumption and criticize Krueger and Perri for not differentiating between transitory and permanent shocks to income. Blundell et al. first generate a new panel dataset on income and consumption by imputing information on consumption from CE data into the Panel Study of Income Dynamics (PSID) and then estimate empirically how consumption reacts to the two kinds of income shocks. Their results show that household consumption does not react at all to transitory income shocks, but that it is only partially insured against permanent shocks. Contrary to the assumptions of Krueger and Perri, they do not find the degree of insurance to change over time. Blundell et al. show that during their period under review it is a change in the composition of aggregate income inequality − from permanent to transitory − that drives the response of consumption inequality.

It has to be noted that Blundell et al. (2008) only examine the period 1980−1992. It is plausible that changes in the degree of consumption insurance cannot be detected if the observation period is relatively short. The first and foremost contribution of this paper is to demonstrate that the results of Blundell et al. break down when the observation period is prolonged. By examining PSID data up to 2010 it becomes possible to show that both the insurance against permanent and against transitory shocks improve significantly at the aggregate level. Thus, changes in the capability of households to insure against income shocks also contribute to the development of consumption inequality over time. Second, I use a new imputed measure for consumption proposed by Attanasio and Pistaferri (2014) which allows to check if the results of Blundell et al. are robust to other measures of household consumption.

In general, evidence on consumption inequality is scarce mainly due to data restrictions. Up to now, the literature has heavily relied on consumption data from the CE. However, the quality of CE data has recently been under discussion. This paper circumvents CE-related problems by exploiting information on consumption from the PSID collected between 1999 and 2011. This information is used to impute a measure of consumption for all sample years of the PSID following the example of Attanasio and Pistaferri (2014). The resulting dataset is a household panel that includes information on income and consumption which is needed to study the effects of transitory and permanent income shocks on consumption.

The empirical framework of Blundell et al. (2008) is used to identify the size of transitory and permanent income shocks and the consumption insurance parameters. This framework is parsimonious and flexible – it allows the variances of the shocks as well as the insurance parameters to change over time. I use their techniques to check if the size of transitory and permanent income inequality has changed and whether the degree of insurance against permanent and transitory shocks has remained constant over the last thirty years.

The imputation procedure of Attanasio and Pistaferri (2014) yields a consumption variable that shows only a slight increase in consumption inequality compared to the drastic increase in income inequality during the same period of time. The minimum distance estimation of empirical covariance relationships shows that the variance of transitory shocks to household income increases significantly whereas the variance of permanent shocks has been rather flat over the last three decades. Moreover, the parameters indicating insurance against income shocks also change substantially over time. The insurance against both permanent and transitory shocks improves. Thus, the type of shock that is better insured becomes more important over time and any shock to household income translates less and less into consumption over time. The combination of these two phenomena can explain why consumption inequality does not react much to income inequality.

The paper is organized as follows: Section 2 gives an overview over the sources of data and the imputation procedure while Section 3 introduces the methodological framework. The results are presented in Section 4 whereas Section 5 discusses them in the light of the related literature. Finally, Section 6 concludes.

2. THE DATA

One major problem encountered when trying to study empirically the response of consumption to permanent and transitory income changes is the lack of panel data on income *and* consumption. Although containing some panel elements, the Consumer Expenditure Survey that provides information on household income and consumption is primarily a repeated cross-section dataset. The Panel Study of Income Dynamics — a panel dataset renowned for high-quality information on household income — includes information only on food expenditure, but not on other consumption items for most of the time. The majority of studies concerned with consumption inequality therefore uses information from CE data (e.g., Fisher, Johnson, & Smeeding, 2013; Meyer & Sullivan, 2013a). However, the quality of CE data has recently been under discussion. It has been shown that CE data and tables from the National Income and Product Accounts (NIPA) on aggregate consumption diverge over time. The CE Survey seems to suffer from an increasingly worsened coverage of nondurable consumption. Therefore, Aguiar and Bils (2015) as well as Attanasio et al. (2015) argue that the use of raw data from the CE yields biased results on consumption inequality. Meyer and Sullivan (2013b), in contrast, state that the largest expenditure categories in the CE are measured well and that most of the differences to NIPA data stem form definitional differences.

Attanasio and Pistaferri (2014) have recently shown how to circumvent CE-related problems by exploiting information from the PSID on consumption collected between 1999 and 2011. They use this information to impute consumption "backwards" for all sample years. Since their procedure offers a possibility to create a panel dataset that includes information on household income and consumption without the need to make use of CE data, I will follow their example in the remainder of this paper and generate a dataset for the years 1978–2010.

2.1. The Panel Study of Income Dynamics

The Michigan Panel Study of Income Dynamics (PSID) is the world's longest running household panel dataset. Since its start in 1968, it has collected very detailed information on household income as well as on socioeconomic characteristics, household composition, and health status. Interviews have been conducted yearly until 1996 and biennially since 1997. For most of the time information on consumption expenditure has been confined to a small number of variables on food expenditure (food at home, restaurant meals, and value of food stamps). Since 1999, though, the PSID has started to collect more detailed information on nondurable consumption, namely expenditure on household utilities, gasoline, car maintenance, transportation, health, education, and child care. These variables sum up to around 70% of NIPA nondurable consumption. In 2005, the PSID added further categories like expenditure on clothing, vacation, and entertainment. Blundell, Pistaferri, and Saporta-Eksten (2015) have shown that the new PSID consumption variables align well with aggregate NIPA data and do not seem to suffer from shrinking coverage.

My sample includes all the years between 1978 and 2011. Households with a head who is not in working age (i.e., younger than 25 or older than 65 years) were dropped from the dataset. The central income variable used in the analysis is household net income since it is the type of income that determines household consumption and savings. To create a variable for household net income, information on federal and state tax payments are necessary which are not available in the PSID in many cases. They therefore have to be simulated with the help of NBER TaxSim (Appendix A contains further information on sample selection, tax simulation, and the construction of the central variables). All income variables are first deflated using Consumer Price Index variables from the U.S. Bureau of Labor Statistics and then equivalence weighted according to the modified OECD scale. The final sample comprises 12,030 households and 130,852 observations.

2.2. The Imputation Procedure

Attanasio and Pistaferri (2014) have recently shown how to use the new PSID variables on nondurable consumption to create a consistent panel dataset that includes income and consumption. They first pool all new consumption expenditure variables that are continuously available for the period 1999–2011 to create a measure of "net consumption" $N_{i,t}$ for household i in year t. Attanasio and Pistaferri then regress this indicator on a set of variables which are available for all years in the PSID according to:

$$\ln N_{i,t} = Z'_{i,t}\beta + p'_t\gamma + g\left(F_{i,t};\theta\right) + u_{i,t} \tag{1}$$

$Z_{i,t}$ denotes observable socioeconomic characteristics, p_t is a set of different prices, and $F_{i,t}$ stands for consumption variables which are available for all years in the broad sample (i.e., food consumption). Note that all of the variables used here need to be available for all sample years in order to be able to impute consumption backwards.[1] The imputed value for total household consumption $\widehat{C_{i,t}}$ is then equal to the sum of the consumption variables that are continuously available ($F_{i,t}$) and the predictions for net consumption $\left(\widehat{N_{i,t}}\right)$:

$$\widehat{C_{i,t}} = F_{i,t} + \exp\left\{Z'_{i,t}\widehat{\beta} + p'_t\widehat{\gamma} + g\left(F_{i,t}; \widehat{\theta}\right)\right\} \tag{2}$$

For further details on the variables included and the regression results see Appendix B.

Attanasio and Pistaferri (2014) argue that this procedure has three important advantages compared to other approaches. First of all, there is no need to rely on information from the CE which is valuable in the light of the debates on data quality. Second, due to the availability of some consumption variables over the whole time span, it is possible to control for preference heterogeneity to some extent. Finally, compared to other methods, imputation quality can be assessed conveniently for the last decade by comparing the forecasts with actual PSID values. Appendix B also includes a figure that shows that the variance of the change in consumption between periods does not differ substantially between imputed data and actual data for the years 1998–2010. This reassures that the imputation procedure captures the dynamics of consumption well.

3. METHODOLOGICAL FRAMEWORK

3.1. The Income Process

The empirical framework of this paper is built around the seminal work of Blundell et al. (2008). The income process of the model is specified in a well-known permanent-transitory fashion — the log of real household net

---

1. The PSID did not collect information on food expenditure in 1988 and 1989. Thus, total consumption expenditure cannot be imputed in these years.

income $Y_{i,t}$ can be separated into a part that is explained by observable household characteristics $X_{i,t}$ and two unexplained components:

$$\log Y_{i,t} = X'_{i,t}\varphi_t + P_{i,t} + v_{i,t} \tag{3}$$

The first of these components $P_{i,t}$ collects all shocks to income that exert a permanent influence on household income whereas the latter $v_{i,t}$ includes all shocks that only affect $Y_{i,t}$ temporarily. Therefore, $P_{i,t}$ is modeled as a random walk with serially uncorrelated innovations $\zeta_{i,t}$:

$$P_{i,t} = P_{i,t-1} + \zeta_{i,t} \tag{4}$$

This assures that permanent innovations to household income $\zeta_{i,t}$ do not vanish over time. The transitory component, on the contrary, needs to be modeled in a way that the effect of the innovations on household income disappears after some time. Hence, $v_{i,t}$ is represented by an MA(q)-process where the innovations $\varepsilon_{i,t}$ are also serially uncorrelated:

$$v_{i,t} = \varepsilon_{i,t} + \sum_{j=1}^{q} \theta_j \varepsilon_{i,t-j} \tag{5}$$

The order q of the MA-process is a priori unknown and will be estimated empirically.

As the two residual components are of main interest, the remainder of this paper is concerned with residual income $y_{i,t}$ and the growth in residual income $\Delta y_{i,t}$:

$$y_{i,t} = \log Y_{i,t} - X'_{i,t}\varphi_t = P_{i,t} + v_{i,t} \tag{6}$$

$$\Delta y_{i,t} = \zeta_{i,t} + \Delta v_{i,t} \tag{7}$$

The variable $\Delta y_{i,t}$ is also needed to identify the order q of the MA-process. By assumption, the innovations $\zeta_{i,t}$ and $\varepsilon_{i,t}$ are mutually uncorrelated. Then, all covariances of $\Delta y_{i,t}$ and $\Delta y_{i,t+s}$ with $s > q+1$ are equal to zero, whereas for $s \le q+1$ all covariances need to be significantly different from zero. The order q can, thus, be identified by estimating Cov($\Delta y_{i,t}$, $\Delta y_{i,t+s}$) for $s = 1, \ldots, T-t$ and checking at which value for s the covariances cease to be significantly different from zero. Table 1 depicts the autocovariances for $s = 0, 1, 2, 3$ for the years 1979–1996. After 1996, the frequency of PSID data is biennial so that first differences of income cease to be available.

Table 1. Variance and Autocovariance of Income Growth.

Year	$\mathrm{Var}(\Delta y_{i,t})$	$\mathrm{Cov}(\Delta y_{i,t},\ \Delta y_{i,t+1})$	$\mathrm{Cov}(\Delta y_{i,t},\ \Delta y_{i,t+2})$	$\mathrm{Cov}(\Delta y_{i,t},\ \Delta y_{i,t+3})$
1978	–	–	–	–
1979	0.1123***	−0.0375***	−0.0004	−0.0036
1980	0.1069***	−0.0464***	0.0031	−0.0019
1981	0.1183***	−0.0463***	−0.0034	0.0033
1982	0.1188***	−0.0484***	−0.0010	−0.0002
1983	0.1243***	−0.0482***	−0.0001	−0.0011
1984	0.1225***	−0.0503***	−0.0012	0.0001
1985	0.1471***	−0.0494***	−0.0075*	−0.0009
1986	0.1367***	−0.0500***	−0.0036	−0.0028
1987	0.1316***	−0.0515***	0.0058*	−0.0027
1988	0.1354***	−0.0575***	−0.0039	−0.0016
1989	0.1320***	−0.0445***	−0.0017	0.0017
1990	0.1303***	−0.0479***	−0.0045	−0.0037
1991	0.1375***	−0.0537***	−0.0017	0.0039
1992	0.1738***	−0.0782***	−0.0034	−0.0014
1993	0.2029***	−0.0833***	0.0017	0.0023
1994	0.1857***	−0.0683***	−0.0106*	–
1995	0.1792***	−0.0649***	–	–
1996	0.1915***	–	–	–

Note: $*p < 0.05$, $**p < 0.01$, $***p < 0.001$.

The values in Table 1 show that – as expected – the variances of the first difference of residual income are positive and significantly different from zero. The first autocovariance of income change is always negative and significantly different from zero. The second and the third autocovariance are very close to zero, sometimes positive and sometimes negative. Statistically, they cannot be distinguished from being zero in nearly all cases. This pattern is in line with $q = 0$, that is, with a transitory income component that is a simple idiosyncratic shock and does not show any moving average-behavior. Thus, PSID data in my sample can be described best by the following income process:

$$\log Y_{i,t} = X'_{i,t}\varphi_t + P_{i,t} + \varepsilon_{i,t} \qquad (8)$$

This income process has often been used for PSID data (e.g., Heathcote et al., 2010). It is a special case of the more general income process of Blundell et al. (2008) since there is no difference between the transitory shock $v_{i,t}$ and the transitory innovation $\varepsilon_{i,t}$.

3.2. The Response of Consumption to Income Shocks

The second central equation in the model of Blundell et al. (2008) is the equation that describes how transitory and permanent shocks are translated into (residual) household consumption. Blundell et al. (2008) do not want to presuppose any kind of theoretical model, but prefer to allow the amount of insurance to be determined freely with respect to both kinds of income shocks. Hence, two parameters $\phi_{i,t}$ and $\psi_{i,t}$ are introduced that govern how much of the permanent and transitory shocks is transmitted into consumption. Therefore, the change in residual consumption is determined by

$$\Delta c_{i,t} = \phi_{i,t}\zeta_{i,t} + \psi_{i,t}\varepsilon_{i,t} + \xi_{i,t} \tag{9}$$

where $c_{i,t}$ is residual real household consumption, $\phi_{i,t}$ is the parameter for insurance against a permanent income shock, and $\psi_{i,t}$ is the counterpart with respect to a transitory shock. Both parameters theoretically lie between zero and one: If a parameter is zero, the shock does not affect consumption at all. If a parameter is one, the shock fully translates into consumption. If the parameter lies between zero and one, Blundell et al. speak of "partial insurance." Finally, the term $\xi_{i,t}$ allows for unobserved heterogeneity and captures all innovations to residual consumption growth that are not related to income changes.

Economic theory predicts that the reaction of household consumption to income shocks is driven by the state of the financial markets of the economy. In the case of perfect insurance markets, it is assumed that households can buy insurance against any kind of shock and, thus, their consumption does not react at all to transitory or permanent income shocks ($\phi_t = \psi_t = 0$).[2] In a situation where the financial markets allow only self-insurance via a non-contingent bond, households accumulate savings that enable them to buffer temporary shocks to income, but permanent shocks will affect the level of consumption ($\psi_t = 0$, $0 < \phi_t \leq 1$). Finally, when credit markets are imperfect and households face tight borrowing constraints, transitory and permanent shocks will both be fully transmitted into consumption ($\phi_t = \psi_t = 1$).

---

2. While $\phi_{i,t}$ and $\psi_{i,t}$ denote the individual insurance of a household, ϕ_t and ψ_t denote the population average. All estimated parameters are population averages.

Since the consumption variable used is imputed, it·is very likely that it is measured with error. Blundell et al., therefore, expand Eq. (9) so that it allows for measurement error in $c_{i,t}$. Thus, for estimation the following variant of Eq. (9) will be used:

$$\Delta c_{i,t} = \phi_{i,t}\zeta_{i,t} + \psi_{i,t}\varepsilon_{i,t} + \xi_{i,t} + u^c_{i,t} - u^c_{i,t-1} \qquad (10)$$

where $u^c_{i,t}$ stands for the measurement error in consumption in period t.

The advantage of this framework is its flexibility — both the variances of transitory and permanent shocks as well as the insurance parameters are allowed to change over time. Due to this fact, the framework can also be used to analyze whether the prediction of Krueger and Perri (2006) on the development of consumption inequality can be confirmed by the data. Their model assumed that financial markets react endogenously to increasing income inequality by extending credit supply. Thus, they assume that over time the level of insurance to income shocks increases. As they do not differentiate between transitory and permanent shocks to income, it is not possible to tell which one of the two parameters needs to decrease, but it is clear that if the mechanism that Krueger and Perri (2006) describe is present, a decrease in either ϕ_t or ψ_t needs to be found.

On the other hand, Blundell et al. (2008) stress the fact that it is the kind of shock that determines the evolution of consumption inequality. They explain the lack of a response of consumption inequality to the rise in income inequality by an ever larger fraction of well-insured transitory shocks. If their result for the 1980s is a general finding then one should find (i) $\phi_t > \psi_t$, that is, transitory shocks are better insured than permanent shocks, and (ii) ϕ_t and ψ_t do not vary over time.

It has to be noted that these are clearly extreme characterizations of the transmission of income inequality to consumption inequality. Of course, both explanations can be present at the same time and work together.

3.3. Minimum Distance Estimation of the Model Parameters

The model parameters are estimated by collecting the variances, covariances, and autocovariances of $\Delta y_{i,t}$ and $\Delta c_{i,t}$ for all t and then minimizing the distance between the empirical covariances and the parameters predicted by the parametric income-consumption model. Thus, it first needs to be analyzed what the two central Eqs. (8) and (10) imply for the empirical variances and covariances. Specifying the income process with $q=0$ has the consequence that only the first autocovariance of income growth is different from zero:

$$\text{Var}(\Delta y_{i,t}) = \text{Var}(\zeta_{i,t}) + \text{Var}(\varepsilon_{i,t}) + \text{Var}(\varepsilon_{i,t-1})$$

$$\text{Cov}(\Delta y_{i,t}, \Delta y_{i,t+1}) = -\text{Var}(\varepsilon_{i,t})$$

$$\text{Cov}(\Delta y_{i,t}, \Delta y_{i,t+s}) = 0 \quad \forall s > 1$$

The first autocovariance of income change identifies the variance of the transitory shocks and together with $\text{Var}(\Delta y_{i,t})$ also the variance of permanent income shocks can be identified. Hence, variances and autocovariances of the change in residual income suffice in general to identify $\text{Var}(\varepsilon_{i,t})$ and $\text{Var}(\zeta_{i,t})$. However, adding also the consumption moments helps to improve the estimation.

The autocovariances of the change in residual consumption have a similar structure. Due to the consumption-martingale property, changes in consumption today are related to changes in the past or the future only via measurement error. The autocovariances of Eq. (10) can be summarized by:

$$\text{Var}(\Delta c_{i,t}) = \phi_t^2 \text{Var}(\zeta_{i,t}) + \psi_t^2 \text{Var}(\varepsilon_{i,t}) + \text{Var}(\xi_{i,t}) + \text{Var}(u_{i,t}^c) + \text{Var}\left(u_{i,t-1}^c\right)$$

$$\text{Cov}(\Delta c_{i,t}, \Delta c_{i,t+1}) = -\text{Var}\left(u_{i,t}^c\right)$$

$$\text{Cov}(\Delta c_{i,t}, \Delta c_{i,t+s}) = 0 \quad \forall s > 1$$

The autocovariance with respect to $t+1$ identifies the variance of measurement error in consumption $\text{Var}(u_{i,t}^c)$, but the variance of unobserved heterogeneity in consumption growth $\text{Var}(\xi_{i,t})$ can only be identified if the insurance parameters ϕ_t and ψ_t are known.

To identify ϕ_t and ψ_t, the covariances between income and consumption changes are of crucial importance. The covariances between $\Delta c_{i,t}$ and $\Delta y_{i,s}$ are as follows:

$$\text{Cov}(\Delta c_{i,t}, \Delta y_{i,t}) = \phi_t \text{Var}(\zeta_{i,t}) + \psi_t \text{Var}(\varepsilon_{i,t})$$

$$\text{Cov}(\Delta c_{i,t}, \Delta y_{i,t+1}) = -\psi_t \text{Var}(\varepsilon_{i,t})$$

$$\text{Cov}(\Delta c_{i,t}, \Delta y_{i,t+s}) = 0 \quad \forall s > 1 \text{ and } s < 0$$

It can be seen that the three sets of second moments $\text{Cov}(\Delta y_{i,t}, \Delta y_{i,t+s})$, $\text{Cov}(\Delta c_{i,t}, \Delta c_{i,t+s})$, and $\text{Cov}(\Delta c_{i,t}, \Delta y_{i,t+s})$ for all t and s suffice to identify the key model parameters ϕ_t, ψ_t, $\text{Var}(\zeta_{i,t})$, $\text{Var}(\varepsilon_{i,t})$, $\text{Var}(u_{i,t}^c)$, and $\text{Var}(\xi_{i,t})$. As in principle all parameters of the model are allowed to vary over time, this method enables us to analyze how much consumption inequality is driven by changes in the insurance parameters and how much by changes in the income shock variances.[3]

Note that the covariance relationships are set up for annual data. As PSID data has a biennial frequency after 1997, the procedure has to be slightly adjusted. The first differences $\Delta c_{i,t}$ and $\Delta y_{i,t}$ cease to be available and it has to be relied on second seasonal differences $\Delta_2 c_{i,t} = c_{i,t} - c_{i,t-2}$ and $\Delta_2 y_{i,t} = y_{i,t} - y_{i,t-2}$. However, this change does not cause major problems to the model. Appendix C contains more details on the estimation process and shows how to ensure identification of the parameters with biennial data.

4. RESULTS

Fig. 1 shows the development of income and consumption inequality over time where inequality is measured as the standard deviation of log-variables. In line with much of the literature, income and consumption inequality are both increasing over time, but inequality of imputed consumption increases far less than the inequality of household net income. This is not only true for overall income and consumption inequality represented by solid lines, but also for their residual measures, that is, the share of inequality that cannot be explained by observable characteristics, which are depicted by the dotted lines.

To generate income and consumption residuals an OLS-regression is run that controls for a set of observable characteristics including the number of persons in the household, employment status, and education of head (and spouse if present), state of residence, ethnicity, sex and age of the household head, and presence of other income earners in the household. The effect of most right-hand side variables is allowed to vary with the respective year. R^2 for the income regression is 0.574, for the consumption regression it is 0.746 showing that a larger amount of household consumption can be explained by observable characteristics.

---

3. Since there is no economic intuition why $\text{Var}(\xi_{i,t})$ should vary over time, this parameter is treated as stationary.

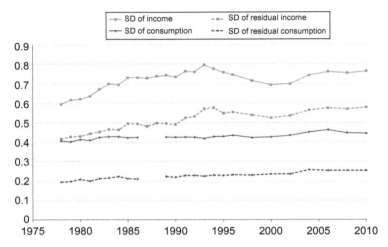

Fig. 1. Inequality of Household Income and Consumption, Overall and Residual.

It can also be seen in Fig. 1 that the increase in overall income inequality is nearly fully driven by an increase in residual income inequality. Overall income inequality increases by 0.167 log-points between 1978 and 2010 whereas residual income inequality increases by 0.161. Residual consumption inequality even increases faster than overall inequality. Overall consumption inequality rises by 0.038 log-points while residual inequality rises by 0.059 over the same time span. That is why the analysis in the following is concentrated on the residual measures of income and consumption that are the driving forces of the increase in overall income and consumption inequality in the last three decades.

4.1. Results of the Minimum Distance Estimation

Fig. 2 depicts the development of $\mathrm{Var}(\zeta_{i,t})$ and $\mathrm{Var}(\varepsilon_{i,t})$ at the aggregate level and the respective 95% confidence bands as estimated by the minimum distance procedure (additional estimation results and standard errors can also be found in Table C1). It can be seen at first glance that the variance of transitory innovations which affect net income only in the respective year is always larger in magnitude compared to the variance of permanent innovations whose effect on household income is lasting. Moreover, the transitory variance is increasing steadily over time whereas

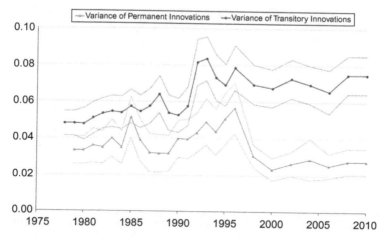

Fig. 2. Variance of Permanent and Transitory Innovations over Time with 95-Percent Confidence Intervals.

it is harder to detect a general trend for the variance of permanent innovations. The latter increases during the first half of the 1980s but decreases again to the initial level by the end of the 1980s. In the 1990s, the permanent variance increases substantially, but then drops below the starting level in 1998 and stays there until the end of the sample period. In total, the variance of permanent innovations is more or less flat or even slightly decreasing so that on average the difference in the levels of $\text{Var}(\zeta_{i,t})$ and $\text{Var}(\varepsilon_{i,t})$ is increasing over time.

Fig. 2 gives a first hint why consumption inequality does not increase as strongly as income inequality does. The composition of overall income inequality changes over time and the transitory part becomes more and more dominant. In case transitory shocks are easier to insure than permanent shocks, consumption will not be affected as much by an increase in the size of the former as by an increase in permanent shocks of the same magnitude. However, this conclusion depends on the size of the insurance parameters. If these were constant over time, a steady increase in transitory inequality and a constant permanent inequality should lead to a steady increase in consumption inequality. If the insurance parameters also changed over time, the development of consumption inequality could be different.

The development of the parameters of insurance against transitory shocks (ψ_t) and permanent shocks (ϕ_t) is shown in Fig. 3. To ease computation, both parameters have not been estimated separately for every single

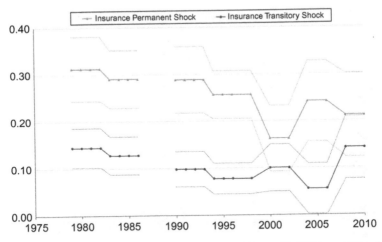

Fig. 3. Development of Insurance Parameters over Time with 95-Percent Confidence
Intervals.

year, but time groups of around 4 years have been used (1979–1982,
1983–1986, 1990–1993, 1994–1998, 1999–2002, 2003–2006, 2007–2010).
These groups should suffice to determine general trends over time.
Estimates and standard errors for ϕ_t and ψ_t are also listed in Table 2.

Fig. 3 reveals some remarkable results: First, as expected above and also
found by other studies, the insurance parameter ϕ_t always lies above ψ_t.
This means that transitory shocks to income affect consumption to a lesser
degree than permanent shocks to income in all years. Second, the insurance
parameters are not constant over time at all. The insurance against permanent income shocks decreases steadily in the last three decades. Although
there is a substantial drop in the period 2000–2002 which seems to be an
outlier, the overall trend is a continuous decrease. In total, ϕ_t decreases
from 0.3126 to 0.2115 between 1978 and 2010. The insurance against transitory income shocks also shows a steady decrease for most of the observation period. ψ_t declines from 0.1443 to 0.0549 between 1978 and 2006.
Thus, the capability of households to insure against any kind of income
shock improves during the 1980s, the 1990s and most of the 2000s. Third,
the improvement in insurance is also statistically significant. Estimated
coefficients in the later periods lie outside the confidence bands of the initial
period for both insurance parameters.

Finally, insurance against transitory income shocks jumps up drastically
in the final period (2007–2010). This result could be explained by the

Table 2. Insurance Parameters (Standard Errors in Parentheses).

	1979–1982	1983–1986	1990–1993	1994–1998	1999–2002	2003–2006	2007–2010
ϕ_t	0.3126	0.2904	0.2883	0.2562	0.1625	0.2415	0.2115
	(0.0349)	(0.0314)	(0.0362)	(0.0260)	(0.0358)	(0.0439)	(0.0456)
ψ_t	0.1443	0.1275	0.0979	0.0773	0.0998	0.0549	0.1423
	(0.0215)	(0.0207)	(0.0190)	(0.0168)	(0.0255)	(0.0273)	(0.0339)

financial crisis that has an effect on credit supply and makes it harder to insure income shocks. Such an effect, though, should not only increase ψ_t, but also ϕ_t. In general, the results of the insurance parameters in the final period should be seen with some caution. The variances of both income shocks cannot be identified separately for 2008 and 2010 so it has to be assumed that $\text{Var}(\zeta_{2008}) = \text{Var}(\zeta_{2010})$ and $\text{Var}(\varepsilon_{2008}) = \text{Var}(\varepsilon_{2010})$. It is possible that this assumption influences the estimated insurance coefficients in that period. Thus, unless further years of data become available, it is not possible to assess properly how the financial crisis affects consumption insurance possibilities. However, regardless of whether the results of the final period are included or not, the main finding of Fig. 3 is that consumption insurance improves over time.

4.2. Robustness

The robustness of the findings can be assessed by varying (i) the kind of variables used as well as (ii) the observations included in the sample. The first set of robustness tests tries to figure out by how much the results depend upon the imputed consumption variable. Two kinds of alternative consumption variables are logical candidates: the actual values for total household consumption of food that are available for the whole sample and the actual values for household nondurable consumption which are available from 1998 onward.

Using only food consumption allows to check whether another consumption variable that is available for the whole sample period also yields an improvement in consumption insurance over time. This route has already been followed by Hall and Mishkin (1982) in a first pioneering empirical contribution on the effect of permanent and transitory income changes on consumption. However, an important difference to nondurable consumption arises which has already been pointed out by Blundell et al. (2008): the food consumption variable only captures a part of total nondurable consumption expenditure, and the fraction of food consumption to total consumption can change over time. The estimated parameters for consumption insurance will then be a product of the true parameter and the elasticity of food consumption with respect to total consumption expenditure (e.g., $\widehat{\phi}_t = \beta_t \phi_t$, where β_t is the mentioned elasticity). If household incomes and the standard of living increase on average since the 1980s, β_t decreases over time. Then, the estimated parameters $\widehat{\phi}_t$ and $\widehat{\psi}_t$ will automatically decrease as well even if the true insurance parameters are constant. Combining a decreasing β_t and decreasing insurance parameters yields a stronger decrease than in the benchmark case. Thus, it can be expected that estimated insurance parameters will decrease more strongly over time when food consumption is used instead of the imputed variable for nondurable consumption. Moreover, since $\beta_t < 1$, the parameters found should also be smaller.

Fig. 4 shows estimated parameters for the aggregate sample when only food consumption is used and compares them with the results of the imputed consumption variable. Moreover, the figure includes confidence intervals around the benchmark values. The qualitative development is similar to the benchmark case and as expected before, the parameters show larger decreases quantitatively. However, the estimated parameters are not smaller than those in the benchmark case, but mostly larger. This counterintuitive finding can be explained by the nature of the imputed

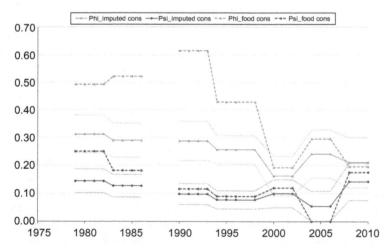

Fig. 4. Robustness Test – Insurance Parameters When Food Consumption Is Used as Variable of Interest (95-Percent Confidence Intervals around Benchmark Values).

consumption variable: As the benchmark consumption variable has been imputed, its variance is smaller in level compared to actual data. Since one of the main identifying equations for the insurance parameters is

$$\text{Var}(\Delta c_{i,t}) = \phi_t^2 \text{Var}(\zeta_{i,t}) + \psi_t^2 \text{Var}(\varepsilon_{i,t}) + \text{Var}(\xi_{i,t}) + \text{Var}(u_{i,t}^c) + \text{Var}(u_{i,t-1}^c)$$

it is clear that $\hat{\phi}_t$ and $\hat{\psi}_t$ will increase when $\text{Var}(\Delta c_{i,t})$ increases and the income shock variances are held constant. This effect can explain why the level of the insurance parameters is higher when actual data for food consumption is used. However, the finding that the insurance parameters decrease more strongly over time in Fig. 4 is exactly in line with expectations and backs the benchmark results.

The actual values for nondurable consumption that are available for the period 1998–2010 can be used to assess whether the estimated insurance coefficients for this period differ from the benchmark results. Again, the variances for the actual consumption variable are larger, compared to imputed data. Hence, the level of the estimated coefficients should be higher compared to the benchmark case, but the change over time should be comparable. Fig. 5 depicts the development of ϕ_t and ψ_t for the periods 2000–2002, 2004–2006, 2008–2010. For ψ_t the results are in line with expectations: the level of insurance against transitory shocks is a bit lower (i.e., the estimated parameters are higher), but all values are inside the confidence intervals and the change over time is parallel to the benchmark results. For ϕ_t, the result is at least qualitatively similar to the benchmark case: the insurance parameter first increases in 2004 and then decreases back in 2008. Quantitatively, though, the level of ϕ_t in the initial period (2000–2002) seems to be a bit too low to be in line with the benchmark case. This deviation could be due to the fact that only a short spell of observations is available for the actual consumption variable compared to the imputed data. Moreover, the years 2000–2002 are the initial period for the sample of actual consumption, but not for the benchmark case. In general, this robustness test also shows that the level of consumption insurance varies over time and thereby supports the previous findings.

I have also experimented with generating a new imputed consumption variable by using the additional consumption expenditure variables that the PSID added in 2005 (clothing, vacation, and entertainment). This broadens the "net consumption" variable $N_{i,t}$, but requires to drop all observations from the years 1999–2003 to rerun the imputation procedure. The results can be found in Fig. D1 which shows that estimated parameters for the 2005-consumption variable are extremely close to the benchmark

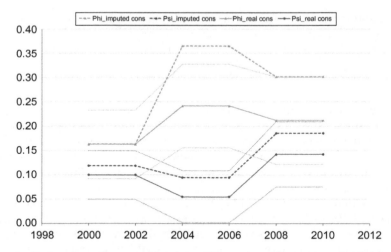

Fig. 5. Robustness Test — Insurance Parameters When Actual Nondurable Consumption Is Used for the Years 1998—2010 (95-Percent Confidence Intervals around Benchmark Values).

case. The reason for this finding is that the new expenditure categories are relatively small compared to the variables that were already part of the imputation procedure before. Thus, the imputation procedure and the minimum distance estimation do not produce results that differ significantly from the benchmark findings when the additional expenditure categories are taken into account.

The second set of robustness tests varies the amount of observations included in the dataset to check whether the results depend on sample selection. A possible criticism of the analysis could be that the results and especially the imputation procedure are biased because the sample includes the years of the financial crisis that differ systematically from the rest of the years. To rule out this possibility, I have rerun the imputation procedure after dropping all observations from the years 2008 and 2010. Fig. D2 shows a comparison of this robustness check with the benchmark results. Aside from small deviations in the years 2004—2006 which constitute the final period for the new sample, the two trends hardly differ. Hence, the main results of the analysis do not seem to be driven by the inclusion of the years of the financial crisis.

Many comparable studies exclude the SEO-subsample of the PSID that was introduced to collect information on poorer households in the United States. Fig. D3 compares estimated insurance parameters for the benchmark and for a sample that excludes the SEO-subsample. Moreover, the benchmark sample requires four observations on income for a household to be included in the dataset. This leads to a dataset consisting of a relatively high number of households with only few observations. To control that the results are not driven by this arbitrary choice, Fig. D4 depicts the benchmark case and a sample that excludes households with less than 30 observations on income and consumption. Figs. D3 and D4 both show that the variations in sample selection do not lead to substantially different insurance parameters. Most estimated parameters lie within the confidence bands of the benchmark estimation. In general, the key findings of the paper seem to be very robust with respect to changes in the consumption variable and the sample selection.

5. DISCUSSION

Fig. 2 shows that transitory shocks to household net income increase in size over time while permanent shocks are roughly constant. Fig. 3, though, makes clear that a changing composition of income shocks — from less insurable permanent to transitory shocks — is not enough to explain the development of consumption inequality in the last three decades. The ability of households to insure their consumption expenditures against shocks to income changes as well. Both, insurance against transitory and against permanent shocks improve significantly over time (at least until 2006). By combining the evidence from the two figures, it becomes obvious why the dramatic increase in income inequality is not mirrored in consumption inequality. The two explanations offered in the literature are present at the same time: transitory shocks become more important as suggested by Blundell et al. (2008), but the insurability of all income shocks also improves over time as suggested by Krueger and Perri (2006).

How do my findings relate to the results of Blundell et al. (2008)? The robustness tests have revealed that the estimated level of consumption insurance is very sensitive to the kind of consumption variable used.[4]

---

4. It is, therefore, surprising that the quantities estimated by Blundell et al. (2008), who also use an imputed consumption variable, have received so much attention (e.g., Kaplan & Violante, 2010). On these grounds, this paper focuses on the trends of consumption insurance parameters over time which seem to be relatively robust to changes in the consumption variable.

Hence, the different level of consumption insurance found by Blundell et al. can to some degree be explained by the fact that they use a different imputation procedure. On the other hand, Fig. 3 shows that although the degree of insurance against shocks is changing substantially over the course of the three decades, the level of ϕ_t and ψ_t in the initial years is relatively stable. Both series are decreasing, but the differences in parameters are relatively small compared to the change over the whole sample period. The insurance against permanent income shocks does not differ significantly from its initial level until the year 2000, whereas the insurance against transitory shocks is already significantly different from 1990 onward. Hence, these results do not need to be seen as a direct contradiction to the observations of Blundell et al. (2008) who find constant parameters in their study that covered the years between 1979 and 1992.[5] Indeed, my analysis rather indicates that their result for the 1980s is a relatively robust finding. The result breaks down, though, when observations for the years 1993−2010 are added.

An important discussion in the literature on income and consumption inequality is on how to distinguish consumption insurance from superior information. If an individual knows that her income will decrease at some point in the future, she is able to accumulate savings before so that at the point in time the income shock hits, it will have no effect on the consumption level. Usually, the econometrician does not have information on foreseen shocks and, therefore, classifies the lack of response to the shock as a sign for well-functioning consumption insurance mechanisms. This point has been made very clear by Primiceri and van Rens (2009) who argue that most of the permanent income shocks are foreseen since consumption inequality does not react appropriately to increasing permanent income shocks. However, they also cannot identify information and insurance separately as data on income expectations are needed for that. Kaufmann and Pistaferri (2009) use an Italian dataset that contains subjective income expectations to distinguish foreseen and unforeseen shocks from each other. They can show that a huge part of transitory and about a third of permanent income shocks are indeed foreseen. For a detailed overview of the insurance versus information debate see Meghir and Pistaferri (2011).

---

5. Note, however, that Blundell et al. (2008) do not find the value of ψ_t to be significantly different from zero whereas it is statistically significant for all years in my sample.

Can the results of this paper potentially be explained by superior information? Due to the limitations of the data used, I have not been able to differentiate between insurance and information. Thus, it is important to keep in mind that everything that is identified as consumption insurance could also be a sign of superior information. The level of insurance found for both kinds of shocks is relatively high and a part of what is identified as "insurance" is probably information. However, concerning the development over time it is hard to argue that there is a trend in superior information in the last 30 years. It seems implausible that households have significantly more information on their stochastic income processes today compared to the 1980s or that the income shocks itself have become more predictable. Thus, the main finding of the paper, that consumption insurance improves over time, cannot be explained by superior information.

Krueger and Perri (2006) hypothesized that an expansion of credit supply is the reason for the trend in consumption inequality. The empirical framework of this paper, though, does not allow to identify the exact channel through which consumption insurance improves. Hence, I am not able to verify the credit supply-hypothesis within my analysis, but there is one finding which is very well in line with it: as discussed above, the insurance parameter against transitory shocks increases substantially in the period 2007—2010. In case this finding is not a statistical artifact driven by a final period-problem, it can be explained by a drying up of credit induced by the financial crisis. However, Blundell et al. (2015) have recently challenged the view that credit is the most important source of consumption insurance. They find that the majority of insurance is explained by intra-family labor supply. If this is true, a trend in intra-family labor supply, for example, by increased female labor force participation, could also produce an improvement in consumption insurance over time. Thus, credit supply and family labor supply both offer plausible explanations for the observed increase in the households' ability to buffer shocks to income. Future research, therefore, needs to be concerned with ways to identify and differentiate between the precise channels that affect consumption insurance parameters.

6. CONCLUSION

This paper has analyzed the joint development of income and consumption inequality in the United States over the last 30 years. By using a new method for imputing consumption into PSID data developed by Attanasio and Pistaferri (2014), a panel dataset that contains income and consumption is created. This data is used to analyze how much consumption reacts to transitory and permanent shocks to income and whether this reaction has changed over the course of the past three decades. Many other papers before have found that consumption inequality does not seem to react very much to increases in income inequality and the reasons for this phenomenon are still under debate. While Krueger and Perri (2006) believe that the ability of households to insure consumption against income shocks has improved due to a better credit supply, Blundell et al. (2008) argue that it is the changing composition of income shocks that determines consumption inequality.

The results of this paper show that inequality of imputed consumption is also characterized by a relatively small increase since the 1980s whereas income inequality rises steadily over the same time span. The minimum distance estimation of the model parameters shows that both explanations contribute to the development of consumption inequality. On the one hand, the composition of shocks to income changes over time. The variance of transitory shocks increases constantly while the variance of permanent shocks is rather flat. On the other hand, the capability of households to insure their consumption against income shocks improves over time. The ability to buffer both permanent and transitory shocks increases so that shocks to household income are transmitted into consumption to a lesser extent. Taken together, these two developments explain why consumption inequality is relatively flat even in the face of increasing income inequality.

This paper contributes to the literature on consumption inequality by showing that the result of Blundell et al. (2008) that only changes in transitory and permanent income shocks determine the development of consumption inequality is driven by the choice of the sample period. When longer time spans are analyzed, also the parameters indicating the households' insurance against income shocks fluctuate and affect the evolution of consumption inequality. The findings in the paper are well in line with the theory of Krueger and Perri (2006) that credit supply determines consumption insurance. However, the recent insight of Blundell et al. (2015) that family labor supply explains most of the insurance against income shocks can as well explain the trends observed. Future research in this area should aim at identifying the importance of the different channels of consumption insurance and investigate how the importance of these channels evolves over time.

REFERENCES

Aguiar, M., & Bils, M. (2015). Has consumption inequality mirrored income inequality? *American Economic Review, 105*(9), 2725–2756.

Attanasio, O., Hurst, E., & Pistaferri, L. (2015). *The evolution of income, consumption, and leisure inequality in the United States, 1980–2010* (pp. 100–140). Chicago, IL: University of Chicago Press.

Attanasio, O., & Pistaferri, L. (2014). Consumption inequality over the last half century. Some evidence using the new PSID consumption measure. *American Economic Review Papers & Proceedings, 104*(5), 122–126.

Blundell, R., Pistaferri, L., & Preston, I. (2008). Consumption inequality and partial insurance. *American Economic Review, 98*(5), 1887–1921.

Blundell, R., Pistaferri, L., & Saporta-Eksten, I. (2015). Consumption inequality and family labor supply. *American Economic Review, forthcoming*. Retrieved from https://www.aeaweb.org/forthcoming/output/accepted_AER.php

Chamberlain, G. (1984). Panel data. In Handbook of econometrics (Vol. 2, pp. 1247–1318). Amsterdam, North-Holland: Elsevier.

Feenberg, D., & Coutts, E. (1993). An introduction to the TAXSIM model. *Journal of Policy Analysis and Management, 12*(1), 189–194.

Fisher, J. D., Johnson, D. S., & Smeeding, T. M. (2013). Measuring the trends in inequality of individuals and families: Income and consumption. *American Economic Review Papers & Proceedings, 103*(3), 184–188.

Hall, R. E., & Mishkin, F. S. (1982). The sensitivity of consumption to transitory income: Estimates from panel data on households. *Econometrica, 50*(2), 461–481.

Heathcote, J., Perri, F., & Violante, G. L. (2010). Unequal we stand: An empirical analysis of economic inequality in the United States, 1967–2006. *Review of Economic Dynamics, 13*(1), 15–51.

Kaplan, G., & Violante, G. L. (2010). How much consumption insurance beyond self-insurance? *American Economic Journal: Macroeconomics, 2*(4), 53–87.

Kaufmann, K., & Pistaferri, L. (2009). Disentangling insurance and information in intertemporal consumption choices. *American Economic Review Papers & Proceedings, 99*(2), 387–392.

Krueger, D., & Perri, F. (2006). Does income inequality lead to consumption inequality? Evidence and theory. *The Review of Economic Studies, 73*(1), 163–193.

Meghir, C., & Pistaferri, L. (2011). Earnings, consumption and life cycle choices. In D. Card & O. Ashenfelter (Eds.), *Handbook of labor economics* (Vol. 4, Pt. B, pp. 773–854). Amsterdam, North-Holland: Elsevier.

Meyer, B. D., & Sullivan, J. X. (2013a). Consumption and income inequality and the great recession. *American Economic Review Papers & Proceedings, 103*(3), 178–183.

Meyer, B. D., & Sullivan, J. X. (2013b). *Consumption and income inequality in the U.S. since the 1960s.* Working Paper.

Primiceri, G. E., & van Rens, T. (2009). Heterogeneous life-cycle profiles, income risk and consumption inequality. *Journal of Monetary Economics, 56*(1), 20–39.

APPENDIX A: SAMPLE SELECTION AND VARIABLE CONSTRUCTION

After merging all observations of the PSID waves between 1978 and 2011, the Latino and the Immigrant subsample are dropped. Since both are available only for some years of the sample, their inclusion would change the sample composition for these years substantially and make comparisons to other years more difficult. Especially, the imputation procedure would yield erroneous results if the Immigrant sample was not left out in the regression and the results were projected onto years before 1996.

As the main focus of the analysis is to identify the households' response to income shocks stemming from labor market risk, households with a head who is not in working age (i.e., where the head is younger than 25 or older than 65) are excluded from the sample. Moreover, observations are dropped when income or consumption values are drastic outliers. Income outliers are those values where household net income increases by more than 500% or by less than −80% compared to the period before. Observations where household net income, household food expenditure, or the sum of all expenditure variables that were added in 1999 (household utilities, gasoline, car maintenance, transportation, health, education, and child care) is less than $100 a year are also identified as outliers and excluded. Households with a missing value for the educational attainment of the household head are dropped as well.

Finally, households that have less than four observations on household net income are excluded. This is done to prevent increases in income variation stemming from households that are only part of the dataset for one or two periods and for which there are no continuous observations on first differences. The decision to exclude those with exactly less than four observations is, of course, somewhat arbitrary. The reason is that four periods (i.e., three first differences) suffice to identify the key parameters of the study. However, robustness tests are conducted to see by how much the results depend on this decision. Table A1 summarizes how many observations are dropped in the process of sample selection.

One of the two central variables of the paper is household net income. To construct an accurate measure of annual household net income all top-coded income values in the PSID are set to missing. All income values that report weekly or monthly earnings are adjusted to annual values. Some of

Table A1. Number of Total Observations in the Dataset by Step of Sample Selection.

Reason for Exclusion	# Dropped	# Remain
Initial sample		205,860
Latino and Immigrant subsample	16,272	189,588
Head not in working age	40,652	148,936
Income and consumption outliers	4,718	144,218
No information on head's education	3,500	140,718
Too few income observations	9,866	130,852

these adjusted values are unrealistically high so that they have to be dropped from the sample. Household net income is then defined as total family money minus the federal and state tax payments of head and wife and the federal tax payments of other family unit members.

Since federal tax payments are only available in the PSID up to 1991 and state taxes are not available at all, the variables have to be simulated. The simulation is realized with the help of NBER TaxSim (Feenberg & Coutts, 1993). Unfortunately, it is not possible to simulate tax payments for other family unit members since there is too little information available in the PSID. Thus, federal tax payments of other family unit members can only be deducted up to 1991. However, as this variable is usually very small or zero, household net income should not be affected too much by this change in definition.

Household net income and consumption expenditure are then deflated using the corresponding Consumer Price Index (CPI) variables taken from the U.S. Bureau of Labor Statistics and, thus, are referring to prices of the year 1979. All variables are also equivalence weighted by the modified OECD scale to control for differences in family composition. All income variables of the PSID are referring to the previous year. I follow most of the literature by also treating consumption expenditure variables as referring to the previous year. Hence, yearly income data is available for the years 1978–1996 and biennial data for the years 1998, 2000, 2002, 2004, 2006, 2008, and 2010. (Imputed) Consumption data is available for the same years except for 1987 and 1988 where food consumption variables were not collected.

APPENDIX B: THE IMPUTATION PROCEDURE

Imputation quality of the procedure by Attanasio and Pistaferri (2014) depends on the validity of the regression Eq. (1). I have tried to mirror the imputation procedure of Attanasio and Pistaferri as closely as possible. However, due to slight differences in sample selection and the treatments of outliers and top-coded income values, minor differences in the regression results can be expected. Table B1 summarizes and compares the regression results of Attanasio and Pistaferri and of this paper.

From a qualitative perspective nearly all point estimates of the two regressions share the same algebraic sign. The only important difference is that the ethnicity dummies (*White*, *Black*) are not statistically significant in the A&P-sample, but in my sample. The dummy *Black* has a negative impact on net consumption in this paper while it is very small, but positive in the sample of Attanasio and Pistaferri. Quantitatively, most of the values are rather close to the results of Attanasio and Pistaferri. Except for the ethnicity dummies only the variable for the family size and the dummy for home ownership show larger discrepancies. However, the comparison shows that there are no systematic differences between the regression results of Attanasio and Pistaferri (2014) and the results of this paper.

Table B1. Comparison of Regression Results.

	A&P (2014)	This Paper
Hours worked/100	0.0057***	0.0072***
Family size	0.1250***	0.0877***
Education dummy 1	−0.4343***	−0.4687***
Education dummy 2	−0.3252***	−0.3382***
Education dummy 3	−0.1815***	−0.1683***
White	0.0373	0.0604**
Black	0.0059	−0.0502**
CPI	0.0088***	0.0057**
CPI_Food at home	−0.0092***	−0.0068***
CPI_Food away	−0.0057***	−0.0047***
CPI_Rent	0.0086***	0.0075***
Food consumption	0.0859***	0.0626***
Food consumption^2	−0.0026***	−0.0015***
Food consumption^3	0.0254***	0.0134***
Home owner dummy	0.3271***	0.2053***
N	26,815	28,830
R^2	0.5058	0.5396

Note: $*p < 0.05$, $**p < 0.01$, $***p < 0.001$.

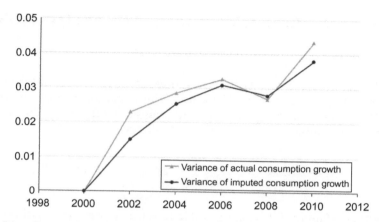

Fig. B1. Imputation Quality: Changes in the Variance of Consumption Growth for Actual and Imputed Data.

Since this paper extensively uses the first difference of consumption $\Delta c_{i,t}$, every test of imputation quality should check how well the imputation procedure captures the change in consumption expenditure between periods compared to actual data. Fig. B1, therefore, shows the development of $\text{Var}(\Delta c_{i,t})$ for imputed and actual consumption for the years where both are available. As the imputed variable only explains a part of the variance of actual consumption, the absolute level of the variance is necessarily lower. Thus, Fig. B1 focuses on the change of $\text{Var}(\Delta c_{i,t})$ over time and sets the level in the year 2000 equal to zero. The figure shows that the development of the variance of consumption growth is extremely close for the two variables of consumption. This reassures that the imputed variable also measures the dynamics of consumption reasonably well. Finally, the robustness test in Section 4.2 using the actual consumption values for the years 1998–2010 also shows that the imputed values are reasonably close to the true values (see Fig. 5).

APPENDIX C: MINIMUM DISTANCE ESTIMATION

Treatment of Biennial Data

For the years after 1996 yearly observations cease to be available and the dataset changes to a biennial frequency. Thus, first differences cannot be constructed and I have to rely on second (seasonal) differences. The second difference of residual income is defined as follows:

$$\Delta_2 y_{i,t} = y_{i,t} - y_{i,t-2} = P_{i,t} + \varepsilon_{i,t} - (P_{i,t-2} + \varepsilon_{i,t-2})$$
$$= \zeta_{i,t} + \zeta_{i,t-1} + \varepsilon_{i,t} - \varepsilon_{i,t-2}$$

Using this definition it is again possible to set up covariance relationships. Note that due to the biennial structure $\text{Cov}(\Delta_2 y_{i,t}, \Delta_2 y_{i,t+s})$ is only available for $s = 0, 2, 4, \ldots$. The structure of the resulting covariances is very similar to the case of yearly data:

$$\text{Var}(\Delta_2 y_{i,t}) = \text{Var}(\zeta_{i,t}) + \text{Var}(\zeta_{i,t-1}) + \text{Var}(\varepsilon_{i,t}) + \text{Var}(\varepsilon_{i,t-2})$$
$$\text{Cov}(\Delta_2 y_{i,t}, \Delta_2 y_{i,t+2}) = -\text{Var}(\varepsilon_{i,t})$$
$$\text{Cov}(\Delta_2 y_{i,t}, \Delta_2 y_{i,t+s}) = 0 \quad \forall s > 2$$

Unfortunately, the single yearly variance of permanent innovations $\text{Var}(\zeta_{i,t})$ cannot be identified, only the sum of the variance in year t and the previous year $(\text{Var}(\zeta_{i,t}) + \text{Var}(\zeta_{i,t-1}))$ can be determined. Thus, I have to assume that the variances are equal for the respective years. The variance of growth in residual income therefore becomes:

$$\text{Var}(\Delta_2 y_{i,t}) = 2\text{Var}(\zeta_{i,t}) + \text{Var}(\varepsilon_{i,t}) + \text{Var}(\varepsilon_{i,t-2})$$

Hence, the depicted variances in the years after 1996 always represent arithmetic means of two years. However, this should suffice to identify a broad trend in the permanent component.

The second difference of residual consumption is defined as

$$\Delta_2 c_{i,t} = c_{i,t} - c_{i,t-2} = (c_{i,t} - c_{i,t-1}) + (c_{i,t-1} - c_{i,t-2}) = \Delta c_{i,t} + \Delta c_{i,t-1}$$
$$= \phi_{i,t}\zeta_{i,t} + \phi_{i,t-1}\zeta_{i,t-1} + \psi_{i,t}\varepsilon_{i,t} + \psi_{i,t-1}\varepsilon_{i,t-1} + \xi_{i,t} + \xi_{i,t-1} + u_t^c - u_{t-2}^c$$

Assuming that the insurance coefficients do not differ for t and $t-1$, the following expression results:

$$\Delta_2 c_{i,t} = \phi_{i,t}\left(\zeta_{i,t} + \zeta_{i,t-1}\right) + \psi_{i,t}\left(\varepsilon_{i,t} + \varepsilon_{i,t-1}\right) + \xi_{i,t} + \xi_{i,t-1} + u_t^c - u_{t-2}^c$$

For the variances and covariances this implies (again assuming also that $\mathrm{Var}(\zeta_t) = \mathrm{Var}(\zeta_{t-1})$, $\mathrm{Var}(\varepsilon_t) = \mathrm{Var}(\varepsilon_{t-1})$, and $\mathrm{Var}(\xi_t) = \mathrm{Var}(\xi_{t-1})$):

$$\mathrm{Var}\left(\Delta_2 c_{i,t}\right) = \phi_t^2(2\mathrm{Var}(\zeta_t)) + \psi_t^2(2\mathrm{Var}(\varepsilon_t)) + 2\mathrm{Var}(\xi_t) + \mathrm{Var}\left(u_t^c\right) + \mathrm{Var}\left(u_{t-2}^c\right)$$

$$\mathrm{Cov}\left(\Delta_2 c_{i,t}, \Delta_2 c_{i,t+2}\right) = -\mathrm{Var}\left(u_t^c\right)$$

$$\mathrm{Cov}\left(\Delta_2 c_{i,t}, \Delta_2 c_{i,t+s}\right) = 0 \quad \forall\, s > 2$$

as well as

$$\mathrm{Cov}\left(\Delta_2 c_{i,t}, \Delta_2 y_{i,t}\right) = \phi_t(2\mathrm{Var}(\zeta_t)) + \psi_t \mathrm{Var}(\varepsilon_t)$$

$$\mathrm{Cov}\left(\Delta_2 c_{i,t}, \Delta_2 y_{i,t+2}\right) = -\psi_t \mathrm{Var}(\varepsilon_t)$$

$$\mathrm{Cov}\left(\Delta_2 c_{i,t}, \Delta_2 y_{i,t+s}\right) = 0 \quad \forall\, s > 2 \text{ and } s < 0$$

The structure of the covariance relationships is analogous to the case of annual data. Thus, all important parameters can also be identified when only biennial data is available.

Estimation Procedure

For every household in the dataset, the following column vector of observations containing the first and second differences of residual consumption and income is collected:

$$x_i = (\Delta c_{i,1979}, \Delta c_{i,1980}, \ldots, \Delta c_{i,1986}, \Delta c_{i,1990}, \ldots, \Delta c_{i,1996}, \Delta_2 c_{i,1998}, \ldots, \Delta_2 c_{i,2010},$$

$$\Delta y_{i,1979}, \Delta y_{i,1980}, \ldots, \Delta y_{i,1996}, \Delta_2 y_{i,1998}, \ldots, \Delta_2 y_{i,2010})'$$

For households that are present in the dataset throughout the whole sample period without missing observations, this yields 22 observations on consumption growth and 25 observations on income growth. Hence, $\dim(x_i) = 47$. Missing values of income or consumption growth are set equal to zero. To control for missing values another vector d_i of the same dimension is constructed for every household in the dataset. d_i contains ones in years where the observations are non-missing and zeros for years with missing values, respectively.

With the help of x_i and d_i a symmetric 47×47-matrix M can be set up:

$$M = \left(\sum_i x_i x_i' \right) \otimes \left(\sum_i d_i d_i' \right)$$

where $\otimes$ represents an elementwise division. M contains estimates of all variances, covariances, and autocovariances of income and consumption growth:

$$M = \begin{pmatrix}
\mathrm{Var}(\Delta c_{i,1979}) & & & \\
\mathrm{Cov}(\Delta c_{i,1979}, \Delta c_{i,1980}) & & & \\
\vdots & & & \\
\mathrm{Cov}(\Delta c_{i,1979}, \Delta_2 c_{i,2008}) & \cdots & \mathrm{Var}(\Delta_2 c_{i,2008}) & \\
\mathrm{Cov}(\Delta c_{i,1979}, \Delta_2 c_{i,2010}) & \cdots & \mathrm{Cov}(\Delta_2 c_{i,2008}, \Delta_2 c_{i,2010}) & \mathrm{Var}(\Delta_2 c_{i,2010}) \\
\mathrm{Cov}(\Delta c_{i,1979}, \Delta y_{i,1979}) & \cdots & \mathrm{Cov}(\Delta_2 c_{i,2008}, \Delta y_{i,1979}) & \mathrm{Cov}(\Delta_2 c_{i,2010}, \Delta y_{i,1979}) \\
\mathrm{Cov}(\Delta c_{i,1979}, \Delta y_{i,1980}) & \cdots & \mathrm{Cov}(\Delta_2 c_{i,2008}, \Delta y_{i,1980}) & \mathrm{Cov}(\Delta_2 c_{i,2010}, \Delta y_{i,1980}) \\
\vdots & & \vdots & \vdots \\
\mathrm{Cov}(\Delta c_{i,1979}, \Delta_2 y_{i,2008}) & \cdots & \mathrm{Cov}(\Delta_2 c_{i,2008}, \Delta_2 y_{i,2008}) & \mathrm{Cov}(\Delta_2 c_{i,2010}, \Delta_2 y_{i,2008}) \\
\mathrm{Cov}(\Delta c_{i,1979}, \Delta_2 y_{i,2010}) & \cdots & \mathrm{Cov}(\Delta_2 c_{i,2008}, \Delta_2 y_{i,2010}) & \mathrm{Cov}(\Delta_2 c_{i,2010}, \Delta_2 y_{i,2010})
\end{pmatrix}$$

$$\left.\begin{matrix}
\mathrm{Var}(\Delta y_{i,1979}) & & & & \\
\mathrm{Cov}(\Delta y_{i,1979}, \Delta y_{i,1980}) & \mathrm{Var}(\Delta y_{i,1980}) & & & \\
\cdots \quad \vdots & \vdots & & & \\
\mathrm{Cov}(\Delta y_{i,1979}, \Delta_2 y_{i,2008}) & \mathrm{Cov}(\Delta y_{i,1980}, \Delta_2 y_{i,2008}) & \cdots & \mathrm{Var}(\Delta_2 y_{i,2008}) & \\
\mathrm{Cov}(\Delta y_{i,1979}, \Delta_2 y_{i,2010}) & \mathrm{Cov}(\Delta y_{i,1980}, \Delta_2 y_{i,2010}) & \cdots & \mathrm{Cov}(\Delta_2 y_{i,2008}, \Delta_2 y_{i,2010}) & \mathrm{Var}(\Delta_2 y_{i,2010})
\end{matrix}\right)$$

For the minimum distance estimation the matrix M is half-vectorized according to $m = vech\ (M)$ so that the resulting vector m is of dimension $\frac{47*48}{2} = 1,128$ and contains all unique second moments of the data:

$$m = \begin{pmatrix} \mathrm{Var}\left(\Delta c_{i,1979}\right) \\ \mathrm{Cov}\left(\Delta c_{i,1979}, \Delta c_{i,1980}\right) \\ \vdots \\ \mathrm{Cov}\left(\Delta c_{i,1979}, \Delta_2 y_{i,2010}\right) \\ \vdots \\ \mathrm{Var}\left(\Delta y_{i,1979}\right) \\ \mathrm{Cov}\left(\Delta y_{i,1979}, \Delta y_{i,1980}\right) \\ \vdots \\ \mathrm{Var}\left(\Delta_2 y_{i,2010}\right) \end{pmatrix}$$

The estimation procedure minimizes the distance between the empirical second moments in the vector m and a vector $f(\theta)$ that contains the predictions of the parametric income model for these moments. The vector $f(\theta)$ is a function of the vector θ that contains the parameters of the income model that I seek to estimate $(\phi_t, \psi_t, \mathrm{Var}(\zeta_{i,t}), \mathrm{Var}(\varepsilon_{i,t}), \mathrm{Var}\left(u_{i,t}^c\right), \mathrm{Var}(\xi_i))$:

$$f(\theta) = \begin{pmatrix} \phi_{1979}^2 \mathrm{Var}\left(\zeta_{i,1979}\right) + \psi_{1979}^2 \mathrm{Var}\left(\varepsilon_{i,1979}\right) + \mathrm{Var}(\xi_i) + \mathrm{Var}\left(u_{i,1979}^c\right) + \mathrm{Var}\left(u_{i,1978}^c\right) \\ - \mathrm{Var}\left(u_{i,1979}^c\right) \\ \vdots \\ 0 \\ \vdots \\ \mathrm{Var}(\zeta_{1979}) + \mathrm{Var}(\varepsilon_{1979}) + \mathrm{Var}(\varepsilon_{1978}) - \mathrm{Var}(\varepsilon_{1979}) \\ \vdots \\ 2\mathrm{Var}(\zeta_{2009-2010}) + \mathrm{Var}(\varepsilon_{2010}) + \mathrm{Var}(\varepsilon_{2008}) \end{pmatrix}$$

Equally weighted minimum distance (EWMD) estimates the parameter vector θ by

$$\min_{\theta}(m - f(\theta))'(m - f(\theta))$$

JOHANNES LUDWIG

Standard errors for θ can be estimated as shown by Chamberlain (1984):

$$\widehat{\text{Var}\left(\hat{\theta}\right)} = (G'G)^{-1}G'VG(G'G)^{-1}$$

where $G = \frac{\partial f(\theta)}{\partial \theta'}\Big|_{\theta = \hat{\theta}}$ and V is the variance–covariance matrix of m.

Estimation Results

Table C1. Additional Results of the Minimum Distance Estimation – Standard Errors in Parentheses.

Var(ζ_t)				Var(ε_t)			
		1992	0.0430	$t = 1978-1979$	0.0479	1992	0.0815
			(0.0055)		(0.0034)		(0.0065)
$t = 1979-1980$	0.0333	1993	0.0490	1980	0.0475	1993	0.0835
	(0.0038)		(0.0064)		(0.0044)		(0.0061)
1981	0.0359	1994	0.0436	1981	0.0508	1994	0.0731
	(0.0047)		(0.0063)		(0.0044)		(0.0063)
1982	0.0348	1995	0.0507	1982	0.0533	1995	0.0691
	(0.0045)		(0.0071)		(0.0042)		(0.0058)
1983	0.0399	1996	0.0565	1983	0.0544	1996	0.0786
	(0.0051)		(0.0071)		(0.0043)		(0.0062)
1984	0.0348	1997–1998	0.0306	1984	0.0537	1998	0.0694
	(0.0045)		(0.0031)		(0.0045)		(0.0055)
1985	0.0513	1999–2000	0.0234	1985	0.0572	2000	0.0675
	(0.0057)		(0.0031)		(0.0047)		(0.0052)
1986	0.0390	1901–1902	0.0265	1986	0.0544	2002	0.0727
	(0.0058)		(0.0033)		(0.0045)		(0.0054)
1987	0.0321	2003–2004	0.0288	1987	0.0575	2004	0.0695
	(0.0052)		(0.0057)		(0.0048)		(0.0053)
1988	0.0317	2005–2006	0.0253	1988	0.0639	2006	0.0656
	(0.0052)		(0.0034)		(0.0051)		(0.0061)
1989	0.0317	2007–2010	0.0277	1989	0.0538	2008–2010	0.0749
	(0.0049)		(0.0036)		(0.0049)		(0.0053)
1990	0.0397			1990	0.0525		
	(0.0051)				(0.0047)		
1991	0.0395	Var(ξ_t)	0.0038	1991	0.0574		
	(0.0054)		(0.0004)		(0.0054)		

APPENDIX D: ROBUSTNESS

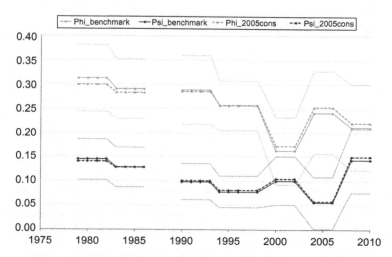

Fig. D1.   Robustness Test: Insurance Parameters When Consumption Variable of 2005 Is Used (95-Percent Confidence Intervals around Benchmark Values).

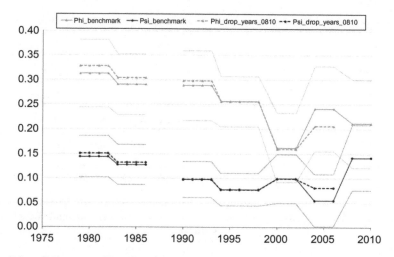

Fig. D2.   Robustness Test: Insurance Parameters When Observations of the Years 2008 and 2010 Are Dropped (95-Percent Confidence Intervals around Benchmark Values).

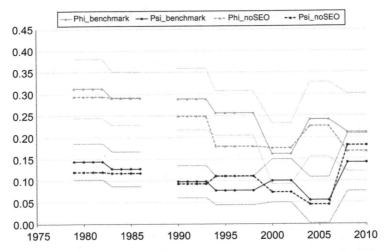

Fig. D3. Robustness Test: Insurance Parameters When SEO-Subsample Is Dropped (95-Percent Confidence Intervals around Benchmark Values).

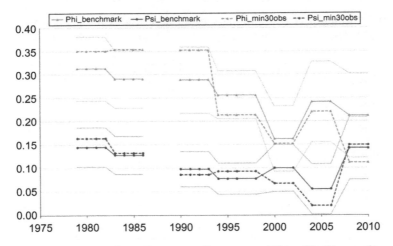

Fig. D4. Robustness Test: Insurance Parameters When 30 Observations per Household Are Required (95-Percent Confidence Intervals around Benchmark Values).

THE ROLE OF ESTABLISHMENTS AND THE CONCENTRATION OF OCCUPATIONS IN WAGE INEQUALITY [☆]

Elizabeth Weber Handwerker[a] and
James R. Spletzer[b]

[a]U.S. Bureau of Labor Statistics
[b]U.S. Census Bureau

[☆]We are grateful to seminar participants at the IZA Workshop on Inequality, the American Economic Association Annual Meetings, the University of Maryland, the Economic Policy Institute, the Bureau of Labor Statistics, the Michigan Labor Lunch, the Upjohn Institute, the NBER Summer Institute, George Washington University, the Society of Government Economists meetings, the Society of Labor Economists meetings, the Berkeley Labor Lunch, and the Center for Economic Studies at the Census Bureau for comments on earlier versions of this work, with special thanks to Katherine Abraham, David Card, Erica Groshen, John Haltiwanger, Henry Hyatt, David Levine, Stephen Machin, and Anne Polivka for particularly helpful comments. We also thank two anonymous referees and the editors, Lorenzo Cappellari, Solomon Polachek, and Konstantinos Tatsiramos, for helpful comments that have improved this paper. Research assistance from Lowell Mason is gratefully acknowledged. Much of the research in this paper was undertaken while both authors were at the Bureau of Labor Statistics. Any opinions and conclusions herein are those of the authors and do not necessarily reflect the views or policies of the U.S. Bureau of Labor Statistics or the U.S. Census Bureau. The research in this paper does not use any confidential Census Bureau information.

Inequality: Causes and Consequences
Research in Labor Economics, Volume 43, 167–193
Copyright © 2016 by Emerald Group Publishing Limited
All rights of reproduction in any form reserved
ISSN: 0147-9121/doi:10.1108/S0147-912120160000043013

ABSTRACT

This paper uses the microdata of the Occupational Employment Statistics (OES) Survey to assess the contribution of occupational concentration to wage inequality between establishments and its growth over time. We show that occupational concentration plays an important role in wage determination for workers, in a wide variety of occupations, and can explain some establishment-level wage variation. Occupational concentration is increasing during the 2000–2011 time period, although much of this change is explained by other observable establishment characteristics. Overall, occupational concentration can help explain a small amount of wage inequality growth between establishments during this time period.

Keywords: Wage inequality; establishments; occupational concentration; employers; employer–employee microdata

JEL classifications: J31; D31; L11; D22; M12; M50

1. INTRODUCTION

Growing inequality – of incomes, compensation, and wages – has been one of the dominant features of the U.S. labor market over the last several decades. An enormous and growing literature has documented and attempted to explain this growing inequality and its many sources. A recent strand of the literature documents that much of the increasing inequality across workers is due to increasing inequality across employers – see, for example, Card, Heining, and Kline (2013), Barth, Bryson, Davis, and Freeman (2014), and Song, Price, Guvenen, Bloom, and von Wachter (2015). We build on this new strand of the literature in three ways: by bringing new U.S.-linked employer–employee data to the inequality literature, by showing the importance of establishment effects in the widening distribution of wages, and by pursuing the hypothesis that the growing divergence of wages between establishments results from a changing distribution of occupations between workplaces.

An enormous literature has examined the composition and sources of growing inequality, using data on individual workers and their characteristics. This work has addressed the changing composition of the workforce and changing returns to education and experience (Bound & Johnson, 1992; Katz & Murphy, 1992; Lemieux, 2006), and the growing inequality within education and skill groups (Juhn, Murphy, & Pierce, 1993; Katz & Autor, 1999).

Growing inequality has been attributed to many sources. These include the differential impact of technology on differing portions of the worker skill distribution, referred to as 'Skill-Biased Technology Change' (Acemoglu, 2002; Autor & Dorn, 2013; Autor, Katz, & Kearney, 2008; Juhn et al., 1993), changing labor market institutions such as declining unionization levels (Lemieux, 2008), the declining real value of the minimum wage (Card & DiNardo, 2002; Lee, 1999), and the growing fraction of workers subject to performance-based pay from their employers (Lemieux, MacLeod, & Parent, 2009). Although these explanations for growing inequality are concerned with the policies and incentives faced by employers, this literature uses worker microdata with little if any information on the businesses employing these workers.

A second, smaller literature has used employer data to study growing wage inequality from the perspective of businesses. This work builds on the evidence showing that establishments play an important role in determining individual wages (Abowd, Kramarz, & Margolis, 1999; Bronars & Famulari, 1997; Groshen, 1991; Lane, Salmon, & Spletzer, 2007). Several authors have used employer microdata to study growing variability in earnings in the United States from the mid-1970s to the early 2000s, and have found that the increasing variability is due more to variation between establishments than to variation within establishments (Davis & Haltiwanger, 1991; Dunne, Foster, Haltiwanger, & Troske, 2004). This early literature has largely relied on combining measures of total variation in wages from worker microdata with measures of establishment mean wages from employer microdata. A new and growing literature, cited in the first paragraph above, uses matched employer−employee microdata to study inequality, and documents the importance of employers and the role of worker sorting between employers.

There is no clear explanation for why wage inequality between employers in the United States has been increasing. The forces that affect the overall distribution of wages − such as skill-biased technological changes, labor market institutions, and employer-specific pay policies − will have differential impacts on different employers. In addition, the wage distribution between employers will be affected by the sorting of workers among employers. While Card et al. (2013) find that increased assortativeness in the matching of highly paid workers and higher-paying employers is an important part of increasing wage variability in West Germany, Barth et al. (2014) find that increased sorting of workers (by education) to establishments in the U.S. has little impact on the overall divergence in pay between establishments in the United States.

In this paper, we study another form of worker sorting between establishments: the concentration of occupations. We document that establishments have become more concentrated in occupational employment during the 2000−2012 time period. This concentration of occupations at the establishment level could be related to changes in the distribution of wages in two ways. First, the overall polarization of employment, as discussed by Autor et al. (2008) and Autor and Dorn (2013), shifts the overall distribution of occupations. These authors describe how routine, middle-wage occupations in the United States have been partially replaced by technology or by trade for goods made elsewhere. When employment in these middle-wage occupations falls, occupational concentration economy-wide will increase, and the overall variance of wages will increase. In this context, occupational concentration at the establishment-level is a particular form of the link between changes in the overall occupational distribution and wage inequality.

A second link between occupational-concentration and greater dispersion of wages at the establishment level can also arise from employers' workforce policies. Establishments will become more concentrated in the occupations they employ when they contract out certain types of work in order to cut compensation costs, buffer their core work force from fluctuations in demand, or benefit from scale economies in specialty services (Abraham & Taylor, 1996). Contracting out particularly low-paid occupations, such as janitors and security guards, is a way for businesses to avoid sharing rents with these low-wage workers, as shown by Dube and Kaplan (2010). Goldschmidt and Schmieder (2015) find that outsourcing of cleaning, security, and logistics workers can account for 10% of increasing wage dispersion in Germany.

To examine empirically whether the large between-establishment component of increasing wage inequality in the United States is due to changes in the occupational composition of establishments, we use the microdata of the Occupational Employment Statistics (OES) Survey. The OES data are collected from a large annual survey of establishments, and contain information both on establishment characteristics and on the wage and occupational distributions of the employees within surveyed establishments. The OES data allow us to decompose increasing wage inequality in the United States into its within- and between-establishment components using a single source of wage information. These data also allow us to assess the impact of changing establishment characteristics (industry, size, and location) on the overall distribution of wages and in particular, on the between-establishment component of variation. In addition, OES data allow us to assess the contribution of the changing distribution of employment by occupation within establishments on the wage distribution.

This paper's main findings are fourfold. First, we confirm with the OES data that nearly all of the recent increase in wage inequality is between establishments rather than within establishments. Second, we show that the composition of occupations within establishments plays an important role in wage determination for workers, in a wide variety of occupations. Third, we show evidence of secular change in establishment-level occupational composition during the 2000–2011 time period, although much of this change can be fully explained by observable establishment characteristics. Fourth, we show that our measures of establishment-level occupational composition help explain growing wage inequality between establishments, but the estimated magnitude is small.

2. THE MICRODATA OF THE OES SURVEY

We use the microdata of the OES Survey, conducted by the Bureau of Labor Statistics. This survey is designed to measure occupational employment and wages in the United States by geography and industry, and is the only such survey of its size and scope. The OES covers all establishments in the United States except for those in agriculture, private households, and unincorporated self-employed workers without employees. Every year, approximately 400,000 private and local government establishments are selected for this survey. They as asked to report the number of employees in each occupation paid within specific wage intervals.[1]

An abridged version of an OES survey form is shown in Fig. 1. This survey form is a matrix, with occupations on the rows and wage intervals on the columns. For large establishments, the survey form lists 50–225 detailed occupations; these occupations pre-printed on the survey form are selected based on the industry and the size of the establishment. Small establishments receive a blank survey form and write in descriptions of the work done by their employees. These employer-provided descriptions are coded into occupations by staff in state labor agencies (as part of the OES Federal-State partnership). Many large employers also provide payroll data to BLS using their own job categories and titles, which are then coded into occupations by staff in state labor agencies. Wage intervals on the OES survey form are given in both hourly and annual nominal dollars, with annual earnings being 2,080 times the hourly wage rates.

---

1. In the early years of our panel, the OES data were collected in October, November, and December. Starting in November 2002, data collection for 200,000 establishments occurs in November and data collection for 200,000 establishments occurs in May. The OES survey is not designed to produce time series statistics. We use the methodology described in Abraham and Spletzer (2010) to reweight the data to November or May benchmarks of total employment by detailed industry and by broad industry and establishment size groups from the Quarterly Census of Employment and Wages (QCEW). Abraham and Spletzer (2010) also describe how to create OES occupation and industry categories that are consistent over time.

OCCUPATIONAL TITLE AND DESCRIPTION OF DUTIES	NUMBER OF EMPLOYEES IN SELECTED WAGE RANGES (Report Part-time Workers According to an Hourly Rate)												
Hourly (part-time or full-time)	A under $7.50	B $7.50–9.49	C $9.50–11.99	D $12.00–15.24	E $15.25–19.24	F $19.25–24.49	G $24.50–30.99	H $31.00–39.24	I $39.25–49.74	J $49.75–63.24	K $63.25–79.99	L $80.00 and over	T Total Employment
Annual (full-time only)	under $15,600	$15,600–19,759	$19,760–24,959	$24,960–31,719	$31,720–40,039	$40,040–50,959	$50,960–64,479	$64,480–81,639	$81,640–103,479	$103,480–131,559	$131,560–166,399	$166,400 and over	
	A	B	C	D	E	F	G	H	I	J	K	L	T
Architects, Except Landscape and Naval - Plan and design structures, such as private residences, office buildings, theaters, factories, and other structural property. 17-1011													
	A	B	C	D	E	F	G	H	I	J	K	L	T
Landscape Architects - Plan and design land areas for such projects as parks and other recreational facilities, airports, highways, hospitals, schools, land subdivisions, and commercial, industrial, and residential sites. 17-1012													
	A	B	C	D	E	F	G	H	I	J	K	L	T
Cartographers and Photogrammetrists - Collect, analyze, and interpret geographic information provided by geodetic surveys, aerial photographs, and satellite data. Research, study, and prepare maps and other spatial data in digital or graphic form. May work with Geographic Information Systems (GIS). 17-1021													
	A	B	C	D	E	F	G	H	I	J	K	L	T
Surveyors - Make exact measurements and determine property boundaries Provide data relevant to the shape, contour, gravitation, location, elevation, or dimension of land or land features on or near the earth's surface. 17-1022													

Fig. 1. OES Survey Form (Abridged).

To calculate average wages, the OES program obtains the mean of each wage interval every year from the National Compensation Survey (NCS). These mean wages are then assigned to all employees in that wage interval.

The OES cannot measure inequality in the top percentiles of the wage distribution. Earnings of individuals at the very top of the wage distribution are reported in an open-ended interval in the OES — the uppermost interval in the recent OES surveys is "$166,400 and over" (the ranges of the intervals vary by year — see Handwerker & Spletzer, 2014, for more information). Averaged across 1998 to May 2012, the uppermost interval contains roughly 1.3% of employment.

We impose only two restrictions on our OES data. First, we delete data collected from federal, state, and local governments, and second, we delete the 22% of the remaining establishments with imputed data. On average, we have data from roughly 275,000 establishments per year.

Two possible concerns about using OES data for studying inequality are the collection of wage data in intervals, and whether inequality measures in an establishment survey such as the OES mimic what we know from commonly used household surveys such as the Current Population Survey (CPS). In our earlier work (Handwerker & Spletzer, 2014), we compare wage data in the OES with wage data from the outgoing rotation groups of the CPS, and have two main findings. First, we show that the interval nature of wage collection in the OES has essentially no impact on measures of overall wage inequality trends. We show this by putting the CPS wage data through the filter of the OES wage intervals, demonstrating that the continuous CPS wage data and the intervalized CPS wage data show extremely similar wage inequality trends. Second, we show that the reweighted OES data can be used to broadly replicate basic CPS wage inequality trends, beginning in 1998. Overall wage distributions in each year are similar, as well as overall variance trends and variance trends by industry and occupation groups. In both the OES and the CPS, industry groups alone explain 15–17% of wage variation, although industry groups explain slightly more of the variation in the (employer-reported) OES than in the (employee-reported) CPS.

Our earlier work comparing wage inequality trends in CPS and OES microdata provides several reasons to focus on the importance of occupations and establishments for understanding inequality. We find that occupational groups alone explain more of the variation in wages in the OES (about 40%) than these same variables explain in the CPS (about 30%). This phenomenon was also noted by Abraham and Spletzer (2009), who attribute it to more accurate reporting of occupation by employers who answer the OES than by individuals who answer the CPS. We also find that the amount of wage variance explained by occupation is growing more quickly in the OES than in the CPS. Furthermore, we show that establishment effects, found in the OES but not the CPS data, explain more of wage variation than any other single variable in the OES.

3. THE ROLE OF ESTABLISHMENTS

As highlighted in the introduction, many recent studies find that establish- ments (or firms) play an important role in determining wage inequality. Most comparable to our work is Barth et al. (2014), hereafter BBDF, who link together several large Census Bureau datasets (individual data from the CPS and Census, establishment data from the Longitudinal Business Database, and wage record data from nine states) to study the roles of employers and worker sorting between employers in wage inequality. They find major roles for industries and unexplained establishment effects in wage inequality and its growth, with smaller roles for geography and worker sort- ing. We compare several measures of wage inequality in the OES data to the findings of BBDF, before extending this work with measures of occupations and occupational concentration, which were not available to BBDF.

Fig. 2 shows the decomposition of the total wage variance in the OES into its within- and between-establishment components. Over the

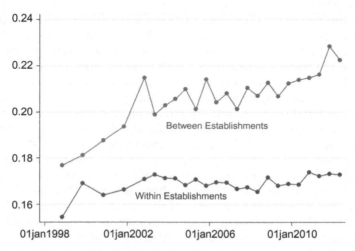

Fig. 2. Variance between and within Establishments in the OES. *Note*: This figure computed from the combined 1998–May 2012 panels of the Occupational Employment Survey, private-sector only.

period of Fall 1999 through November 2011, 55% of wage variance is between establishments, while 92% of the growth in overall wage variance from Fall 1999 to November 2011 is between establishments. BBDF estimate that 46–49% of variance in log earnings is between establishments, with 68% of variance growth during 1992–2007 between establishments.[2] Examining only employees who do not change jobs, they find 79% of the growth in earning variance is between establishments. Although the OES data we use cover a different period than those used in BBDF, we find similar estimates of both the between-establishment component of wage variance and the growth of this component. Table 1 shows the decomposition by industry groups.

We follow BBDF in examining the factors that contribute to the average wage levels by establishment. Using data from November 2007, and letting subscript "*j*" index the establishment, we estimate the amount of establishment-level wage variance explained by the industry, geographic state, and size of establishments, using the regression equation

$$\ln(\text{wage}_j) = \alpha \text{Industry}_j + \beta \text{State}_j + \chi \text{EstabSize}_j + \varepsilon_j \tag{1}$$

Results of this estimation are shown in the first two columns of Table 2. The first row of this table uses a set of 13 Broad Industry Groups,[3] and shows that using these groups alone, we can explain 30% of the variation in establishment-level wages — more than the 20% of establishment-level earnings variation that BBDF explain for 2007 using one-digit industry.

---

2. Other authors of related studies have focused on wages within manufacturing industries, and here also we find broadly consistent results. Davis and Haltiwanger (1991) find that 50–58% of wage variance in manufacturing is between plants, and 48% of variance growth in manufacturing is between plants. Dunne et al. (2004) find that 53–69% of wage variance in manufacturing is between establishments, and 90% of variance growth in manufacturing is between establishments. Barth, Bryson, Davis, and Freeman (in an earlier working paper version of their 2014 paper) find that on average 62% of variance in manufacturing is between establishments, and 27% (0.034/0.125 in Table 2) of variance growth in manufacturing is between establishments. We find in the OES data from 1999–2011 that on average 48% of manufacturing wage variance is between establishments, while 73% of the growth in manufacturing wage variance is between establishments.

3. These groups were devised to use common industry groupings for OES data collected in the 1990s, using the SIC industry classification system, and OES data collected beginning in 2002, using the NAICS industry classification system. OES data for 2000 and 2001 were recoded so they can be analyzed with either system.

Table 1. Variance of Log Real Hourly Wage and Its Growth by Industry Group, OES Fall 1999–November 2011 Averages and Growth.

Industry Group	Average Logged Wage Variance	Percent within Establishments	Percent between Establishments	Overall Logged Wage Variance Growth	Percent within Establishments	Percent between Establishments
Mining	0.2878	54.9	45.1	0.0670	28.2	71.8
Retail Trade	0.2340	64.0	36.0	-0.0158	43.7	55.7
Wholesale, Trans, Util	0.3175	56.6	43.4	0.0127	66.1	33.1
Construction	0.2480	55.2	44.8	0.0069	29.0	71.0
Manufacturing	0.3081	52.5	47.5	0.0579	26.9	73.1
Information	0.3741	50.9	49.1	0.0534	12.5	87.5
Finance & Real Estate	0.3975	55.2	44.8	0.0270	-34.8	135.2
Prof & Bus Services	0.4526	39.8	60.2	0.0465	12.7	87.3
Educ Services	0.3418	69.2	30.8	0.0707	55.4	44.6
Health & Social Assist	0.3659	59.8	40.2	0.0497	0.6	99.6
Arts & Entertainment	0.2979	60.9	39.1	0.0614	15.3	84.5
Food % Lodging	0.1306	68.7	31.3	-0.0102	84.3	15.7
Other Services	0.2823	44.6	55.4	0.0408	0.7	99.3
All Industries	0.3764	45.0	55.0	0.0514	8.2	91.8

Table 2. R^2 Values from Establishment-Level Regressions of November 2007 OES Data.

Level of Industry Detail	Establishment-Level Regressors				
	Industry Alone	Industry + Geography + Establishment Size	Industry + Geography + Estab Size + Occupational Group Herfindahl	Industry + Geography + Estab Size + Detailed Occupation Herfindahl	"Establishment Effect"
Industry Groups	0.30	0.37	0.43	0.44	0.56
Two-digit NAICS	0.40	0.48	0.51	0.51	0.49
Three-digit NAICS	0.50	0.56	0.58	0.58	0.42
Four-digit NAICS	0.57	0.62	0.63	0.63	0.37
Five-digit NAICS	0.60	0.65	0.66	0.66	0.34

Notes: These are R^2 values from establishment level regressions for November 2007 OES data, of the form $\ln(\text{wage}_j) = \alpha \text{Industry}_j + \beta \text{State}_j + \chi \text{EstabSize}_j + \varepsilon_j$, using establishment size and benchmark weights. "Establishment effects" are calculated as residuals, based on the greatest R^2 value on each line.

We also follow BBDF in using successively more detailed industry classifications in explaining establishment-level wage variation. In the second
row of the table, we use two-digit NAICS codes and show that this level of
industry detail explains 40% of establishment-level wages. This is less than
the 49% of establishment-level earnings variation that BBDF explain using
two-digit NAICS codes. However, while BBDF find that four-digit NAICS
codes can explain only 52% of establishment-level earnings variation, we
find somewhat larger effects in that four-digit NAICS codes can explain
57% of establishment-level wage variation, and five-digit NAICS codes
(not reported in BBDF) can explain 60% of establishment-level wage variation. Adding in state-level geographic variables and establishment size variables, we can explain 65% of establishment-level wage variation, while
BBDF explain 58% of establishment-level earnings variation with similar
variables. The conclusion from this analysis, and also from BBDF's similar
analysis, is that a sizable amount of establishment-level wage variation
remains unexplained by observable characteristics.

BBDF conclude their analysis with a call for more research into the link
between the establishments where people work and the determinants of
their pay. In the remainder of this paper, we demonstrate that one factor in
this link is the distribution of employment by occupation within establishments — a measure not available in the data used by BBDF. We show that
this measure is related to individual wages, and also that it plays a role in
explaining differences in earnings between establishments.

4. OCCUPATIONAL CONCENTRATION: A LINK
BETWEEN ESTABLISHMENTS AND OCCUPATIONS

4.1. Measuring Occupational Concentration

We use Herfindahl indices to measure the distribution of employment by
occupation within establishments. In the rest of this paper, we shall refer to
these Herfindahl indices as occupational concentration. Such indices are
occupation-neutral, without any ranking of occupations by skill or wage
levels. We use the structure of the Standard Occupational Classification
(SOC) system to compute two establishment-level indices:

$$H_j^{801} = \sum_{k=1}^{801} \left(\frac{\text{Employment in Occupation } k \text{ in Establishment } j}{\text{Employment in Establishment } j} \right)^2 \quad (2a)$$

$$H_j^{22} = \sum_{k=1}^{22} \left(\frac{\text{Employment in Occupation } k \text{ in Establishment } j}{\text{Employment in Establishment } j} \right)^2 \quad \text{(2b)}$$

The first establishment-level index uses all 801 detailed civilian occupations at the six-digit level of the SOC system. This index varies from 1/801, or 0.001 (equal representation of all occupations), to 1 (perfect concentration). The second establishment-level index uses the 22 major occupational categories at the two-digit level of the SOC system included in the OES. This index varies from 1/22, or 0.045 (equal representation of all categories), to 1 (perfect concentration).

The categories of occupations that are separated in definition (2a) but collapsed in definition (2b) include occupations that perform related tasks, but can be paid very different wage levels. For example, dentists (occupation 29-1020) and dental hygienists (occupation 29-2021) are in the same broad two-digit occupational category (29), but are paid very different wages. We use two different Herfindahls to measure whether the relationship between wages and our measures of occupational concentration are sensitive to the level of occupational aggregation in our data.

The average establishment (employment-weighted) has $H^{22} = 0.545$ and $H^{801} = 0.354$. In the underlying data, the average establishment (employment-weighted) has 5.60 two-digit occupational categories and 19.25 six-digit detailed occupations. Quite naturally these descriptive statistics vary by size class. Large establishments (those with more than 500 employees) have, on average, 11.85 two-digit occupational categories and 65.61 six-digit detailed occupations.

We next examine these two occupational concentration measures for specific occupations studied by Abraham and Taylor (1996) and Dey, Houseman, and Polivka (2010) in their work on outside contracting by employers. We restrict our data to establishments that employ janitors, and compare trends in our occupational concentration measures for these establishments to trends in janitorial services industry employment (this latter measure is calculated from the same OES data for NAICS 561720). The correlation between Herfindahl indices and the fraction of janitors working in the janitorial services industry over time is about 0.8 for both our H^{22} and H^{801} indices, with p values <0.0001. We do the same for accountants, estimating employment in NAICS 54121. The correlations here are lower, at 0.40 for H^{22} and 0.46 for H^{801}, with p values of 0.064 and 0.033, respectively. These examples show that our Herfindahl measures of occupational concentration are related to patterns of employment in industries linked to particular occupations.

The key question for our analysis is whether these establishment-level measures of occupational concentration can help explain the growth in wage inequality. For this to occur, occupational concentration measures must be related to wages, and either this relationship is strengthening over time, or measures of occupational concentration are increasing over time. We examine each of these in turn.

4.2. Relationships between Occupational Concentration Measures and Wages

We use regressions to show that both Occupational Concentration measures are strongly and significantly related to individual wages, across all occupations. We document this for individual worker i, employed by establishment j, with and without controlling for employees' occupations and establishments' industries, geographic states, and sizes, using the regression:

$$\ln(\text{wage}_{ijt}) = \alpha \text{ Occupational Concentration Group}_{jt} + dX_{ijt} + \varepsilon_{ijt} \qquad (3)$$

where Occupational Concentration Group is a vector of indicator variables calculated by rounding values of the establishment-level Herfindahls to the nearest hundredth. Control variables X include the survey date, occupation fixed effects, industry fixed effects, state fixed effects, and establishment size (we use fixed effects for establishment size classes as well as a continuous measure of establishment size).

The relationships between wages and our measures of occupational concentration are shown graphically in Fig. 3. The left panels of Fig. 3 give the raw data from regressions without controls for establishment or individual characteristics X, and the right panels show the wages for each group after controlling for observable characteristics. The top graphs labeled "detailed Herfindahl" show H^{801}, and the bottom graphs labeled "group Herfindahl" show H^{22}. The raw data clearly show that higher Herfindahl indices of occupational concentration are associated with lower wages. This negative relationship remains, albeit much smaller in magnitude, when we include controls for observable employee and employer characteristics.[4]

---

4. It is possible that the particularly low and high values of occupational concentration in Fig. 3 are due to the absence of occupational heterogeneity in small establishments. However, the changes in slope at the extremes of the horizontal axis in Fig. 3 remain when we drop establishments with less than 25 employees from our estimating regressions.

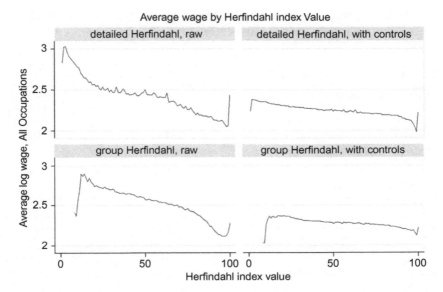

Fig. 3. Relationships between Wages and Occupational Concentration. *Notes*: The average wages plotted here are the set of α coefficients from regressions of the form Ln(wage$_{ijt}$) = α Occupational Concentration Group$_{jt}$ + δX_{ijt} + ε_{ijt}, where Occupation Concentration Groups are formed by rounding each Occupation Concentration variable to the nearest hundredth, and X includes survey date fixed effects, occupation fixed effects, broad industry groups, state fixed effects, and establishment size (we use fixed effects for establishment size classes as well as a continuous measure of establishment size). All unimputed OES private-sector data from Fall 1999 to May 2012 are used in the regressions. Each regression is based on about 43,511,000 occupation − wage interval observations.

This negative relationship between wages and occupational concentration is quantified in Table 3, where the underlying regressions are of the form

$$\ln(\text{wage}_{ijt}) = \alpha \text{ Occupational Concentration}_{jt} \\ + \beta \text{ Occupational Concentration}_{jt} \times \text{Date}_t + dX_{ijt} + \varepsilon_{ijt} \quad (4)$$

where Occupation Concentration is now a continuous variable (rather than a vector of group indicators) and Date$_t$ is a measure of continuous time. When we restrict $\beta = 0$ so that we estimate the relationships in Fig. 3, estimates of the coefficients α from these regressions − with and without

Table 3.   Regressions of Log Wages on Measures of Occupational
Concentration.

	(1)	(2)	(3)	(4)
Panel A: Herfindahl of occupational concentration at the broad occupational level (H^{22})				
Occupational Concentration	−0.655	−0.399	−0.167	−0.222
[*t*-stat]	[− 1940.1]	[− 87.29]	[− 625.01]	[− 80.54]
Occupational Concentration*Date		−0.055		0.012
[*t*-stat]		[− 56.41]		[20.12]
R^2	0.08	0.08	0.67	0.67
Controls for:				
Survey Date Fixed Effects	Yes	Yes	Yes	Yes
Six-Digit Occupation Effects			Yes	Yes
Industry, Size, State			Yes	Yes
Panel B: Herfindahl of occupational concentration at the detailed occupational level (H^{801})				
Occupational Concentration	−0.548	−0.236	−0.181	−0.175
[*t*-stat]	[− 1605.9]	[− 51.22]	[− 661.78]	[− 63.78]
Occupational Concentration*Date		−0.067		−0.001
[*t*-stat]		[− 67.89]		[− 2.20]
R^2	0.06	0.06	0.67	0.67
Controls for:				
Survey Date Fixed Effects	Yes	Yes	Yes	Yes
Six-Digit Occupation Effects			Yes	Yes
Industry, Size, State			Yes	Yes

Notes: These are regressions of the form $Ln(wage_{ijt}) = \alpha$ Occupational Concentration$_{jt} + \beta$ Occupational Concentration$_{jt}$*Date$_t + \delta X_{ijt} + \varepsilon_{ijt}$, where X includes survey date fixed effects, occupation fixed effects, broad industry groups, state fixed effects, and establishment size (we use fixed effects for establishment size classes as well as a continuous measure of establishment size). All unimputed OES private-sector data from Fall 1999 to May 2012 are used in the regressions. Each regression is based on about 43,511,000 occupation − wage interval observations, reweighted to benchmarks of employment by industry and establishment size.

additional controls − show that increased occupational concentration is significantly associated with lower wages. Estimates of the coefficient β (shown here in decade units of time) in column 2 of Table 3 show that the negative relationship between individual wages and the establishment's occupational concentration has significantly strengthened over time, although this time effect declines dramatically when control variables are added (column 4 of Table 3).

We repeat these regressions within each detailed occupation in the OES separately (omitting occupation from the set of X variables). We find that this negative relationship between the occupational concentration of employing establishments and wages for individual workers exists within a wide variety of occupations, using either measure of occupational concentration, with and without other establishment controls. Without controls, occupations with negative and statistically significant relationships (at the $p < 0.05$ level) between wages and occupational concentration account for 61.5% of all employment, and including those with negative but not statistically significant relationships increases this figure to cover 71.0% of all employment. (Similar figures for the detailed measure of occupational concentration are 63.4% and 73.0% of all employment.) The addition of industry, state, and establishment size controls makes little difference to these percentages. These relationships are similar in magnitude for occupations in different parts of the wage distribution. Overall, occupation-specific versions of the α coefficients from Eq. (4) have close to 0 correlation with the log wages of each occupation.

Since Occupational Concentration is defined at the establishment-level, we return to the framework of Eq. (1) and ask how much of the wage variance between establishments can be explained by the occupational concentration measures. In the November 2007 data, a regression of average establishment wages on the broad occupational Herfindahl index has an R^2 value of 0.13, and a regression on the detailed occupation Herfindahl index also has an R^2 value of 0.09. When we add Occupational Concentration to other variables explaining establishment-level wages in column 2 of Table 2, we find that the additional explanatory power of Occupational Concentration falls as the level of detail in industry classification rises. When industry is classified into only 13 broad groups, adding Occupational Concentration variables increases the amount of wage variance explained from 37% to 44% (see column 4 of Table 2). However, when industry is classified at the very detailed five-digit NAICS level, adding Occupational Concentration variables only increases the amount of wage variance explained from 65% to 66%. Nonetheless, even with such detailed measures of industry, Occupational Concentration continues to increase the amount of establishment-level wage variance explained.

4.3. Trends in Occupational Concentration Measures

We now turn to time trends in occupational concentration measures. Finding that occupational concentration has increased during the 1999–2012 time period would be a general indication of increased sorting of particular kinds of work between establishments. Furthermore, observing changes in both broad and detailed occupational concentration would be an indication of a changing type of work done by an establishment. For example, a manufacturing plant that outsources its janitors would show increasing occupational concentration for both indices. In contrast, observing changes in detailed occupational concentration without similar changes in broad occupational concentration would be an indication that an establishment is changing the specific occupations they employ (perhaps changing production processes or purchasing inputs from certain very specific tasks), but not changing the overall type of work done at that establishment.

Fig. 4 shows the time trend in mean values for both measures of occupational concentration, from 1999 to 2012. In the left panels which reflect the raw data, we see some evidence of increases in mean values of both measures, although these measures are generally higher in the November OES

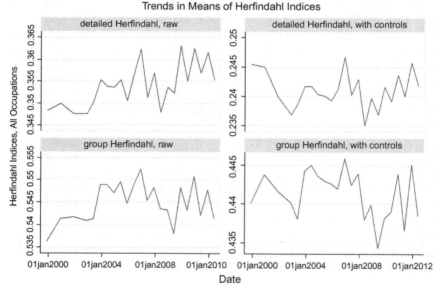

Fig. 4. Trends in Means of Occupational Concentration. *Notes*: These are plots of coefficients α from regressions Occupational Concentration$_{jt} = \alpha$ Date$_t + \delta X_{jt} + \varepsilon_{jt}$, where X includes survey date fixed effects, broad industry groups, state fixed effects, and establishment size (we use fixed effects for establishment size classes as well as a continuous measure of establishment size). All unimputed OES private-sector data from Fall 1999 to May 2012 are used in the regressions. Each regression is based on about 3,576,000 establishment-date observations.

panels than the May panels. However, looking closely at the magnitude of the vertical axis, we conclude that any increases in occupational concentration are economically small. For example, the broad measure increases from roughly 0.535 to 0.550, and the detailed measure increases from roughly 0.35 to 0.36.

In the right panels of the figure, we examine trends in mean values of occupational concentration after controlling for establishment characteristics, plotting coefficients α from regressions

$$\text{Occupational Concentration}_{jt} = \alpha \text{Date}_t + \delta X_{jt} + \varepsilon_{jt} \tag{5}$$

These regression results are given in Table 4. The simple specification in column 1 shows the increasing time trend, with a statistically significant coefficient. In results not shown, we add controls only for detailed occupation. These results are similar to those shown in column 1. This suggests that these increases in occupational concentration are not due only to changes in the overall occupational distribution, such as the changes due to employment polarization (as described by Autor & Dorn, 2013; Autor, Katz, & Kearney, 2006). However, after controlling for changes in other factors (particularly controlling for industry), results in column 2 show no increase in mean values of Occupation Concentration measures.

Table 4 also gives regression results for time trends in employment in particularly concentrated establishments; those with occupational concentration measures of 0.8 or higher. Here again, a simple specification in column 3 shows an increasing time trend in employment in highly occupational concentrated establishments. After controlling for changes in other factors, column 4 continues to show a small but statistically significant increase in employment at highly concentrated establishments using the detailed-occupation Herfindahl, but not when using the broad-occupation Herfindahl measure of occupational concentration.[5]

---

5. Our empirical analysis to this point work has focused on measures of occupational concentration at the establishment level, because establishments are the sampling unit of the OES. However, the OES does contain the Employer Identification Number (EIN) which identifies firms for Federal tax reporting purposes. Using these EINs to identify firms, we find that the relationship between EIN-level occupational concentration and wages is very similar to the results described above. Results for time trends with EIN-level occupational concentration measures are somewhat weaker than described above, which suggests that multi-establishment employers are segregating different occupations into different establishments.

Table 4. Changes in Occupational Concentration Over Time.

	Overall		Indicator for Values above 0.8	
	(1)	(2)	(3)	(4)
Panel A: Herfindahl of occupational concentration at the broad occupational level (H^{22})				
Date (in decade units of time)	0.003	−0.002	0.011	−0.002
[t-stat]	[23.81]	[−28.16]	[61.04]	[−15.85]
R^2	0.00	0.42	0.00	0.34
Controls for:				
Six-Digit Occupation Effects		Yes		Yes
Industry, Size, State		Yes		Yes
Panel B: Herfindahl of occupational concentration at the detailed occupational level (H^{801})				
Date (in decade units of time)	0.008	−0.0001	0.037	0.002
[t-stat]	[73.08]	[−7.77]	[62.06]	[17.22]
R^2	0.00	0.45	0.00	0.26
Controls for:				
Six-Digit Occupation Effects		Yes		Yes
Industry, Size, State		Yes		Yes

Notes: These are coefficients α from regressions of the form Occupational Concentration$_{jt} = \alpha \text{Date}_t + \delta X_{jt} + \varepsilon_{jt}$, where X includes broad industry groups, state fixed effects, and establishment size (we use fixed effects for establishment size classes as well as a continuous measure of establishment size). All unimputed OES private-sector data from Fall 1999 to May 2012 are used in the regressions. Each regression is based on about 43,511,000 occupation-wage cells from 3,576,000 establishment-date observations, reweighted to benchmarks of employment by industry and establishment size.

5. CHANGES IN WAGE INEQUALITY OVER TIME

The strong relationship between establishment-level occupational concentration and wages, together with some evidence for growth in this relationship as well as growth in occupational concentration (although both of these latter disappear once we control for observables), suggests that changes in occupational concentration over time may explain some of the growth in wage inequality. In this section, we conduct a reweighting exercise in order to understand how much of increasing wage inequality in the OES from Fall 1999 to November 2011 can be attributed to changes in the employment composition of observable characteristics such as industry, establishment size, geography, and occupation, as well as our measures of occupational concentration. We use the method of DiNardo, Fortin, and Lemieux (1996), hereafter DFL,[6] to calculate counterfactual wage distributions based on the OES wage intervals, as well as counterfactual variance estimates.

An example may illustrate what we hope to learn from this reweighting exercise. We know that there has been employment polarization during the last 10–20 years: see Autor et al. (2006), Goos and Manning (2007), Goos, Manning, and Salomons (2009), and Abraham and Spletzer (2010). Using the OES data, and defining "jobs" by industry and occupation, Abraham and Spletzer show that the share of both low-wage and high-wage jobs has risen from 1996 to 2004, whereas the share of middle-wage jobs has fallen (employment growth has polarized). These changes in the distribution of occupations should lead to increased wage inequality. The reweighting exercise allows us to hold constant the employment composition of occupations and industries at their 1999 values when calculating the variance of log real hourly wages in 2011, and the resulting counterfactual wage variance quantifies the magnitude of polarized employment growth on the increasing wage variance.

We run DFL-type reweightings for the observable characteristics of broad industry groups (for comparability between the 1999 data, collected using SIC, and the 2011 data, collected using NAICS), state, establishment size, occupation (at the three-digit SOC code level), and our two measures of occupational concentration. These measures of occupational concentration are entered into the reweighting as categorical variables by dividing them into groups at the first decimal place. We run these reweightings for all possible sub-sets of these six variables – a total of 63 possible combinations. Noting that BBDF find that much more of between-establishment earnings growth over time can be explained with more detailed industry measures, we repeat this exercise, using detailed industry at the four-digit NAICS instead of the broad industry groups. However, in order to use the more detailed industry measure, we must begin the reweighting exercise with data from Fall 2000, when NAICS coding is first available in the OES data, instead of Fall 1999. For clarity, we present here only the results of

---

6. The DiNardo et al. (1996) methodology of creating counterfactual distributions for a later year if observable characteristics were held fixed at their distribution in an earlier year is to (1) combine the data for the earlier and later years and run a probit regression of the probability that an observation with a particular set of observable characteristics came from the earlier year and then (2) use the predicted values from this probit regression to create new weights for each observation in the later year.

the reweighting exercise using the more detailed industry data, but the conclusions of the two exercises are very similar.

The top panel of Table 5 documents some basic descriptive statistics of the wage distribution. The variance of ln wages in 2000 is 0.3520, and increases to 0.4018 in 2011. The between-establishment variance rises from 0.1884 in 2000 to 0.2288 in 2011.

Results of reweightings for each observable characteristic alone are shown in rows 1–6 of the bottom panel of Table 5, with reweightings for selected combinations of these characteristics shown in rows 7–12. As shown in Table 5, occupation (at the three-digit SOC level) and industry (at the four-digit NAICS code level) are the variables which alone explain the largest amount of overall wage variance growth from Fall 2000 to November 2011. Reweighting observations in November 2011 to the Fall 2000 distribution of three-digit occupations (row 4) would reduce overall ln wage variance in 2011 from the measured variance of 0.4018 to 0.3853, a decrease representing 33% of ln wage variance growth from Fall 2000 to November 2011. Row 4 also shows a decrease of 41% of ln wage variance growth between establishments. Changes in the distributions of employment by detailed industry (row 1) and geographic states (row 2) can also explain some of overall ln wage variance growth as well as ln wage variance growth between establishments. Changes in the distributions of employment by occupational concentration alone (rows 5 and 6) explain almost none of overall ln wage variance growth, although they do explain some of the growth of wage variance between establishments.

Reweighting by multiple characteristics simultaneously does not always increase the overall amount of ln wage variance growth explained – using all of our possible reweighting variables (row 7 of Table 5), results in less overall variance explained than using only State, Occupation, and Occupational Concentration (rows 8 and 9). Combining groups of characteristics to reweight to their Fall 2000 distributions, we find that the greatest amount of overall ln wage variance explained (38%) is the combination shown in row 8. This is a combination of State, Occupation, and both Herfindahl indices of Occupational Concentration. Surprisingly, this combination does not include detailed industry – all of the explanatory power of detailed industry to explain overall ln wage variance growth has been absorbed by the combination of State and Occupation. This combination of reweighting characteristics can also explain 50% of the growth in the between-establishments component of ln wage variance growth from Fall 2000 to November 2011. We find nearly identical results when we use only the Broad Occupational Category Herfindahl index (row 9) or, in results

Table 5. Results for DFL-Style Reweightings of November 2011 Establishment and Employee Characteristics to Their Fall 2000 Distributions.

2000 ln wage var: 0.3520	2000 Btw estab var: 0.1884	2000 Wtn estab var: 0.1637
2011 ln wage var: 0.4018	2011 Btw estab var: 0.2288	2011 Wtn estab var: 0.1729
Increase: 0.0497	Increase: 0.0405	Increase: 0.0093

Variances After Reweighting 2011 Data to 2000 Chars:

	NAICS4	State	Size	Occup	Herf-22	Herf-801	Overall		Between Estabs		Within Estabs	
							Var	Explained (%)	Var	Explained (%)	Var	Explained (%)
1.	Y						0.3915	21	0.2192	24	0.1723	7
2.		Y					0.3985	7	0.2267	5	0.1718	12
3.			Y				0.4050	−7	0.2299	−3	0.1751	−24
4.				Y			0.3853	33	0.2123	41	0.1731	−2
5.					Y		0.4012	1	0.2256	8	0.1756	−28
6.						Y	0.4025	−1	0.2267	5	0.1758	−31
7.	Y	Y		Y	Y	Y	0.3879	28	0.2107	45	0.1772	−46
8.		Y	Y	Y	Y	Y	0.3831	38	0.2086	50	0.1744	−16
9.		Y		Y	Y	Y	0.3831	38	0.2090	49	0.1741	−13
10.		Y		Y			0.3835	37	0.2113	43	0.1723	7
11.	Y	Y		Y	Y		0.3840	36	0.2077	52	0.1763	−36
12.	Y	Y		Y		Y	0.3841	36	0.2102	46	0.1739	−10

Note: See Section 5 for a detailed explanation of this table.

not shown, when we use only the Detailed Herfindahl index. Removing both measures of Occupational Concentration from this reweighting, as shown in row 10, has little impact on the amount of overall ln wage variance growth explained, but it reduces the amount of the growth in the between-establishments component of ln wages that can be explained (from 50% to 43%).

The combination of characteristics that best explains the between-establishments component of ln wage variance growth between Fall 2000 and November 2011 is shown in row 11 of Table 5. This combination includes detailed industry as well as State, Occupation, and both measures of Occupational Concentration. Combined, reweighting these variables to their Fall 2000 distributions can explain 52% of the between-establishments component of the growth in ln wage variance during this time period. Without either measure of Occupational Concentration, no combination of reweighting characteristics can explain more than 46% of the between-establishments component of the growth in ln wage variance during this time period (shown in row 12).

Overall, the reweighting exercise presented in Table 5 shows that Occupational Concentration — by either of our measures — has at most a small role in explaining the overall growth in variance between 2000 and 2011. However, Occupational Concentration variables can explain a portion of the growth in the between-establishments component of the ln wage variance growth during this period that cannot be explained by other available individual or establishment-level variables.

We have examined the sensitivity of the results in Table 5 to the choice of specific start and end dates (reweighting 2011 data to the distribution of explanatory variables in 2000). Focusing on similar stages of the business cycle, we have reweighted 2007 data to 2000 distributions, and we have reweighted 2011 data to 2003 distributions. These exercises do not change our substantive conclusion that occupational concentration variables have a small amount of explanatory power for explaining the rise in total variance and somewhat more power to explain the rise in between-establishment variance.

6. DISCUSSION AND CONCLUSION

In this paper, we examine the concentration of occupations by establishment and what this concentration means for individual wages and for the distribution of wages within and between establishments. Occupational concentration is a particular form of worker sorting to establishments, which has not been well examined in the United States before. We document increases in occupational concentration that do not appear to be driven by the changing distribution of occupations (employment polarization), but do appear to be largely explained by other establishment characteristics, such as industry. One potential explanation for these changes is that they may result from establishments increasingly specializing in particular tasks, and contracting out other tasks, as described by Abraham and Taylor (1996), Dube and Kaplan (2010), and Goldschmidt and Schmieder (2015). We find that more concentrated establishments pay lower wages, even after controlling for employee occupation, geography, establishment size, and very detailed measures of establishment industry. The relationship between increased concentration of occupations and lower wages holds within a variety of occupations, including both low-wage and high-wage occupations.

Many authors have noted the large and growing role of employers in wage inequality. We find in our data that more than half of wage dispersion and 92% of the recent growth in wage dispersion is between establishments rather than within establishments. We find that occupational concentration can explain as much as 13% of establishment-level wage variation in the year 2007. Combining occupational concentration with other establishment-level measures, such as detailed industry and establishment size, we can explain as much as 66% of all establishment-level wage variation. Combining occupational concentration with individual and establishment level characteristics, we can explain as much as 52% of the growth in wage inequality between establishments over the 2000–2011 period. However, the contribution of occupational concentration by itself to the growth in between-establishment wage inequality is small.

REFERENCES

Abowd, J. M., Kramarz, F., & Margolis, D. (1999). High wage workers and high wage firms. *Econometrica, 67*, 251–334.

Abraham, K. G., & Spletzer, J. R. (2009). New evidence on the returns to job skills. *American Economic Review Papers and Proceedings, 99*(2), 52–57.

Abraham, K. G., & Spletzer, J. R. (2010). Are the new jobs good jobs? In K. G. Abraham, J. R. Spletzer, & M. Harper (Eds.), *Labor in the new economy*. Chicago, IL: University of Chicago Press.

Abraham, K. G., & Taylor, S. K. (1996). Firms' use of outside contractors: Theory and evidence. *Journal of Labor Economics*, *14*(3), 394–424.

Acemoglu, D. (2002). Technical change, inequality, and the labor market. *Journal of Economic Literature*, *40*(1), 7–72.

Autor, D. H., & Dorn, D. (2013). The growth of low-skill service jobs and the polarization of the US labor market. *American Economic Review*, *103*(5), 1553–1597.

Autor, D. H., Katz, L. F., & Kearney, M. S. (2006). The polarization of the U.S. labor market. *American economic association annual meeting papers and proceedings*, 189–194.

Autor, D. H., Katz, L. F., & Kearney, M. S. (2008). Trends in U.S. wage inequality: Re-assessing the revisionists. *Review of Economics and Statistics*, *90*(2), 300–323.

Barth, E., Bryson, A., Davis, J. C., & Freeman, R. (2014). *It's where you work: Increases in earnings dispersion across establishments and individuals in the U.S.* NBER Working Paper No. 20447.

Bound, J., & Johnson, G. (1992). Changes in the structure of wages in the 1980's: An evaluation of alternative explanations. *The American Economic Review*, *82*(3), 371–392.

Bronars, S. G., & Famulari, M. (1997). Wage, tenure, and wage growth variation within and across establishments. *Journal of Labor Economics*, *15*, 285–317.

Card, D., & DiNardo, J. E. (2002). Skill-biased technological change and rising wage inequality: Some problems and puzzles. *Journal of Labor Economics*, *20*(4), 733–783.

Card, D., Heining, J., & Kline, P. (2013). Workplace heterogeneity and the rise of West German wage inequality. *Quarterly Journal of Economics*, *128*(3), 967–1015.

Davis, S. J., & Haltiwanger, J. (1991). *Wage dispersion between and within U.S. manufacturing plants.* Brookings Papers on Economic Activity, 115–200.

Dey, M., Houseman, S., & Polivka, A. (2010). What do we know about contracting out in the United States? Evidence from household and establishment surveys. In K. G. Abraham, J. R. Spletzer, & M. J. Harper (Eds.), *Labor in the new economy* (Vol. 2010, pp. 267–304). Chicago: University of Chicago Press.

DiNardo, J., Fortin, N. M., & Lemieux, T. (1996). Labor market institutions and the distribution of wages, 1973–1992: A semiparametric approach. *Econometrica*, *64*(5), 1001–1044.

Dube, A., & Kaplan, E. (2010). Does outsourcing reduce wages in the low-wage service occupations? Evidence from Janitors and Guards. *Industrial and Labor Relations Review*, *63*(2), 287–306.

Dunne, T., Foster, L., Haltiwanger, J., & Troske, K. R. (2004). Wage and productivity dispersion in United States manufacturing: The role of computer investment. *Journal of Labor Economics*, *22*(2), 397–429.

Goldschmidt, D., & Schmieder, J. F. (2015). *The rise of domestic outsourcing and the evolution of the German wage structure.* NBER Working Paper No. 21366.

Goos, M., & Manning, A. (2007). Lousy and lovely jobs: The rising polarization of work in Britain. *Review of Economics and Statistics*, *89*(1), 118–133.

Goos, M., Manning, A., & Salomons, A. (2009). Job polarization in Europe. *American Economic Review Papers and Proceedings*, *99*(2), 58–63.

Groshen, E. L. (1991). Sources of intra-industry wage dispersion: How much do employers matter? *The Quarterly Journal of Economics*, *106*(3), 869–884.

Handwerker, E. W., & Spletzer, J. R. (2014). Measuring the distribution of wages in the United States from 1996–2010 with the occupational employment survey. *Monthly Labor Review, May*.

Juhn, C., Murphy, K. M., & Pierce, B. (1993). Wage inequality and the rise in returns to skill wage inequality and the rise in returns to skill. *The Journal of Political Economy, 101*(3), 410–442.

Katz, L. F., & Autor, D. H. (1999). Changes in the wage structure and earnings inequality. In O. Ashenfelter & D. Card (Eds.), *Handbook of labor economics* (Vol. 3A, pp. 1463–1555). Amsterdam: Elsevier.

Katz, L. F., & Murphy, K. M. (1992). Changes in relative wages, 1963–1987: Supply and demand factors. *The Quarterly Journal of Economics, 107*(1), 35–78.

Lane, J. I., Salmon, L. A., & Spletzer, J. R. (2007). Establishment wage differentials. *Monthly Labor Review, 130*(3).

Lee, D. (1999). Wage inequality in the United States during the 1980s: Rising dispersion or falling minimum wage? *The Quarterly Journal of Economics, 114*(3), 977–1023.

Lemieux, T. (2006). Increasing residual wage inequality: Composition effects, noisy data, or rising demand for skill? *American Economic Review, 96*(3), 461–498.

Lemieux, T. (2008). The changing nature of wage inequality. *Journal of Population Economics, 21*(1), 21–48.

Lemieux, T., MacLeod, W. B., & Parent, D. (2009). Performance pay and wage inequality. *Quarterly Journal of Economics, 124*(1), 1–49.

Song, J., Price, D. J., Guvenen, F., Bloom, N., & von Wachter, T. (2015). *Firming up inequality.* NBER Working Paper No. 21199.

INEQUALITY AND CHANGES IN TASK PRICES: WITHIN AND BETWEEN OCCUPATION EFFECTS [☆]

Nicole Fortin[a] and Thomas Lemieux[b]

[a]UBC and IZA
[b]UBC and IZA, NBER

ABSTRACT

This paper seeks to connect changes in the structure of wages at the occupation level to measures of the task content of jobs. We first present a simple model where skills are used to produce tasks, and changes in task prices are the underlying source of change in occupational wages. Using Current Population Survey (CPS) wage data and task measures

[☆]We would like to thank an anonymous referee and participants to the IZA Workshop on Inequality for useful comments. Some of the material presented in this paper was previously circulated in an earlier draft of the paper entitled "Occupational Tasks and Changes in the Wage Structure" (joint with Sergio Firpo). We would also like to thank the Social Sciences and Humanities Research Council of Canada and the Bank of Canada Fellowship Program for research support.

Inequality: Causes and Consequences
Research in Labor Economics, Volume 43, 195–226
ISSN: 0147-9121/doi:10.1108/S0147-912120160000043014

from the O*NET, we document large changes in both the within and between dimensions of occupational wages over time, and find that these changes are well explained by changes in task prices likely induced by technological change and offshoring.

Keywords: Wage inequality; tasks; occupations; offshoring; technological change

JEL classifications: J24; J31

1. INTRODUCTION

Earlier studies of changes in inequality and the wage structure have focused on explanations such as changes in the return to traditional measure of skills like education and experience (e.g., Katz & Murphy, 1992) or institutions (e.g., DiNardo, Fortin, & Lemieux, 1996). The role of de-industrialization or foreign competition had been explored in some early studies such as Murphy and Welch (1991), Bound and Johnson (1992), and Freeman (1995). However, until recently little attention had been paid to the potential role of occupations in changing wage inequality.

This situation has changed dramatically in recent years. Starting with the highly influential work of Autor, Levy, and Murnane (2003), the literature has increasingly paid more attention to the role of tasks and occupations in changes in the wage structure. There is now a growing body of work recently summarized by Acemoglu and Autor (2011) that goes beyond the standard model of skills and wages to formally incorporate the role of tasks and occupations in changes in the wage distribution. Despite this recognition of the importance of occupations, there is still limited work exploring explicitly how changes in returns to tasks or occupations have contributed to changes in the overall wage structure. The main contribution of this paper is to help close this gap by directly connecting changes over time in the occupational wage structure to measures of occupational task content.

The paper is organized as follows. In Section 2, we present a simple model where returns to a variety of skills differ by occupations. This model provides a rationale for connecting the task content of occupations with wage setting in these occupations. In Section 3, we introduce measures of task content computed from the O*NET data, and explain how we link these measures to various sources of changes in task prices, such as technological change and offshoring. Section 4 documents changes in the level and dispersion of wages across occupations, and shows that these changes are connected to our measures of the task content of jobs. We conclude in Section 5.

2. WAGE SETTING IN OCCUPATIONS

This section relies heavily on Firpo, Fortin, and Lemieux (2011), who use a similar model to perform an exhaustive decomposition of changes in the wage structure from the late 1970s to recent years. They focus on the contribution of occupational tasks, using measures such as the O*NET, in overall changes in wage inequality. In Firpo et al. (2011), the key mechanism involved is changes in task prices which affect the whole pricing structure for each occupation, and then contributes to overall changes in wage inequality. Their decomposition approach allows them to aggregate the impact of all changes in occupation pricing toward the overall wage distribution. In this paper, we focus instead on the implicit first step in this approach, that is, the effect of changes in task prices on the occupational wage structure.

To fix ideas, it is useful to remember that, until recently, the wage inequality literature has generally followed a traditional Mincerian approach, where wages are solely determined on the basis of (observed and unobserved) skills. Equilibrium skill prices depend on supply and demand factors that shape the evolution of the wage structure over time. Underlying changes in demand linked to factors such technological change and offshoring can certainly have an impact on the allocation of labor across industry and occupations, but ultimately wage changes are only linked to changes in the pricing of skills. Acemoglu and Autor (2011) refer to this approach as the "canonical model" that has been used in many influential studies, such as Katz and Murphy (1992).

There is increasing evidence that the canonical model does not provide a satisfactory explanation for several important features of the evolution of the wage structure observed over the last few decades. This is discussed in detail in Acemoglu and Autor (2011), who mention, among other things, two important shortcomings of the canonical model. First, predictions from this model are always monotone in skills, thus it cannot account for differential changes in inequality in different parts of the distribution, such as the "polarization" of changes in wages illustrated in Fig. 1. Second,

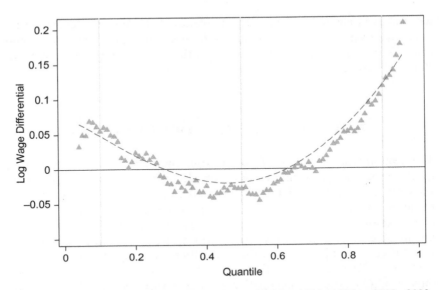

Fig. 1. Changes in Real Log Wages by Percentile Men 1983–1985 to 2000–2002.

the model does not provide insight into the contribution of occupations to changes in the wage structure because it does not draw any distinction between "skills" and "tasks". Acemoglu and Autor (2011) address these shortcomings by proposing a Ricardian model of the labor market where workers use their skills to produce tasks, and get systematically allocated to occupations (i.e., tasks) on the basis of comparative advantage.[1]

We follow Acemoglu and Autor (2011) by introducing a distinction between skills and tasks in our wage setting model. Unlike Acemoglu and Autor (2011), however, we do not attempt to solve the full model of skills, tasks, and wages by modeling how workers choose occupations, and how supply and demand shocks affect wages in general equilibrium. One advantage of our partial equilibrium approach is that we do not have to impose restrictive assumptions to solve the model. For instance, Acemoglu and Autor (2011) have to work with only three skill groups (but many occupations/tasks) to obtain interesting predictions from their model. As a result, the law of one price holds within each skill group in the sense that wages are equalized

---

1. Note that since different tasks are being performed in different occupations, we can think of these two concepts interchangeably.

across occupations, conditional on skill. This is a strong prediction that is not supported by the data, and that we relax by allowing for a large number of skill categories.[2]

A number of recent papers on skills, tasks, and wages, most notably Boehm (2015), Burstein, Morales, and Vogel (2015), and Cortes (2016), also propose models in which the law of one price does not hold. These papers all find that changes in task prices play an important role in changes in U.S. wage inequality, which is consistent with our own findings. While we use a partial equilibrium model here, the results in Boehm (2015), Burstein et al. (2015), and Cortes (2016) all suggest that changes in task prices remain important even after accounting for general equilibrium effects and the endogenous sorting of workers into occupations.[3]

Assume that an occupation j involves producing a task or occupation-specific output Y_j which is one input in the firm's production function. Workers are characterized by a k-dimension set of skills $S_i = [S_{i1}, S_{i2}, ..., S_{iK}]$. Some of these skills (like education and experience) are observed by the econometrician, others (like ability and motivation) are not. The amount of occupation-specific task Y_{ij} produced by worker i in occupation j is assumed to linearly depend on skill:

$$Y_{ij} = \sum_{k=1}^{K} \alpha_{jk} S_{ik} \qquad (1)$$

where the productivity of skills α_{jk} is specific to occupation j. Firms then combine tasks to produce final goods and services according to the production function $Q = F(Y_1, ..., Y_J)$, where Y_j (for $j = 1, ..., J$) is the total amount of (occupation-specific) tasks produced by all workers i allocated to occupation j.[4]

---

2. See, for instance, Heckman and Scheinkman (1987) and Gibbons, Katz, Lemieux, and Parent (2005) for evidence of occupational wage differences among workers with similar observed and unobserved productive characteristics.

3. Burstein et al. (2015) are able to solve their model in general equilibrium by making the strong assumption that efficiency units workers provide in each task follow a Frechet distribution. This provides a closed-form solution for the selection effects linked to occupational (or task) choices (Roy model). Boehm (2015) and Cortes (2016) provide empirical evidence that changes in task prices remain large even after controlling for these selection effects.

4. This specification is also closely related to the "skill-weights" approach of Lazear (2009) where different jobs require the use of different linear combinations of skills.

Under the assumption that wages are set competitively, workers are paid for the value of tasks they produce. Worker i who produces Y_{ij} units of occupation-specific task j is thus paid a wage of $p_{jt}Y_{ij}$, where p_{jt} is the market price of each unit of task Y_{ij} produced at time t. We also allow wages to depend on year and occupation-specific factors δ_t and c_j, where δ_t could capture, for instance, general productivity shocks, while c_j could be thought as reflecting compensating wage differentials.[5]

This yields the wage equation:

$$w_{ijt} = \delta_t + c_j + p_{jt}Y_{ij} \equiv \delta_t + c_j + p_{jt} \sum_{k=1}^{K} \alpha_{jk}S_{ik} \tag{2}$$

As in Acemoglu and Autor (2011), a critical assumption embedded into Eq. (2) is that the mapping of skills into tasks (the parameters α_{jk} in the wage equation) does not change over time, while task prices p_{jt} are allowed to change over time. This means that, in this model, the effect of demand factors such as technological change and offshoring solely goes through changes in task prices. In this setting, technological change and offshoring provide a way for firms of producing the same tasks at a lower price. Take, for instance, the case of call center operators who use their skills to produce consumer service tasks (check customer accounts, provide information about products, etc.). When these tasks are simple, like providing one's balance on a credit card, the call center operators can be replaced by computers now that voice recognition technology is advanced enough. In the case of more complex tasks such as IT support, computers are not sophisticated enough to deal with customers but these tasks can now be offshored to lower paid workers in India. In these examples, the quantity of task produced by call center operators of a given skill level does not change, but the wage associated with these tasks changes in response to technological change and offshoring. At the limit, if the task price in an occupation becomes low enough the occupation will simply disappear, which is the way Acemoglu and Autor (2011) model the impact of "routine-biased" technological change.

In other cases, the assumption that the mapping between skills and tasks is constant over time may be unrealistic. For instance, in highly technical or professional occupations where cognitive skills are important for

---

5. Compensating wage differentials are one possible way why wages are not equalized across tasks (or occupations) in the Acemoglu and Autor (2011) model.

producing tasks, advances in computing likely enable workers with a given set of skills to produce more tasks than they used to. In this example, when wages increase for these workers, Eq. (2) would suggest that task prices have increased, while the underlying explanation may instead be productivity changes linked to changes in the α_{jk}'s. Since p_{jt} and α_{jk} enter multiplicatively in Eq. (2), it is not possible to empirically distinguish the impact of changes in these two factors.

Burstein et al. (2015) also make the point that it is not possible to empirically distinguish changes in pure task prices from technological changes that affect the mapping between skills and task output. They refer to the sum of these two factors as "task shifters". For the sake of simplicity, we refer to these task shifters as changes in task prices, but acknowledge this could also reflect occupation-specific productivity effects. If these two sources of change are positively correlated, our estimates would overstate the true contribution of changes in task prices. This would happen, for instance, if routine occupations that are negatively affected by technological change were also easier to offshore. But regardless of whether we label the sources of between- and within-occupation wage changes as task shifters or changes in task prices, the ultimate goal of this paper is to quantify the magnitude of these changes and see to what extend they are connected with the task measures we construct using the O*NET data.

When task prices are allowed to vary across occupations in a completely unrestricted way, it is difficult to interpret the contribution of changes in task prices to changes in inequality in an economically meaningful way. Following Yamaguchi (2012), we assume that task prices are systematically linked to a limited number of task content measures available in data sets like the Dictionary of Occupational Titles or the O*NET. The idea is that two different occupations where the task content measure for, say, "routine work" is the same will be equally affected by "routine-biased" technological change.

We use a set of five task content measures from the O*NET, described in detail in the next section; they enter in the following linear specification for task prices:

$$p_{jt} = \pi_{0t} + \sum_{h=1}^{5} \pi_{ht} T_{jh} + \mu_{jt} \tag{3}$$

where T_{jh} are the task content measures. These task content measures are assumed to be time invariant for two reasons. First, it has proven difficult to construct consistent measures of the task content of occupations over time because of data limitations (see, e.g., Autor, 2013). More importantly, we use the task content measures as an economically interpretable way of reducing the dimension of the occupational space. Results would be hard to interpret if the way in which task content characterized occupations was also changing over time.[6] Since the T_{jh}'s do not change over time, changes in task prices p_{jt} are solely due to change in the parameters π in Eq. (3). These parameters can be interpreted as the returns to task content measures T_{jh} in the task pricing equations.

The effect of changes in π_{ht} on changes in the wage distribution is complex. To see this, consider the wage equation obtained by substituting Eq. (3) into (2):

$$w_{ijt} = \delta_t + c_j + \left[\pi_{0t} + \sum_{h=1}^{5} \pi_{ht} T_{jh} + \mu_{jt} \right] \sum_{k=1}^{K} \alpha_{jk} S_{ik} \qquad (4)$$

Since task prices and skills enter multiplicatively into the wage equation, a change in task prices linked to changes in the π_{ht} parameters has an impact on both the between- and within-group dimensions of inequality. For instance, even if the α_{jk} parameters were the same in all tasks/occupations, changes in π_{ht} would increase wage dispersion between occupations as long as average skills (e.g., education, one of the elements of the skill vector S_i) varied across occupations. Furthermore, since some dimensions of skills are unobserved, changes in π_{ht} also affect within-occupation inequality even after controlling for observable skills like education and experience.

Firpo et al. (2011) use this empirical model as a guide to carry a full decomposition of overall changes in inequality. In this paper, we instead focus on the connection between the task content measures and changes in the within- and between-occupation wage dispersion. This is motivated by the fact that there are large differences in the changes in the level and dispersion of wages across occupations as shown below.

---

6. Note that Yamaguchi assumes that the parameters α_{jk} are also functions of the task content variables T_{jh}, something we do not do since we would then need to be more specific about the way we introduce the K observed and unobserved skill components (corresponding of each parameter α_{jk}). More importantly, the question of whether or not the T_{jh}'s should be allowed to change over time in this setting is just a more structured way of thinking about the implications of possible changes in α_{jk}, an issue that we have already discussed.

The main objective of this paper is to look at the connection between these wage changes and measures of the task content of occupations. With this in mind, we next introduce our key measures of task content based on the O*NET data.

3. DATA

3.1. Occupational Measures of Technological Change and Offshoring Potential

Like many recent papers (Crinò, 2010; Goos & Manning, 2007; Goos, Manning, & Salomons, 2010) that study the task content of jobs, and in particular their offshorability potential, we use the O*NET data to compute our measures of technological change and offshoring potential.[7] We first produce indexes for all three-digit occupations available in the CPS, noting that previously available indexes did not cover the complete set of occupations.[8] Our construction of an index of potential offshorability follows the pioneering work of Jensen and Kletzer (2007) (JK, thereafter) while incorporating some of the criticisms of Blinder (2007). The main concern of Blinder (2007) is the inability of the objective indexes to take into account two important criteria for non-offshorability: (a) that a job needs to be performed at a specific U.S. location and (b) that the job requires face-to-face personal interactions with consumers. We thus pay particular attention to the "face-to-face" and "on-site" categories in the construction of our indexes.

In the spirit of Autor et al. (2003), who used the Dictionary of Occupational Titles (DOT) to measure the routine versus non-routine, and cognitive versus non-cognitive aspects of occupations, JK use the information available in the O*NET, the successor of the DOT, to construct their measure. The O*NET content model organize the job information into a structured system of six major categories: worker characteristics, worker

---

7. Available from National Center for O*NET Development.
8. Blinder (2007) did not compute his index for Category IV occupations (533 occupations out of 817), which are deemed impossible to offshore. Although, Jensen and Kletzer (2007) report their index for 457 occupations, it is not available for many blue-collar occupations (occupations SOC 439199 and up).

requirements, experience requirements, occupational requirements, labor market characteristics, and occupation-specific information.

Like JK, we focus on the "occupational requirements" of occupations, but we add some "work context" measures to enrich the "generalized work activities" measures. JK consider 11 measures of "generalized work activities," subdivided into five categories: (1) on information content: getting information, processing information, analyzing data or information, documenting/recording information; (2) on internet-enabled: interacting with computers; (3) on face-to-face contact: assisting or caring for others, performing or working directly with the public, establishing or maintaining interpersonal relationships; (4) on the routine or creative nature of work: making decisions and solving problems, thinking creatively; and (5) on the "on-site" nature of work: inspecting equipment, structures or material.

We also consider five similar categories, but include five basic elements in each of these categories. Our first category "Information Content" regroups JK categories (1) and (2). It identifies occupations with high information content that are likely to be affected by ICT technologies; they are also likely to be offshored if there are no mitigating factor.[9] Fig. A1 shows that average occupational wages in 2000–2002 increase steadily with the information content. Our second category "Automation" is constructed using some work context measures to reflect the degree of potential automation of jobs and is similar in spirit to the manual routine index of Autor et al. (2003). The work context elements are: degree of automation, importance of repeating same tasks, structured versus unstructured work (reverse), pace determined by speed of equipment, and spend time making repetitive motions. The relationship between our automation index and average occupational wages displays an inverse U-shaped left-of-center of the wage distribution. We think of these first two categories as being more closely linked to technological change, although we agree with Blinder (2007) that there is some degree of overlap with offshorability. Indeed, the information content is a substantial component of JK's offshorability index.

Our three remaining categories "face-to-face contact", "on-site job" and "decision-making" are meant to capture features of jobs that cannot be offshored, and that they capture the non-offshorability of jobs. Note, however, that the decision-making features were also used by Autor et al. (2003) to

---

9. Table A1 lists the exact reference number of the generalized work activities and work context items that make up the indexes.

capture the notion of non-routine cognitive tasks. Our "face-to-face contact" measure adds one work activity "coaching and developing others" and one work context "face-to-face discussions" element to JK's face-to-face index. Our "on-site job" measure adds four other elements of the JK measure: handling and moving objects, controlling machines and processes, operating vehicles, mechanized devices, or equipment, and repairing and maintaining mechanical equipment and electronic equipment (weight of 0.5 to each of these last two elements). Our "decision making" measure adds one work activity "developing objectives and strategies" and two work context elements, "responsibility for outcomes and results" and "frequency of decision making" to the JK measure. The relationship between these measures of offshorability (the reverse of non-offshorability) and average occupational wages are displayed in Fig. A1. Automation and no-face-to-face contact exhibit a similar shape. Not on-site is clearly U-shaped, and no-decision-making is steadily decreasing with average occupational wages.

For each occupation, O*NET provides information on the "importance" and "level" of required work activity and on the frequency of five categorical levels of work context.[10] We follow Blinder (2007) in arbitrarily assigning a Cobb-Douglas weight of two thirds to "importance" and one third to "level" in using a weighed sum for work activities.[11] For work contexts, we simply multiply the frequency by the value of the level.

Each composite TC_{jh} score for occupation j in category h is, thus, computed as

$$TC_{jh} = \sum_{k=1}^{A_h} I_{jk}^{2/3} L_{jk}^{1/3} + \sum_{l=1}^{C_h} F_{jl} * V_{jl} \tag{5}$$

where A_h is the number of work activity elements and C_h the number of work context elements in the category TC_h, $h = 1, \ldots, 5$.

---

10. For example, the work context element "frequency of decision-making" has five categorical levels: (1) never, (2) once a year or more but not every month, (3) once a month or more but not every week, (4) once a week or more but not every day, and (5) every day. The frequency corresponds to the percentage of workers in an occupation who answer a particular value. For this element, 33 percent of sales manager answer (5) every day, while that percentage among computer programmers is 11 percent.
11. In contrast, Acemoglu and Autor (2011) do not include the "level" values in the construction of their indexes.

To summarize, we compute five different measures of task content using the O*NET: (i) the information content of jobs, (ii) the degree of automation of the job and whether it represents routine tasks, (iii) the importance of face-to-face contact, (iv) the need for on-site work, and (v) the importance of decision making on the job.

3.2. Wage Data

The empirical analysis is based on data from Outgoing Rotation Group (ORG) Supplements of the Current Population Survey. For conciseness in this paper, we focus only on men who were arguably more affected by the decline in manufacturing than women. Further some of the task measures introduced above, in particular the "not on-site" measure, offer a better characterization of men's non-offshorable blue-collar jobs than women's. In other work where we consider women's wages separately, we find that different task measures have relatively more important effects for women than for men. For example, given that clerical occupations are female-dominated occupations, our "information content" measure gathers more explanatory power for women than for men.[12] The important distinctions between men's and women's wages arising from substantial occupational segregation warrant separate analyzes by gender and extended discussions that are beyond the scope of this paper.

Here, we limit out our attention to male wage changes over the 1983–1985 to 2000–2002 period, a time period where both factors of interest, technological change and offshoring, were likely having significant impacts on male wages. This choice of years is also driven by data consistency issues since there is a major change in occupation coding in 2003 when the CPS switches to the 2000 Census occupation classification. This makes it harder to compare detailed occupations from the 1980s or 1990s to those in the post-2002 data. To obtain large enough samples at the occupation level, we pool three years of CPS data at both the start and end periods.

The data files were processed as in Lemieux (2006), who provides detailed information on the relevant data issues. The wage measure used is an hourly wage measure computed by dividing earnings by hours of work

---

12. Minimum wages are another important consideration that needs to be considered when analyzing women's wages.

for workers not paid by the hour. For workers paid by the hour, we use a direct measure of the hourly wage rate. CPS weights are used throughout the empirical analysis.

4. EMPIRICAL TEST OF THE OCCUPATIONAL WAGE SETTING MODEL

4.1. Simple Implications for Means and Standard Deviations

We first discuss the implication of our wage setting model for the mean and standard deviation of occupational wages, which are arguably the simplest measures of between- and within-occupation wage dispersion. Later in the section, we expand the analysis to consider the entire distribution of occupational wages summarized by deciles. We begin by illustrating the fact that, in wage Eq. (2), changes in task prices p_{jt} have an impact on both the level and dispersion of wages across occupations. For instance, let the average wage in occupation j at time t be

$$\overline{w}_{jt} = \delta_t + c_j + p_{jt}\overline{Y}_{jt} \tag{6}$$

The standard deviations of wages are

$$\sigma_{jt} = p_{jt}\sigma_{Y,jt} \tag{7}$$

where $\sigma_{Y,jt}$ is the standard deviation in tasks Y_{ij}, which in turns depends on the within-occupation distribution of skills S_{ik}. Since changes in both $\overline{w}_{jt}$ and σ_{jt} are positively related to changes in task prices p_{jt}, we expect these two changes to be correlated across occupations.

To see this more formally, assume that the within-occupation distribution of skills, S, and thus the distribution of task output, Y, remains constant over time (we discuss the assumption in more detail below). It follows that $\overline{Y}_{jt} = \overline{Y}_j$ and $\sigma_{Y,jt} = \sigma_{Y,j}$ for all t. Using a first-order approximation of Eqs. (6) and (7) and differencing yields:

$$\Delta\overline{w}_j \approx \Delta\delta + \overline{Y} \cdot \Delta p_j \tag{8}$$

and

$$\Delta\sigma_j \approx \overline{\sigma_Y} \cdot \Delta p_j \tag{9}$$

where $\overline{Y}(\overline{\sigma_Y})$ is the average of $\overline{Y}_j(\sigma_{Y,j})$ over all occupations j. Since the variation in Δp_j is the only source of variation in $\Delta\overline{w}_j$ and $\Delta\sigma_j$, the correlation between these two variables should be equal to one in this simplified model. In practice, we expect the correlation to be fairly large and positive, but not quite equal to one because of sampling error (in the estimates values of $\Delta\overline{w}_j$ and $\Delta\sigma_j$), approximation errors, etc.

A second implication of the model is that since task prices p_{jt} depend on the task content measures T_{jh} (see Eq. (3)), these tasks content measures should help predict changes in task prices Δp_j, and thus $\Delta\overline{w}_j$ and $\Delta\sigma_j$. Differencing Eq. (3) over time we get:

$$\Delta p_j = \Delta\pi_0 + \sum_{h=1}^{5} \Delta\pi_h T_{jh} + \Delta\mu_j \tag{10}$$

and, thus:

$$\Delta\overline{w}_j = \varphi_{w,0} + \sum_{h=1}^{5} \varphi_{w,h} T_{jh} + \xi_{w,h} \tag{11}$$

and

$$\Delta\sigma_j = \varphi_{\sigma,0} + \sum_{h=1}^{5} \varphi_{\sigma,h} T_{jh} + \xi_{\sigma,h} \tag{12}$$

where $\varphi_{w,0} = \Delta\delta + \overline{Y} \cdot \Delta\pi_0$; $\varphi_{w,h} = \overline{Y} \cdot \Delta\pi_h$; $\xi_{w,h} = \overline{Y} \cdot \Delta\mu_j$; $\varphi_{\sigma,0} = \overline{\sigma_Y} \cdot \Delta\pi_0$; $\varphi_{\sigma,h} = \overline{\sigma_Y} \cdot \Delta\pi_h$; $\xi_{\sigma,h} = \overline{\sigma_Y} \cdot \Delta\mu_j$. One important implication of the model highlighted here is that the coefficients $\varphi_{w,h}$ and $\varphi_{\sigma,h}$ in Eqs. (11) and (12) should be proportional since they both depend on the same underlying coefficients $\Delta\pi_h$.

4.2. Empirical Evidence for Means and Variances

We provide evidence that these two implications are supported in the data in the case of men over the 1983–1985 to 2000–2002 period, a time period where there was substantial labor market polarization as shown in Fig. 1. Note that, despite our large samples based on three years of pooled CPS data, we are left with a small number of observations in many occupations when we work at the three-digit occupation level. In the analysis presented here, we thus focus on occupations classified at the two-digit level (40 occupations) to have a large enough number of observations in each occupation.[13] All the estimates reported here (correlations and regression models) are weighted using the proportion of workers in the occupation. The raw correlation between the changes in average wages and standard deviations is large and positive (0.48).

We then run regression models for Eqs. (11) and (12) using our five O*NET task content measures as explanatory variables. The regression results are reported in columns 1–4 of Table 1. Columns 1 and 2 show the estimated models for $\Delta \overline{w}_j$ and $\Delta \sigma_j$, respectively, when all five task measure variables are included in the regression. The adjusted R^2's of the regressions are equal to 0.49 and 0.72 for each model, respectively, indicating that our task content measures capture a large fraction of the variation in changes in the level ($\Delta \overline{w}_j$) and dispersion ($\Delta \sigma_j$) of wages over occupations. Since some of the coefficients are imprecisely estimated, we also report in columns 3 and 4 estimates from separate regressions for each task content measure. The task content measures are highly significant, and the sign of the coefficient estimates is generally the same in the models for changes in average wages and standard deviations. This strongly supports the prediction of our wage setting models that the estimated effect of the task content measures should be proportional in the models for average wages and standard deviations.

Note also that, in most of the cases, the sign of the coefficients conforms to expectations. As some tasks involving the processing of information may be enhanced by ICT technologies, we would expect a positive relationship between our "information content" task measure and changes in task prices. On the other hand, to the extent that technological change allows

---

13. Though there is a total of 45 occupations at the two-digit level, we combine five occupations with few observations to similar but larger occupations. Specifically, occupation 43 (farm operators and managers) and 45 (forestry and fishing occupations) are combined with occupation 44 (farm workers and related occupations). Another small occupation (20, sales-related occupations) is combined with a larger one (19, sales workers, retail and personal services). Finally, two occupations in which very few men work (23, secretaries, stenographers, and typists, and 27, private household service occupations) are combined with two other larger occupations (26, other administrative support, including clerical, and 31, cleaning services, respectively).

Table 1. Estimated Effect of Task Requirements on Average Wages and Standard Deviations Men, 1983–1985 to 2000–2002, Two-Digit Occupations.

Tasks Entered:	Raw Changes				Reweighted Changes			
	Together		Separately		Together		Separately	
Dep. variable:	Average (1)	Std Dev (2)	Average (3)	Std Dev (4)	Average (5)	Std Dev (6)	Average (7)	Std Dev (8)
Information content	0.007	0.005	0.024***	0.025***	−0.025**	0.006	−0.009	0.021***
	(0.013)	(0.006)	(0.009)	(0.004)	(0.011)	(0.007)	(0.007)	(0.005)
Automation/routine	−0.035**	−0.012*	−0.055***	−0.032***	−0.017	−0.012	−0.022**	−0.026***
	(0.013)	(0.006)	(0.010)	(0.006)	(0.012)	(0.008)	(0.009)	(0.007)
No on-site work	0.004	0.014***	0.021***	0.018***	0.002	0.015***	0.003	0.017***
	(0.007)	(0.003)	(0.005)	(0.003)	(0.006)	(0.004)	(0.005)	(0.003)
No face-to-face	−0.035*	0.014*	−0.062***	−0.030***	−0.017	0.022**	−0.022*	−0.019**
	(0.017)	(0.008)	(0.012)	(0.009)	(0.016)	(0.010)	(0.011)	(0.010)
No decision making	0.010	−0.016*	−0.037***	−0.030***	−0.011	−0.013	−0.004	−0.022***
	(0.019)	(0.009)	(0.012)	(0.007)	(0.017)	(0.011)	(0.010)	(0.008)
Adj. R^2	0.488	0.715	—	—	0.211	0.530	—	—

Notes: All models are estimated by running regressions of the occupation-specific changes in average wages and standard deviations on the task content measures. The models reported in all columns are weighted using the fraction of observations in each occupation in the base period (1983–1985). In columns 5–8, the data are reweighted so that the distribution of characteristics in each occupation and time period is the same as in the overall sample (for both periods pooled). See the text for more detail. Standard errors in parentheses.

firms to replace workers performing these types of tasks with computer-driven technologies, we would expect a negative effect for the "automation/routine" measure.

Although occupations in the middle of the wage distribution may be most vulnerable to technological change, some also involve relatively more "on-site" work (e.g., repairmen) and may, therefore, be less vulnerable to offshoring. We also expect workers in occupations with a high level of "face-to-face" contact, as well as those with a high level of "decision making" to do relatively well in the presence of offshoring. Since these last three variables capture non-offshorability, they are entered as their reverse in the regression and we should expect their effect to be negative. In columns 3 and 4, the estimated coefficients are generally of the expected sign except for the "not-on-site" task.

One potential issue with these estimates is that we are only using the raw changes in $\overline{w}_{jt}$ and σ_{jt} that are unadjusted for differences in education and other characteristics. Part of the changes in $\overline{w}_{jt}$ and σ_{jt} may thus be due to composition effects or changes in the return to underlying characteristics (like education) that are differently distributed across occupations. To control for these confounding factors, we reweight the data using simple logits to assign the same distribution of characteristics to each of the 40 occupations in the two time periods.[14]

This procedure allows us to relax the assumption that the distribution of skills S is constant over time (within each occupation). Strictly speaking, we can only adjust for observable skills like education and experience. To deal with unobservables, we could then invoke an ignorability assumption to ensure that, conditional on observable skills, the distribution of unobservable skills is constant over time. A more conservative approach is to view the specifications where we control for observable skills as a robustness check.

The results reported in columns 5–8 indeed suggest that the main findings discussed above are robust to controlling for observables. Generally speaking, the estimated coefficients have smaller magnitudes but rarely change sign relative to the models reported in column 1–4. Overall, the results presented here strongly support the predictions of our wage setting model.

---

14. We use a set of five education dummies, nine experience dummies, and dummies for marital status and race as explanatory variables in the logits. The estimates are used to construct reweighting factors that are used to make the distribution of characteristics in each occupation-year the same as in the overall sample for all occupations (and time periods).

4.3. Quantiles of the Occupational Wage Structure

One disadvantage of using the standard deviation (or the variance) as a measure of wage dispersion is that it fails to capture the polarization of the wage distribution that has occurred since the late 1980s. As a result, we need an alternative way of summarizing changes in the wage distribution for each occupation that is yet flexible enough to allow for different changes in different parts of the distribution. We do so by estimating linear regression models for the changes in wages at each decile of the wage distribution for each occupation. As we now explain in more detail, the intercept and the slope from these regressions are the two summary statistics we use to characterize the changes in the wage distribution for each occupation.

We now extend our approach by looking at all quantiles of the wage distribution for each occupation. Consider $F_{jt}(\cdot)$, the distribution of effective skills $\sum_{k=1}^{K} \alpha_{jk}S_{ik}$ provided by workers in occupation j at time t. Under the admittedly strong assumption that the distribution of skills supplied to each occupation is stable over time (and we normalize skills to have a mean of zero within each occupation), we can write the qth quantile of the distribution of wages in occupation j at time t as:

$$w_{jt}^q = \overline{w}_{jt} + p_{jt}F_j^{-1}(q) \tag{13}$$

Taking differences over time yields

$$\Delta w_j^q = \Delta\overline{w}_j + \Delta p_j F_j^{-1}(q) \tag{14}$$

Solving for $F_j^{-1}(q)$ in Eq. (13) in the base period $t=0$, and substituting into Eq. (14) yields

$$\Delta w_j^q = \Delta\overline{w}_j - \frac{\Delta p_j}{p_{j0}}\overline{w}_{j0} + \frac{\Delta p_j}{p_{j0}}w_{j0}^q \tag{15}$$

or

$$\Delta w_j^q = a_j + b_j w_{j0}^q \tag{16}$$

where $a_j = \Delta\overline{w}_j - \frac{\Delta p_j}{p_{j0}}\overline{w}_{j0}$ and $b_j = \frac{\Delta p_j}{p_{j0}}$.

Interestingly, the coefficient on the base-period wage quantile w_{j0}^q is simply the change in the task price p_{jt} expressed in relative terms. This suggests a very simple way of estimating relative changes in task prices in each occupation. First compute a set of wage quantiles for each occupation in a base and an end period. Then simply run a regression of changes in quantiles on base-period quantiles. The slope coefficient of the regression, b_j, provides a direct estimate of the relative change in task price, $\frac{\Delta p_j}{p_{j0}}$.

Our simple wage setting model is highly parametrized since changes in wages in a given occupation are only allowed to depend on task prices p_{jt}. While this parsimonious specification provides a simple interpretation for changes in occupational wages, actual wage changes likely depend on other factors. For instance, Autor, Katz, and Kearney (2008) show that the distribution of wage residuals has become more skewed over time (convexification of the distribution). This can be captured by allowing for a percentile-specific component λ^q which leads to the main regression equation to be estimated in the first step of the empirical analysis:

$$\Delta w_j^q = a_j + b_j w_{j0}^q + \lambda^q + \varepsilon_j^q \tag{17}$$

where we have also added an error term ε_j^q to capture other possible, but unsystematic, departures from our simple task pricing model.

A more economically intuitive interpretation of the percentile-specific error components λ^q is that it represents a generic change in the return to unobservable skills of the type considered by Juhn, Murphy, and Pierce (1993). For example, if unobservable skills in a standard Mincer-type regression reflect unmeasured school quality, and that school quality is equally distributed and rewarded in all occupations, then changes in the return to school quality will be captured by the error component λ^q.

In the second step of the analysis, we link the estimated intercepts and slopes ($\hat{a}_j$ and $\hat{b}_j$) to measures of the task content of each occupation, as we did in the case of the mean and standard deviation earlier.

The second step regressions are

$$\hat{a}_j = \gamma_0 + \sum_{h=1}^{5} \gamma_{jh} T_{jh} + \mu_j \tag{18}$$

and

$$\hat{b}_j = \beta_0 + \sum_{h=1}^{5} \beta_{jh} T_{jh} + \nu_j \tag{19}$$

4.4. Occupation Wage Profiles: Results

We now present the estimates of the linear regression models for within-occupation quantiles (Eq. (17)), and then link the estimated slope and intercept parameters to our measures of task content from the O*NET. We refer to these regressions as "occupation wage profiles".

Before presenting our main estimates, consider again the overall changes in the wage distribution illustrated in Fig. 1. Consistent with Autor, Katz, and Kearney (2006), Fig. 1 shows that 1983–1985 to 2000–2002 changes in real wages at each percentile of the male wages distribution follow a U-shaped curve. The figure shows wages at the very top increased much more than wages in the middle of the distribution, resulting in increased top-end inequality. By contrast, inequality in the lower half of the distribution increased during the second half of the 1980s, but decreased sharply in the 1990s as wages at the bottom grew substantially more than those in the middle of the distribution. For the whole 1983–1985 to 2000–2002 period, there was a clear decline in lower-end wage inequality.

Note that, despite our large samples based on three years of pooled data, we are left with a small number of observations in many occupations when we work at the three-digit occupation level. In the analysis presented in this section, we thus focus on occupations classified at the two-digit level (40 occupations) to have a large enough number of observations in each occupation. This is particularly important given our empirical approach where we run regressions of change in wages on the base-period wage. Sampling error in wages generates a spurious negative relationship between base-level wages and wage changes that can be quite large when wage percentiles are imprecisely estimated.[15]

In principle, we could use a large number of wage percentiles, w_{jt}^q, in the empirical analysis. But since wage percentiles are strongly correlated for small differences in q, we only extract the nine deciles of the within-occupation wage distribution, that is, w_{jt}^q for $q = 10, 20, \ldots, 90$. Finally, all the regression estimates are weighted by the number of observations (weighted using the earnings weight from the CPS) in each occupation.

Fig. 2(a) presents the raw data used in the analysis. The figure plots the 360 observed changes in wages (9 observation for each of the 40 occupations) as a function of the base wages. The most noticeable feature of

---

15. The bias could be adjusted using a measurement-error corrected regression approach, as in Card and Lemieux (1996), or an instrumental variables approach.

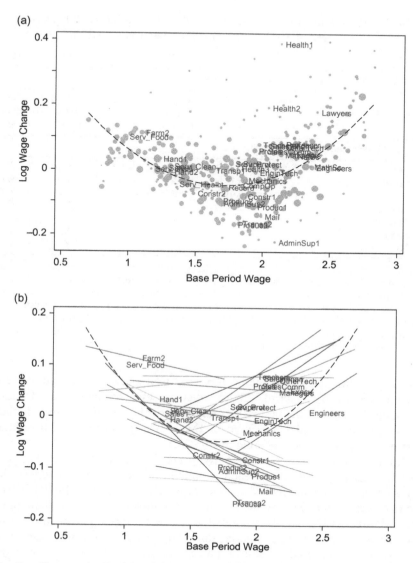

Fig. 2. Changes in Real Log Wages by Decile Men 1983–1985 to 2000–2002. (a) Raw Change by Two-Digit Occupation and (b) Fitted Change in Top 25 Two-Digit Occupations.

Table 2.   Regression Fit of Models for 1983–1985 to 2000–2002 Changes
in Wages at Each Decile, by Two-Digit Occupation.

	(1)	(2)	(3)	(4)	(5)	(6)
Panel A. Models without controls for observables						
Adj. R^2	−0.0002	0.6120	0.0128	0.6421	0.9544	0.8522
Curvature in residuals	0.211	0.131	0.186	0.107	0.003	0.037
	(0.015)	(0.009)	(0.016)	(0.009)	(0.004)	(0.006)
Panel B. Models with controls for observables						
Adj. R^2	0.0189	0.3643	0.0641	0.4457	0.8610	0.6842
Curvature in residuals	0.196	0.164	0.133	0.102	0.003	0.069
	(0.016)	(0.012)	(0.017)	(0.012)	(0.006)	(0.009)
Occupation dummies		X		X	X	X
Decile dummies			X	X	X	
Base wage	X				X	X
Occ*base wage					X	X

Notes: Regression models estimated for each decile (10th, 20th, ..., 90th) of each two-digit occupation. Three hundred and sixty observations used in all models (40 occupations, 9 observations per occupation). Models are weighted using the fraction of observations in the two-digit occupation in the base period. Panel A shows the results when regressions are estimated without any controls for observables. Panel B shows the results when the distribution of observables (age, education, race, and marital status) in each occupation is reweighted to be the same as the overall distribution over all occupations.

Fig. 2(a) is that wage changes exhibit the well-known U-shaped pattern documented by Autor et al. (2006) which we also see in Fig. 1. Broadly speaking, the goal of the first part of the empirical analysis is to see whether the simple linear model presented in Eq. (17) helps explain a substantial part of the variation documented in Fig. 2(a).

Table 2 shows the estimates from various versions of Eq. (17). We present two measures of fit for each estimated model. First, we report the adjusted R^2 of the model. Note that even if the model in Eq. (17) was the true wage determination model, the regressions would not explain all of the variations in the data because of the residual sampling error in the estimated wage changes. The average sampling variance of wage changes is 0.0002, which represents about 3 percent of the total variation in wage changes by occupation and decile. This means that one cannot reject the null hypothesis that sampling error is the only source of residual error (i.e., the model is "true") whenever the R^2 exceeds 0.97.

The second measure of fit consists of looking at whether the model is able to explain the U-shaped feature of the raw data presented in Fig. 2(a). As a reference, the estimated coefficient on the quadratic term in the fitted (quadratic) regression reported in Fig. 2(a) is equal to 0.211. For each estimated model, we run a simple regression of the residuals from the fitted quadratic regression on a linear and quadratic term in the base wage to see whether there is any curvature left in the residuals that the model is unable to explain.

One potential concern with this regression approach is that we are not controlling for any standard covariates, which means that we may be overstating the contribution of occupations in changes in the wage structure. For instance, workers with high levels of education tend to work in high wage occupations. This means that changes in the distribution of wages in high wage occupation may simply be reflecting changes in the return to education among highly educated workers. Changes in the distribution of education, or other covariates, may also be confounding the observed changes in occupational wages.

As in the case of the means and variances, we address these issues by reweighting the distribution of covariates in each occupation at each time period so that it is the same as in the pooled distribution with all occupations and time periods (1983−1985 and 2000−2002 combined). This involves computing 80 separate logits (40 occupations times two years) to perform a DiNardo et al. (1996) reweighting exercise. The various quantiles of the wage distribution for each occupation are then computed in the reweighted samples. The covariates used in the logits are a set of five education dummies, nine experience dummies, and dummies for race and marital status. The unadjusted models are reported in Panel A of Table 2, while the estimates that adjust for the covariates by reweighting are reported in Panel B. Since the results with and without the adjustment are qualitatively similar, we focus our discussion on the unadjusted estimates reported in Panel A.

As a benchmark, we report in column 1 the estimates from a simple model where the only explanatory variable is the base wage. This model explains essentially none of the variation in the data as the adjusted R^2 is essentially equal to 0 (−0.0002). This reflects the fact that running a linear regression on the data reported in Fig. 2(a) yields a flat line. Since the linear regression cannot, by definition, explain any of the curvature of the changes in wages, the curvature parameter in the residuals (0.211) is exactly the same as in the simple quadratic regression discussed above.

In column 2, we only include the set of occupation dummies (the a_j's) in the regression. The restriction imbedded in this model is that all the wage deciles within a given occupation increase at the same rate, that is, there is no change in within-occupation wage dispersion. Just including the occupation dummies explains more than half of the raw variation in the data

(R^2 of 0.61), and about a third of the curvature. The curvature parameter declines from 0.211 to 0.131 but remains strongly significant.

Column 3 shows that only including decile dummies (the λ^{q}'s) explains essentially none of the variation or curvature in the data. This is a strong result as it indicates that using a common within-occupation change in wage dispersion cannot account for any of the observed change in wages. Furthermore, adding the decile dummies to the occupation dummies (column 4) only marginally improves the fit of the model compared to the model with occupation dummies only in column 2. This indicates that within-occupation changes in the wage distribution are highly occupation-specific, and cannot simply be linked to a pervasive increase in returns to skill "à la" Juhn et al. (1993).[16]

By contrast, the fit of the model improves drastically once we introduce occupation-specific slopes in column 5. The adjusted R^2 of the model jumps to 0.9544, which is quite close to the critical value for which we cannot reject the null hypothesis that the model is correctly specified, and that all the residual variation is due to sampling error. The curvature parameter now drops to 0.003 and is no longer statistically significant. In other words, we are able to account for all the curvature in the data using occupation-specific slopes. Note also that once the occupation-specific slopes are included, decile dummies play a more substantial role in the regressions, as evidenced by the drop in the adjusted R^2 between column 5 (decile dummies included) and 6 (decile dummies excluded).

The results reported in Panel B where we control for standard covariates are generally similar to those reported in Panel A. In particular, the model with decile dummies and occupation-specific slopes (column 5) explains most of the variation in the data and all of the curvature. Note that the R^2 is generally lower than in the models where we do not control for covariates. This indicates that the covariates reduce the explanatory power of occupations by relatively more than they reduce the residual variation unexplained by occupational factors. In other words, this reflects the fact

---

16. This finding is also consistent with the evidence that within-group inequality did not increase much during the 1990s, at least in the MORG data we are using here (Lemieux, 2006). We show in Fig. 2(b) below that within-occupation inequality increased in some occupations but decreased in others. Thus, just looking at average changes across occupations (as captured by decile dummies) shows little change in within-occupation inequality as it hides important, but offsetting, changes in different occupations.

that occupational affiliation is strongly correlated with observable skill measures (see, e.g., Gibbons et al., 2005).

We next illustrate the fit of the model by plotting occupation-specific regressions for the 25 largest occupations in Fig. 2(b).[17] While it is not possible to see what happens for each and every occupation on this graph, there is still a noticeable pattern in the data. The slope for occupations at the bottom end of the distribution tends to be negative. Slopes get flatter in the middle of the distribution, and generally turn positive at the top end of the distribution. In other words, it is clear from the figure that the set of occupational wage profiles generally follow the U-shaped pattern observed in the raw data.

We explore this hypothesis more formally by estimating the regression models in Eqs. (18) and (19) that link the intercepts and slopes of the occupation wage change profiles to the task content of occupations. The results are reported in Table 3. In the first two columns of Table 3, we include task measures separately in the regressions (one regression for each task measure). To adjust for the possible confounding effect of overall changes in the return to skill, we also report estimates that control for the base (median) wage level in the occupation.

To get a better sense of how these task measures vary across the occupation distribution, consider again Fig. A1, which plots the values of the task index as a function of the average wage in the (three-digit) occupation. The "information content" and "decision making" measures are strongly positively related to wages. Consistent with Autor et al. (2003), the "automation" task follows an inverse U-shaped curve. To the extent that technological change allows firms to replace workers performing these types of tasks with computer-driven technologies, we would expect both the intercept and slope of occupations with high degree of automation to decline over time.

But although occupations in the middle of the wage distribution may be most vulnerable to technological change, they also involve relatively more on-site work (e.g., repairmen) and may, therefore, be less vulnerable to off-shoring. The last measure of task, face-to-face contact, is not as strongly related to average occupational wages as the other task measures. On the one hand, we expect workers in occupations with a high level of face-to-face contact to do relatively well in the presence of offshoring. On the other

---

17. To avoid overloading the graph, we exclude 15 occupations that account for the smallest share of the workforce (less than 1 percent of workers in each of these occupations).

Table 3. Estimated Effect of Task Requirements on Intercept and Slope of Wage Change Regressions by Two-Digit Occupation.

Tasks Entered:	Separately		Together					
	Intercept	Slope	Intercept			Slope		
Dep. Variable:	(1)	(2)	(3)	(4)	(5)	(6)	(7)	(8)
Information content	0.048***	0.037**	0.004	0.028**	-0.002	0.018	-0.002	0.004
	(0.015)	(0.016)	(0.015)	(0.014)	(0.012)	(0.015)	(0.014)	(0.022)
Automation/routine	-0.068***	-0.058***	-0.039**	-0.050***	-0.035***	-0.029*	-0.019	-0.034*
	(0.012)	(0.014)	(0.016)	(0.013)	(0.011)	(0.016)	(0.014)	(0.020)
No on-site work	0.025***	0.034***	0.004	0.007	0.006	0.027***	0.025***	0.028***
	(0.006)	(0.005)	(0.008)	(0.007)	(0.006)	(0.008)	(0.007)	(0.010)
No face-to-face	-0.068***	-0.072***	-0.044***	-0.005	0.025	0.006	-0.024	-0.029
	(0.015)	(0.015)	(0.021)	(0.019)	(0.016)	(0.020)	(0.020)	(0.029)
No decision making	-0.066***	-0.048**	0.026	-0.019	-0.044**	-0.049**	-0.013	-0.007
	(0.019)	(0.021)	(0.023)	(0.021)	(0.017)	(0.023)	(0.022)	(0.029)
Base wage	Yes	Yes	No	Yes	Yes	No	Yes	Yes
Reweighted	No	No	No	No	Yes	No	No	Yes
Adj. R^2	–	–	0.377	0.599	0.557	0.747	0.807	0.674

Notes: All models are estimated by running regressions of the 40 occupation-specific intercepts and slopes (estimated in specification (5) of Table 2) on the task measures. The models reported in all columns are weighted using the fraction of observations in each occupation in the base period. The intercepts and slopes used in columns 3 and 6 are based on the regression models in Panel B of Table 2 where observables (age, education, race, and marital status) are reweighted to be as in the overall distribution for all occupations. The models reported in all other columns rely on the estimates of Panel A that do not control for observables.

hand, since many of these workers may have relatively low formal skills such as education (e.g., retail sales workers), occupations with a high level of face-to-face contact may experience declining relative wages if returns to more general forms of skills increase.

The strongest and most robust result in Table 3 is that occupations with high level of automation experience a relative decline in both the intercept and the slope of their occupational wage profiles. The effect is statistically significant in six of the eight specifications reported in Table 3. The other "technology" variable, information content, has generally a positive and significant effect on both the intercept and the slope, as expected, when included by itself in columns 1 and 2. The effect tends to be weaker, however, in models where other tasks are also controlled for (columns 3–8).

The effect of the tasks related to the offshorability of jobs is reported in the last three rows of the table. Note that since "on-site," "face-to-face," and "decision making" are negatively related to the offshorability of jobs, we use the reverse of these tasks in the regression to interpret the coefficients as the impact of offshorability (as opposed to non-offshorability). As a result, we expect the effect of these adjusted tasks to be negative. For instance, the returns to skill in jobs that do not require face-to-face contacts will likely decrease since it is now possible to offshore these types of jobs to another country.

The results for the task content measures linked to offshoring are mixed. As expected, the effect of "no face-to-face" and "no decision making" is generally negative. By contrast, the effect of "not-on-site work" is generally positive, which is surprising. One possible explanation is that the O*NET is not well suited for distinguishing whether a worker has to work on "any site" (i.e., an assembly line worker), versus working on a site in the United States (i.e., a construction worker).

On balance, most of the results reported in Table 3 are consistent with our expectations. More importantly, the task measures explain most of the variation in the slopes (R^2 of 0.75–0.81), though less of the variation in the intercepts (R^2 of 0.38–0.60). This suggests that we can capture most of the effect of occupations on the wage structure using only a handful of task measures, instead of a large number of occupation dummies. The twin advantage of tasks over occupations is that they are a more parsimonious way of summarizing the data, and are more economically interpretable than occupation dummies.

We draw two main conclusions from Table 3. First, as predicted by the model of Section 2, the measures of task content of jobs tend to have a similar impact on the intercept and the slope of the occupational profiles. Second, tasks account for a large fraction of the variation in the slopes and intercepts over occupations and the estimated effect of tasks are generally consistent with our theoretical expectations. Taken together, this suggests that occupational characteristics as measured by these five task measures can play a substantial role in explaining the U-shaped feature of the raw data illustrated in Fig. 1.

5. CONCLUSION

In this paper, we study the contribution of occupations to changes in the wage structure. We present a simple model of skills, tasks, and wages, and use this as a motivation for estimating models for the changes in both between- and within-occupation dispersion of wages between 1983−1985 and 2000−2002. We then look at whether measures of the task content of work linked to technological change and offshoring can help explain changes in occupational wages, as summarized by means, variances, and occupation-specific wage percentiles.

One main finding is that a limited number of task content measures (five measures linked to technological change and offshoring) can explain most of the variation in means, variances, and occupation-specific wage percentiles. The estimated effects generally conform to expectations. In particular, occupations that exhibit a high level of automation/routine tend to experience a relative decline in both the level and dispersion of wages. This is consistent with task prices in these occupations being reduced over time as a consequence of routine-biased technological change. Likewise, jobs that are more offshorable because of a lack of face-to-face interactions and decision-making opportunities also tend to experience a decline in task prices. From a more methodological point of view, our findings suggests that a simple model of skills, tasks, and wages where occupational wages are summarized by a single occupation-specific task price does a good job accounting for the large changes in the occupation wage structure that happened in the 1980s and 1990s.

REFERENCES

Acemoglu, D., & Autor, D. H. (2011). Skills, tasks, and technologies: Implications for employment and earnings. In O. Ashenfelter & D. Card (Eds.), *Handbook of economics* (Vol. IV, pp. 1043−1171). Amsterdam: North Holland.

Autor, D. H. (2013, January). *The "Task Approach" to labor markets: An overview*. NBER Working Paper No. 18711.

Autor, D. H., Katz, L. F., & Kearney, M. S. (2006). The polarization of the U.S. labor market. *American Economic Review, 96*, 189–194.

Autor, D. H., Katz, L. F., & Kearney, M. S. (2008). Trends in U.S. wage inequality: Revising the revisionists. *Review of Economics and Statistics, May*.

Autor, D. H., Levy, F., & Murnane, R. J. (2003). The skill content of recent technological change: An empirical exploration. *Quarterly Journal of Economics, 118*(4), 1279–1333.

Blinder, A. (2007). *How many U.S. jobs might be offshorable?* Center for Economic Policy Studies Working Discussion Paper No. 142, Princeton University.

Boehm, M. (2015). *The price of polarization: Estimating task prices under routine-biased technical change*. University of Bonn Working Paper.

Bound, J., & Johnson, G. (1992). Changes in the structure of wages in the 1980s: An evaluation of alternative explanations. *American Economic Review, 82*(3), 371–392.

Burstein, A., Morales, E., & Vogel, J. (2015, January). *Accounting for changes in between-group inequality*. NBER Working Paper No. 20855.

Card, D., & Lemieux, T. (1996). Wage dispersion, returns to skill, and black white wage differentials. *Journal of Econometrics, 74*(2), 319–361.

Cortes, G. M. (2016). Where have the middle-wage workers gone? A study of polarization using panel data. *Journal of Labor Economics, 34*(1), 63–105.

Crinò, R. (2010). *Service offshoring and white-collar employment. Review of Economic Studies, 77*(2), 595–632.

DiNardo, J., Fortin, N. M., & Lemieux, T. (1996). Labor market institutions and the distribution of wages, 1973–1992: A semiparametric approach. *Econometrica, 64*, 1001–1044.

Firpo, S., Fortin, N. M., & Lemieux, T. (2011). *Occupational tasks and changes in the wage structure*. IZA Discussion Paper No. 5542.

Freeman, R. B. (1995). Are your wages set in Beijing? *Journal of Economic Perspectives, 9*(3), 15–32.

Gibbons, R., Katz, L. F., Lemieux, T., & Parent, D. (2005). Comparative advantage, learning, and sectoral wage determination. *Journal of Labor Economics, 23*(4), 681–724.

Goos, M., & Manning, A. (2007). Lousy and lovely jobs: The rising polarization of work in Britain. *Review of Economics and Statistics, 89*(1), 118–133.

Goos, M., Manning, A., & Salomons, A. (2010). *Recent changes in the European employment structure: The roles of technological change, globalization and institutions*. Discussion Paper no. 1016, Center for Economic Performance, LSE, London.

Heckman, J., & Scheinkman, J. (1987). The importance of bundling in a Gorman-Lancaster model of earnings. *Review of Economic Studies, 54*(2), 243–255.

Jensen, J. B., & Kletzer, L. G. (2007). Measuring the task content of offshorable services jobs, tradable services and job loss. In K. Abraham, M. Harper, & J. Spletzer (Eds.), *Labor in the new economy*. Chicago, IL: University of Chicago Press. Peterson Institute for International Economics.

Juhn, C., Murphy, K., & Pierce, B. (1993). Wage inequality and the rise in returns to skill. *The Journal of Political Economy, 101*, 410–442.

Katz, L. F., & Murphy, K. M. (1992). Changes in relative wages, 1963–1987: Supply and demand factors. *Quarterly Journal of Economics, 117*(5), 914–940.

Lazear, E. P. (2009). Firm-specific human capital: A skill-weights approach. *Journal of Political Economy, 117*(5), 914–940.

Lemieux, T. (2006). Increasing residual wage inequality: Composition effects, noisy data, or rising demand for skill? *American Economic Review, 96*(3), 461–498.

Murphy, K. M., & Welch, F. (1991). The role of international trade in wage differentials. In M. Kosters (Ed.), *Workers and their wages* (pp. 39–69). Washington, DC: American Enterprise Institute Press.

Yamaguchi, S. (2012). Tasks and heterogeneous human capital. *Journal of Labor Economics, 30*(1), 1–53.

APPENDIX

Table A1. O*NET 13.0 – Work Activities & Work Context.

A. Characteristics Linked to Technological Change/Offshorability[a]

Information Content

4.A.1.a.1	Getting Information (JK)
4.A.2.a.2	Processing Information (JK)
4.A.2.a.4	Analyzing Data or Information (JK)
4.A.3.b.1	Interacting with Computers (JK)
4.A.3.b.6	Documenting/Recording Information (JK)

Automation/Routinization

4.C.3.b.2	Degree of Automation
4.C.3.b.7	Importance of Repeating Same Tasks
4.C.3.b.8	Structured versus Unstructured Work (reverse)
4.C.3.d.3	Pace Determined by Speed of Equipment
4.C.2.d.1.i	Spend Time Making Repetitive Motions

B. Characteristics Linked to Non-Offshorability

Face-to-Face

4.C.1.a.2.1	Face-to-Face Discussions
4.A.4.a.4	Establishing and Maintaining Interpersonal Relationships (JK,B)
4.A.4.a.5	Assisting and Caring for Others (JK,B)
4.A.4.a.8	Performing for or Working Directly with the Public (JK,B)
4.A.4.b.5	Coaching and Developing Others (B)

On-Site Job

4.A.1.b.2	Inspecting Equipment, Structures, or Material (JK)
4.A.3.a.2	Handling and Moving Objects
4.A.3.a.3	Controlling Machines and Processes
4.A.3.a.4	Operating Vehicles, Mechanized Devices, or Equipment
4.A.3.b.4	Repairing and Maintaining Mechanical Equipment (*0.5)
4.A.3.b.5	Repairing and Maintaining Electronic Equipment (*0.5)

Decision Making

4.A.2.b.1	Making Decisions and Solving Problems (JK)
4.A.2.b.2	Thinking Creatively (JK)
4.A.2.b.4	Developing Objectives and Strategies
4.C.1.c.2	Responsibility for Outcomes and Results
4.C.3.a.2.b	Frequency of Decision Making

[a](JK) indicates a work activity used in Jensen and Kletzer (2007), (B) a work activity used or suggested in Blinder (2007).

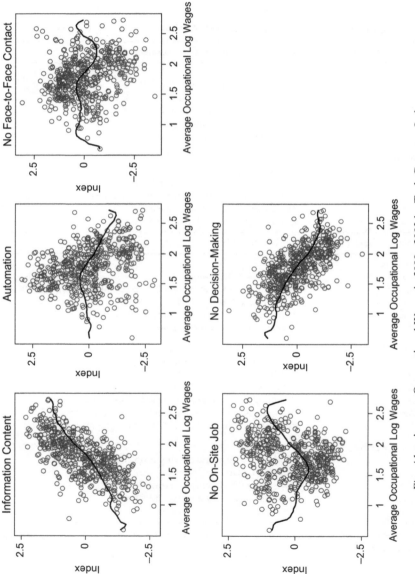

Fig. A1. Average Occupational Wages in 2000–2002 by Task Category Indexes.

INTERGENERATIONAL TRANSMISSION OF SKILLS AND DIFFERENCES IN LABOR MARKET OUTCOMES FOR BLACKS AND WHITES [☆]

Tsunao Okumura[a] and Emiko Usui[b]

[a] Yokohama National University
[b] Hitotsubashi University

[☆] For helpful comments and suggestions, we would like to thank two anonymous referees, as well as Joseph Altonji, Lorenzo Cappellari, Hidehiko Ichimura, Seik Kim, Hideo Owan, Solomon Polachek, Kathryn Shaw, Konstantinos Tatsiramos, and participants in meetings held at Hitotsubashi University, IZA, Keio University, Oakland University, Osaka University, the Trans-Pacific Labor Seminar (TPLS), the University of Michigan, and the University of Tokyo, and at annual meetings of the North American Econometric Society, the European Association of Labour Economists, the Japanese Economic Association, and the Society of Labor Economists. Remaining errors are our own. An earlier version of the article was circulated under the title "Intergenerational Correlations of Skills." This research is supported by JSPS grants 22000001 (Usui) and 15H05692 (Okumura and Usui).

Inequality: Causes and Consequences
Research in Labor Economics, Volume 43, 227–286
ISSN: 0147-9121/doi:10.1108/S0147-912120160000043015

ABSTRACT

This paper investigates, theoretically and empirically, differences between blacks and whites in the United States concerning the intergenerational transmission of occupational skills and the effects on sons' earnings. The father—son skill correlation is measured by the correlation coefficient (or cosine of the angle) between the father's skill vector and the son's skill vector. The skill vector comprises an individual's occupational characteristics from the Dictionary of Occupational Titles (DOT). According to data from the U.S. National Longitudinal Survey of Youth (NLSY79), white sons earn higher wages in occupations that require skills similar to those of their fathers, whereas black sons in such circumstances incur a wage loss. A large portion of the racial wage gap is explained by the father—son skill correlation. However, a significant unexplained racial wage gap remains at the lower tail of the wage distribution.

Keywords: Multidimensional skills; intergenerational transmission; occupational characteristics; black—white differences

JEL classifications: J62; J24; J15

1. INTRODUCTION

Skill disparities between black and white Americans have historically been substantial, a fact attributable to the difficulties that blacks have faced as a result of racial segregation and discrimination. Although the skill gaps between the two groups — as measured by educational attainment and test scores — declined in the 1970s and 1980s due to school desegregation and improvements in school quality for blacks, significant gaps remain, and they are important determinants of earnings differences between blacks and whites.[1] In light of the fact that parents often pass skills and traits onto their children through environment and education, it is essential in this context to estimate to what extent black—white differences in parents' skills contribute to the black—white differences in skills and earnings among their children.

---

1. See Altonji and Blank (1999) for a comprehensive survey of the literature concerning black-white differences in the U.S. labor market.

The seminal work of Neal and Johnson (1996) shows that scores on the Armed Forces Qualification Test (AFQT), a measure of cognitive skills, explain much of the wage gap between black and white young adults. Their results suggest that the black—white wage gap primarily reflects a difference in cognitive skills that exists before young men enter the labor market. To clarify the source of this skill gap, Neal (2006) presents an intergenerational model to demonstrate that the black—white difference in the parents' costs of investing in their children's skill acquisition can contribute to the black—white gaps in skills and wages among children. However, recent empirical studies have found that cognitive skills are not the only skill dimensions that are important in determining wages (Bacolod & Blum, 2010; Ingram & Neumann, 2006). For example, Bacolod and Blum (2010) find that the wage returns to cognitive and people skills more than doubled during the 1968—1990 period, with cognitive skills becoming more complementary to motor skills and especially people skills.

In this paper, we first extend Neal's (2006) intergenerational model to encompass cognitive, people, and motor skills, along with skills associated with physical strength. We then investigate how the black—white differences in the fathers' cost of investing in cognitive skills affect their sons' skill attainment and earnings. For the empirical analysis, we pair information about fathers and sons from the U.S. National Longitudinal Survey of Youth (NLSY79) with the occupational characteristics from the Dictionary of Occupational Titles (DOT) to construct multidimensional skill vectors for fathers and sons. First, we find that white sons earn higher wages in occupations that require skills similar to their fathers' skills, whereas black sons in such circumstances incur a wage loss. This finding implies a positive transfer of skill-related human capital for whites but not for blacks. Second, we find that a significant portion of the black—white wage gap is attributable to the wage premium earned by white sons and the wage penalty incurred by black sons for working in occupations that require skills similar to their fathers' occupations.

We begin by extending the human capital models of Becker and Tomes (1976) and Laband and Lentz (1983) to a model in which fathers and sons invest in two types of human capital: T *skills* that represent cognitive skills, and M *skills* that represent other skills such as people skills, motor skills, and physical strength. For each individual, we construct a skill vector that is composed of the individual's T skills and M skills. We measure the closeness between the father's and the son's skill vectors by the cosine of the angle between these two vectors. The model predicts that an increase in skill inheritance from fathers to sons leads to a greater skill correlation between them, because of the cost savings for sons from "inheriting" part of their fathers' skills.

We then apply the model to examine black—white differences in the effects of the fathers' relative costs of investing in their T skills as compared to their M skills on the sons' skill combinations and earnings. First, we assume that the relative returns to T skills as compared to M skills increased from the fathers' to the sons' generation. We do this because empirical studies such as Ingram and Neumann (2006) have found a large rise in the returns to mathematical and verbal ability since the early 1980s and a steady decline in the returns to manual skills.[2] Second, we assume that black fathers paid a greater relative cost to acquire T skills as compared to M skills than did white fathers, and that black sons' costs of investing in T skills declined, even though some black sons still pay a greater cost to acquire T skills. These assumptions reflect school segregation and difficulties that blacks experienced in accessing quality schools before the Supreme Court ruling on *Brown v. Board of Education* in 1954. Afterwards, however, the black—white disparity in costs of investing in cognitive skills gradually narrowed for blacks because of school desegregation and improvements in school quality for blacks, as documented in Guryan (2004), Neal (2006), Reber (2010), and Johnson (2014), among others.[3] We then present how the black—white differences in the fathers' costs of investing in cognitive skills and the increase over time in the returns to cognitive skills contribute to differences between black and white sons in the skill combinations and earnings. The model predicts that white sons who work in occupations requiring skill sets similar to those of their fathers earn higher wages because they inherit part of their fathers' skill sets, thus reducing the costs of acquiring skills that pay higher wages. However, among blacks, sons who earn higher wages are those who work in occupations requiring skill sets different from those of their fathers. Because of their fathers' higher costs involved in acquiring cognitive skills, the skills sets that the black sons inherit from their fathers are away from those that pay higher wages to the sons. For this reason, the black sons have to acquire different skill sets from those of

---

2. The chronology of these findings overlaps the years in our NLSY79 sample, where information for fathers is from the 1970s and for sons is from the 1990s. Also, see Katz and Autor (1999) and Murnane, Willett, and Levy (1995) regarding the rise in the returns to schooling and cognitive skills.

3. The NLSY79 respondents (sons) were born in the years 1957—64, and therefore after the 1954 Supreme Court ruling. However, about half of the fathers in the NLSY79 sample were born in the 1930s, and therefore received their formal education before the 1954 Supreme Court ruling, i.e., the period when segregation and discrimination were more severe in the U.S.

their fathers in order to seek higher wages. The wage gap between black and white sons is therefore attributable to (1) white sons' wage gains resulting from their cost savings from the intergenerational skill transfer, (2) black sons' wage loss resulting from their costs in moving away from their fathers' occupations, and (3) black sons' wage loss resulting from working in occupations that require skills similar to their fathers'. The model also predicts that when there is complementarity between cognitive skills and other skills in the returns to wages for fathers and sons (see Bacolod and Blum (2010)), the black–white difference in the fathers' costs of investing in cognitive skills further widens the black–white wage gap for sons.

These predictions from the theoretical model are then compared with the empirical analysis using the sample of fathers and sons from the NLSY79, which includes fathers who were in their forties during the 1970s and sons (NLSY79 respondents) who were in their late twenties to late thirties in 1993 and 2000. For each individual, we construct a multidimensional skill vector by measures of skill requirements drawn from the Dictionary of Occupational Titles (DOT). The DOT characterizes each occupation's requirements, using ranges of cognitive skills, people skills, motor skills, and skills associated with physical strength. Skill correlation between father and son is measured by the cosine of the angle of their respective skill vectors. Specifically, we compute the correlation coefficient between the father's skill vector and the son's skill vector.

We establish three facts about the distribution of father–son skill correlation. First, in a hypothetical situation where father–son pairs are randomly matched, the median of the distribution of skill correlation is positive for blacks but it is close to zero for whites. Second, the skill correlation for actual father–son pairs, which goes beyond the skill correlation under random matching of fathers and sons, is greater for whites than for blacks. Third, the correlation coefficients among whites are higher in families with highly educated fathers; however, among blacks the correlation coefficients are higher for not only those families with highly educated fathers but also for those families with the least educated fathers. These facts imply that father–son skill correlation for blacks arises from the limited skill sets available to them, whereas the skill correlation for whites arises from fathers' and sons' choosing similar occupations from a wider variety of skill sets.

We then estimate the sons' wage effects of skill-related human capital transfers (obtained from working in occupations that require skills similar to those of their fathers) and of nepotism (obtained from working in the same occupation as their fathers). Neal and Johnson (1996) find that differences in cognitive skills explain much of the wage gap between black and white men, yet a significant unexplained wage gap remains. We therefore include as regressors in Neal and Johnson's wage equation (1) the correlation coefficient between the father's and the son's skill vectors, (2) a dummy for whether father and son work in the same occupation, and (3) fathers' education and DOT skill variables.

We present the following four findings and discuss their implications. First, white sons earn a wage premium for working in occupations requiring skills similar to their fathers', whereas black sons in such circumstances incur a wage penalty. This implies a positive skill transfer from fathers to sons for whites, but an insufficient skill acquisition for black sons due to their fathers' greater costs of investing in cognitive skills. Second, by including the correlation coefficient between father−son skill vectors in the wage regression, the unexplained black−white wage gap, after controlling for cognitive skills, is reduced to 30 percent. A significant portion of the black−white wage gap is therefore attributable to the wage premium earned by white sons and the wage penalty paid by black sons for working in occupations that require skills similar to their fathers'. Third, from the quantile wage regression, we find that the black−white wage gap in the middle of the wage distribution for sons arises from the black−white differences in the effect of skill transfer from their fathers, whereas the black−white wage gap in the lower tail of the wage distribution arises from the unexplained black−white wage gap. This result indicates that blacks in the lower tail of the wage distribution are hampered in achieving economic success by unexplained difficulties (such as discrimination), while blacks in the middle of the wage distribution are hampered by the negative effect of skill transfer from their fathers. Fourth, evidence of nepotism for sons is found in whites, since they earn higher wages for working in the same occupation as their fathers.

The paper proceeds as follows. Section 2 presents an intergenerational model with multidimensional skills. Section 3 describes the data used in the analysis and includes descriptive statistics for the NLSY79 sample. Section 4 measures the multidimensional-skill correlation between a father and a son, and Section 5 examines sons' economic returns or penalties from working in occupations similar to those of their fathers. Section 6 concludes the paper.

2. MODEL OF INTERGENERATIONAL SKILL TRANSFER

The seminal works of Ishikawa (1975) and Becker and Tomes (1976) study the intergenerational transmission of human capital from parent to child.

Laband and Lentz (1983) extend those intergenerational models to include a son following his father's occupation. They show that when a son adopts a father's occupation, part of the cost of schooling is saved, but a cost for personal training is incurred. When the personal-training cost is less than the school-training cost, the son works in the same job as his father.

Extending these previous studies, we consider the intergenerational transmission of skills that are multidimensional, and we measure the father–son skill correlation by the angle (or cosine of the angle) of the multidimensional skill vectors between father and son. In our model, each family has one father and one son. The father chooses the amount of his skills to maximize his utility. A portion of those skills is then inherited by the son. The son's skill holdings are the sum of his inherited and personally acquired skills. Given his inherited skills, the son chooses the amount of skills that he personally acquires in order to maximize his utility. Because of inherited skills, father and son tend to show similar combinations of skills.[4]

For simplicity, we set up a model of a two-dimensional skill transfer. Each occupation requires a skill vector (T, M), where T stands for cognitive skills and M stands for other skills, such as people skills, motor skills, and physical strength. Let the father's initial skill endowment be $(0, 0)$, and the father invests in a skill vector $\Psi_F = (T_F, M_F)$. An x portion of the father's skill vector is transferred to the son by means of the educational environment at home and/or genes $(0 \leq x \leq 1)$.[5] The son's skill holdings are determined by (1) the father's transfer to him of (xT_F, xM_F) and (2) his own investment (T^*, M^*). Thus, the son's skill vector is

$$\Psi_S = (T_S, M_S) = (xT_F + T^*, xM_F + M^*) \tag{1}$$

where T_F, M_F, T^*, and M^* are nonnegative. Wages are based on a skill vector: $\omega_F(T_F, M_F)$ for the father and $\omega_S(T_S, M_S)$ for the son, which are

---

4. In an alternative analysis, we assumed that an altruistic father maximizes family utility (which consists of the father's and the son's combined utilities) *à la* Ishikawa (1975) and Becker and Tomes (1976). An altruistic father chooses his skills not only to increase his own wages but also to increase his son's wages by transferring his skills to the son. Therefore, parental altruism enhances intergenerational skill correlation. Altruism introduces additional complications but does not change the main results. Details are available from the authors upon request.

5. In our analysis, we do not separate nature and nurture effects, but adoption data have been used in other studies to separate these effects on education, income, and/or behavioral outcomes (Björklund, Lindahl, and Plug, 2006; Sacerdote, 2007).

strictly increasing in each argument and are concave. The cost of investing in skills depends on the amount invested by each individual: $\gamma_F(T_F, M_F)$ for the father and $\gamma_S(T^*, M^*)$ for the son, which are strictly increasing in each argument and are convex.

The father solves the following problem:

$$\max_{\{T_F, M_F, c_F\}} u_F(c_F)$$
$$\text{subject to}: 0 \leq c_F \leq \omega_F(T_F, M_F) - \gamma_F(T_F, M_F) \tag{2}$$

and the son solves the following problem:

$$\max_{\{T^*, M^*, c_S\}} u_S(c_S)$$
$$\text{subject to}: (T_S, M_S) = (xT_F + T^*, xM_F + M^*) \tag{3}$$
$$0 \leq c_S \leq \omega_S(T_S, M_S) - \gamma_S(T^*, M^*)$$

where c_F is the father's consumption and u_F is his utility, while c_S is the son's consumption and u_S is his utility. Fig. 1 illustrates the father's and son's equilibrium skill vectors.[6] The horizontal axis represents T skills, and the vertical axis represents M skills. The father acquires the skill vector Ψ_F, so that at point $\Psi_F = (T_F, M_F)$ the father's iso-wage and iso-cost curves are tangent to each other. Since the son inherits an x portion of the father's skills, the origin of the son's iso-cost curve is (xT_F, xM_F). However, the origin of the son's iso-wage curve is $(0, 0)$. The son acquires the skill vector Ψ_S, so that at point $\Psi_S = (T_S, M_S)$ the son's iso-wage and iso-cost curves are tangent to each other.

---

6. Under the assumption of interior solutions, the first-order conditions for the father's problem (2) and the son's problem (3) are described as:

$$\begin{cases} \dfrac{\partial \omega_F(T_F, M_F)}{\partial T_F} = \dfrac{\partial \gamma_F(T_F, M_F)}{\partial T_F}, & \dfrac{\partial \omega_F(T_F, M_F)}{\partial M_F} = \dfrac{\partial \gamma_F(T_F, M_F)}{\partial M_F}, \\ \dfrac{\partial \omega_S(T_S, M_S)}{\partial T^*} = \dfrac{\partial \gamma_S(T^*, M^*)}{\partial T^*}, & \dfrac{\partial \omega_S(T_S, M_S)}{\partial M^*} = \dfrac{\partial \gamma_S(T^*, M^*)}{\partial M^*}, \\ (T_S, M_S) = (xT_F + T^*, xM_F + M^*), & \\ c_F = \omega_F(T_F, M_F) - \gamma_F(T_F, M_F), & c_S = \omega_S(T_S, M_S) - \gamma_S(T^*, M^*). \end{cases}$$

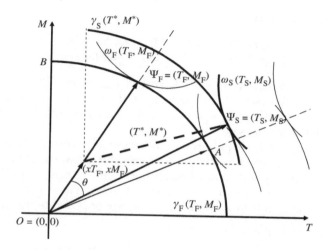

Fig. 1. Model of Intergenerational Skill Transfer.

To measure the skill correlation between father and son, we compute the cosine of the angle between the father's skill vector $\Psi_F = (T_F, M_F)$ and the son's skill vector $\Psi_S = (T_S, M_S)$. Let θ be the angle between these two skill vectors. Then

$$\cos \theta = \frac{T_F T_S + M_F M_S}{\sqrt{T_F^2 + M_F^2}\sqrt{T_S^2 + M_S^2}} \qquad (4)$$

To solve explicitly for equilibrium, the wage function is given by the Cobb–Douglas form:

$$\omega_F(T_F, M_F) = T_F^\delta M_F^{1-\delta} \quad \text{for the father } (\delta \in (0, 1))$$
$$\omega_S(T_S, M_S) = \sqrt{T_S M_S} \quad \text{for the son} \qquad (5)$$

The assumption of complementarity between skills in the returns to wages is supported empirically by Bacolod and Blum (2010), who find evidence of complementarity between cognitive and people skills, between cognitive and motor skills, and between motor skills and physical strength during specified time periods in the United States.

The cost function is specified as

$$\begin{aligned}
\gamma_F(T_F, M_F) &= a_F T_F^2 + b M_F^2 \quad \text{for the father} \\
\gamma_S(T^*, M^*) &= a_S T^{*2} + b M^{*2} \quad \text{for the son}
\end{aligned} \tag{6}$$

where a_F, a_S, and b are positive. The cost of acquiring skills for the father and the son is represented by the sum of the square of T and M skills invested by each individual, which are weighted by a_F and b for the father and by a_S and b for the son.[7]

After solving for the equilibrium outcomes, we formulate four propositions that will be applied to study the relationship between (1) black−white differences in the father's cost of acquiring cognitive skills and (2) black−white differences in the son's economic outcomes. These propositions are stated and discussed below, and their proofs are provided in the appendix.

P1. Effect of skill inheritance (x).

This proposition examines the effects of skill inheritance (x) on the father−son skill correlation ($\cos\theta$) and on the son's wage (ω_S):

$$\begin{cases}
\text{P1(i)} : \partial\cos\theta/\partial x \geq 0 \text{ (the equality holds if } a_S/(1-\delta) = a_F/\delta) \\
\text{P1(ii)} : \partial\omega_S(T_S, M_S)/\partial x > 0.
\end{cases}$$

P1(i) states that skill inheritance (x) causes a skill correlation between father and son. We use Fig. 1 as an example to illustrate this proposition. In Fig. 1, the origin of the son's iso-wage curve is $(0, 0)$, whereas that of the son's iso-cost curve is (xT_F, xM_F). Point A is the point at which the son's iso-wage and iso-cost curves are tangent to each other in the case of no skill inheritance ($x = 0$). When x is positive, as shown in Fig. 1, the vector (xT_F, xM_F) is on the father's skill vector Ψ_F and is above the line OA. As a result, the son's skill vector Ψ_S is above the line OA; specifically, Ψ_S lies between vector Ψ_F and line OA. Since the angle between Ψ_F and Ψ_S is smaller than the angle between Ψ_F and OA, it

---

7. Note that the wage elasticity of T_S and M_S is fixed to $1/2$ for the son in Eq. (5); and the cost parameter of M skills is fixed to b for both father and son in Eq. (6). We make this simplification because the objective is to analyze the effects on the equilibrium outcomes of the relative costs of T skills compared to those of M skills (i.e., a_F/b for the father and a_S/b for the son), when the returns to T skills are greater in the son's generation than in the father's generation ($\delta < 1/2$), which will be assumed later in Eq. (9).

follows that skill inheritance induces a skill correlation between father and son. P1(ii) shows that the inheritance of higher-degree skills raises the son's wages because of the son's greater cost savings in obtaining skills.

From P1(i) and P1(ii), if x varies and all else is held constant, there will be a positive relationship between the father–son skill correlation $(\cos \theta)$ and the son's wages (ω_S).[8]

P2. Effect of son's cost of investing in T skills (a_S).

This proposition studies the effect of the son's cost of investing in T skills (a_S) on the father–son skill correlation $(\cos \theta)$ and on the son's wage (ω_S):

$$\begin{cases} \text{P2(i)} : \partial\cos\theta/\partial a_S > 0, & \text{if } a_S/(1-\delta) < a_F/\delta \\ \text{P2(ii)} : \partial\omega_S(T_S, M_S)/\partial a_S < 0 \end{cases}$$

We use Fig. 1 to illustrate P2(i). When $a_S/(1-\delta) < a_F/\delta$, the slope of the son's skill vector (M_S/T_S) is smaller than that of the father's (M_F/T_F), as can be seen in Fig. 1.[9] When the son's cost of investing in T skills increases, his acquisition of both T and M skills decreases; the decline in his acquisition of T skills is larger than that of M skills. Thus, the slope of the son's skill vector (M_S/T_S) increases and the angle between the son's and the father's skill vectors is smaller. P2(ii) shows that an increase in the son's cost of investing in T skills reduces his holdings of T and M skills and, consequently, his wages.

From P2(i) and P2(ii), we see that if the son's cost of investing in T skills varies and all else is held constant, there will be a negative relationship between the father–son skill correlation and the son's wages when $a_S/(1-\delta) < a_F/\delta$.

P3. Effect of father's cost of investing in T skills (a_F).

---

8. In the model, we assume that the degree of skill transfer x is identical between T and M skills. However, we can relax this assumption so that the father's T and M skills are transferred to the son at x_1 and x_2, respectively. In this case, the son's skill vector is $\Psi_S = (T_S, M_S) = (x_1 T_F + T^*, x_2 M_F + M^*)$. P1 holds if the son's endowment $(x_1 T_F, x_2 M_F)$ is located in the area enclosed by OA, OB, and *arc AB* in Fig. 1.
9. In the section below, in which we study black-white differences in sons' economic outcomes, we assume that the relative value of returns to the costs of acquiring T skills compared to those of M skills is greater for the son $\left(\frac{0.5/a_S}{0.5/b}\right)$ than for the father $\left(\frac{\delta/a_F}{(1-\delta)/b}\right)$; that is, $a_S/(1-\delta) < a_F/\delta$.

This proposition studies the effect of the father's cost of investing in T skills (a_F) on the father–son skill correlation ($\cos \theta$) and on the son's wage (ω_S):

$$\begin{cases} \text{P3(i)} : \partial\cos \theta/\partial a_F < 0, \text{if } a_S/(1 - \delta) < a_F/\delta \\ \text{P3(ii)} : \partial\omega_S(T_S, M_S)/\partial a_F \leq 0 \text{ (the equality holds if } x = 0). \end{cases}$$

P3(i) shows that a son whose father paid a higher cost to invest in T skills chooses a skill vector further away from the father's skill vector, if $a_S/(1 - \delta) < a_F/\delta$, as shown in Fig. 1. When the father's cost of investing in T skills increases, the decline in his acquisition of T skills (T_F) is greater than that of M skills (M_F), so that the slope of the father's skill vector (M_F/T_F) increases. Subsequently, through father–son skill transfer, the decline in the son's inheritance of T skills (xT_F) is greater than that of M skills (xM_F). To compensate for the decline in the son's inheritance of T skills (xT_F), the son increases his T skill acquisition (T^*), such that the slope of his skill-acquisition vector (M^*/T^*) decreases. As a result, the angle between the father's skill vector (T_F, M_F) and the son's skill vector (T_S, M_S) is wider.

P3(ii) shows that if a father pays a higher cost to invest in T skills, then the son's wages are negatively affected. This is because higher costs reduce the father's skill holdings, and subsequently reduce the son's skill holdings through father–son skill transfer.

From P3(i) and P3(ii), we see that if the father's cost of investing in T skills varies and all else is held constant, the relationship between the father–son skill correlation and the son's wages is positive when $a_S/(1 - \delta) < a_F/\delta$.

P4. Effect of complementarity between T and M skills on son's wage.

P3(ii) shows that the high cost for the father to invest in T skills reduces the son's wages through father–son skill transfer. P4 further shows that its effect on the son's wages is enhanced when there is complementarity between T and M skills in the returns to wages for father and son:

$$\frac{\partial\omega_S(T_S, M_S)}{\partial a_F} \leq \frac{\partial\omega_S(T_S, M_S)}{\partial T_S}\frac{\partial T_S}{\partial a_F} \leq \frac{\partial\omega_S(T_S, M_S)}{\partial T_S}\frac{\partial T_S}{\partial T_F}\frac{\partial T_F}{\partial a_F} \leq 0 \qquad (7)$$

where the equalities hold if x is equal to zero. Because of complementarity between T and M skills in the father's wage, the father's high cost of investing in T skills inhibits not only his acquisition of T skills but also his acquisition of complementary M skills.[10] Having inherited fewer T

---

10. Since the iso-wage curve is Cobb-Douglas and the iso-cost curve is elliptical, an increase in a_F decreases M_F. That is, the income effect of a_F on M_F dominates its substitution effect.

and M skills, the son's holdings of such skills are smaller. Because of complementarity between T and M skills in the son's wage, the son's smaller holdings of both skills depress his wage more than the smaller holdings of only T skills. In Eq. (7), the quantity $\frac{\partial \omega_S(T_S, M_S)}{\partial T_S} \frac{\partial T_S}{\partial T_F} \frac{\partial T_F}{\partial a_F}$ represents the son's wage decline when (i) an increase in a_F reduces only the son's T skills through a decrease in the father's T skill transfer, and (ii) the effect of complementary M skills for father and son on the son's wages is ignored. Also, the quantity $\frac{\partial \omega_S(T_S, M_S)}{\partial T_S} \frac{\partial T_S}{\partial a_F}$ represents the son's wage decline when (i) an increase in a_F reduces only the son's T skill acquisition, and (ii) the effect of complementary M skills for only the son is ignored. The numerical results in Appendix B.4 show that the former quantity explains only 30–75 percent of the total decline of the son's wages $\left(\frac{\partial \omega_S(T_S, M_S)}{\partial a_F} \right)$, and the latter quantity explains only 50–75 percent. Therefore, skill complementarity augments the decline in the son's wage.

Propositions P1, P2, P3, and P4 are now used to understand the effect on the son's economic outcomes of black–white differences in the father's cost of investing in cognitive skills. Consider three types of families: the B1-type and the B2-type, which are black, and the W-type, which is white. Assume that fathers in the B1 and B2 families pay a higher cost than fathers in W families to invest in cognitive skills (T). However, the cost of investing in these skills is lower for sons in B2 families than in B1 families because B2 families reflect the improvement in school quality for blacks during the 1970s and 1980s, as documented by Hedges and Nowell (1998) and Neal (2006), among others.[11] In contrast, W-type families pay a lower cost to invest in cognitive skills (T) than do black families, and their cost structure is the same across generations. In particular, costs to the three family types of investing in cognitive skills (T) are defined by the following relation:

$$a_F^{B1} = a_F^{B2} \geq a_S^{B1} > a_S^{B2} = a_F^{W} = a_S^{W} \tag{8}$$

where the superscripts indicate the three family types: B1, B2, and W. We then assume that for returns to cognitive skills (T) in Eq. (5),

$$\delta < 1/2 \tag{9}$$

---

11. Neal (2006) documents the fact that significant improvements in school quality for blacks during the 1970s and 1980s in the U.S. decreased the gap in black-white skills, as measured by test scores among U.S. youth during that period. However, he also shows that this skill gap increased again during the 1990s, suggesting the possibility of persistent barriers to skill development among more recent cohorts of black youth. Since the NLSY79 samples individuals born between 1957 and 1964, we explore the determinants of the black-white skill gap for those earlier cohorts, not the more recent cohorts.

This assumption indicates that returns to cognitive skills (T) are greater in the son's generation, which accords with the rise in returns to cognitive skills that occurred during the 1980s (see Bacolod & Blum, 2010; Ingram & Neumann, 2006; Katz & Autor, 1999; Murnane et al., 1995; among others).[12]

Finally, we assume that the degree of skill inheritance x has the same distribution for all family types.

We now present three predictions, which will be examined in the empirical sections 4 and 5:

1. *A comparison between sons within white families*: The cost of investing in T skills is the same for father and son, but x varies for each father–son pair. Thus, only P1 applies, and there will be a positive relation between the father–son skill correlation and the son's wages within white families. As a result, white sons who work in jobs requiring skills similar to those of their fathers earn higher wages than those who do not.

2. *A comparison between sons of B1 and B2 black families*: Eqs. (8) and (9) imply that $a_S^I/(1-\delta) < a_F^I/\delta$ where I = B1 and B2. Therefore, by P2,

$$E\left[\cos\theta^{B1}\right] > E\left[\cos\theta^{B2}\right] \quad \text{and} \quad E\left[\omega_S^{B1}\right] < E\left[\omega_S^{B2}\right] \tag{10}$$

where the operator $E[\cdot]$ indicates the conditional mean of each type (indicated by a superscript). A son in a B1 family, who pays a cost just as high as his father did to invest in T skills, works in an occupation similar to his father's; however, this son receives lower wages when compared to a son in a B2 family, who pays less than his father to acquire T skills. Thus, between B1 and B2 families, there is a negative relation between the father–son skill correlation and the son's wages.[13]

3. *A comparison between sons of white families and B2 black families*: Sons in B2 black families and in white families pay the same cost to invest in

---

12. Bacolod and Blum (2010), for example, find that the returns to working in occupations that require cognitive skills increased fourfold, based on the 1968–1990 Current Population Survey.

13. P2 and Eqs. (8) and (9) imply that for any given $x \in [0, 1]$, $\cos\theta^{B1} > \cos\theta^{B2}$ and $\omega_S^{B1} < \omega_S^{B2}$ because a_S varies. On the other hand, by reasoning similar to the first prediction for white families, there will be a positive relation within each black family type (B1 or B2) between the father–son skill correlation and the son's wages because x varies. Therefore, within black families comprising B1 and B2 families, there will be a negative (positive) relation between the father–son skill correlation and the son's wages, if the variations in $\cos\theta$ and ω_S are greater (smaller) across B1 and B2 families than within each black family type. Details are available from the authors upon request. We will examine which relation holds for black families in the empirical sections 4 and 5.

T skills $\left(a_{\mathrm{S}}^{\mathrm{B2}}=a_{\mathrm{S}}^{\mathrm{W}}\right)$, but B2 black fathers pay a higher cost to invest in T skills than do white fathers $\left(a_{\mathrm{F}}^{\mathrm{B2}}>a_{\mathrm{F}}^{\mathrm{W}}\right)$. Comparing these two family types enables us to study the effects of the insufficient investment in cognitive skills for black fathers on the earnings of the later generation. By P3, since $a_{\mathrm{S}}^{1}/(1-\delta)<a_{\mathrm{F}}^{1}/\delta$, where $\mathrm{I}=\mathrm{B2}$ and W,

$$E\left[\cos\theta^{\mathrm{B2}}\right]<E\left[\cos\theta^{\mathrm{W}}\right] \quad \text{and} \quad E\left[\omega_{\mathrm{S}}^{\mathrm{B2}}\right]\leq E\left[\omega_{\mathrm{S}}^{\mathrm{W}}\right] \tag{11}$$

where the equality holds if x is equal to zero. Compared to white sons, black sons in B2-type families work in occupations requiring skill combinations that differ from those of their fathers, and they earn lower wages. This wage gap between B2-type black sons and white sons is attributable to the difference in skills obtained by their fathers, because the costs to acquire skills are the same for both sets of sons $\left(a_{\mathrm{S}}^{\mathrm{B2}}=a_{\mathrm{S}}^{\mathrm{W}}\right)$. Neal (2006) shows that the black–white difference in the fathers' cost of investing in cognitive skills influences their sons' human capital gap and thus their wage gap. Our explanation follows his argument. However, as P4 implies, when there is skill complementarity, the black–white difference in the father's costs of investing in cognitive skills widens the black–white gap in the son's attainment of both cognitive and other complementary skills, resulting in further widening of the black–white wage gap.

From Eqs. (10) and (11), the B1 black son receives the lowest wage, the B2 black son the second lowest, and the white son the highest $\left(E\left[\omega_{\mathrm{S}}^{\mathrm{B1}}\right]<E\left[\omega_{\mathrm{S}}^{\mathrm{B2}}\right]\leq E\left[\omega_{\mathrm{S}}^{\mathrm{W}}\right]\right)$. That is, wages of black sons are lower than those of white sons. Skill correlations between father and son are greater for both white and B1 black families than for B2 black families; however, the relative magnitudes of the skill correlations are indeterminate between white and B1 black families $\left(E\left[\cos\theta^{\mathrm{W}}\right]>E\left[\cos\theta^{\mathrm{B2}}\right]\right.$ and $\left.E\left[\cos\theta^{\mathrm{B1}}\right]>E\left[\cos\theta^{\mathrm{B2}}\right]\right)$.

In the empirical sections that follow, the skill components will be represented by 39 occupational characteristics from the Dictionary of Occupational Titles (DOT). We thus expand the number of skill components from two to $N(=39)$. The father's skill vector is expressed as

$$\Psi_{\mathrm{F}}=\left(\psi_{\mathrm{F}}^{1},\psi_{\mathrm{F}}^{2},...,\psi_{\mathrm{F}}^{N}\right)$$

where $\psi_{\mathrm{F}}^{1}, \psi_{\mathrm{F}}^{2}, ..., \psi_{\mathrm{F}}^{N}$ are the father's skill components. Similarly, the son's skill vector is expressed as

$$\Psi_{\mathrm{S}}=\left(\psi_{\mathrm{S}}^{1},\psi_{\mathrm{S}}^{2},...,\psi_{\mathrm{S}}^{N}\right)$$

where $\psi_{\mathrm{S}}^{1}, \psi_{\mathrm{S}}^{2}, ..., \psi_{\mathrm{S}}^{N}$ are the son's skill components. The model uses the cosine of the angle θ between the two skill vectors Ψ_{F} and Ψ_{S}, which measures the closeness of the direction of the two skill vectors.[14] However, in the empirical analysis below, we compute the correlation coefficient between the two vectors because it is a more widely used statistic for assessing correlations.[15]

3. DATA AND DESCRIPTIVE STATISTICS

3.1. Dictionary of Occupational Titles (DOT)

We draw on information about occupational characteristics from the fourth edition (1977) and revised fourth edition (1991) of the U.S. Department of Labor's Dictionary of Occupational Titles (DOT). Using guidelines supplied by the *Handbook for Analyzing Jobs*, the Department of Labor examiners evaluated more than 12,000 occupations along objective and subjective dimensions, including work functions, general

---

14. Several occupational-distance measures have been developed to identify transferability of skills across occupations. Shaw (1984, 1987) measured the distance between two occupations by the frequency with which workers switch between the two occupations. A high probability of such movement implies greater similarity in occupational skills. More recently, Poletaev and Robinson (2008) used a distance measure based on the factor-score change to define similar occupations. Like our study, Gathmann and Schönberg (2010) use a measure of one minus the cosine.

15. The cosine of the angle θ between Ψ_F and Ψ_S is defined as

$$\cos \theta = \frac{\Psi_F \cdot \Psi_S}{\|\Psi_F\| \|\Psi_S\|} = \frac{\sum_{n=1}^{N} \psi_F^n \psi_S^n}{\sqrt{\sum_{n=1}^{N} (\psi_F^n)^2} \sqrt{\sum_{n=1}^{N} (\psi_S^n)^2}}$$

On the other hand, the correlation coefficient between between Ψ_F and Ψ_S is defined as

$$r = \frac{\sum_{n=1}^{N} \left(\psi_F^n - \frac{1}{N} \sum_{n=1}^{N} \psi_F^n \right) \left(\psi_S^n - \frac{1}{N} \sum_{n=1}^{N} \psi_S^n \right)}{\sqrt{\sum_{n=1}^{N} \left(\psi_F^n - \frac{1}{N} \sum_{n=1}^{N} \psi_F^n \right)^2} \sqrt{\sum_{n=1}^{N} \left(\psi_S^n - \frac{1}{N} \sum_{n=1}^{N} \psi_S^n \right)^2}}$$

Wonnacott and Wonnacott (1979) explain that the correlation coefficient between the two vectors is identical to the cosine, except that the former uses the deviation from the mean.

educational development, worker aptitudes, temperaments, interests, physical strength, and environmental conditions.[16] The DOT characteristics represent not only skills related to education (e.g., reasoning ability, mathematical ability, and language development), but also skills related to individuals' personality traits (e.g., adaptability to dealing with people and preference for activities involving business contacts with people) and to their motor aptitude (e.g., ability to perceive forms and spaces). The data in the fourth edition of the DOT (1977) were collected between 1966 and 1976, while those in the revised fourth edition of the DOT (1991) were collected between 1978 and 1990. The 1977 DOT skill measures therefore describe occupations in the 1970s (which overlap with fathers' occupations in our study), while the 1991 measures describe occupations in the 1980s (overlapping with the sons' occupations).[17] All DOT variables are standardized to have a mean of 0 and a standard deviation of 1 in the 1971 CPS distribution. The textual definitions of DOT variables are used to identify four broad skill categories: cognitive skills, people skills, motor skills, and physical strength.[18] The DOT variables are described in detail in Table A1.

---

16. The DOT has been used for job-matching applications, occupational and career guidance, employment counseling, and labor-market information services.

17. Since DOT job codes are more detailed than census occupational codes, they are mapped to the 1970 census occupational codes at the three-digit level. Following Autor, Levy, and Murnane (2003), we use the April 1971 Current Population Survey issued by the National Academy of Sciences (1981), in which experts assign individual DOT job codes to each of the 60,441 workers in the sample. The DOT measures are rescaled so that higher values denote higher requirements, and are transformed into percentile values corresponding to their ranks in the 1971 distribution of skill input. Then, they are standardized to a mean of 0 and a standard deviation of 1. The 1971 CPS sampling weights are used to calculate the means of each DOT characteristic by occupation and gender. In cases where an occupation cell exclusively contains men or women, the cell mean is assigned to both genders. To verify that our results are robust to plausible alternative selections of the DOT variables, we use raw DOT scores in a separate analysis, results of which are qualitatively identical.

18. These skill classifications are also used by Bacolod and Blum (2010), who analyze changes in skill requirements and skill returns in the U.S. On the other hand, Ingram and Neumann (2006) use a factor analysis on the DOT data from the revised fourth edition (1991) to identify a parsimonious set of dimensions: intelligence, fine motor skill, coordination, and strength (which is negatively related to people skills). We also implement a factor analysis to corroborate our choice of skill categories. Most of our skill categorizations are consistent with the grouping from the factor analysis.

3.2. National Longitudinal Survey of Youth 1979 (NLSY79)

This survey is sponsored by the Bureau of Labor Statistics of the U.S. Department of Labor, which gathers information at multiple points in time on individuals who were aged between 14 and 22 in 1979 when they were first surveyed. In addition to its cross-sectional sample, we include respondents from the supplemental sample of blacks but do not include those from the supplemental samples of Hispanics, economically disadvantaged whites, or military personnel. This procedure ensures that our samples are representative of both black and white populations.[19]

To obtain skill measures for NLSY79 fathers, we match fathers' occupations at the three-digit level when the sons (respondents) were aged 14 to the fourth edition of the DOT and let DOT skills stand for the fathers' skills.[20] For sons, a match of occupation is incorporated in both the fourth edition (1977) and the revised fourth edition (1991), but the results are similar in the two editions. Therefore, we report those from the fourth edition of the DOT (1977).[21]

---

19. To construct indicators for white and black, we follow Neal (2004, 2006), who constructed the white indicator to match the census definition of white. Thus, respondents who report being Asian are excluded in the sample. Also, our sample includes sons from all birth years, as in Neal (2006).

20. In 1979, the respondents were asked two questions regarding their father's occupation: (1) father's occupation when the respondent was age 14 and (2) father's occupation in the job he held the longest in 1978. The information on father's occupation when the respondent was age 14 is a more appropriate measure in our study, because the fathers presumably have a greater influence on the child's development (and skill acquisition) when the child is younger (age 14) than when the child is older (in 1978). Therefore, in constructing the father's occupation variable, we use the father's occupation when the respondent was age 14; but if this information is missing, we use the father's occupation in 1978. We obtain similar results when we do the other way around: i.e., when we use the father's occupation in 1979, and if this information is missing, we use the father's occupation when the respondent was age 14. For the respondent's occupation, we use his occupation at the current/most recent job held since the last interview (CPS job). If the respondents worked for more than one employer (i.e., held multiple occupations), the CPS jobs are the jobs at which they report working the most hours during the last week (or the jobs at which they worked most recently).

21. We assume that the workers hold occupations that match their traits and personalities. This assumption corresponds to the assignment model of interpersonal interaction developed by Borghans, ter Weel, and Weinberg (2008). Their model indicates that a worker's behavior is determined by job circumstances and the worker's personality, and that a worker with a comparative advantage in a certain behavior will be assigned to the job which demands that behavior more. They empirically test and confirm these model implications. Alternatively, Borghans, ter Weel, and Weinberg (2014) and Okumura and Usui (2014) find that self-reported sociability measures have a large and positive association with their people-task measures from the DOT.

Following studies by Neal and Johnson (1996) and Neal (2006), we use the Armed Forces Qualification Test (AFQT) as a measure of cognitive skills for sons (respondents). The AFQT, a battery of tests of basic numeracy and literacy, is used by the military for enlistment, screening, and job assignments. It was administered to almost the entire NLSY79 sample. Wigdor and Green (1991) find that the AFQT does not underpredict military job performance for blacks and is not otherwise biased with respect to blacks or whites. Test scores have been age-standardized, such that they have a mean of 0 and a standard deviation of 1.

3.3. Descriptive Statistics

We provide facts regarding the differences in the black–white skill gap between fathers and sons in the NLSY79 sample. Table 1 presents means and standard deviations of demographic characteristics and occupational skills of fathers and sons. We have information about fathers at one point in time, but for sons we have multiple-year observations, and we report the means and standard deviations for the 1993 and 2000 waves.[22] In the 1993 wave, sons (i.e., NLSY79 respondents) were aged between 28 and 36, and, on average, 11 years younger than their fathers were when the information on the latter's occupations was available. Education levels are: 12.5 years for white fathers, 10.4 for black fathers, 13.5 for white sons, and 12.6 for black sons. There is a greater increase in education level across the two generations for blacks than for whites, although black sons' education level remains lower than that of white sons.[23]

---

22. In the 1993 wave, the response rate excluding the deceased is the highest after the 1990 wave. The 2000 wave is the last year in which the respondent's occupation is coded with the three-digit 1970 census occupation codes. As reported in Table 1, the sample size is 1,854 for white fathers and 715 for black fathers; here, we use fathers for whom we have valid information on their education and occupation, and whose sons were interviewed in the 1993 wave. The sample size is 1,752 for white sons and 601 for black sons in the 1993 wave; here, we use sons for whom we have valid information on fathers' education and occupation and who themselves reported valid information on their education and occupation.
23. Similarly, relative to whites, the proportion of blacks who work in professional or managerial occupations increases from fathers to sons. The percentage of whites working for pay is 95.2 percent for fathers and 97.1 percent for sons, while the percentage of blacks working for pay is lower: 90.0 percent for fathers and 90.3 percent for sons.

Table 1. Comparison of Means and Standard Deviations of Selected Variables.

Variable	Father				Son, 1993 Wave				Son, 2000 Wave			
	Whites		Blacks		Whites		Blacks		Whites		Blacks	
	Mean	SD	Mean	SD	Mean	SD	Mean	SD	Mean	SD	Mean	SD
Age	43.126	6.768	42.853	7.270	32.094	2.294	31.816	2.267	39.133	2.304	38.926	2.274
Education	12.494	3.331	10.442	3.281	13.506	2.628	12.588	2.253	13.659	2.731	12.735	2.291
Experience					10.926	3.942	9.121	4.162	17.646	4.669	14.938	5.646
Log(wage)					2.429	0.519	2.109	0.499	2.639	0.578	2.256	0.517
Cognitive skills												
Math	0.316	0.839	−0.360	0.767	0.257	0.837	−0.265	0.849	0.377	0.829	−0.138	0.898
Reasoning	0.305	0.816	−0.362	0.757	0.259	0.847	−0.271	0.881	0.379	0.815	−0.124	0.904
Language	0.205	0.828	−0.440	0.725	0.168	0.839	−0.327	0.851	0.273	0.814	−0.204	0.873
General Learning	0.269	0.798	−0.329	0.652	0.226	0.796	−0.234	0.795	0.322	0.788	−0.115	0.820
Verbal	0.184	0.880	−0.468	0.741	0.171	0.888	−0.300	0.872	0.278	0.866	−0.199	0.906
Numerical	0.289	0.821	−0.369	0.739	0.243	0.821	−0.232	0.819	0.327	0.806	−0.114	0.824
Creative Activity	0.350	0.703	−0.175	0.801	0.286	0.749	−0.135	0.826	0.387	0.687	−0.029	0.826
Plan Activity	0.312	0.961	−0.172	0.700	0.236	0.905	−0.116	0.690	0.393	0.955	0.040	0.838
Data	0.376	0.866	−0.303	0.868	0.332	0.902	−0.225	0.902	0.464	0.884	−0.064	0.975
People skills												
Deal with People	−0.101	0.860	−0.422	0.755	−0.079	0.843	−0.317	0.787	0.009	0.846	−0.201	0.822
Talking, Hearing	−0.050	0.839	−0.409	0.772	0.016	0.814	−0.285	0.808	0.116	0.799	−0.178	0.823
Communicate Data	−0.076	0.834	−0.469	0.670	−0.009	0.810	−0.268	0.805	0.042	0.788	−0.205	0.775
Business Contact	−0.112	0.872	−0.241	0.626	−0.096	0.868	−0.191	0.688	−0.053	0.887	−0.134	0.738
Good of People	−0.305	0.806	−0.484	0.697	−0.241	0.758	−0.219	0.764	−0.240	0.769	−0.280	0.764
People	0.136	0.864	−0.304	0.746	0.107	0.832	−0.208	0.805	0.213	0.814	−0.078	0.826

Motor skills												
Motor Coordination	0.015	0.693	0.138	0.591	−0.078	0.691	−0.093	0.666	−0.107	0.682	−0.105	0.634
Form Perception	0.181	0.720	−0.139	0.681	0.130	0.684	−0.205	0.665	0.153	0.666	−0.139	0.667
Spatial Perception	0.477	0.748	0.350	0.699	0.387	0.743	0.103	0.710	0.436	0.734	0.233	0.710
Finger Dexterity	−0.083	0.748	−0.184	0.645	−0.133	0.721	−0.273	0.656	−0.166	0.711	−0.313	0.607
Manual Dexterity	−0.039	0.896	0.294	0.681	−0.089	0.896	0.091	0.749	−0.139	0.915	−0.023	0.779
Eye-Hand-Foot Coord.	0.149	0.845	0.488	0.847	0.098	0.808	0.271	0.846	0.092	0.790	0.280	0.851
Precisely Set Limits	0.035	0.819	0.107	0.769	0.018	0.778	0.022	0.739	−0.054	0.770	−0.049	0.746
Make Judgments	0.398	0.779	0.182	0.756	0.348	0.759	0.053	0.724	0.371	0.746	0.090	0.750
Perform Variety of Duties	−0.004	0.684	−0.135	0.692	0.005	0.652	−0.151	0.636	0.036	0.637	−0.115	0.638
Things	0.132	0.891	0.182	0.745	0.030	0.863	−0.049	0.776	0.010	0.867	−0.022	0.780
Physical strength												
Strength	0.117	0.859	0.614	0.654	0.039	0.876	0.417	0.826	−0.044	0.882	0.306	0.824
Climbing	0.192	0.914	0.319	0.914	0.137	0.883	0.223	0.900	0.074	0.830	0.149	0.836
Stooping	0.096	0.828	0.432	0.825	0.063	0.829	0.229	0.843	0.001	0.801	0.165	0.814
Reaching	−0.214	0.894	0.260	0.576	−0.248	0.893	0.067	0.760	−0.359	0.916	−0.063	0.824
Seeing	0.113	0.717	0.191	0.619	0.066	0.704	0.037	0.676	0.019	0.705	0.027	0.668
N	1,854		715		1,752		601		1,594		564	

Note: The numbers in the table are the means of the row variables conditional on column segments of the sample. The DOT data are matched to the individuals' 1970 census occupation.

The DOT cognitive- and people-skill variables increase between the 1993 and 2000 waves for both white and black sons. For white sons in the 2000 wave, the variables are slightly higher than those for their fathers, but this is not the case in the 1993 wave. For black sons, the variables are higher in both waves, and in the 2000 wave are about 0.2 points higher than those for their fathers. The increase in these DOT skills for blacks parallels their growth in education levels. However, just as white sons continue to have, on average, a higher educational level than black sons, white sons in the 2000 wave continue to have higher DOT scores for both cognitive and people skills than black sons.

Most of the DOT motor-skill variables and all of the DOT physical-strength variables decline from fathers to sons for both whites and blacks. This decline is greater for blacks than whites; in particular, the decrease in "manual dexterity" and "strength" is especially large for blacks. Although the black−white gaps in the DOT physical-strength variables narrow from fathers to sons, these scores remain higher for blacks than for whites in the 2000 wave.

In summary, black−white skill gaps narrowed between fathers and sons in the NLSY79 sample, but significant black−white skill gaps remain among sons.

4. SKILL CORRELATION BETWEEN FATHER AND SON

We begin this section by showing that each of the DOT skills is related between father and son for both whites and blacks. We then study differences between blacks and whites in the overall skill correlation by computing the correlation coefficient between the father's and the son's skill vectors.

4.1. Correlation by Each Skill Component

In Table 2, we display the correlation matrix of father−son skills separately for whites and blacks, with information for sons taken from the 1993 wave. The on- and off-diagonal correlations are large and positive within the categories of cognitive and people skills. The on-diagonal correlations within the category of motor skills are somewhat large and positive, but

Table 2. Correlation Matrix of Father–Son DOT Skills.

Whites — Father (rows) × Son (columns)

	[C]					[P]				[M]				[Ph]
Father	Educ.	Math	Reas.	Lang.	General learning	Talk	Deal w/ people	Comm. data	Business contact	Manual dexterity	Eye-hand-foot	Form percep.	Precisely set limits	Strength
Education	0.476	0.244	0.283	0.318	0.293	0.262	0.256	0.309	0.068	-0.208	-0.214	0.030	-0.189	-0.283
[C] Math	0.369	0.208	0.210	0.236	0.220	0.181	0.160	0.183	0.013	-0.121	-0.125	0.051	-0.113	-0.195
Reason	0.418	0.237	0.256	0.284	0.262	0.220	0.183	0.228	0.009	-0.144	-0.148	0.045	-0.133	-0.236
Language	0.434	0.228	0.246	0.284	0.259	0.229	0.207	0.245	0.040	-0.162	-0.163	0.026	-0.156	-0.243
General learning	0.427	0.238	0.254	0.285	0.274	0.225	0.203	0.244	0.033	-0.158	-0.149	0.046	-0.155	-0.239
[P] Talk	0.306	0.158	0.196	0.233	0.198	0.225	0.191	0.227	0.074	-0.141	-0.116	0.005	-0.141	-0.193
Deal w/people	0.284	0.150	0.186	0.215	0.195	0.212	0.203	0.224	0.091	-0.138	-0.110	-0.002	-0.152	-0.183
Comm. data	0.318	0.174	0.207	0.239	0.222	0.227	0.209	0.244	0.088	-0.146	-0.129	0.004	-0.162	-0.208
Business contact	0.043	0.032	0.055	0.062	0.052	0.100	0.094	0.094	0.098	-0.050	-0.018	-0.005	-0.051	-0.063
[M] Manual dexterity	-0.228	-0.140	-0.154	-0.179	-0.165	-0.160	-0.150	-0.170	-0.073	0.123	0.083	0.009	0.120	0.169
Eye-hand-foot	-0.257	-0.143	-0.155	-0.180	-0.154	-0.196	-0.177	-0.197	-0.084	0.121	0.131	-0.012	0.108	0.191
Form percep.	0.117	0.044	0.044	0.036	0.033	0.008	0.002	0.011	-0.053	0.026	-0.014	0.088	0.005	-0.015
Precisely set limits	-0.202	-0.115	-0.146	-0.166	-0.162	-0.170	-0.166	-0.175	-0.090	0.120	0.074	0.025	0.145	0.134
[Ph] Strength	-0.358	-0.211	-0.236	-0.266	-0.243	-0.243	-0.219	-0.258	-0.071	0.159	0.142	-0.027	0.149	0.251

Table 2. (Continued)

| | | | | | Son | | | | | | | | | |
| | | [C] | | | | | [P] | | | | [M] | | | | [Ph] |
Father		Educ.	Math	Reas.	Lang.	General learning	Talk	Deal w/ people	Comm. data	Business contact	Manual dexterity	Eye-hand-foot	Form percep.	Precisely set limits	Strength
Blacks															
	Education	0.294	0.172	0.188	0.191	0.191	0.220	0.222	0.240	0.126	-0.105	-0.131	0.074	-0.101	-0.195
[C]	Math	0.207	0.157	0.177	0.185	0.183	0.120	0.113	0.142	0.053	-0.053	-0.043	0.120	-0.053	-0.144
	Reason	0.227	0.203	0.225	0.226	0.230	0.149	0.151	0.171	0.082	-0.068	-0.048	0.137	-0.035	-0.177
	Language	0.217	0.191	0.216	0.230	0.231	0.174	0.168	0.190	0.108	-0.080	-0.089	0.111	-0.051	-0.188
	General learning	0.215	0.199	0.228	0.227	0.239	0.177	0.181	0.202	0.107	-0.101	-0.089	0.114	-0.055	-0.196
[P]	Talk	0.133	0.161	0.174	0.172	0.172	0.131	0.116	0.140	0.097	-0.070	-0.052	0.088	-0.018	-0.157
	Deal w/ people	0.115	0.148	0.164	0.173	0.171	0.148	0.156	0.157	0.135	-0.119	-0.086	0.029	-0.057	-0.166
	Comm. data	0.149	0.176	0.184	0.200	0.202	0.173	0.183	0.181	0.160	-0.159	-0.120	0.039	-0.060	-0.203
	Business contact	0.037	0.080	0.069	0.081	0.091	0.048	0.078	0.090	0.085	-0.078	-0.056	-0.005	-0.039	-0.104
[M]	Manual dexterity	-0.074	-0.056	-0.063	-0.067	-0.086	-0.075	-0.098	-0.076	-0.090	0.050	0.101	-0.019	0.016	0.070
	Eye-hand-foot	-0.146	-0.105	-0.093	-0.145	-0.115	-0.128	-0.134	-0.126	-0.094	0.105	0.109	-0.007	0.047	0.136
	Form percep.	0.155	0.113	0.122	0.142	0.127	0.060	0.085	0.095	0.036	-0.067	-0.018	0.084	-0.035	-0.141
	Precisely set limits	0.052	-0.020	-0.047	-0.035	-0.063	-0.085	-0.066	-0.070	-0.079	0.054	0.088	0.044	0.041	0.046
[Ph]	Strength	-0.214	-0.187	-0.211	-0.216	-0.220	-0.188	-0.218	-0.221	-0.143	0.133	0.100	-0.083	0.077	0.200

Notes: The sons' information is taken from the 1993 wave. See Table A1 for a detailed description of the DOT skill variables. [C] stands for cognitive skills, [P] for people skills, [M] for motor skills, and [Ph] for physical strength.

the off-diagonal correlations are smaller and take both positive and negative values. Most correlations between father and son are greater for whites than for blacks.

Table 3 presents estimates of the effect of fathers' DOT skill variables on the corresponding DOT skill variables of the sons, using the sons' sample between 1990 and 2000 (separately for blacks and whites). The regressions include sons' education, a quadratic in sons' AFQT score, a cubic in sons' labor-market experience, sons' place of residence, fathers' education, a dummy for whether father and son work in the same occupation, and year dummies. Most of the DOT skill variables (including cognitive, people, and motor skills and physical strength) for white fathers have a large positive and significant relationship with the corresponding DOT skill variables of the white sons. Black fathers' motor-skill variables have a positive and significant relationship with the corresponding motor-skill variables for black sons. The magnitudes of these associations are about the same as those of the associations of white fathers' motor-skill variables with those for white sons. Although several cognitive-skill and people-skill variables for black fathers have a positive and significant association with the black sons, all the physical-strength variables for black fathers have a small and insignificant association with the black sons. We then include a term that interacts the father's DOT skill variable with the son's labor-market experience in the regression model, using the sons' sample between 1979 and 2000. The coefficients for this term are positive for most DOT skill variables for white father–son pairs, but are positive only for a few black father–son pairs (not reported). This indicates that sons' occupational skills draw closer to their fathers' skills over time for whites but not for blacks.

In sum, each of the fathers' skill sets is positively linked to the sons' corresponding skill set, but the link is stronger for whites than for blacks.

4.2. Overall Skill Correlation

To measure skill correlation between father and son, Table 4 reports the mean and standard deviation of the correlation coefficient of the father's and the son's skill vectors. The individual's skill vector is composed of the DOT skill variables listed in Table A1, and Table 4 presents the correlation

Table 3.   Effect of Father's DOT Skills on Son's DOT Skills.

Independent Variables: Separate Regression for Each DOT Skill	Whites	Blacks	Independent Variables: Separate Regression for Each DOT Skill	Whites	Blacks
Cognitive Skills			Motor Skills		
Father's Math	0.049***	0.006	Father's Spatial Perception	0.056***	0.089***
	(0.019)	(0.031)		(0.019)	(0.031)
Father's Reason	0.044**	0.029	Father's Manual Dexterity	0.033*	0.063**
	(0.019)	(0.032)		(0.020)	(0.032)
Father's General Intelligence	0.048***	0.057*	Father's Eye-Hand-Foot Coordination	0.043**	0.061**
	(0.018)	(0.033)		(0.018)	(0.028)
Father's Verbal	0.056***	0.060*	Father's Form Perception	0.043**	0.048*
	(0.019)	(0.035)		(0.018)	(0.029)
Father's Plan Activity	0.054***	−0.006	Father's Finger Dexterity	0.036*	0.073**
	(0.017)	(0.027)		(0.019)	(0.030)
Father's Make Evaluations	0.042**	0.052*	Father's Precisely Set Limits	0.077***	0.081***
	(0.018)	(0.030)		(0.018)	(0.028)
Father's Data	0.060***	0.024	Father's Things	0.041**	0.075**
	(0.020)	(0.029)		(0.018)	(0.031)
People Skills			Physical Strength		
Father's Dealing with People	0.069***	0.090**	Father's Strength	0.072***	0.056
	(0.018)	(0.033)		(0.019)	(0.037)
Father's Talking/Hearing	0.068***	0.039	Father's Climbing	0.085***	0.042
	(0.018)	(0.029)		(0.019)	(0.028)
Father's Communicate Data	0.052***	0.063*	Father's Stooping	0.054***	0.015
	(0.018)	(0.038)		(0.019)	(0.028)
Father's Business Contact	0.084***	0.037	Father's Reaching	0.054***	0.018
	(0.021)	(0.037)		(0.019)	(0.045)
Father's People	0.046***	0.074***	Father's Seeing	0.069***	0.048
	(0.018)	(0.028)		(0.018)	(0.031)

Notes: This table presents estimates of the effect of the father's DOT skill variables (row variable) on the son's corresponding DOT skill variables using the NLSY79 sample between 1990 and 2000. Regressions include son's education, a quadratic in son's AFQT score, a cubic in son's labor-market experience, son's place of residence, father's education, a dummy for whether father and son work in the same occupation, and year dummies. Robust standard errors clustered at the individual level are in parentheses. *$p < 0.1$, **$p < 0.05$, ***$p < 0.01$.

Table 4. Means and Standard Deviations of the Correlation Coefficient of Father–Son Skill Vectors.

Father's Education	Whites						Blacks					
	Correlation Coefficient All Father–Son Pairs		Correlation Coefficient Exclude Pairs in Same Occupation		Fraction of Father–Son Pairs in Same Occupation		Correlation Coefficient All Father–Son Pairs		Correlation Coefficient Exclude Pairs in Same Occupation		Fraction of Father–Son Pairs in Same Occupation	
	Mean	SD	Mean	SD	Mean	SD	Mean	SD	Mean	SD	Mean	SD
1993 Wave												
Less than high school	0.191	0.512	0.143	0.486	0.056	0.231	0.297	0.484	0.266	0.472	0.042	0.201
	N=467		N=441		N=467		N=313		N=301		N=313	
High school	0.153	0.516	0.102	0.486	0.058	0.234	0.143	0.463	0.129	0.453	0.016	0.127
	N=647		N=611		N=647		N=209		N=206		N=209	
Some college	0.163	0.525	0.110	0.496	0.059	0.236	0.019	0.461	0.019	0.461	0.000	0.000
	N=232		N=218		N=232		N=43		N=43		N=43	
College	0.265	0.478	0.234	0.464	0.040	0.195	0.252	0.510	0.214	0.493	0.049	0.219
	N=406		N=391		N=406		N=36		N=34		N=36	
Total	0.191	0.509	0.146	0.485	0.053	0.225	0.216	0.484	0.192	0.471	0.030	0.170
	N=1,752		N=1,661		N=1,752		N=601		N=584		N=601	
2000 Wave												
Less than high school	0.172	0.521	0.114	0.489	0.066	0.249	0.228	0.514	0.196	0.499	0.040	0.196
	N=434		N=405		N=434		N=292		N=280		N=292	
High school	0.169	0.530	0.103	0.494	0.073	0.261	0.059	0.492	0.033	0.473	0.027	0.161
	N=592		N=551		N=592		N=200		N=195		N=200	
Some college	0.188	0.536	0.142	0.514	0.053	0.225	-0.044	0.440	-0.044	0.440	0.000	0.000
	N=212		N=201		N=212		N=39		N=39		N=39	
College	0.331	0.468	0.287	0.450	0.061	0.240	0.267	0.489	0.203	0.456	0.080	0.275
	N=356		N=334		N=356		N=33		N=31		N=33	
Total	0.210	0.519	0.154	0.491	0.066	0.248	0.147	0.507	0.117	0.490	0.034	0.182
	N=1,594		N=1,491		N=1,594		N=564		N=545		N=564	

Notes: The numbers in the table are means and standard deviations of the column variables conditional on row segments. The correlation coefficient between the father's skill vector and the son's vector is computed using all the DOT skill variables. See Table A1 for a detailed description of the DOT skill variables.

coefficient for using all the DOT skills (39 variables).[24] Data for sons are taken from the 1993 and 2000 waves (reported separately by year and race).

For white fathers and sons in the 1993 wave, skill correlation rises as fathers' education increases, from 0.153 for fathers with high-school education to 0.265 for fathers with college education. In the 2000 wave, the skill correlations for fathers with high-school education and college education increase to 0.169 and to 0.331, respectively.[25]

In the 1993 wave, 5.3 percent of white fathers and sons work in the same occupation, and these pairs raise the correlation coefficients because their correlation coefficients are one. When we exclude these father–son pairs, the correlation coefficient drops by 0.046; the correlation coefficient then ranges between 0.102 and 0.234 and continues to increase with the father's education level. Skill correlation remains even when father–son pairs who work in the same occupation have been excluded.

For black fathers and sons in the 1993 wave, skill correlation is 0.297 for fathers with less-than-high-school education, 0.143 for those with a high-school education, 0.019 for those with some college education, and 0.252 for those with college education. Sons of the least educated (less-than-high-school) and the most highly educated (college-educated) black fathers work in occupations similar to their fathers'.[26] In general, there is a greater skill correlation within those white and black families with highly educated fathers. There is also a skill correlation for black families with the least-educated fathers. Between the 1993 and 2000 waves, skill correlation within white families has increased, but skill correlation for black families has declined; in particular, skill correlation for black families with fathers with high-school education is reduced from 0.143 in the 1993 wave to 0.059 in the 2000 wave.

To get a better understanding of skill correlation between father and son, the cumulative distribution functions (c.d.f.) of the correlation

---

24. In an alternative analysis, by assuming that a subset of DOT variables measures a single skill, we construct a cognitive-skill index that is derived from the first component of the principal component analysis on DOT cognitive skills (for textual definitions, see Table A1). Likewise, we construct a people-skill index, a motor-skill index, and a physical-strength index. We then compute the correlation coefficient of these indices between father and son. The results using this measure are similar to those presented in this paper.

25. Note that the proportion of white sons who work in the same occupation as their fathers also increases from 5.3 percent in 1993 to 6.6 percent in 2000, whereas for black sons, the corresponding numbers are 3.0 percent in 1993 and 3.4 percent in 2000.

26. The correlation coefficient remains high for these groups in the 2000 wave: 0.228 for fathers with less-than-high-school education and 0.267 for those with college education.

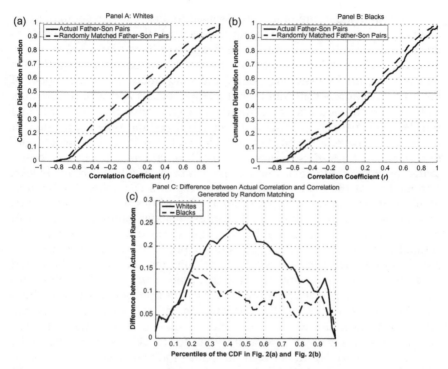

Fig. 2. Distribution of Correlation Coefficients for Father−Son Pairs: (a) whites, (b) blacks, and (c) difference between actual correlation and correlation generated by random matching.

Notes: The sons' information is taken from the 1993 wave. The correlation coefficient between father−son skill vectors is computed using the DOT skill variables listed in Table A1. Fig. 2(c) takes the difference between the actual correlation coefficient and the randomly matched correlation coefficient by the percentiles of the CDF in Fig. 2(a) for whites and Fig. 2(b) for blacks.

coefficient between father and son for whites in the 1993 wave are shown in Fig. 2(a) and for blacks in Fig. 2(b). The c.d.f. distribution, represented by the solid line, is skewed toward the left for both whites and blacks, suggesting positive skill correlations.[27]

---

27. The median of the distribution of the correlation coefficient is 0.252 for whites and 0.258 for blacks, while the mean is 0.193 for whites and 0.219 for blacks.

Even if individuals are randomly assigned to different skill combinations, however, skill correlation may occur, especially if the skill sets available to them are limited. To consider this, we compute skill correlations that will be observed under random allocation. Specifically, we construct hypothetical father—son pairs by matching fathers and sons randomly from the pool of the NLSY79 father—son sample (but keeping blacks and whites separate), and then we compute the correlation coefficients between these father and son. We repeat these simulations a hundred times and take the average of the generated correlation coefficients. The c.d.f. distribution of the correlation coefficient for these randomly matched father—son pairs is represented by the dotted line in Fig. 2(a) for whites and in Fig. 2(b) for blacks. The median of the distribution of the correlation coefficient for the randomly matched father—son pairs is 0.011 for whites but 0.199 for blacks; this implies a positive skill correlation even under random matching of fathers and sons for blacks but not for whites. The differences between the actual father—son pairs (solid line) and the randomly matched father—son pairs (dotted line) represent skill correlations that go beyond those that occur under random matching of fathers and sons. Fig. 2(c) plots this difference by the percentile of the c.d.f. distribution (separately for whites and blacks). Relative to the distribution of the randomly matched father—son pairs, the actual distribution is skewed more toward the left, and the skewness is greater for whites than for blacks. We therefore find a large positive correlation between the skills of actual father—son pairs for whites. In contrast, for blacks, the actual distribution of correlation coefficients makes a rather small parallel rightward shift from the correlations generated by random matching; this implies that skill sets available to black fathers and sons are limited, and that the correlations of skills across generations for blacks are closer to a random matching.

5. ECONOMIC RETURNS TO FATHER—SON SKILL CORRELATION

The theoretical analysis of Laband and Lentz (1983) offers two reasons for occupational following. First, sons inherit name-brand loyalty capital from their fathers, where value is maximized when sons work in the same occupation as their fathers, the so-called "nepotism." Second, sons receive a direct transfer of career-related human capital by way of informal "on-the-job training" from their fathers. Lentz and Laband (1989) and Laband and Lentz (1992) test evidence for nepotism versus transfer of career-related human capital in two professions, those of doctors and lawyers. In their 1989 paper, they found evidence of the transmission of career-related human capital for lawyers, because lawyers' sons who follow in their parents' occupational footsteps receive an earning premium only if their parents talk about their careers with them. In contrast, in their 1992 paper, they found evidence of nepotism among doctors.

The model in Section 2 predicts that skills transfer not only from fathers to sons who work in their fathers' occupations but also to sons who work in occupations requiring skills similar to those of their fathers. Specifically, skill transfer (x) enables sons to hold more skills and earn higher wages; sons therefore benefit from working in positions that require skills similar to those of their fathers (see P1). However, from the analysis on the effects of the fathers' and sons' costs of investing in cognitive skills (a_F and a_S) on the sons' wages, the model also predicts that sons earn lower wages when they work in occupations that require skills similar to those of their fathers, for whom the costs of investing in cognitive skills were higher (see P2 and P3). As the model predicts an opposite relationship between the sons' wages and the father–son skill correlation, we now examine which effect is more dominant for whites and blacks.

Using the NLSY79 sample, we identify the wage effects of both nepotism and the transfer of skill-related human capital by including (1) a dummy for whether father and son work in the same occupation, and (2) the correlation coefficient between father–son skill vectors as regressors in the wage regression model posited by Neal and Johnson (1996). Consider the following wage regression:

$$\omega_S = \alpha_0 B + \alpha_1 W \times r + \alpha_2 B \times r + \alpha_3 W \times \mathbf{1}_{occ} + \alpha_4 B \times \mathbf{1}_{occ} + X\Gamma + \varepsilon \qquad (12)$$

where ω_S is the log of the son's wage; B is an indicator for black; W is an indicator for white; r is the correlation coefficient between father–son skill vectors; $\mathbf{1}_{occ}$ is an indicator of whether the son and the father work in the same occupation; X includes controls for the son's AFQT score and its square, son's age, father's education, and father's DOT skill variables; ε is an error term; and α_0, α_1, α_2, α_3, α_4, and Γ represent the coefficients of the respective variables in the wage regression. We include the father's DOT skill variables in the wage regression to control for the father's skill vectors.[28]

---

28. All wages are measured in 1990 dollars. The observations in which the wage is below \$2 or above \$100 in 1990 dollars are eliminated from the analysis.

Table 5. OLS Estimates of Wage Equation.

Variables	1993 Wave			1996 Wave	1998 Wave	2000 Wave
	(1)	(2)	(3)	(4)	(5)	(6)
Blacks	−0.091***	−0.051*	−0.015	−0.005	−0.023	−0.052*
	(0.026)	(0.027)	(0.032)	(0.032)	(0.031)	(0.030)
Whites × Correlation Coefficient (r)			0.080***	0.035	0.032	0.063**
			(0.026)	(0.027)	(0.028)	(0.030)
Blacks × Correlation Coefficient (r)			−0.102**	−0.113**	−0.109**	−0.038
			(0.045)	(0.049)	(0.045)	(0.047)
Whites × 1(Same Occupation as Father)			0.146**	0.109	0.052	0.064
			(0.062)	(0.077)	(0.060)	(0.070)
Blacks × 1(Same Occupation as Father)			0.095	0.102	0.143	0.071
			(0.124)	(0.100)	(0.107)	(0.088)
Father's Education		0.013***	0.013***	0.013***	0.012**	0.012**
		(0.004)	(0.004)	(0.005)	(0.005)	(0.005)
Controls for Father's Skills	No	Yes	Yes	Yes	Yes	Yes
R^2	0.203	0.236	0.247	0.260	0.272	0.278
N	2,137	2,137	2,137	2,149	2,070	1,978

Notes: The correlation coefficient between the father's skill vector and the son's vector is computed using all the DOT skill variables. See Table A1 for a detailed description of the DOT skill varibles. All regressions include son's AFQT score and its square, and age. The specifications in Columns 2–6 add father's education and father's DOT skill variables. Robust standard errors are in parentheses. *$p < 0.1$, **$p < 0.05$, ***$p < 0.01$.

In the above wage regression, the coefficients α_1 and α_2 reflect the returns to working in occupations that require skills similar to those of the fathers for white and black sons, respectively. When the coefficients are positive, the sons receive a pay premium for working in jobs that require skills similar to their fathers', but when the coefficients are negative, the sons incur a wage penalty. On the other hand, the coefficients α_3 and α_4 reflect the nepotism effect, which measures the wage premium that white and black sons, respectively, receive from working in the same occupation as their fathers.

Table 5 reports the mean regression estimates of Eq. (12) for the 1993, 1996, 1998, and 2000 waves, separately. In the 1993 wave, the coefficient on skill correlation for whites α_1 is 0.080 (0.026), while that coefficient for blacks α_2 is −0.102 (0.045), with both being significant at the 5 percent level (Table 5, Column 3). White sons thus earn higher wages when they work in jobs similar to those of their fathers. However, black sons earn less when they work in jobs similar to those of their fathers. In other words, white sons receive a wage premium resulting from the positive skill transfer from their fathers, while black sons receive lower wages because the effect of their fathers' limited skill acquisition dominates the effect of positive skill transfer.[29] There is weak evidence for nepotism, as the coefficient on nepotism for whites α_3 is 0.146 (0.062) and that coefficient for blacks α_4 is 0.095 (0.124), which are both positive, but significant at the 5 percent level only for whites.

In the specification of the mean regression without the skill correlation terms, the coefficient on black α_0 is −0.051 (0.027) for the 1993 wave (Table 5, Column 2), which is negative and significant. In contrast, the specification that includes the skill correlation terms takes a coefficient α_0 of −0.015 (0.029) (Table 5, Column 3), which is small in magnitude and insignificant. This result indicates that skill transfer from fathers to sons explains nearly 70 percent of the black−white wage gap, after controlling for cognitive skills. Although much of the black−white wage gap is explained by differences in cognitive skills among sons, as Neal and Johnson (1996) found,[30] a significant portion of the remaining black−white wage gap is attributable to the differences in the wage premium earned by white sons and the wage penalty paid by black sons for working in occupations that require skills similar to their fathers'.[31]

For the mean regression estimates of Eq. (12) for the 1996 and 1998 waves (Table 5, Columns 4 and 5, respectively), we find similar results to those for the 1993 wave (Table 5, Column 3). Specifically, the coefficient

---

29. We examine whether the effects of skill correlation on wages differ depending on the father's occupation (white-collar, blue-collar, and other, as defined in Bjerk (2007)). The coefficient on skill correlation is 0.009 (0.035) for whites whose fathers work in the blue-collar sector and −0.165 (0.049) for blacks whose fathers work in the blue-collar sector. However, the coefficient on skill correlation is positive for sons whose fathers work in the white-collar sector, regardless of race: specifically, 0.195 (0.041) for whites and 0.339 (0.133) for blacks. Since the proportion of blacks whose fathers work in the white-collar sector is only 8.6 percent, while it is 34.5 percent for whites, the overall skill-correlation effect is negative for blacks, as shown in Table 5, Column 3. We further examine the effects of skill correlation on wages for fathers with a higher school education or less. The results that restrict the sample to fathers with a high school education or less are similar to those that use all the fathers (Table 5, Column 3 and Fig. 3), except for the coefficient estimate on White × r. Specifically, the OLS estimate is 0.023 (0.032) for the sample that restricts fathers to those with a high school education or less, while it is larger and 0.080 (0.026) for the sample that uses all the fathers. This result implies that white sons whose fathers have a lower education level receive a smaller positive skill transfer from their fathers.

30. We confirm this finding of Neal and Johnson (1996) by using our sample; the coefficient on black is −0.091 (0.026) for the case in which the sons' AFQT score is included in the mean regression (Table 5, Column 1), while it is −0.313 (0.025) for the case where it is not included.

31. The reduction in the black-white wage gap, which results from including the correlation coefficient in the wage regression, is approximately equal to the difference between $\alpha_1 = 0.080$ and $\alpha_2 = -0.102$, multiplied by the average correlation coefficient (around 0.2).

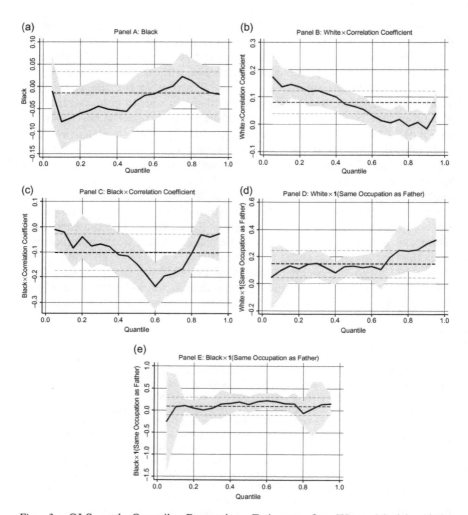

Fig. 3. OLS and Quantile Regression Estimates for Wage Model: 1993.
(a) Black, (b) white × correlation coefficient, (c) black × correlation coefficient,
(d) white × 1(same occupation as father), and (e) black × 1(same occupation as father).
Notes: The correlation coefficient between the father's skill vector and the son's vector
is computed using all the DOT skill variables. See Table A1 for a detailed description
of the DOT skill varibles. All regressions include son's AFQT score and its square,
age, father's education, and father's DOT skill variables. The quantile regression
estimates are the solid curve, the shaded grey area depicts the 90 percent confidence
interval for the quantile regression estimates. The dashed line depicts the OLS
estimate, and the two light dotted lines is the 90 percent confidence interval for the
OLS estimate. Robust standard errors are used to compute confidence intervals.

on black α_0 is negative but small in magnitude and insignificant, whereas the coefficient on skill correlation for blacks α_2 is significantly negative and as large as that of the 1993 wave: -0.113 (0.049) in the 1996 wave and -0.109 (0.045) in the 1998 wave. However, for the 2000 wave (Table 5, Column 6), the coefficient on black α_0 is -0.052 (0.030), which is significant and large in magnitude; and the coefficient on skill correlation for blacks α_2 is -0.038 (0.047), which is insignificant and small in magnitude. Therefore, the explanation for the black–white wage gap may differ between pre-1998 and 2000, a point which we discuss further later in this section.

Fig. 3 presents a visual summary of the quantile regression results for the 1993 wave, which illustrates how changes in skill transfer are related to the changes in wages not only in the middle of the wage distribution but also in its tails. This method is useful because disadvantaged blacks are typically overrepresented in the lower tail of the wage distribution, and so we examine whether there are differential effects among blacks. For each of the coefficients on α_0, α_1, α_2, α_3, and α_4, we plot the 19 distinct quantile regression estimates for each quantile, ranging from 0.05 to 0.95 as the solid curve. The shaded grey area represents a 90 percent confidence interval for the quantile regression estimates. The dashed line in each figure shows the OLS estimate, and the two light dotted lines represent the 90 percent confidence interval for the OLS estimate.[32]

For whites, the coefficients on skill correlation α_1 are significantly positive and largest at the lower tail of the wage distribution, and continue to be significantly positive until the 55th quantile of the wage distribution but thereafter become smaller and less significant (Fig. 3(b)). Meanwhile, for whites, the nepotism effects α_3 are positive, and become larger and more significant toward the upper tail of the wage distribution (Fig. 3(d)).

On the other hand, for blacks, the coefficients on skill correlation α_2 are negative throughout the entire wage distribution (Fig. 3(c)). In particular, between the 40th and 80th quantiles of the wage distribution, the coefficients on skill correlation for blacks α_2 are significantly negative, while the coefficients on black α_0 are significantly negative at the lower tail of the wage distribution – specifically, in the 10th and 20th quantiles of the wage

---

32. In the lowest tenth percentile of the wage distribution, 57.7 percent are blacks, while in the highest tenth percentile of the wage distribution, 15.4 percent are blacks. Therefore, whites are sufficiently represented in the lowest tenth percentile of the wage distribution and blacks in the highest tenth percentile of the wage distribution.

distribution (Fig. 3(a)).[33] It follows that the black—white wage gap in the middle of the wage distribution arises from the differences in the effects of skill transfer from fathers, whereas the wage gap in the lower tail of the wage distribution arises from other, unexplained black—white differences not controlled for in the wage regression.[34] These results indicate that blacks in the lower tail of the wage distribution are hampered in achieving economic success because of unexplained difficulties (such as discrimination), while blacks in the middle of the wage distribution are hampered because of the negative effect of skill transfer from their fathers.

The model in Section 2 provides an explanation for these empirical findings. Black fathers in both B1 and B2 families paid a greater cost to invest in cognitive skills (T skills) than white fathers. Because of the difficulty that blacks experienced in accessing quality schools before the Supreme Court's decision in *Brown v. Board of Education* in 1954 and the civil rights legislation of the mid-1960s, the black fathers faced greater difficulty than white fathers in obtaining quality education and cognitive skills when they were young. Such costs have declined in the sons' generation for B2 families because those blacks had greater freedom in choosing their residential communities and schools. However, B1 black sons continue to pay costs as high as their fathers paid, because they continue to face the difficulty of obtaining quality education and developing cognitive skills (potentially due to discrimination). The model predicts that the B1 black sons work in jobs similar to those of their fathers and receive significantly low wages, whereas the B2 black sons work in different jobs and receive low wages compared to those of white sons (but not as low

---

33. Using a semi-parametric procedure developed by DiNardo, Fortin, and Lemieux (1996) for estimating counterfactual distributions, O'Neill, Sweetman, and Van de gaer (2006) specify the wage model as in Neal and Johnson (1996), and find that differences in cognitive skills cannot fully explain the black-white wage gap at the lower end of the wage distribution.
34. We obtain similar qualitative results for the quantile regressions when other waves between 1990 and 2000 are used; specifically, the coefficients on skill correlation for whites α_1 are positive at the lower tail of the wage distribution, the coefficients on skill correlation for blacks α_2 are negative at the middle of the wage distribution, and the coefficients on black α_0 are negative at the lower tail of the wage distribution. We show the quantile regression results for the 1993 wave because that wave provides the clearest results. Furthermore, to deal with multiple siblings in the NLSY, we estimate the OLS and quantile regressions by clustering the standard errors at the family level. The standard errors are similar to those reported in the paper. We also conduct robustness checks by restricting the sample to full-time/full-year employment, the results of which show patterns similar to the estimates in Table 5 and Fig. 3. These results are all available from the authors upon request.

as the B1 black sons) $\left(E\left[\omega_S^{B1}\right] < E\left[\omega_S^{B2}\right] \leq E\left[\omega_S^{W}\right]\right)$. The B1 black sons therefore incur a wage loss because they have to choose skill sets from those as limited as their fathers. The B2 black sons pay a price when they seek higher wages, because they have to move away from their fathers' occupation in order to do so, a move which incurs the cost of acquiring different skill sets than those they may have inherited from their fathers. In contrast, white fathers and sons who both pay lower costs to invest in cognitive skills work in similar jobs and receive higher wages. White sons therefore receive a wage gain from the positive skill transfer from their fathers.

Lastly, we assess how the racial differences in skill correlation between father and son contribute to the racial wage gap of sons between 1993 and 2000. According to Table 4, from 1993 to 2000 the average skill correlation increased for whites from 0.191 to 0.210, but decreased for blacks from 0.216 to 0.147. Meanwhile, for both blacks and whites, the coefficients on skill correlation in the 2000 wave, as shown in Table 5, Column 6, are smaller in magnitude than those in the 1993 wave. We therefore can see that the average skill correlation changed in the direction of improving the sons' economic outcomes for both whites and blacks, but the coefficient on skill correlation changed in the direction of benefiting blacks but not whites. Following Smith and Welch (1989), Heckman, Lyons, and Todd (2000), and Barr and Lin (2015), we decompose the change in the sons' black−white wage gap between 1993 and 2000 into the changes due to (i) changing characteristics, and (ii) changing returns to characteristics, and we do this in three steps. Step 1: Separately by race and year, we estimate the wage regression of Eq. (12): $\omega_{S,t}^{I} = \gamma_0 + \gamma_1 r_t^{I} + \gamma_2 \mathbf{1}_{occ}^{I} + X_t^{I}\Gamma_t^{I} + \varepsilon_t^{I}$ for $I = B, W$ and $t = 1993, 2000$. Step 2: We obtain $\bar{z}^{W}$ and $\bar{z}^{B}$, which respectively denote the mean vectors of the white and black characteristics included as independent variables in the wage regression; and γ^{W} and γ^{B} which respectively denote the associated vectors of the coefficients. Step 3: We decompose the change in log white wages minus log black wages between 1993 and 2000 $\left(= \left(\bar{\omega}_{2000}^{W} - \bar{\omega}_{2000}^{B}\right) - \left(\bar{\omega}_{1993}^{W} - \bar{\omega}_{1993}^{B}\right) = 0.068 \right)$ as:

$$\left[\left(\bar{z}_{2000}^{W}\gamma_{2000}^{W} - \bar{z}_{2000}^{B}\gamma_{2000}^{B}\right) - \left(\bar{z}_{1993}^{W}\gamma_{1993}^{W} - \bar{z}_{1993}^{B}\gamma_{1993}^{B}\right)\right]$$

$$= \left[\left(\bar{z}_{2000}^{W} - \bar{z}_{2000}^{B}\right) - \left(\bar{z}_{1993}^{W} - \bar{z}_{1993}^{B}\right)\right]\gamma_{1993}^{B} \qquad \text{Main Effect}$$

$$+ \left(\bar{z}_{2000}^{W} - \bar{z}_{1993}^{W}\right)\left(\gamma_{1993}^{W} - \gamma_{1993}^{B}\right) \qquad \text{Race Interaction Effect}$$

$$+ \left(\bar{z}_{2000}^{W} - \bar{z}_{2000}^{B}\right)\left(\gamma_{2000}^{B} - \gamma_{1993}^{B}\right) \qquad \text{Year Interaction Effect}$$

$$+ \bar{z}_{2000}^{W}\left[\left(\gamma_{2000}^{W} - \gamma_{2000}^{B}\right) - \left(\gamma_{1993}^{W} - \gamma_{1993}^{B}\right)\right] \qquad \text{Race − Year Interaction Effect}$$

Table 6. Total Contribution of Skill Correlation between Father–Son and Nepotism to Change in the Relative Wage Gap: Comparison between: 1993 and 2000.

Panel A: Log Wage	Coef.	SE	N
Current Year: 2000			
White (A)	2.630	0.015	1,453
Black (B)	2.246	0.023	525
Base Year: 1993			
White (C)	2.418	0.013	1,579
Black (D)	2.101	0.022	558
Panel B: Log Wage Gap			
Current Year (A−B)	0.385	0.028	
Base Year (C−D)	0.317	0.025	
Change in Log Wage Gap (A−B)−(C−D)	0.068	0.038	
Panel C: Detailed Decomposition			
Main Effect			
Correlation Coefficient (r)	−0.007	0.005	
1(Same Occupation as Father)	0.001	0.003	
Race Interaction Effect			
Correlation Coefficient (r)	0.001	0.004	
1(Same Occupation as Father)	0.000	0.002	
Year Interaction Effect			
Correlation Coefficient (r)	0.003	0.004	
1(Same Occupation as Father)	−0.002	0.005	
Race−Year Interacton Effect			
Correlation Coefficient (r)	−0.021	0.017	
1(Same Occupation as Father)	0.000	0.012	

The main effect measures the change in the wage gap predicted by the change in the characteristics of whites relative to blacks from 1993 to 2000, valued at 1993 black return values. The race-year interaction effect measures the change in the wage gap that occurs because the relative returns to characteristics of blacks and whites changed between 1993 and 2000, valued at 2000 white characteristic values.

Table 6, Panel C presents the detailed decomposition results only for the skill correlation r and nepotism 1_{occ}.[35] First, the main effect of skill correlation r is negative but fairly small (−0.007), and so it played a minor role in

---

35. Results for the other variables are available from the authors upon request.

closing the wage gap. Second, the race-year interaction effect of skill correlation r is -0.021, and so the changes in the returns to skill correlation r move in the direction of closing the black—white wage gap. Third, the race interaction effect and year interaction effect both take positive values but their effects are small (0.001 and 0.003, respectively). Therefore, although the skill correlation r served to close the black—white wage gap between 1993 and 2000 (by -0.024), the overall change in the racial log wage gap widened by 0.068 log points between 1993 and 2000, since the changes in other factors widened the racial wage gap.[36]

6. CONCLUDING REMARKS

This paper examines how fathers' occupational skills affect sons' occupational decisions and earnings. We present a model of intergenerational multidimensional-skill transmission that extends a model of univariate human capital into a model of multidimensional human capital. The vector of skill sets for an individual comprises his occupational characteristics from the Dictionary of Occupational Titles (DOT). The correlation coefficient of the father—son skill vectors measures the closeness of the direction of these vectors. Skill correlation is found for father—son pairs, and the correlation (which goes beyond random assignment) is greater for whites than for blacks.

White sons earn a wage premium for working in occupations that require skills similar to those of their fathers, whereas black sons in such circumstances incur a wage penalty. We also find evidence for nepotism when white sons earn a wage premium for working in the same occupation as their fathers.

Although black—white skill gaps significantly narrowed from fathers to sons in the NLSY79 sample, the skill and wage gaps have persisted between black and white sons. Black sons who have skill sets as limited as their fathers work in occupations that require skills similar to those of their fathers, and they earn significantly lower pay. Even black sons who can

---

36. Alternatively, we decomposed the change in the black-white sons' wage gap between 1993 and 1998. Although the magnitude of the change in the black-white sons' wage gap is only 0.036 between 1993 and 1998, we obtained the same conclusion, namely, that skill correlation worked in the direction of closing the black-white wage gap. Note, however, that the wage gap may arise from selective attribution and sample differences between the two waves. These results are available from the authors upon request.

choose from a wider variety of skill sets than their fathers incur the cost of acquiring these skill sets, and they earn low pay. Because these black sons, unlike white sons, cannot fully benefit from positive skill transfer from their fathers, this results in a wage disparity between the black and white sons.

REFERENCES

Altonji, J. G., & Blank, R. M. (1999). Race and gender in the labor market. In O. Ashenfelter & D. Card (Eds.), *Handbook of labor economics* (Vol. 3C). Amsterdam: Elsevier Science.

Autor, D. H., Levy, F., & Murnane, R. J. (2003). The skill content of recent technological change: An empirical exploration. *Quarterly Journal of Economics*, *118*(4), 1279–1333.

Bacolod, M., & Blum, B. S. (2010). Two sides of the same coin: U.S. "Residual Inequality" and the gender gap. *Journal of Human Resources*, *45*(1), 197–242.

Barr, T., & Lin, C. (2015). A detailed decomposition of synthetic cohort analysis. *Economics Letters*, *127*(C), 76–80.

Becker, G. S., & Tomes, N. (1976). Child endowments, and the quantity and quality of children. *Journal of Political Economy*, *84*(4), S143–S162.

Bjerk, D. (2007). The differing nature of black-white wage inequality across occupational sectors. *Journal of Human Resources*, *42*(2), 398–434.

Björklund, A., Lindahl, M., & Plug, E. (2006). The origins of intergenerational associations: Lessons from Swedish adoption data. *Quarterly Journal of Economics*, *121*(3), 999–1028.

Borghans, L., ter Weel, B., & Weinberg, B. A. (2008). Interpersonal styles and labor market outcomes. *Journal of Human Resources*, *43*(4), 815–858.

Borghans, L., ter Weel, B., & Weinberg, B. A. (2014). People people: Social capital and the labor market outcomes of underrepresented groups. *Industrial and Labor Relations Review*, *67*(2), 287–334.

DiNardo, J., Fortin, N. M., & Lemieux, T. (1996). Labor market institutions and the distribution of wages 1973–1992: A semi-parametric approach. *Econometrica*, *64*(5), 1001–1044.

Gathmann, C., & Schönberg, U. (2010). How general is human capital? A task-based approach. *Journal of Labor Economics*, *28*(1), 1–49.

Guryan, J. (2004). Desegregation and black dropout rates. *American Economic Review*, *94*(4), 919–943.

Heckman, J. J., Lyons, T. M., & Todd, P. E. (2000). Understanding black-white wage differentials, 1960–1990. *American Economic Review*, *90*(2), 344–349.

Hedges, L. V., & Nowell, A. (1998). Black-white test score convergence since 1965. In C. Jencks & M. Phillips (Eds.), *The black-white test score gap*. Washington, D.C: Brookings Institution Press.

Ingram, B. F., & Neumann, G. R. (2006). The returns to skill. *Labour Economics*, *13*(1), 35–59.

Ishikawa, T. (1975). Family structures and family values in the theory of income distribution. *Journal of Political Economy*, *83*(5), 987–1008.

Johnson, R. C. (2014). *Long-run impacts of school desegregation and school quality on adult attainments*. NBER Working Paper No. 16664.

Katz, L., & Autor, D. H. (1999). Changes in the wage structure and earnings inequality. In O. Ashenfelter & D. Card (Eds.), *Handbook of labor economics* (Vol. 3A). Amsterdam: Elsevier Science.

Laband, D. N., & Lentz, B. F. (1983). Like father, like son: Toward an economic theory of occupational following. *Southern Economic Journal, 50*(2), 474–493.

Laband, D. N., & Lentz, B. F. (1992). Self-recruitment in the legal profession. *Journal of Labor Economics, 10*(2), 182–201.

Lentz, B. F., & Laband, D. N. (1989). Why so many children of doctors become doctors. *Journal of Human Resources, 24*(3), 396–413.

Murnane, R. J., Willett, J. B., & Levy, F. (1995). The growing importance of cognitive skills in wage determination. *Review of Economics and Statistics, 77*(2), 251–266.

National Academy of Science, Committee on Occupational Classification and Analysis. (1981). Dictionary of DOT scores for 1970 census categories (4th ed.). ICPSR Document No. 7845. Ann Arbor, MI.

Neal, D. A. (2004). The measured black-white wage gap among women is too small. *Journal of Political Economy, 112*(1), S1–S28.

Neal, D. A. (2006). Why has black-white skill convergence stopped? In E. Hanushek & F. Welch (Eds.), *Handbook of economics of education.* Amsterdam: Elsevier Science.

Neal, D. A., & Johnson, W. R. (1996). The role of pre-market factors in black-white wage differences. *Journal of Political Economy, 104*(5), 869–895.

Okumura, T., & Usui, E. (2014). Do parents' social skills influence their children's sociability? *The B.E. Journal of Economic Analysis and Policy, 14*(3), 1081–1116.

O'Neill, D., Sweetman, O., & Van de gaer, D. (2006). The impact of cognitive skills on the distribution of the black-white wage gap. *Labour Economics, 14*(3), 343–356.

Poletaev, M., & Robinson, C. (2008). Human capital specificity: Evidence from the dictionary of occupational titles and displaced worker surveys, 1984–2000. *Journal of Labor Economics, 26*(3), 387–420.

Reber, S. J. (2010). School desegregation and educational attainment for blacks. *Journal of Human Resources, 45*(4), 893–914.

Sacerdote, B. (2007). How large are the effects from changes in family environment? A study of Korean American adoptees. *Quarterly Journal of Economics, 121*(1), 119–158.

Shaw, K. (1984). A formulation of the earnings function using the concept of occupational investment. *Journal of Human Resources, 19*(3), 319–340.

Shaw, K. (1987). Occupational change, employer change and the transferability of skills. *Southern Economic Journal, 53*(3), 702–719.

Smith, J. P., & Welch, F. R. (1989). Black economic progress after myrdal. *Journal of Economic Literature, 27*(2), 519–564.

U.S. Department of Labor, Employment and Training Administration. (1977). *Dictionary of occupational titles* (4th ed.). Washington, D.C.

U.S. Department of Labor, Employment and Training Administration. (1991). *Dictionary of occupational titles* (Rev. 4th ed.). Washington, D.C.

Wigdor, A. K., & Green, B. F. (1991). *Performance assessment for the workplace* (Vol. 2). Technical issues. Washington, D.C.: National Academy Press.

Wonnacott, R. J., & Wonnacott, T. H. (1979). *Econometrics* (2nd ed.). New York, NY: John Wiley & Sons.

APPENDIX A

Table A1. Definitions of the Variables from the *Dictionary of Occupational Titles* (DOT).

Variable	DOT Job Component	Description
		Cognitive-Skill Variables
Relation to Data	Worker Function	Complexity at which worker performs job in relation to data, from highest to lowest: Synthesizing, Coordinating, Analyzing, Compiling, Computing, Copying, Comparing.
Reasoning	GED	General educational development (GED) in reasoning required for job, ranging from being able to apply logical or scientific thinking to wide range of intellectual and practical problems, to being able to apply commonsense understanding to carry out simple instructions.
Mathematics	GED	GED in mathematics required for job, from knowledge of advanced calculus, modern algebra and statistics; algebra, geometry and shop math; to simple addition and subtraction.
Language	GED	GED in language required for job, from reading literature, writing editorials and speeches, and conversant in persuasive speaking and debate; to reading at rate of 95–120 words per minute or vocabulary of 2,500 words and writing and speaking simple sentences.
Specific Vocational Preparation	SVP	SVP is the amount of time required to learn the techniques, acquire the information, and develop the facility needed for average performance in a specific job-worker situation.
General Learning	Aptitude	Ability to "catch on" or understand instructions and underlying principles; ability to reason and make judgments.
Verbal	Aptitude	Ability to understand meaning of words and to use them effectively. Ability to comprehend language, to understand relationships between words, and to understand meanings of whole sentences and paragraphs.
Numerical	Aptitude	Ability to perform arithmetic operations quickly and accurately.

Table A1. (Continued)

Variable	DOT Job Component	Description
Clerical Perception	Aptitude	Ability to perceive pertinent detail in verbal or tabular material. Ability to observe differences in copy, to proofread words and numbers, and to avoid perceptual errors in arithmetic computation. A measure of perception which is required in many industrial jobs even when the job does not have verbal or numerical content.
Plan Activity	Temperaments	Adaptability to accepting responsibility for the direction, control or planning of an activity.
Make Evaluations	Temperaments	Adaptability to making generalizations, evaluations, or decisions based on sensory or judgmental criteria.
Creative Activity	Interest Factor	A preference for activities of an abstract and creative nature versus a preference for activities of a routine, concrete, organized nature.
Esteem of Others	Interest Factor	A preference for activities resulting in prestige or the esteem of others versus a preference for activities resulting in tangible productive satisfaction.
People-Skills Variables		
Relation to People	Worker Function	Complexity at which worker performs job in relation to people, from highest to lowest: Mentoring, Negotiating, Instructing, Supervising, Diverting, Persuading, Speaking-Signaling, Serving. Taking Instructions-Helping.
Deal with People	Temperaments	Adaptability to dealing with people beyond giving and receiving instructions.
Influence People	Temperaments	Adaptability to influencing people in their opinions, attitudes or judgments about ideas or things.
Interpret Feelings	Temperaments	Adaptability to situations involving the interpretation of feeling, ideas or facts in terms of personal viewpoint.
Talking and/or Hearing	Physical Demands	Presence or absence of talking and/or hearing.
Communicate Data	Interest Factor	A preference for activities concerned with the communication of data versus a preference for activities for dealing with things and objects.
Business Contact	Interest Factor	A preference for activities involving business contact with people versus a preference for activities of a scientific and technical nature.
Work for the Good of People	Interest Factor	A preference for working for the presumed good of people versus a preference for activities that are carried on in relation to processes, machines, and techniques.

Table A1. (*Continued*)

Variable	DOT Job Component	Description
		Motor-Skills Variables
Relation to Things	Worker Function	Complexity at which worker performs job in relation to things: Setting-Up, Precision Working, Operating-Controlling, Driving-Operating, Manipulating, Tending, Feeding-Offbearing, Handling.
Finger Dexterity	Aptitude	Ability to move fingers, and manipulate small objects with fingers, rapidly or accurately.
Motor Coordination	Aptitude	Ability to coordinate eyes and hands or fingers rapidly and accurately in making precise movements with speed. Ability to make a movement response accurately and swiftly.
Manual Dexterity	Aptitude	Ability to move the hands easily and skillfully. Ability to work with the hands in placing and turning motions.
Eye-Hand-Foot Coordination	Aptitude	Ability to move the hand and foot coordinately with each other in accordance with visual stimuli.
Spatial Perception	Aptitude	Ability to think visually of geometric forms and to comprehend the two-dimensional representation of three-dimensional objects. Ability to recognize the relationships resulting from the movement of objects in space.
Form Perception	Aptitude	Ability to perceive pertinent detail in objects or in pictorial or graphic material. Ability to make visual comparisons and discriminations and see slight differences in shapes and shadings of figures and widths and lengths of lines.
Color Discrimination	Aptitude	Ability to match or discriminate between colors in terms of hue, saturation, and brilliance. Ability to identify a particular color or color combination from memory and to perceive contrasting color combinations.
Precisely Set Limits	Temperaments	Adaptability to situations requiring the precise attainment of set limits, tolerances, or standards.
Repetitive Work	Temperaments	Adaptability to performing repetitive work, or to continuously performing the same work, according to set procedures, sequence, or pace.
Make Judgments	Temperaments	Adaptability to making generalizations, judgments, or decisions based on measurable or verifiable criteria.

Table A1. (*Continued*)

Variable	DOT Job Component	Description
Perform Variety of Duties	Temperaments	Adaptability to performing a variety of duties, often changing from one task to another of a different nature without loss of efficiency or composure.
Under Stress	Temperaments	Adaptability to performing under stress when confronted with emergency, critical, unusual, or dangerous situations; or in situations in which working speed and sustained attention are make or break aspects of the job.

Physical-Strength Variables

Variable	DOT Job Component	Description
Strength	Physical Strength	Strength rating reflects the estimated overall strength requirement of the job (expressed by: sedentary, light, medium, heavy, and very heavy).
Climbing	Physical Strength	Indicate the presence or absence of climbing (climbing and/or balancing).
Stooping	Physical Strength	Indicate the presence or absence of stooping (stooping, kneeling, crouching, and/or crawling).
Reaching	Physical Strength	Indicate the presence or absence of reaching (reaching, handling, fingering and/or feeling).
Seeing	Physical Strength	Indicate the presence or absence of seeing.

Notes: Aptitudes (specific capacities or abilities required of an individual in order to facilitate the learning of some task or job duty) have been rated for each occupation, using a five-point scale. The quantiles for rating aptitudes are based on whether the segment of the population possessing the particular aptitude is within: the top 10 percent of the population, the top one-third except for the top 10 percent, the middle third, the lowest third except for the bottom 10 percent, and the lowest 10 percent. Temperaments are coded 1 for the presence of a given temperament and 0 for its absence. Bipolar interest factors signify interests, tastes, and preferences for certain kinds of activities that are entailed in job performance. These interest factors are indicated by 1, 0, and −1.

APPENDIX B: PROOFS OF PROPOSITIONS P1, P2, P3, AND P4

Except for P3(i), the propositions are proved analytically. P3(i) is solved numerically for various parameter values, because the derivative of $\cos\theta$ with respect to a_F is too complicated to solve analytically. The numerical results for P4 are also provided.

B.1. Proof of Proposition P1

Proof of P1(i): When the wage and cost functions are defined as in Eqs. (5) and (6), the first-order conditions in Note 5 become the following:

$$\delta T_F^{\delta-1} M_F^{1-\delta} = 2a_F T_F \tag{B.1}$$

$$(1-\delta)T_F^{\delta} M_F^{-\delta} = 2b M_F \tag{B.2}$$

$$\frac{1}{2}T_S^{-1/2} M_S^{1/2} = 2a_S T^* \tag{B.3}$$

$$\frac{1}{2}T_S^{1/2} M_S^{-1/2} = 2b M^* \tag{B.4}$$

$$(T_S, M_S) = (xT_F + T^*, xM_F + M^*) \tag{B.5}$$

Because of the functional forms of the wage and cost functions, there is no corner solution. By Eqs. (B.3)–(B.5), we have

$$\frac{M_S}{T_S} = \frac{xM_F + M^*}{xT_F + T^*} = \frac{a_S}{b}\frac{T^*}{M^*} \tag{B.6}$$

$$16a_S b T^* M^* = 1 \tag{B.7}$$

By Eqs. (B.6) and (B.7), we have

$$16a_S b^2 T^* x M_F + b - 16^2 a_S^3 b^2 T^{*3}(x T_F + T^*) = 0 \qquad \text{(B.8)}$$

We take the total derivative of Eq. (B.8) with respect to x and T^*; then

$$\frac{dT^*}{dx} = -\frac{T^*\left(M_F - 16a_S^2 T^{*2} T_F\right)}{x M_F - 16a_S^2 T^{*2}3 x T_F - 16a_S^2 T^{*2}4T^*} = -\frac{T^* T_F\left(\dfrac{M_F}{T_F} - \dfrac{a_S}{b}\dfrac{T^*}{M^*}\right)}{x M_F - \dfrac{a_S}{b}\dfrac{T^*}{M^*}(3 x T_F + 4T^*)}$$

$$= \frac{T^* T_F\left(\dfrac{M_F}{T_F} - \dfrac{M_S}{T_S}\right)}{2M_S + M^* + \dfrac{M_S}{T_S} T^*}$$

$$\text{(B.9)}$$

where the second and third equalities hold because of Eqs. (B.7) and (B.5), respectively. Therefore,

$$\frac{dT^*}{dx} \gtreqless 0 \qquad \text{if } \frac{M_F}{T_F} \gtreqless \frac{M_S}{T_S} \qquad \text{(B.10)}$$

By Eqs. (B.7) and (B.10), it follows that

$$\frac{dM^*}{dx} \lesseqgtr 0 \qquad \text{if } \frac{M_F}{T_F} \gtreqless \frac{M_S}{T_S} \qquad \text{(B.11)}$$

Thus, by Eqs. (B.6), (B.10), and (B.11),

$$\frac{d\left(\frac{M_S}{T_S}\right)}{dx} \gtreqless 0 \qquad \text{if } \frac{M_F}{T_F} \gtreqless \frac{M_S}{T_S} \qquad \text{(B.12)}$$

Eq. (B.12) represents the finding that if the slope of the son's skill vector (M_S/T_S) is smaller (or larger) than that of the father's (M_F/T_F), as in Fig. 1, then with an increase in x, the slope of the son's skill vector increases (or decreases). As a result, as x increases, the slope of the son's skill vector gets close to that of the father's, that is, $\partial \cos \theta / \partial x \geq 0$.

Furthermore, we show:

Lemma 1. $\partial \cos \theta / \partial x = 0$ and $\cos \theta = 1$, if $a_S / (1 - \delta) = a_F / \delta$.

Proof of Lemma 1: By Eqs. (B.1) and (B.2),

$$\frac{(1 - \delta)/b}{\delta/a_F} = \left(\frac{M_F}{T_F}\right)^2 \tag{B.13}$$

Suppose that

$$\frac{a_S}{1 - \delta} = \frac{a_F}{\delta} \tag{B.14}$$

Then, by Eqs. (B.6), (B.13), and (B.14),

$$\left(\frac{M_F}{T_F}\right)^2 = \left(\frac{M^*}{T^*}\right)\left(\frac{M_S}{T_S}\right) \tag{B.15}$$

Because of Eq. (B.5), we can claim the following:

Claim 2: *If either* $\dfrac{M_F}{T_F} \gtreqless \dfrac{M^*}{T^*}$ *or* $\dfrac{M_F}{T_F} \gtreqless \dfrac{M_S}{T_S}$, *then* $\dfrac{M_F}{T_F} \gtreqless \dfrac{M_S}{T_S} \gtreqless \dfrac{M^*}{T^*}$.

By Claim 2, Eq. (B.15) is equivalent to

$$\frac{M_F}{T_F} = \frac{M^*}{T^*} = \frac{M_S}{T_S} \tag{B.16}$$

Thus, by Eqs. (B.12), Lemma 1 holds. That is, the father's skill vector and the son's skill vector have the same direction. ∎

Proof of P1(ii): By Eqs. (B.5) and (B.9),

$$\frac{dT_S}{dx} = T_F + \frac{dT^*}{dx} = \frac{T_F(2M_S + M^*) + T^* M_F}{2M_S + M^* + \frac{M_S}{T_S} T^*} > 0 \tag{B.17}$$

By Eqs. (B.5), (B.7), and (B.9),

$$\frac{dM_S}{dx} = M_F + \frac{dM^*}{dx} = \frac{M_F\left(2M_S + \frac{M_S}{T_S}T^*\right) + M^* T_F \frac{M_S}{T_S}}{2M_S + M^* + \frac{M_S}{T_S}T^*} > 0 \tag{B.18}$$

By Eqs. (B.17) and (B.18),

$$\frac{\partial \omega_S}{\partial x} = \frac{1}{2}(T_S M_S)^{-1/2}\left(M_S \frac{dT_S}{dx} + T_S \frac{dM_S}{dx}\right) > 0 \qquad \blacksquare$$

B.2. Proof of Proposition P2

Proof of P2(i): We now prove:

Lemma 3. $\partial\cos\theta/\partial a_S \gtreqqless 0$, if $\frac{a_S}{1-\delta} \lesseqqgtr \frac{a_F}{\delta}$

First, we make this claim:

Claim 4: $\frac{M_F}{T_F} \gtreqqless \frac{M_S}{T_S}$, if and only if $\frac{a_S}{1-\delta} \lesseqqgtr \frac{a_F}{\delta}$.

Proof of Claim 4: (i) Suppose that $\frac{a_S}{1-\delta} \lesseqqgtr \frac{a_F}{\delta}$. By Eqs. (B.6) and (B.13), $\left(\frac{M_F}{T_F}\right)^2 \gtreqqless \left(\frac{M^*}{T^*}\right)\left(\frac{M_S}{T_S}\right)$. Therefore, because of Claim 2, $\frac{M_F}{T_F} \gtreqqless \frac{M_S}{T_S} \gtreqqless \frac{M^*}{T^*}$.

(ii) Suppose that $\frac{M_F}{T_F} \gtreqqless \frac{M_S}{T_S}$. Then by Claim 2, $\frac{M_F}{T_F} \gtreqqless \frac{M_S}{T_S} \gtreqqless \frac{M^*}{T^*}$. Thus, $\left(\frac{M_F}{T_F}\right)^2 \gtreqqless \left(\frac{M^*}{T^*}\right)\left(\frac{M_S}{T_S}\right)$. Therefore, by Eqs. (B.6) and (B.13), $\frac{a_S}{1-\delta} \lesseqqgtr \frac{a_F}{\delta}$. $\blacksquare$

Second, we show that if a_S increases, then the slope of the son's skill vector (M_S/T_S) also increases. By Eqs. (B.6) and (B.7),

$$\frac{d\left(\frac{M_S}{T_S}\right)}{da_S} = 32 a_S T^{*2}\left(1 + \frac{a_S}{T^*}\frac{dT^*}{da_S}\right) \tag{B.19}$$

We take the total derivative of Eq. (B.8) with respect to a_S and T^*; we then have

$$\frac{a_S}{T^*}\frac{dT^*}{da_S} = \frac{xM_F - 16 a_S^2 T^{*2} 3 T_S}{16 a_S^2 T^{*3} - \left(xM_F - 16 a_S^2 T^{*2} 3 T_S\right)} = \frac{1}{\dfrac{16 a_S^2 T^{*3}}{xM_F - 16 a_S^2 T^{*2} 3 T_S} - 1} \tag{B.20}$$

By Eqs. (B.6) and (B.7),

$$xM_F - 16a_S^2 T^{*2} 3T_S = M_S - M^* - 3\frac{a_S T^*}{bM^*} T_S = -2M_S - M^* < 0 \qquad (B.21)$$

By Eqs. (B.20) and (B.21),

$$-1 < \frac{a_S}{T^*}\frac{dT^*}{da_S} < 0 \qquad (B.22)$$

By Eqs. (B.19) and (B.22),

$$\frac{d\left(\frac{M_S}{T_S}\right)}{da_S} > 0 \qquad (B.23)$$

Therefore, if the slope of the son's skill vector is initially smaller (or larger) than that of the father's, as in Fig. 1, that is, if $\frac{M_F}{T_F} > \frac{M_S}{T_S}$ $\left(\text{or } \frac{M_F}{T_F} < \frac{M_S}{T_S}\right)$, then as a_S increases, the slope of the son's skill vector moves closer to (or further away from) that of the father's and thus $\cos\theta$ increases (or decreases). That is,

$$\frac{\partial\cos\theta}{\partial a_S} \gtrless 0 \quad \text{if } \frac{M_F}{T_F} \gtrless \frac{M_S}{T_S} \qquad (B.24)$$

The proof that $d\cos\theta/da_S = 0$ if $M_F/T_F = M_S/T_S$ is immediate. (The proof is available from the authors upon request.) Therefore, by Eq. (B.24),

$$\frac{\partial\cos\theta}{\partial a_S} \gtrless 0 \quad \text{if } \frac{M_F}{T_F} \gtrless \frac{M_S}{T_S} \qquad (B.25)$$

Because of Claim 4 and Eq. (B.25), Lemma 3 holds. Therefore, P2(i) holds. ∎

Proof of P2(ii): By Eqs. (B.7) and (B.22),

$$\frac{dM^*}{da_S} = -\frac{1}{16a_S^2 bT^*}\left(1 + \frac{a_S}{T^*}\frac{dT^*}{da_S}\right) < 0 \qquad (B.26)$$

By Eqs. (B.22) and (B.26),

$$\frac{\partial\omega_S}{\partial a_S} = \frac{\omega_S}{2}\left(\frac{1}{T_S}\frac{dT^*}{da_S} + \frac{1}{M_S}\frac{dM^*}{da_S}\right) < 0 \qquad ∎$$

B.3. Proof of Proposition P3

Proof of P3(i): We numerically prove P3(i). In Fig. C1, the white region shows the region of the parameter space (a_S, a_F) that satisfies $\partial \cos \theta / \partial a_F < 0$, given the parameters $x = 1/2$, $b = 1$, and $\delta = 1/4$, $1/2$, and $3/4$. The straight line dividing the black and white regions represents $a_S/(1 - \delta) = a_F/\delta$ and describes $\cos \theta = 1$ and $\partial \cos \theta / \partial a_F = 0$. The white region above the straight line satisfies $a_S/(1 - \delta) < a_F/\delta$. Therefore, Fig. C1 shows that P3(i) holds. For other parameter values, we also obtain $\partial \cos \theta / \partial a_F < 0$ in the regions where $a_S/(1 - \delta) < a_F/\delta$. The results are available from the authors upon request.

Proof of P3(ii): First, we define the terms $T_{F,1}$, $M_{F,1}$, and $T_{F,2}$ as follows:

$$T_{F,1} = T_F + \frac{dT_F}{da_F} da_F; \quad M_{F,1} = M_F + \frac{dM_F}{da_F} da_F; \quad \text{and}$$

$$T_{F,2} = \frac{T_F}{M_F} M_{F,1} = T_F + \frac{T_F}{M_F} \frac{dM_F}{da_F} da_F \tag{B.27}$$

Because $M_{F,1}/T_{F,2} = M_F/T_F$, the vector $(T_{F,2}, M_{F,1})$ is on the vector (T_F, M_F).

Second, given $T_{F,1}$, $M_{F,1}$, and $T_{F,2}$, we next define $\left(T_j^*, M_j^*\right)$ and $(T_{S,j}, M_{S,j})$ for $j = 1, 2$, which satisfy

$$\frac{1}{2} T_{S,j}^{-1/2} M_{S,j}^{1/2} = 2 a_S T_j^*; \quad \frac{1}{2} T_{S,j}^{1/2} M_{S,j}^{-1/2} = 2 b M_j^*; \quad \text{and}$$

$$(T_{S,j}, M_{S,j}) = \left(x T_{F,j} + T_j^*, x M_{F,1} + M_j^*\right) \tag{B.28}$$

(This is similar to the way that (T^*, M^*) and (T_S, M_S) satisfy Eqs. (B.3)–(B.5).) Reasoning in a way similar to our use of Eqs. (B.3)–(B.5) to prove Eqs. (B.6) and (B.7), we can now use Eq. (B.28) to show that, for $j = 1$ and 2, it is true that

$$\frac{M_{S,j}}{T_{S,j}} = \frac{x M_{F,1} + M_j^*}{x T_{F,j} + T_j^*} = \frac{a_S}{b} \frac{T_j^*}{M_j^*} \quad \text{and} \quad 16 a_S b T_j^* M_j^* = 1 \tag{B.29}$$

Third, we now prove that

$$\omega_S \left(T_{S,1}, M_{S,1}\right) \leq \omega_S \left(T_{S,2}, M_{S,2}\right) \leq \omega_S (T_S, M_S) \quad \text{if } da_F > 0 \tag{B.30}$$

$$\omega_S \left(T_{S,1}, M_{S,1}\right) \geq \omega_S \left(T_{S,2}, M_{S,2}\right) \geq \omega_S (T_S, M_S) \quad \text{if } da_F < 0 \tag{B.31}$$

where these equalities hold if $x = 0$.

(i) *The proof that $\omega_S(T_{S,2}, M_{S,2}) \leq \omega_S(T_S, M_S)$ if $da_F > 0$ (the equality holds if $x = 0$) in Eq. (B.30):*

The proof is organized in three steps. Step 1 characterizes the father's skill vector (T_F, M_F). Step 2 shows that an increase in a_F reduces M_F skills. This is because the iso-wage curve is Cobb–Douglas and the iso-cost curve is elliptical; the income effect of a_F on M_F thus dominates its substitution effect. As a result, $(T_{F,2}, M_{F,1}) = h(T_F, M_F)$ for $h \in (0,1)$. Step 3 concludes by using Step 2 and P1(ii).

Step 1: By Eqs. (B.1) and (B.2),

$$T_F = \frac{1}{2} a_F^{-(1+\delta)/2} b^{-(1-\delta)/2}(1-\delta)^{(1-\delta)/2} \delta^{(1+\delta)/2}, \quad \text{and}$$

$$M_F = \frac{1}{2} a_F^{-\delta/2} b^{-(1-\delta/2)}(1-\delta)^{1-\delta/2} \delta^{\delta/2}$$

(B.32)

Step 2: By Eq. (B.32), $dM_F/da_F < 0$. Because (i) the vector $(T_{F,2}, M_{F,1})$ is on the vector (T_F, M_F), (ii) $da_F > 0$, and (iii) $dM_F/da_F < 0$, it follows that $(T_{F,2}, M_{F,1}) = h(T_F, M_F)$ for $h \in (0,1)$.

Step 3: The first, second, and fourth equalities in (B.33) hold because of Eq. (B.28), Step 2, and Eq. (B.5), respectively, while the third inequality holds because of P1(ii):

$$\begin{aligned}
\omega_S(T_{S,2}, M_{S,2}) &= \omega_S(xT_{F,2} + T_2^*, xM_{F,1} + M_2^*) \\
&= \omega_S(hxT_F + T_2^*, hxM_F + M_2^*) \\
&\leq \omega_S(xT_F + T^*, xM_F + M^*) \\
&= \omega_S(T_S, M_S)
\end{aligned}$$

(B.33)

where $h \in (0,1)$ and the equality in the inequality holds if $x = 0$.

(ii) *The proof that $\omega_S(T_{S,1}, M_{S,1}) \leq \omega_S(T_{S,2}, M_{S,2})$ if $da_F > 0$ (the equality holds if $x = 0$) in Eq. (B.30):*

The proof is organized in four steps. Step 1 shows that an increase in a_F reduces both T_F and M_F skills because of the complementarity between these skills, but the decrease in the T_F skill $(= T_F - T_{F,1})$

is greater than the decrease in the M_F skill multiplied by $T_F/M_F(=T_F - T_{F,2})$ because of the substitution effect between these skills. Therefore, the new origin of the son's cost function ($xT_{F,1}$, $xM_{F,1}$) satisfies this inequality: $xT_{F,1} < xT_{F,2}$. Steps 2 and 3 show that the son's skills $T_{S,1}$ and $M_{S,1}$ associated with ($xT_{F,1}$, $xM_{F,1}$) as the origin of his cost function are smaller than $T_{S,2}$ and $M_{S,2}$ associated with ($xT_{F,2}$, $xM_{F,1}$) as the origin, respectively. Step 4 concludes.

Step 1: By Eq. (B.32),

$$\frac{dT_F}{da_F} < \frac{T_F}{M_F}\frac{dM_F}{da_F} < 0 \tag{B.34}$$

Because $da_F > 0$ and because of Eqs. (B.27) and (B.34), $T_{F,1} < T_{F,2}$. Therefore,

$$\begin{aligned}
(T_{F,1}, M_{F,1}) &= (kT_{F,2}, M_{F,1}) \quad \text{for } k \in (0,1), \quad \text{and} \\
(T_{F,2}, M_{F,1}) &= (kT_{F,2}, M_{F,1}) \quad \text{for } k = 1
\end{aligned} \tag{B.35}$$

Step 2: By Eqs. (B.28) and (B.35),

$$\begin{cases}
T_{S,1} = xT_{F,1} + T_1^* = xkT_{F,2} + T_1^* & \text{for } k \in (0,1) \\
T_{S,2} = xT_{F,2} + T_2^* = xkT_{F,2} + T_2^* & \text{for } k = 1
\end{cases} \tag{B.36}$$

When we substitute Eq. (B.36) into Eq. (B.29), for $j = 1, 2$, (such that if $j = 1$, then $k \in (0,1)$; and if $j = 2$, then $k = 1$), it then follows that

$$\frac{M_{S,j}}{T_{S,j}} = \frac{xM_{F,1} + M_j^*}{xkT_{F,2} + T_j^*} = \frac{a_S}{b}\frac{T_j^*}{M_j^*} \quad \text{and} \quad 16a_S b T_j^* M_j^* = 1 \tag{B.37}$$

In Appendix B.1, in the proof of P1(i), we used Eqs. (B.6) and (B.7) to obtain Eq. (B.9). Similarly, we now use Eq. (B.37) to obtain this equation:

$$\frac{dT_j^*}{dk} = -\frac{16a_S^2 T_j^{*3} x T_{F,2}}{2M_{S,j} + M_j^* + \frac{M_{S,j}}{T_{S,j}}T_j^*} \leq 0 \tag{B.38}$$

where the equality in the inequality holds if $x=0$. Hence, by Eqs. (B.36) and (B.38),

$$\frac{\mathrm{d}T_{\mathrm{S},j}}{\mathrm{d}k} = xT_{\mathrm{F},2} + \frac{\mathrm{d}T_j^*}{\mathrm{d}k} = \frac{xT_{\mathrm{F},2}\left(2M_{\mathrm{S},j} + M_j^*\right)}{2M_{\mathrm{S},j} + M_j^* + \frac{M_{\mathrm{S},j}}{T_{\mathrm{S},j}}T_j^*} \geq 0 \qquad (\text{B.39})$$

where the equality in the inequality holds if $x=0$. Thus, by Eqs. (B.36) and (B.39),

$$T_{\mathrm{S},1} \leq T_{\mathrm{S},2} \text{ (the equality holds if } x=0) \qquad (\text{B.40})$$

Step 3: Because of Eqs. (B.28) $(M_{\mathrm{S},j} = xM_{\mathrm{F},1} + M_j^*$ for $j=1,\ 2)$, (B.37), and (B.38), it follows that $\frac{\mathrm{d}M_{\mathrm{S},j}}{\mathrm{d}k} = \frac{\mathrm{d}M_j^*}{\mathrm{d}k} = -\frac{1}{16a_{\mathrm{S}}bT_j^{*2}}\frac{\mathrm{d}T_j^*}{\mathrm{d}k} \geq 0$, where the equality in the inequality holds if $x=0$. Therefore,

$$M_{\mathrm{S},1} \leq M_{\mathrm{S},2} \text{ (the equality holds if } x=0) \qquad (\text{B.41})$$

Step 4: By Eqs. (B.40) and (B.41),

$$\omega_{\mathrm{S}}\left(T_{\mathrm{S},1}, M_{\mathrm{S},1}\right) \leq \omega_{\mathrm{S}}\left(T_{\mathrm{S},2}, M_{\mathrm{S},2}\right) \text{ (the equality holds if } x=0) \qquad (\text{B.42})$$

By Eqs. (B.33) and (B.42), we conclude that Eq. (B.30) holds.

(iii) *The proof of Eq. (B.31)*:

The proof is constructed along lines similar to the proof of Eq. (B.30) in (i) and (ii).
We conclude that P3(ii) holds.   ∎

B.4. Proof of Proposition P4

We prove that
(i) $\dfrac{\partial \omega_{\mathrm{S}}(T_{\mathrm{S}},\ M_{\mathrm{S}})}{\partial a_{\mathrm{F}}} \leq \dfrac{\partial \omega_{\mathrm{S}}(T_{\mathrm{S}},\ M_{\mathrm{S}})}{\partial T_{\mathrm{S}}}\dfrac{\partial T_{\mathrm{S}}}{\partial a_{\mathrm{F}}}$ and

(ii) $\dfrac{\partial \omega_S(T_S, M_S)}{\partial T_S} \dfrac{\partial T_S}{\partial a_F} \leq \dfrac{\partial \omega_S(T_S, M_S)}{\partial T_S} \dfrac{\partial T_S}{\partial T_F} \dfrac{\partial T_F}{\partial a_F} \leq 0,$

where these equalities hold if $x=0$. We use the variables $T_{F,1}$, $M_{F,1}$, $T_{F,2}$, T_j^*, M_j^*, $T_{S,j}$, and $M_{S,j}$ for $j=1$, 2; these variables are defined in Appendix B.3, in the proof of P3(ii).

(i) *The proof that* $\dfrac{\partial \omega_S(T_S, M_S)}{\partial a_F} \leq \dfrac{\partial \omega_S(T_S, M_S)}{\partial T_S} \dfrac{\partial T_S}{\partial a_F}$ *(the equality holds if $x=0$).*

First, we prove that $\partial M_S/\partial a_F \leq 0$ for two cases: Case (1) where $da_F > 0$ and Case (2) where $da_F < 0$.

In Case (1) where $da_F > 0$: Because of Eq. (B.28) and Step 2 in Part (i) of the proof of P3(ii) in Appendix B.3, it follows that $M_{S,2} = x M_{F,1} + M_2^* = h x M_F + M_2^*$ for $h \in (0,1)$. By reasoning similar to Step 3 in Part (i) of the proof of P3(ii) in Appendix B.3, we have $h x M_F + M_2^* \leq x M_F + M^* = M_S$, where the equality in the inequality holds if $x=0$. Hence,

$$M_{S,2} \leq M_S \text{ (the equality holds if } x=0) \tag{B.43}$$

By Eqs. (B.41) and (B.43),

$$M_{S,1} \leq M_S \text{ (the equality holds if } x=0) \tag{B.44}$$

By the definitions of $T_{F,1}$, $M_{F,1}$, and $M_{S,1}$ in Eqs. (B.27) and (B.28), Eq. (B.44) implies

$$\frac{\partial M_S}{\partial a_F} \leq 0 \text{ (the equality holds if } x=0) \tag{B.45}$$

In Case (2) where $da_F < 0$: The proof of Eq. (B.45) is constructed along lines similar to the proof of Case (1) where $da_F > 0$. Therefore, Eq. (B.45) holds for both Cases (1) and (2). Accordingly, because $\partial \omega_S(T_S, M_S)/\partial M_S > 0$ and Eq. (B.45) holds, it follows that:

$$\frac{\partial \omega_S(T_S, M_S)}{\partial a_F} = \frac{\partial \omega_S(T_S, M_S)}{\partial T_S} \frac{\partial T_S}{\partial a_F} + \frac{\partial \omega_S(T_S, M_S)}{\partial M_S} \frac{\partial M_S}{\partial a_F} \leq \frac{\partial \omega_S(T_S, M_S)}{\partial T_S} \frac{\partial T_S}{\partial a_F} \tag{B.46}$$

where the equality in the inequality holds if $x=0$.

(ii) *The proof that* $\dfrac{\partial \omega_S(T_S,\,M_S)}{\partial T_S}\dfrac{\partial T_S}{\partial a_F} \leq \dfrac{\partial \omega_S(T_S,\,M_S)}{\partial T_S}\dfrac{\partial T_S}{\partial T_F}\dfrac{\partial T_F}{\partial a_F} \leq 0$ *(the equalities hold if* $x = 0$*)*.

The proof is organized in seven steps. In Step 1, we define $(T_{S,3}, M_{S,3})$ and then document that $T_{S,3} - T_S = \frac{\partial T_S}{\partial T_F}\frac{\partial T_F}{\partial a_F}$ and $T_{S,1} - T_S = \partial T_S / \partial a_F$ where $T_{S,1}$ is defined as in Eq. (B.28). In Step 2, we characterize $(T_{S,3},\,M_{S,3})$. In Step 3, we show that $T_{S,1}$ is smaller than $T_{S,3}$. In Step 4, we show that $T_{S,3}$ is smaller than T_S. In Steps 5 and 6, we combine Steps 1–4 to show that $\partial T_S / \partial a_F \leq \frac{\partial T_S}{\partial T_F}\frac{\partial T_F}{\partial a_F} \leq 0$. In Step 7, we conclude.

Step 1: We define $T_{F,1}$ in Eq. (B.27). Given $T_{F,1}$ and M_F, we define (T_3^*, M_3^*) and $(T_{S,3},\,M_{S,3})$, which satisfy:

$$\frac{1}{2}T_{S,3}^{-1/2}M_{S,3}^{1/2} = 2a_S T_3^*, \quad \frac{1}{2}T_{S,3}^{1/2}M_{S,3}^{-1/2} = 2b M_3^* \quad \text{and}$$

$$(T_{S,3}, M_{S,3}) = (xT_{F,1} + T_3^*, xM_F + M_3^*) \tag{B.47}$$

By the definitions of $T_{F,1}$ and $T_{S,3}$,

$$\frac{\partial T_S}{\partial T_F}\frac{\partial T_F}{\partial a_F} = T_{S,3} - T_S \tag{B.48}$$

Since we define $(T_{F,1},\,M_{F,1})$ in Eq. (B.27), and then define $T_{S,1}$ in Eq. (B.28),

$$\frac{\partial T_S}{\partial a_F} = T_{S,1} - T_S \tag{B.49}$$

Step 2: Reasoning in a way similar to our use of Eq. (B.28) to prove Eq. (B.29), we can use Eq. (B.47) to show that

$$\frac{M_{S,3}}{T_{S,3}} = \frac{xM_F + M_3^*}{xT_{F,1} + T_3^*} = \frac{a_S}{b}\frac{T_3^*}{M_3^*} \quad \text{and} \quad 16a_S b T_3^* M_3^* = 1 \tag{B.50}$$

Step 3: We prove that $\partial T_S / \partial a_F \leq \frac{\partial T_S}{\partial T_F}\frac{\partial T_F}{\partial a_F} \leq 0$ for two cases: Case (1) where $da_F > 0$ and Case (2) where $da_F < 0$.

In Case (1) where $da_F > 0$: Because of Eqs. (B.27) and (B.34), $M_F = lM_{F,1}$ for $l > 1$. Therefore, by Eqs. (B.29) and (B.50), for $j = 1, 3$ (such that if $j = 1$, then $l = 1$; and if $j = 3$, then $l > 1$), it then follows that

$$\frac{M_{S,j}}{T_{S,j}} = \frac{xlM_{F,1} + M_j^*}{xT_{F,1} + T_j^*} = \frac{a_S}{b}\frac{T_j^*}{M_j^*} \quad \text{and} \quad 16a_SbT_j^*M_j^* = 1 \tag{B.51}$$

We used Eq. (B.37) to obtain Eq. (B.39). Similarly, we now use Eq. (B.51) to obtain the following equation:

$$\frac{dT_{S,j}}{dl} = \frac{xT_j^*M_{F,1}}{2M_{S,j} + M_j^* + \frac{M_{S,j}}{T_{S,j}}T_j^*} \geq 0 \tag{B.52}$$

where the equality in the inequality holds if $x = 0$. Therefore,

$$T_{S,1} \leq T_{S,3} \quad \text{(the equality holds if } x = 0\text{)} \tag{B.53}$$

Step 4: Because of Eqs. (B.27) and (B.34), $T_{F,1} = qT_F$ for $q \in (0,1)$. Therefore, by Eq. (B.50),

$$\frac{M_{S,3}}{T_{S,3}} = \frac{xM_F + M_3^*}{xqT_F + T_3^*} = \frac{a_S}{b}\frac{T_3^*}{M_3^*} \quad \text{and} \quad 16a_SbT_3^*M_3^* = 1 \tag{B.54}$$

We used Eq. (B.37) to obtain Eq. (B.40). Similarly, we now use Eqs. (B.6), (B.7), and (B.54) to obtain this equation:

$$T_{S,3} \leq T_S \text{ (the equality holds if } x = 0\text{)} \tag{B.55}$$

Step 5: By Eqs. (B.48), (B.49), (B.53), and (B.55),

$$\frac{\partial T_S}{\partial a_F} \leq \frac{\partial T_S}{\partial T_F}\frac{\partial T_F}{\partial a_F} \leq 0 \quad \text{(the equalities holds if } x = 0\text{)} \tag{B.56}$$

Step 6: In Case (2) where $da_F < 0$: The proof of Eq. (B.56) is constructed along lines similar to the proof in Steps 3–5.

Step 7: Because $\partial\omega_S(T_S, M_S)/\partial T_S > 0$ and Eq. (B.56) holds,

$$\frac{\partial\omega_S(T_S, M_S)}{\partial T_S}\frac{\partial T_S}{\partial a_F} \leq \frac{\partial\omega_S(T_S, M_S)}{\partial T_S}\frac{\partial T_S}{\partial T_F}\frac{\partial T_F}{\partial a_F} \leq 0 \quad \text{(the equalities hold if } x = 0\text{)}$$

$$(B.57)$$

By Eqs. (B.46) and (B.57), P4 holds. ∎

B.4.1 Numerical Results for P4
Let

$$R1 = \frac{\dfrac{\partial\omega_S(T_S, M_S)}{\partial T_S}\dfrac{\partial T_S}{\partial a_F}}{\dfrac{\partial\omega_S(T_S, M_S)}{\partial a_F}} \quad \text{and} \quad R2 = \frac{\dfrac{\partial\omega_S(T_S, M_S)}{\partial T_S}\dfrac{\partial T_S}{\partial T_F}\dfrac{\partial T_F}{\partial a_F}}{\dfrac{\partial\omega_S(T_S, M_S)}{\partial a_F}}$$

Fig. C2(a) displays the ratios $R1$ and $R2$ on an (a_S, a_F) plane, given $x = 1/2$, $\delta = 1/4$, and $b = 1$. Fig. C2(b) displays these ratios when a_S is set to one and Fig. C2(c) displays them when a_F is set to one. Both ratios $R1$ and $R2$ are smaller than unity and $R1$ is greater than $R2$, which support Eq. (7) because $\partial\omega_S(T_S, M_S)/\partial a_F < 0$. The ratio $R1$ is in the range of $0.5 - 0.75$, whereas the ratio $R2$ is in the range of $0.3 - 0.75$, unless a_F and a_S are close to zero. For other parameter values, we obtain the same conclusion; the results are available from the authors upon request.

APPENDIX C

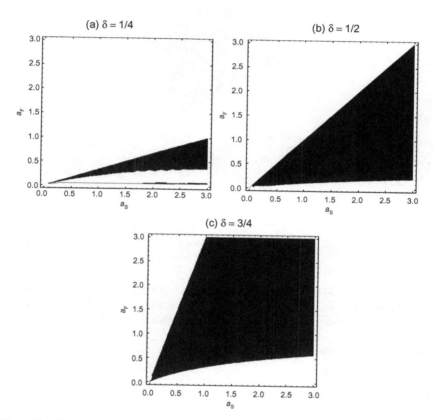

Fig. C1. Region of Parameter Space (a_S, a_F) Satisfying $\partial \cos\theta/\partial a_F < 0$ in Proposition P3(i).

Notes: The black region indicates the region of the parameter space (a_S, a_F) that satisfies $\partial \cos\theta/\partial a_F \geq 0$, and the white region indicates the region that satisfies $\partial \cos\theta/\partial a_F < 0$. The straight line dividing the black and white regions is $\delta/a_F = (1-\delta)/a_S$, and the white region above the straight line satisfies $\delta/a_F < (1-\delta)/a_S$. The parameter values are set as: $x = 1/2$ and $b = 1$.

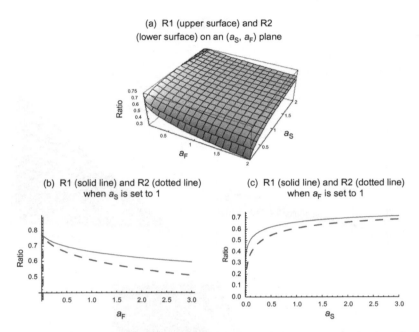

Fig. C2. Ratios $R1$ and $R2$ in Proposition P4. (a) $R1$ (upper surface) and $R2$ (lower surface) on an (a_S, a_F) plane. (b) $R1$ (solid line) and $R2$ (dotted line) when a_S is set to 1. (c) $R1$ (solid line) and $R2$ (dotted line) when a_F is set to 1.

Notes: Ratios $R1$ and $R2$ are defined as:

$$R1 = \frac{\dfrac{\partial \omega_S(T_S, M_S)}{\partial T_S}\dfrac{\partial T_S}{\partial a_F}}{\dfrac{\partial \omega_S(T_S, M_S)}{\partial a_F}} \quad \text{and} \quad R2 = \frac{\dfrac{\partial \omega_S(T_S, M_S)}{\partial T_S}\dfrac{\partial T_S}{\partial T_F}\dfrac{\partial T_F}{\partial a_F}}{\dfrac{\partial \omega_S(T_S, M_S)}{\partial a_F}}.$$

The parameter values are set as: $x = 1/2$, $\delta = 1/4$, and $b = 1$.

THE COLLEGE WAGE PREMIUM OVER TIME: TRENDS IN EUROPE IN THE LAST 15 YEARS ☆

Elena Crivellaro

The Organisation for Economic Co-operation and Development OECD

ABSTRACT

While there has been intense debate in the empirical literature over the evolution of the college wage premium in the United States, its evolution in Europe has received little attention. This paper investigates the causes of the evolution of the college wage premium in 12 European countries from 1994 to 2009, assessing the relevance of the supply factor as a

☆I am grateful to Giorgio Brunello, Elena Meschi, Mario Padula, Steve Pischke, Guglielmo Weber, Daniel Horn and two anonymous referees for valuable suggestions. I thank conferences and seminars participants at the IZA Workshop on Inequality – causes and consequences 2015, the SOLE conference 2014, RES Conference 2014, EALE Conference 2013, Workshop on Educational Governance, Trondheim 2013, PhD Workshop in Empirical Economics, Potsdam 2013, ESPE Conference 2012, at LSE Labour Workshop and at University of Padova PhD Seminars for helpful comments. The financial support from the Italian Ministry of University and Research is gratefully acknowledged. The paper is part of the FIRB 2008 project on 'The economic effects of demographic ageing'. Errors are my own. E-mail: elena.crivellaro[at]oecd.org

Inequality: Causes and Consequences
Research in Labor Economics, Volume 43, 287–328
ISSN: 0147-9121/doi:10.1108/S0147-912120160000043016

determinant of the college wage premium. *I use cross-country variation in relative supply, demand, and labour market institutions to examine their effects on the trend in wage inequality. I address possible concerns of endogeneity of the relative supply using an IV strategy exploiting the differential legislations of university autonomy and their variations over time. Results show that the strong increase in the relative supply that European countries have experienced has decreased the college wage premium. The most relevant institution is the minimun wage, which significantly decreases college wage premium.*

Keywords: College wage premium; inequality; relative supply

JEL classifications: J24; J31; I24

1. INTRODUCTION

In the last two decades there has been a huge increase in the average years of attained education, and the proportion of young people enroled into higher education has risen significantly in all developed countries. Over the 1997–2010 period, the proportion of graduates in the 25–64 age brackets increased by more than 60 per cent in Italy, Spain and Portugal and the United Kingdom, and by over 40 per cent in the Sweden, France and Norway, thanks also to European policies (i.e. Lisbon 2000) aimed at increasing participation in higher education.[1] This 'boom' in education can be interpreted as a supply shock to European labour market and is likely to have substantially affected the structure of wage differentials.

Many contributions in the literature dealing with the United States have noticed a growing college wage premium over time and a greater college premium implies greater inequality. The underlying causes of increasing inequality are highly debated among labour economists. While there are two leading explanations – skill biased technical change (SBTC) and labour market institutions[2] – the role of the supply of college graduates in

---

1. See OECD (2012).
2. 'Institutions' are noncompetitive forces acting on the labour market, such as labour unions, minimum wage, product and labour market regulations, taxes and subsidies and social norms. All these factors can affect the shape of wage distribution, including earnings inequality.

determining changes in the returns to a college education has yet to be explored in depth. Many empirical studies such as Katz and Murphy (1992), Card and Lemieux (2001) and Taber (2001) found SBTC to be the driving force behind rising wage inequality: this conclusion stems from the observation that the relative supply of high-skilled workers and the skill premium can only increase together if the relative demand for high-skilled workers also increases at the same time. There is substantial evidence in support to the fact that skill differentials in the United States have increased considerably in the last two decades. Between 1961 and 1979, returns to a college education (compared to a high school degree) rose from 61% to 82% despite the huge increase in the number of college graduates. The trend in Europe is less clear.[3] Rising returns have been observed for Portugal, Denmark and Italy, constant returns have been found in the United Kingdom and Germany, and falling returns for Sweden and Austria (at the beginning of 2000). However, most of this evidence refers to the period until the end of the 1990s with little attention being dedicated to the development of this phenomenon successively. Evidence on the evolution of the college wage premium and skill differentials in Europe is more scarce. Recent evidence of the impact of the increasing supply of graduates on their wage is available for the United Kingdom: Walker and Zhu (2008) are interested in how the college premium has varied over time, across subjects of study, wage distribution and two different cohorts. They show that up to 2000 there is almost no evidence of declining returns to college following the surge in participation in higher education. However, beyond 2002 they find suggestive evidence of modestly declining wage premia for graduates. Furthermore, only very few studies deal with the relation between wage inequality and education. Using UK data, Harmon, Oosterbeek, and Walker (2003) find that returns to schooling are higher for those at the very top of the wage distribution compared to those at the very bottom. Martins and Pereira (2004) have provided descriptive evidence showing that in the mid-1990s, in 15 European countries, returns to education at the upper quantiles significantly exceeded those at lower quantiles, that is, increasing education increases within wage inequality.

---

3. Katz and Murphy (1992) analyse changes in wage inequality over 25 years, from 1963 to 1987, in the United States, concluding that the rising in the relative demand for more skilled workers is 'a key component of any consistent explanation for rising inequality and changes in the wage structure over the last 25 years'.

Given that in the last two decades the demand for higher education has seen sheer expansion, it is interesting to investigate whether or not the returns are changing. It is reasonable to assume that changes in educational participation rates across cohorts will also imply changes in the ability—education relationship. If the ability composition changes, it can have an impact on estimated returns to education and to degrees. Reasoning with a simple supply and demand framework, an increase in the supply of highly educated workers would cause a decline in their wages. The demand for college graduates may be rising dramatically but if the supply keeps up with the demand, college wages will not increase.

Nevertheless, the supply and demand framework alone cannot account for empirical puzzles such as the one in the United States. Thus, if these inequality trends are not primarily explained by market-driven changes in the supply and demand for skills, it is possible that episodic institutional shocks are also a relevant factor. Changes in institutional factors such as the minimum wage have contributed to the evolution in the wage differential between college and non-college educated workers.[4] Goldin and Katz (2007) combine the usual supply-demand framework with institutional rigidities and alterations in order to understand returns to education in the United States in the past century.

DiNardo, Fortin, and Lemieux (1996) find that, in addition to supply and demand factors, de-unionization and declining minimum wages are important in explaining wage inequality. Using variation in the minimum wage across regions, Lee (1999) shows that not only is minimum wage negatively correlated with rising inequality at the top end of wage distribution but it can also explain much of the increase in the dispersion at the lower end of the wage distribution.

Europe may differ from the United States in this case: in fact, the presence of stronger institutions has helped and continues to help moderate the changes to the college wage premium in European countries. Machin (1997) and Dickens, Machin, and Manning (1999) find that in the United Kingdom, higher union density and higher minimum wages, respectively, reduce wage inequality. Manacorda (2004) and Edin and Holmlund (1995), studying Italy and Sweden, respectively, find that wage setting institutions are important for wage inequality. Koeniger, Leonardi, and Nunziata (2007) use panel data on institutions in OECD countries to assess the quantitative

---

4. See Fortin and Lemieux (1997) for a review of the effect of labour market institutions on the wage structure.

relationship between institutions and male wage inequality. Their findings show that labour market institutions do matter: the employment protection index, unemployment benefit, union density and minimum wage have a significant negative association with wage inequality within countries.

While (increasing) US wage inequality is extensively documented in the literature, there is less evidence on the (non-increasing) European wage dispersions. The difference in the pattern of college wage premium between the United States and Europe may be due to their different markets and institutions. When technological progress generates a higher relative demand for skilled labour, competitive markets increase wage differentials across skill groups in the United States, while in Europe compressed and rigid wage differentials have reduced inequality.[5] This paper fills this gap in the literature, investigating the evolution of the college wage premium in Europe over the period 1994–2009. It explores which dimensions of inequality are changing and which shifts in demand and supply and/or changes in wage setting institutions are responsible for this trend.

Hence, I assess the pattern of the college wage premium as a result of the recent expansion in graduation rates. Defining the role of the supply of college graduates on the college wage premium is important for its implications on higher-education policy and evolution of wage inequality. I aggregate individual data in cells identified by country, time, birth cohort and gender to obtain information on the college wage premium. The main novelty of this paper is that I address possible concerns of endogeneity of relative supply, in the college wage premium equation by using an instrumental variable strategy, which is something that has never been done before in the literature dealing with college wage premium. By exploiting the differential legislations of tertiary education institutions, namely the degree of university autonomy in different countries, and their variation over time, I am able to estimate the causal effect of relative supply on the wage premium. There is evidence that both market and non-market factors play a role in explaining inequality. More specifically, college wage premium appears to be negatively correlated to changes in relative supply and positively correlated with the relative demand index. Institutional constraints, such as minimum wage and unions play a minor role. Additionally, the effect of relative supply is more important for males and

5. See Levy and Murnane (1992) and Bertola and Ichino (1995).

for countries which have faced a stronger and faster increase in higher education graduation rates.

The paper is organized as follows: Section 2 presents the data used and describes the raw trends in wage changes, education differentials and wage inequalities. Section 3 is dedicated to the empirical framework. Sections 4 and 5 show the results of the trends in between-education-group wage inequality and the potential explanations for these evolutions in addition to some robustness checks. Section 6 concludes.

2. DATA AND AGGREGATE TRENDS

I use a unique dataset, merging the European Survey of Income and Living Condition (EUSILC) and European Community Household Panel (ECHP) to assess returns to college and wage inequality in Europe from 1994 to 2009.[6] The ECHP is a survey of 15 countries in the European Union from 1994 up to 2001.[7] The EUSILC is a collection of timely and comparable multidimensional microdata covering EU countries, starting in 2004 and ending in 2009, for a total of six waves. These surveys share many features, which makes it possible to harmonize the variables of interest.[8]

One advantage of these data is that they provide information for an overall period of 15 years within which I can observe a total of 12 European countries: Austria, Belgium, Germany, Denmark, Spain, Finland, France, Greece, Ireland, Italy, Portugal and the United Kingdom. For each country in the sample, I only consider the sub-sample of individuals who reside in the country of birth (more than 94 per cent of the total in 2009) because EUSILC data do not report the country of origin.[9]

The reference sub-sample focuses on native male and female working employees (self-employed are excluded) between 25 and 50 years old. This

---

6. This paper is not the first one using ECHP and EUSILC as a single data source (see, e.g. Naticchioni, Ragusa, & Massari, 2014; Goos, Manning, & Salomons, 2009).

7. The advantage of the ECHP over country-specific panel datasets consists in the homogeneity of the sampling procedures and of the questionnaires across countries which allow a high level of cross-country comparability.

8. See 'Comparative EU statistics on Income and Living Conditions: Issues and Challenges' available at www.ceps:lu=publihc_viewer:cfm?tmp=122. When aggregating sample weights are used.

9. In principle selecting only native workers may lead to issues bias estimates, thus these estimates should be interpreted as a lower bound of the real effect.

age framework allows to compare the youngest college graduates with their non-graduate counterparts and to avoid selection bias due to retirement and pensions.

I use net annual earnings in the reference sub-sample of all wage and salary workers in the public and private sector. All measures of wages in the paper are adjusted and deflated using the Purchasing Power Parity PPP (base Euro 15 = 1) to take into account different costs of living and to allow for comparison among years.

Educational attainments are measured by the highest level of education completed, based on ISCED levels, common to all countries and whose information is available in all datasets.[10]

Therefore, I define high-skilled workers as workers with at least some higher education (i.e. tertiary or post-secondary non-tertiary education) and low-skilled people as those with high school diplomas. As standard in the literature, the college wage premium is defined as the ratio of wage rates between college and high school graduates. For the sake of this analysis, I take the microdata and I group them into cells defined by time, country, year of birth cohort and gender. To control for aggregate labour supply and demand conditions, I use data from the OECD, EUKLEMS and ILO.[11] In particular, for the supply index, an indicator of gender-specific relative supply of college graduates with respect to high school diplomates, I use OECD data on the relative skill endowment, measured in terms of educational attainment.[12] For the construction of the demand index (à la Katz and Murphy), an indicator of the relative demand for high-skilled workers, I use data from EUKLEMS on the share of hours worked by high-skill workers relative to low skill workers. In investigating

---

10. The two surveys record differently information about schooling and sometimes not even consistently through time. ECHP only displays information about the highest earned qualification, and provides an education variable in three levels: low-middle-high skills (i.e. low, secondary, post-secondary-tertiary). They correspond to 0–2, 3 and 4–6 ISCED levels, respectively. EUSILC contains information on both earned qualifications (highest ISCED level achieved) and on ages at which individuals left school. ISCED states for international standard classification of education, it is an instrument implemented by the European Union for compiling internationally comparable educational statistics. It was designed by the UNESCO in the early 1970s to serve 'as an instrument suitable for assembling, compiling and presenting statistics of education both within individual countries and internationally' (UNESCO, 1997). See http://www.http://epp.eurostat.ec.europa.eu for further details.
11. Detailed information can be found in Appendix B.
12. The ratio of college graduates over high school graduates is a standard measure of the relative supply of graduates in each country.

the evolution of wage inequality institutions are another potential explanation of the trend in the college wage gap.[13] Institutional data are provided
by OECD and ILO.[14] These are yearly data, measuring wage bargaining
institutions, strictness of employment protection legislation, minimum
wage, union density and public sector employment.

2.1. Relative Wage Changes, Education Differentials and Wage Inequality

Over recent decades, tertiary education attainment has more than doubled
in most European countries. The strong increase in participation rates
in Europe is evident from Fig. 1, which shows the recent history of the

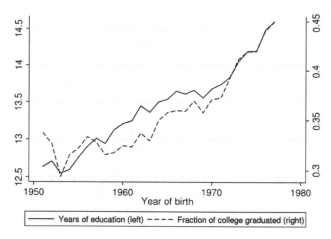

Fig. 1. Increasing Trend in Higher Education by Cohorts.
Source: Author's computations on EUSILC and ECHP data.

---

13. Traditionally in the literature, the institutional features that are considered to be important
for wage formation are: unions and bargaining institutions, wage regulation and welfare benefits, and labour market policies. A common finding of the studies that have investigated the
effects of institutions on wage dispersion is that the interactions between supply, demand and
institutions can take several routes altering both the between and the within structure of wages.
See, for example, Brunello, Comi, and Lucifora (2000) and Barth and Lucifora (2006).
14. Detailed information on institutional data used in the empirical analysis can be found in
Appendix B.

percentage of each cohort currently undertaking higher education and the average amount of years of education achieved by each cohort. The figure confirms the increasing trend in education attainment in Europe over time, showing that the average years of education achieved and the fraction of college graduates have increased by year of birth. For people born in 1955 the average number of years of education completed was almost 13.5 years, and the percentage of higher educated (i.e. high-skilled people) of that cohort was 30%; these numbers are almost 15 and 45% for the 1975 cohort.

Over the period, mean real income by educational group has changed differently across countries and educational groups. However, the generally increasing trends in education patterns are fairly similar across many European countries. Fig. 2 shows the trend of relative supply of college graduates to high school graduates separately by gender; the trend is constantly increasing over time for both men and women in European countries.

Panel A of Table 1 reports individual level descriptive statistics of education and income for the two dataset used. The percentage of people achieving different degrees, together with the average years of education achieved and the log of wages are shown for both men and women. Educational achievement is increasing over time in Europe, for both men and women. The other stylized fact that emerges is that women are overtaking men in college attainment.

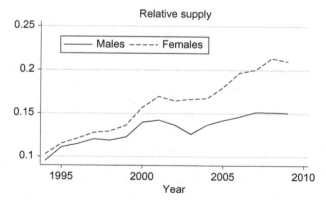

Fig. 2. Evolution of Relative Supply.
Source: Author's computations on OECD data.

Table 1.   Descriptive Statistics.

	Males		Females	
	ECHP	EUSILC	ECHP	EUSILC
Panel A: Demographics				
College graduates	0.30	0.32	0.39	0.43
High school graduates	0.36	0.42	0.36	0.39
High school drop outs	0.34	0.25	0.26	0.18
Years of education	12.69	13.60	13.11	14.20
Log wage	9.52	9.97	9.23	9.66
N	100,591	148,018	77,622	132,085
Panel B: Education premium				
College wage premium	1.64	1.54	1.55	1.45
College wage premium (age groups)				
Age 25–30	1.35	1.19	1.43	1.30
Age 31–36	1.58	1.44	1.56	1.48
Age 37–40	1.67	1.61	1.58	1.48
Age 41–45	1.70	1.68	1.63	1.54
Age 46–50	1.76	1.71	1.64	1.61
College wage premium (birth cohorts)				
Year Birth < 1950	1.67		1.49	
Year Birth 1950–1954	1.66	1.57	1.63	1.61
Year Birth 1955–1959	1.67	1.61	1.53	1.60
Year Birth 1960–1964	1.66	1.57	1.55	1.59
Year Birth 1965–1969	1.56	1.51	1.54	1.50
Year Birth 1970–1974	1.38	1.43	1.49	1.47
Year Birth 1975–1979	1.19	1.28	1.32	1.36
Year Birth > 1980		1.16		1.26

Source: Author's computations on EUSILC and ECHP DATA.
Notes: ECHP data cover the period 1994–2001, EUSILC data the period 2004–2009.

Looking at the trend in the college wage premium in Europe, Fig. 3 shows that its evolution has been very similar among European countries, with the exception of the United Kingdom. It is possible to observe a stable and slightly decreasing trend for the college wage premium for both men and women, with women receiving, in some cases, a slightly higher premium. The pattern observed would suggest that the huge influx of college graduates has saturated the demand for this type of worker, continuously reducing their potential comparative advantage and eroding the differences between peers with degrees and high school diplomas. This trend in the evolution of college wage premium is remarkably different from what is observed in the United States where wage dispersion has increased sharply

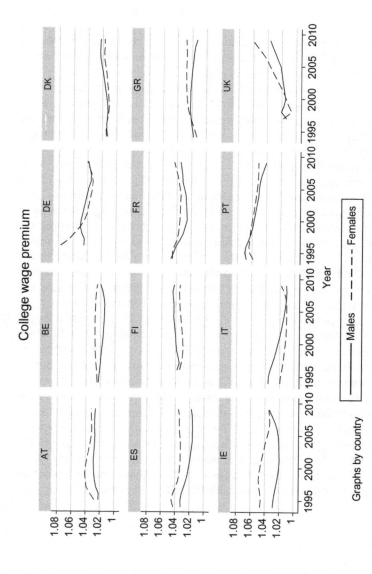

Fig. 3. Evolution of College Wage Premium by Country.
Source. Author's computations on EUSILC and ECHP data.

over time. European institutional rigidities have always been seen as the principal explanation for the differences in wage inequality between Europe and United States.[15] A possible explanation of the non-increasing trend in Europe compared to the increasing trend in the United States may lie in the different production structures characterizing the two continents: the strong leading effect of SBTC in the United States could be much lower in Europe because of the lack of high-skill intense sectors.

Moreover, the evolution over time of the college wage premium could be due to both different dynamics of cohort-specific relative wages as well as changes in the composition of employment by cohort. This means that the relative wage may vary across cohorts and, more specifically, that younger cohorts can experience higher wage gaps. Panel B of Table 1 shows the evolution of the education premium, a measure of between-groups-wage inequality. It measures the college wage premium, that is, the ratio of the earnings of college graduates to the earnings of high school graduates. The trend in the education premium seems to be decreasing slightly for both men and women from different age groups although these differences are not significant. Additionally, since different age group workers are imperfect substitutes in production and that relative supplies of different age groups are not all trending at the same rate, one would expect cohort effects to play some role in explaining the pattern of wage gaps across age groups and over time. Therefore, aggregating data controlling for year of birth cohorts, it is possible to notice striking differences between cohorts: younger cohorts have, on average, lower premia, reflecting a combination of both age differences and of the overall decline in average real earnings in Europe. This pattern is documented and analysed, for the United States, the United Kingdom and Canada, by Card and Lemieux (2001). It would be interesting to investigate how the college wage premium has varied across subjects studied as relative premia can also differ according to a college graduate's field of study. Generally, the most technical and quantitatively focused disciplines (such as engineering, computer science, economics and finance) tend to have the largest education premia, while the less quantitative arts and humanities disciplines tend to have much smaller education premia, and this would be consistent with the SBTC hypothesis.[16]

---

15. See Bertola and Ichino (1995).
16. Recent studies by Walker and Zhu (2011) and Webber (2014) find that the economic returns, for both for the United Kingdom and the United States, are higher for STEM-related majors (i.e. sciences, technology, engineering and maths).

3. EMPIRICAL FRAMEWORK

I draw on the standard model in the literature, which is presented in Appendix A, to analyse the leading proximate causes of overall and between-group wage inequality.[17]

Understanding the sources of the variation in the college wage premium means using a model where wage premia are determined not only by the interaction of market forces, namely, supply and demand of various kind of labour but also by labour market institutions (wage setting norms, unionization, minimum wages) that can reconcile patterns in the skill premium when supply–demand forces alone fail explaining the evolution of wage differentials (see Goldin and Katz, 2007; Lemieux, 2006). Taking the standard supply and demand framework to the data, the equation of interest is the following:

$$\ln w = \rho \left(\frac{\alpha_{hct}}{\alpha_{lct}} \right) - \frac{1}{\sigma} \ln \left(\frac{H_{ct}}{L_{ct}} \right) \tag{1}$$

where the variable of interest, w, represents the relative wage of skilled to unskilled workers. The relative wage of different educational groups is generally used as a measure of between-group inequality. $(\frac{H_{ct}}{L_{ct}})$ represents the relative supply of skilled versus unskilled labour, and $(\frac{\alpha_{hct}}{\alpha_{lct}})$ the SBTC.

As is frequently done in the literature, to control for changes in demand conditions, I proxy the relative demand shift, with a demand index, time trends and a measure of technology – R&D intensity.[18,19]

The idea is that all these measures increase relative productivity in the skill-intensive sectors; I thus expect a positive coefficient in my estimations. The standard model allows both supply and demand for skills to grow exogenously. With exogenous variation in the demand of skills, the theory predicts that the wage premium should vary inversely with the relative supply of skills. In the absence of institutional constraints, the wage premium goes up or down depending on whether demand grows faster than supply, or vice versa. Since demand and supply alone cannot explain the complete

---

17. Katz and Murphy (1992). This model assumes competitive markets and full employment.
18. This demand index is similar to the demand index used by Katz and Murphy (1992) which is based on the changes in the relative employment.
19. Ratio of R&D expenditure over value added in the manufacturing sector measured every year in each country.

trend of college wage premium, institutions are added to the model as additional proximate causes of wage inequality (see Goldin & Katz, 2007). Institutions may ease or limit the operation of market forces.[20]

Taking the theoretical framework to the data, I estimate the following augmented model that includes a vector of labour market institutions as control variables:

$$\ln\left(\frac{w_{cta}^H}{w_{cta}^L}\right) = \gamma_0 + \gamma_1 D_{ct} + \gamma_2 \ln\left(\frac{H_{ct}}{L_{ct}}\right) + \gamma_3 X_{ct} + \gamma_4 G + \tau_t + \mu_c + \eta_a + \varepsilon_{cta} \quad (2)$$

where X_{ct} is a vector of labour market institutions, namely, union density, minimum wage, employment protection and a measure of public sector employment.[21] The coefficient γ_2 provides an estimate for $1/\sigma$, that is the inverse of the elasticity of substitution between skilled groups. D_{ct} is the relative demand indicator and τ_t, μ_c and η_a are time country and birth cohorts fixed effects (for five-year birth cohorts), respectively. G is a gender dummy equal to 1 for males and to 0 for females. This equation suggests an explanation of relative wage movements comprising both market and institutional factors.

To get efficient estimates and to avoid underestimation of standard errors that can emerge in case of wage premium persistence, standard errors are bootstrapped using clustering at country level. Using the United States as reference, the model above suggests that the competitive wage of a particular type of workers depends positively on the average rate of technical change — meaning a positive effect on the wage ratio of SBTC, negatively on their relative supply change and positively on their relative product-demand shift (that is associated to the technical change).

Concerning institutional factors, the effect is less straightforward. The impact of institutions is generally concentrated in specific parts of the wage distribution. Institutions may affect wage differentials in various ways, also depending on the elasticity of labour supply and across demographic

---

20. In this literature labour market institutions are introduced as a deviation from the competitive norm. Indeed, some consensus has emerged on the fact that both institutions and interactions institutions-shocks can matter in explaining unemployment trends and, as a consequence, wage premia. For example, Blanchard and Wolfers (2000) show that in Europe institutions can be responsible for the cross-sectional variation in unemployment across countries while exogenous shocks can explain the general increase in unemployment.

21. Detailed information on the sources of the institutional data is contained in Appendix B.

groups. Moreover, institutions have different effects across industries by changing the incentives for capital investment and thus indirectly affecting wage inequality. Unions increase the wage rates of their members above the level they would achieve in the absence of representation, thus favouring low-skilled workers and inducing inequality to decline. The problem with this argument is that it ignores the effects of union wage policy on non-union wages. If a set of jobs usually performed by a particular type of worker is unionized and the employer forced to pay higher wages, the supply of labour to all other jobs done by that type of worker will increase together with a reduction in wages. Therefore, it is not clear if the average wage for the group rises or falls with the increase in union representation. Additionally, white-collar workers at the higher end of the wage distribution may be very unionized − for example, this is the case of some professional orders in Italy − making it hard to establish the effect of unions on the wage premium. By setting an explicit threshold for the lowest wage rate paid, the presence of a statutory minimum wage tends to reduce wage dispersion. Minimum wage can impact the wage distribution in several ways: firstly, by preventing employers from hiring workers with productivity below the minimum wage. Secondly, by preventing firms from pushing down wages for workers with low bargaining power and reducing heterogeneity at the bottom. Additionally, a minimum wage increase leads to an increase in wages for workers paid at the minimum wage level, a weaker increase for workers with wages slightly above the minimum wage (spillover effects) and has little or no effect on high-paid workers.[22] Thanks to its regressive nature, this measure is likely to have a stronger effect at the bottom rather than at the top of the wage distribution.

Employment protection policies are often associated with a more compressed wage structure. They protect unskilled more than skilled workers and thus have a negative effect on the wage ratio.[23]

In turn, accepting the hypothesis that the effects of institutions on the outside option of workers are mostly in favour of the unskilled, I would expect aggregate institutional measures to have a negative impact on the relative wage. They improve the outside option of employers for low-skilled groups, strengthening their bargaining position and compressing the skill wage differentials.

22. Charnoz, Coudin, and Gaini (2011).
23. See Boeri and Jimeno (2005).

In addition to this standard set of labour market institutions, I add a measure of public sector pervasiveness — relative percentage of the population working on the public sector. Since public sector employment is perceived as safer and offering more benefits, the more risk-averse individuals sort into public sector employment.[24] The idea is that public sector employment may have acted to offset the widening wage inequality seen in recent years and to narrow the college wage premium.[25]

Since it is plausible that market and institutional factors alter the wage distribution both across skill groups and across age groups, data are aggregated by country, year of the survey and year of birth cohorts.

While this model, including cross-country differences in the role of labour institutions, does a reasonable job in accounting for trends in skill premium, some questions are left unsolved.

A first concern of this model is that relative skill supply is predetermined, thus labour supply of each group is inelastic. This assumption may no longer hold. Previous literature focuses on the relationship between relative supply and college wage premium without considering the potential endogeneity of the relative supply. Failure to take this issue into consideration could result in OLS estimation of the effect of relative supply on college wage premium being inadequate ($\hat{\gamma}_2$ is biased). Theoretically, the bias is negative ($\text{plim}_{n \to \infty} \hat{\gamma}_2 < \gamma_2$) if the errors are negatively correlated or if relative supply is measured with error, and positive otherwise. The assumption that the relative supply of workers is predetermined is plausible in the very short run, whereas, it is reasonable to suppose that, in the long run, the fraction of workers that choose to become more educated responds both to innovations increasing the relative demand for more educated labour and ability premia.

From the individual point of view, given the existing set of possibilities for accessing education, a worker can choose whether to undertake education and to what extent, in order to maximize his/her lifetime earnings (i.e. as well as in relation to the relative wages expected). Therefore, a significant relationship between education attainment — relative supply — and some individual outcomes may simply result from some unobserved heterogeneity determining both variables.

---

24. This is shown to be the case in Germany by Pfeifer (2011).
25. However, it seems to be the case that workers at the lower tail of the wage distribution benefit more from public sector employment than workers at the upper tail of the wage distribution. Actually, there is evidence that there can be a wage penalty for highly qualified employees — see, for example, Melly (2005).

Similarly, there may be concerns with regard to some unobserved country-specific factor that shifts the relative demand for skilled workers, leading to higher relative wages and higher relative employment, and confounding the estimation of the inverse substitution elasticity. To overcome these concerns I use an instrumental variable strategy. I exploit data on the reforms affecting the university system as an instrumental variable for the aggregate relative supply ratio. In particular, I use an index measuring university autonomy in several domains.[26] This empirical strategy exploits the differences across countries in accessibility to tertiary education due to changes in institutions and legislations.[27]

Another possible issue is the potential endogeneity of the relative demand index: hours worked can be jointly determined with wages, thus

---

26. The domains of university autonomy are: budget, recruitment, organization, logistic, courses organization, self-evaluation and development plans. The data used here have been kindly provided by Daniele Checchi, Elena Meschi and Michela Braga, who in Braga, Checchi, and Meschi (2013) have constructed a dataset on school reforms occurred in the last century in 18 countries in Europe. See Appendix B for details about the data and the reforms.

27. Another issue to address is immigration. It is likely that, since immigrants, on average, are less educated than natives, changes in immigration flows during years affected the relative skill supplies, having as well an impact on college wage premium. Hence, it is important to understand how much of the change in skill supplies have come from changes in immigration and how much is stemming from changes in the native population. The first and most common presumption is that immigration greatly increases the premium to skill, as immigrants increase the supply of less educated people. However, following the reasoning of Goldin and Katz (2007) for the United States, immigration is found not to be so relevant in determining the relative skill supplies having a modest impact on the wage premium. The main reason can be found in the change of the educational distribution of more recent migrants: in the recent period immigrants can be distributed at both the very top or the very bottom of the educational ladder. Goldin and Katz (2007) found that immigration had only a minor impact on the growth in the relative supply of the college graduates and a moderate impact on the high school graduates workers relative to the supply in the 1980–2005 period. To avoid problems stemming from the possible misreporting of educational information about migrants, I select my sample on native people. However, in many European countries, in particular in many countries belonging to the subgroup of the 'low relative supply countries' migration is a very important and massive phenomenon. It is possible, that it has an effect on the relative supply of college graduates and thus on college wage premium. This is the case of Italy and the United Kigdom. To check my results, even if related only to native people, are not biased by the high proportion of migrants existing in some countries, I control for yearly immigration rate by country, and this does not change much the results. Additionally, as a further robustness check, I control for relative migration (i.e. share of college graduate migrants over non-college graduates migrants) in the countries for which these date are available. Results are in line with previous findings.

determining supply-induced demand. To overcome this potential pitfall, I use a proxy measure for relative demand: time trends and a measure of technology – R&D intensity. Results are proven to be robust also using only R&D intensity and time trends as proxy for relevant demand.[28]

4. ESTIMATION RESULTS

The different evolutions of wage distributions are also driven by different labour market structures and the dissimilar interactions between economic shocks and institutions in the countries analysed. To investigate the proximate causes of inequality, I regress the college wage premium on a set of variables including proxy for relative demand and supply and some institutional indicators. The idea is to identify which are the main drivers and whether they act differently from the ones involved in the American scenario. The standard OLS estimation results are presented in Table 2.

Results show that institutions matter together with demand and supply factors. The first column of Table 2 uses the original specification of Katz and Murphy (1992) – baseline specification in the tables – with only relative demand and supply measures included as explanatory variables, in addition to country fixed effects, year of birth fixed effects and time fixed effects, gender and survey dummies. I then add some measure of institutional constraints in each column to estimate the 'full' model. In column 2, I add controls for minimum wage, employment protection legislation and union density. Column 3 incorporates an alternative measure of the relative demand – R&D intensity. Finally, in the last column, I add the percentage of people working in the public sector. The coefficients for the relative supply and relative demand variables are negative and significant for relative supply, positive for the relative demand index. The coefficient of the relative supply index is slightly higher, in absolute value, than the relative demand indicator in the baseline and in the richer specifications (−0.0124 vs. 0.0089). The alternative measure of demand, R&D intensity, has a positive and significant effect although it is very low.[29] The negative and

---

28. Results are omitted but available upon request.
29. In order to make these results comparable with others in the literature, referring to Autor, Katz, and Kearney (2008), I also included a time trend as a proxy for the demand for high-skilled workers: a positive coefficient would be interpreted as a sign of SBTC. What I find is that the sign is not always positive neither significant, confirming the lower effect of the demand in contrast to the relative supply.

Table 2. The College Wage Premium – Pooled Countries.

	(1)	(2)	(3)	(4)
Relative supply	−0.0119***	−0.0124***	−0.0131***	−0.0134***
	(0.0039)	(0.0039)	(0.0038)	(0.0039)
Relative demand	0.0054	0.0089**	0.0080**	0.0079*
	(0.0036)	(0.0042)	(0.0040)	(0.0041)
Males	−0.0024***	−0.0024***	−0.0024***	−0.0024***
	(0.0003)	(0.0003)	(0.0003)	(0.0003)
Minimum wage		−0.0160**	−0.0195***	−0.0183**
		(0.0068)	(0.0071)	(0.0071)
EPS		−0.0000	−0.0003	−0.0003
		(0.0004)	(0.0004)	(0.0004)
Union density		−0.0000	−0.0000	−0.0000
		(0.0000)	(0.0000)	(0.0000)
R&D intensity			0.0006***	0.0006***
			(0.0002)	(0.0002)
Public employees				−0.0058
				(0.0073)
R-squared	0.147	0.149	0.154	0.155
Observations	1,686	1,686	1,686	1,686

Notes: The table reports OLS estimates of the evolution of wage inequality. The dependent variable is college wage premium. All regressions include a full set of country, year, survey and birth cohort dummies. Clustered standard errors using bootstrap in parentheses. *$p < 0.1$, **$p < 0.05$, ***$p < 0.01$. EPL denotes employment protection legislation. Column (1) shows the baseline model – à la Katz and Murphy, column (2) adds labour market institutions. Columns (3) and (4) add, respectively R&D intensity and the % of public employment.

significant coefficient of the dummy for male is not surprising. It is well known that, on average, there is much more selection into education for women rather than for men. A higher college wage premium for women is a common finding in the literature.[30] Institution constraint coefficients are expected to have mainly a negative sign, since these policies should affect unskilled more than skilled workers. A one per cent increase in the minimum wage lowers the college wage premium by around 1.6%: thus revealing that increases in the minimum wage provide a valid explanation for the slowdown in the positive trend in wage premia in Europe over the period. Although negatively correlated with wage inequality, the effect of union density is almost zero. Employment protection legislation does not seem to

---

30. See Goldin, Katz, and Kuziemko (2006).

matter. Public sector employment is negatively but not significantly corre-lated with wage inequality.[31] Consequently, it seems that in European countries an important determinant of the non-increasing trend in college wage premium is the strong increase in the relative supply. Comparing these estimates to the United States, it is evident that in Europe demand plays a much smaller role in boosting wage inequality. This may be due to the different sectorial composition of the European production sector, which is generally characterized by a lower technology intensity with respect to the American production sector.

4.1. Assessing the Endogeneity Bias

As mentioned in the previous section, although this model does a good job in capturing the general trend of the college wage premium, it suffers from a potential endogeneity problem. In the very short run, the supply of skills and labour market institutions may be treated as given. However, in the long run, the growth of supply and the changes in the skill premium can be jointly determined.

To assess the potential endogeneity of the relative supply, that is the relative share of the labour force with tertiary education relative to the share of the labour force with a high school diploma, I use an instrumental variable strategy.[32]

In particular, I use an index measuring the expansion of university autonomy as instrument.[33] Educational reforms can be considered

---

31. Unemployment could also be a part of the story, as argued in Autor et al. (2008): selection into unemployment could shift to the right the distribution of unobserved skills and of wages. However, adding unemployment rate and relative unemployment of skilled to unskilled people to the wage inequality regression does not change remarkably the results. Results are omitted but are available upon request.

32. A common way of addressing this issue is to use different characteristics of the institutional structure of the education system as instruments for the educational attainment. Institutional reforms are generally seen as formal rules affecting the assignment of the endogenous variable (in this case relative supply) in a way interrelated to the outcome (i.e. college wage premium) (see also Hanushek & Woessmann, 2012).

33. The expansion in university index measures autonomy at tertiary level in the following dimensions: budget, recruitment, organization, logistic, courses organization, self-evaluation and development plans. Allowing greater autonomy to university implies greater differentia-tion in admission curricula, resource availability, and attractiveness for best researchers (see Braga et al., 2013) for further details.

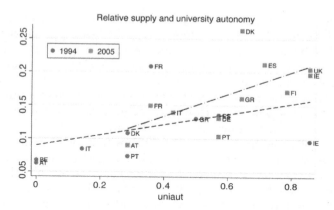

Fig. 4. University Autonomy and Relative Supply.
Source: Author's computations on OECD data on relative supply and
institutional data from Braga et al. (2013).

structural reforms, and as such they require a sufficiently long period to
yield results. For this reason I impute the level of university autonomy to
the relative supply five years later.

For this IV methodology to work, the university autonomy instrument
must satisfy three conditions, being (a) university autonomy is correlated
with relative supply (first-stage relevance); (b) university autonomy is
uncorrelated with the econometric error e (second-stage independence); and
(c) university autonomy has no impact on college wage premium other than
through its first-stage impact on relative supply (second-stage exclusion).

University autonomy is shown to be positively associated with student
achievement. Fig. 4 provides graphical evidence in support of the relevance
of the instrument: it shows the existence of a positive relation between
increasing university autonomy and the relative supply.[34] The graph depicts
the association between the level of university autonomy and the relative
supply measured after five years, in 1994 and 2005. It is easy to notice the
presence of a positive gradient between the two variables. Moreover, it is
evident that in time countries have experienced an increase in university
autonomy, followed by an increase in the relative supply.

---

34. Since 1980 European countries implemented reforms generally aimed at increasing the
degree of autonomy given to higher education institutions. This degree of autonomy varied
enormously between countries and between the university and non-university sectors.

Reforms increasing university autonomy are generally viewed positively and they influence the relative supply via the following mechanism: it is thought that by involving more competition, these reforms improve the quality of the tertiary institution, thus increasing college participation. The main benefits of university autonomy are several but the main one concerns efficiency gains in the production of education through greater competition in the provision of schooling. However, the drawback is that this process could increase social stratification.[35] All the different aspects of university autonomy considered in the index are features that increase the efficiency of the institutions, thus lowering costs, and, in a general equilibrium framework, a reduction of the universities' cost curve is the flip side of an increase in the supply curve of graduates. While other policies such as the ones inducing selectivity or those enclosing student financing or educational expenditures may be endogenous − potentially driven by the demand or by the wealth of the country − university autonomy can reasonably be assumed to be uncorrelated with the disturbances of the 'inequality equation'. Since there have been some trends in these reforms increasing decentralization and autonomy of decision-making in schools and university over time and across countries, there is no implication that this is driven by demand for a particular type of skilled/unskilled individuals or by systematic differences in economic and cultural systems.[36] Additionally, this has been true despite the alternance of different political parties, which generally have divergences in the ideal distribution of educational attainment of a country.[37] Overall, these results suggest that these reforms on different aspects of university autonomy identify an authentic source of exogenous variation across years and countries: they have an exogenous impact on college enrolment/relative supply, are expected to impact the relative wage only through college enrolment and do not suffer from reverse causality.

By pooling countries, I exploit the fact that the timing of reforms concerning university autonomy varies across countries and by doing so it is possible to disentangle tertiary education reform from cohort fixed effects. A key assumption here is that we can treat the pooled data from multiple countries

---

35. Braga et al. (2013).

36. See also Hanushek and Woessmann (2012).

37. Different political parties have different opinions with respect to what is the appropriate skill composition in the domestic labour force, as well as about the desirable degree of social differentiation. Both the degree of skill composition and of social differentiation depend heavily on the distribution of educational attainment in the population, which can be modified by policy interventions − such as policy reforms (see also Braga et al., 2013).

Table 3. First Stage – Pooled Countries.

	(1)	(2)	(3)
University autonomy	0.112***	0.106***	0.099***
	(0.006)	(0.006)	(0.009)
Institutions	No	No	Yes
Year FE	Yes	Yes	Yes
Birth cohorts FE	Yes	Yes	Yes
Country FE	No	Yes	Yes
R-squared	0.219	0.377	0.732
Observations	1,182	1,182	1,182
F-statistics	127.61	48.93	162.76
F-statistics p-value	0.000	0.000	0.000

Notes: The table reports first-stage estimates of the IV estimation for wage inequality. The dependent variable is relative supply of graduates. An index measuring the level of university autonomy by country and year is used as instrument. Included but not shown are all the exogenous controls such as relative demand, males and survey dummies. Clustered standard errors using bootstrap in parenthesis. $*p < 0.1$, $**p < 0.05$, $***p < 0.01$.

as one population and therefore treat the timing of the natural experiment in different countries as regional variation in the timing in the same way as US researchers would use state-by-state variation in implementation.

Table 3 shows first-stage estimates of the IV strategy for the relative supply: relative supply is regressed on all the exogenous controls plus the indicator measuring the variation in university autonomy reforms, measured five years before. The underlying assumption is that it takes an average of five years in order for these reforms to take action, be implemented and affect the relative supply.[38] In all the specifications, the instrument measuring the expansion in university autonomy is shown to be a good explanatory variable for aggregate relative supply: the coefficient is always positive and significant confirming the evidence depicted in Fig. 4, suggesting that exposure to reforms improving university autonomy tends to lead to a higher relative supply of graduates. Therefore, the level of tertiary education in a particular year and in a specific country is reasonably deemed to be affected by the level of institutional set-up of tertiary education, measured by the degree of university autonomy, five years before.

38. Five years is the standard length of a university cycle. Moreover, this mismatch increase as well the validity of the instrument used as it avoids any problem of reverse causality. For this reason the sample observed is partially reduced and delimited to the year 2005, since the data on the tertiary education institutions arrive up to 2005.

Table 4.   2SLS Estimates of Wage Inequality — Pooled Countries.

	Baseline Model		+ Labour Market Institutions	
	OLS	IV	OLS	IV
Relative supply	−0.017**	−0.043**	−0.018**	−0.049**
	(0.006)	(0.015)	(0.006)	(0.016)
Relative demand	−0.004	0.003	−0.001	0.005
	(0.003)	(0.005)	(0.004)	(0.005)
Males	−0.003***	−0.003***	−0.003***	−0.003***
	(0.000)	(0.000)	(0.000)	(0.001)
Minimum wage			−0.020*	−0.033**
			(0.009)	(0.011)
EPS			0.001	0.001
			(0.001)	(0.001)
Union density			−0.000	−0.000*
			(0.000)	(0.000)
Angrist−Pischke F test		92.659		99.759
R-squared	0.135	0.110	0.137	0.108
Observations	1,182	1,182	1,182	1,182

Notes: OLS and IV estimates of wage inequality are reported. The sample is reduced to the period 1994−2005. The dependent variable is college wage premium. Relative supply is instrumented by an indicator measuring university autonomy. All regressions include a full set of country, year, survey and birth cohort dummies. Clustered standard errors using bootstrap in parenthesis. *$p < 0.1$, **$p < 0.05$, ***$p < 0.01$.

At the bottom of the table, I report the F-statistic of the excluded instruments. It oscillates between 48 and 162, well above the conventional threshold of 10 for strong instruments. Thus, there should be no concerns about potential biases in the second stage due to the use of weak instruments.

The second-stage results are presented in Table 4. I compare OLS and IV estimates of the college wage premium, replacing relative supply with the university autonomy instrument. More specifically, columns 1 and 2 show the baseline specification where college wage premium is regressed on a demand index and a supply index. Columns 3 and 4 add labour market institutions such as minimum wage, EPL and union density as additional controls.[39] The estimated IV coefficients of relative supply are negative,

---

39. The richer specification, that is the one including the other controls used in the OLS estimations, such as the, public employment and R&D intensity, has been omitted since these variables do not appear relevant.

strongly significant and larger in magnitude than the OLS. OLS estimates give a relative supply coefficient of −0.018, while IV estimates are substantially larger in both the specifications (−0.043 and −0.049), implying a positive bias. The Angrist−Pischke robust F-statistics for excluded instruments confirm that the instrument is a strong predictor of the relative supply as I already know from the regressions in Table 3. Additionally, in the IV estimates, the sign and the significance of the coefficients of the labour market institutions are very close to what has been found in the original OLS estimates. Institutions play a minor role in this reduced sample. Again, the most relevant institution is the minimum wage, which has a negative and significant effect − of a very similar size of the OLS one on the college wage premium. Collective bargaining instruments seem not to be relevant in compressing the college wage premium, as their effect is almost zero.

A few conclusions can be drawn from this set of estimates. First, there is clear empirical evidence that relative supply has a negative effect on college wage premium in Europe: being exposed to a higher relative supply of graduates has caused a reduction in the college wage premium, that is, the relative advantage of the relatively higher educated people. Second, the comparison between OLS and IV estimates suggests that the OLS estimates are upward biased. The story behind these results could be the following: relatively more college graduates should earn relatively less, due to increased supply. The increase in supply may also have an indirect effect through a compositional effect on unobserved ability. Average quality (ability) of college graduates could decrease relatively to high school graduates' ability, due to the expansion of relative supply, and this may result in lower wage premia but this is mere speculation because I do not have any measure to control for ability.

5. ROBUSTNESS CHECKS

To check the validity of my results I have run a series of robustness checks. Firstly, to avoid potential issues stemming from sample selection bias that might affect female labour force participation, I ran the analysis separately for men and women. A prominent stylized fact in this literature has been that the college wage premium for women is higher than the college wage premium for men: see, for example, Mincer and Polachek (1974), Chiappori, Iyigun, and Weiss (2009) and Goldin et al. (2006). The general conclusion is that 'women receive a higher increase in wages than men when they acquire college or advanced degrees'.[40] However, more recent data seem to contradict these findings: Peña (2006) offers only evidence from outside the United States to support the claim that the college wage premium is higher for men and Hubbard (2011), for the United States argues the gender difference in the college wage premium has dwindled over time, and there has been no female advantage in the college wage premium for at least a decade.[41]

Following Olivetti and Petrongolo (2008), neglecting selection into employment may lead to serious bias in the estimation of women's wage equations. Results of both OLS and 2SLS are shown in Tables 5 and 6.

Table 5.   OLS Estimates – Males and Females.

	Males		Females	
	(1)	(2)	(3)	(4)
Relative supply	−0.0190***	−0.0213***	−0.0075	−0.0094**
	(0.0060)	(0.0065)	(0.0045)	(0.0044)
Relative demand	0.0126**	0.0099**	−0.0011	0.0061
	(0.0050)	(0.0049)	(0.0055)	(0.0060)
R&D intensity		0.0004*		0.0007***
		(0.0002)		(0.0003)
Minimum wage		−0.0136		−0.0220**
		(0.0094)		(0.0094)
EPL		−0.0009**		0.0003
		(0.0003)		(0.0006)
Union density		−0.0001		−0.0000
		(0.0000)		(0.0001)
Public employees		0.0079		−0.0137
		(0.0085)		(0.0117)
R-squared	0.180	0.193	0.108	0.119
Observations	822	822	864	864

Notes: The table reports OLS estimates of the evolution of wage inequality separately by gender. The dependent variable is college wage premium. All regressions include a full set of country, year, survey and birth cohort dummies. Clustered standard errors using bootstrap $*p < 0.1$, $**p < 0.05$, $***p < 0.01$. EPS denotes employment protection legislation. Columns (1) and (3) show the baseline model – à la Katz and Murphy, columns (2) and (4) add labour market institutions, R&D intensity and the % of public employment.

---

40. Chiappori et al. (2009) look at white workers aged 25–54 in the United States during years 1975–2004 using CPS data.
41. This suggests that other forces, such as the non-market benefits of college education or the (non-pecuniary) costs of attending college, are driving relative changes in college attendance of men and women.

Table 6. College Wage Premium for Males and Females — Instrumental Variable Estimates.

	(1) Relative Supply (FS)	(2) CWP (OLS)	(3) CWP (2SLS)
Panel A: Males			
University autonomy	0.060***		
	(0.007)		
Relative demand	0.054*	0.010	0.013*
	(0.026)	(0.005)	(0.006)
Relative supply		−0.012*	−0.041
		(0.006)	(0.029)
Controls	Yes	Yes	Yes
Angrist–Pischke *F* test			23.956
R-squared			0.200
Observations	582	582	582
F-statistics			
F-statistics *p*-value	0.000		
Panel B: Females			
University autonomy	0.117***		
	(0.010)		
Relative demand	0.029	0.006	0.004
	(0.037)	(0.010)	(0.007)
Relative supply		−0.003	0.009
		(0.007)	(0.018)
Controls	Yes	Yes	Yes
Angrist–Pischke *F* test			56.246
R-squared	0.826	0.121	0.113
Observations	600	600	600
F-statistics	104.596		
F-statistics *p*-value	0.000		

Notes: The table reports first-stage estimates, OLS and 2SLS estimations for wage inequality for the two subsamples of men (Panel A) and women (Panel B). The dependent variable is relative supply of graduates in the first column and college wage premium (CWP) in columns 2 and 3. The index of university autonomy is the instrument. All the exogenous controls of the full specification are included, in particular institutions (EPL, minimum wage, union density), country, year, birth cohort and survey dummies. Clustered standard errors using bootstrap in parenthesis. $*p < 0.1$, $**p < 0.05$, $***p < 0.01$.

Table 5 presents OLS estimates of wage inequality separately for males and females. Columns (1) and (3) reproduce the baseline model, whereas columns (2) and (4) add the whole set of controls. Results are in line with previous findings, with relative supply negatively and significantly correlated with college wage premium and relative demand positively associated.

The role of relative supply and demand is much stronger for men: the effect of supply is almost double than for women while the effect of the demand is significant only for males. These results are in line with the literature dealing with sample selection and gender wage gap. Specification (1) of Table 5 reveals that university autonomy is significantly associated with relative supply in the first stage. This effect appears stronger for women. A possible explanation is that women in this period have seen a much higher increase in relative supply than men. Specifications (2) and (3) show the OLS and the second-stage estimates, respectively. The second-stage estimates of the wage inequality model confirm previous findings: institutionally induced changes in relative supply are negatively and significantly related, and affect college wage premium for men. These results are a confirmation of the existence of stronger non-random selection for women into employment: women who are employed tend to have relatively high-wage characteristics.

Additionally, since the focus of this paper is on the role of the supply in the evolution of college wage premium, I differentiate between countries with a high (initial) relative supply of graduates and countries with low (initial) relative supply of graduates, measured at the beginning of the period analysed, that is in 1994. Denmark, Finland, Ireland, Spain, France and Belgium are countries that were experiencing high percentage of people achieving higher education in the 1990s. On the other hand, countries, such as Italy, the UK, Portugal, Germany, Greece and Austria had lower graduate rates at the beginning of the period analysed. Looking at the values of this ratio in 1994, I divide the set of countries into two regions: countries with a high or low relative supply of graduates as in 1994. Countries characterized by a lower stock of highly educated individuals experienced even higher growth in attainment levels, thus suggesting a catching-up phenomenon. Certainly, the evolution of the relative supply trend has differed in the two sets of countries, therefore, I expect differences in the evolution of the college wage premia as well: Fig. 5 shows that college wage premium has evolved very differently among countries with a high and low relative supply of graduates. The college wage premium in high relative supply countries has been decreasing slowly over time, while in low relative supply countries it has been experiencing a fast growing trend. I replicate the analysis separately for the two sets of countries and I show supportive evidence of what has been found pooling the countries, in both the OLS and 2SLS estimates. Still, there is evidence of a negative and significant effect of relative supply on the college wage premium, and this is true also correcting for the endogeneity of labour supply. The negative effect of relative supply is higher in countries with a low relative supply of graduates. Results of OLS estimates are shown in Table 7: the coefficient of the relative supply

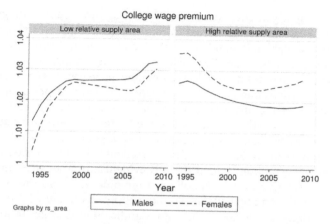

Fig. 5. Evolution of College Wage Premium in the Two Set of Countries.
Source: Author's computations on EUSILC and ECHP DATA.

Table 7. OLS Estimates – High and Low Relative Supply Countries.

	High Relative Supply Countries		Low Relative Supply Countries	
Relative supply	−0.0082**	−0.0073**	−0.0255**	−0.0216*
	(0.0037)	(0.0035)	(0.0111)	(0.0115)
Relative demand	0.0070	0.0177*	0.0059	0.0069
	(0.0063)	(0.0096)	(0.0061)	(0.0075)
Males	−0.0021***	−0.0020***	−0.0027***	−0.0027***
	(0.0003)	(0.0003)	(0.0005)	(0.0005)
R&D intensity		0.0009***		0.0005
		(0.0003)		(0.0006)
Minimum wage		0.0208		−0.0280***
		(0.0165)		(0.0097)
EPL		0.0012		−0.0012
		(0.0008)		(0.0008)
Union density		0.0000		0.0000
		(0.0000)		(0.0002)
Public sector employment		−0.0540***		−0.0420
		(0.0164)		(0.0427)
R-squared	0.194	0.215	0.129	0.135
Observations	948	948	738	738

Notes: The table reports OLS estimates of the evolution of wage inequality. The dependent variable is college wage premium. All regressions include a full set of country, year, survey and birth cohort dummies. Clustered standard errors using bootstrap *p < 0.1, **p < 0.05, ***p < 0.01. EPS denotes employment protection legislation. Columns (1) and (3) show the baseline model – à la Katz and Murphy, columns (2) and (4) add labour market institutions, R&D intensity and the % of public employment.

indicator is slightly higher in countries with a lower supply of graduates (−0.022 vs. −0.007). Countries with a high relative supply of skilled workers present a higher and significant relative demand indicator in the baseline and in the richer specifications, whereas in countries with a lower relative supply, the standard relative demand measure does not appear to be a significant determinant of wage inequality. Table 8 presents the first-stage estimates of the effect of tertiary education reforms, namely the estimated coefficients on the instrument in the regression of relative supply. In this case too, instruments appear strong and significant, and robust F test statistics support the relevance of the instruments. Table 9 compares results of OLS and IV estimates. Again there is evidence of a negative and significant effect of relative supply on college wage premium, and this is true also correcting for the endogeneity of labour supply. Estimated IV coefficients of relative supply are negative, strongly significant and larger in magnitude than the OLS for low relative supply countries, however, this is not the case for high relative supply countries. According to these estimates, the OLS coefficient of relative supply is −0.009 in the preferred specification in high relative supply countries, and −0.057 in countries with a low relative supply of graduates. The IV estimates are substantially larger in low relative supply countries and in both the specifications (−0.093 in the baseline model and −0.101 in the richer specification), implying a positive

Table 8. Relative Supply Equation: First Stage.

	High Relative Supply Countries		Low Relative Supply Countries	
University autonomy	0.113***	0.174***	0.077***	0.066***
	(0.015)	(0.015)	(0.009)	(0.013)
Institutions	No	Yes	No	Yes
Year FE	Yes	Yes	Yes	Yes
Birth cohorts FE	Yes	Yes	Yes	Yes
Country FE	Yes	Yes	Yes	Yes
R-squared	0.596	0.664	0.779	0.784
Observations	648	648	534	534
F-statistics	43.15	81.62	142.85	132.44
F-statistics *p*-value	0.000	0.000	0.000	0.000

Notes: The table reports first-stage estimates of the IV estimation for wage inequality. The dependent variable is relative supply of graduates. The set of tertiary education reforms are the instruments. All the exogenous controls such as dummy for males, relative demand and institutions. All regressions include a full set of country, year, survey and birth cohort dummies. Clustered standard errors using bootstrap in parenthesis. $*p < 0.1$, $**p < 0.05$, $***p < 0.01$.

Table 9. 2SLS Estimates — High and Low Relative Supply Countries.

	Baseline Model		+ Labour Market Institutions	
	OLS	IV	OLS	IV
Panel A: High relative supply countries				
Relative supply	−0.007	−0.019	−0.009*	−0.009
	(0.004)	(0.016)	(0.004)	(0.014)
Relative demand	0.006	0.009	0.008	0.008
	(0.008)	(0.009)	(0.013)	(0.013)
Institutions			Yes	Yes
Angrist−Pischke *F* test		59.578		99.534
R-squared	0.194	0.184	0.201	0.201
Observations	648	648	648	648
Panel B: Low relative supply countries				
Relative supply	−0.056*	−0.093*	−0.057*	−0.101*
	(0.025)	(0.045)	(0.024)	(0.050)
Relative demand	0.007	0.011	0.011	0.016*
	(0.007)	(0.007)	(0.007)	(0.008)
Institutions			Yes	Yes
Angrist−Pischke *F* test		20.393		13.267
R-squared	.148	.140	.149	.137
Observations	534	534	534	534

Notes: OLS and IV estimates of wage inequality are reported. The sample is reduced to 1994−2005. The dependent variable is college wage premium. Relative supply is instrumented by a set of indicators measuring university autonomy. All regressions include a dummy for males and a full set of country, year, survey and birth cohort dummies. Clustered standard errors using bootstrap in parenthesis. $*p < 0.1, **p < 0.05, ***p < 0.01$.

bias. In addition, I have also run pooled regressions removing one country at time. In this case too, excluding one country at time, results are in line with the ones obtained pooling all countries together.[42]

6. CONCLUSIONS

While there has been intense debate about the contribution of the increase of higher education participation to the widening wage inequality in the United States, its evolution in Europe has been given little attention.

---

42. Results are omitted but are available upon request.

This paper aims at analysing changes in the wage premium associated with a college degree using a large European dataset obtained harmonizing two different sources. More specifically, I am interested in how the college premium has evolved across time. I try to offer some insights into this topic by looking at the supply and demand for skills. This paper assesses the importance of relative supply factors as determinant of the college wage premium by analysing the effects of the recent strong increase in participation rates on returns to college and inequality in Europe. Identifying the role of relative supply of college graduates on the college wage premium is important for its implication on higher education policy and enhancing the accessibility to higher education. I have constructed a dataset which covers 15 years and exploited cross-country variation in relative supply, demand and labour market institutions to look at their effects on the trend in the college wage gap.

Observing the evolution of the college wage premium, a striking difference emerges with respect to the American scenario. A potential explanation of the observed declining/stable trend in the college wage premium in Europe is indeed the increase in educational attainment over the period and the low leading effect of the demand. The fall in the skill premium is intuitively the first outcome of a classic supply and demand effect. In particular, it could be that the demand was not able to compensate for the increase in the labour supply of skilled workers. To check whether this is the case, I look at the potential sources of wage inequality, including supply and demand factors as well as institutional indicators. I address possible concerns of endogeneity of relative supply by an instrumental variable strategy exploiting the variation over time and over countries of university autonomy. Results show that demand and supply factors explain a lot of the variation, and that institutions are not the main driver: the estimates reveal the important effect of the increased relative supply on the evolution of college wage premium while relative demand appears to play a minor role. The minimum wage is an institutional constraint deserving more attention. The main policy implication of these findings is that increasing accessibility to tertiary education in Europe can not only lower the disparities among different education groups but can also lower college wage premia, possibly due to the implied changes in ability composition across education groups. Moreover, the institutional explanation holds as well; it is apparently possible to protect low-skilled workers against market forces by establishing proper institutions, specifically those concerning minimum wages.

REFERENCES

Autor, D. H., Katz, L. F., & Kearney, M. S. (2008). Trends in U.S. wage inequality: Revising the revisionists. *The Review of Economics and Statistics, 90,* 300–323.

Barth, E., & Lucifora, C. (2006). *Wage dispersion, markets and institutions: The effects of the boom in education on the wage structure.* IZA Discussion Papers No. 2181. Institute for the Study of Labor (IZA).

Bertola, G., & Ichino, A. (1995). Wage inequality and unemployment: United States versus Europe. In NBER *Macroeconomics Annual 1995, Volume 10,* National Bureau of Economic Research, Inc., NBER chapters, pp. 13–66.

Blanchard, O., & Wolfers, J. (2000). The role of shocks and institutions in the rise of European unemployment: The aggregate evidence. *Economic Journal, 110,* C1–33.

Boeri, T., & Jimeno, J. F. (2005). The effects of employment protection: Learning from variable enforcement. *European Economic Review, 49,* 2057–2077.

Braga, M., Checchi, D., & Meschi, E. (2013). Educational policies in a long-run perspective. *Economic Policy, 28,* 45–100.

Brunello, G., Comi, S., & Lucifora, C. (2000). *The college wage gap in 10 European countries: Evidence from two cohorts.* IZA Discussion Papers No. 228. Institute for the Study of Labor (IZA).

Card, D., & Lemieux, T. (2001). Can falling supply explain the rising return to college for younger men? A cohort-based analysis. *The Quarterly Journal of Economics, 116,* 705–746.

Charnoz, P., Coudin, E., & Gaini, M. (2011). *Decreasing wage inequality in France 1976–2004: Another French exception?* Technical Report 6, INSEE Working Paper.

Chiappori, P.-A., Iyigun, M., & Weiss, Y. (2009). Investment in schooling and the marriage market. *American Economic Review, 99,* 1689–1713.

Dickens, R., Machin, S., & Manning, A. (1999). The effects of minimum wages on employment: Theory and evidence from Britain. *Journal of Labor Economics, 17,* 1–22.

DiNardo, J., Fortin, N. M., & Lemieux, T. (1996). Labor market institutions and the distribution of wages, 1973–1992: A semiparametric approach. *Econometrica, 64,* 1001–1044.

Edin, P., & Holmlund, B. (1995). *The Swedish wage structure: The rise and fall of solidarity wage policy?* National Bureau of Economic Research, Inc., NBER chapters, pp. 307–344.

Eurydice. (2000). Two decades of reform in higher education in Europe: 1980 onwards. *Eurydice Thematic Studies.* Retrieved from http://www.mp.gov.rs/resursi/dokumenti/dok174-eng%20Reform_higher.pdf

Fortin, N. M., & Lemieux, T. (1997). Institutional changes and rising wage inequality: Is there a linkage? *Journal of Economic Perspectives, 11,* 75–96.

Goldin, C., & Katz, L. F. (2007). *The race between education and technology: The evolution of U.S. educational wage differentials, 1890 to 2005.* NBER Working Papers No. 12984. National Bureau of Economic Research, Inc.

Goldin, C., Katz, L. F., & Kuziemko, I. (2006). The homecoming of American college women: The reversal of the college gender gap. *Journal of Economic Perspectives, 20,* 133–156.

Goos, M., Manning, A., & Salomons, A. (2009). Job polarization in Europe. *American Economic Review Papers and Proceedings,* American Economic Association, *99*(2), 58–63.

Hanushek, E., & Woessmann, L. (2012). Do better schools lead to more growth? Cognitive skills, economic outcomes, and causation. *Journal of Economic Growth, 17,* 267–321.

Harmon, C., Oosterbeek, H., & Walker, I. (2003). The returns to education: Microeconomics. *Journal of Economic Surveys*, *17*, 115−156.

Hubbard, W. H. J. (2011). The phantom gender difference in the college wage premium. *Journal of Human Resources*, *46*, 568−586.

Katz, L. F., & Autor, D. H. (1999). Changes in the wage structure and earnings inequality. In *Handbook of Labor Economics* (Vol. 3, pp. 1463−1555). Amsterdam, North-Holland: Elsevier.

Katz, L. F., & Murphy, K. M. (1992). Changes in relative wages, 1963−1987: Supply and demand factors. *The Quarterly Journal of Economics*, *107*, 35−78.

Koeniger, W., Leonardi, M., & Nunziata, L. (2007). Labor market institutions and wage inequality. *Industrial and Labor Relations Review*, *60*, 340−356.

Lee, D. (1999). Wage inequality in the United States during the 1980s: Rising dispersion or falling minimum wage? *Quarterly Journal of Economics*, *114*(3), 977−1023.

Lemieux, T. (2006). Increasing residual wage inequality: Composition effects, noisy data, or rising demand for skill? *American Economic Review*, *96*, 461−498.

Leuven, E., Oosterbeek, H., & van Ophern, H. (2004). Explaining international differences in male wage inequality by differences in demand and supply of skill. *Economic Journal*, *144*, 478−498.

Levy, F., & Murnane, R. J. (1992). U.S. earnings levels and earnings inequality: A review of recent trends and proposed explanations. *Journal of Economic Literature*, *30*, 1333−1381.

Machin, S. (1997). The decline of labour market institutions and the rise in wage inequality in Britain. *European Economic Review*, *41*, 647−657.

Manacorda, M. (2004). Can the scala mobile explain the fall and rise of earnings inequality in Italy? A semiparametric analysis, 1977−1993. *Journal of Labor Economics*, *22*, 585−613.

Martins, P. S., & Pereira, P. T. (2004). Does education reduce wage inequality? Quantile regression evidence from 16 countries. *Labour Economics*, *11*, 355−371.

Melly, B. (2005). Public-private sector wage differentials in Germany: Evidence from quantile regression. *Empirical Economics*, *30*, 505−520.

Mincer, J., & Polachek, S. (1974). Family investments in human capital: Earnings of women. In *Marriage, family, human capital, and fertility*. National Bureau of Economic Research, Inc., NBER chapters, pp. 76−110.

Naticchioni, P., Ragusa, G., & Massari, R. (2014). Unconditional and conditional wage polarization in Europe. IZA Discussion Papers 8465, Institute for the Study of Labor (IZA).

OECD. (2012). *Education at a glance 2012: OECD indicators*. Paris: OECD Publishing.

Olivetti, C., & Petrongolo, B. (2008). Unequal pay or unequal employment? A cross-country analysis of gender gaps. *Journal of Labor Economics*, *26*, 621−654.

Peña, X. (2006). Assortative matching and the education gap. Borradores de Economia 427. Banco de la Republica de Colombia.

Pfeifer, C. (2011). Risk aversion and sorting into public sector employment. *German Economic Review*, *12*, 85−99.

Taber, C. R. (2001). The rising college premium in the eighties: Return to college or return to unobserved ability? *Review of Economic Studies*, *68*, 665−691.

UNESCO. (1997). *International standard classification of education 1997*. Retrieved from http://www.uis.unesco.org/Library/Documents/isced97-en.pdf

Walker, I., & Zhu, Y. (2008). The college wage premium and the expansion of higher education in the UK. *Scandinavian Journal of Economics, 110*, 695–709.

Walker, I., & Zhu, Y. (2011). Differences by degree: Evidence of the net financial rates of return to undergraduate study for England and Wales. *Economics of Education Review, 30*, 1177–1186.

Webber, D. A. (2014). The lifetime earnings premia of different majors: Correcting for selection based on cognitive, noncognitive, and unobserved factors. *Labour Economics, 28*, 14–23.

APPENDIX A: THEORETICAL FRAMEWORK

Following the conventional conceptual framework of this literature, I model the relative wage dynamics as a combination of supply and demand factors and labour market institutions.[43]

From a theoretical perspective there is the need to account separately for the relative wage of two types of workers. Consider an extended version of the CES production function with two labour inputs that are imperfect substitutes: low educated (or unskilled) and high educated (or skilled). Assume that firms in each economy use the following simple production function where output depends on employment:

$$Y_{ct} = e^{\phi_{ct}} N_{ct} \qquad (3)$$

with Y being the total output produced, N the employment in efficiency units, c the country, t the time and ϕ a country- and time-specific productivity shock, a parameter denoting total factor productivity.

Employment is made by two groups of workers, skilled and unskilled labour, which are employed according to

$$N_{ct} = [(e^{\alpha_{lct}} L_{ct})^\rho + (e^{\alpha_{hct}} H_{ct})^\rho]^{1/\rho} \qquad (4)$$

α is an efficiency parameter indicating the productivity of a particular type of worker (L, H) in country c at time t, it is an index of the technological efficiency of a worker as it is factor augmenting technical change parameter capturing changes in input quality over time. H_{ct} and L_{ct} are the quantities employed of college equivalent (skilled labour) and high school equivalent (unskilled labour).

It is assumed that the economy is at full employment, that means the total effective aggregate labour supply of each labour group is employed in the industries of the economy. Another assumption is that H_{ct} and L_{ct} are

---

43. In their paper, Katz and Murphy (1992) used a demand and supply of skills framework to analyse the change in wage inequality over time. The same framework has then been used by Katz and Autor (1999), Goldin and Katz (2007) and Leuven, Oosterbeek, and van Ophern (2004) to look at differences in skills groups across countries. All these studies focus exclusively on demand side modelling.

exogenous. That is the aggregate supply does not depend on its relative average wage.

$\rho = 1 - 1/\sigma$ is a time-invariant production parameter, where σ is the aggregate elasticity of substitution between labour inputs. The low quality and high quality workers are gross substitutes if $\sigma < 1$ and $\rho > 0$, whereas they are gross complements if $\sigma < 1$ and $\rho > 0$.

Skill neutral technological progress raises both $e^{\alpha_{lct}}$ and $e^{\alpha_{hct}}$ by the same proportion. Whereas, skill-biased technical changes involve the increase of $\frac{e^{\alpha_{hct}}}{e^{\alpha_{lct}}}$.

Competitive labour markets are assumed, so college equivalent and high school workers are paid their marginal products, then profit maximization with respect to N_{ict} (with $i = L, H$) yields to

$$w_{ict} = e^{\phi_{ct} + \alpha_{ict}} \left[\frac{N_{ict}}{N_{ct}} \right]^{\rho - 1}$$

where w_{ict} is the real wage for labour input i in country c at time t.

In other terms, efficient utilization of different skill groups requires that the relative wages are equated to the relative marginal products. The relative wage of high-skill to low skill workers can be written as

$$w = \frac{w_{ct}^H}{w_{ct}^L} = \left(\frac{e^{\alpha_{hct}}}{e^{\alpha_{lct}}} \right)^{(\sigma - 1)/\sigma} \left(\frac{H_{ct}}{L_{ct}} \right)^{-(1/\sigma)} \tag{5}$$

which is equal to:

$$\ln w = \rho \left(\frac{\alpha_{hct}}{\alpha_{lct}} \right) - \frac{1}{\sigma} \ln \left(\frac{H_{ct}}{L_{ct}} \right) \tag{6}$$

The relative wage of different educational groups is generally used as a measure of between-groups inequality. $\left(\frac{H_{ct}}{L_{ct}} \right)$ represents the relative supply of skilled versus unskilled labour, and $\left(\frac{\alpha_{hct}}{\alpha_{lct}} \right)$ the skill-bias technological change. This can be rewritten as

$$\ln \left(\frac{w_{ct}^H}{w_{ct}^L} \right) = \frac{1}{\sigma} \left[D_t - \ln \left(\frac{H_{ct}}{L_{ct}} \right) \right] \tag{7}$$

where D_t indexes relative demand shifts which favour high-skilled workers and it is measured in log quantity units.

Eq. (6) can lead to a very simple and intuitive demand-supply interpretation. Given a skill-bias technical change, the substitution effect is such that the skill premium increases when there is a scarcity of skilled relative to unskilled workers.

Relative demand changes can be due to shifts in product demand, SBTC and non-neutral changes in the relative changes in relative prices/quantities of non-labour inputs, so marginal productivity and elasticity.

The relative demand is shifted by the bias of the technological change:

$$\frac{\partial \ln w}{\partial \left(\frac{\alpha_{hct}}{\alpha_{lct}} \right)} = \frac{\sigma - 1}{\sigma}$$

This means that, given the relative supply, if there is skill-biased technological change (i.e. technological shock shifting the demand line outward) the wage premium will increase.

Similarly, for a given 'skill bias', $\left(\frac{\alpha_{hct}}{\alpha_{lct}} \right)$, an increase in the relative supplies $\left(\frac{H_{ct}}{L_{ct}} \right)$ lowers relative wages with elasticity σ.

Following the reasoning above, the evidence of a negative relationship between college premium and relative supply of skills in the recent period in Europe can be interpreted as an increase in the relative supply of college skills, under the assumption of stable demand's conditions. In short, there are the main forces that operates in this framework: the relative supply and the relative demand of more-educated workers. When these two forces fail in explaining the wage differentials, the pattern can be reconciled by institutional factors such as change in union density/strength and wage setting policies. Labour market institutions, indeed, differently alter the outside option of skilled and unskilled workers thus affecting wage differential as well as relative labour demand.

APPENDIX B: DATA APPENDIX

College wage premium: It is defined as the ratio of wage rates between college and high school graduates. I obtain college wage premium data at the birth cohort-country-year level from the European Community Household Panel (ECHP) and the European Union Survey on Income and Living Conditions (EUSILC). The ECHP started in 1994 and lasted until 2001 and reports wages in national currencies, while the EUSILC covers 2004–2009 and contains wages in Euros.

Relative supply index: This index is created using OECD data. It is a measure of relative supply and it is calculated separately by gender in each country, yearly, as the ratio of college graduates to high school graduates (ISCED 5/ISCED 3).

Relative demand index: This index is created using EUKLEMS data. It is a measure of relative demand and it is calculated for each country, yearly, considering hours worked by high-skilled persons engaged (share in total hours) by industries relative to hours worked by middle-skilled workers.

R&D intensity: Data are drawn from the OECD-STAN database which provides information on imports, R&D and value added in the manufacturing sector from 1973 to 2009. Using these data I manage to build a proxy for technology using the ratio of R&D over total value added in manufacturing, by year for all countries.

Minimum wage: This is the ratio of the statutory minimum wage to the median wage in each country. The measure is provided by the OECD. Germany, Denmark, Finland and Italy have no statutory minimum wage.

Employment protection legislation (EPL): The employment protection legislation consists on a set of norms and procedures followed in case of dismissal of redundant workers. The OECD indicators of employment protection are synthetic indicators of the strictness of regulation on dismissals and the use of temporary contracts. These indicators are compiled from 21 items covering three different aspects of employment protection: Individual dismissal of workers with regular contracts, additional costs for collective dismissals and regulation of temporary contracts. Range {0, 6} increasing with strictness of employment protection.

Net union density: Union density expresses union membership as a proportion of the eligible workforce. Normally, union density rates are standardised by the calculation of union membership as a proportion of the wage and salary earners in the same year (preferably on the basis of some annual average year data). The data are drawn from the ILO website.

Public sector employment: Data are collected from the laborsta.ilo.org website (ILO). These are data covering all employment of general governmental sector plus employment of publicly owned enterprises and companies. It covers all persons employed directly by those institutions. Based on this data, I compute an index of 'public sector employment' by calculating the percentage of public employees over total working population, yearly, by country.

To address any further concern regarding the presence of endogeneity, I then implement an IV strategy. The potentially endogenous relative supply variable is instrumented using the 'tertiary education institutional set-up' variables. Data are taken from Braga et al. (2013) and contains information about the degree of university autonomy in the different countries.

The reforms carried out in Europe since 1980 generally aimed at increasing the autonomy of the higher education institutions, particularly in the case of the universities, in relation to the planning and delivery of higher education. However, the degree of autonomy given to higher education institutions varied enormously between countries and between the university and non-university sectors.

Index of university autonomy measures autonomy at tertiary level in the following dimensions: budget, recruitment, organization, logistic, courses organization, self-evaluation and development plans. This data is taken from Braga et al. (2013) who used Eurydice (2000) 'Two decades of reforms in higher education in Europe: 1980 onwards' (p. 91) as source. It is a continuous measure from 0 to 1, which is simply a normalized sum of indexes characterizing seven separate dimensions (budget, recruitment, organization, logistic, courses organization, self-evaluation and development plans), which are then rescaled in order to retain unitary variation.

Full autonomy in the different areas is understood as meaning that the institutions are able to: freely spend any income derived from government grants, fees and contracts; decide on the employment of academic staff and their salaries (even if all legal requirements for minimum qualifications and minimum salaries have to be met); be responsible for internal management without the obligation to include specific external members on governing boards or similar bodies; own buildings and equipment used for teaching purposes; freely change course structure and content; determine when and how to assess the quality of their educational provision and, finally, determine any policy significantly affecting the institution's future development. The majority of countries studied have a high degree of autonomy over a wide range of their activities. Course planning is the area where most of the countries suffered restrictions in institutional autonomy, followed by development planning, budget spending and employment of teaching staff. Self-evaluation is the area where all countries except the French Community of Belgium, Denmark, Greece and France had full autonomy. Countries where universities had (and have) the least autonomy are Germany, France and Austria.

APPENDIX C

Table C1. Timing of Reforms on University Autonomy and Degree of Autonomy Enjoyed by Higher Education Institutions.

Country	Budget Spending	Recruitment	Organization	Logistic	Course Planning	Self-Evaluation	Development Planning
Austria	1993*	1993*	1993	None	1997*	1993	None
Belgium (fr)	1998	1995	Pre-1980*	1991	1994	Pre-1980*	None
Belgium (nl)	1996	1996	1996*	Pre-1980*	1995*	Pre-1980*	None
	1991*	1991*	1991*	1991*	1991*	1991	1991*
	1994*	1994*	1994*	1994*	1994*	1994	1994*
Germany	None	None	Pre-1980	Pre-1980*	Pre-1980*	1990	Pre-1980
Denmark	1993	Pre-1980	1993	1993*	Pre-1980	1992*	1993*
Finland	1988–1994	Pre-1980	1986	1988	Pre-1980*	Pre-1980	1997
	1991	1991	1991	1991	1991*	1991	1991
France	Pre-1980*	None	1984*	1989*	Pre-1980*	1989*	1984
Greece	1997*	1982*	1982	Pre-1980	1982	1997*	1982*
Ireland	Pre-1980	Pre-1980	Pre-1980	Pre-1980	Pre-1980	Pre-1980	Pre-1980
Italy	1983	1998*	1989	1993	1990*	1993	none
Spain	1983	1988*	1983	1983	1983*	1991	1983
Portugal	1988	1988*	1988*	1997	1989	1994	1997
	Pre-1980	Pre-1980	Pre-1980	Pre-1980	Pre-1980	Pre-1980	Pre-1980
UK	1992	1992	1992	1992	1992	1992	1992

Source: Eurydice (2000, p. 91).

Notes: The table shows the years in which relevant legislations in the main areas of university autonomy change, implementing full autonomy, for the different countries analysed. The asterisk indicates that institutional autonomy is not complete but is determined by a framework of rules and conditions laid down by the government or any other authority.

RISING WAGE INEQUALITY, REAL WAGE STAGNATION AND UNIONS [☆]

Stephen Machin

University College London and Centre for Economic Performance, London School of Economics

ABSTRACT

Labour markets across the globe have recently been characterized by rising wage inequality, real wage stagnation or both. Most academic work to date considers each in isolation, but the research in this paper attempts to pull them together, arguing that higher wage inequality takes on an added significance if real wages of the typical worker are not growing, and showing that inequality rises and real wage slowdowns have gone hand-in-hand with one another due to wages decoupling from productivity in the United States and United Kingdom. The lack of growth of real

[☆]I would like to thank an anonymous referee, Christian Dustmann and Hank Farber, together with participants at the IZA workshop on 'Inequality: Causes and Consequences' in March 2015 and the 'The German Labour Market in a Globalized World' conference in Nuremburg in April 2015, for a number of helpful comments.

Inequality: Causes and Consequences
Research in Labor Economics, Volume 43, 329–354
ISSN: 0147-9121/doi:10.1108/S0147-912120160000043017

wages at the median in the United States is also shown to be linked to the declining influence of trade unions.

Keywords: Rising wage inequality; real wage stagnation; unions

JEL classifications: I20; I21; I28

1. INTRODUCTION

A by now large academic research literature has studied the trend of rising wage inequality, and its drivers, that has characterized the labour markets of many developed countries over the past four decades. This work first began with studies of the two countries where rising wage gaps took off first — the United States and United Kingdom — and now there is a huge literature focussing on the evolution of wage structures in many more settings and time periods.[1]

Whilst the rising gap between the highest and lowest paid has received close attention, less commonly studied are the changing patterns of real wage growth that have accompanied rising wage inequality. In fact, it is less well known that real wages of the typical (median) worker have stagnated in a number of countries for some time. For example, as will be shown below, real wages have not grown much at the median in the United States since the late 1970s. Median real wages in Germany have barely grown since the mid-1990s. More recently, many countries have been characterized by historically weak levels of real wage growth.

When median real wage changes have been studied, they have mostly been considered in isolation from increased wage inequality (one recent exception looking at overall income is Kenworthy, Nolan, Roser, Smeeding, & Thewissen, 2015). In this paper, I consider the two together, presenting evidence on how they have evolved through time in different countries. Further, for the United States, where wage inequality has risen and real wage growth for the typical worker has stalled for quite a long time, I look at them in the particular context of the long-run demise of trade unions.

The findings of the paper show that rising wage inequality takes on an increased significance when coupled with a recognition that real wage

---

1. For reviews of this work see the *Handbook of Labor Economics* chapters by Katz and Autor (1999) and Acemoglu and Autor (2010).

performance has been weak. This is because real wage stagnation has resulted in lack of improvement in living standards which makes inequality matter more. For the United States, this seems to have been magnified by the significantly reduced role that trade unions now play in the process of wage determination, as compared to the time when wage inequality started to rise.

The rest of the paper is structured as follows. In Section 2, I first describe international patterns of changing wage inequality and then present evidence on real wage stagnation. Section 3 considers how they can be connected to one another by showing that increased wage inequality is a reason why growth in median wages has fallen significantly behind productivity and overall compensation. Section 4 considers union decline and how it relates to real wage stagnation in the United States. Section 5 offers some conclusions, as well as highlighting possible future research directions that can be taken with the aim of more closely integrating research on real wage evolutions and wage inequality trends.

2. RISING WAGE INEQUALITY AND REAL WAGE STAGNATION

This section of the paper presents descriptive evidence on what has happened to wage inequality and to growth in the real wages of the median worker in a number of OECD countries who have consistently defined data through time.

2.1. Rising Wage Inequality

Table 1 shows trends in the 90–10 wage ratio for male full-time workers between 1980 and 2013 (or the most recently available year). It reports information for the seven countries in the OECD.Stat database that have consistently defined data for all these years.

Consider first the patterns for the United Kingdom and United States, as shown in the bottom two rows of the table. Both countries see continually rising 90–10 ratios from 1980 to 2013. In the 1980 the 90th percentile full-time man in the United States was paid 3.6 times as much as the 10th percentile full-time man in 1980, with this rising to 4.4 by 1990, to 4.8 by 2000 and to its highest level over this period of 5.4 by 2013. Thus, the 90–10 wage ratio rose by 50 per cent over the 33 years covered in the table.

Table 1.   Trends in the 90−10 Male Full-Time Weekly Wage Ratio, 1980−2013.

	90−10 Wage Ratio			
	1980	1990	2000	2013
Australia	2.7	2.7	3.1	3.6
Finland	2.4	2.6	2.5	2.6[a]
France	3.4	3.4	3.3	3.2[b]
Japan	2.6	2.8	2.8	2.9
Sweden	2.0	2.0	2.4	2.4[a]
UK	2.7	3.3	3.5	3.7
US	3.6	4.4	4.8	5.4

Notes: 90−10 male full-time weekly wage ratio. From OECD.Stat database. All countries with data for 1980, 1990, 2000 and 2013.
[a]Denotes 2012.
[b]Denotes 2010.

In the United Kingdom there was also a significant rise that also occurred through the decades, going from 2.7 in 1980 to 3.7 by 2013, or a 37 per cent increase in wage inequality as measured by the 90−10 metric.

In the 1980s the other five countries shown in the table show little in the way of changes. However, as time progresses the 90−10 wage ratios increase in almost all of them, producing a level of wage inequality at the end of the time period that is higher than it was at the start. This is true even in the Scandinavian countries in the table, albeit with smaller increases from a lower level. The only country out of the seven not characterized by a higher 90−10 at the end is France.

Columns (1) and (2) of Table 2 show the evolution of the same measure of wage inequality for all countries that have data between 2000 and 2013 (or the most recently available year close to then). Looking at this narrower time window enables consideration of a much larger number of countries, with nineteen countries (including the original seven from Table 1) having consistently defined data.

It is evident from the numbers in columns (1) and (2) of Table 2 that the vast majority of countries experienced rising wage inequality in the 2000s. The overall 90−10 ratio is higher in the 2013 (or nearest) time period in 15 out of the 19 countries. Indeed, some countries experienced very sizable increases in the 90−10 wage ratio over this time period − for example, there are big increases in Ireland, Korea, New Zealand and Poland, where the 2000s rise is just as big as the US increase. Only in four countries − France, Hungary, Italy and Sweden − is there no increase in wage

Table 2. Trends in the 90−10, 90−50 and 50−10 Male Full-Time Weekly Wage Ratio, 2000−2013.

	90−10 Wage Ratio		90−50 Wage Ratio		50−10 Wage Ratio	
	2000 (1)	2013 (2)	2000 (3)	2013 (4)	2000 (5)	2013 (6)
Australia	3.1	3.6	1.8	2.1	1.7	1.8
Belgium	2.4	2.5[a]	1.7	1.8[a]	1.4	1.4[a]
Canada	3.5	3.7	1.7	1.9	2.0	2.0
Czech Rep	3.5	3.7	2.0	1.9	1.8	1.9
Denmark	2.5	2.9[a]	1.7	1.7[a]	1.5	1.7[a]
Finland	2.5	2.6[a]	1.7	1.8[a]	1.5	1.5[a]
France	3.3	3.2[b]	2.1	2.1[b]	1.6	1.5[b]
Germany	3.0	3.4[a]	1.8	1.9[a]	1.7	1.8[a]
Hungary	5.2	4.2	2.4	2.5	2.2	1.7
Ireland	3.4	4.2	1.9	2.1	1.8	2.0
Italy	2.5	2.4[a]	1.7	1.6[a]	1.5	1.5[a]
Japan	2.8	2.9	1.7	1.8	1.6	1.6
Korea	4.1	4.7	2.0	2.2	2.0	2.1
New Zealand	2.7	3.2	1.8	2.0	1.5	1.6
Poland	3.8	4.7[a]	2.0	2.2[a]	2.0	2.1[a]
Sweden	2.4	2.4[a]	1.7	1.7[a]	1.4	1.4[a]
Switzerland	2.5	2.7[b]	1.7	1.9[b]	1.4	1.4[b]
UK	3.5	3.7	1.9	2.0	1.8	1.8
US	4.8	5.4	2.2	2.4	2.1	2.2

Notes: 90−10 male full-time weekly earnings ratio. From OECD.Stat database. All countries with data for 2000 and 2013.
[a]Denotes 2012.
[b]Denotes 2010.

inequality. And even here, only Hungary sees a significant fall, with wage inequality close to unchanged in the other three countries.[2]

Columns (3) and (4) of the table show numbers for upper tail wage inequality measured by the 90−50 ratio and columns (5) and (6) for lower

---

2. Note that, other than them being defined for male full-timers, these wage ratios are not adjusted for the changing composition of wage earners through time. Some studies note that this can matter in that composition-adjusted trends may be different. Lemieux (2006), for example, reports that a significant fraction of the growth in US wage inequality can be explained by an increase in education and experience levels through time. The issue is relevant for some European countries as well, for example as shown for Spain by Carrasco, Jimeno, and Ortega (2015) and for France by Verdugo (2014) where there was a large expansion of the level of education in the 1990s and the 2000s. In this setting of sizable compositional changes this can explain the stability or maybe even a decline at constant composition of wage inequality in these countries.

tail wage inequality measured by the 50−10 ratio (the product of the 90−50 and the 50−10 is equal to the overall 90−10 ratio). In 15 of the 19 countries, upper tail inequality rises between 2000 and 2013. In the four non-risers, the 90−50 is essentially flat.

The 50−10 numbers in columns (5) and (6) show that lower tail wage inequality rose in nine of the 19 countries was essentially flat in nine and fell substantially in one, Hungary. That lower tail wage inequality fell there seems very likely to be because of the very big minimum wage increases that took place in the 2000s (see Harasztosi & Lindner, 2014).[3]

From the patterns described in this section, it therefore seems that rising wage inequality has been a prominent feature of the labour market of most developed countries in the recent past. In most countries, overall wage inequality rose, in a few countries it remained flat and it is rare (and with special circumstances) to see reductions in wage inequality in labour markets in the 2000s. The central tendency points to rising wage inequality in contemporary labour markets.

2.2. Real Wage Stagnation

Less frequently studied than wage inequality trends has been the growth of real wages at different points in the wage distribution through time. Unfortunately the online OECD database used above does not break the ratios down to allow separate analysis of different percentiles, so it is necessary to look at country-specific sources to do so.

Fig. 1 shows the growth in the real weekly wage of the 10th, 50th and 90th percentile full-time workers and the growth in the hourly wage for all workers at the same percentiles in the United States from 1980 to 2013. This comes from Current Population Survey (CPS) data where median wages are deflated by the Consumer Price Index (CPI).[4] The patterns of

---

3. Note that the 90−50 rose in Hungary so that all the fall in the overall 90−10 ratio is due to narrowing wage inequality in the lower half of the distribution. The monthly minimum wage rose very significantly in the 2000s, going in nominal terms from 25,500 forint in 2000 to 98,000 forint in 2013, with some particularly big hikes taking place in 2001, 2002 and 2011. Thus, the monthly minimum expressed as a percentage of average monthly gross earnings rose significantly from 29.1 per cent in 2000 to 41.7 per cent by 2013 (*Source*: Hungarian Central Statistical Office STADAT database).

4. More specifically, the source is the CPS Merged Outgoing Rotation Groups monthly data available from the National Bureau of Economic Research.

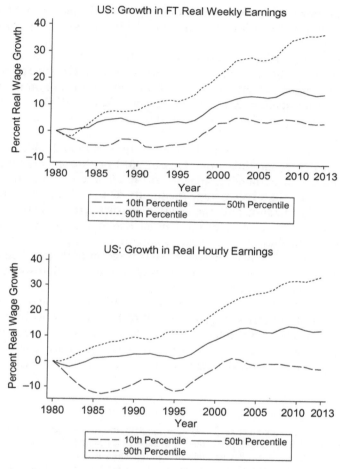

Fig. 1. Real Wage Growth at the 10th, 50th and 90th Percentile in the United States, 1980–2013. *Source*: Own calculations from Current Population Survey Merged Outgoing Rotation Group (CPS MORG) data.

rising wage inequality already shown are evident from the fanning out of the wage distribution resulting from higher wage growth at the 90th and lower wage growth at the 10th percentile compared to the median. But what is striking is that real wage growth of the median – or typical – worker is almost flat and it barely grows over the entire period. This is true for the full-time weekly wage and the hourly wage. Thus, real wage growth at the median is more or less stagnant over the period when wage inequality rapidly rose.

Real wage stagnation starts later, but is a feature of other countries with rising wage inequality as well. Fig. 2 shows real wage growth at 15th, 50th and 85th percentile in Germany from 1990 to 2008 (drawing on numbers in Dustmann, Fitzenberger, Schoenberg, & Spitz-Oener, 2014).[5] The fanning out of real wage growth is again seen, but growth at the median is again almost flat.

The UK real wage growth pattern at the 10th, 50th and 90th percentiles is shown in Fig. 3, the time from 1988 to 2013 (with numbers taken from Gregg, Machin, & Fernández-Salgado, 2014b). There is again the fanning out that characterizes rising wage inequality as the 90th percentile grows faster than the median and the median in turn grows faster than the 10th percentile.[6] In the case of the United Kingdom, however, real wage growth at the median is quite healthy at roughly 2 per cent a year until the mid-2000s. After that, however, real wage growth slows and turns negative in the economic downturn from 2008 onwards that was triggered by the global financial crash.

This downturn period has been characterized by weak real wage growth in most countries. Fig. 4 uses OECD data to show average real hourly wage growth from 2008 to 2013 in 26 countries. Almost everywhere real wage growth is relatively weak. In fact, the only countries that achieve real wage growth in the region of 2 per cent a year all have

---

5. The reason why Dustmann et al. (2014) show the 85th and 15th percentiles, rather than the more widely used 90th and 10th percentiles, is because of topcoding of earnings issues in their data that spread further down the distribution than the 90th percentile.

6. Notice that the 10th percentile for full-timers in the upper Figure grows almost as much as the 50th percentile over the period considered. There is more of a gap for hourly wages in the lower figure on inclusion of part-time workers. This feature of faster rising upper as compared to lower tail wage inequality is because much of the rise in lower tail wage inequality that occurred in the United Kingdom took place in the 1980s, after which the 10th percentile did not fall back as much. Machin (2011) shows that both lower and upper tail wage inequality grew rapidly in the United Kingdom in the 1980s, but that most of the subsequent increases in the 1990s and 2000s were driven by rising wage gaps between the 90th and 50th percentiles. In addition, the national minimum wage that was introduced in 1999 played a role in keeping wage growth up in the lower part of the wage distribution in the 2000s and actually narrowed lower tail wage inequality in the economic downturn since 2008.

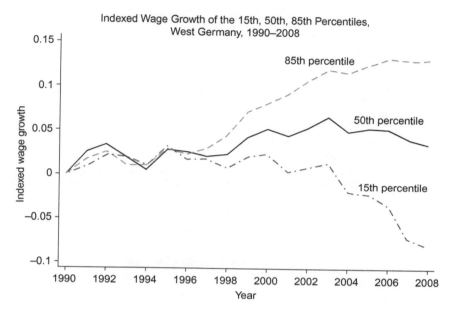

Fig. 2. Real Wage Growth at the 15th, 50th and 85th Percentiles in Germany, 1990–2008. *Source*: Reproduced from Dustmann et al. (2014). *Notes*: Calculations based on SIAB Sample for West German Full-Time Workers between 20 and 60 years of age. The figure shows the indexed (log) real wage growth of the 15th, 50th and 85th percentiles of the wage distribution, with 1990 as the base year. Nominal wages are deflated using the consumer price index (1995 = 100) provided by the German Federal Statistical Office.

special circumstances one can associate with that growth. Poland was the only European country not to formally do into recession during the downturn. Australia also did not fall into recession aided by the mining boom it experienced due to massive increases in demand for iron and steel from China for construction projects (Downes, Hanslow, & Tulip, 2014). Norway has been protected from recession by its oil reserves and, in the most recent downturn, the same was true of Canada where Alberta's oil boom also enhanced economic performance, so holding up real wages.

Thus, it seems that, as wage inequality levels in most countries are at their peak level for the last 30 or 40 years, real wage stagnation is also

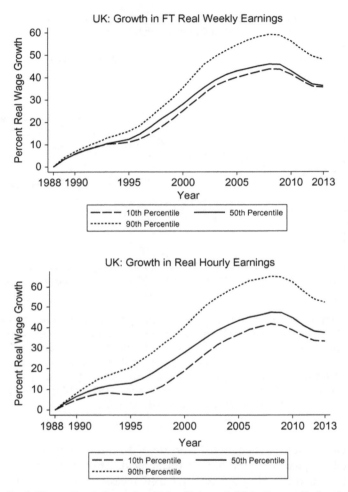

Fig. 3. Real Wage Growth at the 10th, 50th and 90th Percentile in the United Kingdom, 1988–2013. *Source*: Updated New Earnings Survey/Annual Survey of Hours and Earnings (NES/ASHE) numbers from Gregg, Machin, and Fernandez-Salgado (2014a), Gregg et al. (2014b).

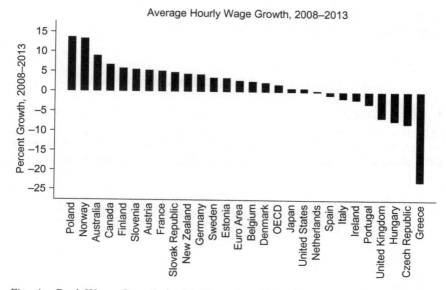

Fig. 4. Real Wage Growth in 26 Countries, 2008–2013. *Source*: From OECD Employment Outlook, 2014.

the order of the day. The two put together obviously have the implication that as inequality is rising, lack of growth of real wages of the typical worker is resulting in stalled living standards. In the next section I consider how the two patterns are related owing to the fact that gains from productivity do not seem to have been shared out equally amongst workers through time.

3. GROWTH IN REAL WAGES, PRODUCTIVITY AND INEQUALITY

Rising wage inequality takes on an increased significance when coupled with a recognition that real wage performance has been weak. Not only is the relative position of typical workers deteriorating relative to those further up the distribution, their absolute lot is not improving either. A key defining feature of this, as will be shown in this section of the paper, is that wages have over time become decoupled from productivity and that, in tandem with this, rising inequality has proven to be a key factor. To demonstrate this, US and UK data are analysed.

3.1. Productivity and Total Compensation Growth

The top two solid — black and grey — lines in Figs. 5 and 6 show trends in aggregate productivity (GDP per hour) and hourly compensation per worker between 1980 and 2013 in the United States (Fig. 5) and between 1988 and 2013 in the United Kingdom (Fig. 6).[7] The figure shows the

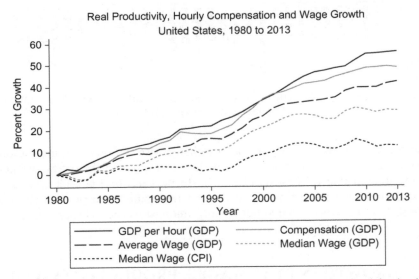

Fig. 5.   The Decoupling of Average and Median Wages from Productivity in the United States, 1980–2013. *Sources*: GDP per hour and hourly compensation data from OECD.Stat. Average and hourly wages from the Current Population Survey Merged Outgoing Rotation Groups. *Note*: Productivity is measured as GDP per hour and compensation, average and median wages are hourly.

---

7. The reason for the UK start year of 1988 is because the Consumer Price Index (CPI) was initially collected then and, as will be discussed shortly, this is needed to define the real consumer wage.

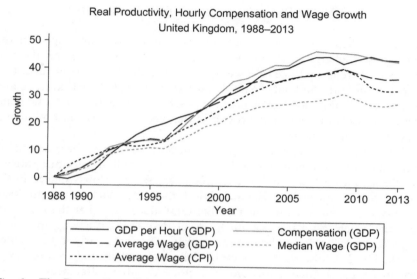

Fig. 6. The Decoupling of Average and Median Wages from Productivity in the United Kingdom, 1988–2013. *Sources*: GDP per hour and hourly compensation data from OECD.Stat. Average and hourly wages from New Earnings Survey/Annual Survey of Hours and Earnings. *Note*: Productivity is measured as GDP per hour and compensation, average and median wages are hourly.

trends in each tend to map on each other quite well over time, with compensation mostly tracking productivity quite well in the United States, with a bit of divergence from the early 2000s, and tracking well in the United Kingdom over the whole 1988–2013 time period.[8,9]

---

8. The modest drop back of compensation growth from productivity growth in the United States over this time period reflects that labour's share of GDP (=compensation/GDP) also showed a modest fall (for longer run patterns, looking at business sector productivity and compensation growth from 1947 to 2010, see Fleck, Glaser, & Sprague, 2011). The almost one-to-one mapping of compensation growth and productivity growth between 1988 and 2013 in the United Kingdom is because, unlike most countries where labour's share falls through time (see Karabarbounis & Neiman, 2014) the United Kingdom has unusually seen labour's share to be more or less flat in these years. If the start year is extended further back, there is a bit more divergence as labour's share fell in the United Kingdom in the 1980s.
9. For these two countries, similar patterns of change are seen if only business sector productivity (corporate gross value added per hour) and compensation are considered.

3.2. The Decoupling of Wages from Productivity

However, when one includes plots of average and median wages on the same growth charts — as shown by the various dashed lines on the two figures — there is evidence of lower growth in both of these over time. It is clear that in both the United States and United Kingdom that average and median wages have not grown as much as labour productivity or total compensation. In turn, real wage growth at the median is lower in both countries than at the average.

Whilst these two features are present in both countries, there are differences that are worth noting as well. First, the real median consumer wage — the black shortdashed line in the figures — grows very slowly indeed in the United States. Its growth is much lower than the real median producer wage (the median wage deflated by the GDP deflator rather than the CPI deflator) which in turn grows much slower than the real average producer wage. Second, the decoupling of the median starts very early in the United States. Third, whilst there is a wedge between median and average wage growth in the United Kingdom, the price deflator differences are less marked than in the United States.[10]

3.3. Wage Decoupling and Wage Inequality

Why has this decoupling of average wages from productivity and compensation, and the further decoupling of median wages from average wages, taken place? The two wedges between median and average wage growth, and between average wage growth and compensation growth, are inherently related to inequality. Consider first the lower rate of growth of average wages compared to overall compensation. The lower growth in the wage means that non-wage compensation must have been rising faster. Faster growth in non-wage compensation was identified in one of the few earlier studies of compensation inequality undertaken by Pierce (2001). He noted that, between 1981 and 1997 in the United States, non-wage components of compensation — specifically employer costs for paid leave, pensions and health insurance — grew faster for higher wage workers than

---

10. These differences due to price deflators are not the focus here, but they likely reflect terms of trade effects (see Pessoa & Van Reenen, 2013; for more discussion of the UK–US differences and Mishel, 2012; for discussion of the US terms of trade wedge).

the wage parts so that compensation inequality rose faster than wage inequality through time.

This pattern has continued since the time period considered in Pierce's work.[11] As Figs. 5 and 6 show the continued faster growth in non-wage labour costs has taken a growing share of the productivity growth achieved. The reasons for the gap between compensation growth and average wage growth because of this are, however, different in the two countries. In the United States it is now largely due to the health insurance component of non-wage labour costs growing faster. In the United Kingdom it is largely due to pension costs growing rapidly. Of course, both of these non-wage benefits (health and pensions) accrue more to workers who are paid more, and so there is a clear connection between rising inequality and this faster growth in non-wage compensation.

The more direct route whereby wage inequality has had an effect on the slowdown of wage growth for the median worker is through the other wedge that is clear to see in Figs. 5 and 6, namely the wedge between growth in average and median wages. The opening of the gap between average and median wages is because of rising wage inequality. As top earners had faster wage growth that pulled the average wages up at a faster rate than the median wages (of the middle or typical worker).

Longer run inequality increases have therefore gone hand-in-hand with slowing and stagnant real wage performance at the median as the median has fallen behind the average over time. The fast growth in the average to median wage ratio is shown for the United States and United Kingdom between 1980 and 2013 in Fig. 7 (for both hourly wages and full-time weekly wages).[12] There is a very clear trend upwards in the ratio of the average to median wages, revealing that part of the reason for the slowing down of wage growth at the median is because an increasing share of the gains from productivity have gone to workers further up the wage distribution.

4. REAL WAGE GROWTH AND UNION DECLINE

This section moves on to consider the extent to which slowing, or stagnant, real wage growth relates to the sharp declines in union coverage and

---

11. See Pierce's (2010) update of the earlier work to cover the period up to 2007.
12. For this ratio the data can be pushed back further to 1980 in the United Kingdom as there is no need for the consumer price index deflator.

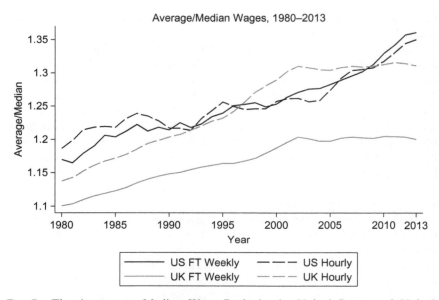

Fig. 7. The Average to Median Wage Ratio in the United States and United Kingdom, 1980–2013. *Source*: From CPS MORG and NES/ASHE data used in Figs. 1 and 3.

membership that has also occurred in the United States over the past 40 years as real wages have stagnated. Other work has established that trade union decline has been a factor that accounts for part of the rise in wage inequality in the United States and United Kingdom, and that part of this connection is due to changing composition. The main interest here is the extent to which union decline correlates with the real wage growth trends shown in the previous sections of the paper.[13] Put differently, the empirical work asks whether union decline has been an associated factor in the stagnation of median real wages in the United States?

---

13. For studies of union decline and rising wage inequality in the United States see Freeman (1980, 1982) and Card (1996, 2001) and for the United Kingdom see Gosling and Machin (1995) and Machin (1997). That part of the union connection is due to compositional changes is studied in DiNardo, Fortin, and Lemieux's (1996) decomposition of the US wage distribution.

4.1. Spatial Variations in Median Real Wage Growth

To study evolutions of real wage growth and unionization through time, the analysis looks at spatial changes. This is considered for the United States, looking at changes across states over time, based upon Current Population Survey data. Whilst median real wage growth has been sluggish in the United States since 1980, there are significant geographical differences. For example, the overall median full-time weekly wage rises by a meagre 13 per cent in real terms between 1980 and 2013. But the spatial range is quite wide. In Massachusetts, the state with the fastest real wage growth, the median full-time weekly wage rate grew by 51 per cent; in Montana, the state with the slowest real wage growth, it fell by 5 per cent.[14]

4.2. Real Wage Growth and Unionization

Fig. 8 plots median real wage growth between 1980 and 2013 for US states against changes in the level of union collective bargaining coverage.[15] The figure shows that union coverage fell in all states over this time period, but by more in some states than in others.[16] The plot against real wage growth reveals a very clear, statistically significant, negative gradient. Real wage growth at the median was significantly slower in states where the rate of unionization fell by more.

It is, however, possible that these associations are masking compositional changes that may have occurred over time in the characteristics of people working in the union and non-union sectors. This may reflect different characteristics of the workforce over time (e.g. more women working,

---

14. Forty-eight states are considered here as Alaska, Hawaii and the District of Columbia are excluded from the empirical analysis. The union coverage data is the proportion of workers covered by collective bargaining in the state, from the website run by Barry Hirsch and David Macpherson: http://www.unionstats.com/

15. The proportion of workers covered by collective bargaining in the United States fell from 0.26 in 1980 to 0.12 by 2013.

16. Larger falls occurred in states with higher levels of unionization at the start, resulting in convergence of unionization rates across states over time. For example, a regression of the 1980–2013 change in union coverage on the 1980 level across 48 states produced an estimated coefficient (and associated standard error) on the 1980 level of −0.471 (0.059). Thus, states with a 10 percentage point higher level of union coverage in 1980 experienced a −4.7 percentage point bigger fall in coverage rates by 2013. The same pattern is true if data on union density (the proportion of workers who are union members) was used, rather than coverage.

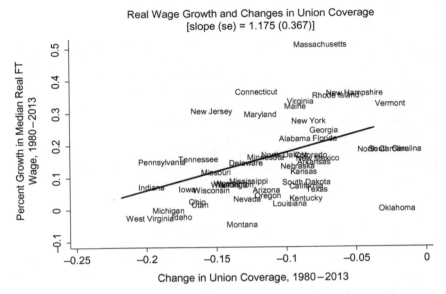

Fig. 8. Median Real Wage Growth and Changes in Union Coverage, US States, 1980–2013. *Sources*: Median real full-time wage growth from CPS MORG data, union coverage from the website run by Barry Hirsch and David Macpherson: http://www.unionstats.com/.

or workers now having higher education levels), or perhaps sectoral differences. To study the extent to which this is true, it is possible to also standardize for the changing composition of workers and to also look within broad sectors over time.

This is considered in Table 3, for hourly wages and for full-time weekly wages. The table first shows state-level regression estimates of median real wage growth on changes in union coverage between 1980 and 2013 that are analogous to the upper Fig. 8 plot, for real hourly wages in column (1) and for full-time weekly wages in column (3). In the upper panel the latter thus reproduces the slope of the line (=1.175) of the chart of Fig. 8. This suggests a 10 percentage point bigger fall in unionization was associated with 12 per cent lower real wage growth over the 1980–2013 time period.[17] For hourly wages — in column (1) of the table — the magnitude is close

---

17. If union density was used instead of coverage the slope was very similar at 1.086 (with an associated standard error of 0.351).

Table 3. Median Real Wage Growth and Changes in Unionization in US States (1980–2013).

	Changes in Median Real Wage Growth and Union Coverage, 48 US States, 1980–2013			
	Real hourly wage growth		Real FT weekly wage growth	
	Raw wage (1)	Composition-adjusted wage (2)	Raw wage (3)	Composition-adjusted wage (4)
A. All				
Change in union coverage	1.122 (0.351)***	0.698 (0.234)***	1.175 (0.367)***	0.668 (0.247)***
R-squared	0.18	0.19	0.18	0.16
B. Manufacturing				
Change in union coverage	1.433 (0.446)***	0.840 (0.266)***	1.435 (0.472)***	0.646 (0.276)**
R-squared	0.15	0.15	0.14	0.08
C. Non-manufacturing				
Change in union coverage	0.760 (0.391)*	0.538 (0.254)**	0.870 (0.398)**	0.573 (0.279)**
R-squared	0.09	0.12	0.11	0.11

Notes: Robust standard errors in parentheses. The composition-adjusted wages come from the residuals in separate regressions by year of log(wages) on age, age squared, four education dummies (advanced degree, bachelor degree, some college and high school diploma — omitted category is high school graduates) and two race dummies (black and other — omitted category is white). The 1980 and 2013 estimates are shown in Tables A1 and A2 of the appendix.

*Denotes statistical significance at the 10 per cent level, ** at the 5 per cent level and *** at the 1 per cent level.

with an estimated coefficient of 1.122 suggesting an 11 per cent lower growth in wages for a 10 percentage point bigger unionization fall.

One might worry that the changing composition of the workforce could be driving this. To net out composition effects to do with age, gender, race and education, individual-level wage regressions were estimated for each year and then composition-adjusted relative wage growth were computed across states from the residuals from the regressions. The actual microdata regressions for each year are reported in the tables in the appendix and do reveal what are reasonably well-known changes in wage premia related to the included characteristics (e.g. rising wage differentials by age and education, or falling gender wage differentials through time).

Results from the composition-adjusted wage growth equations are given in columns (2) and (4) of Table 3. The estimated effects are clearly moderated, suggesting part of the sizable estimates already discussed reflect composition changes, but the estimated connection between residual wage growth and changes in union coverage remains significant. For hourly wages and full-time weekly wages, respectively, a 10 percentage point bigger fall in coverage predicts slower wage growth of 6.98 and 6.68 per cent between 1980 and 2013.

Another issue with the results so far could be that in the past higher unionization rates were typically associated with some sectors, most notably manufacturing which has declined very sharply through time. In Panels B and C of the table, results are therefore reported within manufacturing and non-manufacturing. The effects remain significant in all cases, suggesting that union decline was associated with lower real wage growth within both sectors over time. Interestingly, the magnitudes of the estimated coefficients are larger for manufacturing real wage growth across states than for non-manufacturing.

The final empirical issue considered in this section is to consider what happens if additional variables related to technical changes that have been connected to rising wage inequality in other work are included in the state wage growth regressions. Table 4 thus shows results where changes in the R&D stock (measured relative to state GDP) and the proportions of workers using computers are added to Table 3 specifications.[18]

---

18. The computer use variable is constructed from the Current Population Survey supplements of October 1984 and 2003 CPS. The Research and Development (R&D) intensity measures are generated using R&D expenditure divided by nominal GDP for the years 1977 and 2007. Both of these come from the state-level data used in Lindley and Machin's (2014) analysis of spatial changes in labour market inequality.

Table 4. Median Real Wage Growth and Changes in Unionization in US States (1980–2013) – Adding Technical Change Variables.

| | Changes in Median Real Wage Growth and Union Coverage, 48 US States, 1980–2013 | | | |
| | Real hourly wage growth | | Real FT weekly wage growth | |
	Raw wage (1)	Composition-adjusted wage (2)	Raw wage (3)	Composition-adjusted wage (4)
A. All				
Change in union coverage	1.144 (0.322)***	0.707 (0.221)***	1.207 (0.325)***	0.681 (0.233)***
Change in R&D/GDP	4.209 (1.681)***	1.882 (0.939)**	5.161 (1.660)***	2.302 (0.963)**
Change in computer use	0.670 (0.404)*	0.342 (0.269)	0.637 (0.432)	0.349 (0.276)
R-squared	0.18	0.29	0.40	0.29
B. Manufacturing				
Change in union coverage	1.493 (0.455)***	0.853 (0.276)***	1.505 (0.461)***	0.661 (0.289)**
Change in R&D/GDP	5.571 (1.837)***	1.364 (1.287)	6.876 (1.754)***	1.315 (1.517)
Change in computer use	−0.237 (0.069)	0.026 (0.365)	−0.175 (0.192)	−0.095 (0.446)
R-squared	0.29	0.17	0.34	0.10
C. Non-manufacturing				
Change in union coverage	0.788 (0.345)**	0.553 (0.231)**	0.905 (0.340)**	0.589 (0.253)**
Change in R&D/GDP	5.036 (1.481)***	2.590 (0.870)***	5.655 (1.472)	3.015 (0.903)***
Change in computer use	0.794 (0.409)*	0.367 (0.266)	0.711 (0.429)*	0.503 (0.276)*
R-squared	0.35	0.29	0.39	0.32

Notes: Robust standard errors in parentheses. The composition-adjusted wages come from the residuals in separate regressions by year of log (wages) on age, age squared, four education dummies (advanced degree, bachelor degree, some college and high school diploma – omitted category is high school graduates) and two race dummies (black and other – omitted category is white). The 1980 and 2013 estimates are shown in Tables A1 and A2 of the appendix.

*Denotes statistical significance at the 10 per cent level, ** at the 5 per cent level and *** at the 1 per cent level.

The results in Table 4 show that technology improvements related to R&D and computers have gone hand-in-hand with faster state-specific increases in real wage growth. However, and of most interest for this paper, their additional inclusion does not drive away the connection with union coverage. Thus, the empirical finding that states where collective bargaining coverage has fallen by more have also seen significantly slower real wage growth remains intact.

5. CONCLUSIONS

In this paper a focus is placed upon the empirical study of two dimensions of changing wage structures that have occurred in different labour markets over the last 40 years or so. The first is rising wage inequality, which over time, and to varying extents, has become a feature of the labour markets of many industrialized countries. The second is the pattern of slowing real wage growth for the typical worker, which has also come to characterize many modern labour markets, especially more recently.

Empirical evidence from a number of sources is drawn upon to show rising wage inequality takes on an increased significance when coupled with a recognition that real wage performance has been weak, because the two are connected to one another in certain dimensions. One aspect of this is that real wage stagnation has resulted in lack of improvement in living standards which makes inequality matter more. A second is that over time inequality has driven a wedge between average wages and median wages so that the gains from productivity growth have become increasingly unequally distributed. For the United States, real wage stagnation at the median, which has now been a stubborn feature of the labour market since the late 1970s, has been magnified by the significantly reduced role that trade unions now play in the process of wage determination.

There are a number of future research directions that this paper suggests. One is that studying connections between real wage growth at the median and wage inequality trends in a broader range of countries than was possible here. A second would be to look at whether the slowing and stalling of real wage growth are related to union decline in other countries where the role of unions has also diminished over time (the two obvious countries to first study here are Germany and the United Kingdom). Finally, a third is to better understand how productivity gains are shared out across the wage distribution, from both a theoretical and an empirical perspective, so as to gain a better understanding of how real wage changes map into wage inequality trends.

REFERENCES

Acemoglu, D., & Autor, D. (2010). Skills, tasks and technologies: Implications for employment and earnings. In O. Ashenfelter & D. Card (Eds.), *Handbook of labor economics* (Vol. 4). Amsterdam: Elsevier.

Card, D. (1996). The effects of unions on the structure of wages. *Econometrica, 64*, 957–979.

Card, D. (2001). The effect of unions on wage inequality in the U.S. labor market. *Industrial and Labor Relations Review, 54*, 296–315.

Carrasco, R., Jimeno, J., & Ortega, A. (2015). Returns to skills and the distribution of wages: Spain 1995–2010. *Oxford Bulletin of Economics and Statistics, 77*, 542–565.

DiNardo, J., Fortin, N., & Lemieux, T. (1996). Labor market institutions and the distribution of wages, 1973–1992: A semi-parametric approach. *Econometrica, 64*, 1001–1044.

Downes, P., Hanslow, K., & Tulip, P. (2014). *The effect of the mining boom on the Australian economy*. Federal Reserve Bank of Australia Discussion Paper 2014-08.

Dustmann, C., Fitzenberger, B., Schoenberg, U., & Spitz-Oener, A. (2014). From sick man of Europe to economic superstar: Germany's resurgent economy. *Journal of Economic Perspectives, 28*, 167–188.

Fleck, S., Glaser, J., & Sprague, S. (2011). The compensation-productivity gap: A visual essay. *Monthly Labor Review, 134*, 57–69.

Freeman, R. (1980). Unionism and the dispersion of wages. *Industrial and Labor Relations Review, 34*, 3–23.

Freeman, R. (1982). Union Wage Practices and Wage Dispersion Within Establishments. *Industrial and Labor Relations Review, 36*, 3–21.

Gosling, A., & Machin, S. (1995). Trade unions and the dispersion of earnings in British establishments, 1980–90. *Oxford Bulletin of Economics and Statistics, 57*, 167–184.

Gregg, P., Machin, S., & Fernández-Salgado, M. (2014a). Real wages and the big squeeze. *Economic Journal, 124*, 408–432.

Gregg, P., Machin, S., & Fernández-Salgado, M. (2014b). The squeeze on real wages – And what it might take to end it. *National Institute Economic Review, 228*, R3–16.

Harasztosi, P., & Lindner, A. (2014). *Who pays for the minimum wage?* University of California at Berkeley mimeo.

Karabarbounis, L., & Neiman, B. (2014). The global decline of the labor share. *Quarterly Journal of Economics, 129*, 61–103.

Katz, L., & Autor, D. (1999). Changes in the wage structure and earnings inequality. In O. Ashenfelter & D. Card (Eds.), *Handbook of labor economics* (Vol. 3). North Holland: Elsevier.

Kenworthy, L., Nolan, B., Roser, M., Smeeding, T., & Thewissen, S. (2015). *Rising inequality and living standards in OECD countries: How does the middle fare?* mimeo.

Lemieux, T. (2006). Increasing residual wage inequality: Composition effects, noisy data or rising demand for skill? *American Economic Review, 96*, 461–498.

Lindley, J., & Machin, S. (2014). Spatial changes in labour market inequality. *Journal of Urban Economics, 79*, 121–138.

Machin, S. (1997). The decline of labour market institutions and the rise in wage inequality in Britain. *European Economic Review, 41*, 647–658.

Machin, S. (2011). Changes in UK wage inequality over the last forty years. In P. Gregg & J. Wadsworth (Eds.), *The labour market in winter*. Oxford: Oxford University Press.

Mishel, L. (2012). The wedges between productivity and median compensation growth. Economic Policy Institute. Issue Brief #330.

Pessoa, J., & Van Reenen, J. (2013). *Wage growth and productivity growth: The myth and reality of 'decoupling'*. Centre for Economic Performance Discussion Paper 1246.

Pierce, B. (2001). Compensation inequality. *Quarterly Journal of Economics, 116*, 1493–1525.

Pierce, B. (2010). Recent trends in compensation inequality. In K. Abraham, J. Spletzer, & M. Harper (Eds.), *Labor in the new economy*. Chicago, IL: University of Chicago Press.

Verdugo, G. (2014). The great compression of the French wage structure, 1969–2008. *Labour Economics, 28*, 131–144.

APPENDIX

Table A1. Log(Full-Time Weekly Wage) Equations, 1980 and 2013.

| | Log(Hourly Wage) | | | | | |
| | All | | Manufacturing | | Non-manufacturing | |
	1980 (1)	2013 (2)	1980 (3)	2013 (4)	1980 (5)	2013 (6)
Age	0.061 (0.001)	0.069 (0.001)	0.050 (0.001)	0.057 (0.001)	0.063 (0.001)	0.070 (0.001)
Age^2/100	−0.065 (0.001)	−0.067 (0.001)	−0.052 (0.001)	−0.053 (0.001)	−0.068 (0.001)	−0.068 (0.002)
Male	0.399 (0.002)	0.282 (0.004)	0.394 (0.004)	0.248 (0.011)	0.385 (0.003)	0.278 (0.004)
Black	−0.118 (0.004)	−0.142 (0.007)	−0.143 (0.007)	−0.182 (0.019)	−0.106 (0.005)	−0.136 (0.008)
Other race	−0.059 (0.007)	−0.037 (0.007)	−0.137 (0.012)	−0.123 (0.018)	−0.032 (0.008)	−0.027 (0.008)
Advanced degree	0.433 (0.005)	0.839 (0.007)	0.564 (0.013)	1.082 (0.019)	0.437 (0.006)	0.820 (0.007)
Bachelor degree	0.284 (0.005)	0.541 (0.006)	0.349 (0.007)	0.672 (0.014)	0.281 (0.004)	0.526 (0.006)
Some college	0.098 (0.003)	0.181 (0.005)	0.121 (0.006)	0.209 (0.012)	0.100 (0.004)	0.177 (0.006)
High school dropout	−0.208 (0.003)	−0.288 (0.009)	−0.203 (0.005)	−0.256 (0.019)	−0.219 (0.004)	−0.295 (0.010)
R-squared	0.37	0.35	0.44	0.43	0.36	0.34
Sample size	121,101	74,846	32,894	9,986	88,207	64,860

Source: From Current Population Survey Merged Outgoing Rotation Group (CPS MORG) data.

Notes: The dependent variable is the log(weekly wage) for full-time workers in 2013 prices (deflated by the consumer price index). Allocated wages and hours are excluded. The omitted reference groups are: female (for gender); white (for race); high school graduate (for education). Robust standard errors in parentheses.

Table A2. Log(Hourly Wage) Equations, 1980 and 2013.

| | Log(Full-Time Weekly Wage) | | | | | |
| | All | | Manufacturing | | Non-manufacturing | |
	1980 (1)	2013 (2)	1980 (3)	2013 (4)	1980 (5)	2013 (6)
Age	0.060 (0.001)	0.064 (0.001)	0.050 (0.001)	0.054 (0.001)	0.059 (0.001)	0.065 (0.001)
$Age^2/100$	−0.065 (0.001)	−0.063 (0.001)	−0.052 (0.001)	−0.051 (0.001)	−0.065 (0.001)	−0.064 (0.001)
Male	0.353 (0.002)	0.228 (0.003)	0.363 (0.004)	0.222 (0.010)	0.328 (0.003)	0.219 (0.004)
Black	−0.089 (0.004)	−0.109 (0.006)	−0.121 (0.007)	−0.171 (0.017)	−0.076 (0.003)	−0.101 (0.006)
Other race	−0.037 (0.006)	−0.023 (0.006)	−0.122 (0.012)	−0.091 (0.016)	−0.010 (0.007)	−0.016 (0.007)
Advanced degree	0.404 (0.005)	0.804 (0.006)	0.529 (0.013)	0.996 (0.012)	0.417 (0.006)	0.795 (0.006)
Bachelor degree	0.274 (0.005)	0.522 (0.005)	0.332 (0.007)	0.623 (0.013)	0.277 (0.004)	0.514 (0.005)
Some college	0.084 (0.003)	0.171 (0.005)	0.115 (0.006)	0.191 (0.011)	0.088 (0.003)	0.171 (0.005)
High school dropout	−0.200 (0.003)	−0.205 (0.005)	−0.203 (0.005)	−0.241 (0.016)	−0.201 (0.004)	−0.198 (0.008)
R-squared	0.37	0.37	0.43	0.43	0.35	0.36
Sample size	148,580	95,284	35,308	10,482	113,272	84,442

Source: From Current Population Survey Merged Outgoing Rotation Group (CPS MORG) data.
Notes: The dependent variable is the log(hourly wage) in 2013 prices (deflated by the consumer price index). Allocated wages and hours are excluded. The omitted reference groups are: female (for gender); white (for race); high school graduate (for education). Robust standard errors in parentheses.

IS THERE AN ADVANTAGE TO WORKING? THE RELATIONSHIP BETWEEN MATERNAL EMPLOYMENT AND INTERGENERATIONAL MOBILITY ☆

Martha H. Stinson[a] and Peter Gottschalk[b]

[a]U.S. Census Bureau
[b]Boston College

☆We would like to thank two anonymous referees, Jonathan Rothbaum, Gary Benedetto, Graton Gathright, Christopher Wignall, and Mahdi Sundukchi for helpful comments and suggestions. Any views expressed on statistical, methodological, technical, or operational issues are those of the authors and not necessarily those of the U.S. Census Bureau. All data used in this paper are confidential. The U.S. Census Bureau supports external researchers' use of some of these data through the Research Data Center network (www.census.gov/ces). For public-use data, please visit www.sipp.census.gov/sipp/ and click "Access SIPP Synthetic Data."

Inequality: Causes and Consequences
Research in Labor Economics, Volume 43, 355–405
ISSN: 0147-9121/doi:10.1108/S0147-912120160000043018

ABSTRACT

We investigate the question of whether investing in a child's development by having a parent stay at home when the child is young is correlated with the child's adult outcomes. Specifically, do children with stay-at-home mothers have higher adult earnings than children raised in households with a working mother? The major contribution of our study is that, unlike previous studies, we have access to rich longitudinal data that allows us to measure both the parental earnings when the child is very young and the adult earnings of the child. Our findings are consistent with previous studies that show insignificant differences between children raised by stay-at-home mothers during their early years and children with mothers working in the market. We find no impact of maternal employment during the first five years of a child's life on earnings, employment, or mobility measures of either sons or daughters. We do find, however, that maternal employment during children's high school years is correlated with a higher probability of employment as adults for daughters and a higher correlation between parent and daughter earnings ranks.

Keywords: Human capital; child development; female labor supply

JEL classifications: J13; J22; J24

1. INTRODUCTION

The rise in the labor force participation rate of women, including women with young children, has led to a sharp increase in the proportion of children being raised by working parents.[1] As a result, parents have increasingly relied on purchased inputs, such as day care, as substitutes for the time they would have devoted to their children had they been stay-at-home parents. Whether the increased reliance on market inputs has had a long-term effect on these children is the question we investigate in this paper.

A large body of literature has found a range of results on the impact of a mother working. Some studies have shown that the children of working mothers have lower mean outcomes on a variety of indicators of later

---

1. A Bureau of Labor Statistics report (2013) shows a steady increase in the number of employed women with children under the age of six, ranging from 33% in 1975 to 43% in 1982 to 58% in 2012.

success, such as reading and math scores in early elementary school (Baker, Gruber, & Milligan, 2008; Ruhm, 2004; Waldfogel, Han, & Brooks-Gunn, 2002) while others have found limited or no effect (Baker & Milligan, 2010; Blau & Grossberg, 1992; Dustmann & Schonberg, 2012). But this evidence on short-term impacts, such as test scores in school, is not evidence on adult outcomes, such as labor supply or earnings. Our paper fills this gap by using the Survey of Income and Program Participation (SIPP) linked to administrative tax data. Together, the survey and tax records form a longitudinal data set that is sufficiently long to allow us to measure the mother's work history before the child was born, during the preschool years (0–5 years old), and throughout the K-12 education period, as well as the child's earnings 30 years after birth. These rich data allow us to examine the relationship between the mother's work history and the child's adult labor market outcomes directly rather than having to rely on intermediary child outcomes as predictors of the child's adult outcome.

As with all papers in this literature, estimating the causal impact of the mother's work behavior on the child's adult outcomes is challenging since maternal employment is almost certainly endogenous. High-ability mothers presumably command a higher wage in the labor market and, hence, are more likely to work. However, they may also be more likely to have high-ability children. This will produce a spurious correlation between the mother's work behavior when the child is young and the child's adult earnings. We follow the literature by first estimating models that condition on a rich set of observables, including family income at various ages of the child and summary measures of each parent's lifetime earnings, and then estimating a within-mother fixed effects model that relies on variation in maternal employment across siblings and an IV model that uses geographic variation in female labor force participation and child care costs to instrument for maternal employment.[2]

While our estimation techniques are traditional, the outcomes we are able to study are unique in the literature on maternal employment. We investigate whether the mother working when her child was young impacts how much the child earned in his early thirties; whether the child was more or less likely to work himself between the time he turned 18 and the year 2012;

---

2. We estimate log linear earnings regressions on the parents' earnings histories using REML. These random effects are not the typical random effects used by economists but rather are predicted values resulting from solutions to Henderson (1953) mixed effects equations. See Searle, Casella, and McCulloch (1992) for details. Appendix A summarizes this literature.

how mobile the child was in the earnings distribution relative to where his parents were ranked when he was young and when he was a teenager.

We find few significant effects of a mother working on her child's adult earnings and find a positive correlation between mother and child employment status only for daughters and only for maternal employment when the daughter is in her late teens. We find that if both the mother and father contribute to family earnings when the child is young, there is no impact on the correlation between parental earnings rank and child earnings rank and hence mobility is largely unaffected. If both parents work and contribute to family earnings when the child is a teenager, the correlation between a daughter's earnings and the parents' joint earnings increases. Thus for a teenage girl, having an employed mother seems to be associated with lower levels of mobility. We suspect this is at least partly a labor supply issue. Daughters with employed mothers are more likely to be employed themselves and this fact alone will push these daughters higher in the rank ordering of earnings, above the segment of women in their thirties who earn nothing because they are engaged in full-time child care, and closer to the same part of the earnings distribution as their parents. Taken together, these results seem to suggest that maternal employment when a child is preschool age has few long-term effects on the child's labor market outcomes. Maternal employment when a child is in high school is correlated with future labor supply decisions of daughters, and this may be mostly through the effect of imitation: daughters who see their mothers working are more likely to make similar labor market choices.

Our results are consistent with several possible interpretations. First, it may indeed be true that mothers who stay at home with young children are no more effective at producing human capital for their children than mothers who work outside the home and use bought inputs to invest in their children's future human capital. An alternative explanation for the lack of a clear relationship between mothers' employment and their children's future earnings is that there is unobserved heterogeneity in the mother's relative productivity in the market and in the home. Mothers who are relatively productive in the home become stay-at-home mothers. Those relatively productive in the market work outside the home and buy market goods that are inputs into their children's human capital production functions. While each mother is making the optimal choice for her child, the expected future income of children with working mothers is no higher than the expected future income of children raised by stay-at-home mothers. Unobserved heterogeneity in child raising skills and market skills may mask the effect of the mother's work choice on the child's future income.

Finally, measurement error in home production may mask the impact of mothers' work decisions on children's outcomes. The implicit assumption in many papers, including this one, is that there is a one-to-one relationship between increases in market work and decreases in home production. However, evidence from time use studies suggests even working mothers continue to invest large amounts of maternal time in their children, compensating for working outside the home by doing less housework and having less personal time (Bianchi, 2000; Sandberg & Hofferth, 2001).

Our paper proceeds as follows: first, we discuss the relevant literature and our contributions. Second, we present a simple analytical framework that focuses on the factors that influence the parent's decision about whether to invest their own time in the development of their child's human capital or to rely more heavily on bought inputs. Third, we describe our statistical methods for handling endogenous mother labor force participation and for estimating intergenerational mobility. Fourth, we describe our data and present our results. We conclude with an assessment of what we learn from this work.

2. LITERATURE REVIEW

Our study builds on the vast literature that considers the effects of family circumstances on the outcomes of children. This includes much recent literature that has focused on whether early childhood investment (or negative shocks) produces effects that can be measured later in life (see Almond & Currie, 2010 for a summary). It also includes the literature on intergenerational mobility which focuses on whether children do better or worse than their parents, usually in terms of earnings, and what influences this outcome (see Jantti & Jenkins, 2015 for a recent review). We tie these literatures together by considering the impact of maternal employment when a child is very young on long range outcomes that include mobility. If, in fact, as Conti and Heckman (2012) suggest, investments early in life are more effective at producing good long term outcomes for children than investments later in life, we might expect that maternal employment at young ages will be more related to children's adult outcomes than maternal employment at older ages.

The benefit of early investment in children is supported by many studies that find small negative effects of maternal employment in the first five years of a child's life on early childhood educational outcomes. For example,

Bernal and Keane (2010), Berger, Hill, and Waldfogel (2005), Ruhm (2004), Baker et al. (2008), Han, Waldfogel, and Brooks-Gunn (2001), Waldfogel et al. (2002), and Gregg, Washbrook, Propper, and Burgess (2005) all find small negative impacts of maternal employment during preschool years on cognitive test scores in early elementary school. Likewise, Blau and Grossberg (1992) and James-Burdumy (2005) find negative effects of employment in the first year of the child's life. Baker and Milligan (2010) is an exception and find no effect of early maternal employment. Blau and Currie (2006) find a positive effect of maternal employment on school-age children if those children participate in high quality after school care.

The major drawback of these studies is that they are only able to follow children for a relatively short amount of time. Only Ruhm (2008) follows children as far as age 11. He finds mixed results of maternal employment depending on the education of the mother. We build on these studies by extending the time horizon many years forward and considering whether these early differences in children's test scores translate into long-run benefits.

Time spent at home by the mother when the child is young provides more opportunity for direct parental involvement in child human capital production but comes at the cost of lower family income. Since the effect of parental income on child development is generally found to be positive (see Baum, 2003; Blau, 1999; Dahl & Lochner. 2012), it is not clear a priori what the net effect of maternal employment will be. However, the estimated income effects in these studies are quite small. Thus, it is possible that the effects of the loss in income when the mother stays at home are offset by the benefits of the mother's direct input into the child's training. It is also possible that maternal income loss does not affect early childhood outcomes but does have a longer lasting effect as children age. If the mother is absent from the labor market for a significant number of years and reduces her earnings potential by lowering her experience levels, family resources may be lower when the child is in high school or college, when purchased inputs are more important. Many maternal employment studies may not extend long enough to capture the full effect. Our study is able to consider the combined effects of family income and maternal time at home by controlling for both types of inputs at every age of the child.

Interest in longer run outcomes has given rise to recent papers using European data to follow children late into high school, with heavy reliance on changes in maternity leave laws to identify the effects of maternal employment. Rasmussen (2010), Liu and Skans (2010), Carneiro, Loken, and Salvanes (2011), Dustmann and Schonberg (2012), and Bettinger,

Haegeland, and Rege (2014) all use variation in maternal employment caused by changes in length of time and cash benefits allowed for maternity leave in Denmark, Sweden, Norway, Germany, and Norway, respectively, to estimate the effect on child high school GPA and graduation rates. Dunifon, Hansen, Nicholson, and Nielsen (2013) also use Danish administrative data to estimate the casual effect of mothers working on high school outcomes. The results of these studies are mixed, with Rasmussen (2010) and Dustmann and Schonberg (2012) finding no effects of maternal employment, Liu and Skans (2010), Carneiro et al. (2011), and Bettinger et al. (2014) finding benefits to mothers staying home, and Dunifon et al. (2013) finding positive effects of mothers working. We build on these newer studies by considering outcomes for children after they have entered the labor market and (most likely) finished their schooling.

Intergenerational mobility is another long-run outcome that has generated particular interest recently, partly due to work that has begun to exploit administrative data to study intergenerational mobility in the United States. Chetty, Hendren, Kline, Saez, and Turner (2014, hereafter CHKST) use Internal Revenue Service (IRS) tax returns to look at children born between 1971 and 1993 and their parents. They rank children based on family income at age 30 and rank their parents based on income in the years the child was age 12–16. These data are used to estimate the rank-rank correlation which is the slope coefficient from an OLS regression of child rank on parent rank. Their estimates are in the range of .3, meaning that for every percentile higher the family is located in the earnings distribution, the child will be approximately a third of a percentile higher in his or her adult earnings distribution. Thus compared to a child from a family that was in the 50th percentile of the earnings distribution, a child from a family in the 80th percentile would be predicted to be nine percentiles higher in the adult earnings distribution. Recent work by Rothbaum (2015), using similar linked Census Survey-SSA-IRS data to ours, shows that in addition to family income, family demographics are also highly correlated with a child's adult earnings rank. In particular, parental education and race are significant predictors of child rank, even after controlling for parental earnings. We build on these analyses by estimating a rank-rank correlation model that considers the direct effect of maternal employment and the composition of family earnings on the rank outcome of the child. This model allows us to test whether the same level of family earnings has a different correlation with child earnings if the mother contributes part of the earnings versus if the father earns everything alone.

3. ANALYTICAL FRAMEWORK

3.1. Endogeneity Concerns in a Basic Model

We consider our question about the impact of maternal employment in the framework of a static utility maximization problem where mothers get utility from consumption and child human capital. Mothers make choices about the optimal amounts of these two commodities by choosing amounts of time to spend at home with their children and in paid employment, conditional on the wage they are able to earn in the labor market, their child human capital production abilities, the earnings of their husband, and the husband's inputs into child human capital development.[3] The optimal amount of consumption and child human capital that is the solution to the utility maximization problem stipulates that the marginal utility of the marginal increase in child human capital will equal the cost of that increase, the mother's foregone wages which translate into foregone consumption. Likewise, market inputs into the child's human capital production function will be expanded until the marginal gain is equal to the marginal cost, subject to the amount of money available to spend given the mother's labor supply decision and money earned by other household members. A mother will work until the marginal return of an additional hour would not buy adequate market goods to replace her time in the production of child human capital. Likewise, a mother will spend time with her child until the increase in child human capital is too small to compensate for the lost consumption. Thus labor supply will vary across mothers in a cross section due to differences in the wage a mother can earn, differences in the mother's child raising ability, differences in the mother's utility from child human capital, and differences in the utility of consumption. Parents who are highly productive in the labor market will tend to substitute away from own time spent with children toward purchased inputs which include day care arrangements and also extra activities such as SAT prep classes, music lessons, academic enrichment activities, and transportation to these activities. Other parents who earn less in the labor market but are equally

---

3. In a dynamic framework, a mother will base her labor supply decisions not only on the current period wage but also on the effect of working this period on future wages. This makes the utility maximization problem more complicated but does not change the fundamental trade-off the mother faces between producing child human capital and earning money for consumption.

productive in child care will stay at home with their children since their opportunity cost of staying home is lower.

Ideally we would like to estimate how much money a woman needs to earn to compensate for lost time at home working in child human capital production. However, this is not straightforward because child human capital also has a genetic component and we expect a positive correlation between parent and child ability, independent of time inputs. Since parent ability is largely unobserved and is correlated with labor market participation, there is likely to be a spurious correlation between working and child outcomes. Considering how to hold unobserved ability constant is thus the thrust of any econometric specification that uses covariation in maternal work choices and eventual labor market outcomes of the child.

Another confounding factor in measuring the return to maternal time investment is the ability and earnings of the father, which because of the time period we are considering, we treat as exogenous.[4] A father's unobserved ability both helps to determine his earnings and exacerbates the problem of unmeasured genetic transmission of ability to the child. The father's earnings in turn produce variation in the mother's work choices due to income constraints. If the father's earnings are sufficiently high that the marginal benefit of additional consumption has been driven below the benefit of increased child human capital, the mother will choose not to work. If we could control for men and women's abilities, we could compare high-earning men who have wives who stay at home to men with working wives who together earn the same amount and could estimate the maternal time/earnings trade-off in relation to eventual child outcomes. A negative relationship between women working and child outcomes would mean that family income needs to rise in order to compensate for the mother being gone from home. However without such controls, any type of marriage sorting pattern that tends to link women of a particular ability level to men of a particular ability level (e.g., assortative mating) causes this comparison to break down. Taken together, these issues make it essential to also account for father unobserved ability and family income in addition to mother unobserved ability when estimating returns to the mother's time at home.

---

4. In a more recent time period, this assumption would likely be unrealistic, but in the late 1970s and early 1980s, we think it unlikely that men significantly reduced their hours or chose to stay home due to child care responsibilities with any frequency.

3.2. Identification Strategies

Consider the following linearized version of the relationship between the child's adult earnings, Y_{it}, and the mother's employment status, W_i:

$$Y_{it} = X_{it}\beta + \gamma W_i + \theta_i + \eta_{it} \tag{1}$$

where X_{it} represents time-varying characteristics of the child, θ_i represents time-invariant unobserved child characteristics, and η_{it} is a time specific unobservable characteristic of the child. Given the growing consensus that the effects of parental inputs are largest when the child is young (see Conti & Heckman, 2012), we include a set of interactions between the child's age and the mother's employment status. This allows us to test the effect of working at different points during childhood. We define the age categories to correspond to the common educational periods of a child's life in the United States: preschool age $0-5$, elementary school age $6-10$, middle school age $11-13$, and high school age $14-18$.

The key to obtaining consistent estimates of γ, the effect of a mother working at various ages of her child, on the child's adult outcomes, is to address the potential endogeneity between the mother's work pattern, W_i, and the child's unobserved θ_i. In other words, we need to find variation in parent work patterns that is independent of the child's unobservable traits. We describe three methods that we employ, each commonly used in the literature on maternal employment.

3.2.1. Control on Observables
First, we control for observable parent characteristics including age of the mother when the child was born, education levels for both parents, and estimates of parental ability created from statistical measures of each parent's work history. We also include average family earnings during the same childhood periods defined above. To create parental ability estimates, we stack annual earnings measures and parental characteristics and use a mixed effects model of the following form to estimate separate earnings equations for mothers and fathers:

$$Y^m = X^m\beta + Z\theta^m + \eta \tag{2}$$

$$Y^f = X^f\beta + Z\theta^f + \eta \tag{3}$$

We describe mixed effects models in detail in Appendix A. These models are more general than the fixed effects or random effects models common in the econometrics literature. In particular, they do not impose orthogonality between X and Z and they not only provide $\hat{\beta}$ but also $\tilde{\theta}^m$ and $\tilde{\theta}^f$. We treat the predicted values of the random effects for the parents of each child i, $\tilde{\theta}_i^m$, and $\tilde{\theta}_i^f$, as measures of mother and father unobserved ability in the formal labor market. By definition they are centered at zero and rank mothers and fathers relative to each other in terms of earnings that are not explained by characteristics included in X. Thus using these predicted random effects allows us to control for observed ability (education) and unobserved ability (variation in earnings not explained by education) of the parents when estimating child earnings equations.[5] For fathers we use all earnings years from 1978 to 2012 to estimate these effects. For mothers, we use earnings from years between when the youngest child turned 11 and 2012 in order to try to mitigate the impact of unobserved part-time work which deflates earnings in a way unrelated to ability.[6] We control for parent age, race, education, labor force experience, calendar year, and firm characteristics such as industry and firm size in X^f and X^m. More detail about the firm characteristics data is given in Section 4. For a relatively small group of mothers and fathers, we are unable to predict a random effect because they have no history of paid employment during the time period we use to estimate the mixed effect models. This is not a case of missing data but rather structural zeros due to lack of participation in the labor market. We control for this circumstance in our regressions by including indicators for whether each parent has a predicted random effect.

In addition to estimating Eq. (1) for the full sample, we also address the issue of the endogeneity of parental work by limiting the sample to subgroups that are more homogeneous and less likely to differ in unobservable

---

5. A more traditional fixed effect estimate from a parent's earnings equation would not have allowed us to separate the effect of parent education and unobserved characteristics in the child earnings equation as the fixed effect would have contained the effect of education as well as any unobservable, time-invariant characteristics.
6. In other words, if a mother earns only 25,000 in a year, it is necessary to know whether she worked full-time or only a few hours a week in order to determine whether she is a low-skill, low-paid worker or a high-skill, high-paid worker. However since we do not have any information about number of hours worked in our administrative data on earnings, we are unable to distinguish between these two alternatives. In order to avoid lumping these different types of workers together, we restrict ourselves to a time period in a woman's life when labor supply is more likely to be uniform in terms of hours worked.

ways. In our first sub-sample, we compare parents with the same labor force attachment before their first child was born by restricting our sample to children whose fathers worked continuously when the child was between the ages of 1 and 5 and mothers who were working before the child was born. This sub-sample is potentially more homogenous than our original sample because it contains women who were all working the year before their child was born and hence had at least some labor market attachment. The effect of working after the child is born is then identified from variation in the mothers' decisions about whether to quit work or stay employed. Since all the fathers were steadily employed as well, the women's alternatives are similar to each other.

We also restrict our original sample to oldest children whose fathers worked continuously when the children were between the ages of 1 and 5 and whose mothers were working before the children were born. As with the previous sub-sample, these mothers were already employed and faced the decision of whether to stay home or work after having a baby, but in this case they were making the decision for the first time, with no other children to take into consideration. This sub-sample is again a more homogenous group because the mothers all had only one child after the baby was born.

We also use the birth of a younger sibling to identify potentially exogenous variation in the mother's labor supply. For example, consider a mother who works when she has only one child. If she has an additional child, she may leave the labor market since time at home now serves two children. Hence, working parents may decrease their labor market activity when the second child is born. To take advantage of this potential change in mothers' work decisions, we limit the sample to oldest children whose mothers and fathers had strong labor force attachment when they had only one child. Among these, we then further restrict the sample to oldest children who had younger siblings born before the oldest turned 5. These are the families who may limit their labor market activity when the second child is born, potentially impacting the older child.

Variation due to changes in family size, however, is only exogenous if parental decisions about spacing between births are unrelated to unobserved maternal ability. If high-ability mothers who are more likely to work tend to space their children differently in order to diminish child care costs for preschoolers, the birth of the second child does not represent an exogenous impact on mother labor supply. For example, a mother may delay a second birth because she cannot afford the child care for two children at once or she may shorten the interval between births in order to have fewer total years when she needs full-day child care and to take advantage of a lower marginal child care cost for the second child in the form of sibling discounts. Since controlling for endogenous fertility decisions is beyond the scope of our paper, we interpret these results with caution.

Finally, we consider whether characteristics of the mother's employer have any impact on child outcomes. Our hypothesis is that some types of work are more flexible and family-friendly than others and hence mothers working at some types of firms might be better able to balance work and home responsibilities. Thus two mothers earning the same amount of money but working in two different industries or firm size-classes might have different amounts of time to spend with their children. For example, if larger firms provide more family-oriented benefits and higher earnings for the same number of hours worked, we might expect to see an impact on children. Likewise, if the mother works in the retail industry and has few benefits and low earnings per hour worked, this may also have an impact. We investigate this possibility by including indicators for maternal employment by broad industry and firm size categories (see Section 4 for details on how these categories are created).

3.2.2. Instrumental Variables
We also use IV methods to control for endogeneity of mother's work attachment when the child is young. State-year-level female labor force participation rates, per capita counts of child care facilities, and averages of payroll per employee at child care facilities are used as instruments. These variables represent local conditions faced by mothers that may cause exogenous shifts in their labor supply if geographic location is not correlated with mother and child unobserved ability. Our hypothesis is that if child care is more plentiful or cheaper or working is more common among a woman's peers, then she will be more likely to work.

3.2.3. Variation in Maternal Employment across Siblings
Following the literature, we also control for time-invariant attributes of the family. These mother fixed effects models use only within-mother variation in maternal work to see if siblings' adult outcomes depend on whether the mother worked during their formative years.[7] To estimate this model, we use the sub-sample of children with same gender siblings who were also

---

7. In this model, mother and father fixed effects are not separately identifiable because both siblings had the same mother and father. This is due to our method of linking parents and children that requires us to observe children living with both their biological parents.

born between 1978 and 1982 and hence have earnings histories stretching to their thirties. Thus we use sons who had brothers born in this five year window and daughters who had sisters born in the same time period (see Section 4 for details). The advantage of these restrictions is that family conditions besides the mother's employment status are likely to be quite similar for both siblings. The disadvantage is that these restrictions produce a small sample both for sons and daughters and hence this estimation strategy may suffer from lack of precision. It is also the case that if unobservable child characteristics that impact child outcomes are associated with maternal labor supply, this model will produce biased results. Thus if a mother is less likely to work when the second child is young because that child has a disability, the effect of her employment on the earnings of her children will be biased upward.

3.2.4. Logistic Models
We use logistic regressions to estimate models predicting the probability of annual employment from the child's 18th year to calendar year 2012. For these models, we use the same parental controls and family earnings measures as in the previous models and continue to interact maternal employment with age categories for the child.

3.2.5. Rank-Rank Correlation Models
Our final analysis uses our longitudinal earnings history to estimate rank-rank correlations between parent and child earnings in the same manner as CHKST (2014). We first calculate average couple earnings when the child is age 1−5 and age 14−18. Next we rank fathers of children in our sample on the basis of couple earnings relative to all SIPP 1984, 1990−1993, and 1996 panel male respondents born in the same birth cohort and ever having children. We divide men into cohorts born between 1923−1929, 1930−1935, 1936−1940, 1941−1947, 1948−1950, 1951−1955, and 1956−1966. A man without a spouse in the comparison group has couple earnings equal to his own earnings. The same is true for men in our sample and men in the comparison group who have nonemployed spouses. For sons and daughters, we calculate average earnings between age 28 and 30 and rank them relative to other same gender SIPP respondents born between 1978 and 1982.

After obtaining each child's and each couple's rank, we regress the child's rank on the couple's rank. We do this analysis both for couple average earnings when the child is age 1−5 and for average earnings when the child is age 14−18 in order to compare the impact of the mother working at different ages of the child. We include an indicator for whether the couple earnings include maternal earnings or not and also interact this maternal employment indicator with the couple's rank. The maternal employment indicator provides an estimate of the direct effect of the mother working on the child's rank. The interaction tests whether the correlation with child rank changes if some of the family rank was determined by money earned by the mother. Thus, we are able to compare two families of the same rank where one family obtained all its earnings through the father and the other obtained its earnings through both the father and the mother. A significant main effect indicates that maternal employment is associated with different levels of child rank, regardless of couple earnings. A significant interaction term indicates that the earnings source matters for the child's mobility outcome. A positive sign on the interaction means children of working mothers have earnings that are more closely correlated to their parents' earnings, that is, the children are less mobile. This would indicate that maternal employment provided an advantage for children in high-ranked families. A negative sign on the interaction means that children of working mothers are more mobile, which would indicate that maternal employment provided an advantage for children from low-ranked families. The relative magnitudes of the main effect and the interaction provide evidence on whether additional family earnings, added by the mother and leading to a higher couple rank, overcome any deficit in expected child rank due to the direct impact of maternal employment.

4. DATA

We use a previously unexploited source of data, the SIPP linked to the Social Security Administration (SSA) and Internal Revenue Service (IRS) Detailed Earnings Record Extract (DER) which contains W-2 earnings records from 1978 to 2012. These linked data provide the two essential pieces necessary to study our question. From the survey, we obtain links between parents and children and from the DER, we obtain a longitudinal history of labor market outcomes that spans much of the lives of the family members. For our sample, we select children born between 1978 and 1982 because, for this group, we can observe parents' earnings from the year of the child's birth forward, and, at the same time, the children turn 30 by the end of our earnings time series in 2012. We also selected children who were observed to be living with both of their biological parents during a SIPP panel between 1984 and 1996, at which point they ranged in age from

5 to 18 years old.[8] For children with step-parents, the SIPP does not interview the nonresident biological parent and thus we are unable to obtain a W-2 earnings history for this parent. This prevents us from calculating total family earnings prior to the survey and for this reason we exclude children with step-parents from our analysis. We also exclude children where either parent was less than 16, the mother was 50 or older, or the father was 56 or older at the time of the child's birth, out of concern for data error in the survey-reported family relationships. Finally, we require that average family earnings when the child was age 1–5 be positive. This restricts our sample to families where at least one parent worked at least one year when the child was preschool age.

We rely on the W-2 earnings to measure labor force participation and earnings for all family members before, during, and after the survey. We follow parents' earnings and labor force participation from the birth of the child and construct annual measures of maternal and paternal employment and total family earnings to age 18 of the child. Children are also followed forward through 2012, and we construct the same labor force participation and earnings variables for them. Unfortunately we do not observe final schooling outcomes or eventual family formation decisions of the child because the SIPP panel ends before any child is older than 22 years old and we have no available administrative data for these topics.

Our linked survey-administrative database is an internal data product created by the Census Bureau and is called the SIPP Gold Standard File (GSF). It contains all SIPP respondents from the 1984, 1990, 1991, 1992, 1993, 1996, 2001, 2004, and 2008 SIPP panels. For a subset of the questions asked by the survey, consistent variables are created across all nine panels. For the panels we use in this paper, the Census Bureau asked each SIPP respondent at the time of the survey to provide a Social Security Number (SSN). SSA then compared demographic information (name, sex, and date of birth) from the survey reports and the Numident, an administrative database containing demographic information collected upon issuance of

---

8. For the 1984 panel, we imposed one additional restriction and took only children who were born in 1978 and 1979. This restriction ensured that the kids were at least five years old at the beginning of the SIPP panel and that the family had not broken up during the first five years of the child's life. For the 1990 panel, kids range in age from 12 to 8, for the 1991 panel ages 13–9, for the 1992 panel ages 14–10, for the 1993 panel ages 15–11, and for the 1996 panel ages 18–14. An 18-year-old child living with his or her parents in a SIPP panel conducted in the 2000s will not be 30 by 2012 so we did not use children from any later SIPP panels.

the SSN. If a respondent's name and demographics were deemed to match between the two sources, the SSN was declared valid. For individuals where a validated SSN was obtained, they were then linked to IRS and SSA administrative data on earnings, OASDI, and SSI benefits.[9] For individuals where no validated SSN was obtained, we multiply-impute their earnings history to create four separate data sets with no missing values, called completed implicates. Results for this paper were obtained by running the regression models separately on each implicate and then combining the results using the standard Rubin formulae.[10] Quite simply, the reported regression coefficients are the average calculated across all four implicates and the standard errors are a weighted average of the average variance of each coefficient and the between-implicate variance. Exact formulae are given in Appendix B. In our sample, 18.6% of sons had missing SSNs, with 10.2% of their fathers, and 11.3% of their mothers also having missing SSNs. The corresponding percentages for daughters were 21.3%, 11.2%, and 11.8%, respectively.

Parent and child relationships are taken from the household roster compiled at the time of the interview.[11] From the survey, we also make use of the mother's self-reported fertility history to determine if the child was the oldest, youngest, or a middle child. We use self-reported race of both the parents and the children and the self-reported education of

---

9. The SIPP GSF is the base file used to create the SIPP Synthetic Beta (SSB), a public-use product that uses data synthesis methods to protect the confidentiality of the linked data and provide access outside secure Census facilities.

For more information on the SSB and how to use these data, see http://www.census.gov/programs-surveys/sipp.html and click on Methodology and SIPP Synthetic Beta Data Product.

10. The more common practice is to drop observations containing missing data. This has the disadvantage of reducing sample size and potentially introducing bias into the sample if individuals who are missing their SSNs are different from those who are not. Due to these concerns, we prefer to handle the missing data problem by imputation. We have also run all the regression models in the paper dropping observations with missing SSNs. The results are noisier but otherwise give the same conclusions in terms of sign and significance of the coefficients.

11. In the 1984–1993 SIPP panels, the relationship between a child and one parent is reported in the core data files by including the parent person number on the child's record. Most commonly, this parent identifier links to the mother. The second parent's information must be obtained from the topical module that reports household relationships in a matrix form, that is, person A's relation to person B, person C, etc. Beginning in 1996, links to both parents are included on a child's record in the core files and the topical module is not necessary for defining the parent-child relationship.

the parents. For date of birth, we use the date recorded in the Numident, preferring this as the more reliable measure instead of the survey self-report. We define a person as working in a given year if he or she has positive W-2 annual earnings, and we create years of labor force experience measures by summing these work indicators over time. Mother's age at birth of the child is the difference between the mother and child administrative birth dates.

Our final data source is the Longitudinal Business Database (LBD) which is a research version of the Census Business Register, edited to be longitudinally consistent over time. These data contain industry, firm size, and payroll information for almost all of the businesses in the United States from 1976 to 2012. Firms are identified by an Employer Identification Number (EIN) which in turn links to the W-2 record of an individual worker. Utilizing this SSN-EIN link, we merge LBD data about firm characteristics onto the earnings histories of mothers and fathers in our sample and create an annual summary that measures percentage of earnings during the year in each firm size and industry category. We use these for three purposes. First, annual measures of firm size and industry sector serve as control variables in the parent mixed effects models that we use to estimate the random parent effect that proxies for ability. For individuals without SSNs, we are unable to match them to the LBD because we do not yet have a methodology to multiply impute assignment to a particular firm. For the parent earnings equations, we assign earnings-year observations without firm size or industry information to a "missing" category.

Second, we divide mothers who were employed when their children were age 1−5 into groups based on industry classification and firm size. Mothers who worked in the agriculture, forestry, fishing, mining, utilities, construction, manufacturing, wholesale trade, or transportation sectors are assigned to the production industry group. Mothers who worked in the information, finance, insurance, real estate, professional, scientific, technical, management, administration, education, healthcare, public service, or government sectors are assigned to the skilled services group. Mothers who worked in the retail, arts, accommodations, food services, or other services sectors are assigned to the unskilled services group. Mothers with self-employment are assigned to the self-employment group. We assign firm size groups in a similar manner. Mothers who worked at firms with 1−50 employees are assigned to the small firm group; 51−500 employees is the medium firm group; and over 500 employees is the large firm group. Mothers may be assigned to more than one industry and firm size group if they have jobs in different industries and/or at different firms during the period their child was age 1–5.[12] We include these indicators in one child earnings regression in order to capture the effect of the mother being employed and allow that effect to vary by type of employment. We drop children whose mothers do not have valid SSNs since the LBD variables have not been imputed.

Finally we use the LBD to calculate the number of child care businesses (NAICS code = 62441) per capita and average payroll per employee at these businesses by state for every year from 1978 to 2012. We merge this onto each parent's annual records using the state of the employer (EIN) where they worked in a year. If a parent worked at more than one employer we merge earnings-weighted average state values. If the state of the employer was unknown either due to missing information in the LBD or failure to link to the LBD due to missing parental SSN, then we used a state-female population weighted national average. These variables become the instruments in our IV estimation. For each child, we create a measure of local conditions for each age from 1 to 18 by choosing the state-level variables merged to the father's record for the appropriate year, or if they are missing, the mother's. If both parents are missing, we are then forced to use the population weighted national average. Just over 20% of sons at age 1 have parents with missing state of employment and so have the population weighted national average assigned.

In Tables 1a and 1b, we show summary statistics for our sample of sons and daughters. Of the almost 7,000 boys in our sample, 8% are black, 38% are the first-born child of their mother, and their mother's average age at the time of their birth was 26.8 years.[13] Among these sons, 51% had mothers with no more than a high school degree, and 46% had fathers with a high school degree or less. Average total mother and father earnings when the son was age five or under was approximately $62,000 in 2012 dollars.[14] At age 30, average total earnings of these sons was around $46,000 in 2012 dollars, and average labor force experience was 12.6 years.

---

12. This includes assigning the mother to the missing firm characteristics group if any of her employers did not match to the LBD. Being in the missing group means that a mother had an SSN and matched to the W-2 records but the employer identifier from the tax records could not be found in the Census firm data. Therefore, being in the missing group does not preclude the mother from also being in other industry and firm size groups if she had other W-2 employers who do match to the LBD.

13. Each completed implicate has a slightly different sample size. In all tables, we report the sample size of the smallest of the four implicates.

14. While this number for total family earnings may seem high, we remind the reader that our sample of boys comes from parents who remain together in the same household till the son is at least five years old and more often in his early teens.

Table 1a. Summary Statistics for Sons.

N	Overall		Mother – No Work		Mother – Some Work		Mother – All Work	
	Mean 6,982	St. dev.	Mean 1,855	St. err. for mean	Diff 2,878	T-stat for diff	Diff 2,221	T-stat for diff
Black	0.08	0.27	0.04	0.20	0.04	5.11	0.07	8.06
Oldest child	0.38	0.49	0.30	0.46	0.08	6.02	0.15	9.85
Youngest child	0.28	0.45	0.27	0.45	0.01	0.93	0.02	1.70
Age of mother at birth	26.84	5.08	27.25	5.35	-0.89	-5.76	-0.14	-0.85
Age of father at birth	29.35	5.81	30.09	6.17	-1.23	-6.91	-0.73	-3.96
Younger sibling before age 5	0.51	0.50	0.56	0.50	-0.05	-3.17	-0.09	-5.76
Mother educ. indicators								
High school or less	0.51	0.50	0.61	0.49	-0.07	-5.04	-0.21	-13.45
Some college	0.28	0.45	0.23	0.42	0.05	3.81	0.10	7.43
College or more	0.21	0.41	0.17	0.37	0.03	2.23	0.10	8.10
Father educ. indicators								
High school or less	0.46	0.50	0.48	0.50	0.00	0.18	-0.07	-4.33
Some college	0.26	0.44	0.24	0.43	0.03	2.12	0.04	3.03
College or more	0.28	0.45	0.29	0.45	-0.03	-2.26	0.03	1.80
Mother no random effect	0.06	0.24	0.14	0.35	-0.10	-11.82	-0.13	-15.14
Mother random effect	-0.01	0.77	0.08	0.83	-0.16	-6.21	-0.05	-2.15
Father no random effect	0.01	0.08	0.02	0.12	-0.01	-3.89	-0.01	-4.78
Father random effect	0.00	0.61	0.06	0.64	-0.06	-3.29	-0.12	-6.31
Average family earnings								
Son ages 1–5	61,895	84,640	54,352	48,676	1,388	0.69	21,160	8.79
Son ages 6–10	75,558	121,461	63,658	66,850	11,287	3.19	22,215	10.65
Son ages 11–13	84,112	137,508	71,882	87,700	11,092	3.20	23,414	6.07
Son ages 14–18	91,897	130,536	81,793	132,170	8,394	2.11	20,472	5.01
Age 30+ positive earnings	0.86	0.34	0.86	0.34	0.00	-0.30	0.00	-0.20

Age 30 earnings ($2012)	45,606	52,598	45,081	45,608	−403	−0.25	2,162	1.24
Age 30 yrs labor force exp.	12.63	3.18	12.39	3.31	0.21	2.21	0.46	4.59
Mother work year before birth	0.61	0.49	0.29	0.45	0.33	24.01	0.60	48.26
Mother work age 0	0.54	0.50	0.16	0.37	0.36	29.00	0.73	68.28
Mother work age 1	0.50	0.50						
Mother work age 2	0.51	0.50						
Years mother work age 3–5	1.63	1.32						
Years mother work age 6–10	3.28	1.96	1.59	1.74	1.76	33.43	3.02	66.70
Years mother work age 11–13	2.19	1.19	1.53	1.34	0.67	17.73	1.18	33.97
Years mother work age 14–18	3.88	1.80	3.04	2.12	0.88	14.96	1.52	27.78
Years father work age 1–5	4.48	1.27	4.02	1.77	0.59	12.97	0.71	15.87

Sample is boys who were: 1. born between 1978 and 1982; 2. living with both biological parents at time of SIPP panel (1984, 1990–1993, 1996); Means for overall sample; Means for sons with No Work mothers; Diff = Mean (Some Work mothers) − Mean (No Work mothers); Diff = Mean (All Work mothers) − Mean (No Work mothers).

To see whether there are observable differences between sons with working mothers and those whose mothers stay home, we divide our sample into three groups: (1) sons with mothers who never worked when the son was age 5 and under; (2) sons with mothers who worked some years when the son was age 5 and under; (3) sons with mothers who worked all years when the son was age 5 and under. Hereafter we refer to these groups as No Work, Some Work, and All Work. We report means for sons in the No Work group and the differences in means between the Some Work group and the No Work group and between the All Work group and the No Work group. These comparisons highlight observable differences in a single dimension while allowing us to differentiate between different types of maternal working patterns. For most characteristics, sons in the Some Work and All Work groups are different from sons in the No Work group in statistically significant ways. They are more likely to be black, oldest children, have younger fathers, and less likely to have siblings under the age of 5. Their mothers are more educated but have lower random effects. However the No Work mothers are more likely to have no random effects because they never worked for pay after the youngest child reached age 11 and hence have no W-2 work history in the years we used to predict a random effect. Mothers who work when their sons are preschool age continue to work more years throughout the son's school-age years. Sons in the All Work group have higher family earnings on average when they are preschool age and sons in both the All Work and Some Work groups have higher family earnings on average when they are school age. The differences for father's education are more muted. Sons in the All Work group are more likely to have a father with at least some college whereas most of the differences in education levels for the Some Work group are not significant. However fathers of sons in both the All Work and Some Work groups have lower random effects on average and are more likely to have no W-2 employment history and hence no predicted random effect. There are no statistically significant differences in average son earnings between the No Work group and either of the Work groups but sons in the All Work group have worked, on average, about half a year longer by age 30 than sons in the No Work group.

In Table 1b, we report the same summary statistics for our sample of daughters. The most noteworthy thing about this table is that our sample of approximately 6,700 daughters looks remarkably similar to the sample of sons in Table 1a in almost every respect. Race, oldest child status, mother age at birth of daughter, parental education, average combined parent earnings when the daughter was under 5, and percentages of mothers

Table 1b. Summary Statistics for Daughters.

N	Overall		Mother – No Work		Mother – Some Work		Mother – All Work	
	Mean 6,704	St. dev.	Mean 1,852	St. err. for mean	Diff 2,694	T-stat for diff	Diff 2,129	T-stat for diff
Black	0.09	0.28	0.05	0.21	0.03	4.71	0.08	8.91
Oldest child	0.38	0.49	0.32	0.46	0.07	4.60	0.12	7.72
Youngest child	0.28	0.45	0.26	0.44	0.03	2.02	0.04	2.64
Age of mother at birth	26.77	5.06	27.35	5.27	-1.20	-7.73	-0.30	-1.85
Age of father at birth	29.30	5.90	30.23	6.15	-1.64	-9.11	-0.85	-4.50
Younger sibling before age 5	0.51	0.50	0.57	0.49	-0.06	-4.28	-0.12	-7.69
Mother educ. indicators								
High school or less	0.52	0.50	0.63	0.48	-0.11	-7.80	-0.21	-13.44
Some college	0.28	0.45	0.23	0.42	0.06	4.31	0.08	5.44
College or more	0.21	0.40	0.14	0.35	0.06	5.29	0.13	10.53
Father educ. indicators								
High school or less	0.46	0.50	0.51	0.50	-0.05	-3.03	-0.08	-5.38
Some college	0.27	0.44	0.23	0.42	0.05	3.97	0.06	4.53
College or more	0.27	0.44	0.26	0.44	-0.01	-0.46	0.02	1.58
Mother no random effect	0.07	0.25	0.15	0.36	-0.10	-10.38	-0.13	-15.52
Mother random effect	0.00	0.76	0.10	0.84	-0.18	-7.09	-0.07	-2.91
Father no random effect	0.01	0.07	0.01	0.11	-0.01	-2.87	-0.01	-3.76
Father random effect	0.01	0.61	0.09	0.67	-0.09	-4.69	-0.13	-6.30
Avg. family earnings								
Daughter ages 1–5	61,097	55,842	57,185	62,970	-4,283	-2.44	17,258	8.31
Daughter ages 6–10	73,705	94,113	65,076	78,554	2,761	1.28	23,143	6.72
Daughter ages 11–13	81,709	100,765	72,293	76,977	6,242	2.25	21,185	7.18
Daughter ages 14–18	91,486	254,053	85,508	403,572	2,120	0.21	15,910	1.61
Age 30 + positive earnings	0.84	0.37	0.82	0.39	0.02	1.89	0.04	3.14
Age 30 earnings ($2012)	35,090	38,800	35,784	42,867	-2,534	-1.84	1,012	0.69

Table 1b. *(Continued)*

N	Overall		Mother – No Work		Mother – Some Work		Mother – All Work	
	Mean 6,704	St. dev.	Mean 1,852	St. err. for mean	Diff 2,694	T-stat for diff	Diff 2,129	T-stat for diff
Age 30 yrs labor force exp.	12.53	3.08	12.02	3.42	0.57	5.83	0.88	8.80
Mother work year before birth	0.61	0.49	0.29	0.45	0.32	22.61	0.61	48.63
Mother work age 0	0.54	0.50	0.17	0.38	0.33	25.29	0.73	67.21
Mother work age 1	0.49	0.50	0	0	0.43	45.53	1	0
Mother work age 2	0.51	0.50	0	0	0.47	49.33	1	0
Years mother work age 3–5	1.62	1.31	0	0	1.63	86.04	3	0
Years mother work age 6–10	3.24	1.97	1.47	1.72	1.88	35.60	3.16	70.48
Years mother work age 11–13	2.17	1.21	1.45	1.34	0.76	19.90	1.28	36.66
Years mother work age 14–18	3.84	1.81	2.91	2.12	1.01	17.10	1.61	28.95
Years father work age 1–5	4.48	1.28	4.04	1.77	0.56	12.18	0.69	15.31

Sample is girls who were: 1. born between 1978 and 1982; 2. living with both biological parents at time of SIPP panel (1984, 1990–1993, 1996); Means for overall sample; Means for daughters with No Work mothers; Diff = Mean (Some Work mothers) − Mean (No Work mothers); Diff = Mean (All Work mothers) − Mean (No Work mothers).

who worked are very similar on average to sons. Similar trends hold that daughters in the All Work and Some Work groups also have more highly educated mothers compared to the No Work group; slightly more educated fathers; and fathers with lower unobserved ability. The only major dissimilarity between the genders is in average earnings at age 30, where the mean is lower for daughters than sons. This is true despite sons and daughters having similar levels of work experience. We expect this result is probably due in part to unobserved labor supply differences. Daughters may work fewer hours per week at age 30 than sons due to child care responsibilities. Unfortunately our administrative data do not contain labor supply measures so we cannot differentiate among various potential causes of lower earnings.

While our data set clearly expands our knowledge by providing the long time series on earnings necessary to observe the mother's labor market attachment when the child was young and to observe the child's labor market outcomes 30 years later, like all data sets, this one has limitations. Like many previous studies, we are also not able to control for quality of purchased child care services. Furthermore, we cannot determine what happens to family structure after the end of the survey nor observe any other child outcomes besides labor market participation and earnings. There are currently no published weights for this sample because it is drawn from five different SIPP panels and hence our sample is not nationally representative and our estimates cannot be interpreted as applying broadly. We also have no sub-annual information on labor supply and no occupation information because the W-2 records we receive do not contain dates worked, hours, or occupation. However, there is much to recommend these data. Our sample size is relatively large, we have long histories of earnings which are potentially more reliable than self-reports about earnings and work decisions from the far past, and we know a great deal about the history of the family over a time period that covers the important early years of a child's life.

5. RESULTS

5.1. Child Earnings at Age 30 and Older

We begin in Table 2 with our first results from earnings regressions for sons. This sample of sons includes any who met our original sample restrictions and had positive earnings in at least one year at age 30 or older, which reduces our sample by about 900 boys. This leaves us with 6,035 sons with

16,598 years of positive earnings at age 30 or older.[15] In column 1, we show results from our most restrictive regression which, in addition to mother work indicators, includes only the following son characteristics: age, age squared, black, oldest child, youngest child, mother's age at birth of the son, and year indicators for 2008 through 2011. We specify the mother work variables as indicators for working when the son was age 0 and between the ages of 1−5, 6−10, 11−13, and 14−18. The maternal work indicator for age 0 helps to account for mother heterogeneity as it also captures the mother's work decisions in the part of the year before the child was born. Given the differences we observed in Tables 1a and 1b between mothers who work some years and mothers who work all years when their children are age 1−5, we split the work indicator for this age range into two components: work some years (i.e., between 1 and 4 years) and work all years (i.e., work 5 years).[16] None of the coefficients on the mother's work indicators are significant. However, the coefficient on years of father working when the son was 1−5 is significant and positive. In column 2, we add controls for parent education, random parent effects from our parent earnings regressions, indicators for parents who had no random effects because they had no work histories during the time period used to estimate the mixed model equations, and average family earnings when the son was 1−5, 6−10, 11−13, and 14−18. With these controls, neither mother's nor father's work coefficients are significant. This implies that the initial positive coefficient on father's work when the son was 1−5 was capturing correlated unobservables.

The next two columns show slightly different results for daughters. In neither column 3 or 4 is the father's years of work when the daughter was 1−5 statistically significant. In column 3, the indicator on mother working some years when her daughter is age 1−5 is negative and significant. Even when we add parental controls, the coefficient on mother working some when the child was a preschooler remains negative and significant although it has decreased in magnitude. We also stratified by mother's education in order to allow all coefficients to vary by education, and find that the negative effects of the mother working are confined to mothers with a high school degree or less. We conclude from this that these regressions may not adequately control for differences in father and mother underlying ability.[17]

To further highlight the impact of the parent observable characteristics, we also report the coefficients on the parent education indicators and

---

15. These sample sizes are from the smallest completed data implicate.
16. For example, the All Work mothers are more likely to have a college degree.
17. Results available from the authors.

Table 2. Log Annual W-2 Earnings of Children at Age 30 and Older.

Parental Work Variables	Sons		Daughters	
	(1) Simple	(2) Full controls	(3) Simple	(4) Full controls
Mother work age 0	0.015	0.011	0.049	0.036
	(0.036)	(0.038)	(0.044)	(0.045)
Mother work some years age 1−5	−0.048	−0.015	−0.117*	−0.098*
	(0.039)	(0.039)	(0.047)	(0.048)
Mother work all years age 1−5	−0.027	−0.012	−0.062	−0.082
	(0.049)	(0.050)	(0.056)	(0.056)
Mother work age 6−10	−0.047	−0.023	−0.017	0.006
	(0.051)	(0.049)	(0.062)	(0.064)
Mother work age 11−13	−0.036	−0.029	0.022	0.018
	(0.053)	(0.053)	(0.060)	(0.062)
Mother work age 14−18	0.081	0.082	0.097	0.040
	(0.058)	(0.071)	(0.061)	(0.070)
Years father work age 1−5	0.046***	0.026	0.000	−0.031
	(0.012)	(0.026)	(0.014)	(0.029)

Parental Controls					
Mother	High school degree		0.105		0.009
			(0.058)		(0.058)
Mother	Some college		0.080		0.155*
			(0.062)		(0.073)
Mother	College degree		0.125		0.104
			(0.072)		(0.075)
Mother	Graduate degree		0.226*		0.187
			(0.089)		(0.099)
Father	High school degree		0.117*		0.136*
			(0.056)		(0.055)
Father	Some college		0.212**		0.160**
			(0.070)		(0.061)
Father	College degree		0.262***		0.316***
			(0.076)		(0.072)
Father	Graduate degree		0.403***		0.323***
			(0.084)		(0.089)
Mother	No random effect		0.175		0.031
			(0.109)		(0.084)
Mother	Random effect		0.062**		0.083**
			(0.020)		(0.026)
Father	No random effect		−0.098		0.049
			(0.231)		(0.324)
Father	Random effect		0.180***		0.088*
			(0.031)		(0.039)
N children-years		16,598	16,598	15,165	15,165
N children		6,035	6,035	5,588	5,588

Sample is children who were: 1. born between 1978 and 1982; 2. living with both biological parents at time of SIPP panel (1984, 1990−1993, 1996); 3. had positive earnings at age 30 or older. Other regression controls not reported in all columns: age, age squared, black, oldest child, youngest child, mother age at child birth, year indicators (2008−2011; 2012 excluded year); in columns 2 and 4: log of average family earnings child age 1−5, age 6−10, age 11−13, age 14−18 in levels, squared, cubed. Standard errors in parentheses.
*$p < .05$; **$p < 0.01$; ***$p < 0.001$.

random parent effects in Table 2. As we expected, parental education is a very strong predictor of future child earnings, as are both parent random effects. Interestingly, father education has the strongest impact on both sons and daughters. Having a father with a graduate degree predicts the son's earnings to be 40% higher than the earnings of a son with a father without a high school degree. The equivalent comparison is 32% for daughters. In comparison, the magnitude of the impact of the parental random effect is much smaller. A one standard deviation increase above the mean in the mother's random effect predicts a 4.8% increase in the son's earnings and a 6.3% increase in the daughter's earnings. The impact of the father's random effect is larger, with a one standard deviation increase above the mean predicting 11% higher earnings for the son and 5.4% higher for daughters. These coefficients lead us to conclude that much of the correlation in parent-child earnings is due to correlation in education levels and unobserved factors such as ability.

In Table 3, we reestimate the model on several sub-samples in an effort to further control for unobserved differences in families that may be correlated with both maternal work decisions and children's outcomes. In the first column, we restrict the sample to children of parents with strong labor force attachment prior to having a child in order to compare families where the mother was working the year before the child was born.[18] The only coefficient that is significantly different from zero is the coefficient on mothers who work when the son is 14–18. Interestingly, the coefficient is positive, indicating that sons have higher expected earnings when they become adults if their mothers worked when they were teenagers.

In column 2, we further restrict the sample to oldest child so the mother is facing the decision for the first time of whether to use her own time or bought inputs in the child's human capital production function. Imposing this restriction has little impact on the coefficients but the smaller sample size increases the standard errors. As a result, none of the coefficients on parental work are statistically significant.

Finally in column 3, we further restrict the sample to children who had a younger sibling born before the oldest child turned 5. If different mothers face different costs of going back to work after having a second child then the arrival of the second child could provide some exogenous variation in mother employment. However, in this sample also, none of the work variables are statistically different from zero.

---

18. We restrict the sample to sons and daughters of mothers who were working the year before the child was born and fathers who worked every year from when the child was born to age 5.

Table 3.   Log Annual W-2 Earnings of Children at Age 30 and Older, Restricted Samples.

Parental Work Variables	Sample 1	Sample 2	Sample 3
Sons			
Mother work age 0	0.011	0.107	
	(0.063)	(0.088)	
Mother work some years age 1−5	−0.017	−0.055	
	(0.062)	(0.094)	
Mother work all years age 1−5	−0.003	−0.047	−0.055
	(0.067)	(0.099)	(0.080)
Mother work age 6−10	0.009	0.044	−0.015
	(0.077)	(0.107)	(0.147)
Mother work age 11−13	−0.043	−0.056	−0.050
	(0.070)	(0.097)	(0.112)
Mother work age 14−18	0.205*	0.224	−0.016
	(0.103)	(0.153)	(0.165)
N sons-years	8,884	4,380	2,296
N sons	3,256	1,596	844
Daughters			
Mother work age 0	0.067	0.064	
	(0.057)	(0.086)	
Mother work some years age 1−5	−0.061	0.028	
	(0.081)	(0.113)	
Mother work all years age 1−5	−0.041	0.045	0.070
	(0.085)	(0.129)	(0.102)
Mother work age 6−10	0.011	−0.005	−0.129
	(0.092)	(0.114)	(0.223)
Mother work age 11−13	−0.094	−0.108	0.076
	(0.091)	(0.122)	(0.211)
Mother work age 14−18	0.140	0.144	0.075
	(0.125)	(0.156)	(0.241)
N daughters-years	8,007	3,863	2,012
N daughters	3,012	1,441	740

Column 1: original sample restricted to mother worked year before birth, father worked every year child age 1−5; Column 2: column 1 sample restricted to oldest children; Column 3: original sample restricted to mother worked at child age 1, father worked every year child age 1−5, oldest child, younger sibling born before child is 5. Other regression controls not reported: mother/father education categories (same as in Table 2), mother/father predicted random effects from parental earnings equations, mother/father indicators for no random effect, age, age squared, black, oldest child, youngest child, mother age at child birth, year indicators (2008−2011; 2012 excluded year), log of average family earnings child age 1−5, age 6−10, age 11−13, age 14−18 in levels, squared, cubed. Standard errors in parentheses.
*$p <.05$; **$p < 0.01$; ***$p < 0.001$.

In Table 4, we present results from models where we control for mother employer characteristics. Here, we find that the indicators for maternal employment by industry category are all positive for sons but not statistically significant. In contrast, maternal employment in the service sectors groups is negative for daughters while production and self-employment are positive. However, these results are also not significant. We do see a significant negative correlation between the mother working at a large firm when her son is age 1−5 and son earnings as an adult. More research is needed to see what factors might be driving this result. One possibility is that the large firms that tended to employee mothers of young children in the late 1970s and early 1980s were often large retail chains which did not provide the benefits and higher pay often associated with large firms.

In Table 5, we show results from an IV estimation in which state-year-level female labor force participation, child care centers per capita, and average payroll per employee at child care centers are the excluded instruments. Again there are no mother work coefficients that are statistically significant for sons or for daughters. We test for weak instruments using the standard F-test that measures the joint significance of the excluded exogenous variables in the first-stage regression. While these variables are often significant, the F-statistic is not sufficiently high to alleviate concerns about weak instruments.[19]

Thus far we have controlled for observables, implicitly assuming that the remaining unobservables were random. We now relax this assumption by presenting estimates of models that include fixed effects. In Table 6, we use variation in mother work choices across brothers and across sisters to identify the effect of maternal employment at young ages. Again none of the coefficients are significantly different from zero.

In summary, these results lead us to believe that there is no significant correlation between mothers' labor force participation and their children's adult earnings, once we have controlled for parental characteristics correlated with mother, father, and child ability levels. There may be a number of reasons for this result. Perhaps our sample is too small, perhaps we have not been able to adequately identify exogenous variation in mother labor supply, or perhaps our annual measure of labor supply is too coarse to pick up effects. It is also possible that there truly are no effects of mother employment once we account for family earnings. If mothers are truly

---

19. Stock, Wright, and Yogo (2002) argue that only values of 10 or higher reliably mean there is not a weak instrument problem.

Table 4. Log Annual W-2 Earnings of Children at Age 30 and Older, Mother Firm Characteristic Variables Included.

Parental Work Variables	Sons	Daughters
	Full controls	Full controls
Mother work age 0	0.023	0.035
	(0.039)	(0.041)
Mother work age 1−5: production sectors	0.022	0.016
	(0.041)	(0.044)
Mother work age 1−5: skilled service sectors	0.072	−0.013
	(0.043)	(0.044)
Mother work age 1−5: unskilled service sectors	0.068	−0.062
	(0.037)	(0.046)
Mother work age 1−5: self-employment	0.104	0.027
	(0.058)	(0.068)
Mother work age 1−5: small firm	−0.044	−0.049
	(0.038)	(0.047)
Mother work age 1−5: medium firm	−0.042	0.008
	(0.040)	(0.039)
Mother work age 1−5: large firm	−0.166***	−0.047
	(0.043)	(0.051)
Mother work age 1−5: missing firm characteristics	0.011	0.040
	(0.048)	(0.067)
Mother work age 6−10	−0.016	−0.004
	(0.051)	(0.058)
Mother work age 11−13	−0.027	0.022
	(0.054)	(0.061)
Mother work age 14−18	0.061	0.040
	(0.071)	(0.071)
Years father work age 1−5	0.018	−0.024
	(0.027)	(0.028)
N children-years	15,266	13,864
N children	5,474	5,035

Original sample, restricted to children with mothers with valid SSNs. Production sectors include: agriculture/forestry/fishing, mining, utilities, construction, manufacturing, wholesale, transportation. Skilled service sectors include: information, finance/insurance/real estate, professional/scientific/technical, management, administration, education, healthcare, public service/government. Unskilled service sectors include: retail, arts, accommodation/food services, other. Small-sized firms have 1−50 employees. Medium-sized firms have 51−500 employees. Large-sized firms have 501 or more employees. Employers that did not match to Census firm data are classified as missing firm characteristics. Other regression controls not reported: mother/father education categories (same as in Table 2), mother/father predicted random effects from parental earnings equations, mother/father indicators for no random effect, age, age squared, black, oldest child, youngest child, mother age at child birth, year indicators (2008−2011; 2012 excluded year), log of average family earnings child age 1−5, age 6−10, age 11−13, age 14−18 in levels, squared, cubed. Standard errors in parentheses.
*$p < .05$; **$p < 0.01$; ***$p < 0.001$.

Table 5. IV Estimate: Log Annual W-2 Earnings of Children at Age 30 and Older.

Parental Work Variables	*F*-stat				
	Full controls	Implicate 1	Implicate 2	Implicate 3	Implicate 4
Sons					
Mother work age 0	0.934	2.402	1.821	1.618	1.995
	(3.767)				
Mother work some years age 1−5	1.120	1.017	1.323	1.192	0.991
	(3.141)				
Mother work all years age 1−5	1.324	1.605	1.616	2.118	2.004
	(4.186)				
Mother work age 6−10	−0.873	3.598	3.569	3.964	4.655
	(3.064)				
Mother work age 11−13	−6.297	0.267	0.542	0.271	0.521
	(10.237)				
Mother work age 14−18	−3.105	0.621	0.622	0.934	1.259
	(7.319)				
Years father work age 1−5	0.047				
	(0.439)				
N sons-years	16,598				
N sons	6,035				
Daughters					
Mother work age 0	3.372	1.534	1.250	1.609	1.046
	(21.384)				
Mother work some years age 1−5	−0.300	1.151	1.066	1.175	0.897
	(3.496)				
Mother work all years age 1−5	−2.698	1.803	1.915	2.182	1.927
	(17.622)				
Mother work age 6−10	2.042	1.498	1.303	0.716	1.511
	(7.688)				
Mother work age 11−13	−0.664	1.892	2.173	2.247	2.164
	(8.019)				
Mother work age 14−18	0.666	1.331	0.927	1.067	1.412
	(10.396)				
Years father work age 1−5	−0.031				
	(0.421)				
N daughters-years	15,165				
N daughters	5,588				

Sample is children who were: 1. born between 1978 and 1982; 2. living with both biological parents at time of SIPP panel (1984, 1990−1993, 1996); 3. had positive earnings at age 30 or older. Other regression controls not reported in both columns: mother/father education categories (same as in Table 2), mother/father predicted random effects from parental earnings equations, mother/father indicators for no random effect, age, age squared, black, oldest child, youngest child, mother age at child birth, year indicators (2008−2011; 2012 excluded year), log of average family earnings child age 1−5, age 6−10, age 11−13, age 14−18 in levels, squared, cubed. Excluded instruments are: female labor force participation rate in state of employment at child age 1, 5, 10, 14; number of child care establishments per capita in state of employment at child age 1 and 2; average ratio of payroll to employment at child care establishments in state of employment at child age 1 and 2. *F*-stat reports significance of excluded instruments in each first-stage regression, for each completed implicate. Standard errors in parentheses.
*$p < .05$; **$p < 0.01$; ***$p < 0.001$.

Table 6. Log Annual W-2 Earnings of Children at Age 30, Mother Fixed Effects.

Parental Work Variables	Sons	Daughters
Mother work age 0	−0.142	0.033
	(0.127)	(0.148)
Mother work some years age 1−5	0.092	0.304
	(0.197)	(0.227)
Mother work all years age 1−5	−0.075	−0.072
	(0.339)	(0.441)
Mother work age 6−10	0.358	0.200
	(0.226)	(0.273)
Mother work age 11−13	−0.063	0.101
	(0.230)	(0.250)
Mother work age 14−18	0.070	−0.150
	(0.304)	(0.428)
Years father work age 1−5	0.257	0.060
	(0.162)	(0.258)
N children	1,130	925
N mothers	554	450

Original sample restricted to sons with brothers also born between 1978 and 1982 or daughters with sisters also born between 1978 and 1982; mother fixed effects included. Other regression controls not reported: oldest child, mother age at child birth, year indicators (2008−2011; 2012 excluded year), log of average family earnings child age 1−5, age 6−10, age 11−13, age 14−18 in levels, squared, cubed. Standard errors in parentheses.
*$p < .05$; ** $p < 0.01$; ***$p < 0.001$.

optimizing when choosing their hours of employment and their hours at home, one would expect that they would work until the benefit from additional income arising from another unit of time spent at a job would be equal to the benefit of additional production of child human capital from another unit of time spent at home and the net effect of working would be zero.

5.2. Child Employment from Age 18 Till Early Thirties

While mothers' decisions about whether to work when their children are young may not have an impact on the quality of the jobs the children get when they are adults, mothers may nonetheless be role models, influencing their children so that they are more likely to work if their mothers do. To explore this possibility, we reestimate some of our models with adult labor force participation as the dependent variable.

To explore this intergenerational link, Table 7 shows the results of a logistic regression using presence of W-2 earnings as an annual indicator for employment between the age of 18 and age in 2012, which ranged from 30 to 34. In our first simple model, analogous to column 1 in Table 2, we see that the mother working when the son was between the ages of 14 and 18 is correlated with an increased likelihood of the son working after the age of 18. However when we add parental controls in column 2, we see that this correlation is no longer statistically significant. Here we see different results for sons and daughters. In columns 3 and 4, the mother and father working when the daughter is high school age are both correlated with an increased probability of the daughter working as an adult. We conclude that the influence of the mother (or father) as a role model is stronger with daughters than sons in regards to employment. This is not surprising given the relatively high percentages of men in their twenties and thirties who work and the still common phenomenon of women taking time off from the formal labor market when raising young children. Sons are a more homogeneous group than daughters in terms of their expectations about whether they will work and hence are less influenced by maternal example. Daughters, on the other hand, may shape their beliefs about the feasibility and desirability of employment outside the home by watching their mothers.

5.3. Intergenerational Mobility

Finally, we report measures of intergenerational mobility in Tables 8 and 9. In these tables, the outcome of interest is the child's rank in his or her adult earnings distribution. The focus is on the role of family earnings rank in predicting the child's rank and whether parental composition of family earnings matters. We consider family earnings rank in two different time periods in order to determine whether family rank from early childhood or from the high school years is a better predictor of adult rank.

We show several different specifications of the rank-rank correlation model. In the first column of both Tables 8 and 9, we show the simplest model which includes only family average earnings rank, either from the child's preschool years or the child's high school years, and indicators for maternal employment. In the second column, we add controls for demographic characteristics: an indicator for whether the child is black, age of the mother at birth of the child, age of the father at birth of the child, and

Table 7. Annual Labor Force Participation of Children at Age 18 and Older.

Parental Work Variables	Sons		Daughters	
	(1) Simple	(2) Full controls	(3) Simple	(4) Full controls
Mother work age 0	1.057	1.024	1.086	1.051
	(0.066)	(0.062)	(0.057)	(0.056)
Mother work some years age 1−5	0.909	0.920	1.015	1.023
	(0.055)	(0.061)	(0.071)	(0.070)
Mother work all years age 1−5	0.941	0.897	1.059	1.022
	(0.082)	(0.084)	(0.084)	(0.082)
Mother work age 6−10	0.990	0.968	1.093	1.084
	(0.077)	(0.078)	(0.075)	(0.080)
Mother work age 11−13	1.128	1.066	1.166*	1.133
	(0.082)	(0.085)	(0.087)	(0.084)
Mother work age 14−18	1.348***	1.125	1.348***	1.189*
	(0.100)	(0.115)	(0.102)	(0.101)
Years father work age 1−5	1.153***	1.046	1.098***	1.072*
	(0.019)	(0.038)	(0.021)	(0.035)

Parental Controls				
Mother	High school degree		1.125	1.129
			(0.085)	(0.090)
Mother	Some college		1.095	1.229*
			(0.092)	(0.103)
Mother	College degree		1.057	1.103
			(0.113)	(0.133)
Mother	Graduate degree		1.019	1.064
			(0.132)	(0.164)
Father	High school degree		1.151	1.100
			(0.093)	(0.088)
Father	Some college		1.235*	1.048
			(0.106)	(0.095)
Father	College degree		1.107	1.199
			(0.125)	(0.130)
Father	Graduate degree		1.166	1.085
			(0.152)	(0.136)
Mother	No random effect		0.906	0.935
			(0.111)	(0.099)
Mother	Random effect		1.038	1.026
			(0.033)	(0.039)
Father	No random effect		0.882	1.337
			(0.262)	(0.457)
Father	Random effect		1.015	0.936
			(0.050)	(0.045)
N children-years			104,568	100,671
N children			6,982	6,704

Sample is children who were: 1. born between 1978 and 1982; 2. living with both biological parents at time of SIPP panel (1984, 1990−1993,1996). Other regression controls not reported in all columns: age, age squared, black, oldest child, youngest child, mother age at child birth, year indicators (1996−2011; 2012 excluded year); in columns 2 and 4: log of average family earnings child age 1−5, age 6−10, age 11−13, age 14−18 in levels, squared, cubed; Exponentiated coefficients, standard errors in parentheses.
*$p < .05$; **$p < 0.01$; ***$p < 0.001$.

Table 8. Family-Child Earnings Rank Correlation – Family Earnings Measured When Child Was Age 1–5.

	Sons				Daughters			
	(1) Simple	(2) Add controls	(3) Controls + interactions	(4) Full	(5) Simple	(6) Add controls	(7) Controls + interactions	(8) Full
(1) Family average earnings rank, child age 1–5	0.187*** (0.015)	0.116*** (0.018)	0.130*** (0.023)	0.120*** (0.027)	0.140*** (0.016)	0.070*** (0.015)	0.061*** (0.020)	0.044* (0.024)
(2) Mother work all years, child age 1–5	−3.372*** (1.028)	−2.384* (1.082)		−2.297 (2.081)	0.795 (1.079)	1.024 (1.130)		−2.299 (2.507)
(3) Interaction btw. family earnings rank and mother work all years, child age 1–5			−0.035* (0.018)	−0.003 (0.033)			0.027 (0.017)	0.060 (0.036)
(4) Mother work some years, child age 1–5	−1.436* (0.859)	−0.936 (0.868)		−0.495 (1.653)	−0.728 (1.132)	−0.557 (1.194)		−1.767 (1.990)
(5) Interaction btw. family earnings rank and mother work some years, child age 1–5			−0.017 (0.016)	−0.009 (0.030)			0.001 (0.019)	0.028 (0.032)

Father and mother earnings are summed and averaged over the first five years of the child's life. Families are grouped and ranked relative to groups of families from the SIPP (1984, 1990–1993, 1996 panels) defined by the father's birth cohort. Child (son, daughter) earnings are averaged over age 28–30 and children are ranked relative to other children of the same gender and birth cohort. Reported coefficients are from a regression of child earnings rank on family earnings rank. Controls included in columns 2–4: mother age at child birth, father age at child birth, indicator for black, mother and father education indicators (high school degree, some college, college degree, graduate degree; no high school degree is the excluded case). Standard errors in parentheses.

*$p < .05$; **$p < 0.01$; ***$p < 0.001$.

Table 9. Family-Child Earnings Rank Correlation – Family Earnings Measured When Child Was Age 14–18.

	Sons				Daughters			
	(1) Simple	(2) Add controls	(3) Controls + interactions	(4) Full	(5) Simple	(6) Add controls	(7) Controls + interactions	(8) Full
(1) Family average earnings rank, child age 14–18	0.219*** (0.014)	0.153*** (0.016)	0.146*** (0.027)	0.160*** (0.040)	0.209*** (0.016)	0.127*** (0.016)	0.066* (0.028)	0.062 (0.041)
(2) Mother work any years, child age 14–18	0.967 (1.052)	0.798 (1.042)		1.207 (1.999)	2.767** (1.154)	3.281** (1.185)		−0.285 (2.107)
(3) Interaction btw. family earnings rank and mother work any years, child age 14–18			0.009 (0.022)	−0.009 (0.040)			0.074*** (0.024)	0.078* (0.043)

Father and mother earnings are summed and averaged over the years the child is age 14–18. Families are grouped and ranked relative to groups of families from the SIPP (1984, 1990–1993, 1996 panels) defined by the father's birth cohort. Child (son, daughter) earnings are averaged over age 28–30 and children are ranked relative to other children of the same gender and birth cohort. Reported coefficients are from a regression of child earnings rank on family earnings rank. Controls included in columns 2–4: mother age at child birth, father age at child birth, indicator for black, mother and father education indicators (high school degree, some college, college degree, graduate degree; no high school degree is the excluded case). Standard errors in parentheses.
*p <.05; **p < 0.01; ***p < 0.001.

mother and father three-category education indicators.[20] In the third column, we again include the demographic characteristics but drop the maternal employment indicators and instead interact maternal employment with family earnings rank in order to test whether the presence of maternal earnings changes the correlation between family and child rank. Finally in the fourth column, we include all the controls from the previous columns: demographic characteristics, indicators for maternal employment, and interactions between maternal employment and family earnings rank.

In the first row of Table 8, we report the correlation between family earnings rank when the child was preschool age and child rank as an adult across all our different specifications. For sons, the correlation ranges from .19 to .12, meaning that for every percentile higher in the earnings distribution the family ranks, the son is predicted to rank between 12% and 19% of a percentile higher.[21]

In the second row, the indicator for maternal employment in all five preschool years is negative and significant for sons but only before we include the interaction term with family earnings rank (columns 1 and 2 vs. 4). The interaction term between maternal employment in all five preschool years and family rank, reported in row 3, is negative and significant when it is included by itself (column 3) but is not significant when the indicator for maternal employment is included (column 4). Looking at the full specification in column 4, the point estimates indicate that maternal employment in all preschool years has a direct negative impact on the son's adult earnings rank but no effect on the correlation between family earnings rank and

---

20. Education indicators are mother high school degree of less, mother some college, mother college degree or higher, father high degree or less, father some college, father college degree or higher.

21. The range of our rank-rank correlation estimates is lower than the .3 found by CHKST (2014). There are two likely reasons for this difference — one having to do with the type of data we use and one having to do with our sample of individuals. First, we use only earnings and not total family income to measure our correlations because we have only W-2 records filed by employers with SSA/IRS on behalf of individual employees and not Form 1040 records filed by couples with IRS to report income for tax purposes. While income is a better measure of general well-being, we feel it is also important to consider specifically how children fare in the labor market relative to their parents. Second, our families are all intact families with both biological parents present at the time of the interview. Thus our families are likely somewhat advantaged relative to the sample used by CHKST and this may contribute to higher estimates of mobility. Given these differences, our highest correlation estimate of .22 for family earnings during high school and son earnings as an adult is closer than might have been expected to the CHKST estimate.

child earnings rank. However, the standard errors are high enough that we cannot say the main effect of maternal employment is significantly different from zero. If the mother worked only some years when the son was age 5 and under, there is no evidence of an impact on the son's earnings rank as an adult, either through a main effect or through an interaction with family earnings rank. Considered together, these results lead us to conclude that maternal employment does not have an impact on the mobility of sons relative to their parents' place in the family earnings distribution when the son was very young.

Columns 5–8 show the results for daughters. Here we see that family earnings rank is the only statistically significant predictor of daughter earnings rank as an adult. Maternal employment when the daughter is age 1–5, both all years and some years, is neither significant nor is the interaction of maternal employment and family earnings rank. As with sons, it appears that maternal employment at very young ages does not impact the mobility of daughters.

In general, daughters have a much lower correlation between family earnings rank and their own rank as adults, beginning at .14 and dropping to .04 after all controls are included. We hypothesize that this may again be a labor supply issue. Unlike the earnings regressions from Section 5.1, the rank-rank correlation model does not drop individuals with zero earnings but rather assigns them to the bottom of the distribution. Daughters may be choosing not to participate in the formal labor market when they are in their thirties and hence will rank very low in the earnings distribution. Because of this possibility, for daughters, we would ideally like to have family earnings at age 30 in order to see how their adult family earnings rank is correlated with their parents' earnings rank. However since we have no data on marital status or the identity of a spouse for individuals after the end of the SIPP data collection period, we are unable to test this hypothesis at this time.

In Table 9, we show results from models that estimate the correlation between the family earnings rank when the child is in high school and the child's earnings rank as an adult. Here we find different results than in Table 8. While we find no significant effects of maternal employment during high school on sons, we do see a positive correlation for daughters. If the mother worked during this time period of the daughter's life, the correlation between family and daughter earnings rank increased. We again hypothesize that this is the result of different labor supply decisions, on average, by daughters of employed mothers. If the mother worked when the daughter was in high school, the daughter is more likely to work and will consequently be ranked higher in the earnings distribution. This causes the correlation between her rank and her parents' rank to more than double (baseline correlation is .062 (row 1, column 8) and the interaction term is .078 (row 3, column 8)). This result substantiates what we found in Section 5.2 and leads us to conclude that maternal employment when the daughter is too young to remember or to understand any alternative has less impact than maternal employment at a point when the daughter is beginning to make her own educational and career choices. However these results do not provide us with a complete picture of the effects of maternal employment on daughter intergenerational mobility. Since we cannot rank daughters on the basis of family income, we do not know how they truly compare to their parents in the overall family earnings distribution.

6. CONCLUSION

Given the dramatic increase in labor force participation of mothers with young children, it is not surprising that considerable attention has been paid to possible impacts on later outcomes of the children of these newly working mothers. Did these children benefit or were they harmed when mothers went to work and spent less time with them?

A very standard human capital model predicts that if mothers' work decisions were constrained by social norms or discrimination, then relaxing these constraints would lead some mothers to enter the labor market and substitute bought inputs for own time raising their children. If these mothers place value on better outcomes for their children then their decision to increase their labor force participation would lead to better outcomes for their children. While the argument is straightforward, the evidence is at best mixed. The existing literature spans the spectrum. Some studies show that children of working mothers have better outcomes than children of stay-at-home moms, while others report no difference or even mild declines.

A major limitation of all these studies has been that they cover relatively short time periods. Children's outcomes can only be measured at best through high school. In this paper, we are able to overcome this major impediment through the use of linked survey-administrative data. Our ability to link W-2 earnings data to mothers and children allows us to measure parental input and adult outcomes of children many years apart.

With these data, we were able to estimate standard models that deal explicitly with the endogeneity of the parents' work decisions. Before controlling for correlated unobservables across generations, we find statistically significant correlations between the mother's work decisions and the child's labor outcome as an adult. However, once we control for endogeneity, these correlations largely disappear.

This finding is consistent with two possible interpretations. First, mother's inputs into the child's human capital production function when the child is very young may have little impact on the child's outcomes 30 years later. This explanation could be consistent with the large literature by Heckman and others that shows that early childhood investments do have an impact on children's pre-teen outcomes. Our ability to look at adult outcomes for the children suggests that these early childhood interventions may not have long-term impacts.

An alternative interpretation of our empirical finding is that there is heterogeneity both in production functions and in mother's input. Some children benefit more from having a stay-at-home mom while others benefit more from having a working mother who buys child-rearing goods and services. Mothers may also differ in their child-rearing and market skills. This heterogeneity in production functions and in mother's skills may vary not only over children but also across time. For example, a mother may be particularly skilled at raising her children when they are very young but not when they are teenagers. This heterogeneity in production functions and mother's skills would lead to heterogeneity in optimal outcomes. Comparing outcomes of children with stay-at-home mothers with the outcomes of children of working mothers would show no difference even though mothers' work decisions did have an impact.

Our estimates of intergenerational mobility based on the rank correlation approach used by Chetty et al. (2014) tell a mixed story. The mobility of a son relative to his parents does not appear to be affected by maternal employment at any age. For a daughter, we see that her earnings are more closely tied to her parents earnings (i.e., she is less mobile) if her mother worked during the daughter's high school years. We hypothesize that this is a labor supply issue, with daughters more likely to work in general if their mothers did. The impact of changing from not employed to employed on the daughter's place in the rank ordering of earnings is large enough to significantly impact the mobility estimate. More work is needed to disentangle the sample selection effects of which mothers and children are working, whether this is different for sons and daughters, and how this relates to mobility measures.

It is also important to remember that the birth years we study, 1978–1982, are early enough that the majority of women with young children in the United States were not employed. According to the Bureau of Labor Statistics (2013), only 44% of women with children under age 6 were part of the labor force in 1978 and only 39% were actually employed. Working mothers from that time period may have been a different group than working mothers today and hence we caution that our results may not generalize to the current generation of mothers with young children. Certainly larger U.S. economic trends such as stagnant male wages and declining marriage rates play a role in the reasons women work today and advances in technology that allow more flexible working hours and job locations make working a different experience for today's mothers. All of these may also alter the impact of working on children. Whether maternal employment continues to have minimal impact on children's labor market outcomes will be a topic of continuing research interest as the children of the 1980s, 1990s, and 2000s age and their work histories become available.

REFERENCES

Abowd, J. M., Benedetto, G., & Stinson, M. H. (2013). *The creation and use of the SIPP synthetic beta.* Census Working Paper. Retrieved from http://www.census.gov/programs-surveys/sipp/methodology/sipp-synthetic-beta-data-product.html

Almond, D., & Currie, J. (2010). Human capital development before age 5. In O. Ashenfelter & D. Card (Eds.), Handbook of labor *economics* (Vol. 4B, pp. 1315−1486).

Baker, M., Gruber, J., & Milligan, K. (2008). Universal child care, maternal labor supply, and family well-being. *Journal of Political Economy, 116*(4), 709−745.

Baker, M., & Milligan, K. (2010). Evidence from maternity leave expansions of the impact of maternal care on early child development. *Journal of Human Resources, 45*(1), 1−32.

Baum, C. L. (2003). Does early maternal employment harm child development? An analysis of the potential benefits of leave-taking. *Journal of Labor Economics, 21*(2), 409−448.

Berger, L. M., Hill, J., & Waldfogel, J. (2005). Maternity leave, early maternal employment, and child health and development in the U.S. *Economic Journal, 115*(501), 29−47.

Bernal, R., & Keane, M. P. (2010). Quasi-structural estimation of a model of child care choices and child cognitive ability production. *Journal of Econometrics, 156*(1), 164−189.

Bettinger, E., Haegeland, R., & Rege, M. (2014). Home with mom: The effects of stay-at-home parents on children's long-run educational outcomes. *Journal of Labor Economics, 32*(3), 443−467.

Bianchi, S. (2000). Maternal employment and time with children: Dramatic change or surprising continuity? *Demography, 37*(4), 401−414.

Blau, D. (1999). The effect of income on child development. *Review of Economics and Statistics, 81*(2), 201−276.

Blau, D., & Currie, J. (2006). Preschool, day care, and after school care: Who is minding the kids? In E. Hanushek & F. Welch (Eds.), *Handbook of the economics of education.* Amsterdam: Elsevier.

Blau, F., & Grossberg, A. (1992). Maternal labor supply and children's cognitive development. *Review of Economics and Statistics, 74*(3), 474–481.

Bureau of Labor Statistics. (2013). *Women in the labor force: A databook.* Retrieved from www.bls.gov/cps/wlf-databook-2013.pdf

Carneiro, P. M., Loken, K. V., & Salvanes, K. G. (2011). *A flying start or no effect? Long-term outcomes for mother and child.* IZA Discussion Paper No. 6930, Institute for the Study of Labor, Bonn.

Chetty, R., Hendren, N., Kline, P., Saez, E., & Turner, N. (2014). *Is the United States still a land of opportunity? Recent trends in intergenerational mobility.* NBER Working Paper No. 19844. National Bureau of Economic Research, Cambridge, MA.

Conti, G., & Heckman, J. (2012). *The economics of child-well being.* IZA Discussion Paper No. 6930, Institute for the Study of Labor, Bonn.

Dahl, G. B., & Lochner, L. (2012). The impact of family income on child achievement: Evidence from the earned income tax credit. *American Economic Review, 102*(5), 1927–1956.

Dunifon, R., Hansen, A. T., Nicholson, S., & Nielsen, L. P. (2013). *The effect of maternal employment on children's academic performance.* NBER Working Paper No. 19364. National Bureau of Economic Research, Cambridge, MA.

Dustmann, C., & Schonberg, U. (2012). Expansions in maternity leave coverage and children's long-term outcomes. *American Economic Journal: Applied Economics, 4*(3), 190–224.

Gregg, P., Washbrook, E., Propper, C., & Burgess, S. (2005). The effects of a mother's return to work decision on child development in the UK. *The Economic Journal, 115*, F48–F80.

Han, W.-J., Waldfogel, J., & Brooks-Gunn, J. (2001). The effects of early maternal employment on later cognitive and behavioral outcomes. *Journal of Family and Marriage, 63*(2), 336–354.

Henderson, C. R. (1953). Estimation of variance and covariance components. *Biometrics, 9*, 226–252.

James-Burdumy, S. (2005). The effect of maternal labor force participation on child development. *Journal of Labor Economics, 23*(1), 177–211.

Jantti, M., & Jenkins, S. P. (2015). Income mobility. In A. B. Atkinson & F. Bourguignon (Eds.), *Handbook of income distribution* (Vol. 2, pp. 807–935). Amsterdam: Elsevier.

Liu, Q., & Skans, O. N. (2010). The duration of paid parental leave and children's scholastic performance. *The B. E. Journal of Economic Analysis and Policy, 10*(1), 1–33.

Rasmussen, A. W. (2010). Increasing the length of parents' birth-related leave: The effect on children's long-term educational outcomes. *Labour Economics, 17*(1), 91–100.

Rothbaum, J. L. (2015). *Parent characteristics and the geography of mobility.* Working Paper from Federal Reserve System Community Development Research Conference on Economic Mobility. Retrieved from https://www.stlouisfed.org/community-development/economic-mobility-conference-2015/conference-materials

Rubin, D. B. (1987). *Multiple imputation for nonresponse in surveys.* New York, NY: Wiley.

Ruhm, C. (2004). Parental employment and child cognitive development. *Journal of Human Resources, 39*(1), 155–192.

Ruhm, C. (2008). Maternal employment and adolescent development. *Labour Economics, 15*, 958–983.

Sandberg, J. L., & Hofferth, S. L. (2001). Changes in children's time with parents: United States 1981–1997. *Demography, 38*(3), 423–436.

Searle, S., Casella, G., & McCulloch, C. (1992). *Variance components*. New York, NY: Wiley.
Stock, J. H., Wright, J. H., & Yogo, M. (2002). A survey of weak instruments and weak identi-
    fication in generalized method of moments. *Journal of Business and Economic Statistics,*
    20, 518–529.
Waldfogel, J., Han, W. J., & Brooks-Gunn, J. (2002, May). The effects of early maternal
    employment on child cognitive development. *Demography, 39*(2), 369–393.

APPENDIX A

In this appendix, we describe the prediction of the mother and father random effects that we use to control for unobserved heterogeneity of both parents in the child's equations. Our goal in predicting these effects is to exploit the long earnings history from the administrative data for each parent in order to create a measure of unobserved labor market heterogeneity, beyond what could be observed in terms of education and labor force experience of the parent. We treat these as random effects and estimate them using a mixed effects model. While such models are common in the statistics literature, especially biostatistics, they are not as common in the economics literature. Therefore, we begin by briefly presenting the mixed model and then we explain why the mixed effects model does not suffer from some of the same problems that economists typically associate with random effects. We end with a brief description of our estimation and prediction method.

A.1. Mixed Model

In their classic text on random and mixed effects models, Searle, Casella, and McCulloch (1992) begin by defining factor variables as information that classifies the data into categories. These factor variables have effects on variables of interest to a researcher and these effects can be either fixed or random. The authors define fixed effects as those which are "attributable to a finite set of levels of a factor that occur in the data." Random effects are unobserved factors with an infinite set of levels "of which only a random sample occur in the data." In each case, there are multiple observations for each factor. For example, the data may be on housing prices which vary by city, neighborhood, and block. Heterogeneity occurs at each level. The heterogeneity within blocks can be treated as random since the quality of homes has infinite support.

Note that the distinction in the statistics literature between random and fixed effects is based on whether the heterogeneity distribution is fully captured by covariates in the data (i.e., fixed effects) or whether the data only provides a sample of the heterogeneity distribution that has infinite support.

In our data, we treat mothers' and fathers' unobserved personal earnings heterogeneity, θ, as random because there is an infinite number of types of

mothers and fathers — the support for the unobserved heterogeneity is infinite. Therefore, the heterogeneity for the group of mothers and fathers present in our data is only a finite sample of all possible values. In contrast, we
treat the unobserved heterogeneity associated with different levels of education as fixed since there is a finite and relatively small number of levels of
education, each with its own heterogeneity component. If the unobserved
heterogeneity distribution is fully captured by the observed education then
this form of heterogeneity is fixed. Note that the distinction between the
parental heterogeneity, which is random, and the educational heterogeneity, which is fixed, does not require any assumption about the independence
of the unobserved heterogeneity.

One particularly appealing characteristic of mixed effects models is that
both fixed and random effects can be included. For example, when estimating an earnings equation, one can include a set of dummies for a particular
characteristic such as education that capture the mean of the heterogeneity
distribution across time for individuals. These fixed effects control for time
invariant attributes of the individual. A person random effect can also be
included that captures the dispersion around this conditional mean. This
is in contrast with the standard fixed effects models where a person-level
effect will soak up the effect of all time-invariant person characteristics.

A.2. Estimation

The models we first estimate are a set of parental earnings models with parental characteristics such as age, labor force experience, race, education,
and year time dummies included as explanatory variables. We estimate
separate models for mothers and fathers but they are not qualitatively different. To aid the flow of our description, we use mothers as our example
in what follows. Everything can be equivalently applied to fathers. First let
I be the total number of mothers in the sample with T observations each
for a total of $N = I*T$ observations. Let Y_i be a $T x 1$ vector of annual earnings measures for mother i and let X_i be a $T x k$ matrix of explanatory variables with coefficient vector β with dimensions $k x 1$. Let d_i be a $1 \times I$ design
matrix of the effects associated with mother i and θ be the $I x 1$ matrix of
person effects such that $d_i \theta = \theta_i$. Finally let η_i be the $T x 1$ vector of residuals.
The linear model for mother i is given by

$$Y_i = X_i \beta + d_i \theta + \eta_i$$

and then stacked across all mothers to become

$$Y = X\beta + Z\theta + \eta \tag{A.1}$$

$$Z = \begin{bmatrix} d_1 \\ \vdots \\ d_I \end{bmatrix} = \begin{bmatrix} 1 & 0 & \cdots & 0 \\ 0 & 1 & \cdots & 0 \\ \vdots & \vdots & \ddots & \vdots \\ 0 & 0 & \cdots & 1 \end{bmatrix}, \quad \theta = \begin{bmatrix} \theta_1 \\ \vdots \\ \theta_I \end{bmatrix}, \quad Y = \begin{bmatrix} Y_1 \\ \vdots \\ Y_I \end{bmatrix}, \quad X = \begin{bmatrix} X_1 \\ \vdots \\ X_I \end{bmatrix}, \quad \eta = \begin{bmatrix} \eta_1 \\ \vdots \\ \eta_I \end{bmatrix}$$

Statisticians call Z the design matrix of the effects θ. It is merely a set of dummies that assign θ_i from the θ vector to the ith mother.

This model described by Eq. (A.1) can be treated as what Greene calls the least squares dummy variable (LSDV) model (p. 466) with the following commonly made assumptions:[22]

$$\eta \sim N(0, R)$$

$$R = \sigma_\eta^2 I$$

where β and θ are called fixed effects in the statistics literature if the unobservable and observable factors in the population ($\theta_1...\theta_I$ and $X_1...X_I$) are finite and cover all possible values in the population.

The standard normal equations for the OLS estimator are

$$\begin{bmatrix} Z'Z & Z'X \\ X'Z & X'X \end{bmatrix} \begin{bmatrix} \theta \\ \beta \end{bmatrix} = \begin{bmatrix} Z'Y \\ X'Y \end{bmatrix} \tag{A.2}$$

which are familiar to most economists. These can be solved to yield

---

22. In all our descriptions here, we will assume that the variance structure of the model error, η, is defined as $R = \sigma_\eta^2$ but this assumption can be changed to a more complicated variance structure without substantially changing the model descriptions presented here.

$$\beta = \left[X'(I - Z(Z'Z)^{-1}Z')X \right]^{-1} \left[X'(I - Z(Z'Z)^{-1}Z')Y \right]$$

$$\theta = \left[Z'(I - X(X'X)^{-1}X')Z \right]^{-1} \left[Z'(I - X(X'X)^{-1}X')Y \right]$$

using the general rules for obtaining solutions for partitioned regressions (Greene, p. 179). One characteristics of the LSDV method is that the solutions for (θ, β) do not impose orthogonality between Z and X. In the terms used in the econometrics literature, one does not need to assume that the time invariant unobservables are independent of the $X's$.

The term "random effects" has a different meaning in the econometrics literature where unobserved heterogeneity is treated as a random effect in the following sense:

$$Y = X\beta + \theta + \eta$$
$$\eta \sim N\left(0, \sigma_\eta^2 I\right)$$
$$\theta \sim N(0, \sigma_\theta^2 I)$$
$$\mathrm{cov}(\theta, \eta) = 0, \mathrm{cov}(X, \eta) = 0, \mathrm{cov}(X, \theta) = 0$$

$$\Omega = \mathrm{var}(y_i) = \begin{bmatrix} \sigma_\eta^2 + \sigma_\theta^2 & \sigma_\theta^2 & \cdots & \sigma_\theta^2 \\ \sigma_\theta^2 & \sigma_\eta^2 + \sigma_\theta^2 & \cdots & \sigma_\theta^2 \\ \vdots & \vdots & \ddots & \vdots \\ \sigma_\theta^2 & \sigma_\theta^2 & \cdots & \sigma_\eta^2 + \sigma_\theta^2 \end{bmatrix}$$

$$R = \begin{bmatrix} \Omega & 0 & \cdots & 0 \\ 0 & \Omega & \cdots & 0 \\ \vdots & \vdots & \ddots & \vdots \\ 0 & 0 & \cdots & \Omega \end{bmatrix}$$

In this model, the random effect is merely treated as a portion of the error term. The identity of the mother imposes additional structure on the variance/covariance matrix of the error term. This type of model does not estimate θ directly but rather estimates σ_θ^2. The solution for fixed effects, β, is

$$\beta = \left(X'R^{-1}X\right)^{-1}X'R^{-1}Y$$

which is the standard GLS estimator. There is no $X'Z$ term in this model because of the assumption of orthogonality between the random effects and the observed characteristics in the X vector.[23]

In contrast to these two methods, mixed effects models allow θ to be treated as a random effect but also allow $\hat{\theta}_i$ to be predicted for each mother in the sample. These methods were pioneered by Henderson, a biostatistician interested in estimating genetic models that predicted milk production of cows as a function of the identity of their sires and dames. The goal of his models was to be able to predict parent effects for the milk production of a child cow, with the intent of identifying which bulls sired the best milk-producing daughters. He began with the same model as above, namely,

$$Y = X\beta + Z\theta + \eta$$

along with the assumptions (Searle, Casella, & McCulloch, p. 275)

$$\begin{bmatrix} \theta \\ Y \end{bmatrix} \sim N\left(\begin{bmatrix} 0 \\ X\beta \end{bmatrix}, \begin{bmatrix} G & GZ' \\ ZG & V \end{bmatrix} \right)$$

$$\text{var}(Y) = V = ZGZ' + R$$
$$R = \sigma_\eta^2 I$$
$$\text{var}(\theta) = G = \sigma_\theta^2 I$$
$$\text{cov}(Y,\theta) = ZG$$

Henderson shows that the pdf of the joint distribution is given by:

$$f(y,\theta) = f(y|\theta)f(\theta) = \frac{\exp\left\{ -\tfrac{1}{2}\left[(y-X\beta-Z\theta)'R^{-1}(y-X\beta-Z\theta) + \theta'G^{-1}\theta\right] \right\}}{(2\pi)^{1/2(N+I)}|R|^{1/2}|G|^{1/2}}$$

(A.3)

23. The widely used Hausman test is in fact a test of whether $X'Z=0$ and the frequent rejection of this hypothesis has left most economists skeptical of using random effects.

By taking partial derivatives of Eq. (A.3) with respect to β and θ, Henderson arrived at what are now known as the mixed model equations (MME) (Searle, Casella, & McCulloch, p. 276).

$$\begin{bmatrix} X'R^{-1}X & X'R^{-1}Z \\ Z'R^{-1}X & Z'R^{-1}Z+G^{-1} \end{bmatrix} \begin{bmatrix} \hat{\beta} \\ \hat{\theta} \end{bmatrix} = \begin{bmatrix} X'R^{-1}Y \\ Z'R^{-1}Y \end{bmatrix} \qquad (A.4)$$

The important thing to notice in these equations is that $X'R^{-1}Z \neq 0$, and hence the standard economist concern about imposing orthogonality between the characteristics in X and the design of the random effects matrix is no longer an issue.

It is also informative to compare Eq. (A.4) to Eq. (A.2), the normal equations for the LSDV model. Without G^{-1} in the bottom right cell, the MME are simply the maximum likelihood versions of the normal equations for the LSDV model. As $|G| \to \infty$, the MME converge to the normal equations. Thus, the LSDV model is a special case of the mixed effect model.

In estimating our mixed effect model, we use Restricted Maximum Likelihood (REML). The basic concept of REML estimation is to maximize a marginal likelihood. A set of linear error contrast equations are created that do not include β and these are used to create a likelihood function that contains only σ_η^2 and σ_θ^2 from the variance matrices G and R (Searle et al., 1992). These parameters are called variance components and are estimated by maximizing this marginal likelihood. Using these estimates of G and R, the mixed model equations are solved to give estimates for the fixed effects, $\hat{\beta}$, and then to predict the random effects, $\hat{\theta}$. For samples of our size and earnings equations with simple random effects, the Stata version of REML for mixed effects models (xtmixed) is sufficient to generate $\hat{\theta}_i$ for each parent in our sample in a computationally feasible amount of time.

APPENDIX B

Rubin first proposed multiple imputation as a way to handle missing data problems. In his seminal book (Rubin, 1987), he advocates applying any given imputation method multiple times to create many replacement values for missing data. This approach produces multiple copies of the data set, each copy having its missing values replaced with one of the sets of imputed values. The need for this arises from the fact that extra variability is introduced by the missing data. This variability needs to be taken into account or else the confidence intervals generated for statistics produced using the data will be too small, that is, parameters will be determined to be significant too often. By generating multiple data sets or implicates, the user can run a standard analysis on each one and then calculate the within-implicate variance (standard variance measure) and the between-implicate variance (variance across the implicates). The total variance formula then has two components which take account of the standard measure of variance and the variance introduced by the imputation. Formally, for a set of statistics $q^{(\ell)}$ (such as a mean or regression coefficient), calculated for each $\ell = 1,...,m$ completed data implicate, a single point estimate, $\bar{q}_m$, and variance measure, T_m, are created using the following formula:

Average across implicates : $\displaystyle \bar{q}_m = \sum_{\ell=1}^{m} \frac{q^{(\ell)}}{m}$

Variance across implicates : $\displaystyle b_m = \sum_{\ell=1}^{m} \frac{\left(q^{(\ell)} - q_m\right)\left(q^{(\ell)} - q_m\right)'}{m-1}$

Variance on each implicate file : $u^{(\ell)} = u\left(q^{(\ell)}\right)$

Average variance across implicates : $\displaystyle \bar{u}_m = \sum_{\ell=1}^{m} \frac{u^{(\ell)}}{m}$

Total variance : $\displaystyle T_m = \bar{u}_m + \left(1 + \frac{1}{m}\right) b_m$

Degrees of freedom : $\displaystyle \nu_m = (m-1) \left(1 + \frac{u_m}{\left(1 + \frac{1}{m}\right) b_m}\right)^2$

For details on the imputation models used to create the implicates used in this paper, see Abowd, Benedetto, and Stinson (2013).

DOES INCOME INEQUALITY IN EARLY CHILDHOOD PREDICT SELF-REPORTED HEALTH IN ADULTHOOD? A CROSS-NATIONAL COMPARISON OF THE UNITED STATES AND GREAT BRITAIN [☆]

Richard V. Burkhauser[a,b,c,d], Markus H. Hahn[d],
Dean R. Lillard[a,b,e] and Roger Wilkins[d]

[a]*DIW Berlin*
[b]*NBER*
[c]*Cornell University*
[d]*The University of Melbourne*
[e]*Ohio State University*

[☆]We gratefully acknowledge comments from seminar participants at the University of Wisconsin-Madison, University of Kentucky, Ohio State University, and participants at the SOEP Data Users Conference (2012), Understanding Society Data Users Conference (2013), and the IZA Workshop on Inequality: Causes and Consequences (2015). We also thank two anonymous referees and Lorenzo Capellari, Solomon Polachek, and Konstantinos Tatsiramos for their comments on an earlier version of this paper, and Heather Laurie for valuable information and advice on the British Household Panel Study.

Inequality: Causes and Consequences
Research in Labor Economics, Volume 43, 407–476
Copyright © 2016 by Emerald Group Publishing Limited
All rights of reproduction in any form reserved
ISSN: 0147-9121/doi:10.1108/S0147-912120160000043019

ABSTRACT

We use Cross-National Equivalent File (CNEF) data from the United States and Great Britain to investigate the association between adults' health and the income inequality they experienced as children up to 80 years earlier. Our inequality data track shares of national income held by top income percentiles from the early 20th century. We average those data over the same early-life years and merge them to CNEF data from both countries that measure self-reported health of individuals between 1991 and 2007. Observationally, adult men and women in the United States and Great Britain less often report being in better health if inequality was higher in their first five years of life. Although the trend in inequality is similar in both countries over the past century, the empirical association between health and inequality in the United States differs substantially from the estimated relationship in Great Britain. When we control for demographic characteristics, measures of permanent income, and early-life socio-economic status, the health−inequality association remains robust only in the U.S. sample. For the British sample, the added controls drive the coefficient on inequality toward zero and statistical insignificance.

Keywords: Income inequality; self-reported health; early-life conditions

JEL classifications: I14; I31; H51

1. INTRODUCTION

A substantial empirical literature investigates how health varies with income inequality within and across countries. These studies rest on a theoretical framework that remains underdeveloped but that generally argues that health inequality might be statistically associated with income inequality in one of several ways. In his review, Deaton (2003) outlines three mechanisms commonly cited in the empirical literature. Deaton observes (and most researchers recognize) that the correlation between health and income inequality may be a statistical artefact. Known as the "absolute income hypothesis," if income allows individuals to produce better health but with declining marginal product, then a dollar will produce greater health among low-income than high-income individuals. But this association is an artefact, not directly due to inequality in the distribution of income. Deaton also notes that health might also be correlated with income inequality because the causality runs in the opposite direction — either directly (i.e., people in better health produce more income) or through third variables (e.g., healthier people get better education and then earn more). Deaton and others observe that income inequality might plausibly affect health indirectly if inequality affects how much societies spend on public goods that are health inputs (Deaton, 2003; Subramanian & Kawachi, 2004). A correlation will arise if societies with less inequality allocate a greater share of public goods to health inputs — a mechanism that finds mixed support in empirical studies. Araujo, Ferreira, Lanjouw, and Özler (2008) report evidence of more spending on health-related public goods in more equal municipalities. Mayer and Sarin (2005) find states with greater income inequality spend more on public health. More broadly, this type of mechanism may link health with inequality through public resources that affect violent crime, social capital, and trust.

The theory linking health with relative income inequality rests on the well-established fact that stress (psychological or physical) produces hormonal and physical responses in (primates) humans that, when sustained, degrade health (Sapolsky, Alberts, & Altmann, 1997). Under the assumption that exposure to income inequality increases stress, this theory implies that within group income inequality matters but, as Deaton (2003) notes, except in rare cases, it is practically impossible to know what defines a person's relevant reference group. Consequently, this mechanism is difficult to empirically test. However, some research tries to explore directly whether variation in income inequality explains variation in measures of mental health (Weich, Lewis, & Jenkins, 2002). That study finds evidence that runs against the presumed inequality–(mental) health relationship — higher income individuals experience worse mental health when income inequality is higher.

More broadly, the empirical literature reports mixed evidence on the relationship between health outcomes and income inequality. Further, the evidence varies across countries (see, e.g., Deaton, 2003, 2013; Pickett & Wilkinson, 2015; Wilkinson & Pickett, 2006; for reviews of this literature). In general, older studies are more likely to report statistically significant associations that imply that better health is negatively related to greater income inequality, whereas only a minority of more recently published studies report evidence supporting such an association.

A conceptual weakness of most studies of this relationship is their focus on contemporaneous health and income inequality, when theories

of the structural drivers of health typically focus on accumulated life
experiences. A limited number of studies have consequently appealed to
this type of evidence and the underlying processes that dictate how health
evolves to rationalize model specifications that include measures of income
inequality in earlier years. Blakely, Kennedy, Glass, and Kawachi (2000)
relate U.S. Current Population Survey (CPS) data on individuals' self-
reported health in 1995 and 1997 to state-level measures of income inequality
measured contemporaneously and at several intervals up to 18 years in the
past. They conclude that contemporaneous self-rated health may be more
strongly associated with income inequality experienced up to 15 years previously than with income inequality measured contemporaneously. Mellor
and Milyo (2003) also relate CPS data on individuals' self-reported health to
state-level measures of income inequality measured between 5 and 29 years in
the past. However, in their models that control for regional fixed-effects, current health is uncorrelated with past income inequality. Karlsson, Nilsson,
Lyttkens, and Leeson (2010) relate 2006 cross-sectional data on self-assessed
health, activities of daily living, and country life expectancy in 19 countries to
contemporaneous Gini coefficients and to the Gini coefficient from (around)
1990. They find no consistent evidence of an association between health and
income inequality but find some correlation in high-income countries.

de Vries, Blane, and Netuveli (2013) draw on 2006−2007 English
Longitudinal Study of Aging, Survey of Health Ageing and Retirement in
Europe, and Health and Retirement Study data covering 16 countries to
examine the association between current physical functioning of people
aged 50 and over and income inequality, as measured by the mean of
the Gini coefficient, over the period from 1960 to 2006. They find a negative correlation between their measures of increased physical functioning
and their inequality measure. But because they only measure physical functioning in one year, they rely on cross-country variation in averaged
income inequality to estimate the association. In addition, they find no relationship between self-reported health and average income inequality.

In Lillard, Burkhauser, Hahn, and Wilkins (2015), we focus on this
subset of the health/income inequality literature that attempts to link current health to early-life events but with an important difference. The studies
discussed above relate health in the current calendar year to inequality
measured in a past calendar year (or an average of past calendar years).
We use a more life-cycle approach and relate currently reported heath as
an adult in a given year to the inequality each adult experienced when he
or she was the same age. We do so by investigating the link in the United
States between self-reported health as an adult and national income

inequality experienced as a child. We find that U.S. men and women are less likely to report being in better health as adults if inequality was higher in their first five years of life. Here, we use that same data on self-reported health from the Panel Study of Income Dynamics (PSID) together with data on self-reported health from the British Household Panel Survey (BHPS) from the same calendar years to explore how the adult health—early-life inequality association in the United States compares with the same association in Great Britain.

While we do not develop an economic model linking adult health to early-life inequality, we follow a series of empirical studies that suggest that early-life conditions play a role. Evidence suggests that later-life health and mortality are associated with childhood health conditions (Case, Fertig, & Paxson, 2005; Elo & Preston, 1992; Hayward & Gorman, 2004); adult achievement, employment, and health are associated with childhood poverty (Duncan, Ziol-Guest, & Kalil, 2010, 2013); and that the productivity of medical resources plausibly varies with the age at which a person receives those inputs (Currie & Rossin-Slater, 2015; Wüst, 2012). While this evidence is not directly about early-life inequality, it supports the hypothesis that an adult's health may have been affected by early-life inequality if this inequality affected the level and mix of resources their household had to produce health when they were young. At the same time, this evidence also leaves open the possibility that any measured association only reflects omitted variables because early-life inequality might simply proxy for conditions people faced in early childhood that affect health.

A small literature suggests some mechanisms that might generate a connection between adult health and income inequality experienced in early life. For example, Araujo et al. (2008) and Deaton (2013) suggest that income inequality is associated with the allocation of public goods related to health, such as immunizations and the provision of subsidized medical care. Given the non-rivalrous and non-excludable nature of such public goods, this line of reasoning suggests that, irrespective of family resources, children will get fewer health inputs if they grow up during periods of greater income inequality. In principle, these mechanisms can operate in response to local or national income inequality.

In this study, we explore whether the association observed in the U.S. data is also present in Great Britain. As in Lillard et al. (2015), our analysis exploits panel data on self-reported health along with data that consistently track the share of taxable income held by the top 1 percent of tax units since the early 20th century (Piketty & Saez, 2003; Atkinson, 2005). In contrast to the survey-based income inequality data used in existing studies, the long tax-based time series allows us to relate current health over long periods of individuals' lives, including at very old ages, to the share of taxable income held by top income groups during critical and very early periods of each individual's life. In the two countries, this measure of inequality follows a similar trend over the last century.

With these data, we explore whether the current health of adults, as measured in the PSID and BHPS, varies systematically and independently with income inequality experienced at lags of up to 80 years. We do so by estimating models of self-reported health in the PSID and BHPS data, including controls for income and demographic characteristics, and including as an explanatory factor the income share of the top 1 percent over the first five years of life. The data on self-reported health that we use span the period 1991–2007, while the income share variable is available for all individuals born in 1913 or later. This "early-life inequality" variable is fixed and the same for all individuals within a country who were born in the same year. Thus, the effects of early-life inequality are essentially identified by parameterizing the effects of birth year. Clearly, a limitation of this approach is that income inequality does not vary across individuals living in different geographical sub-divisions. Because our measure only varies across birth-years, it is potentially correlated with other factors that have evolved in similar ways, resulting in omitted variable bias in our models. However, we simply lack good long-run time-series data on many of such factors, including medical technology and spending on health. Our models do, however, include time trend, permanent income, and family background controls, which collectively will account for many of these trends.

We find that, despite similar trends in inequality in the two countries, the association between adults' self-reported health and the early-life inequality they experienced differs. When we estimate the simple correlation between adult health and early-life inequality, we find that, in the United States and Great Britain, men and women are less likely to report being in better health as adults if inequality was higher in their first five years of life. However, only in the United States is the association robust when we control for demographics, current and past economic status, and time trends. When we control for those factors in the British sample, the association is not robust. We also show that the lack of an association in the British sample does not result because we limited the sample to the same calendar years. When we use all available data in all calendar years, we continue to find a robust adult health-early-life inequality correlation in the United States but no association in the British data.

2. DATA

We use data from the United States Panel Study of Income Dynamics (PSID) and the British Household Panel Study (BHPS) samples of the Cross-National Equivalent Files (CNEF). The CNEF reworks data from each of these surveys so they are comparable across countries.[1] From each wave of these surveys, we draw data on self-reported health, post-government household size-adjusted income, age, sex, parents' educational attainment (PSID only), and parents' occupation (BHPS only). The household income measure is a measure that CNEF labels "post-government" income because it adds government transfer income to gross household (market) income and subtracts income taxes. We adjust post-government household income for household size assuming a scale elasticity of 0.5. In both samples, we exclude respondents aged 20 or younger in the year they report their health status.

The CNEF data are, in many ways, ideal for this analysis because each survey follows individuals from the year they first participate until they die or attrit from the sample. In the PSID, the family head (or a designated proxy) reports data for all family members. The BHPS interviews all adult household members (aged 16 and above). Both surveys follow and interview children when they leave their parental homes to live independently. From 1968 to 1997, the PSID administered the survey annually. Since 1997, it does so biennially. The BHPS has been administered annually since 1991.

We restrict our U.S. sample to U.S.-born respondents who belong to the PSID's Survey Research Center (SRC) sample. We include all SRC respondents in the original households and all members of those households (and their spouses) who participated in any PSID survey from 1984 to 2009. From this sample, we retain respondents with valid information on self-reported health and our control variables.[2] We construct our control variables using data from the 1970–2009 surveys, and include each person's contemporaneous household size and income as well as that person's retrospectively reported information on the education of his or her mother and father.

---

1. For more details, see Burkhauser, Butrica, Daly, and Lillard (2001), Frick, Jenkins, Lillard, Lipps, and Wooden (2007), Burkhauser and Lillard (2005, 2007) and http://cnef.ehe.osu.edu/
2. Lillard et al. (2015) report that the estimated correlation between inequality and health does not vary when one includes or excludes PSID respondents in the Survey of Economic Opportunity and Latino subsamples.

We restrict our Great Britain sample to British-born respondents who belong to the original BHPS sample and all their descendants who participated in the BHPS. We limit this sample to respondents for whom we observe valid data in any of the 1991–2009 surveys.

However, because the purpose of this paper is to compare outcomes in the United States with outcomes in Great Britain, in the body of the paper we report findings from subsamples of these two data sets, comprising the years between 1991 and 2007 when both the PSID and the BHPS surveyed their populations. This includes all years from 1991 to 1996 and every other year from 1997 through 2007 (except 1999). We begin with 1991 because that is the first wave of the BHPS. We drop BHPS data from 1998, 2000, 2002, 2004, and 2006 because the PSID did not administer surveys in those years. We drop 1999 in both the PSID and BHPS because the health questions on the 1999 BHPS survey substantially differ from the set they ask in other years. To characterize income inequality, we use the top income data series from Piketty and Saez (2003) for the United States and from Atkinson (2005) for Great Britain for 1913 through 2009.[3] We next describe these data. Appendix A provides additional information about the variables we use.

2.1. Dependent Variable

Our dependent variable measures each adult's self-reported health. While, on multiple surveys, the PSID and the BHPS ask respondents about their health, the two surveys ask slightly different questions and offer respondents slightly different response categories.

---

3. The two top income data series we use include estimates for years after publication of Piketty and Saez (2003) and Atkinson (2005). These are available from the World Top Incomes Database (http://www.wid.world/). While the BHPS is a random sample of Great Britain, the Atkinson (2005) top income series is for the United Kingdom and it is not possible to separate Ireland and later Northern Ireland from the United Kingdom top income series. While the United Kingdom is not a perfect geographical match for Great Britain, Ireland and later Northern Ireland were relatively small parts of the Gross Domestic Product of the United Kingdom over the period of our analysis. For instance, Maddison (2001) estimates that in 1913 the GDP of Ireland made up only 5.3 percent of total GDP of the United Kingdom. Atkinson (2005) reports that the Republic of Ireland was no longer included in top income shares for the United Kingdom in 1921. In that year and henceforth only Northern Ireland was included along with England, Scotland, and Wales.

On the 1984—2009 surveys, the PSID asks:

Would you say your (or wife's/husband's/friend's) health in general is ...

On the 1991—2009 surveys, the BHPS asks:

Please think back over the last 12 months about how your health has been. Compared to people of your own age, would you say that your health has on the whole been ...

While both surveys ask respondents to pick one of five Likert-scale categories that best describes their current health, the category descriptors are somewhat different. For the PSID, the category labels are "Excellent," "Very Good," "Good," "Fair," and "Poor," while in the BHPS the category labels are "Excellent," "Good," "Fair," "Poor," and "Very Poor."

The two surveys also differ because they collect these data from different sample members. The PSID respondent is usually the household head so he or she rates his or her own current health and, if relevant, the current health of his or her spouse. The BHPS interviews every household member who is aged 16 or older.

Given these differences, it is reasonable to wonder if the data measure comparable underlying health across the two countries. A large literature establishes that self-reported health correlates well with measured health (see Idler & Benyamini, 1997; Jürges, Avendano, & Mackenbach, 2008; Miilunpalo, Vuori, Oja, Pasanen, & Urponen, 1997; Sacker, Wiggins, Bartley, & McDonough, 2007; van Doorslaer & Jones, 2003). And although one might be concerned about measurement error in proxy health reports, when we drop all U.S. observations for whom we have only a proxy health report, results do not qualitatively change (results available on request).

Table 1 reports the distribution of men's and women's current health status across the five health status categories drawn from our PSID and BHPS subsamples of adults. In both countries, respondents are least likely to report health in the lowest two categories and most likely to report their health in the fourth category. Within each country, fewer women report health in the highest category. Relative to their British counterparts, self-reported health of U.S. men and women is skewed toward the lower response categories. The fraction of people who report health in the bottom three categories is higher in the United States than in Britain. If one combines responses in the top two categories, a smaller fraction of U.S. than British men and women report health in the top categories.

Table 1. Distribution of Self-Reported Current Health
Status — Native-Born Adults Aged 21 and Older (%).

United States			Great Britain		
Current health status	Men	Women	Current health status	Men	Women
Poor (1)	3.12	3.17	Very poor (1)	1.71	2.11
Fair (2)	8.15	9.32	Poor (2)	5.87	7.49
Good (3)	24.98	28.20	Fair (3)	19.00	21.24
Very good (4)	36.17	36.60	Good (4)	46.94	47.65
Excellent (5)	27.58	22.70	Excellent (5)	26.48	21.50
N (person-years)	36,522	41,238	N (person-years)	38,329	44,101

Sources: Same-years subsamples of PSID (1991–2007) and BHPS (1991–2007).
Note: Numbers in parentheses refer to coding of variable.

2.2. Income Inequality

We take advantage of a relatively new measure of income inequality that is based on administrative tax records. Such data are available for 28 countries, including the United States and Great Britain, and researchers have used these data to measure the share of all reported income held by various percentiles of tax units.[4] As with any such data, there are breaks in each country's top income data over time and differences in the types of taxable income that are taxed and the tax units across countries. For instance, the U.S. tax unit is the family. For Great Britain, the tax unit varies over time. From 1913 to 1989, taxes are measured for families. In 1990 and all subsequent years, Great Britain's tax unit is the person.

In the United States, we can measure income inequality as either the share of taxable income held by the top 1 percent (with or without capital gains) or the top 0.1 percent (with or without capital gains) of all tax units. In Lillard et al. (2015), we show that our results are not sensitive to either our choice of top income group or the inclusion or exclusion of capital gains. There are fewer top income data options for Great Britain, and even the data series that do exist do not have values for every year. Here, we focus solely on the top 1 percent series without capital gains in both countries. We impute income share values in some years for Great Britain

---

4. For reviews of the top income data and the literatures using these data, see Atkinson et al. (2011) and Alvaredo, Atkinson, Piketty, and Saez (2013a, 2013b). The World Top Income Database can be accessed at: http://www.wid.world/

because the data are missing. To impute, we use a simple average and straight-line interpolation between bracketing years for which values are available.[5] We then compute each respondent's birth year (as survey year minus current age) and average the top income shares observed in the first five years of each person's life — that is, from each person's birth year to the year he or she turned 4.

As a measure of income inequality, the tax record data are imperfect. The share of taxable income held by a given percentile varies with who is taxed, and the data are not adjusted for tax evasion and tax avoidance. Further, because the data measure national income inequality, it only varies temporally and may reflect trends in other factors that also temporally vary, such as changes in medical technology. While it might be preferable to use other measures of inequality, such as the Gini coefficient, these measures cannot be constructed with the tax record data.

Overall, these shortcomings are more than counter-balanced by three attractive features of tax record data. First, the administrative data measure income for samples that, over time, are more consistent in whom they include than other data sets — because the data include all taxes paid and all tax-paying units. Second, the data cover more years than other time-series researchers commonly use. For example, researchers often use CPS data to construct Gini coefficients for the United States, but data on incomes of families of two or more are only available for the period 1947–present and data on incomes of consistently defined households are available only from 1967.[6] Third, because the top income share data cover so many years, we can produce averages of inequality over various years. This feature helps to mitigate problems that might arise from associations between health and specific historical events (e.g., World War II). Finally, while in principle a broader inequality measure such as the Gini coefficient is preferable to a measure of the income share of the top 1 percent, Leigh (2007) shows a strong positive correlation between a country's Gini coefficient and its top income share over those years in which both measures are available. Our explanatory variable is therefore likely to be capturing movements in inequality more broadly defined.

Fig. 1 reports a rolling five-year average of top income share levels in each year from 1913 to 2009. For both the United States and Great Britain, they form a U-shaped pattern — dramatic declines over the first

---

5. A detailed discussion of the imputation procedure is provided Appendix A.
6. See www.census.gov/hhes/www/income/data/historical/inequality/

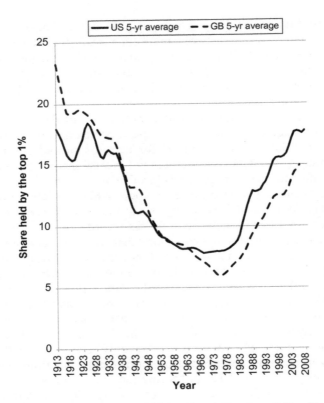

Fig. 1. Share of Taxable Income Held by Top 1 Percent of Tax Units, United States and Great Britain, 1913–2009. *Source*: Top 1 percent income series without taxable realized capital gains from Piketty and Saez (2003) and Atkinson (2005). Authors' calculations of mean annual value of top 1 percent share over first five years of life of those born in years between 1913 and 2006.

part of the 20th century, a levelling off in the second half of the century after World War II, then increases, especially between the 1980s and the start of the Great Recession in 2007. While our five-year average smooths some variation away, plenty remains.

2.3. Other Control Variables

To account for differences in health that vary with other observable characteristics, we control for sex, age, race, time, "permanent" income, and parents' education (United States) or occupation (Great Britain). We estimate separate models for men and women. To control for age, we define and categorize each respondent into one of 13 five-year age categories from age 21 to age 80 and older in the current year. We exclude 20-year-olds from the first group so it only includes people aged 21–24. The omitted category includes everyone aged 80 and older.

We control for time because, even though our sample period is short, medical technology changed substantially over the periods examined. To allow for different time trends, we specify several different models that alternately control for time with a linear trend, a quadratic trend, or indicator variables for survey years in the 1990s (relative to surveys from 2000 to 2007) in our same-years subsample and in the 1980s and 1990s in our full PSID sample.

To control for the well-established association between health and income (see Preston, 1975 and subsequent related work; Ettner, 1996; Larrimore, 2011), we construct a measure of real "permanent" family income. We use the "post-government" income measure from the Cross-National Equivalent File version of the PSID and BHPS. That measure starts with gross family income from all private sources, adds government transfer income, and subtracts estimated income taxes (based on NBER's tax simulation model for the United States and a similar University of Essex tax simulation model for Great Britain).[7] We adjust for inflation and divide by the square root of the number of family members in that year. Then we average observed income over all years from the first year we observe it (1970 for the United States; 1991 for Great Britain), up to and including the year prior to the year a person reports his or her health status. We exclude income in the most recent year to avoid changes in income that result from changes in health. Because the number of valid observations differs across people, we separately control for the number of years over which we average income. We also create a dummy variable for persons that have zero, negative, or missing permanent incomes.

We use available data to control for childhood socio-economic status that may directly or indirectly determine childhood health, and therefore impact on health in adulthood. We control for mother's and father's education in the U.S. sample and mother's and father's occupation in the British sample. Few existing studies on lagged income inequality and health do so.

---

7. For details on the estimation of post-government income, see http://cnef.ehe.osu.edu/

For the PSID sample, we include two indicators to identify respondents whose fathers completed a college degree or more and fathers who either completed high school or high school plus some vocational education (the reference category is respondents whose fathers did not complete high school). We similarly create two indicators for mothers' education. For the BHPS sample, we create an indicator for respondents whose father worked in a managerial or professional occupation and respondents whose father worked in some other skilled occupation when the respondent was aged 14 years. Here, the reference group is respondents whose father worked in a non-skilled occupation or who did not report an occupation for his father. We similarly create two indicators for mothers' occupation.

While we have data on parents' education for most of our U.S. sample, we do not have data on parents' occupations for a significant and selected subset of our Great Britain sample. In the BHPS, information on parents' occupation only began to be collected in 1998. Hence, this information is missing for persons no longer in the sample in 1998. To retain the integrity of our sample, we keep these individuals in the estimation sample, but control for missing values in parents' occupation with a dummy variable. We also control for missing values in parents' education in the U.S. sample.[8]

We do not include other macro-level controls for two reasons. First, it is difficult to find data consistently measured over the sample period we study. Second, the available macro-control (estimated per capita GDP) increases almost monotonically and almost linearly over our sample period. We explore the robustness of our results to different time trends to try to capture that variation. Despite that analysis, we acknowledge as a limitation of our analysis that our inequality measure only varies over time.

2.4. Sample Selection and Descriptive Statistics

We restrict our sample to native-born adult men and women who are 21 years or older in the year that they report their health and who have complete data on our control variables. Our selection rule drops individuals born before 1913 because 1913 is the first year in which our top income share time series is available in both countries. Although the PSID and

---

8. As a check on the robustness of our results, we estimated each of our main models excluding observations with missing values for parents' education in the United States and parents' occupation in Great Britain. Our findings are not qualitatively different.

BHPS are panel data, we treat the data as pooled cross-sectional measures of health. Some people contribute multiple observations. That fact will matter because our measure of top income shares varies only by birth year. To control for systematic differences in health of people who appear multiple times, we cluster standard errors for all people born in the same calendar year. Our results are robust when we do not cluster standard errors by birth year.

Table 2 reports the distribution of our observations by 10-year birth cohort and age group for both men and women for our same-years subsamples of the United States and Great Britain. In each age range, we observe the current health of up to three cohorts, each of which likely experienced different levels of inequality as children. Each of the 10-year birth cohorts from 1920–1929 through 1970–1979 contributes at least 10 percent of the observations for each sample. The 1913–1919 and 1980–1986 birth cohorts contribute fewer observations because they are shorter (seven years) and, in the case of the 1980–1986 birth cohort, because there are fewer sample years in which the cohort is aged 21 or older. In the case of the 1913–1919 birth cohort (and indeed for subsequent cohorts), deaths also play a role in reducing the number of observations available.

Table 3 reports the means of the independent variables for each of our subsamples. On average, early-life income inequality is lower than average contemporaneous inequality in both countries. This difference reflects the fact that top income shares were relatively low over the 1940s to 1970s in both the United States and Great Britain. The gap between contemporaneous and early-life inequality is, however, greater for the United States, since the top income share has been consistently higher in the United States since the 1970s. In both countries, the mean of our measure of permanent income is higher for men than women. The sample is distributed fairly evenly across a wide range of five-year age groups between 25 and 54, but is less evenly distributed in the younger and older age groups. Approximately 99 percent of the British sample is white, compared with 90 percent of the U.S. sample.

Table 4 isolates the sample of respondents who report being in the lowest two health categories — "Poor" and "Fair" for the United States and "Very Poor" and "Poor" for Great Britain. It presents the proportion reporting these low health values for cells defined by birth cohort and age group. Comparing cells in the same row allows us to see how the share of persons in each birth cohort who report lower health values changes as the cohort ages. Comparing cells in the same column allows us to see how, in

Table 2. Distribution of Same-Years Subsamples by Age Group and Birth Cohort (%).

	Age Group							All Ages
	21–29	30–39	40–49	50–59	60–69	70–79	80+	
The United States								
Men								
Born 1913–1919						1.3	0.8	2.1
Born 1920–1929					3.2	3.7	0.7	7.6
Born 1930–1939				2.8	4.4	1.1		8.3
Born 1940–1949			7.2	8.6	2.1			17.9
Born 1950–1959		9.1	13.9	4.1				27.1
Born 1960–1969	5.6	12.6	4.3					22.5
Born 1970–1979	7.7	4.8						12.5
Born 1980–1986	2.1							2.1
All cohorts	15.3	26.5	25.4	15.6	9.6	6.1	1.5	100.0
Women								
Born 1913–1919						1.8	1.3	3.1
Born 1920–1929					3.2	4.1	0.9	8.2
Born 1930–1939				2.8	4.5	1.3		8.5
Born 1940–1949			6.1	7.3	1.9			15.4
Born 1950–1959		8.6	13.8	4.3				26.6
Born 1960–1969	5.7	12.6	4.4					22.7
Born 1970–1979	8.4	4.4						12.8
Born 1980–1986	2.8							2.8
All cohorts	16.9	25.6	24.3	14.4	9.5	7.2	2.2	100.0
Great Britain								
Men								
Born 1913–1919						2.0	1.0	3.0
Born 1920–1929					4.2	5.0	1.0	10.2
Born 1930–1939				4.5	5.6	1.6		11.8
Born 1940–1949			7.1	8.6	2.3			18.0
Born 1950–1959		7.3	9.5	2.8				19.6
Born 1960–1969	7.5	11.8	3.7					23.0
Born 1970–1979	9.1	3.4						12.5
Born 1980–1986	2.0							2.0
All cohorts	18.6	22.5	20.4	15.8	12.2	8.6	2.0	100.0
Women								
Born 1913–1919						2.6	1.6	4.3
Born 1920–1929					4.2	5.8	1.3	11.4
Born 1930–1939				4.2	5.7	1.6		11.5
Born 1940–1949			6.9	8.4	2.3			17.6
Born 1950–1959		6.7	9.3	2.7				18.7
Born 1960–1969	7.6	11.6	3.7					22.9
Born 1970–1979	8.5	3.2						11.7
Born 1980–1986	2.0							2.0
All cohorts	18.0	21.5	19.9	15.3	12.2	10.1	3.0	100.0

Sources: Same-years subsamples of PSID (1991–2007) and BHPS (1991–2007).
Note: Blank cells are zeros. The total number of person-year observations is 36,522 for U.S. males, 41,238 for U.S. females, 38,329 for British males, and 44,101 for British females. Individuals can appear more than once. In the U.S. samples, on average each of the 5,678 unique males and 6,050 unique females appears 6.4 and 6.8 times, respectively. In the British samples, on average each of the 6,129 unique males and 6,542 unique females appears 6.3 and 6.7 times, respectively.

Table 3. Mean Values of Variables in Same-Years Subsamples.

Variable	United States		Great Britain	
	Men	Women	Men	Women
Income share of top 1% of tax units				
Current year as adult	14.75	14.75	11.75	11.77
	(1.93)	(1.93)	(1.61)	(1.63)
Mean value for years from birth to age 4	10.40	10.48	11.27	11.54
	(3.06)	(3.15)	(4.39)	(4.57)
Log of permanent family income[a]	10.41	10.32	9.22	8.97
	(0.60)	(0.62)	(1.72)	(2.10)
Years used in permanent income measure	5.71	5.82	4.98	4.92
	(3.45)	(3.46)	(3.33)	(3.36)
Age groups				
21−24	0.04	0.06	0.08	0.07
25−29	0.11	0.11	0.10	0.11
30−34	0.13	0.13	0.12	0.11
35−39	0.14	0.13	0.11	0.10
40−44	0.13	0.13	0.10	0.10
45−49	0.12	0.11	0.10	0.10
50−54	0.09	0.08	0.09	0.08
55−59	0.07	0.06	0.07	0.07
60−64	0.05	0.05	0.06	0.06
65−69	0.05	0.05	0.06	0.06
70−74	0.04	0.04	0.05	0.06
75−79	0.03	0.03	0.03	0.04
80 and older	0.02	0.02	0.02	0.03
Race				
White	0.90	0.89	0.988	0.988
Black	0.06	0.08	0.004	0.006
Other	0.04	0.04	0.008	0.006
Parents' education				
Father: BA degree or more	0.17	0.17		
Father: High school degree	0.42	0.42		
Father: Less than high school degree	0.41	0.41		
Mother: BA degree or more	0.12	0.12		
Mother: High school degree	0.56	0.53		
Mother: Less than high school degree	0.32	0.35		
Parents' occupation				
Father: Professional, managerial, technical			0.21	0.21
Father: Skilled and semi-skilled			0.56	0.56
Father: Other or no occupation			0.23	0.23
Mother: Professional, managerial, technical			0.09	0.10
Mother: Skilled and semi-skilled			0.28	0.29
Mother: Other or no occupation			0.63	0.61
N (person-years)	36,522	41,238	38,329	44,101
N (persons)	5,678	6,050	6,129	6,542

Sources: Same-years subsamples of PSID (1991−2007) and BHPS (1991−2007).
Notes: Numbers in parentheses are standard deviations.
[a]A person's permanent family income is the family size-adjusted post-tax post-government transfer income averaged over all years from a person's first year up to 1 year before a person reported his/her health status. We use the estimates of yearly family income in the CNEF data. Yearly income values are adjusted for inflation to 2011 dollars.

Table 4. Percentage Ranking Their Health in the Lowest Two Health Categories, by Age and Birth Cohort.[a]

	Age Group[b]							All Ages
	21–29	30–39	40–49	50–59	60–69	70–79	80+	
United States								
Men								
Born 1913–1919						38.2	44.5	40.9
Born 1920–1929					21.0	31.8	38.9	28.5
Born 1930–1939				18.5	22.1	32.1		22.0
Born 1940–1949			8.9	13.9	17.6			12.2
Born 1950–1959		5.2	8.5	12.0				7.9
Born 1960–1969	3.4	4.6	8.8					5.1
Born 1970–1979	4.0	6.0						4.7
Born 1980–1986	3.3							3.3
All cohorts	3.7	5.1	8.7	14.3	20.9	33.4	41.6	11.1
Women								
Born 1913–1919						35.2	41.0	38.0
Born 1920–1929					24.7	31.1	43.2	30.8
Born 1930–1939				19.3	23.5	34.3		23.6
Born 1940–1949			9.3	15.7	19.6			13.5
Born 1950–1959		6.3	10.3	16.2				9.9
Born 1960–1969	3.7	5.4	9.4					5.7
Born 1970–1979	5.6	7.7						6.3
Born 1980–1986	5.2							5.2
All cohorts	5.0	6.1	9.9	16.6	23.3	32.7	42.0	12.8
Great Britain								
Men								
Born 1913–1919						13.0	13.8	13.3
Born 1920–1929					9.5	12.2	15.7	11.6
Born 1930–1939				8.4	11.5	11.8		10.3
Born 1940–1949			6.2	10.1	9.9			8.5
Born 1950–1959		4.4	8.4	10.0				7.1
Born 1960–1969	4.0	5.0	5.2					4.7
Born 1970–1979	4.7	4.8						4.7
Born 1980–1986	4.3							4.3
All cohorts	4.4	4.8	7.0	9.6	10.5	12.4	14.8	7.5
Women								
Born 1913–1919						19.1	19.3	19.2
Born 1920–1929					10.5	13.8	19.9	13.8
Born 1930–1939				12.1	10.3	13.4		11.4
Born 1940–1949			9.1	11.1	11.1			10.3
Born 1950–1959		6.5	9.0	11.3				8.4
Born 1960–1969	6.3	8.2	10.8					8.0
Born 1970–1979	6.3	7.9						6.7
Born 1980–1986	5.7							5.7
All cohorts	6.2	7.6	9.4	11.4	10.5	15.2	19.6	9.9

Sources: Same-years subsamples of the PSID (1991–2007) and BHPS (1991–2007).
[a]The two lowest categories for the U.S. are "poor" or "fair" health. For Great Britain, they are "very poor" or "poor" health.
[b]The actual ages considered within the age groups have been made consistent across birth cohorts. The actual age groups are 22–27, 32–37, 42–47, 52–57, 62–67, 72–77, and 80–87. The row and column totals only include these ages.

each age group, the share of persons who report worse health differs across birth cohorts — that is, we compare across cohorts the prevalence of low health values when each cohort was the same age. Our scope for comparing cohorts at specific ages varies by birth cohort. For example, the ages over which we observe respondents born in the 1960s range from 22 (in 1991) to 47 (in 2007). To measure as consistently as possible differences in prevalence of low health values associated with membership in each birth cohort (i.e., reading down a given column), we measure the prevalence of low health values for the subset of each birth cohort for whom we can observe their health in the age range listed at the top of each column. Thus, the 21−29 age group column includes only persons aged 22−27, the 30−39 age group column includes only those aged 32−37, and so on.[9]

The pattern of differences in the level of the lowest two health categories reported in the United States and Great Britain by age is not surprising since the stem of the U.S. question asks respondents to rate their health without qualifications while the stem of the British question asks them to rate their health "compared to people of your own age." The age-conditioned responses in Great Britain result in higher reported health problems in the youngest age category relative to the unconditional U.S. responses and progressively lower responses relative to the United States at older ages. Nonetheless, it is reassuring that the percentage reporting worse health increases at older ages in both countries, despite the way the stem question and descriptors attached to the response categories differ in the two surveys. Holding age constant, the pattern is less clear. In the United States, for the cohorts of older men and most of the cohorts of older women (those aged 50 and older), the prevalence of poor health is lower for more recent birth cohorts. In Britain, the pattern is less clear.

3. EMPIRICAL STRATEGY

Our data vary across adults (i) who belong to one of 75 birth cohorts (c) and who report their health in successive calendar years (t). Our self-reported health data, h_{ict}, represent the continuously distributed underlying state of true health, h_{ict}^*, in five categories ranging from poor ($h_{ict} = 1$) to

---

9. However, when we include all people we observe in each age-cohort cell it does not qualitatively affect the results.

excellent ($h_{ict} = 5$). We, therefore, estimate ordered probit models of self-reported health as a function of early-life income inequality, $\hat{I}_c$, as well as various controls, Z_{it}. Thus, the probability individual i belonging to cohort c in year t observed in health state j is modeled as:

$$P\left(h^*_{ict} = h_{ict}(j)\right) = \Pr\left(\mu_{j-1} < \gamma_1 \hat{I}_c + \beta Z_{ict} + \in_{ict} \leq \mu_j\right) \tag{1}$$

where ε_{ict} is a normally distributed error term with mean zero that captures stochastic, individual-specific shocks to health in each period.

We order health categories from poor/very poor (1) to excellent (5). Consequently, if γ_1 statistically differs from zero, we can reject the hypothesis that an adult's current health does not vary with early-life income inequality (holding constant all factors in Z). If γ_1 is negative and statistically differs from zero, we can reject the hypothesis that an adult is not more likely to report being in poorer health when income inequality was greater during early life. We also present mean predicted marginal changes in the probability of reporting each health category of a 1 percent increase in the top percentile income share.

Depending on the specification, the vector Z_{it} includes age group indicators, race indicators, permanent family income, parental education, parental occupation, contemporaneous income inequality as an adult, and a time trend. We estimate a series of models that successively add controls to explore how the association between current adult health and early-life income inequality varies.

Model 1 includes only the top income share averaged over ages 0–4. Model 2 adds a quadratic time trend. Model 3 additionally controls for age using our age-group categories and race using our CNEF indicator variables — "black" and "other," with "white" as the excluded category. Model 4 additionally controls for permanent income, and Model 5 adds controls for father's and mother's education (United States) or parents' occupation (Great Britain).[10]

To check the robustness of the association to a definition of inequality that focuses on the very top of the income distribution, we substitute the income shares of the top 0.1 percent for the income shares of the top 1 percent and estimate the five models with that measure of inequality. Our findings are robust to this change.[11]

---

10. The PSID contains information on parental occupation, but the occupational classification system differs from that for the BHPS and, moreover, changes over time.
11. These results are not reported, but are available on request.

In all our analyses, we cluster standard errors by birth year because the average of income shares experienced in early-life years is the same for all individuals born in the same-years and because many adults contribute multiple observations. We do not use sample weights. Results do not qualitatively change when we use sample weights or when we do not cluster the standard errors.

4. RESULTS

4.1. Main Specifications

Table 5 reports results for U.S. men. Recall that we have ordered reported health from 1 for poor to 5 for excellent health. The estimated coefficient in Model 1 indicates that the simple correlation between adult health and early-life income inequality is negative and statistically significant ($p < .01$). U.S. men are less likely to report being in better health as adults if income inequality was higher in their first five years of life. When we control for time in Model 2, the association between current health and early-life income inequality is almost unchanged (or even slightly larger) and still significant at the 1 percent level.

Model 3 adds controls for age and race. We find that coefficient estimates for these controls have the expected negative association between age and health and that self-assessed health is highest for whites and lowest for blacks. All coefficient estimates are significant at the 1 percent level. But we also find that once we control for age and race, while the coefficient on early-life income inequality remains significant at the 5 percent level, its absolute value falls by 80 percent.

Model 4 adds controls for permanent income. We find that permanent income has the expected positive association with health and is significant at the 1 percent level. Including this control increases the absolute value of our early-life income inequality coefficient but it remains much lower than without controls. It is now significant at the 1 percent level.

Model 5 adds controls for parental education, which partially controls for individual differences in economic resources available in early life. As hypothesized, the coefficient estimates on the parental education variables imply that adult U.S. men report better health if they grew up with better educated parents and hence had access to greater economic resources in early life. Including this control slightly reduces the absolute value of our

Table 5. Ordered Probit Coefficient Estimates for U.S. Men.

Variable	(1)	(2)	(3)	(4)	(5)
Mean top 1% income	−0.1016***	−0.1064***	−0.0208**	−0.0334***	−0.0244**
share when aged 0−4	(0.0058)	(0.0061)	(0.0102)	(0.0103)	(0.0099)
Time trend		−0.0075	0.0894*	0.0829	0.0824
		(0.0598)	(0.0488)	(0.0536)	(0.0536)
Time trend squared		−0.0000	−0.0005*	−0.0005*	−0.0005*
		(0.0003)	(0.0002)	(0.0003)	(0.0003)
Age groups (reference age: 80 years and older)					
21−24			1.1273***	1.2497***	1.1453***
			(0.0991)	(0.1071)	(0.1044)
25−29			1.1230***	1.1369***	1.0405***
			(0.1013)	(0.1074)	(0.1042)
30−34			1.0266***	0.9718***	0.8886***
			(0.1018)	(0.1064)	(0.1032)
35−39			0.9054***	0.8235***	0.7583***
			(0.0977)	(0.1011)	(0.0983)
40−44			0.8421***	0.7206***	0.6685***
			(0.0900)	(0.0941)	(0.0911)
45−49			0.7426***	0.5796***	0.5382***
			(0.0823)	(0.0875)	(0.0846)
50−54			0.6398***	0.4594***	0.4332***
			(0.0735)	(0.0772)	(0.0755)
55−59			0.5317***	0.3351***	0.3206***
			(0.0666)	(0.0691)	(0.0656)
60−64			0.4127***	0.2367***	0.2349***
			(0.0628)	(0.0685)	(0.0658)
65−69			0.3644***	0.2382***	0.2276***
			(0.0664)	(0.0694)	(0.0681)
70−74			0.1843***	0.1340**	0.1294**
			(0.0526)	(0.0570)	(0.0546)
75−79			0.0749	0.0369	0.0341
			(0.0604)	(0.0620)	(0.0633)
Race (reference: white)					
Black			−0.4215***	−0.2224***	−0.1793***
			(0.0512)	(0.0502)	(0.0510)
Other			−0.1714***	−0.0816*	−0.0394
			(0.0557)	(0.0486)	(0.0474)
Log of permanent family income				0.5790***	0.5181***
				(0.0228)	(0.0249)
Years used in permanent measure				0.0016	−0.0021
				(0.0052)	(0.0052)

Table 5. (*Continued*)

Variable	(1)	(2)	(3)	(4)	(5)
Parents' education (reference: less than high school degree)					
Father: BA degree or higher					0.1918***
					(0.0443)
Father: High school degree					0.1060***
					(0.0315)
Mother: BA degree or higher					0.2264***
					(0.0456)
Mother: High school degree					0.1302***
					(0.0302)
N (person-years)	36,522	36,522	36,522	36,522	36,522

Source: Same-years subsample of PSID (1991–2007).

Notes: Robust standard errors in parentheses. Coefficient estimates that statistically differ from zero are denoted by ***, **, and * for *p*-values ≤.01, ≤.05, and ≤.10, respectively. Reference categories include those aged 80 and over and those whose parents did not receive a high school degree. We do not drop observations because of missing values in the log of permanent family income or parental education but rather add three dummy variables that indicate missing values in these variables. The coefficients of these dummy variables are not shown here but are available on request.

early-life income inequality coefficient. It is now significant at the 5 percent level.

Table 6 reports results for U.S. women. Results for women are similar to those of U.S. men. In all five models, women are less likely to report being in better health as adults when they experienced higher average income inequality when aged 0–4. This association statistically differs from zero at the 1 percent significance level in the first four models and at the 5 percent level in Model 5. As was the case for men, the addition of controls dramatically reduces this coefficient's absolute value. Adult women are also more likely to report being in better health if they are younger, white, have greater permanent income, and had access to greater economic resources as a child.

Hence, across all our specifications we find a robust, statistically significant negative relationship between better self-reported health of adult U.S. men (Table 5) and women (Table 6) and the income inequality they experienced in early life.

Tables 7 and 8 respectively report results for British men and women. As in the United States, for British men the simple correlation in Model 1 is negative and statistically significant ($p < .01$). This result does not change when we control for time in Model 2. However, when we control for age

Table 6. Ordered Probit Coefficient Estimates for U.S. Women.

Variable	(1)	(2)	(3)	(4)	(5)
Mean top 1% income	−0.1015***	−0.1071***	−0.0311***	−0.0320***	−0.0216**
share when aged 0−4	(0.0049)	(0.0051)	(0.0100)	(0.0104)	(0.0103)
Time trend		0.0383	0.1198**	0.1161**	0.1217**
		(0.0546)	(0.0472)	(0.0581)	(0.0571)
Time trend squared		−0.0003	−0.0006***	−0.0007**	−0.0007**
		(0.0003)	(0.0002)	(0.0003)	(0.0003)
Age groups (reference age: 80 years and older)					
21−24			0.9923***	1.1016***	1.0020***
			(0.1060)	(0.1144)	(0.1158)
25−29			0.9767***	0.9763***	0.8884***
			(0.1079)	(0.1158)	(0.1172)
30−34			0.9405***	0.8925***	0.8208***
			(0.1034)	(0.1111)	(0.1127)
35−39			0.8609***	0.7715***	0.7184***
			(0.1007)	(0.1082)	(0.1104)
40−44			0.8138***	0.6834***	0.6448***
			(0.0962)	(0.1003)	(0.1030)
45−49			0.7146***	0.5366***	0.5090***
			(0.0885)	(0.0934)	(0.0968)
50−54			0.6234***	0.4055***	0.3985***
			(0.0830)	(0.0878)	(0.0921)
55−59			0.5562***	0.3312***	0.3276***
			(0.0746)	(0.0770)	(0.0814)
60−64			0.4489***	0.2420***	0.2439***
			(0.0829)	(0.0851)	(0.0885)
65−69			0.3255***	0.1744***	0.1732***
			(0.0628)	(0.0576)	(0.0634)
70−74			0.1914***	0.1102*	0.1124*
			(0.0654)	(0.0614)	(0.0672)
75−79			0.1159*	0.0825	0.0886
			(0.0670)	(0.0621)	(0.0638)
Race (reference: white)					
Black			−0.5935***	−0.3122***	−0.2689***
			(0.0511)	(0.0507)	(0.0500)
Other			−0.2142***	−0.1507**	−0.1079*
			(0.0674)	(0.0594)	(0.0578)
Log of permanent family income				0.5425***	0.4730***
				(0.0240)	(0.0232)
Years used in permanent measure				0.0068	0.0025
				(0.0056)	(0.0055)

Table 6. (*Continued*)

Variable	(1)	(2)	(3)	(4)	(5)
Parents' education (reference: less than high school degree)					
Father: BA degree or higher					0.2498***
					(0.0325)
Father: High school degree					0.1420***
					(0.0283)
Mother: BA degree or higher					0.2018***
					(0.0499)
Mother: High school degree					0.1644***
					(0.0313)
N (person-years)	41,238	41,238	41,238	41,238	41,238

Source: Same-years subsample of PSID (1991–2007).

Notes: Robust standard errors in parentheses. Coefficient estimates that statistically differ from zero are denoted by ***, **, and * for p-values $\leq.01$, $\leq.05$, and $\leq.10$, respectively. Reference categories include those aged 80 and over and those whose parents did not receive a high school degree. We do not drop observations because of missing values in the log of permanent family income or parental education but rather add three dummy variables that indicate missing values in these variables. The coefficients of these dummy variables are not shown here but are available on request.

and race in Model 3, the absolute value of the coefficient on early-life inequality falls by 73 percent and the standard error increases so the association is not statistically different from zero at conventional levels of significance ($p < .1$). Adding economic controls for permanent income (Model 4) and parents' occupations (Model 5) does not affect the estimated relationship.

As was the case in the United States, British men are more likely to report being in better health as adults if they are younger and have greater permanent income. Because we limit our sample to those adults born in Great Britain, 98.8 percent of our CNEF sample are coded as white, while only about 0.4 percent are coded as black and 0.8 percent as "other." Those coded as "other" are significantly less likely to report better health at the 1 percent level. This is not the case for blacks, where the coefficient is not significantly different from whites. Men whose fathers worked in professional or managerial occupations, which partially controls for individual differences in economic resources available in early life, are more likely, as adults, to report being in better health. Mother's occupation was not found to be significantly different from zero at conventional levels.

Results for British women in Table 8 are similar to those of British men. In Models 1 and 2, British women are less likely to report being in better

Table 7. Ordered Probit Coefficient Estimates for British Men.

Variable	(1)	(2)	(3)	(4)	(5)
Mean top 1% income	−0.0406***	−0.0444***	−0.0120	−0.0088	−0.0084
share when aged 0−4	(0.0025)	(0.0025)	(0.0099)	(0.0102)	(0.0102)
Time trend		−0.2983***	−0.2726***	−0.3417***	−0.3350***
		(0.0490)	(0.0439)	(0.0473)	(0.0482)
Time trend squared		0.0014***	0.0013***	0.0016***	0.0016***
		(0.0002)	(0.0002)	(0.0002)	(0.0002)
Age groups (reference age: 80 years and older)					
21−24			0.4465***	0.5025***	0.5118***
			(0.1524)	(0.1584)	(0.1571)
25−29			0.4876***	0.5125***	0.5220***
			(0.1467)	(0.1521)	(0.1509)
30−34			0.4780***	0.4974***	0.5051***
			(0.1402)	(0.1458)	(0.1448)
35−39			0.4333***	0.4461***	0.4551***
			(0.1340)	(0.1384)	(0.1368)
40−44			0.4322***	0.4377***	0.4479***
			(0.1277)	(0.1312)	(0.1301)
45−49			0.3686***	0.3517***	0.3632***
			(0.1165)	(0.1209)	(0.1199)
50−54			0.3245***	0.2871***	0.2990***
			(0.1026)	(0.1057)	(0.1054)
55−59			0.2165**	0.1738*	0.1860*
			(0.0946)	(0.0961)	(0.0955)
60−64			0.1797**	0.1646**	0.1750**
			(0.0787)	(0.0821)	(0.0810)
65−69			0.1518**	0.1563**	0.1638**
			(0.0672)	(0.0715)	(0.0716)
70−74			0.0772	0.0771	0.0829
			(0.0499)	(0.0525)	(0.0515)
75−79			0.0317	0.0398	0.0402
			(0.0328)	(0.0339)	(0.0336)
Race (reference: white)					
Black			−0.0339	0.0616	0.0625
			(0.1255)	(0.1398)	(0.1407)
Other			−0.1664***	−0.1731***	−0.1717***
			(0.0575)	(0.0629)	(0.0631)
Log of permanent family income				0.3749***	0.3571***
				(0.0224)	(0.0226)
Years used in permanent measure				0.0077**	0.0068*
				(0.0038)	(0.0040)

Table 7. (*Continued*)

Variable	(1)	(2)	(3)	(4)	(5)
Parents' occupation (reference: other or no occupation)					
Father: Professional, managerial, technical				0.1219***	
					(0.0377)
Father: Skilled and semi-skilled					−0.0135
					(0.0338)
Mother: Professional, managerial, technical				−0.0282	
					(0.0429)
Mother: Skilled and semi-skilled					−0.0286
					(0.0285)
N (person-years)	38,329	38,329	38,329	38,329	38,329

Source: Same-years subsample of BHPS (1991–2007).
Notes: Robust standard errors in parentheses. Coefficient estimates that statistically differ from zero are denoted by ***, **, and * for *p*-values ≤.01, ≤.05, and ≤.10, respectively. Reference categories include those aged 80 and over and those whose parents had other or no occupation. We do not drop observations because of missing values in the log of permanent family income or parental occupation but rather add three dummy variables that indicate missing values in these variables. The coefficients of these dummy variables are not shown here but are available on request.

health as adults when they experienced higher average income inequality when aged 0–4. This association statistically differs from zero at the 1 percent significance level. However, when we control for age and race in Model 3, the absolute value of the coefficient on early-life inequality falls by 80 percent and the standard error increases so the association does not statistically differ from zero. Adding economic controls for permanent income (Model 4) and parents' occupations (Model 5) does not affect the estimated relationship. Adult British women are also more likely to report being in better health if they are younger, have greater permanent income, and grew up with fathers who worked in professional or managerial occupations and hence allowed them to have access to greater economic resources as a child.

The results using PSID–BHPS samples from the same calendar years show that for both U.S. men and women, reported health as an adult is related to inequality experienced when aged 0–4. This result is robust across all five models. We find evidence of a similar association for British men and women in models that estimate only the simple correlation. But the relationship is not robust to controls for demographic and economic factors. While the coefficient on the income inequality variable continues to be negative in these models, it does not statistically differ from zero.

Table 8. Ordered Probit Coefficient Estimates for British Women.

Variable	(1)	(2)	(3)	(4)	(5)
Mean top 1% income	−0.0376***	−0.0407***	−0.0080	−0.0059	−0.0046
share when aged 0−4	(0.0023)	(0.0024)	(0.0080)	(0.0088)	(0.0086)
Time trend		−0.3654***	−0.3273***	−0.3948***	−0.3910***
		(0.0510)	(0.0438)	(0.0475)	(0.0491)
Time trend squared		0.0018***	0.0016***	0.0019***	0.0019***
		(0.0003)	(0.0002)	(0.0002)	(0.0002)
Age groups (reference age: 80 years and older)					
21−24			0.5494***	0.5673***	0.5648***
			(0.1226)	(0.1309)	(0.1305)
25−29			0.5871***	0.5835***	0.5791***
			(0.1195)	(0.1289)	(0.1287)
30−34			0.6048***	0.5989***	0.5917***
			(0.1116)	(0.1197)	(0.1194)
35−39			0.5736***	0.5637***	0.5585***
			(0.1051)	(0.1137)	(0.1130)
40−44			0.5489***	0.5217***	0.5192***
			(0.0992)	(0.1069)	(0.1067)
45−49			0.4745***	0.4111***	0.4121***
			(0.0895)	(0.0952)	(0.0943)
50−54			0.3987***	0.3272***	0.3339***
			(0.0690)	(0.0763)	(0.0756)
55−59			0.3796***	0.3196***	0.3262***
			(0.0637)	(0.0718)	(0.0712)
60−64			0.4188***	0.3762***	0.3837***
			(0.0524)	(0.0584)	(0.0580)
65−69			0.2768***	0.2529***	0.2586***
			(0.0467)	(0.0494)	(0.0491)
70−74			0.2182***	0.2083***	0.2122***
			(0.0440)	(0.0479)	(0.0473)
75−79			0.0746	0.0741	0.0771*
			(0.0453)	(0.0453)	(0.0447)
Race (reference: white)					
Black			0.0394	0.0965	0.1222
			(0.1231)	(0.1322)	(0.1345)
Other			−0.3223***	−0.1964**	−0.1789**
			(0.0844)	(0.0800)	(0.0825)
Log of permanent family income				0.3699***	0.3462***
				(0.0213)	(0.0225)
Years used in permanent measure				0.0078*	0.0072
				(0.0046)	(0.0045)

Table 8.   (*Continued*)

Variable	(1)	(2)	(3)	(4)	(5)
Parents' occupation (reference: other or no occupation)					
Father: Professional, managerial, technical				0.1641***	
				(0.0409)	
Father: Skilled and semi-skilled					0.0673**
					(0.0324)
Mother: Professional, managerial, technical				0.0485	
				(0.0399)	
Mother: Skilled and semi-skilled					0.0332
					(0.0261)
N (person-years)	44,101	44,101	44,101	44,101	44,101

Source: Same-years subsample of BHPS (1991−2007).
Notes: Robust standard errors in parentheses. Coefficient estimates that statistically differ from zero are denoted by ***, **, and * for *p*-values ≤.01, ≤.05, and ≤.10, respectively. Reference categories include those aged 80 and over and those whose parents had other or no occupation. We do not drop observations because of missing values in the log of permanent family income or parental occupation but rather add three dummy variables that indicate missing values in these variables. The coefficients of these dummy variables are not shown here but are available on request.

To gauge the economic significance of the estimated associations, we use the coefficients from each model in Tables 5−8 to compute the mean predicted marginal effect on the probability of reporting a given level of health given a one unit change in experienced inequality. Table 9 presents the mean predicted marginal effects.

In the U.S. samples, the estimates from our preferred Model 5 imply that a one percentage point increase in experienced early-life inequality would reduce the probability that a person reports being in excellent health as an adult by 0.74 percentage points for men and 0.58 percentage points for women. That change would increase the probability a person reports being in poor health as an adult by 0.14 percentage points for men and 0.13 percentage points for women.

As noted above, results from the British samples show that adult health is uncorrelated with early-life inequality. However, when we use the point estimates to compute the mean marginal effects estimates, those predicted effects are considerably smaller in the British samples than they are in the U.S. samples. For example, the Model 5 estimates imply that a one percentage point increase in experienced early-life inequality would reduce the probability that a person reports being in excellent health as an adult by 0.26 percentage points for men and 0.13 percentage points for women.

Table 9.   Mean Predicted Marginal Effects on Current Health of a
1 Percentage Point Increase in Mean Early-Life Income Inequality
(Birth to Age 4), by Model Specification, United States and
Great Britain (1991−2007).

Current Health	(1)	(2)	(3)	(4)	(5)
United States					
Men					
Excellent	−0.0327***	−0.0341***	−0.0066**	−0.0101***	−0.0074**
Very good	−0.0036***	−0.0037***	−0.0007**	−0.0011***	−0.0008**
Good	0.0180***	0.0188***	0.0036**	0.0056***	0.0041**
Fair	0.0117***	0.0122***	0.0024**	0.0037***	0.0027**
Poor	0.0066***	0.0069***	0.0013**	0.0020***	0.0014**
Women					
Excellent	−0.0294***	−0.0309***	−0.0088***	−0.0087***	−0.0058**
Very good	−0.0080***	−0.0084***	−0.0024***	−0.0023***	−0.0015**
Good	0.0178***	0.0188***	0.0054***	0.0054***	0.0036**
Fair	0.0129***	0.0136***	0.0038***	0.0038***	0.0025**
Poor	0.0067***	0.0070***	0.0020***	0.0019***	0.0013**
Great Britain					
Men					
Excellent	−0.0131***	−0.0143***	−0.0039	−0.0028	−0.0026
Good	−0.0000	−0.0000	0.0000	−0.0000	−0.0000
Fair	0.0074***	0.0081***	0.0022	0.0016	0.0015
Poor	0.0040***	0.0044***	0.0012	0.0008	0.0008
Very poor	0.0017***	0.0018***	0.0005	0.0004	0.0003
Women					
Excellent	−0.0108***	−0.0117***	−0.0023	−0.0017	−0.0013
Good	−0.0022***	−0.0024***	−0.0005	−0.0003	−0.0003
Fair	0.0067***	0.0073***	0.0014	0.0010	0.0008
Poor	0.0044***	0.0048***	0.0009	0.0007	0.0005
Very poor	0.0019***	0.0020***	0.0004	0.0003	0.0002
Controls					
Time trend		✓	✓	✓	✓
Age group			✓	✓	✓
Race			✓	✓	✓
Log permanent family income				✓	✓
Parents' education/ occupation					✓

Sources: Same-years subsamples of PSID (1991−2007) and BHPS (1991−2007).
Notes: Results in each column based on mean predicted marginal effects using coefficient estimates from the corresponding columns in Tables 5−8. Sample sizes are $N = 36,522$ for U.S. males, $N = 41,238$ for U.S. females, $N = 38,329$ for British males, and $N = 44,101$ for British females. Coefficient estimates that statistically differ from zero are denoted by ***, **, and * for *p*-values ≤.01, ≤.05, and ≤.10, respectively.

Indeed, it is clear that the lack of statistical significance in the British samples is the result of smaller estimated effects than obtained for the U.S. samples rather than larger standard errors; the standard errors on the ordered probit coefficients are actually quite similar in magnitude to those obtained from the U.S. samples.

4.2. Alternative Specifications

Table 10 reports results from variants of Model 5 that specify time differently and that control for current income inequality. We present results for both the U.S. and British samples but only discuss results for the U.S. sample because it is only in the U.S. sample that there is a statistically significant association between later-life health and early-life inequality. In the

Table 10. Sensitivity of Coefficient Estimates for Early-Life (Aged 0−4) Income Share of Top 1 Percent to Alternative Time Trend Specifications and the Inclusion of the Current Top 1 Percent Income Share.

	United States		Great Britain	
	Men	Women	Men	Women
Quadratic time trend	−0.0244**	−0.0216**	−0.0084	−0.0046
	(0.0099)	(0.0103)	(0.0102)	(0.0086)
Quadratic time trend + current income share	−0.0240**	−0.0214**	−0.0083	−0.0045
	(0.0099)	(0.0104)	(0.0101)	(0.0086)
Linear time trend	−0.0248**	−0.0222**	−0.0065	−0.0018
	(0.0099)	(0.0103)	(0.0106)	(0.0090)
Linear time trend + current income share	−0.0241**	−0.0216**	−0.0069	−0.0020
	(0.0100)	(0.0104)	(0.0105)	(0.0089)
Decade dummies	−0.0203**	−0.0182*	0.0085	0.0112
	(0.0098)	(0.0104)	(0.0090)	(0.0076)
Decade dummies + current income share	−0.0237**	−0.0214**	0.0057	0.0080
	(0.0099)	(0.0105)	(0.0098)	(0.0083)
N (person-years)	36,522	41,238	38,329	44,101

Sources: Same-years subsamples of PSID (1991−2007) and BHPS (1991−2007).
Notes: Robust standard errors in parentheses. Coefficient estimates that statistically differ from zero are denoted by ***, **, and * for p-values $\leq.01$, $\leq.05$, and $\leq.10$, respectively. Coefficient estimates and their standard errors in each of our six specifications are based on Model 5 in Tables 5−8 but using alternative time trend specifications with or without the addition of a current-year measure of the share of income held by the top 1 percent. Current income share is the value of the top 1 percent share in the year health is reported. Values for the quadratic time trend were previously reported in Tables 5−8.

U.S. sample, the estimated coefficient on early-life income inequality is robust to each model specification (of different time trends), and to controlling for current inequality. Also notable is that, in both the U.S. and British samples, the coefficient on current-year top income share (not reported) is unstable across specifications that do and do not control for time trends and age.

As we discussed earlier in reference to Table 2, which shows the distribution of our subsamples by age group and birth cohort, because mortality is non-random, especially with respect to the remaining older people in these birth cohorts at the time they report their health, this may result in biased estimates. There is no ex ante reason to expect the bias to be upward or downward, but in Table 11 we consider this issue by examining the sensitivity of our estimates when we restrict our sample to persons aged 21–69 at the time their health is measured. This restriction has the undesirable effect of reducing the variation in both the explanatory variable (since much of the high-inequality early 20th century is eliminated) and the dependent variable (since self-reported health is much lower among people aged 70 and over).[12] Nonetheless, the broad conclusions remain intact. Indeed, for U.S. men, the coefficient estimates are larger in magnitude for the restricted-age sample, which is consistent with non-random mortality at older ages leading to downward bias in estimated effects of early-life inequality.

In principle, income inequality experienced in childhood at ages beyond five years of age could impact on later-life health. In Table 12, we consider how estimates are impacted by an alternative definition of "early life," being in inequality over the first 15 years from birth. We find that our results are relatively insensitive to whether the early-life age range is 0–4 or 0–14.

4.3. Exploring the Sources of the Different Findings for the United States and Great Britain

In both our U.S. and British subsamples adult men and women are more likely to report being in better health if they are younger, have greater permanent income, and had greater economic resources as a child (as measured by parents' education in the United States and their occupation in

---

12. The age-birth cohort composition of the restricted sample is reported in Table C1, while Table C2 presents the proportion reporting low health by age and birth cohort for the restricted sample.

Table 11. Sensitivity of Coefficient Estimates for Early-Life (aged 0−4) Income Share of Top 1 Percent to Restriction to Persons Aged 21−69 at the Time Health Is Measured.

	(1)	(2)	(3)	(4)	(5)
United States (All ages)					
Men					
Mean top 1% income share	−0.1016***	−0.1064***	−0.0208**	−0.0334***	−0.0244**
when aged 0−4	(0.0058)	(0.0061)	(0.0102)	(0.0103)	(0.0099)
Women					
Mean top 1% income share	−0.1015***	−0.1071***	−0.0311***	−0.0320***	−0.0216**
when aged 0−4	(0.0049)	(0.0051)	(0.0100)	(0.0104)	(0.0103)
United States (21−69 years old)					
Men					
Mean top 1% income share	−0.0928***	−0.1020***	−0.0375***	−0.0468***	−0.0379***
when aged 0−4	(0.0056)	(0.0058)	(0.0103)	(0.0107)	(0.0105)
Women					
Mean top 1% income share	−0.0875***	−0.0976***	−0.0350***	−0.0309***	−0.0203*
when aged 0−4	(0.0052)	(0.0054)	(0.0107)	(0.0116)	(0.0114)
Great Britain (All ages)					
Men					
Mean top 1% income share	−0.0406***	−0.0444***	−0.0120	−0.0088	−0.0084
when aged 0−4	(0.0025)	(0.0025)	(0.0099)	(0.0102)	(0.0102)
Women					
Mean top 1% income share	−0.0376***	−0.0407***	−0.0080	−0.0059	−0.0046
when aged 0−4	(0.0023)	(0.0024)	(0.0080)	(0.0088)	(0.0086)
Great Britain (21−69 years old)					
Men					
Mean top 1% income share	−0.0354***	−0.0421***	−0.0121	−0.0087	−0.0074
when aged 0−4	(0.0034)	(0.0035)	(0.0102)	(0.0105)	(0.0104)
Women					
Mean top 1% income share	−0.0273***	−0.0329***	−0.0084	−0.0068	−0.0054
when aged 0−4	(0.0025)	(0.0027)	(0.0084)	(0.0093)	(0.0091)
Controls					
Time trend		✓	✓	✓	✓
Age group			✓	✓	✓
Race			✓	✓	✓
Log permanent family income				✓	✓
Parents' education/occupation					✓

Sources: Same-years subsamples of PSID (1991−2007) and BHPS (1991−2007).
Notes: Robust standard errors in parentheses. Coefficient estimates that statistically differ from zero are denoted by ***, **, and * for *p*-values ≤.01, ≤.05, and ≤.10, respectively. Coefficient estimates and their standard errors are from model specifications that correspond to those used for Tables 5−8. Sample sizes for all age samples are $N = 36{,}522$ for U.S. males, $N = 41{,}238$ for U.S. females, $N = 38{,}329$ for British males, and N = 44,101 for British females. Sample sizes for 21−69-years-old samples are $N = 33{,}729$ for U.S. males, $N = 37{,}368$ for U.S. females, $N = 34{,}265$ for British males, and $N = 38{,}353$ for British females.

Table 12. Sensitivity of Early-Life Inequality Coefficient Estimates to Alternative Early-Life Age-Ranges.

	(1)	(2)	(3)	(4)	(5)
United States					
Men					
When aged 0–4	−0.1016***	−0.1064***	−0.0208**	−0.0334***	−0.0244**
	(0.0058)	(0.0061)	(0.0102)	(0.0103)	(0.0099)
When aged 0–14	−0.1100***	−0.1122***	−0.0275***	−0.0307***	−0.0243***
	(0.0063)	(0.0065)	(0.0077)	(0.0084)	(0.0084)
Women					
When aged 0–4	−0.1015***	−0.1071***	−0.0311***	−0.0320***	−0.0216**
	(0.0049)	(0.0051)	(0.0100)	(0.0104)	(0.0103)
When aged 0–14	−0.1111***	−0.1137***	−0.0357***	−0.0298***	−0.0216**
	(0.0048)	(0.0050)	(0.0088)	(0.0086)	(0.0086)
Great Britain					
Men					
When aged 0–4	−0.0406***	−0.0444***	−0.0120	−0.0088	−0.0084
	(0.0025)	(0.0025)	(0.0099)	(0.0102)	(0.0102)
When aged 0–14	−0.0457***	−0.0490***	−0.0097	0.0018	0.0019
	(0.0027)	(0.0028)	(0.0085)	(0.0084)	(0.0085)
Women					
When aged 0–4	−0.0376***	−0.0407***	−0.0080	−0.0059	−0.0046
	(0.0023)	(0.0024)	(0.0080)	(0.0088)	(0.0086)
When aged 0–14	−0.0420***	−0.0447***	0.0016	0.0101	0.0117
	(0.0024)	(0.0025)	(0.0075)	(0.0075)	(0.0075)
Controls					
Time trend		✓	✓	✓	✓
Age group			✓	✓	✓
Race			✓	✓	✓
Log permanent family income				✓	✓
Parents' education/ occupation					✓

Sources: Same-years subsamples of PSID (1991–2007) and BHPS (1991–2007).
Notes: Robust standard errors in parentheses. Coefficient estimates that statistically differ from zero are denoted by ***, **, and * for p-values $\leq.01$, $\leq.05$, and $\leq.10$, respectively. Coefficient estimates and their standard errors are from model specifications that correspond to those used for Tables 5–8. Sample sizes are $N = 36{,}522$ for U.S. males, $N = 41{,}238$ for U.S. females, $N = 38{,}329$ for British males, and $N = 44{,}101$ for British females.

Great Britain). Here, we explore the following result — in both countries the simple correlation between adult health and early-life inequality is negative and statistically significant. But, when we control for individual demographic and economic factors, this negative relationship remains robust only in the United States. The question is why. In Fig. 1, the U-shaped trend in taxable income held by the top 1 percent of tax units is remarkably similar in the two countries over the 1913–2006 period. What explains this difference in the relationship between health as an adult and inequality when aged 0–4? To try to provide some insights, we look to differences across the two countries.

Deaton (2013) suggests that income inequality is associated with the allocation of public goods related to health, such as immunizations and the provision of subsidized medical care. If this is the case, the relatively early creation of the National Health Service in Great Britain may explain the difference, since this major British public health initiative may have offset some of the adverse effects of income inequality at younger ages that we find in the United States. Since the British National Health Service did not come into existence until 1948, we would expect that, other things equal, this additional provision of services to all residents of Great Britain would have had an offsetting effect on income inequality for those born in Great Britain in the post-World War II period.

In Table 13, we crudely account for this differential effect by including an interaction term on our inequality at ages 0–4 measure for those born before 1950 and those born in 1950 or later in both the United States and Great Britain. This interaction term is never significant in the British models. Relative to our results in Tables 5–8 (without the interaction term), in Models 1 and 2 it reduces the magnitude of the coefficient on the variable for inequality at younger ages, but this variable remains significant at the 1 percent level. It also reduces the magnitude of this coefficient in the other three models. In the United States, this placebo interaction term is also never significant. As in Great Britain, the addition of this interaction term does reduce the size of the coefficient on the variable for inequality at younger ages in Models 1 and 2, but it remains significant at the 1 percent level. However, in Models 3–5, the size of the coefficient falls in absolute value and turns statistically insignificant for men in Models 3–5 and for women in Model 5.

When we repeat this exercise, but instead focus on 1966, the year that Medicare and Medicaid were implemented in the United States, as expected, adding this interaction term has no impact on the results for men or women in Great Britain. In the United States, it reduces the inequality coefficient in all five models, but its significance remains robust. Hence, at least using this crude measure of the importance of the each country's most important public health initiative, we find no evidence that its inclusion explains the lack of robustness in our British findings, and at best suggests that its inclusion can affect the robustness of our U.S. results.

4.4. Comparing Same-Years Subsample Results with Full-sample Results

Because the focus of this paper is a comparison of the relationship between self-reported health in adulthood and inequality as a child in the United States and Great Britain, we restricted our sample to years when both the PSID and BHPS launched new waves of data. In the top two panels of Table 14, we reproduce the early-life inequality coefficient estimates for the same-years U.S. subsamples first presented in Tables 5 and 6. In the next two panels, we report these coefficient values when we use all waves of PSID data. In all five models, we find a negative relationship that remains significant at the 1 percent level. In this case-study style analysis of the U.S. data, the increase in years of data improves the level of significance to 1 percent in all cases.

In the next four panels, we repeat this exercise for men and women in Great Britain, reproducing the values found in Tables 7 and 8 for our same-years sample and then reporting the values for the inequality at ages 0–4 variable using all available waves of the BHPS (except 1999, which uses a different measure of self-reported health). In this case-study style analysis of the British data, the increase in years of data does not improve the robustness of our findings. The coefficient in Models 3, 4, and 5 remains negative but does not statistically differ from zero.[13]

---

13. We report a full set of results in the appendix. Neither the sign nor statistical significance of the coefficients on our control variables changes much when we estimate the models on the full samples. This is also the case with respect to our findings in the robustness tables, with one exception. In Table 13, when we use 1950 as our placebo year, the coefficient on our inequality variable for the United States returns to being significant at the 5 percent level or better. This is not the case for Great Britain.

Table 13. Sensitivity of Coefficient Estimates for Early-Life (Aged 0–4) Income Share of Top 1 Percent to Major Change in Public Health System for Persons Born before 1950 and 1966.

	(1)	(2)	(3)	(4)	(5)
United States					
Men					
Birth to age 4	-0.0772***	-0.0707***	-0.0221**	-0.0324***	-0.0236**
	(0.0087)	(0.0091)	(0.0099)	(0.0103)	(0.0100)
Birth to age 4 × born before 1966	-0.0170***	-0.0259***	0.0040	-0.0026	-0.0020
	(0.0035)	(0.0041)	(0.0050)	(0.0048)	(0.0047)
Women					
Birth to age 4	-0.0922***	-0.0854***	-0.0328***	-0.0322***	-0.0227**
	(0.0077)	(0.0083)	(0.0100)	(0.0105)	(0.0104)
Birth to age 4 × born before 1966	-0.0066*	-0.0157***	0.0043	0.0006	0.0025
	(0.0035)	(0.0042)	(0.0045)	(0.0046)	(0.0046)
United States (1950 as "placebo")					
Men					
Birth to age 4	-0.0875***	-0.0913***	-0.0162	-0.0233*	-0.0158
	(0.0130)	(0.0137)	(0.0144)	(0.0137)	(0.0128)
Birth to age 4 × born before 1950	-0.0068	-0.0073	-0.0025	-0.0055	-0.0047
	(0.0054)	(0.0058)	(0.0064)	(0.0054)	(0.0053)
Women					
Birth to age 4	-0.1080***	-0.1119***	-0.0369***	-0.0272**	-0.0178
	(0.0108)	(0.0115)	(0.0134)	(0.0139)	(0.0131)
Birth to age 4 × born before 1950	0.0031	0.0023	0.0032	-0.0026	-0.0020
	(0.0047)	(0.0050)	(0.0052)	(0.0049)	(0.0044)
Great Britain					
Men					
Birth to age 4	-0.0423***	-0.0510***	-0.0238	-0.0128	-0.0131
	(0.0091)	(0.0090)	(0.0149)	(0.0149)	(0.0147)
Birth to age 4 × born before 1950	0.0009	0.0038	0.0055	0.0019	0.0022
	(0.0050)	(0.0049)	(0.0047)	(0.0050)	(0.0049)

Table 13. (Continued)

	(1)	(2)	(3)	(4)	(5)
Women					
Birth to age 4	−0.0391***	−0.0466***	−0.0106	0.0036	0.0035
	(0.0071)	(0.0073)	(0.0126)	(0.0137)	(0.0136)
Birth to age 4 × born before 1950	0.0009	0.0034	0.0012	−0.0045	−0.0038
	(0.0038)	(0.0039)	(0.0040)	(0.0044)	(0.0043)
Great Britain (1966 as "placebo")					
Men					
Birth to age 4	−0.0478***	−0.0461***	−0.0105	−0.0071	−0.0065
	(0.0053)	(0.0052)	(0.0100)	(0.0104)	(0.0103)
Birth to age 4 × born before 1966	0.0053	0.0013	−0.0021	−0.0024	−0.0026
	(0.0035)	(0.0033)	(0.0033)	(0.0035)	(0.0035)
Women					
Birth to age 4	−0.0447***	−0.0430***	−0.0032	−0.0024	−0.0005
	(0.0057)	(0.0057)	(0.0084)	(0.0090)	(0.0089)
Birth to age 4 × born before 1966	0.0053	0.0017	−0.0067	−0.0048	−0.0056
	(0.0041)	(0.0042)	(0.0050)	(0.0052)	(0.0052)
Controls					
Time trend		✓	✓	✓	✓
Age group			✓	✓	✓
Race			✓	✓	✓
Log permanent family income				✓	✓
Parents' education/occupation					✓

Sources: Same-years subsamples of PSID (1991–2007) and BHPS (1991–2007).

Notes: Robust standard errors in parentheses. Coefficient estimates that statistically differ from zero are denoted by ***, **, and * for p-values ≤.01, ≤.05, and ≤.10, respectively. Coefficient estimates and their standard errors are from model specifications that correspond to those used for Tables 5–8. Sample sizes are $N = 36,522$ for U.S. males, $N = 41,238$ for U.S. females, $N = 38,329$ for British males, and $N = 44,101$ for British females.

Table 14. Sensitivity of Coefficient Estimates for Early-Life (Aged 0–4) Income Share of Top 1 Percent to using Same-Years Subsamples and Full Country Samples.

	(1)	(2)	(3)	(4)	(5)
United States[a]					
Men (1991–2007 respondents)					
Mean top 1% income share when aged 0–4	-0.1016***	-0.1064***	-0.0208**	-0.0334***	-0.0244**
	(0.0058)	(0.0061)	(0.0102)	(0.0103)	(0.0099)
N (person-years)	36,522	36,522	36,522	36,522	36,522
Women (1991–2007 respondents)					
Mean top 1% income share when aged 0–4	-0.1015***	-0.1071***	-0.0311***	-0.0320***	-0.0216**
	(0.0049)	(0.0051)	(0.0100)	(0.0104)	(0.0103)
N (person-years)	41,238	41,238	41,238	41,238	41,238
Men (1984–2009 respondents – Full sample)					
Mean top 1% income share when aged 0–4	-0.0945***	-0.1053***	-0.0233***	-0.0308***	-0.0221***
	(0.0052)	(0.0058)	(0.0079)	(0.0072)	(0.0075)
N (person-years)	62,389	62,389	62,389	62,389	62,389
Women (1984–2009 respondents – Full sample)					
Mean top 1% income share when aged 0–4	-0.0959***	-0.1047***	-0.0340***	-0.0380***	-0.0283***
	(0.0045)	(0.0048)	(0.0079)	(0.0074)	(0.0074)
N (person-years)	70,347	70,347	70,347	70,347	70,347
Great Britain[b]					
Men (1991–2007 respondents)					
Mean top 1% income share when aged 0–4	-0.0406***	-0.0444***	-0.0120	-0.0088	-0.0084
	(0.0025)	(0.0025)	(0.0099)	(0.0102)	(0.0102)
N (person-years)	38,329	38,329	38,329	38,329	38,329
Women (1991–2007 respondents)					
Mean top 1% income share when aged 0–4	-0.0376***	-0.0407***	-0.0080	-0.0059	-0.0046
	(0.0023)	(0.0024)	(0.0080)	(0.0088)	(0.0086)
N (person-years)	44,101	44,101	44,101	44,101	44,101

Table 14. (*Continued*)

	(1)	(2)	(3)	(4)	(5)
Men (1991–2008 respondents – Full sample)					
Mean top 1% income share when aged 0–4	-0.0428***	-0.0467***	-0.0131	-0.0101	-0.0098
	(0.0024)	(0.0024)	(0.0097)	(0.0100)	(0.0099)
N (person-years)	58,055	58,055	58,055	58,055	58,055
Women (1991–2008 respondents – Full sample)					
Mean top 1% income share when aged 0–4	-0.0405***	-0.0436***	-0.0037	-0.0023	-0.0002
	(0.0022)	(0.0023)	(0.0079)	(0.0085)	(0.0085)
N (person-years)	67,096	67,096	67,096	67,096	67,096
Controls					
Time trend		✓	✓	✓	✓
Age group			✓	✓	✓
Race			✓	✓	✓
Log permanent family income				✓	✓
Parents' education/occupation					✓

Sources: Same-years subsamples of PSID (1984–2009) and BHPS (1991–2008), and full country samples of PSID (1991–2007) and BHPS (1991–2007).

Notes: Robust standard errors in parentheses. Coefficient estimates that statistically differ from zero are denoted by ***, **, and * for *p*-values ≤.01, ≤.05, and ≤.10, respectively. Reference categories include those aged 80 and over, those whose parents did not receive a high school degree.
[a]The following two panels repeat the early-life inequality coefficients and sample sizes N from Tables 5 and 6.
[b]The following two panels repeat the early-life inequality coefficients and sample sizes N from Tables 7 and 8.

5. DISCUSSION AND CONCLUSION

Lillard et al. (2015) find that the health of U.S.-born adult men and women is worse if they experienced higher average levels of income inequality during the early years of their lives. Here, we find similar results for the United States when we restrict the PSID sample to the same calendar years for which BHPS data are available.

Measuring inequality as the average share of income held by the top 1 percent of tax units in each country, we compare the relationship between the self-reported health of U.S. and British adults and the inequality they experienced when aged 0–4. Despite similar trends in inequality in each country over the period from 1913 to 2007, we find quite different relationships between self-reported health and early-life inequality.

In both countries, the simple correlation is negative and statistically different from zero. That is, the unconditional correlation suggests that adults are less likely to report being in better health if inequality was higher in their first five years of life. This association remains statistically significant among U.S. men and women when we control for individual differences in demographic and economic factors and control for time trends. But in Great Britain, the simple association vanishes when we control for similar individual differences in other determinants of health.

There are reasons to be cautious about interpreting these results. The most obvious limitation is our use of an income inequality measure that only varies over time and not across individuals living in different geographical sub-divisions. Because our measure only varies over time, it is probably correlated with trends in many other factors that developed in similar ways to the ones we capture with our income inequality trend measure. Hence, we may have omitted variable bias in our models. For the most part, we simply lack long time-series data on factors such as medical technology, spending on health, and similar inputs to health production. Despite our efforts to crudely capture the introduction of the National Health Service in Great Britain and Medicare/Medicaid in the United States, our results in this regard require caution in their interpretation. The changes in our top income time series may, and even plausibly will, be correlated with the evolution of these other factors.

While it is premature to conclude that health as an adult is adversely affected by exposure to early-life income inequality in the United States, our finding that they are statistically linked is all the more striking given the absence of evidence of such a linkage in Great Britain, using the same models over the same set of years. Future research should focus on understanding the nature of this relationship and the difference we find in it between two countries that have experienced similar top income trends over the last 100 years.

REFERENCES

Alvaredo, F., Atkinson, A. B., Piketty, T., & Saez, E. (2013a). The top 1 percent in inter-national and historical perspective. *Journal of Economic Perspectives, 27*(3), 3–20.

Alvaredo, F., Atkinson, A. B., Piketty, T., & Saez, E. (2013b). *The world top incomes database.* Retrieved from http://topincomes.g-mond.parisschoolofeconomics.eu. Accessed on July 8, 2013.

Araujo, M. C., Ferreira, F. H. G., Lanjouw, P., & Özler, B. (2008). Local inequality and project choice: Theory and evidence from Ecuador. *Journal of Public Economics, 92*, 1022–1046.

Atkinson, A. B. (2005). Top incomes in the UK over the 20th century. *Journal of the Royal Statistical Society Series A, 168*, Pt. 2, 325–343.

Atkinson, A. B., Piketty, T., & Saez, E. (2011). Top incomes in the long run of history. *Journal of Economic Literature, 49*(1), 3–71.

Blakely, T., Kennedy, B., Glass, R., & Kawachi, I. (2000). What is the lag time between income inequality and health status? *Journal of Epidemiology and Community Health, 54*, 318–319.

Burkhauser, R. V., Butrica, B. A., Daly, M. C., & Lillard, D. R. (2001). The cross-national equiva-lent file: A product of cross-national research. In I. Becker, N. Ott, & G. Rolf (Eds.), *Soziale Sicherung in Einer Dynamischen Gesellschaft* (pp. 354–376). Frankfurt: Campus Verlag.

Burkhauser, R. V., & Lillard, D. R. (2005). The contribution and potential of data harmoniza-tion for cross-national comparative research. *Journal of Comparative Policy Analysis, 7*(4), 313–330.

Burkhauser, R. V., & Lillard, D. R. (2007). The expanded cross-national equivalent file: HILDA joins its international peers. *The Australian Economic Review, 40*(2), 1–8.

Butrica, B. A., & Burkhauser, R. V. (1997). *Estimating federal income tax burdens for Panel Study of Income Dynamics (PSID) Families using the national bureau of economic research TAXSIM model.* (Aging Studies Program Paper No. 12). Syracuse, NY: Center for Policy Research Maxwell School of Citizenship and Public Affairs, Syracuse University.

Case, A., Fertig, A., & Paxson, C. (2005). The lasting impact of childhood health and circum-stance. *Journal of Health Economics, 24*, 365–389.

Currie, J., & Rossin-Slater, M. (2015). Early-life origins of life-cycle well-being: Research and policy implications. *Journal of Policy Analysis and Management, 34*(1), 208–242.

Deaton, A. (2003). Health, inequality, and economic development. *Journal of Economic Literature, 41*(1), 113–158.

Deaton, A. (2013). *The great escape: Health, wealth, and the origins of inequality.* Princeton, NJ: Princeton University Press.

de Vries, R., Blane, D., & Netuveli, G. (2013). Long-term exposure to income inequality: Implications for physical functioning at older ages. *European Journal of Ageing,* doi:10.1007/s10433-013-0285-5.

Duncan, G., Kalil, A., & Ziol-Guest, K. M. (2013). Early childhood poverty and adult achievement, employment and health. *Family Matters, 93*, 2735.

Duncan, G., Ziol-Guest, K., & Kalil, A. (2010). Early childhood poverty and adult attainment, behavior and health. *Child Development, 81*(1), 306–325.

Elo, I. T., & Preston, S. H. (1992). Effects of early-life conditions on adult mortality: A review. *Population Index, 58*(2), 186–212.

Ettner, S. L. (1996). New evidence on the relationship between income and health. *Journal of Health Economics, 15*(1), 67–85.

Frick, J. R., Jenkins, S. P., Lillard, D. R., Lipps, O., & Wooden, M. (2007). The Cross-National Equivalent File (CNEF) and its member country household panel studies. Schmollers Jahrbuch. *Journal of Applied Social Science Studies, 127*(4), 627–654.

Hayward, M. D., & Gorman, B. K. (2004). The long arm of childhood: The influence of early-life social conditions on men's mortality. *Demography, 41*(1), 87–107.

Idler, E. L., & Benyamini, Y. (1997). Self-rated health and mortality: A review of 27 community studies. *Journal of Health and Social Behavior, 38*(1), 21–37.

Jürges, H., Avendano, M., & Mackenbach, J. P. (2008). Are different measures of self-rated health comparable? An assessment in five European countries. *European Journal of Epidemiology, 23*, 773–781.

Karlsson, M., Nilsson, T., Lyttkens, C. H., & Leeson, G. (2010). Income inequality and health: Importance of a cross-country perspective. *Social Science and Medicine, 70*, 875–885.

Larrimore, J. (2011). Does a higher income have positive health effects? Using the earned income tax credit to explore the income-health gradient. *Milbank Quarterly, 89*(4), 694–727.

Leigh, A. (2007). How closely do top income shares track other measures of inequality? *The Economic Journal, 117*(524), F619–F633.

Lillard, D. R., Burkhauser, R. V., Hahn, M., & Wilkins, R. (2015). Does early-life income inequality predict self-reported health in later life? Evidence from the United States. *Social Science and Medicine, 128*(3), 347–355.

Lillard, D. R., Christopoulou, R., Goebel, J., Freidin, S., Lipps, O., Snider, K., & KLIPS Team. (2008). *Codebook for the cross-national equivalent file 1970–2008*. Retrieved from http://www.human.cornell.edu/pam/research/centers-programs/german-panel/cnef.cfm

Maddison, A. (2001). The world economy: A millennial perspective. Paris: OECD.

Mayer, S. E., & Sarin, A. (2005). Some mechanisms linking economic inequality and infant mortality. *Social Science and Medicine, 60*, 439–455.

Mellor, J. M., & Milyo, J. (2003). Is exposure to income inequality a public health concern? Lagged effects of income inequality on individual and population health. *Health Services Research, 38*(1), 137–151.

Miilunpalo, S., Vuori, I., Oja, P., Pasanen, M., & Urponen, H. (1997). Self-rated health status as a health measure: The predictive value of self-reported health status on the use of physician services and on mortality in the working-age population. *Journal of Clinical Epidemiology, 50*(5), 517–528.

Pickett, K. E., & Wilkinson, R. G. (2015). Income inequality and health: A causal review. *Social Science and Medicine, 128*(3), 316–326.

Piketty, T., & Saez, E. (2003). Income inequality in the United States 1913–1998. *Quarterly Journal of Economics, 118*(1), 1–38.

Preston, S. H. (1975). The changing relation between mortality and level of economic development. *Population Studies, 29*, 231–248.

Sacker, A., Wiggins, R. D., Bartley, M., & McDonough, P. (2007). Self-rated health trajectories in the United States and the United Kingdom: A comparative study. *American Journal of Public Health., 97*, 812–818.

Sapolsky, R. M., Alberts, S. C., & Altmann, J. (1997). Hypercotisolism associated with social subordinance or social isolation among wild baboons. *Archives of General Psychiatry, 54*, 1137–1143.

Subramanian, S. V., & Kawachi, I. (2004). Income inequality and health: What have we learned so far? *Epidemiologic Review, 26*, 78–91.

van Doorslaer, E., & Jones, A. M. (2003). Inequalities in self-reported health: Validation of a new approach to measurement. *Journal of Health Economics, 22*, 61–87.

Weich, S., Lewis, G., & Jenkins, S. P. (2002). Income inequality and self rated health in Britain. *Journal of Epidemiology and Community Health, 56*, 436–441.

Wilkinson, R. G., & Pickett, K. E. (2006). Income inequality and population health: A review and explanation of the evidence. *Social Science and Medicine, 62*, 1768–1784.

Wüst, M. (2012). Early interventions and infant health: Evidence from the Danish home visiting program. *Labour Economics, 19*, 484–495.

APPENDIX A: DESCRIPTION OF DATA

A.1. Data Sources

Our analysis uses data from the Panel Study of Income Dynamics (PSID) and the British Household Panel Survey (BHPS). It uses data from the respective U.S. and British Cross-National Equivalent Files (CNEF). The CNEF provides internationally harmonized variables that are based on the PSID and the BHPS.

Unlike the BHPS, in most years the PSID only interviews one member in each family. Further, the PSID does not gather information on every member of a family but focuses on family heads and their partners. We follow the PSID terminology and refer to "heads" and "wives." Because important variables such as self-reported health status are only asked with respect to the head and wife of a family, we are forced to restrict our analysis to these family members only.

From the 1970–2009 U.S. CNEF, we extract sex, age, race, post-tax post-transfer family income (labeled "Household Post-Government Income (TAXSIM)") and self-reported health status. We then merge PSID data on the educational attainment of a person's parents (henceforth: father's and mother's education).

The BHPS interviews every family member aged 16 years and older. From the 1991–2008 British CNEF, we extract sex, age, race, post-tax post-transfer family income (labeled "Household Post-Government Income") and self-reported health status. We then merge BHPS data on the occupation of a person's parents (henceforth: father's and mother's occupation).

Finally, we merge the Piketty and Saez (2003) top 1 percent income series without taxable realized capital gains to our U.S. sample. We merge the Atkinson (2005) top 1 percent income series to our British sample. From these series, we create our measures for current and early-life inequality.

A.2. Sample Restrictions

Our U.S. sample consists of family heads aged 21 years and older and their partners aged 21 years and older. It is restricted to the 1984–2009 waves of PSID data, because questions about health status are not asked before

1984. But we are able to use pre-1984 income data for our permanent income measure. We have data for every year until 1997 and then for every other year until 2009.

Our British sample consists of all family members aged 21 and older. We have data for every year from 1991 to 2008. However, we excluded the 1999 wave because the health status question in 1999 is different from that in all other years.

In both our U.S. and British samples, we exclude everyone who is foreign-born, since our measure of early-life inequality only applies to individuals living in the United States or Great Britain when they were children. We also exclude individuals born before 1913 because the U.S. top income series starts in 1913. Although the British top income series goes back as far as 1908, for comparison purposes, we excluded those born before 1913 from our British sample.

The PSID consists of four samples: the SRC sample (1968–2009); the SEO or Census sample (1968–2009); the Latino sample (1990–1995), and the New Immigrant sample (1997–2009). The SEO or Census sample oversamples low-income families in the PSID. We restrict our U.S. analysis to the SRC sample to avoid issues with oversampling.

The BHPS consists of five samples: the original BHPS sample (1991–2008), the European Community Household Panel (ECHP) low-income sample (1997–2001); the Welsh extension (1999–2008); the Scottish extension (1999–2008), and the Northern Ireland extension (2001–2008). All samples apart from the original BHPS sample oversample their members. We restrict our British analysis to the original BHPS sample to avoid issues with oversampling.

In the main paper, we use same-years subsamples, that is, we restrict the U.S. and British samples to years that are available in both the BHPS and the PSID. Because the BHPS starts in 1991, ends in 2008, and asks a different self-reported health question in 1999 and because the PSID is only administered every other year from 1997 onward, we restrict the samples to respondents to surveys in the following years: 1991, 1992, 1993, 1994, 1995, 1996, 1997, 2001, 2003, 2005, and 2007.

A.3. Description of Variables

A.3.1. Self-Reported Health Status (Dependent Variable)
In the PSID, self-reported health status is only asked of family heads and wives. In 1984–2009, the PSID asks: "Would you say your (or head's)

health in general is …" with respect to heads and "Would you say your (or wife's/friend's) health in general is …" with respect to partners. The responses are coded as "Excellent (1)," "Very good (2)," "Good (3)," "Fair (4)," and "Poor (5)."

In 1991–1998 and 2000–2008, the BHPS asks "Please think back over the last 12 months about how your health has been. Compared to people of your own age, would you say that your health has on the whole been …" The responses are coded as "Excellent (1)," "Good (2)," "Fair (3)," "Poor (4)," and "Very poor (5)."

In 1999, the BHPS asks a different question: "In general would you say your health is …" The responses are coded as "Excellent (1)," "Very good (2)," "Good (3)," "Fair (4)," and "Poor (5)."

Table A1 shows the distribution of the BHPS self-reported health status in 1998, 1999, and 2000.

Self-reported health status in 1999 is inconsistent compared to the other years. We, therefore, exclude the 1999 wave from our British sample and, for comparison purposes, from our same-years U.S. subsample.

A.3.2. Year
This variable relates to the current year when a person's interview took place.

Table A1. Distribution of Self-Reported Health Status in the BHPS Data.

	Value Label	1998		2000		Value Label	1999	
		Freq.	%	Freq.	%		Freq.	%
1	Excellent	2,358	21.6	3,310	21.2	Excellent	2,394	15.8
2	Good	5,101	46.8	7,162	45.9	Very good	4,474	30.6
3	Fair	2,263	20.8	3,443	22.1	Good	4,847	31.0
4	Poor	879	8.1	1,246	8.0	Fair	2,414	15.5
5	Very poor	297	2.7	435	2.8	Poor	755	4.8
	Total	10,898		15,596		Total	15,184	
	Missing values							
−9	Missing	6	0.1			Missing	1	0.0
−7	Proxy respondent					Proxy respondent	435	2.8
−1	Not answered	2	0.0	7	0.0	Not answered	3	0.0
	Question text in 1998 and 2000					*Question text in 1999*		

Please think back over the last 12 months about how your health has been. Compared to people of your own age, would you say that your health has on the whole been …

In general would you say your health is …

Source: BHPS codebooks for 1998, 1999, and 2000.

A.3.3. Birth Year
Birth year is defined as the year minus the sample member's age in years.

A.3.4. Time Trend
We create three specifications to model time: a linear time trend (year); a quadratic time trend (year plus year squared), and decade dummies (1980s (only in the full PSID sample), 1990s, 2000s (reference year)). Our preferred specification is the quadratic time trend. The other specifications are included as robustness checks (reported in Table 10 in the main paper and Table B9 in this appendix).

A.3.5. Age Dummies
Rather than using age in years in our regression models, we use age dummies to allow for flexible and non-linear age effects. We create 13 age dummies: 21–24, 25–29, 30–34, 35–39, 40–44, 45–49, 50–54, 55–59, 60–64, 65–69, 70–74, 75–79, and 80 years and older. "80 years and older" is the reference age group.

A.3.6. Race
For the U.S. sample, we use the race variable in the U.S. CNEF and create three race dummies referring to "Whites," "Blacks," and "Others." "Others" contains American Indians, Aleuts, Eskimos, Asians, Pacific Islanders, Hispanics, and Other Ethnicities. We use "Whites" as our reference race.

For the British sample, we use the race variable in the British CNEF and create three race dummies referring to "Whites," "Blacks," and "Others." "Others" contains Indians, Pakistanis, Bangladeshis, Chinese, and Other Ethnicities. We use "Whites" as our reference race.

A.3.7. Permanent Income (Real Permanent Family-Size-Adjusted Post-Government Income)
To construct our U.S. permanent income measure, we first retrieve post-tax post-transfer family income, which in the U.S. CNEF is labeled "Household Post-Government Income (TAXSIM)." All family members contribute to this family income aggregate. It is defined as the "sum of total family income from labor earnings, asset flows, the imputed rental value of owner occupied housing, private transfers, public transfers, and social security pensions minus total household taxes" (Lillard et al., 2008). The method for estimating "Total household taxes" is described in Butrica and Burkhauser (1997).

To construct our British permanent income measure, we first retrieve post-tax post-transfer family income, which in the British CNEF is labeled

"Household Post-Government Income." All family members contribute to this family income aggregate. It is similarly defined to the U.S. income measure.

We adjust this post-tax post-transfer family income measure for inflation, and adjust for the number of family members in that year by dividing by the square root of the number of family members. We exclude persons with negative and zero family incomes. We then average the adjusted annual income of each person's family for all available years of data, up to and including the year that is one year prior to the survey year (when a person reports his or her current health status). When constructing this measure of "permanent" family income, we exclude the year just prior to the year a person reported his or her health status to avoid capturing variation in income that is caused by a person's health status. This derived measure of average family income is a proxy for an individual's permanent income. In our regressions, we use the logarithm of this variable.

A.3.8. Number of Years Used to Create Permanent Income

Our permanent income measure can be averaged over different number of years for each person and for the same person captured in different waves of the data. To control for any bias caused by this averaging procedure, we create a variable that measures the number of years over which we create our average income measure.

A.3.9. Permanent Income Data Missing

We create a dummy variable that is 1 when a person's permanent income data are missing and 0 otherwise. We do so to keep persons that have missing permanent income data in our samples (assigning them a value of zero for permanent income) to avoid selectivity issues that may arise from excluding persons with negative or zero permanent incomes. For example, business owners, who sometimes report negative incomes, are a select group and excluding them could affect our results.

A.3.10. Father's and Mother's Education (PSID)

The PSID first asked about the educational attainment of the head's father and mother in 1968 and first asked about the educational attainment of the wife's father and mother in 1974. Until 1995, the PSID asks: "How much education did your (head's) father/mother have?" and "How much education did your wife's father/mother have?" As is characteristic for the PSID, typically one person, who often is the head, answers on behalf of both the head and the wife. In each wave, only for new heads and new wives is the parents' education obtained, on the assumption that this does not change over time. In 1976 and 1985, the PSID family questionnaire featured a special extended section on wives. In both these years, data on parents' education was collected for all (new and old) wives. In our analysis for 1984–1995, we create three dummy variables for each parent's education: "Bachelor's (BA) degree or higher," "High school degree," and "Less than high school degree."

Beginning in 1997, the PSID changed the way it asks about parents' education to: "Where did your father/mother receive his/her education – in the United States, outside the United States or both?" (question 1). If the parent received any education in the United States, the PSID asks: "How much education did your (Head's) father/mother complete (in the United States)?" (question 2). If the parent received any education outside the United States, the PSID asks: "How many years of school did he/she complete outside of the U.S.?" (question 3) and "What was the highest degree or certificate he/she earned outside the U.S.?" (question 4). Question 4 is not asked in 1999, 2001, and 2003. These questions are only administered to families with new heads or new wives, with the data from the previous years carried forward for existing sample members.

For families administered the post-1995 questions, adjustments need to be made to create consistent and comparable variables. For parents obtaining all education in the United States, we use the responses to question 2 and create the same three dummy variables as before. For parents obtaining all education outside the United States, we use question 4 where possible and use question 3 only when question 4 data are missing. From question 4, we create the three dummy variables ("Bachelor's (BA) degree or higher," "High school degree," and "Less than high school degree") as before. When question 4 data are missing, we create the three dummy variables based on the number of years of schooling reported at question 3. We assume an individual has a bachelor's degree or higher if years of schooling is 15 or more and a high school degree if years of schooling is less than 15 but at least 12. Those with 11 or fewer years of schooling are assumed to be in the "less than high school degree" category.

For parents who completed part of their education outside of the United States, we first combine responses to questions 2, 3, and 4. Responses to question 2 are converted into a number of years of education, assuming 5 years if the parent completed "0–5 grades," 8 years if he completed "6–8 grades," 11 years if he completed "9–11 grades," 12 years if he completed "12 grades," 14 years if he completed "Some college, no degree; Associate's degree," 15 years if he completed "College BA and no advanced degree mentioned," and 17 years if he completed "College, advanced or professional degree, some graduate work; close to receiving degree." We then add this derived "years of U.S. schooling" to "years of non-U.S. schooling" obtained in question 3 to produce "total years of schooling." Responses to question 2 and, where available, question 4, are used in the first instance to ascertain highest educational qualification. Only when question 4 data are missing is the derived "total years of schooling" used, applying the same conversion from years of schooling to education category as applied to parents who obtained all education outside the United States.

To avoid selectivity bias from excluding individuals missing parental education information, we retain these individuals in the estimation sample and include additional dummy variables indicating missing data on parents' education (one for the father and one for the mother).

A.3.11. Father's and Mother's Occupation (BHPS)

The BHPS began administering questions about respondents' parents in 1998. We use the question "Thinking back to when you were 14 years old, what job was your father/mother doing at that time?" Three dummy variables are created, the first equal to 1 if the parent had a professional, managerial, or technical occupation; the second equal to 1 if the parent had a skilled non-manual, skilled manual, or partly skilled occupation; and the third equal to 1 if the parent had an unskilled, armed forces, or unknown occupation, or if a person's father did not work at all, was deceased, or did not live with the respondent. The BHPS did not ask the parental background questions of new respondents that turned 16 in 1998 or later. For these individuals, the parents' occupations when the respondent was aged 14 are directly observed in the data (two waves prior to first interview). In our regressions, we use the third dummy variable, "Other occupation," as the reference group.

Note that, because the BHPS asked the parental background questions only from 1998 onward, parental occupation is missing for pre-1998 respondents who did not respond in 1998. To avoid selectivity bias from excluding these individuals, we retain these individuals in the estimation sample and include an additional dummy variable that is equal to 1 if parental occupations are missing.

A.3.12. Current and Early-Life Inequality (Top Income Shares)

We use the U.S. top 1 percent income series developed by Piketty and Saez (2003) and the British top 1 percent income series developed by Atkinson (2005). We retrieved the data from:

http://www.wid.world/ (Alvaredo et al., 2013a, 2013b).

For the United States, we use the top 1 percent series that started in 1913 and ends in 2009. The series we use excludes realized taxable capital gains.

The British top 1 percent series is discontinuous, with data available only for 1918–1919; 1937; 1949; 1951–1960; 1962–1979; 1981–2007; and 2009. We use linear interpolation to fill the gaps for 1950, 1961, 1980, and 2008, which gives us a continuous series from 1949 to 2009. For the years before 1949, we use information from higher quantiles – the top 0.5% and 0.1% – to fill the remaining gaps. As for the United States, the series we use starts in 1913 and ends in 2009.

Let P_t^x denote the top $x\%$ income share at time t. For example, P_{1948}^1 is the top 1% income share in 1948.

For 1987–1992, we use formula 1:

$$P_t^{0.1} = P_{t-1}^{0.1} + \frac{P_t^{0.5} - P_{t-1}^{0.5}}{P_{1993}^{0.5} - P_{1986}^{0.5}} \left(P_{1993}^{0.1} - P_{1986}^{0.1} \right),$$

starting in $t = 1987$, to impute forward to $t = 1992$.

For 1943–1948, we use formula 2:

$$P_t^1 = P_{t+1}^1 - \frac{P_{t+1}^{0.5} - P_t^{0.5}}{P_{t+1}^{0.5}} P_{t+1}^1,$$

starting in $t = 1948$, to impute backward to $t = 1943$.

For 1938–1942, we use formula 3:

$$P_t^1 = P_{t-1}^1 + \frac{P_t^{0.1} - P_{t-1}^{0.1}}{P_{1943}^{0.1} - P_{1937}^{0.1}} \left(P_{1943}^1 - P_{1937}^1 \right),$$

starting in $t = 1938$, to impute forward to $t = 1942$.

For 1920–1936, we use formula 4:

$$P_t^1 = P_{t-1}^1 + \frac{P_t^{0.1} - P_{t-1}^{0.1}}{P_{1937}^{0.1} - P_{1919}^{0.1}} \left(P_{1937}^1 - P_{1919}^1 \right),$$

starting in $t = 1920$, to impute forward to $t = 1936$.

For 1913–1917, we use formula 5:

$$P_t^1 = P_{t+1}^1 - \frac{P_{t+1}^{0.1} - P_t^{0.1}}{P_{t+1}^{0.1}} P_{t+1}^1,$$

starting in $t = 1917$, to impute backward to $t = 1913$.

Table A2 shows the results of our imputation procedure.

Table A2.   Imputation for the British Top 1% and 0.1% Income Shares.

Year (t)	Top 1% (P_t^1)	Top 0.5% ($P_t^{0.5}$)	Top 0.1% ($P_t^{0.1}$)	Imputation Method Top 1%	Imputation Method Top 0.1%
1913	*24.91*		11.24	Formula 5	
1914	*23.74*		10.71	Formula 5	
1915	*23.87*		10.77	Formula 5	
1916	*23.21*		10.47	Formula 5	
1917	*20.53*		9.26	Formula 5	
1918	19.24	15.46	8.68		
1919	19.59	15.69	8.98		
1920	*18.55*		8.03	Formula 4	
1921	*18.61*		8.08	Formula 4	
1922	*19.69*		9.07	Formula 4	
1923	*19.93*		9.29	Formula 4	
1924	*19.67*		9.05	Formula 4	
1925	*19.38*		8.79	Formula 4	
1926	*19.25*		8.67	Formula 4	
1927	*19.05*		8.49	Formula 4	
1928	*19.11*		8.54	Formula 4	
1929	*18.88*		8.33	Formula 4	
1930	*18.31*		7.81	Formula 4	
1931	*17.61*		7.17	Formula 4	
1932	*17.29*		6.87	Formula 4	
1933	*17.15*		6.75	Formula 4	
1934	*17.19*		6.78	Formula 4	
1935	*17.38*		6.96	Formula 4	
1936	*17.46*		7.03	Formula 4	
1937	16.98	13.07	6.59		
1938	*16.94*		6.57	Formula 3	
1939	*16.55*		6.35	Formula 3	
1940	*15.34*		5.67	Formula 3	
1941	*14.14*		5.00	Formula 3	
1942	*13.14*		4.44	Formula 3	
1943	*12.77*	9.04	4.23	Formula 2	
1944	*12.67*	8.97	4.13	Formula 2	
1945	*13.25*	9.38	4.23	Formula 2	
1946	*14.13*	10.00	4.48	Formula 2	
1947	*13.25*	9.38	4.10	Formula 2	
1948	*12.54*	8.88	3.86	Formula 2	
1949	11.47	8.12	3.45		
1950	*11.18*	8.51	3.59	Linear interpolation	
1951	10.89	7.69	3.21		
1952	10.20	7.15	2.95		
1953	9.72	6.78	2.77		

Table A2. (*Continued*)

Year (*t*)	Top 1% (P_t^1)	Top 0.5% ($P_t^{0.5}$)	Top 0.1% ($P_t^{0.1}$)	Imputation Method Top 1%	Imputation Method Top 0.1%
1954	9.67	6.71	2.72		
1955	9.30	6.48	2.65		
1956	8.75	6.03	2.42		
1957	8.70	5.96	2.37		
1958	8.76	5.98	2.38		
1959	8.60	5.85	2.30		
1960	8.87	6.08	2.45		
1961	*8.65*		*2.37*	Linear interpolation	Linear interpolation
1962	8.43	5.76	2.29		
1963	8.49	5.76	2.23		
1964	8.48	5.77	2.26		
1965	8.55	5.79	2.28		
1966	7.92	5.32	2.04		
1967	7.69	5.11	1.91		
1968	7.54	5.00	1.87		
1969	7.46	4.96	1.85		
1970	7.05	4.59	1.64		
1971	7.02	4.56	1.67		
1972	6.94	4.52	1.61		
1973	6.99	4.59	1.68		
1974	6.54	4.29	1.58		
1975	6.10	3.92	1.40		
1976	5.89	3.75	1.30		
1977	5.93	3.75	1.27		
1978	5.72	3.60	1.24		
1979	5.93	3.76	1.30		
1980	*6.30*		*1.42*	Linear interpolation	Linear interpolation
1981	6.67	4.27	1.53		
1982	6.85	4.40	1.61		
1983	6.83	4.36	1.58		
1984	7.16	4.59	1.67		
1985	7.40	4.83	1.82		
1986	7.55	4.92	1.86		
1987	7.78	5.04	*1.92*		Formula 1
1988	8.63	5.80	*2.33*		Formula 1
1989	8.67	5.90	*2.39*		Formula 1
1990	9.80	6.72	*2.83*		Formula 1
1991	10.32	7.18	*3.08*		Formula 1
1992	9.86	6.74	*2.84*		Formula 1
1993	10.36	7.20	3.09		

Table A2.   (*Continued*)

Year (t)	Top 1% (P_t^1)	Top 0.5% ($P_t^{0.5}$)	Top 0.1% ($P_t^{0.1}$)	Imputation Method Top 1%	Imputation Method Top 0.1%
1994	10.60	7.36	3.10		
1995	10.75	7.49	3.24		
1996	11.90	8.59	4.13		
1997	12.07	8.72	4.15		
1998	12.53	9.11	4.44		
1999	12.51	9.15	4.54		
2000	12.67	9.33	4.64		
2001	12.71	9.28	4.51		
2002	12.27	8.87	4.22		
2003	12.12	8.79	4.23		
2004	12.89	9.40	4.57		
2005	14.25	10.49	5.19		
2006	14.82	11.00	5.55		
2007	15.44	11.60	6.05		
2008	*14.66*		*5.58*	Linear interpolation	Linear interpolation
2009	13.88	10.23	5.11		

Notes: Estimates in bold italics are imputed values. See text for explanation.

From these series we create a measure for current inequality (current top 1 percent income share) and a measure for early-life inequality (top 1 percent income share averaged from birth year to age 4).

APPENDIX B: RESULTS USING FULL COUNTRY SAMPLES

Table B1.   Distribution of Self-Reported Current Health Status in Full Country Samples — Native-Born Adults Aged 21 and Older (%).

United States			Great Britain		
Current health status	Men	Women	Current health status	Men	Women
Poor (1)	2.95	3.18	Very Poor (1)	1.74	2.24
Fair (2)	8.06	9.58	Poor (2)	5.99	7.73
Good (3)	24.62	28.24	Fair (3)	19.62	21.43
Very good (4)	35.93	35.74	Good (4)	47.21	47.72
Excellent (5)	28.44	23.26	Excellent (5)	25.44	20.87
N (person-years)	62,389	70,347	N (person-years)	58,055	67,096

Source: Full samples of PSID (1984–2009) and BHPS (1991–2008).
Notes: Numbers in parentheses refer to coding of variable.

Table B2.   Distributions of Full Country Samples by Age Group and Birth Cohort (%).

	Age Group							Total
	21–29	30–39	40–49	50–59	60–69	70–79	80+	
United States								
Men								
Born 1913–1919					0.5	1.8	0.6	2.9
Born 1920–1929				0.9	4.5	2.6	0.6	8.6
Born 1930–1939			0.8	4.4	3.1	1.0		9.2
Born 1940–1949		2.1	9.2	6.1	2.0			19.3
Born 1950–1959	2.0	13.2	9.7	3.6				28.5
Born 1960–1969	7.1	8.9	3.7					19.6
Born 1970–1979	5.4	4.3						9.7
Born 1980–1986	2.2							2.2
Total	16.7	28.4	23.3	15.0	10.0	5.4	1.2	100.0

Table B2. (*Continued*)

	21−29	30−39	40−49	50−59	60−69	70−79	80+	Total
			Age Group					Total
Women								
Born 1913−1919					0.6	2.4	0.9	3.9
Born 1920−1929				0.9	4.6	2.9	0.8	9.1
Born 1930−1939			0.8	4.4	3.2	1.1		9.4
Born 1940−1949		1.8	7.7	5.3	1.7			16.5
Born 1950−1959	2.1	12.6	9.7	3.7				28.1
Born 1960−1969	7.9	8.8	3.7					20.4
Born 1970−1979	5.9	3.9						9.9
Born 1980−1986	2.8							2.8
Total	18.6	27.2	21.9	14.2	10.0	6.4	1.7	100.0
Great Britain								
Men								
Born 1913−1919						1.4	1.2	2.5
Born 1920−1929					2.9	5.1	1.4	9.4
Born 1930−1939				3.1	5.8	2.4		11.3
Born 1940−1949			4.8	9.2	3.5			17.4
Born 1950−1959		5.0	10.2	4.1				19.2
Born 1960−1969	5.1	12.3	5.5					22.8
Born 1970−1979	9.8	4.9						14.6
Born 1980−1986	2.8							2.8
Total	17.7	22.1	20.4	16.4	12.2	8.8	2.5	100.0
Women								
Born 1913−1919						1.8	1.9	3.6
Born 1920−1929					2.8	5.8	1.9	10.5
Born 1930−1939				2.9	5.9	2.4		11.2
Born 1940−1949			4.6	9.0	3.5			17.1
Born 1950−1959		4.5	9.7	4.0				18.2
Born 1960−1969	5.1	12.1	5.5					22.7
Born 1970−1979	9.3	4.7						14.0
Born 1980−1986	2.7							2.7
Total	17.1	21.3	19.8	15.8	12.2	9.9	3.8	100.0

Sources: Full samples of PSID (1984−2009) and BHPS (1991−2008).

Notes: Blank cells are zeros. The total number of person-year observations is 62,389 for U.S. males, 70,347 for U.S. females, 58,055 for British males, and 67,096 for British females. Individuals can appear more than once. In the U.S. samples, on average each of the 6,521 unique males and 6,839 unique females appears 9.6 and 10.3 times, respectively. In the British samples, on average each of the 6,315 unique males and 6,717 unique females appears 9.2 and 10.0 times, respectively.

Table B3. Mean Values of Variables in the Full Country Samples.

Variable	United States		Great Britain	
	Men	Women	Men	Women
Income share of top 1% of tax units				
Current year as adult	13.82	13.83	12.25	12.28
	(2.60)	(2.60)	(1.60)	(1.61)
Mean value for years from birth to age 4	10.69	10.76	11.00	11.26
	(3.16)	(3.25)	(4.33)	(4.52)
Log of permanent family income[a]	10.37	10.31	9.32	9.08
	(0.47)	(0.50)	(1.55)	(1.94)
Years used in permanent income measure	18.30	18.92	7.40	7.31
	(8.9)	(8.80)	(4.93)	(4.96)
Age groups				
21−24	0.05	0.06	0.08	0.07
25−29	0.12	0.12	0.10	0.10
30−34	0.14	0.14	0.11	0.11
35−39	0.14	0.13	0.11	0.11
40−44	0.13	0.12	0.10	0.10
45−49	0.11	0.10	0.10	0.10
50−54	0.08	0.08	0.09	0.08
55−59	0.07	0.06	0.08	0.07
60−64	0.05	0.05	0.06	0.06
65−69	0.05	0.05	0.06	0.06
70−74	0.03	0.04	0.05	0.06
75−79	0.02	0.02	0.04	0.04
80 and older	0.01	0.02	0.03	0.04
Race				
White	0.90	0.89	0.987	0.987
Black	0.06	0.08	0.005	0.006
Other	0.04	0.03	0.008	0.007
Parents' education				
Father: BA degree or more	0.16	0.16		
Father: High school degree	0.41	0.40		
Father: Less than high school degree	0.44	0.44		
Mother: BA degree or more	0.11	0.11		
Mother: High school degree	0.55	0.52		
Mother: Less than high school degree	0.34	0.37		
Parents' occupation				
Father: Professional, managerial, technical			0.22	0.22
Father: Skilled and semi-skilled			0.55	0.55
Father: Other or no occupation			0.23	0.23
Mother: Professional, managerial, technical			0.10	0.10
Mother: Skilled and semi-skilled			0.29	0.30
Mother: Other or no occupation			0.61	0.59
N (person-years)	62,389	70.347	58,055	67,096
N (persons)	6,521	6,839	6,315	6,717

Sources: Full samples of PSID (1984−2009) and BHPS (1991−2008).
[a]A person's permanent family income is the family size-adjusted post-tax post-government transfer income averaged over all years from a person's first year up to 1 year before a person reported his/her health status. We use the estimates of yearly family income in the CNEF data. Our yearly income values are adjusted for inflation to 2011 dollars. Numbers in parentheses are standard deviations.

Table B4.   Percentage Ranking Their Health in the Lowest Two Health Categories, by Age and Birth Cohort — Full Country Samples.[a]

	Age Group[b]							Total
	21—29	30—39	40—49	50—59	60—69	70—79	80+	
United States								
Men								
Born 1913—1919					29.7	39.5	42.2	39.2
Born 1920—1929				13.9	25.3	32.0	38.7	27.8
Born 1930—1939			11.8	19.6	22.6	31.8		21.3
Born 1940—1949		4.1	8.2	14.0	17.1			10.6
Born 1950—1959	3.6	5.1	8.7	12.9				7.2
Born 1960—1969	3.1	4.6	8.8					4.8
Born 1970—1979	4.0	6.9						5.2
Born 1980—1986	4.7							4.7
Total	3.7	5.1	8.6	15.5	23.1	34.6	40.2	11.1
Women								
Born 1913—1919					38.4	38.3	39.3	38.6
Born 1920—1929				22.0	28.4	31.4	44.6	30.9
Born 1930—1939			14.5	20.1	23.5	32.9		22.3
Born 1940—1949		7.9	9.4	15.8	18.9			12.3
Born 1950—1959	6.4	6.7	10.2	17.2				9.2
Born 1960—1969	4.2	5.5	10.0					5.7
Born 1970—1979	5.6	8.1						6.5
Born 1980—1986	5.5							5.5
Total	5.1	6.5	10.0	17.9	25.7	34.3	41.9	13.0
Great Britain								
Men								
Born 1913—1919						13.0	15.1	14.1
Born 1920—1929					9.5	12.6	14.6	12.1
Born 1930—1939				8.4	11.9	13.3		11.2
Born 1940—1949			6.2	9.8	9.9			8.9
Born 1950—1959		4.4	8.0	10.0				7.5
Born 1960—1969	4.0	5.3	5.8					5.1
Born 1970—1979	4.4	4.6						4.4
Born 1980—1986	4.3							4.3
Total	4.3	4.9	7.0	9.6	10.8	12.9	14.8	7.7

Table B4.   (*Continued*)

	21−29	30−39	40−49	50−59	60−69	70−79	80+	Total
				Age Group[b]				Total
Women								
Born 1913−1919						19.1	20.0	19.6
Born 1920−1929					10.5	15.0	20.1	15.3
Born 1930−1939				12.1	11.3	13.2		11.9
Born 1940−1949			9.1	11.6	11.8			10.9
Born 1950−1959		6.5	9.0	10.8				8.8
Born 1960−1969	6.3	8.3	10.3					8.4
Born 1970−1979	6.5	7.4						6.8
Born 1980−1986	5.3							5.3
Total	6.2	7.8	9.4	11.5	11.2	15.3	20.1	10.2

Sources: Full samples of PSID (1984−2009) and BHPS (1991−2008).

[a]The two lowest categories for the United States are "poor" or "fair" health. For Great Britain, they are "very poor" or "poor" health.

[b]The actual ages considered within the age range-rows have been made consistent across birth-year groups. The actual age groups are 22−27, 32−37, 42−47, 52−57, 62−67, 72−77, and 80−87. The row totals only include these ages.

Table B5.   Ordered Probit Coefficient Estimates for U.S. Men (1984−2009 Full Sample).

Variable	(1)	(2)	(3)	(4)	(5)
Mean top 1% income share when aged 0−4	−0.0945*** (0.0052)	−0.1053*** (0.0058)	−0.0233*** (0.0079)	−0.0308*** (0.0072)	−0.0221*** (0.0075)
Time trend		−0.0487* (0.0273)	0.0225 (0.0241)	0.0293 (0.0271)	0.0220 (0.0273)
Time trend squared		0.0002 (0.0001)	−0.0001 (0.0001)	−0.0002 (0.0001)	−0.0002 (0.0001)
Age groups (reference age: 80 years and older)					
21−24			1.0559*** (0.0894)	1.3496*** (0.0872)	1.2204*** (0.0873)
25−29			1.0547*** (0.0903)	1.2365*** (0.0850)	1.1157*** (0.0843)
30−34			0.9658*** (0.0878)	1.0933*** (0.0824)	0.9884*** (0.0817)
35−39			0.8867*** (0.0818)	0.9886*** (0.0782)	0.8994*** (0.0779)
40−44			0.8001*** (0.0786)	0.8735*** (0.0741)	0.7984*** (0.0731)
45−49			0.7044*** (0.0714)	0.7526*** (0.0659)	0.6882*** (0.0652)

Table B5. (*Continued*)

Variable	(1)	(2)	(3)	(4)	(5)
50−54			0.5861***	0.6091***	0.5589***
			(0.0642)	(0.0596)	(0.0586)
55−59			0.4922***	0.4794***	0.4450***
			(0.0613)	(0.0570)	(0.0548)
60−64			0.3738***	0.3503***	0.3264***
			(0.0598)	(0.0586)	(0.0559)
65−69			0.2650***	0.2375***	0.2176***
			(0.0565)	(0.0559)	(0.0538)
70−74			0.1527***	0.1466***	0.1342***
			(0.0372)	(0.0427)	(0.0416)
75−79			0.0150	0.0256	0.0181
			(0.0562)	(0.0613)	(0.0621)
Race (reference: white)					
Black			−0.4351***	−0.1923***	−0.1569***
			(0.0520)	(0.0529)	(0.0543)
Other			−0.1684***	−0.0861*	−0.0433
			(0.0543)	(0.0519)	(0.0506)
Log of permanent				0.6676***	0.5799***
family income				(0.0275)	(0.0305)
Years used in				−0.0007	−0.0011
permanent				(0.0014)	(0.0015)
measure					
Parents' education (reference: less than high school degree)					
Father: BA					0.1813***
degree or					(0.0446)
higher					
Father: High					0.1158***
school degree					(0.0291)
Mother: BA					0.2240***
degree or					(0.0442)
higher					
Mother: High					0.1289***
school degree					(0.0286)
N (person-years)	62,389	62,389	62,389	62,389	62,389

Source: Full sample of PSID (1984−2009).
Notes: Robust standard errors in parentheses. Coefficient estimates that statistically differ from zero are denoted by ***, **, and * for *p*-values ≤.01, ≤.05, and ≤.10, respectively. Reference categories include those aged 80 and over and those whose parents did not receive a high school degree. We do not drop observations because of missing values in the log of permanent family income or parental education but rather add three dummy variables that indicate missing values in these variables.

Table B6. Ordered Probit Coefficient Estimates for U.S. Women (1984–2009 Full Sample).

Variable	(1)	(2)	(3)	(4)	(5)
Mean top 1% income share when aged 0–4	−0.0959*** (0.0045)	−0.1047*** (0.0048)	−0.0340*** (0.0079)	−0.0380*** (0.0074)	−0.0283*** (0.0074)
Time trend		0.0547** (0.0254)	0.1124*** (0.0224)	0.1103*** (0.0237)	0.1042*** (0.0238)
Time trend squared		−0.0004*** (0.0001)	−0.0006*** (0.0001)	−0.0006*** (0.0001)	−0.0006*** (0.0001)
Age groups (reference age: 80 years and older)					
21–24			0.9135*** (0.0939)	1.1179*** (0.1040)	1.0049*** (0.1063)
25–29			0.9262*** (0.0927)	1.0269*** (0.1017)	0.9233*** (0.1044)
30–34			0.8969*** (0.0890)	0.9524*** (0.0980)	0.8650*** (0.1007)
35–39			0.8371*** (0.0845)	0.8688*** (0.0928)	0.7934*** (0.0963)
40–44			0.7762*** (0.0812)	0.7799*** (0.0885)	0.7199*** (0.0921)
45–49			0.6801*** (0.0752)	0.6501*** (0.0820)	0.6036*** (0.0863)
50–54			0.5780*** (0.0739)	0.5087*** (0.0793)	0.4781*** (0.0838)
55–59			0.5064*** (0.0708)	0.4053*** (0.0748)	0.3835*** (0.0789)
60–64			0.3979*** (0.0691)	0.2865*** (0.0731)	0.2726*** (0.0774)
65–69			0.2749*** (0.0598)	0.1913*** (0.0614)	0.1838*** (0.0659)
70–74			0.1678*** (0.0616)	0.1276** (0.0630)	0.1236* (0.0662)
75–79			0.0921* (0.0549)	0.0714 (0.0575)	0.0702 (0.0587)
Race (reference: white)					
Black			−0.5771*** (0.0460)	−0.2425*** (0.0434)	−0.2129*** (0.0436)
Other			−0.2211*** (0.0703)	−0.1353** (0.0607)	−0.0996* (0.0598)
Log of permanent family income				0.6562*** (0.0272)	0.5618*** (0.0261)
Years used in permanent measure				0.0016 (0.0012)	0.0011 (0.0012)

Table B6.   (*Continued*)

Variable	(1)	(2)	(3)	(4)	(5)
Parents' education (reference: less than high school degree)					
Father: BA degree or higher					0.2298*** (0.0308)
Father: High school degree					0.1221*** (0.0263)
Mother: BA degree or higher					0.1941*** (0.0461)
Mother: High school degree					0.1678*** (0.0291)
N (person-years)	70,347	70,347	70,347	70,347	70,347

Source: Full sample of PSID (1984−2009).
Notes: Robust standard errors in parentheses. Coefficient estimates that statistically differ from zero are denoted by ***, **, and * for *p*-values ≤.01, ≤.05, and ≤.10, respectively. Reference categories include those aged 80 and over and those whose parents did not receive a high school degree. We do not drop observations because of missing values in the log of permanent family income or parental education but rather add three dummy variables that indicate missing values in these variables.

Table B7.   Ordered Probit Coefficient Estimates for British Men (1991−2008 Full Sample).

Variable	(1)	(2)	(3)	(4)	(5)
Mean top 1% income share when aged 0−4	−0.0428*** (0.0024)	−0.0467*** (0.0024)	−0.0131 (0.0097)	−0.0101 (0.0100)	−0.0098 (0.0099)
Time trend		−0.2628*** (0.0385)	−0.2374*** (0.0357)	−0.2611*** (0.0366)	−0.2598*** (0.0368)
Time trend squared		0.0012*** (0.0002)	0.0011*** (0.0002)	0.0012*** (0.0002)	0.0012*** (0.0002)
Age groups (reference age: 80 years and older)					
21−24			0.4813*** (0.1495)	0.5361*** (0.1538)	0.5390*** (0.1539)
25−29			0.4990*** (0.1444)	0.5166*** (0.1482)	0.5210*** (0.1480)
30−34			0.4954*** (0.1366)	0.5042*** (0.1413)	0.5078*** (0.1412)
35−39			0.4366*** (0.1300)	0.4395*** (0.1339)	0.4434*** (0.1331)

Table B7. (*Continued*)

Variable	(1)	(2)	(3)	(4)	(5)
40–44			0.4341***	0.4300***	0.4360***
			(0.1238)	(0.1269)	(0.1267)
45–49			0.3846***	0.3642***	0.3721***
			(0.1126)	(0.1165)	(0.1162)
50–54			0.3297***	0.2885***	0.2976***
			(0.0999)	(0.1030)	(0.1038)
55–59			0.2259**	0.1735*	0.1838**
			(0.0919)	(0.0935)	(0.0936)
60–64			0.2046**	0.1754**	0.1840**
			(0.0803)	(0.0836)	(0.0832)
65–69			0.1728**	0.1655**	0.1723**
			(0.0701)	(0.0745)	(0.0750)
70–74			0.0949**	0.0876*	0.0924*
			(0.0470)	(0.0498)	(0.0495)
75–79			0.0346	0.0403	0.0422
			(0.0374)	(0.0379)	(0.0380)
Race (reference: white)					
Black			0.0321	0.1323	0.1348
			(0.1261)	(0.1394)	(0.1403)
Other			−0.1558**	−0.1565**	−0.1549**
			(0.0657)	(0.0693)	(0.0687)
Log of permanent family income				0.4047***	0.3837***
				(0.0250)	(0.0249)
Years used in permanent measure				0.0038	0.0032
				(0.0029)	(0.0031)
Parents' occupation (reference: other or no occupation)					
Father: Professional, managerial, technical				0.1289***	
					(0.0374)
Father: Skilled and semi-skilled					−0.0161
					(0.0326)
Mother: Professional, managerial, technical				−0.0193	
					(0.0406)
Mother: Skilled and semi-skilled					−0.0237
					(0.0257)
N (person-years)	58,055	58,055	58,055	58,055	58,055

Source: Full sample of BHPS (1991–2008).

Notes: Robust standard errors in parentheses. Coefficient estimates that statistically differ from zero are denoted by ***, **, and * for p-values $\leq$.01, $\leq$.05, and $\leq$.10, respectively. Reference categories include those aged 80 and over and those whose parents had other or no occupation. We do not drop observations because of missing values in the log of permanent family income or parental occupation but rather add three dummy variables that indicate missing values in these variables.

Table B8. Ordered Probit Coefficient Estimates for British Women
(1991−2008 Full Sample).

Variable	(1)	(2)	(3)	(4)	(5)
Mean top 1% income share	−0.0405***	−0.0436***	−0.0037	−0.0023	−0.0002
when aged 0−4	(0.0022)	(0.0023)	(0.0079)	(0.0085)	(0.0085)
Time trend		−0.3657***	−0.3244***	−0.3483***	−0.3510***
		(0.0397)	(0.0342)	(0.0356)	(0.0360)
Time trend squared		0.0018***	0.0016***	0.0017***	0.0017***
		(0.0002)	(0.0002)	(0.0002)	(0.0002)
Age groups (reference age: 80 years and older)					
21−24			0.6635***	0.6782***	0.6824***
			(0.1144)	(0.1220)	(0.1223)
25−29			0.6897***	0.6783***	0.6813***
			(0.1147)	(0.1238)	(0.1240)
30−34			0.7057***	0.6901***	0.6906***
			(0.1086)	(0.1159)	(0.1160)
35−39			0.6517***	0.6348***	0.6353***
			(0.1014)	(0.1095)	(0.1090)
40−44			0.6264***	0.5956***	0.5977***
			(0.0953)	(0.1026)	(0.1027)
45−49			0.5332***	0.4718***	0.4774***
			(0.0847)	(0.0905)	(0.0901)
50−54			0.4707***	0.3948***	0.4052***
			(0.0663)	(0.0736)	(0.0729)
55−59			0.4234***	0.3570***	0.3669***
			(0.0630)	(0.0701)	(0.0693)
60−64			0.4465***	0.3961***	0.4072***
			(0.0549)	(0.0624)	(0.0613)
65−69			0.3253***	0.2954***	0.3044***
			(0.0444)	(0.0478)	(0.0470)
70−74			0.2586***	0.2463***	0.2524***
			(0.0387)	(0.0408)	(0.0405)
75−79			0.1157***	0.1152***	0.1204***
			(0.0430)	(0.0434)	(0.0428)
Race (reference: white)					
Black			−0.0125	0.0374	0.0680
			(0.1200)	(0.1281)	(0.1298)
Other			−0.3022***	−0.1820**	−0.1659**
			(0.0805)	(0.0782)	(0.0818)
Log of permanent family				0.3846***	0.3576***
income				(0.0210)	(0.0225)
Years used in permanent				0.0042	0.0041
measure				(0.0035)	(0.0035)

Table B8. (*Continued*)

Variable	(1)	(2)	(3)	(4)	(5)
Parents' occupation (reference: other or no occupation)					
Father: Professional, managerial, technical				0.1686***	
					(0.0391)
Father: Skilled and semi-skilled					0.0787**
					(0.0316)
Mother: Professional, managerial, technical				0.0594	
					(0.0392)
Mother: Skilled and semi-skilled					0.0398
					(0.0248)
N (person-years)	67,096	67,096	67,096	67,096	67,096

Source: Full sample of BHPS (1991–2008).

Notes: Robust standard errors in parentheses. Coefficient estimates that statistically differ from zero are denoted by ***, **, and * for *p*-values $\leq.01$, $\leq.05$, and $\leq.10$, respectively. Reference categories include those aged 80 and over and those whose parents had other or no occupation. We do not drop observations because of missing values in the log of permanent family income or parental occupation but rather add three dummy variables that indicate missing values in these variables.

Table B9. Sensitivity of Coefficient Estimates for Early-Life (Aged 0−4) Income Share of Top 1 Percent to Alternative Time Trend Specifications and the Inclusion of the Current Top 1 Percent Income Share − Full Country Samples.

	United States		Great Britain	
	Men	Women	Men	Women
Quadratic time trend	−0.0221***	−0.0283***	−0.0098	−0.0002
	(0.0075)	(0.0074)	(0.0099)	(0.0085)
Quadratic time trend + current income share	−0.0221***	−0.0284***	−0.0098	−0.0001
	(0.0075)	(0.0074)	(0.0099)	(0.0084)
Linear time trend	−0.0229***	−0.0312***	−0.0075	0.0030
	(0.0075)	(0.0074)	(0.0103)	(0.0088)
Linear time trend + current income share	−0.0227***	−0.0306***	−0.0077	0.0029
	(0.0075)	(0.0073)	(0.0102)	(0.0087)
Decade dummies	−0.0171**	−0.0230***	0.0078	0.0119
	(0.0072)	(0.0069)	(0.0087)	(0.0074)
Decade dummies + current income share	−0.0197***	−0.0255***	0.0028	0.0086
	(0.0074)	(0.0072)	(0.0096)	(0.0082)
N (person-years)	62,389	70,347	58,055	67,096

Sources: Full samples of PSID (1984−2009) and BHPS (1991−2008).
Notes: Coefficient estimates and their standard errors in each of our six specifications are based on Model 5 in Tables B5−B8 but using alternative time trend specifications with or without the addition of a current-year measure of the share of income held by the top 1 percent. Current income share is the value of the top 1 percent share in the year health is reported. Values for the quadratic time trend were previously reported in Tables B5−B8. Coefficient estimates that statistically differ from zero are denoted by ***, **, and * for *p*-values ≤.01, ≤.05, and ≤.10, respectively.

Table B10. Sensitivity of Coefficient Estimates for Early-Life (Aged 0−4) Income Share of Top 1 Percent to Major Change in Public Health System for Persons Born before 1950 and 1966 − Full Country Samples.

	(1)	(2)	(3)	(4)	(5)
United States					
Men					
Birth to age 4	−0.0880***	−0.0747***	−0.0244***	−0.0309***	−0.0222***
	(0.0076)	(0.0086)	(0.0077)	(0.0072)	(0.0074)
Birth to age 4 × born before 1966	−0.0048	−0.0240***	0.0067	0.0004	0.0008
	(0.0030)	(0.0040)	(0.0048)	(0.0046)	(0.0043)
Women					
Birth to age 4	−0.0970***	−0.0843***	−0.0348***	−0.0379***	−0.0285***
	(0.0066)	(0.0075)	(0.0079)	(0.0075)	(0.0075)
Birth to age 4 × born before 1966	0.0008	−0.0160***	0.0047	−0.0005	0.0009
	(0.0030)	(0.0039)	(0.0040)	(0.0047)	(0.0046)

Table B10. (Continued)

	(1)	(2)	(3)	(4)	(5)
United States (1950 as "placebo")					
Men					
Birth to age 4	−0.0946***	−0.1018***	−0.0327***	−0.0417***	−0.0338***
	(0.0115)	(0.0123)	(0.0114)	(0.0109)	(0.0107)
Birth to age 4 × born before 1950	0.0000	−0.0017	0.0052	0.0060	0.0065
	(0.0046)	(0.0050)	(0.0057)	(0.0053)	(0.0053)
Women					
Birth to age 4	−0.1078***	−0.1124***	−0.0446***	−0.0455***	−0.0362***
	(0.0104)	(0.0109)	(0.0113)	(0.0110)	(0.0104)
Birth to age 4 × born before 1950	0.0058	0.0037	0.0058	0.0041	0.0043
	(0.0045)	(0.0046)	(0.0047)	(0.0046)	(0.0042)
Great Britain					
Men					
Birth to age 4	−0.0452***	−0.0538***	−0.0242	−0.0126	−0.0131
	(0.0089)	(0.0090)	(0.0148)	(0.0144)	(0.0142)
Birth to age 4 × born before 1950	0.0014	0.0041	0.0053	0.0012	0.0016
	(0.0050)	(0.0050)	(0.0051)	(0.0052)	(0.0051)
Women					
Birth to age 4	−0.0450***	−0.0524***	−0.0073	0.0059	0.0066
	(0.0069)	(0.0073)	(0.0115)	(0.0123)	(0.0123)
Birth to age 4 × born before 1950	0.0026	0.0051	0.0018	−0.0040	−0.0033
	(0.0039)	(0.0041)	(0.0039)	(0.0042)	(0.0041)
Great Britain (1966 as "placebo")					
Men					
Birth to age 4	−0.0460***	−0.0449***	−0.0130	−0.0102	−0.0096
	(0.0053)	(0.0054)	(0.0096)	(0.0100)	(0.0099)
Birth to age 4 × born before 1966	0.0024	−0.0013	−0.0002	0.0001	−0.0002
	(0.0032)	(0.0033)	(0.0036)	(0.0038)	(0.0038)
Women					
Birth to age 4	−0.0412***	−0.0401***	0.0008	0.0009	0.0037
	(0.0054)	(0.0055)	(0.0082)	(0.0087)	(0.0086)
Birth to age 4 × born before 1966	0.0005	−0.0026	−0.0063	−0.0044	−0.0053
	(0.0036)	(0.0038)	(0.0046)	(0.0047)	(0.0047)
Controls					
Time trend		✓	✓	✓	✓
Age group			✓	✓	✓
Race			✓	✓	✓
Log permanent family income				✓	✓
Parents' education/occupation					✓

Sources: Full samples of PSID (1984−2009) and BHPS (1991−2008).

Notes: Coefficient estimates and their standard errors are from model specifications that correspond to those used for Tables B5−B8. Sample sizes are $N = 62,389$ for U.S. males, $N = 70,347$ for U.S. females, $N = 58,055$ for British males, and $N = 67,096$ for British females. Coefficient estimates that statistically differ from zero are denoted by ***, **, and * for p-values ≤.01, ≤.05, and ≤.10, respectively.

APPENDIX C: AGE AND HEALTH OF
RESTRICTED-AGE SAMPLES (AGED 21−69)

Table C1. Distribution of Same-Years Subsamples by Age Group and Birth Cohort (Restricting to 21−69 Year Olds) (%).

	Age Group					All Ages
	21−29	30−39	40−49	50−59	60−69	
United States						
Men						
Born 1922−1929					3.4	3.4
Born 1930−1939				3.1	4.7	7.8
Born 1940−1949			7.8	9.3	2.3	19.4
Born 1950−1959		9.9	15.0	4.5		29.3
Born 1960−1969	6.0	13.6	4.7			24.4
Born 1970−1979	8.3	5.2				13.5
Born 1980−1986	2.2					2.2
All cohorts	16.6	28.7	27.5	16.9	10.4	100.0
Women						
Born 1922−1929					3.5	3.5
Born 1930−1939				3.1	4.9	8.0
Born 1940−1949			6.8	8.1	2.1	17.0
Born 1950−1959		9.5	15.2	4.7		29.4
Born 1960−1969	6.3	13.9	4.8			25.1
Born 1970−1979	9.3	4.8				14.1
Born 1980−1986	3.1					3.1
All cohorts	18.6	28.2	26.8	15.9	10.5	100.0
Great Britain						
Men						
Born 1922−1929					4.7	4.7
Born 1930−1939				5.1	6.3	11.4
Born 1940−1949			7.9	9.6	2.6	20.1
Born 1950−1959		8.2	10.7	3.1		21.9
Born 1960−1969	8.3	13.2	4.2			25.7
Born 1970−1979	10.2	3.8				14.0
Born 1980−1986	2.3					2.3
All cohorts	20.8	25.1	22.8	17.7	13.6	100.0
Women						
Born 1922−1929					4.9	4.9
Born 1930−1939				4.9	6.5	11.4
Born 1940−1949			7.9	9.6	2.7	20.2
Born 1950−1959		7.7	10.7	3.1		21.5

Table C1. *(Continued)*

	Age Group					All Ages
	21−29	30−39	40−49	50−59	60−69	
Born 1960−1969	8.8	13.3	4.3			26.3
Born 1970−1979	9.7	3.7				13.5
Born 1980−1986	2.2					2.2
All cohorts	20.7	24.7	22.9	17.6	14.1	100.0

Sources: Same-years subsamples of PSID (1991−2007) and BHPS (1991−2007).
Note: Blank cells are zeros. The total number of person-year observations is 33,729 for U.S. males, 37,368 for U.S. females, 34,265 for British males, and 38,353 for British females. Individuals can appear more than once. In the U.S. samples, on average each of the 5,475 unique males and 5,766 unique females appears 6.2 and 6.5 times, respectively. In the British samples, on average each of the 5,794 unique males and 6,065 unique females appears 5.9 and 6.3 times, respectively.

Table C2. Percentage Ranking Their Health in the Lowest Two Health Categories, by Age and Birth Cohort (Restricting to 21−69 Year Olds).[a]

	Age Group[b]					All Ages
	21−29	30−39	40−49	50−59	60−69	
United States						
Men						
Born 1922−1929					21.0	21.0
Born 1930−1939				18.5	22.1	20.7
Born 1940−1949			8.9	13.9	17.6	12.2
Born 1950−1959		5.2	8.5	12.0		7.9
Born 1960−1969	3.4	4.6	8.8			5.1
Born 1970−1979	4.0	6.0				4.7
Born 1980−1986	3.3					3.3
All cohorts	3.7	5.1	8.7	14.3	20.9	8.9
Women						
Born 1922−1929					24.7	24.7
Born 1930−1939				19.3	23.5	21.9
Born 1940−1949			9.3	15.7	19.6	13.5
Born 1950−1959		6.3	10.3	16.2		9.9
Born 1960−1969	3.7	5.4	9.4			5.7
Born 1970−1979	5.6	7.7				6.3
Born 1980−1986	5.2					5.2
All cohorts	5.0	6.1	9.9	16.6	23.3	10.3

Table C2. (*Continued*)

	Age Group[b]					All Ages
	21−29	30−39	40−49	50−59	60−69	
Great Britain						
Men						
Born 1922−1929					9.5	9.5
Born 1930−1939				8.4	11.5	10.1
Born 1940−1949			6.2	10.1	9.9	8.5
Born 1950−1959		4.4	8.4	10.0		7.1
Born 1960−1969	4.0	5.0	5.2			4.7
Born 1970−1979	4.7	4.8				4.7
Born 1980−1986	4.3					4.3
All cohorts	4.4	4.8	7.0	9.6	10.5	6.8
Women						
Born 1922−1929					10.5	10.5
Born 1930−1939				12.1	10.3	11.1
Born 1940−1949			9.1	11.1	11.1	10.3
Born 1950−1959		6.5	9.0	11.3		8.4
Born 1960−1969	6.3	8.2	10.8			8.0
Born 1970−1979	6.3	7.9				6.7
Born 1980−1986	5.7					5.7
All cohorts	6.2	7.6	9.4	11.4	10.5	8.7

Sources: Same-years subsamples of the PSID (1991−2007) and BHPS (1991−2007).
[a]The two lowest categories for the United States are "poor" or "fair" health. For Great Britain, they are "very poor" or "poor" health.
[b]The actual ages considered within the age groups have been made consistent across birth cohorts. The actual age groups are 22−27, 32−37, 42−47, 52−57, and 62−67. The row and column totals only include these ages.